Communications
in Computer and Information Science 1423

More information about this series at http://www.springer.com/series/7899

Xingming Sun · Xiaorui Zhang ·
Zhihua Xia · Elisa Bertino (Eds.)

Advances in Artificial Intelligence and Security

7th International Conference, ICAIS 2021
Dublin, Ireland, July 19–23, 2021
Proceedings, Part II

Springer

Editors
Xingming Sun 🆔
Nanjing University of Information Science
and Technology
Nanjing, China

Xiaorui Zhang 🆔
Nanjing University of Information Science
and Technology
Nanjing, China

Zhihua Xia 🆔
Jinan University
Guangzhou, China

Elisa Bertino 🆔
Purdue University
West Lafayette, IN, USA

ISSN 1865-0929 ISSN 1865-0937 (electronic)
Communications in Computer and Information Science
ISBN 978-3-030-78617-5 ISBN 978-3-030-78618-2 (eBook)
https://doi.org/10.1007/978-3-030-78618-2

This Springer imprint is published by the registered company Springer Nature Switzerland AG
The registered company address is: Gewerbestrasse 11, 6330 Cham, Switzerland

Preface

The 7th International Conference on Artificial Intelligence and Security (ICAIS 2021), formerly called the International Conference on Cloud Computing and Security (ICCCS), was held during July 19–23, 2021, in Dublin, Ireland. Over the past six years, ICAIS has become a leading conference for researchers and engineers to share their latest results of research, development, and applications in the fields of artificial intelligence and information security.

We used the Microsoft Conference Management Toolkits (CMT) system to manage the submission and review processes of ICAIS 2021. We received 1013 submissions from authors in 20 countries and regions, including the USA, Canada, the UK, Italy, Ireland, Japan, Russia, France, Australia, South Korea, South Africa, Iraq, Kazakhstan, Indonesia, Vietnam, Ghana, China, Taiwan, and Macao, etc. The submissions covered the areas of artificial intelligence, big data, cloud computing and security, information hiding, IoT security, multimedia forensics, encryption and cybersecurity, and so on. We thank our Technical Program Committee (TPC) members and external reviewers for their efforts in reviewing the papers and providing valuable comments to the authors. From the total of 1013 submissions, and based on at least three reviews per submission, the Program Chairs decided to accept 183 papers to be published in three Communications in Computer and Information Science (CCIS) volumes and 122 papers to be published in two Lecture Notes in Computer Science (LNCS) volumes, yielding an acceptance rate of 30%. This volume of the conference proceedings contains all the regular, poster, and workshop papers.

The conference program was enriched by a series of keynote presentations, and the keynote speakers included Michael Scott, MIRACL Labs, Ireland, and Sakir Sezer, Queen's University of Belfast, UK. We enjoyed their wonderful speeches.

There were 49 workshops organized as part of ICAIS 2021 which covered all the hot topics in artificial intelligence and security. We would like to take this moment to express our sincere appreciation for the contribution of all the workshop chairs and their participants. We would like to extend our sincere thanks to all authors who submitted papers to ICAIS 2021 and to all TPC members. It was a truly great experience to work with such talented and hard-working researchers. We also appreciate the external reviewers for assisting the TPC members in their particular areas of expertise. Moreover, we want to thank our sponsors: Association for Computing Machinery; Nanjing University of Information Science and Technology; Dublin City University; New York University; Michigan State University; University of Central Arkansas; Université Bretagne Sud; National Nature Science Foundation of China; Tech Science Press; Nanjing Normal University; Northeastern State University; Engineering

Research Center of Digital Forensics, Ministry of Education, China; and ACM
SIGWEB China.

April 2021   Xingming Sun
                                                    Xiaorui Zhang
                                                    Zhihua Xia
                                                    Elisa Bertino

Organization

General Chairs

Martin Collier	Dublin City University, Ireland
Xingming Sun	Nanjing University of Information Science and Technology, China
Yun Q. Shi	New Jersey Institute of Technology, USA
Mauro Barni	University of Siena, Italy
Elisa Bertino	Purdue University, USA

Technical Program Chairs

Noel Murphy	Dublin City University, Ireland
Aniello Castiglione	University of Salerno, Italy
Yunbiao Guo	China Information Technology Security Evaluation Center, China
Suzanne K. McIntosh	New York University, USA
Xiaorui Zhang	Engineering Research Center of Digital Forensics, Ministry of Education, China
Q. M. Jonathan Wu	University of Windsor, Canada

Publication Chairs

Zhihua Xia	Nanjing University of Information Science and Technology, China
Zhaoqing Pan	Nanjing University of Information Science and Technology, China

Workshop Chair

Baowei Wang	Nanjing University of Information Science and Technology, China

Organization Chairs

Xiaojun Wang	Dublin City University, Ireland
Genlin Ji	Nanjing Normal University, China
Zhangjie Fu	Nanjing University of Information Science and Technology, China

Technical Program Committee Members

Saeed Arif	University of Algeria, Algeria
Anthony Ayodele	University of Maryland, USA
Zhifeng Bao	Royal Melbourne Institute of Technology, Australia
Zhiping Cai	National University of Defense Technology, China
Ning Cao	Qingdao Binhai University, China
Paolina Centonze	Iona College, USA
Chin-chen Chang	Feng Chia University, Taiwan, China
Han-Chieh Chao	Taiwan Dong Hwa University, Taiwan, China
Bing Chen	Nanjing University of Aeronautics and Astronautics, China
Hanhua Chen	Huazhong University of Science and Technology, China
Xiaofeng Chen	Xidian University, China
Jieren Cheng	Hainan University, China
Lianhua Chi	IBM Research Center, Australia
Kim-Kwang Raymond Choo	University of Texas at San Antonio, USA
Ilyong Chung	Chosun University, South Korea
Robert H. Deng	Singapore Management University, Singapore
Jintai Ding	University of Cincinnati, USA
Xinwen Fu	University of Central Florida, USA
Zhangjie Fu	Nanjing University of Information Science and Technology, China
Moncef Gabbouj	Tampere University of Technology, Finland
Ruili Geng	Spectral MD, USA
Song Guo	Hong Kong Polytechnic University, Hong Kong
Mohammad Mehedi Hassan	King Saud University, Saudi Arabia
Russell Higgs	University College Dublin, Ireland
Dinh Thai Hoang	University of Technology Sydney, Australia
Wien Hong	Nanfang College of Sun Yat-sen University, China
Chih-Hsien Hsia	National Ilan University, Taiwan, China
Robert Hsu	Chung Hua University, Taiwan, China
Xinyi Huang	Fujian Normal University, China
Yongfeng Huang	Tsinghua University, China
Zhiqiu Huang	Nanjing University of Aeronautics and Astronautics, China
Patrick C. K. Hung	University of Ontario Institute of Technology, Canada
Farookh Hussain	University of Technology Sydney, Australia
Genlin Ji	Nanjing Normal University, China
Hai Jin	Huazhong University of Science and Technology, China
Sam Tak Wu Kwong	City University of Hong Kong, China
Chin-Feng Lai	Taiwan Cheng Kung University, Taiwan, China
Loukas Lazos	University of Arizona, USA

Yongjun Ren	Nanjing University of Information Science and Technology, China
Arun Kumar Sangaiah	VIT University, India
Di Shang	Long Island University, USA
Victor S. Sheng	University of Central Arkansas, USA
Zheng-guo Sheng	University of Sussex, UK
Robert Simon Sherratt	University of Reading, UK
Yun Q. Shi	New Jersey Institute of Technology, USA
Frank Y. Shih	New Jersey Institute of Technology, USA
Biao Song	King Saud University, Saudi Arabia
Guang Sun	Hunan University of Finance and Economics, China
Jianguo Sun	Harbin University of Engineering, China
Krzysztof Szczypiorski	Warsaw University of Technology, Poland
Tsuyoshi Takagi	Kyushu University, Japan
Shanyu Tang	University of West London, UK
Jing Tian	National University of Singapore, Singapore
Yoshito Tobe	Aoyang University, Japan
Cezhong Tong	Washington University in St. Louis, USA
Pengjun Wan	Illinois Institute of Technology, USA
Cai-Zhuang Wang	Ames Laboratory, USA
Ding Wang	Peking University, China
Guiling Wang	New Jersey Institute of Technology, USA
Honggang Wang	University of Massachusetts Dartmouth, USA
Jian Wang	Nanjing University of Aeronautics and Astronautics, China
Jie Wang	University of Massachusetts Lowell, USA
Jin Wang	Changsha University of Science and Technology, China
Liangmin Wang	Jiangsu University, China
Ruili Wang	Massey University, New Zealand
Xiaojun Wang	Dublin City University, Ireland
Xiaokang Wang	St. Francis Xavier University, Canada
Zhaoxia Wang	A-Star, Singapore
Sheng Wen	Swinburne University of Technology, Australia
Jian Weng	Jinan University, China
Edward Wong	New York University, USA
Eric Wong	University of Texas at Dallas, USA
Shaoen Wu	Ball State University, USA
Shuangkui Xia	Beijing Institute of Electronics Technology and Application, China
Lingyun Xiang	Changsha University of Science and Technology, China
Yang Xiang	Deakin University, Australia
Yang Xiao	University of Alabama, USA
Haoran Xie	The Education University of Hong Kong, China
Naixue Xiong	Northeastern State University, USA

Wei Qi Yan	Auckland University of Technology, New Zealand
Aimin Yang	Guangdong University of Foreign Studies, China
Ching-Nung Yang	Taiwan Dong Hwa University, Taiwan, China
Chunfang Yang	Zhengzhou Science and Technology Institute, China
Fan Yang	University of Maryland, USA
Guomin Yang	University of Wollongong, Australia
Qing Yang	University of North Texas, USA
Yimin Yang	Lakehead University, Canada
Ming Yin	Purdue University, USA
Shaodi You	Australian National University, Australia
Kun-Ming Yu	Chung Hua University, Taiwan, China
Weiming Zhang	University of Science and Technology of China, China
Xinpeng Zhang	Fudan University, China
Yan Zhang	Simula Research Laboratory, Norway
Yanchun Zhang	Victoria University, Australia
Yao Zhao	Beijing Jiaotong University, China

Organization Committee Members

Xianyi Chen	Nanjing University of Information Science and Technology, China
Zilong Jin	Nanjing University of Information Science and Technology, China
Yiwei Li	Columbia University, USA
Yuling Liu	Hunan University, China
Zhiguo Qu	Nanjing University of Information Science and Technology, China
Huiyu Sun	New York University, USA
Le Sun	Nanjing University of Information Science and Technology, China
Jian Su	Nanjing University of Information Science and Technology, China
Qing Tian	Nanjing University of Information Science and Technology, China
Yuan Tian	King Saud University, Saudi Arabia
Qi Wang	Nanjing University of Information Science and Technology, China
Lingyun Xiang	Changsha University of Science and Technology, China
Zhihua Xia	Nanjing University of Information Science and Technology, China
Lizhi Xiong	Nanjing University of Information Science and Technology, China

Leiming Yan	Nanjing University of Information Science and Technology, China
Li Yu	Nanjing University of Information Science and Technology, China
Zhili Zhou	Nanjing University of Information Science and Technology, China

Contents – Part II

Big Data

Cloud Computing and Security

Artificial Intelligence

An Approach Based on Demand Prediction with LSTM for Solving Multi-batch 2D Cutting Stock Problems

Kaimin Pang[1], Bo Zhu[1](✉), Hongshuo Zhang[1], Ning Liu[1], Miao Xu[1], and Lianfu Zhang[2]

[1] Faculty of Mechanical and Electrical Engineering, Kunming University of Science and Technology, Kunming 650500, China
[2] Shenyang Machine Tool (Group) Co., Ltd., Shenyang 110142, China

Abstract. In order to improve the 2D cutting stock under the condition of small batch and multiple batches production, we propose to predict the parts demand of subsequent batches first, and then take advantage of the idea of centralized cutting to integrate the predicted parts demand of multiple batches into a larger scale problem to solve. As a supplement, the shortages of actual parts demand caused by prediction error are settled by compensating cutting as it occurred. A model is built for that and it uses the long short-term memory (LSTM) neural networks to predict parts demand, and solve the integrated cutting problem by the classical method of column generation combined with strip construction. To check the effectiveness of this model, an experiment is exerted on it with some simulated historical parts demand data generated by Monte-Carlo simulation method. The experiment results show that the model predicts the parts demands of subsequent batches accurately, and achieves higher overall material utilization rate than that of cutting for each batch without considering use of surplus materials and inventory-based cutting approach proposed by other researchers.

Keywords: Multiple batches cutting stock problem · Parts demand prediction · Monte-Carlo simulation · Long short-term memory neural networks · Method of column generation combined with strips construction

1 Introduction

Two-Dimensional Rectangular Cutting Stock Problem (2D-CSP) is about how to design layout of needed parts on material bins to achieve the highest material utilization rate, and 2D-CSP often occurs in sheet metal, construction, leather, ceramics and other manufacturing industries. Effectively solving the 2D-CSP can decrease the waste of resources and improve the economic benefits of enterprises [1, 2]. The 2D-CSP problem has been widely and deeply studied in the academic circles, for example, Gilmore and Gomory [3] solved the 2D-CSP by method of integer programming; Christofides and Blazewicz j [4] proposed a mode which using the precise recursive method and dynamic programming; Mundim et al. [5] adopted a new general heuristic algorithm (H4NP) to solve the

X. Sun et al. (Eds.): ICAIS 2021, CCIS 1423, pp. 3–15, 2021.
https://doi.org/10.1007/978-3-030-78618-2_1

2D-CSP. Ma, Liu and Zhou [6] proposed two heuristic algorithms: Column Generation based heuristic algorithm (CGH) and the dynamic programming based heuristic algorithm (IDPH) to solve the multi-cycle 2D-CSP. These studies are focused on the solution algorithm to search the approximate optimal solution from the huge two-dimensional solution space, so as to obtain a higher material utilization rate. At the same time, some scholars carry out research on the actual cutting requirements and scenarios, and put forward some approaches to further improve the material utilization rate from the perspective of the optimal application of the algorithm rather than the algorithm itself. Centralized cutting is such a typical method. Through the integration of multiple cutting tasks with similar requirements (from multiple projects or multiple manufacturing enterprises in the same industry), multiple small-scale problems are merged into a small number of large-scale problems, thus increasing the possibility of complementarity and fit between parts, which is conducive to obtain better layout scheme so as to improve the material utilization rate, and obtain the benefits of reducing equipment input cost and start-up cost. For example, Reinders [7] combines integrated production management with actual cutting system to effectively reduce the cost of Strip Packing (SP) problem. Reinders [8] transformed the multi-period 2D-CSP of wood production into the centralized optimization cutting problem, and effectively reduced the wood use cost through the decision support system. Qin et al. [9] combined with the idea of centralized cutting and proposed a grouping optimization approach based on part samples, which effectively improved the bars utilization rate.

At present, in order to better meet the personalized needs of customers and quickly respond to the market, mass customization, multi batch and small batch production have become the main production mode of manufacturing enterprises, which determines that the production mode of manufacturing enterprises has the following characteristics: there are many cutting batches, similar batch cutting stock requirements, small scale of single batch cutting stock, and unclear parts demand of subsequent batches. In view of such cutting characteristics, it is difficult to obtain a better overall material utilization rate if only optimizing for each batch without considering the use of surplus materials (defined as Batch Cutting Stock). Therefore, some scholars put forward the Inventory-Based Cutting Stock, that is, the surplus materials generated from each cutting are put into the inventory, and the remaining materials in the inventory are preferentially used for each blanking, so that the surplus materials can be used effectively. Relevant researches such as: Kos and Duhovnik [10] considered the inventory of materials and proposed a hybrid genetic algorithm to optimize the Cutting Stock problem of one-dimensional materials by giving priority to the use of inventory surplus; Ayadi o et al. [11] linked the scale of cutting stock batch with the inventory of surplus materials and used a hybrid heuristic, based on the combination of the Bottom Left and Shelf algorithms to solve 2D-CSP problem.

Compared with the horizontal integration of centralized cutting on the parts demand, our idea is to longitudinally integrate the parts demand, and its effectiveness depends on the accuracy of the subsequent batch parts demand prediction. At present, there are many researches on parts demand prediction methods. Among them, Long Short-Term Memory (LSTM) neural networks of deep learning can not only deal with the continuity of

time series information, but also deal with the gradient disappearance and gradient explosion in the process of long-term training, which has significant advantages in solving
the prediction problem. For example, Zhao et al. [12] used the deep structure of LSTM
recurrent neural network to model the temporal and spatial characteristics of traffic, and
then proposed a model based on deep LSTM RNNs and linear regression to predict Traffic Matrix (TM); Petersen, Rodrigues and Pereira [13] constructed a transit travel time
prediction system based on LSTM neural networks, The system takes advantage of the
non-static spatiotemporal correlation existing in the urban public transport network, and
can find complex patterns that cannot be captured by traditional methods; Cortez et al.
[14] proposed an Emergency Events (EV) prediction architecture based on LSTM neural
networks, and proved its effectiveness by comparing with traditional time series analysis and machine learning methods. Xu and Yoneda [15] proposed an automatic coding
multi-task learning model based on LSTM neural networks to predict PM2.5 time series
of multiple locations in the city, and achieved good results. Therefore, we use LSTM
neural networks as the prediction tool to predict the parts demand of subsequent batches.
According to the prediction results, we integrate the cutting tasks according to the idea
of centralized cutting, solve the 2D-CSP problem by the method of column generation
combined with strips construction, and compensate the cutting to solve the problem
that the demand can not be met due to prediction error, and finally achieve the highest
overall material utilization rate. This paper discusses the related theory, constructs the
mathematical model of LSTM-2DCSP, simulates the parts demand data by Monte-Carlo
simulation method, and verifies the effectiveness of the LSTM-2DCSP.

The following parts of this paper include: the second section describes the mathematical model of Two-Dimensional Rectangular Cutting Stock Problem (2D-CSP), the
method of column generation combined with strips construction, and the LSTM neural
networks principle; the third section constructs the LSTM-2DCSP model, and introduces the working process of the model. The fourth section carries on the simulation
experiment research, carries on the analysis to the experimental result; the fifth section
gives the full text conclusion.

2   Description of 2CSV Problem

2.1   Mathematical Model of Two-Dimensional Rectangular Cutting Stock Problem (2D-CSP)

Guillotine cutting is an edge to edge cutting method, which is widely used in the field
of cutting processing [16]. The cutting methods we studied are guillotine cutting, the
materials (bins) and parts (items) are rectangular.

In the 2D-CSP, the length, width and price of each bins are recorded as follows:
L_i, W_i, V_i, (i = 1, 2 ... K); The length and width of each items are recorded as follows:
l_j, w_j, (j = 1, 2 ... M), d_i is the demand of the i − th item. In order to meet the cutting

conditions and minimize the total cost of bins, the following models can be constructed:

$$\min \ ZC = \sum_{K=1}^{K} \sum_{j=1}^{n_k} X_j^k V_K$$

$$s.t \begin{cases} \sum_{k=1}^{K} \sum_{j=1}^{n_k} X_j^k a_{ij}^k \geq d_i, \ i = 1, 2 \ldots K; \ j = 1, 2 \ldots M \\ X_j^k \geq 0 \text{ and integer}, \ k = 1, 2, \ldots M \\ a_j^k \text{ is a kind of layout on the } k - \text{th bin} \end{cases} \tag{1}$$

Among them, ZC is the objective function, which represents the minimum value of the total price of bins; V_K is the price of the $k -$ th bin; k is the number of bin; X_j^k is the number of $k -$ th bin used in j cutting layout; n_K is the total number of cutting plans on the $K -$ th bin; d_i is the demand for the i —th item; a_{ij}^k is the quantity of the $i -$ th item that can be obtained on the $K -$ th bin using the $j -$ th cutting method. In this model, all a_{ij}^k items are generated by the column generation. Each column $a_{.j}^k$ represents a feasible cutting method on the corresponding bins.

2.2 Long Short-Term Memory (LSTM) Neural Networks

Long Short-Term Memory (LSTM) neural networks is a special kind of Recurrent Neural Network (RNN). LSTM can not only effectively deal with the continuity of time series information [17], but also effectively solve the problems of gradient disappearance and gradient explosion in the long sequence training process by adding three information control units in the hidden layer unit.

When the current time is t, the output value h(t) is not only related to the input x(t), but also to the output value h(t − 1) at the previous time. The hidden layer unit A of LSTM can transmit the output state h(t − 1) from the previous time to the next time, and the current output state h(t) is determined by the state h(t − 1) and the current input x(t). LSTM controls the activity of the whole cell by adding three control units (input gate, forget gate and output gate) in the hidden unit layer to determine whether the information is retained. Input gate, forgetting gate and output gate control input state, output state and memory cell state respectively, thus completing the update of the previous state. Its mathematical expression is as follows:

$$i(t) = \sigma (W_{ix}(t)x(t) + W_{ih}(t)h(t - 1) + b_i(t))$$
$$f(t) = \sigma \left(W_{fx}(t)x(t) + W_{fh}(t)h(t - 1) + b_f(t) \right) \tag{2}$$
$$o(t) = \sigma (W_{ox}(t)x(t) + W_{oh}(t)h(t - 1) + b_o(t))$$

$W(t)$ is the weight coefficient matrix, and the weight coefficient matrix of $i(t)$ is $W_{ix}(t)$ in the same order, $b(t)$ is the offset matrix, $b_i(t)$ is the offset matrix of $i(t)$, σ is sigmoid function, tan is hyperbolic tangent function, and state information $C(t)$, hidden layer output $h(t)$ and network output $y(t)$ can be expressed as follows:

$$(t) = f(t)C(t - 1) + i(t)\tan(W_{cx}(t)x(t) + W_{ch}(t)h(t - 1) + b_c(t))$$
$$h(t) = o(t)\tan(C(t) \tag{3}$$
$$y(t) = W_{yh}(t)h(t) + b_y(t)$$

The process of each sequence index position can be summarized as: update the output of forgetting gate, updating the output of input gate, updating cell state, updating output gate output, updating the prediction output of current sequence index.

The Master Production Schedule (MPS) is to determine the specific production quantity of a product in a period, usually in a week. The demand of each items in the next seven days is predicted by LSTM according to the historical simulation data.

3 Two-Dimensional Rectangular Cutting Stock Problem Based on LSTM Prediction Demand (LSTM-2DCSP)

LSTM-2DCSP model aims at minimizing the total value of materials (bins) consumed in the process of multi batch cutting, and carries out the layout from the perspective of multi batch cutting. The historical demand of each part (item) is counted and used as the training set. The LSTM model is constructed to predict the items demand in MPS in the future, and the predicted demand will be centralized. In the process of layout, firstly, the strips generated by the strip construction are used to arrange on each kind of bins, and an initial solution is obtained, which is added to the model. Secondly, the method of column generation is used for iterative solution to obtain the optimal layout.

In this model, according to its own characteristics, LSTM controls the data flow direction through the control gate, circulates the sequence information (the demand of different items) and predicts the demand of different items in the next batch. The prediction results are transformed into constraints, and the strip construction and the method of column generation are used to carry out the layout on bins, so as to obtain the overall optimal layout of the multi batch 2D-CSP. The strip construction method can simplify the Two-Dimensional Rectangular Cutting Stock Problem (2D-CSP) into One-Dimensional Rectangular Cutting Stock Problem (1D-CSP), and the column generation is used to solve the problem, which significantly improves the efficiency of the model.

Based on the 2D-CSP Problem, the predicted demand of the items is added into Eq. 2 as a constraint condition.

$$\min ZC = \sum_{K=1}^{K} \sum_{j=1}^{n_k} X_j^k V_K \tag{4}$$

$$s.t \begin{cases} \sum_{k=1}^{K} \sum_{j=1}^{n_k} X_j^k a_{ij}^k \geq \sum_{w=1}^{s} d_{jw}, \ i = 1, 2 \ldots K; \ j = 1, 2 \ldots M; \ w = 1, 2 \ldots s \\ X_j^k \geq 0 \text{ and integer}, \ k = 1, 2, \ldots M \\ a_j^k \text{ is a kind of layout on the k} - \text{th bin} \end{cases}$$

We assume that a Manufacturing cycle has s days, and there are M kinds of items to be cut. The demand of the j − th items on the w − th day is recorded as the demand d_{jw}, ($w = 1, 2 \ldots s$).

The actual number of items produced must meet the demand for each item. However, there are deviations in the prediction results. When the total predicted demand is lower than the actual total demand, compensation cutting is required to meet the actual demand. Compensation cutting is the arrangement of shortages and missing items independently, with the number of missing items as a constraint.

4   Experimental Results and Analysis

4.1   Experimental Condition

The hardware conditions for calculation and test are: AMD Ryzen7 1700, 3.45 Ghz, CPUGPU: NVIDIA GeForceRTX2060 6G, DDR4 2733 MHz 48G memory, Windows 10 operating system.

4.2   Experimental Data

We have investigated the cutting stock process of a glass manufacturer and obtained the specifications of typical bins and items as shown in Tables 1 and 2.

Table 1. Bins example data

Name of bins	Length	Width	Price
Bin1	3050	2150	150.82
Bin2	3300	2440	185.2
Bin3	2400	1830	101.02
Bin4	2600	2200	131.56

Table 2. Items example data

Name of items	Length	Width
Item1	560	450
Item 2	1200	600
Item 3	980	320
Item 4	360	190

Originally, a great many historical demand data should be prepared to train the LSTM to achieve a satisfactory prediction accuracy. However, we failed to do that for reason of commercial confidentiality. In such a situation, Monte-Carlo simulation method is used to simulate data sets to verify the validity of the proposed model. We create simulation data sets based on a few obtained actual historical demand data, and use them to train and test our model. The demand for each item is assumed to be sinusoidal periodic. In order to make the demand data general, stochastic disturbance team subject to normal distribution are linearly superimposed on the simulated sinusoidal periodic data. The mean and variance of the normal distribution are set as the sample mean and variance of each item, which are calculated from the obtained historical demand data, as shown in Table 3.

10000 pieces of demand data of each kind of items are simulated, among which 7700 pieces are used as training data and 2100 pieces are used as test data. We randomly

Table 3. Data of normal distribution stochastic disturbance team of items

Name of items	Mean	Variance
Item 1	98.33	11.05
Item 2	80.51	6.69
Item 3	89.17	5.53
Item 4	92.67	6.68

select 7 consecutive pieces of data from the remaining 200 pieces of data as the actual parts demand (shown in Table 4).

Table 4. Actual demand data of items

Item name	The first batch	The second batch	The third batch	The fourth batch	The fifth batch	The sixth batch	The seventh batch
Item1	96	102	105	120	100	103	103
Item2	95	102	93	90	91	87	89
Item3	100	107	106	107	104	99	96
Item4	110	105	110	110	113	107	105

4.3 Experimental Process and Result Analysis

Items Demand Prediction Performance Experiment. Accurate prediction of item demand is the core of this model, so the prediction performance of the model is tested by experiments. Aiming at the LSTM-2DCSP model, the influence of its prediction window (i.e. step-size λ) on the prediction performance is studied. The LSTM-2DCSP with $\lambda = 800$, $\lambda = 1300$ and $\lambda = 1800$ was selected for the control experiment.

The Mean Absolute Percentage Error (MAPE), Root Mean Square Error (RMSE) and Coefficient of Determination (R^2 score) are used as the evaluation indexes of the model.

Mean Absolute Percentage Error (MAPE):
MAPE not only calculates the difference between the real value and the predicted value, but also considers the ratio of the difference to the real value.

$$\text{MAPE} = \sum_{t=1}^{n} \left| \frac{y_i - f(x_i)}{y_i} \right| \times \frac{100}{n} \tag{5}$$

Root Mean Square Error (RMSE).

The RMSE is very sensitive to the prediction error, which can well reflect the accuracy of the prediction.

$$\text{RMSE} = \sqrt{\frac{1}{n}\sum_{t=1}^{n}(y_i - f(x_i))^2} \tag{6}$$

Coefficient of Determination (R^2 score)

$$R^2 = 1 - \frac{\sum_{t=1}^{n}(y_i - f(x_i))^2}{\sum_{t=1}^{n}(y_i - mean)^2} \tag{7}$$

The Coefficient of Determination is used to judge the fitting degree of regression equation, and can be used to measure the prediction ability of the model. The larger the Coefficient of Determination is, the better the prediction performance of the model is.

We adjust the prediction window λ of LSTM-2DCSP model to 800,1300 and 1800, and test each of them on the test set. The evaluation indexes of the prediction results of the four items are shown in the Table 5.

Table 5. Evaluation index table of LSTM-2DCSP

λ	Evaluation indexes	Item1	Item 2	Item 3	Item 4
$\lambda = 800$	R^2	0.9691	0.9278	0.8891	0.9163
	RMSE	2.0683	2.0683	2.0683	2.0683
	MAPE	2.0656	2.4699	2.2402	2.1561
$\lambda = 1300$	R^2	0.9677	0.924	0.9182	0.9412
	RMSE	1.9836	1.9836	1.9836	1.9836
	MAPE	1.9892	2.3478	2.1222	2.061
$\lambda = 1800$	R^2	0.9689	0.8995	0.8689	0.9153
	RMSE	2.1406	2.1406	2.1406	2.1406
	MAPE	2.1418	2.5685	2.2923	2.2699

The maximum value of Coefficient of Determination (R^2) is 1. The closer the R^2 to 1, the better the fitting degree of regression line; conversely, the smaller the R^2, the worse the fitting degree of regression line. Through the demand predict performance experiment, it can be seen that the LSTM-2DCSP ($\lambda = 800$, $\lambda = 1300$ and $\lambda = 1800$) has good prediction performance and the overall prediction effect of the four items is the best when $\lambda = 1300$. Compared with three experiments, it is found that the RMSE and MPAE of $\lambda = 1300$ are less than those of $\lambda = 800$ and $\lambda = 1800$.In the LSTM-2DCSP ($\lambda = 1300$) model, the test error of the prediction results of the four items is shown in Fig. 1.

When LSTM deals with the continuity of time series information, it is necessary to add λ data to cells. When λ increases from zero, the relevant data in cells will increase, and its prediction performance will improve continuously. However, the information

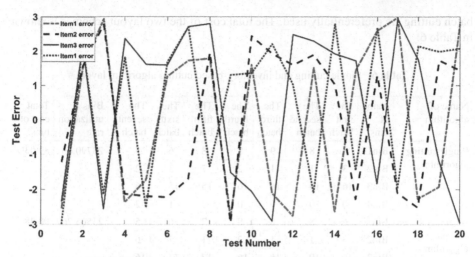

Fig. 1. The test error of the prediction results of the four items

capacity of the hidden layer (the number of hidden units) of LSTM is limited. When λ increases to a certain limit and exceeds its saturation point, the algorithm will appear overfitting, which is not sensitive to the subsequent data, so the prediction performance will decline. In this item demand predication performance experiment, when ($\lambda = 800$), the hidden layer information capacity of LSTM does not reach the saturation point, and its prediction performance is not optimal; when $\lambda = 1800$, the hidden layer information capacity of LSTM network exceeds the saturation point, and the prediction performance is reduced due to overfitting. Therefore, in the use of LSTM-2DCSP, it is necessary to select the appropriate prediction window λ.

LSTM-2DCSP ($\lambda = 1300$) is selected as the experimental model in the Optimization Performance Comparison Experiment.

Optimization Performance Comparison Experiment. In order to verify the effectiveness of the proposed model, a comparative experiment was carried out with Single Cutting (pursuing the optimal cutting of each batch without considering the use of the surplus material in inventory) and Inventory-Based Cutting (pursuing the optimal cutting of each batch, including the surplus material into the inventory and giving priority to the next cutting). The indicators of comparison are the bins utilization rate and the total cost of bins.

Bins utilization rate = total area of items/total area of bins;
Total cost of bins = number of sheets of bins * unit price of bins.

The Single Cutting algorithm performs the layout of seven batches of cutting stock problems, and completes one batch at a time; Inventory-Based Cutting algorithm performs the layout of seven batches of cutting stock problems, and the remaining bins are added to the inventory after each batch cutting is completed, and the remaining bins in the next batch cutting are preferentially used. The total cost of the two layout schemes is shown in Table 6:

Table 6. Single cutting and inventory-based cutting algorithm layout

Name of algorithm	Name of bins	The first batch	The second batch	The third batch	The fourth batch	The fifth batch	The sixth batch	The seventh batch	Bins utilization rate	Total cost of bins
Single cutting algorithm	Bin1	6	8	9	8	8	6	5	23790.66	89.03%
	Bin2	3	1	1	2	7	3	2		
	Bin3	16	19	16	16	15	15	16		
	Bin4	0	0	0	0	2	1	2		
Inventory-based cutting algorithm	Bin1	6	8	8	8	7	6	5	23565.76	90.48%
	Bin2	3	1	1	2	1	7	6		
	Bin3	16	19	16	16	17	14	16		
	Bin4	0	0	1	1	1	2	2		

The LSTM-2DCSP ($\lambda = 1300$) considers cutting from an overall point of view. The Table 7. gives a detailed prediction demand for each layout, in which Item1 produces 731, Item2 651, Item3 715 and Item 4 764. Table 8 shows the specific layout of LSTM-2DCSP ($\lambda = 1300$); Fig. 2 shows the layout of some bins.

Table 7. Item prediction demand data

Item prediction demand							
Item name	The first batch	The second batch	The third batch	The fourth batch	The fifth batch	The sixth batch	The seventh batch
Item1	99	108	113	124	95	98	94
Item2	91	102	99	92	92	87	88
Item3	102	106	103	108	105	96	95
Item4	105	106	115	112	112	110	104

Comparing the actual items demand, we find that Item3 less 4 pieces. Therefore, the less produced items are arranged again. We use a piece of Bin3 for compensated cutting. Bins utilization rate and the total cost of bins of LSTM-2CSV ($\lambda = 1300$) are shown in Table 9.

Through the optimization performance comparison experiment, it is found that the LSTM-2DCSP greatly improves the bins utilization rate compared with Single Cutting and Inventory-Based Cutting Algorithm, and its total cost also decreases with the increase of the bins utilization rate. Compared with Single Cutting, the total cost of bins obtained

Table 8. Specific layout of LSTM-2DCSP ($\lambda = 1300$)

Specification of bins	Number	Bins utilization rate	450*560	600*1200	320*980	190*360
2150*3050	53	98.129	424		689	265
2440*3300	1	98.296	8	2	14	1
2440*3300	1	97.645	20		9	
2440*3300	1	97.521	25	1	2	3
2440*3300	8	98.405	232			72
2440*3300	1	98.584	22			35
2440*3300	2	97.690				230
1830*2400	108	98.361		648		
2200*2600	1	97.559			1	77
2200*2600	1	96.860				81

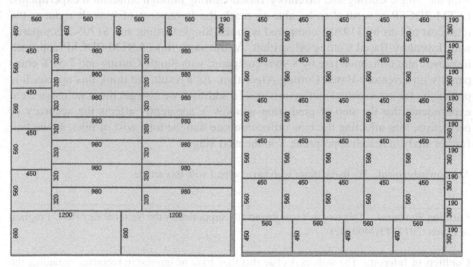

Fig. 2. The layout of some bins.

by LSTM-2DCSP ($\lambda = 1300$) is lower, reducing \$1930.1. LSTM-2DCSP combines the idea of centralized cutting to centralize the demand of items longitudinal and enlarge the solution space of multi-batch two-dimensional cutting stock problem. LSTM-2DCSP is more effective and reasonable than t Inventory-Based Cutting Algorithm which considers inventory separately to expand solution space.

Table 9. Bins utilization rate and the total cost of bins of LSTM-2DCSP ($\lambda = 1300$)

Name of bins	Number	Total cost of bins	Bins utilization rate
Bin1	53	21860.56	97.99%
Bin2	14		
Bin3	109		
Bin4	2		

5 Conclusion

We proposed an approach based on demand prediction with LSTM for solving multi-batch 2D cutting stock problems (LSTM-2DCSP). Inspired by the thought of centralized cutting, the demands of cutting items of the subsequent batches are predicted, based on which an overall layout cutting for these continuous batches is carried out. Compared with the Single Cutting and Inventory-Based Cutting through simulation experiments, LSTM-2DCSP is verified to be able to reach the lower cost of bins. It reduces the total cost of bins by $1930.1 compared with the Single Cutting and $1705.2 compared with Inventory-Based Cutting Algorithm. At the same time, LSTM-2DCSP approach improves bins utilization rate by 8.96% compared with Single Cutting and 7.51% compared with Inventory-Based Cutting Algorithm. As a result, we think this approach is promising for use in actual cutting process. In addition, we also get the conclusion from experiments that the step of prediction window λ apparently affects the accuracy of prediction, thus affecting the bins utilization rate and the total cost of bins, so we will further study to search appropriate λ in the next stage.

Acknowledgement. We thank those who have helped with this article.

Funding *Statement*. This research was financially supported by the National Key R&D Program of China (2017YFB1400301).

Conflicts of Interest. The authors declare that they have no interest in reporting regarding the present study.

References

1. Kenyon, C., Remila, E.: A near-optimal solution to a two-dimensional cutting stock problem. Math. Oper. Res. **25**(4), 645–656 (2000)
2. Yanasse, H.H., Zinober, A.S., Harris, R.G.: Two-dimensional cutting stock with multiple stock sizes. J. Oper. Res. Soc. **42**(8), 673–683 (1991)
3. Gilmore, P.C., Gomory, R.E.: Multistage cutting stock problems of two and more dimensions. Oper. Res. **13**(1), 94–120 (1965)
4. Błażewicz, J., Hawryluk, P., Walkowiak, R.: Using a tabu search approach for solving the two-dimensional irregular cutting problem. Ann. Oper. Res. **41**(4), 313–325 (1993)

5. Mundim, L.R., Andretta, M., Carravilla, M.A., Oliveira, J.F.: A general heuristic for two-dimensional nesting problems with limited-size containers. Int. J. Prod. Res. **56**(1–2), 709–732 (2017)
6. Ma, N., Liu, Y., Zhou, Z.: Two heuristics for the capacitated multi-period cutting stock problem with pattern setup cost. Comput. Oper. Res. **109**(9), 218–229 (2019)
7. Reinders, M.P.: Cutting stock optimization and integral production planning for centralized wood processing. Math. Comput. Model. **16**(1), 37–55 (1992)
8. Reinders, M.P.: Tactical planning for a cutting stock system. J. Oper. Res. Soc. **44**(7), 645–657 (1993)
9. Qin, B., Yan, C.P., Wang, K., Liu, F.: Grouping optimization method of large-scale parts supporting centralized cutting stock. Jisuanji Jicheng Zhizao Xitong/Comput. Integr. Manuf. Syst. CIMS **18**(5), 943–949 (2012)
10. Kos, L., Duhovnik, J.: Cutting optimization with variable-sized stock and inventory status data. Int. J. Prod. Res. **40**(10), 2289–2301 (2002)
11. Ayadi, O., Cheikhrouhou, N., Masmoudi, F., et al.: A new formulation of the two-dimensional cutting-stock problem with consideration of demand planning. Int. J. Adv. Oper. Manag. **4**(1–2), 27–61 (2012)
12. Zhao, J., Qu, H., Zhao, J., Jiang, D.: Towards traffic matrix prediction with LSTM recurrent neural networks. Electron. Lett. **54**(9), 566–568 (2018)
13. Petersen, N.C., Rodrigues, F., Pereira, F.C.: Multi-output bus travel time prediction with convolutional LSTM neural network. Expert Syst. Appl. **120**(4), 426–435 (2019)
14. Cortez, B., Carrera, B., Kim, Y.J., Jung, J.Y.: An architecture for emergency event prediction using LSTM recurrent neural networks. Expert Syst. Appl. **97**(5), 315–324 (2018)
15. Xu, X., Yoneda, M.: Multitask air-quality prediction based on LSTM-autoencoder model. IEEE Trans. Cybern. **99**(10), 1–10 (2019)
16. Cintra, G.F., Miyazawa, F.K., Wakabayashi, Y., Xavier, E.C.: Algorithms for two-dimensional cutting stock and strip packing problems using dynamic programming and column generation. Eur. J. Oper. Res. **191**(1), 61–85 (2008)
17. Hochreiter, S., Schmidhuber, J.: ONG short-term memory. Neural Comput. **9**(8), 1735–1780 (1997)

The Identification of Slope Crack Based on Convolutional Neural Network

Yaoyao Li[1,2], Pengyu Liu[1,2(✉)], Shanji Chen[3], Kebin Jia[1,2], and Tianyu Liu[1,2]

[1] Faculty of Information Technology, Beijing University of Technology, Beijing 100124, China
liupengyu@bjut.edu.cn
[2] Beijing Laboratory of Advanced Information Networks, Beijing 100124, China
[3] Qinghai Nationalities University, Xining 810000, China

Abstract. In the process of construction and operation of mountain roads, slope disasters such as landslide and collapse are often encountered, which seriously affect the transportation infrastructure and safe operation in China. Cracks are the early symptoms of most slope diseases. By monitoring the change trend of cracks, the displacement trajectory of the slope body can be reflected in time, which is of great significance for landslide monitoring and early warning, so the safety detection is concentrated in this stage. In recent years, great progress has been made in deep learning-based computer vision methods, which have the advantages of simple observation method, low cost, wide detection area and sustainable monitoring. In view of this, a pixel level segmentation method of slope cracks based on deep convolutional neural network is proposed in this paper. According to the shape characteristics of slope cracks, a deep convolutional neural network was designed. The network was trained on the self-made slope image data set, and the IOU on the validation set reached 75.26%, which realized the precise segmentation and recognition of cracks. Experimental results show that the model has a good ability to characterize the slope cracks, can accurately extract the slope cracks, and provides a reliable basis for the formulation of slope early warning and disaster relief programs.

Keywords: Slope hazards · Crack · Convolutional neural networks

1 Introduction

In recent years, as the country's overall strength has increased, the construction of large-scale mountain expressways has become more and more intense. Highway slopes in mountainous areas of China are characterized by a large number of slopes, steep slopes and bare surface leakage. Moreover, the internal geology of slopes is complicated, and the development of gaps and stability of slopes are prominent. In the process of construction and operation, the mountain highway is faced with the threat of landslide, debris flow, collapse and other geological disasters, and the slope problem seriously restricts and hinders the further development of the mountain highway in China. Therefore, highway slope stability monitoring has become the focus of engineers and scholars.

© Springer Nature Switzerland AG 2021
X. Sun et al. (Eds.): ICAIS 2021, CCIS 1423, pp. 16–26, 2021.
https://doi.org/10.1007/978-3-030-78618-2_2

Collapse and landslide are the two most common types of highway slope hazards. The creep crack of the potential collapse body is reflected in the collapse and increases with the development of time. Landslide mostly refers to the overall sliding of rock and soil along one or more cracks under the action of external stress. From the movement characteristics of these two geological disasters, it can be seen that cracks are the early symptoms of most slope diseases, and the increase, expansion and evolution of cracks are intuitive reflections of slope instability. Therefore, capturing the changes of cracks can be used as an important reference for real-time monitoring of slope conditions. At present, slope disasters mainly use optical fiber sensing technology [1, 2], three-dimensional laser scanning technology [3] and manual hand-held monitoring instruments as monitoring methods, but three-dimensional laser scanning technology has poor anti-interference, high cost, and slow processing speed; optical fiber sensing Technical construction is difficult and easy to break; manual monitoring requires a lot of manpower and material resources, and the real-time data monitoring cannot be guaranteed.

With the continuous development of deep learning, crack recognition technology based on computer vision becomes possible. Using computer vision technology to process the crack pictures through professional cameras, identify and mark the contours of the crack area, calculate the crack area, count the crack development direction, and constantly monitor the periodic law of slope disaster occurrence, which makes up for the shortcomings of traditional detection methods and is efficient The advantages of high and low cost can play a very helpful role in monitoring and early warning of slope landslides.

2 Related Research

Slope stability has been studied for a hundred years, during which the problem of slope stability has been perplexing scholars. Xue Jinchun [4] used the dynamic cluster analysis method of mathematical statistics to study the calculation parameters of slope stability, and used the dynamic cluster analysis method to analyze the stability of the studied slope; Mohammad et al. [5] studied an antenna sensor that can monitor the growth of fatigue cracks with sub-millimeter resolution, but this method can only be used for a small number of cracks and cannot meet the conditions of large-scale cracks; S Uhlemann et al. [6] proposed a ground-based monitoring technology that uses traditional inclinometers and inclinometers on the ground array to transmit data, but the location of the sensor equipment on the ground array cannot be accurately determined; Xing Zeyuan and others [7] applied three-dimensional laser scanning technology to slope monitoring, but its reflection accuracy and realization of characteristic interest points were low.

In recent years, deep learning has achieved encouraging results in computer vision[8–10], and pixel-level image segmentation algorithms based on deep learning have gradually begun to be used in slope cracks. H. K. Shin et al. [11] and Gibb et al. [12] respectively used convolutional neural networks to detect cracks on the concrete surface, but this method can only complete the location of the crack detection, and cannot complete the measurement of the length and width of the crack; Yamaguchi et al. [13] proposed an image-based filtering model based on the connectivity of the brightness or gray level inside the crack and the shape of the connected area to detect the location of the crack; Nishiyama et al. [14] placed targets on both sides of the crack, and calculated the width of the crack by judging the change in the position of the target. However, the above method has certain limitations in use. The crack detection effect is very sensitive to the unevenness of light. The accuracy of the measurement of fine cracks is poor. Only the detection of the crack area is completed, but the measurement of the crack width is not fully realized. And error analysis.

In summary, the research and design of an algorithm that can accurately and automatically identify slope cracks has great application value for highway safety. Taking into account the outstanding performance of convolutional neural network in the field of image recognition, this article first uses professional cameras to take and screen a large number of slope crack pictures, and under the guidance of geotechnical experts, construct a large-scale slope crack data set. Based on this data set, this paper proposes a slope crack recognition network based on convolutional neural network, which can extract targeted features of slope cracks. The results show that this model has a good effect on slope crack recognition.

3   Fracture Identification Network Model

This section mainly introduces the complete framework, training method and evaluation index of deep convolutional neural network for crack detection.

3.1   Network Framework

In this paper, a deep convolutional neural network with residual network is mainly used. The neural network is mainly composed of input layer, convolution layer, pooling layer, activation function and output layer. The structure of the full convolutional neural network designed in this paper is shown in Fig. 1. Firstly, the shallow layer information is extracted through a 3×3 convolution layer and pooling layer, and then the network is constructed by repeating four modules, each module contains a different number of feature extraction units and a down-sampling unit. Finally, feature classification is realized through convolution, global pooling and full connection layer.

Feature extraction unit mainly use the point by point convolution, expansion random hybrid convolution and channel depth of these four convolution, first using the depth can be separated into 4 standard convolution and point by point convolution, used the jump connection, the residual extraction, finally the hybrid channel random thoughts, disrupted between channels of information, improve the understanding ability of the model. The feature extraction unit is shown in Fig. 2.

First, the down-sampling unit integrates the disrupted channel information through point-by-point convolution, then down-sampling is completed by means of average pooling and maximum pooling, and finally feature extraction is realized by using global pooling and full connection layer. The down-sampling unit is shown in Fig. 3.

Convolutional Layer. The convolutional layer is composed of several convolutional neural units, and the image features can be extracted through the convolution operation of the image and the convolution kernel. Common convolution kernels are 1*1, 3*3, 5*5. Through the convolution operation, dimensionality reduction and feature extraction of the input image can be achieved.

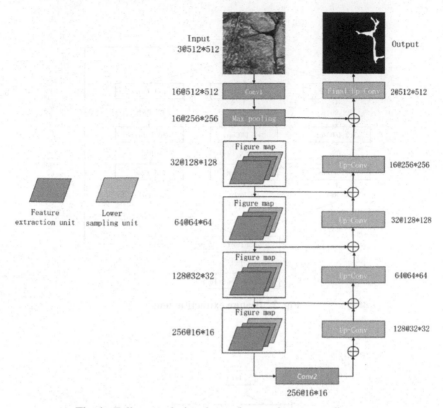

Fig. 1. Fully convolutional neural network structure diagram

Pooling Layer. The pooling layer is also called the down-sampling layer. The pooling layer is sandwiched between successive convolutional layers to compress the amount of data and parameters to avoid overfitting. Common pooling operations include average pooling and maximum pooling. The main functions of the pooling layer are feature invariance and feature dimensionality reduction. Feature invariance is the invariance of feature scale. Translating, rotating, and scaling an image will not affect the feature expression of the image. Feature dimensionality reduction means to retain the main features of the image while reducing the parameters and calculations, avoiding over-fitting and improving the generalization ability of the model.

Fully Connected Layer. The fully connected layer refers to the local features extracted by the previous convolutional layer after dimensionality reduction by the pooling layer, and then recombined into a complete graph through the weight matrix. The fully connected layer converts the two-dimensional feature map output by the convolution into a one-dimensional vector, which plays a role of classification in the entire convolutional neural network.

Relu. The fully connected layer refers to the local features extracted by the previous convolutional layer after dimensionality reduction by the pooling layer, and then recombined

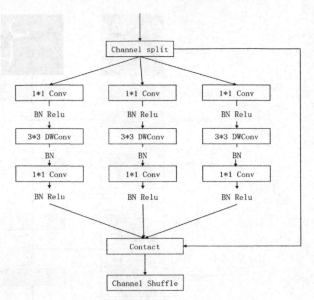

Fig. 2. Feature extraction unit

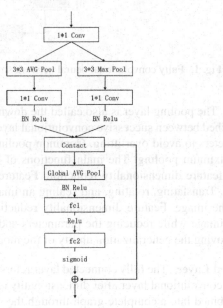

Fig. 3. Down-sampling unit

into a complete graph through the weight matrix. The fully connected layer converts the two-dimensional feature map output by the convolution into a one-dimensional vector, which plays a role of classification in the entire convolutional neural network.

$$f(z) = \max(0, z) \tag{1}$$

ReLU is a function that takes the maximum value, and when the input is greater than 0, the input is equal to the input; When the input is less than 0, the output is 0. The problem of gradient disappearance can be solved by using ReLU function, and the calculation speed is relatively fast.

Residual Block. As the number of network layers increases, the network will degrade, and the loss of the training set will decrease gradually and then tend to saturate. When the network depth is further increased, the training set loss will increase instead. When the network degenerates, the shallow network can achieve better training effect than the deep network, then the residual network can be used.

A residual velocity can be expressed as:

$$H(x) = x + \mathcal{F}(x) \tag{2}$$

The residual block consists of a direct mapping part and a residual part. Where H (x) is the direct mapping part, and F(x) is the residual part, which is generally composed of two or three convolution operations. The structure of residual blocks is shown in Fig. 4.

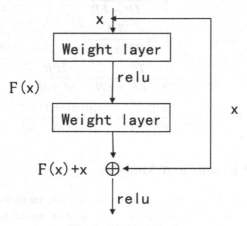

Fig. 4. Residual block

3.2 Training Methods

Loss Function. In this paper, the cross entropy loss function is used to determine the proximity between the actual output and the expected output of the network. As shown in type

$$loss = -\frac{1}{n}\sum_x \left[y ln a + (1 - y) ln(1 - a) \right] \tag{3}$$

Where, X represents the sample, Y represents the actual label, A represents the predicted output, and N represents the total sample amount. The smaller the cross-entropy loss function is, the closer the predicted value of the model is to the real value.

Optimization Algorithm. In this paper, stochastic gradient descent SGD is adopted as the optimization algorithm. By gradient updating each sample, the speed is fast and new samples can be added. Remember to:

$$\theta_{n+1} = \theta_n - \gamma \nabla_\theta L_R(\theta_n) \tag{4}$$

3.3 The Evaluation Index

Semantic segmentation is the process of classifying pixels in an image according to different characteristics. Crack segmentation is to distinguish between cracks and background pixels. Commonly used semantic segmentation performance evaluation indicators include precision (P), recall, F1 score and intersection ratio (IOU) [15–18], where P represents the true positive class in the sample predicted to be the positive class The proportion, R represents the proportion of the positive class in the sample that is correctly predicted, F1 numerically represents the harmonic mean of the two, and IOU refers to the ratio of the intersection and union of the segmentation result and the two sets of true labels.

$$P = \frac{TP}{TP + FP} \tag{5}$$

$$R = \frac{TP}{TP + FN} \tag{6}$$

$$F_1 = \frac{2TP}{2TP + FP + FN} = \frac{2PR}{P + R} \tag{7}$$

$$IOU = \frac{TP}{TP + FN + FP} = \frac{area(SR \cap GT)}{area(SR \cup GT)} \tag{8}$$

4   Experimental Results and Analysis

This section introduces the specific experimental content, including data sets, experimental configuration and model training, visualization of model results, experimental results and analysis.

4.1   Data Set

Data Preparation. In the field of slope, there is no open slope crack image data sets. Therefore, in this paper, image data of slope cracks were taken on site in Shifangshan District, Beijing, and the data set was screened under the guidance of geotechnical experts. Images with no useful information and images with repeated perspectives were deleted to form the initial slope crack data set. There are 312 pieces of this data set with resolutions of 4624*3472, 1920*1080 and 4000*300, respectively.

Construction of Slope Fracture Data Set. Due to the large size of the original data images collected, labelme software will lose a lot of texture details, so the original images need to be segmented into 512*512. There are 638 images after segmentation.

4.2   Experimental Configuration and Model Training

This experiment is carried out under the Windows operating system, using the MxNet framework, and the programming language is python3.6. The data set is divided into three parts: training set, validation set and test set according to the ratio of 8:1:1. The first two are used to build the optimization model, and the latter is used for model performance testing.

In the training process, the adaptive gradient optimization algorithm is selected. When the training parameter is set, the data size of each batch is set to 10, the learning rate is 3e-4, and the default number of iterations is 1000, but it is added in the training process The early stop mechanism stops training when the loss is not reduced for 5 consecutive iterations.

4.3   Experimental Results and Analysis

According to the above data sets and training methods, the convolutional neural network based on VGG16, VGG19 and UNET is trained, and the training results are shown in Table 1.

Table 1. Comparison of network results

Model	P/%	Loss	IOU/%
VGG16	91.32	0.00147	66.49
VGG19	92.61	0.00131	66.85
Unet	94.01	0.000629	73.73
Proposed method	96.89	0.000570	75.26

As can be seen from the table, compared with VGG16, VGG19 and UNET, the IOU of the method proposed in this paper is 75.26%, which has a good effect.

The untrained crack images are used to test the segmentation performance of the model, and the test images A1-A5 are taken as examples to analyze the test performance of the model. The diversity of test data can reflect the overall performance of the model, such as edge extraction ability, detail identification ability, anti-noise ability, etc. Images A1, A3, and A5 contain a lot of noise interference (surface potholes), and the cracks in images A2 and A4 are uneven in thickness, especially the bends are too thin and difficult to be detected. It can be seen from Fig. 5 that the segmentation result of the image is relatively close to the annotation form, indicating that the model has a certain degree of adaptability to actual application scenarios.

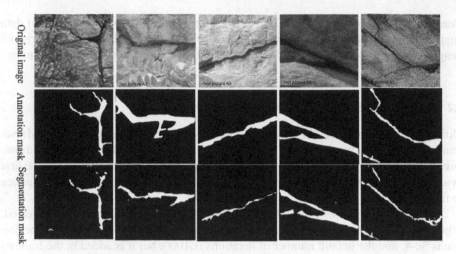

Fig. 5. Display of crack results of test images A1–A5

5   Conclusion

According to the characteristics of slope fractures, based on the deep network structure of convolutional neural network and combined with the self-made data set of slope fractures, this paper proposes a morphological segmentation model suitable for slope fractures, constructs a simulation scene and sets up a simulation experiment. The results show that deep learning has incomparable advantages in slope detection.

The automatic detection and early warning of slope crack can reduce the identification error caused by subjective factors to a great extent, save manpower cost, and have indicative significance to the safety of highway slope.

Although deep learning has made revolutionary progress in computer vision, its application in slope disaster is still in its infancy and exploration stage, and still faces many difficulties and challenges. On the one hand, compared with the traditional identification method [19], the features of the deep semantic segmentation model [20–23] need to be learned from the big data, and the model performance will highly depend on the amount and diversity of training data. However, the amount of slope fracture data constructed in this paper is still insufficient, so more data should be taken in the later work. On the other hand, the detection accuracy of deep semantic segmentation network in this paper still needs to be further improved.

Acknowledgement. This thesis was completed under the careful guidance of my tutor Professor Liu Pengyu. My tutor's profound professional knowledge, rigorous academic attitude and excellent work style had a profound influence on me, which not only enabled me to set a lofty academic goal, but also enabled me to master the truth of dealing with people. Here, I would like to express my high respect and heartfelt thanks to my tutor. Through the writing of this paper, I can systematically and comprehensively master the knowledge related to slope disaster monitoring and in-depth learning, and learn from the valuable experience of many scholars, which is a rare treasure for me. Due to the limited level of this theory, some of the points in the paper are inevitably inadequate, teachers and experts are welcome to criticize and correct.

Funding Statement. This paper is supported by the following funds: National Key R&D Program of China (2018YFF01010100), National natural science foundation of China (61672064), Basic Research Program of Qinghai Province under Grants No. 2021-ZJ-704 and Advanced information network Beijing laboratory (PXM2019_014204_5000 29).

Conflicts of Interest. The authors declare that they have no conflicts of interest to report regarding the present study.

References

1. Fang, W., Zhang, F., Ding, Y., Sheng, J.: A new sequential image prediction method based on LSTM and DCGAN. Comput. Mater. Con. **64**(1), 217–231 (2020)
2. Wang, X.: Design and implementation of landslide concentrator based on multi-sensor information fusion. Southwest Jiaotong University (2019)
3. Zeyuan, X.: The application of 3D laser scanning technology in slope monitoring. Surv. Spatial Geogr. Inf. **43**(06), 222–224 (2020)
4. Xue, J., Li, X., Dong, L.: The clustering unascertained comprehensive identification method of slope stability and its application. Rock Soil Mech. (SI), 293–297 (2010)
5. Mohammad, I., Huang, H.: Monitoring fatigue crack growth and opening using antenna sensors. Smart Mater. Struct. **19**, 055023-1–055023-8 (2010)
6. Uhlemann, S., et al.: Assessment of ground-based monitoring techniques applied to landslide investigations. Geomorphology **253**, 438–451 (2016)
7. Xing, Z.: The application of three-dimensional laser scanning technology in slope monitoring. Surv. Spatial Geogr. Inf. **43**(06), 222–224 (2020)
8. Fang, W., Pang, L., Yi, W.N.: Survey on the application of deep reinforcement learning in image processing. J. Artif. Intell. **2**(1), 39–58 (2020)
9. Gu, B., Xiong, W., Bai, Z.: Human action recognition based on supervised class-specific dictionary learning with deep convolutional neural network features. Comput. Mater. Con. **63**(1), 243–262 (2020)
10. Liu, Y., Gu, X., Huang, L., Ouyang, J., Liao, M., Wu, L.: Analyzing periodicity and saliency for adult video detection. Multimedia Tools Appl. **79**(7–8), 4729–4745 (2020)
11. Shin, H.K., Ahn, Y.H., Lee, S.H., Kim, H.Y.: Digital vision based concrete compressive strength evaluating model using deep convolutional neural network. Comput. Mater. Con. **61**(3), 911–928 (2019)
12. Gibb, S., La, H.M., Louis, S.: A genetic algorithm for convolutional network structure optimization for concrete crack detection. In: 2018 IEEE Congress on Evolutionnary Computation (CEC), Piscataway, pp. 1–8. IEEE (2018)
13. Yamaguchi, T., Nakamura, S., Saegusa, R., Hashimoto, S.: Image-based crack detection for real concrete surfaces. IEEJ Trans. Electr. Electron. Eng. **3**(1), 128–135 (2008)
14. Nishiyama, S., Minakata, N., Kikuchi, T., Yano, T.: Improved digital photogrammetry technique for crack monitoring. Adv. Eng. Inform. **29**(4), 861 (2015)
15. Han, X., Zhao, Z.: Research on surface crack detection method based on computer vision technology. J. Build. Struct. **39**(S1), 418–427 (2018)
16. Wang, N., Zhao, X., Zou, Z., et al.: Autonomous damage segmentation and measurement of glazed tiles in historic buildings via deep learning. Comput. Aided Civil Infrastruct. Eng. **118**, 103291 (2020)
17. Ji, A., Xue, X., Wang, Y., Luo, X., Xue, W.: An integrated approach to automatic pixel-level crack detection and quantification of asphalt pavement. Autom. Constr. **114**, 103176 (2020)

18. Kang, D., Benipal, S.S., Gopal, D.L., Cha, Y.-J.: Hybrid pixel-level concrete crack segmentation and quantification across complex backgrounds using deep learning. Autom. Constr. **118**, 103291 (2020)
19. Wei, T., Faning, D., Yanwen, L., et al.: Application of support vector machine in concrete CT image analysis. J. Hydraul. Eng. **7**, 889–894 (2008)
20. Long, J., Shelhamer, E., Darrell, T.: Fully convolutional networks for semantic segmentation. In: Proceedings of the IEEE Conference on Computer Vision and Pattern Recognition, pp. 3431–3440 (2015)
21. Badrinarayanan, V., Kendall, A., Cipolla, R.: Segnet: a deep convolutional encoder-decoder architecture for image segmentation. IEEE Trans. Pattern Anal. Mach. Intell. **39**(12), 2481–2495 (2017)
22. Ronneberger, O., Fischer, P., Brox, T.: U-net: convolutional networks for biomedical image segmentation. In: Navab, N., Hornegger, J., Wells, W.M., Frangi, A.F. (eds.) MICCAI 2015. LNCS, vol. 9351, pp. 234–241. Springer, Cham (2015). https://doi.org/10.1007/978-3-319-24574-4_28
23. Qayyum, A., Ahmad, I., Iftikhar, M., Mazher, M.: Object detection and fuzzy-based classification using UAV data. Intell. Autom. Soft Comput. **26**(4), 693–702 (2020)

Multi-dimensional Fatigue Driving Detection Method Based on SVM Improved by the Kernel Function

Yilong Sun[1], Jieren Cheng[1,2,3](✉), Minghan Chen[1,2], Manling Zeng[1,2], Zhiwei Fan[1], Jingzheng Sun[1], Jiang Liu[1], Zhuoxian Chen[1], and Yixiu Wang[1]

[1] Hainan University, Haikou 570208, China
[2] School of Compute Science and Cyberspace Security, Hainan University, Haikou 570228, China
[3] Hainan Blockchain Technology Engineering Research Center, Haikou 570228, China

Abstract. Driver fatigue is one of the leading causes of traffic accidents. At present, fatigue driving detection has disadvantages such as low practical application effect and high equipment requirements. This paper proposes a multi-feature point non-invasive fatigue monitoring system based on a support vector machine with a hybrid kernel function. The system detects feature points through a gradient descent tree algorithm based on a cascaded regression and calculates the eye aspect ratio (EAR) and mouth aspect ratio (MAR). The heart rate is obtained through RGB image analysis combined with Euler's video magnification algorithm. Classify facial features to get fatigued. This paper is based on the Logistic and Radial Basis Polynomial Kernel (RBPK) function to improve the support vector machine, which has better learning and generalization. Finally, this paper uses the Driver Drowsiness Detection Dataset and the author's dataset to test. The classification accuracy rate for a single picture is 96.92%. In summary, the system proposed in this paper has a better recognition rate for fatigue driving detection.

Keywords: Driver fatigue · Fatigue detection · Support vector machine

1 Introduction

Traffic accidents cause thousands of people to be injured or even lose their lives every year. According to statistics from the World Health Organization (WHO), fatigued driving causes a considerable part. In this regard, fatigue driving detection technology is also developing rapidly [1]. According to the dimensionality of the acquired feature data, the current fatigue detection methods can be divided into single-dimensional detection and multi-dimensional detection. The researchers [2, 3] proposed an improved method for detecting driver fatigue by calculating the eyelid movement parameter Parcels. The Percols theory's limitations can only be applied under certain conditions. Uncertain conditions such as indoor lighting, changes in light, and head motion will cause detection errors. Researchers have found that when drivers feel tired, they show many facial features, including frequent blinking, yawning, and shaking their heads. The researcher

X. Sun et al. (Eds.): ICAIS 2021, CCIS 1423, pp. 27–40, 2021.
https://doi.org/10.1007/978-3-030-78618-2_3

Sahayad et al. [4] has pointed out that the hybrid fatigue driving detection method's reliability and accuracy that combines multiple methods are much higher than that of the method using a single sensor. Multi-dimensional fatigue driving detection is to classify multiple data items and involve convex quadratic programming problems. C Buchheim et al. [5] studied the ellipsoid boundary to determine the convex quadratic programming problem's boundary. Tao Cai et al. [6] designed the Newton-CG augmented Lagrangian algorithm for the convex quadratic constrained quadratic semi-definite programming, assuming Robin-son constraint norms, healthy second-order sufficient, and other three conditions. The assumptions are relatively strong.

Researchers [7, 8] studied a support vector machine to classify data items in the process of classification and feature selection. In classifying data items, the support vector machine's principle is to put the target vector into a high-dimensional space through nonlinear changes and find the best hyperplane to distinguish data items. Mingze Xia et al. [9] proposed using genetic algorithms to optimize the RBF parameter and error penalty function C, thus achieving better classification of the model.

Qingshuo Zhang et al. [10] proposed multicore support vector machines based on nuclear alignment, which significantly improved the model's training efficiency. The kernel function is an essential part of the support vector machine, which is divided into a linear kernel function and a polynomial kernel function. Different kernel functions determine that the support vector machine has different characteristics. M. Tanveer et al. [11] proposed a novel, precise 1-norm linear programming formula linear kernel function for twin support vector machine (TWSVM), which has good generalization ability. However, it does not have excellent learning ability and good predictive ability. G Sideratos et al. [12] proposed a probabilistic wind power prediction model based on radial basis function neural network (RBFNN), which has good learning ability but does not have a good generalization and prediction ability. VH Moghaddam [13] proposed a new kernel called Hermite orthogonal polynomial, which has good predictive ability but does not have good generalization ability and learning ability. In addition, the emergence of federated learning has greatly improved the accuracy of the fatigue driving model [14, 15].

According to previous scholars' research results, one-dimensional fatigue driving detection is easy for researchers to realize, but the data obtained is more susceptible to interference from indoor lighting and head movement. After multi-dimensional fatigue driving detection combines multiple single-dimensional detection methods reasonably, it can significantly improve detection accuracy in the real environment.

However, a single kernel function often cannot have these characteristics simultaneously, so there is currently a lack of a kernel function that can have multiple characteristics at the same time. At present, few researchers combine multi-dimensional feature data and design a support vector machine that can combine multiple kernel function characteristics to realize a complete set of fatigue testing equipment. To realize the academic vacancy in this area, this paper designs a fatigue driving detection device. The device's processor uses a microcomputer motherboard that provides an open-source software architecture: Raspberry Pi 4 Model B. The photosensitive device uses the infrared sensor of the OV5647 sensory chip. The camera prevents the normal driving activities of the driver from being affected by contact with the driver. Even in the absence of light or low light conditions, the driver's image can be obtained well. Besides, to meet various needs, this article's fatigue driving detection system is also equipped with a Global Navigation Satellite System (GNSS) module of Micro Snow for Global Positioning System (GPS), BeiDou Navigation Satellite System (BDS), and Quasi-Zenith Satellite System (QZSS) multi-satellite system speed measurement and other sensors. For this device, its core is the algorithm part [16]. Based on the concept of multi-dimensional detection, this paper uses a face location algorithm based on a cascaded gradient descent tree to locate and distinguish the driver image's face and obtain the eye aspect ratio (EAR) and mouth aspect ratio (MAR). This paper uses the Euler-based video zoom algorithm to process the face video image. It obtains the driver's heart rate signal without touching the driver, which dramatically reduces the system's intrusiveness (Table 1).

Table 1. Pseudo-code display of fatigue driving proposed in this article

Set the trained support vector machine based on the improved kernel function as $Y = F(X_1, X_2, X_3)$, and X_I represents the different eigenvalues of the input;

Fatigue driving output 1; normal driving output 0.

Input: Image A captured by camera.

While (ture) :

  If (Get the face from A):

    Obtain feature points P_i from the face;

$$EAR = \frac{\|P_2 - P_6\| + \|P_3 - P_5\|}{2\|P_1 - P_4\|};$$

$$MAR = \frac{\|P_{14} - P_{24}\| + \|P_{15} - P_{23}\| + \|P_{16} - P_{22}\| + \|P_{17} - P_{21}\| + \|P_{18} - P_{20}\|}{2\|P_{13} - P_{19}\|};$$

$$\tilde{I}(x,t) \approx f(x + (1 + \alpha)\delta(t));$$

$$Y = F\left(EAR, MAR, \tilde{I}(x,t)\right);$$

    If (y=1):

      M=M+1;

      If(M=4):

        Output("Fatigue driving");

      End

    Else:

      M = 0;

    End

  Else:

    M = 0;

    Break;

  Time. sleep(0.5);

End

Finally, load the collected data into a pre-designed multi-dimensional dataset. Aiming at the problem that supports vector machines cannot have multiple characteristics simultaneously, this paper proposes a hybrid kernel function, which combines a logical kernel function with good generalization and a radial basis polynomial kernel with excellent learning and predictive capabilities [17]. The functions are combined to construct a support vector machine with a hybrid kernel function. The support vector machine based on the improved kernel function has robust learning and prediction capabilities and has good generalization capabilities. Finally, use the improved support vector machine to classify the mixed dataset, and then use the Raspberry Pi 4 Model B and make the corresponding output on the local side [18]. The average total accuracy of the detection of fatigue driving level reached 96.92% in the obtained experimental results. The fatigue detection system can efficiently and accurately detect the driver's fatigue state in real-time without contacting the driver.

2   Fatigue Driving Detection Method Based on Improved Kernel Function Support Vector Machine

This method can obtain the video stream through the camera. After intercepting the pictures in the video stream, the driver's facial feature points are detected based on the gradient descent tree algorithm of cascade regression. Calculate the eye aspect ratio (EAR) and mouth aspect ratio (MAR). The driver's heart rate is obtained by analyzing the RGB image and combining it with the Euler algorithm. The hybrid kernel function using logic type and RBPK type kernel function improves the support vector machine to classify facial features to determine whether they are fatigued. The system can run on low-end development boards, such as Raspberry Pi 4 Model B (Fig. 1).

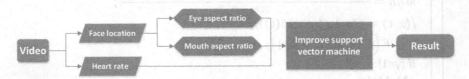

Fig. 1. The flow chart of the fatigue driving detection system of the support vector machine with an improved kernel function

2.1   Multi-dimensional Fatigue Driving Feature Extraction Based on Gradient Descent Cascade Regression Model

Face Location Based on Gradient Descent Tree Algorithm of Cascade Regression. This paper locates the face base on the Gradient Boosting Decision Tree (GBDT) [19]. This algorithm can locate human faces within one millisecond, significantly improving the detection efficiency.

The algorithm lets represent all 68 facial landmarks' coordinates and use the gradient descent tree algorithm to learn each regressor in the cascade. From the image and the facial landmark estimation value, predict and update the vector and add it to the current shape estimate, make the estimated value closer to the right value, complete the purpose of face alignment, and obtain the value of the 68-dimensional facial landmark:

$$\widehat{S}^{(t+1)} = \widehat{S}^{(t)} + r_t(I, \widehat{S}^{(t)}) \tag{1}$$

After achieving face alignment and acquiring the coordinates of 68 facial landmarks, this article selects 32 dimensions of the 68-dimensional coordinates to calculate the eye aspect ratio (EAR) and mouth aspect ratio (MAR) to determine whether the driver is fatigued or not.

Calculation of EAR and MAR. In this paper, 12-dimensional eyes (both eyes) and a 20-dimensional mouth are selected to calculate the opening and closing degree. The calculation formula of EAR [20] is defined as follows, where P_1 to P_6 represents the left eye, P_7 to P_{12} represent the right eye, and the EAR values of the two eyes are calculated separately:

$$EAR = \frac{||P_2 - P_6|| + ||P_3 - P_5||}{2||P_1 - P_4||} \tag{2}$$

The MAR calculation formula is as follows, P_{13} to P_{32} represent the mouth (Fig. 2):

$$MAR = \frac{||P_{14} - P_{24}|| + ||P_{15} - P_{23}|| + ||P_{16} - P_{22}|| + ||P_{17} - P_{21}|| + ||P_{18} - P_{20}||}{2||P_{13} - P_{19}||} \tag{3}$$

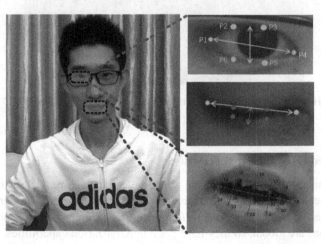

Fig. 2. Schematic diagram of the EAR and MAR (the three pictures on the right represent open eye EAR, closed eye EAR, MAR from top to bottom)

Heart Rate Detection Based on Euler Video Zoom. In addition to calculating EAR and MAR, this article also obtains heart rate as an index for comprehensively judging fatigue driving.

This paper uses Euler's video magnification algorithm to process face video images. Compared with the independent component analysis algorithm, this algorithm does not require the source signal's non-Gaussian independence. It has lower time complexity, which can reduce the time for fatigue driving detection. The algorithm processes video images in the spatial and temporal domains, thereby magnifying subtle changes in the video that are usually invisible or difficult to detect with the naked eye.

In this paper, the G channel with the stronger pulse wave signal among the three frequency channels of RGB in each frame of image magnified on the forehead is detected. The maximum power spectrum corresponding frequency of the signal sequence formed by the average value of the pixels in the G channel's region of interest is used as the heart rate estimation value. The processed heart rate output value $\tilde{I}(x, t)$ is calculated [21]. It can be seen from the following formula that the original small translational motion $\delta(t)$ is amplified to $(1 + \alpha)\delta(t)$ after time-domain band-pass filtering (Fig. 3):

$$\tilde{I}(x, t) \approx f(x + (1 + \alpha)\delta(t)) \tag{4}$$

Fig. 3. Heart rate detection based on Euler video magnification from the forehead

2.2 Improved Logical Kernel Function

The kernel function is the core of the support vector machine. The performance of different kernel functions has its advantages and disadvantages. The performance of the support vector machine is also different due to different kernel functions. Some kernel functions are global, so they have good generalization capabilities. Some kernel functions have good learning ability and predictive ability. Generally speaking, a single kernel function may not have good learning and generalization capabilities. Therefore, this paper combines the logical kernel function with good generalization, and the radial basis polynomial kernel function (RBPK) with excellent learning ability and predictive ability to construct a mixed kern el function support vector machine, which improves based on The support vector machine of kernel function has not only robust learning and prediction ability but also has good generalization ability.

Logistic Kernel Function. The expression of Logistic function is:

$$K(x) = \frac{1}{1 + e^{-ax^2}}, \quad \alpha > 0 \tag{5}$$

The expression of Logistic kernel function is:

$$K(x_i, x_j) = \frac{1}{1 + e^{-a(x_i - x_j)^2}} \tag{6}$$

As long as the kernel function satisfies the Mercer condition, the dot product operation in the high-dimensional space can be converted into the kernel function operation in the input space, thereby avoiding direct calculation in the high-dimensional space and solving the problem of high algorithm complexity.

The literature [22] gives the proof process of the Logistic kernel function as the support vector machine's kernel function (Fig. 4).

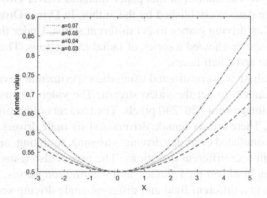

Fig. 4. Graph of logical kernel function

Radial Basis Polynomial Kernel Function (RBPK). The paper [23] defines a kernel function called Radial Basis Polynomial Kernel (RBPK):

$$K(x_i, x_j) = exp\left(\frac{(x_i.x_j)^d}{\sigma^2}\right) d > 0 \tag{7}$$

The paper improves RBPK from two kernel functions, which makes full use of the good predictive ability of the polynomial kernel function and the RBF kernel function's learning ability.

LRBPK Hybrid Kernel Function. By analyzing the logical kernel function's image and the radial basis polynomial kernel function, we can conclude that the logical kernel function has good generalization ability, and the support vector machine whose kernel function is RBPK has good learning and prediction ability. Therefore, to obtain a support vector machine with robust learning and predictive capabilities, and generalization capabilities. The Logical and Radial Basis Polynomial Kernel (LRBPK) mixed kernel function is a mixed kernel function of Logistic and RBPK type kernel functions. LRBPK is used as the kernel function of the improved support vector machine in this system.

According to the lemma, we know that if K_1 and K_2 are kernel functions on $X*X$, and $X \in R$, the constant $a >= 0$, then $K(x, y) = K_1(x, y) + K_2(x, y)$, $K(x, y) = \alpha.K_1(x, y)$ is still the kernel function.

Therefore, the LRBPK hybrid kernel function expression is as follows:

$$K_{LRBPK} = n.K_{logistic} + (1 - n)K_{RBPK} \tag{8}$$

3   Experiment and Result Analysis

3.1   Experimental Background

Dataset Description. The dataset in this paper includes Driver Drowsiness Detection Dataset [24] and the dataset established by the author. In Driver Drowsiness Detection Dataset, subjects play driving games to get different states. Under the guidance of the experimenters, the testers showed a series of facial expressions. The total time of this dataset is about nine and a half hours.

A self-built database was constructed using the experimental device below. Use the OV5647 infrared camera to get the video stream. The video format is 30 frames per second and a color image with 320*240 pixels. The total recording time is 5 h. Contains 12 different testers. There are six female drivers and six male drivers, aged between 18 and 40. The testers simulated everyday driving, yawning, squinting, and sleepiness. And we were shooting in four different directions. The testers also tested without wearing any glasses, wearing black-rimmed glasses, and wearing sunglasses.

We collect data in a different light and different angle driving scenes to simulate a real driving scene. The different light environments are intense light, normal light, low light, and no light. Other angles are divided into front, left, and right sides. The camera's built-in infrared light supplement can display the picture even when there is no light, but it will be different from the usual light environment (Fig. 5).

Fig. 5. Dataset display

Description of Experimental Device. This paper designs and manufactures a fatigued driving detection device composed of Raspberry Pi 4 Model B, OV5647 infrared camera, and various sensors to test the actual driving situation. The device is used to run the fatigue driving detection algorithm proposed in this article and obtain self-built dataset (Fig. 6).

Fig. 6. The overall situation of the equipment. The infrared camera is connected to the Raspberry Pi 4 Model B through the CSI interface. In order to be able to prompt alarm data, the Raspberry Pi is connected with a micro display, LED lights.

Raspberry Pi 4 Model B. The Raspberry Pi 4 Model B selected in this article is a microcomputer motherboard that provides an open-source software architecture. It has a 4-core ARM processor clocked at 1.5 GHz and 4 GB memory, which can run the algorithm model proposed in this article. Its price is not high, and it is easy to mass manufacture similar low-cost devices. It is equipped with 40 GPIO interfaces, which can connect a variety of sensors to facilitate the acquisition of various data. Its built-in Wi-Fi module can transmit data to the server during the experiment, reducing the storage and investment of data related to fatigue driving.

Infrared Camera. This article uses an infrared camera with the sensory chip OV5647. It has a 160-degree viewing angle range, can acquire more images, and can adjust the focus. Equipped with an infrared fill light that can feel ambient light, the camera can reach a visual distance of 2 m at night. It can adapt well to the environment in the car. It can adapt to low-light and no-light environments that are common for driving (Fig. 7).

Fig. 7. OLED display module and GNSS module.

Other Modules. The fatigue driving detection of the actual scene will consider many factors. Fatigued driving is detected only during driving, and the Weixue brand GNSS module is installed for GPS, Beidou satellite navigation system (BDS), and QZSS multi-satellite system speed measurement; considering the need for actual temperature and humidity detection, DHT11 sensor is installed; In order to facilitate the intuitive acquisition of data, this article adds a 0.96-inch OLED screen and so on.

3.2   Experimental Process

First, this article extracts fragments from the dataset. A total of 240 video fragments are removed, each of which is 30 s. According to the subjective judgment method, 113 fatigue video clips, 127 non-fatigue video clips, and the category label (0, 1). This paper randomly samples the video and includes four different angles and three glasses-wearing clips—extract 95 fatigue and 95 non-fatigue video clips, respectively. Divide the video into the training set, and test set equally (Fig. 8).

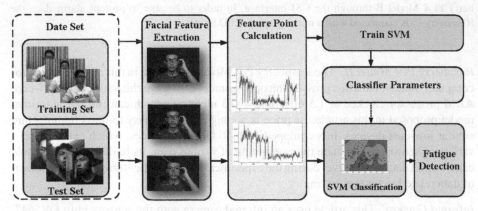

Fig. 8. Experimental flowchart.

One thousand eight hundred pictures were intercepted from the training set and test set and subjectively classified, and 900 images were divided into a training set and test set. Since there are not many data sets, this article conducts Data Augmentation and uses OpenCv to batch flip, adjust brightness, blur, and other processing methods to get 5400 pictures (Fig. 9).

The gradient descent tree algorithm of the cascaded regression is used to obtain the face in the picture, obtain the face's 68-dimensional feature points, and extract the feature values of EAR and MAR. Extract the characteristic value of the heart rate through each video clip. Match the video to the corresponding picture. The three sets of feature value data of the training set are provided to the SVM classifier for training.

Get the training parameters to test the test set. The images in the test group were divided into four groups, each with 675 pictures. In order to ensure the balance between the false alarm rate and the false alarm rate, this article defines the accuracy rate: *Total accuracy* $= 1 - $ *(false alarm rate + false alarm rate)* (Table 2).

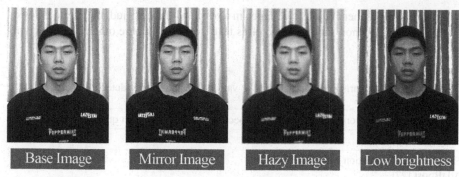

Base Image | Mirror Image | Hazy Image | Low brightness

Fig. 9. Data Augmentation processing result display. Different processing is performed on the fatigue state image data.

Table 2. Precision display

Group	Daytime environment		Night environment		Total accuracy
	False alarm rate	False negative rate	False alarm rate	False negative rate	
1	97.33%	96.15%	97.19%	96.30%	96.92%
2	98.81%	96.30%	97.19%	97.19%	
3	98.07%	95.85%	95.85%	97.63%	
4	97.48%	96.30%	95.70%	97.33%	

It can be seen that the SVM algorithm using the improved kernel function proposed in this paper has better processing results in the false positive rate and can effectively reduce the false-negative rate.

Since the judgment of the picture cannot be intuitively derived from the test in the actual driving environment, this article selects video clips as the continuous monitoring test. However, since the video has a rate of 30 frames per second, this paper establishes 0.5 s as the interval time for fatigue driving judgment. In this article, we have also made relevant calculations based on the blinking frequency of human eyes. According to Sakai's research [25], the average number of blinks per minute (Nob) of people is about 25 times. Blink time (BT) is about 0.2 s. According to the probability, we can know that the likelihood of being recognized as closed eyes when blinking is:

$$P(C) = \frac{Not * BT}{60} = 20.833\% \tag{9}$$

The probability of closing the eyes for 5 consecutive times is:

$$P(FC) = 1 - P(C)^5 = 0.039\% \tag{10}$$

Studies have shown that people's blinking frequency is lower when focusing on driving [26]. The probability of closing the eyes five times will be even lower. In many comparative experiments, this article has also found that the correct rate is better when the fatigue driving judgment occurs five times in a row, and the miss judgment rate is lower. Finally, test with 95 non-fatigue video clips tests set and compare other fatigue driving test data (Table 3).

Table 3. Comparison of the accuracy of various fatigue driving detection methods

Fatigue driving detection method	Inspection quantity	Correct quantity	Correct rate
Method of this article	95	94	98.95%
Fatigue driving detection based on AdaBoost [27]	95	89	93.68%
Fatigue driving detection based on YCbCr color space [28]	95	93	97.89%
Fatigue driving detection based on ASM and HSV color model [29]	95	92	96.84%

It can be seen from the test that the accuracy of this method reaches 98.95%, which exceeds 1.06% of the fatigue driving detection method based on YCbCr color space. In the actual driving process, this article uses the equipment mentioned above to conduct multiple tests. Compared with similar commercial products, our fatigue driving test has a lower false alarm rate and a lower false alarm rate (Fig. 10).

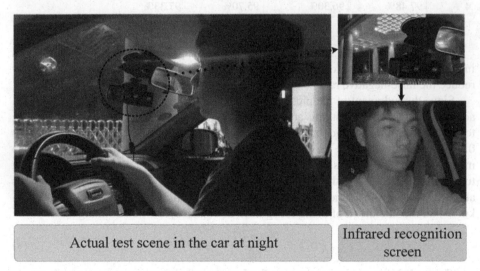

Actual test scene in the car at night

Infrared recognition screen

Fig. 10. Practical Testing. The left side of the picture.is the actual test environment, the upper right is the packaged test equipment, and the lower right is the image of the device identification.

4 Conclusion and Future Directions

This paper proposes a multi-dimensional fatigue driving detection system based on an improved kernel function support vector machine by locating and identifying the EAR, MAR, and heart rate of the face. A new fatigue driving detection framework is constructed by improving the kernel function in the support vector machine. Construct a new dataset and combine the public dataset for training and testing, and get a better recognition rate. Comparing single point feature detection with classic support vector machine detection, it has an absolute accuracy improvement. However, due to the lack of a camera to obtain the heartbeat. In the future, we will improve the shortcomings in this area and use better methods to predict. The author will collect more data sets and strive to build a complete fatigue driving detection system. The streamlined system can be used in mid-range IoT devices. In the future, more features such as human body pressure, steering wheel, and head tracking can be combined to develop a more accurate fatigue driving detection system. Combining with L1-L3 unmanned driving systems is also a follow-up research direction.

Acknowledgement. This work was supported by the Hainan Provincial Natural Science Foundation of China (Grant No. 2019RC041 and 2019RC098), Research and Application Project of Key Technologies for Blockchain Cross-chain Collaborative Monitoring and Traceability for Large-scale Distributed Denial of Service Attacks, National Natural Science Foundation of China (Grant No. 61762033), Opening Project of Shanghai Trusted Industrial Control Platform (Grant No. TICPSH202003005-ZC), and Education and Teaching Reform Research Project of Hainan University (Grant No. hdjy1970).

References

1. Liu, B., Wang, L., Liu, M.: Lifelong federated reinforcement learning: a learning architecture for navigation in cloud robotic systems. IEEE Robot. Autom. Lett. **4**(4), 4555–4562 (2019)
2. Li, L., Xie, M., Dong, H.: A method of driving fatigue detection based on eye location. In: 2011 IEEE 3rd International Conference on Communication Software and Networks, pp. 480–484. IEEE (2011)
3. Shuze, G.: Research on driving fatigue detection system based on ARM platform. Ph.D. thesis (2016)
4. Sahayadhas, A., Sundaraj, K., Murugappan, M.: Detecting driver drowsiness based on sensors: a review. Sensors **12**(12), 16937–16953 (2012)
5. Buchheim, C., Hubner, R., Schobel, A.: Ellipsoid bounds for convex quadratic integer programming. SIAM J. Optim. **25**(2), 741–769 (2015)
6. Tao, C.: Newton-CG augmented lagrangian algorithm for convex quadratic constrained quadratic semidefinite programming. Ph.D. thesis, Beijing University of Technology (2012)
7. Cortes, C., Vapnik, V.: Support-vector networks. Mach. Learn. **20**(3), 273–297 (1995)
8. Ghaddar, B., Naoum-Sawaya, J.: High dimensional data classification and feature selection using support vector machines. Eur. J. Oper. Res. **265**(3), 993–1004 (2018)
9. Xia, M.: Research on product quality prediction system based on improved support vector machine. General Institute of Mechanical Science Research (2020)
10. Zhang, Q.: Method research of multi-core support vector machines. Ph.D. thesis, Beijing Jianzhu University (2020)

11. Tanveer, M.: Robust and sparse linear programming twin support vector machines. Cogn. Comput. **7**(1), 137–149 (2015)
12. Sideratos, G., Hatziargyriou, N.D.: Probabilistic wind power forecasting using radial basis function neural networks. IEEE Trans. Power Syst. **27**(4), 1788–1796 (2012)
13. Moghaddam, V.H., Hamidzadeh, J.: New hermite orthogonal polynomial kernel and combined kernels in support vector machine classifier. Pattern Recognit. **60**, 921–935 (2016)
14. Liu, B., et al.: A real-time contribution measurement method for participants in federated learning. arXiv preprint arXiv:2009.03510 (2020)
15. Liu, B., Wang, L., Chen, X., Huang, L., Xu, C.Z.: Peer-assisted robotic learning: a data-driven collaborative learning approach for cloud robotic systems. arXiv preprint arXiv:2010.08303 (2020)
16. Cheng, J., Zheng, J., Yu, X.: An ensemble framework for interpretable malicious code detection. Int. J. Intell. Syst. (2020)
17. Liu, J., et al.: A novel robust watermarking algorithm for encrypted medical image based on DTCWT-DCT and chaotic map. Comput. Mater. Con. **61**(2), 889–910 (2019)
18. Tang, X., Wang, L., Cheng, J., Chen, J.: Forecasting model based on information-granulated GA-SVR and ARIMA for producer price index. arXiv preprint arXiv:1903.12012 (2019)
19. Kazemi, V., Sullivan, J.: One millisecond face alignment with an ensemble of regression trees. In: Proceedings of the IEEE Conference on Computer Vision and Pattern Recognition, pp. 1867–1874 (2014)
20. Soukupova, T., Cech, J.: Eye blink detection using facial landmarks. In: 21st Computer Vision Winter Workshop, Rimske Toplice, Slovenia (2016)
21. Wan, Z.: Research on heart rate detection based on face video images. Ph.D. thesis (2014)
22. Yang, X.: A support vector machine-based image multi-feature fatigue driving detection method. Ph.D. thesis, Xi'an University of Technology
23. Bhavsar, M.H., Ganatra, A.: Radial basis polynomial kernel (RBPK): a generalized kernel for support vector machine. Int. J. Comput. Sci. Inf. Secur. (IJCSIS) **14**(4) (2016)
24. Weng, C.-H., Lai, Y.-H., Lai, S.-H.: Driver drowsiness detection via a hierarchical temporal deep belief network. In: Chen, C.-S., Lu, J., Ma, K.-K. (eds.) ACCV 2016. LNCS, vol. 10118, pp. 117–133. Springer, Cham (2017). https://doi.org/10.1007/978-3-319-54526-4_9
25. Sakai, T., et al.: Edabased estimation of visual attention by observation of eye blink frequency. Int. J. Smart Sens. Intell. Syst. **10**(2), 296–307 (2017)
26. Ingre, M., Åkerstedt, T., Peters, B., Anund, A., Kecklund, G.: Subjective sleepiness, simulated driving performance and blink duration: examining individual differences. J. Sleep Res. **15**(1), 47–53 (2006)
27. Liu, C., Zhang, X.: Research on fatigue driving warning based on image processing. Appl. Electron. Tech. (8) (2019)
28. Wenteng, K., Kuancheng, M., Jiacai, H., Haibin, L.: Fatigue driving detection based on Gaussian white eye model. Chin. J. Image Graph. **21**(011), 1515–1522 (2016)
29. Xu, Z., He, F., Hua, X., Li, J.: Research on fatigue driving detection system based on adaboost algorithm. Automob. Technol. (005), 17–21 (2019)

Experiments of Federated Learning
for COVID-19 Chest X-ray Images

Bingjie Yan[1], Jun Wang[2], Jieren Cheng[1(✉)], Yize Zhou[3], Yixian Zhang[2],
Yifan Yang[1], Li Liu[1], Haojiang Zhao[2], Chunjuan Wang[1], and Boyi Liu[4]

[1] School of Computer Science and Cyberspace Security, Hainan University,
Haikou 570228, China
[2] School of Information and Communication Engineering, Hainan University,
Haikou 570228, China
[3] School of Science, Hainan University, Haikou 570228, China
[4] University of Chinese Academy of Science, Beijing 100049, China

Abstract. AI plays an important role in COVID-19 identification. Computer
vision and deep learning techniques can assist in determining COVID-19 infection
with Chest X-ray Images. However, for the protection and respect of the privacy
of patients, the hospital's specific medical-related data did not allow leakage and
sharing without permission. Collecting such training data was a major challenge.
To a certain extent, this has caused a lack of sufficient data samples when performing deep learning approaches to detect COVID-19. Federated Learning is an
available way to address this issue. It can effectively address the issue of data
silos and get a shared model without obtaining local data. In the work, we propose
the use of federated learning for COVID-19 data training and deploy experiments
to verify the effectiveness. And we also compare performances of four popular
models (MobileNet_v2, ResNet18, ResNeXt, and COVID-Net) with the federated
learning framework and without the framework. This work aims to inspire more
researches on federated learning about COVID-19.

Keywords: COVID-19 · Federated learning · Chest X-ray image

1 Introduction

The COVID-19 pandemic has caused continuous damage to the health and normal production of people all over the world. Therefore, researches on detecting and diagnosing COVID-19 patients are very meaningful [20, 21]. The clinical manifestations of
COVID-19 infected pneumonia are mainly fever, chills, dry cough, and systemic pain.
A few patients have abdominal symptoms. It is worth noting that there are asymptomatic
patients in the population. So it is necessary to test more people as soon as possible. A
key step in judging and treating COVID-19 is the effective screening of infected patients.
One of the key screening methods is the use of chest X-rays image. Computer vision
and machine learning technology play an important role in this approach. At present,
artificial intelligence, especially deep learning, has become an important technology for

© Springer Nature Switzerland AG 2021
X. Sun et al. (Eds.): ICAIS 2021, CCIS 1423, pp. 41–53, 2021.
https://doi.org/10.1007/978-3-030-78618-2_4

computer-aided medical applications and has achieved remarkable results in medical imaging. Deep learning has made a huge contribution to the classification of chest X-ray radiology in the medical field, and it has become an effective tool for doctors to judge and analyze the condition. To obtain an accurate and robust depth model, the core element is large and widely diverse training data. However, out of the protection and respect of the privacy of patients, the hospital's specific medical-related data did not allow leakage and public research.

Collecting such training data was a major challenge. To a certain extent, this has caused a lack of sufficient data samples when performing deep learning approaches to detect COVID-19. Federated Learning is an available way to address this issue. It can effectively address the issue of data silos and get a shared model without obtaining local data. In the paper, we firstly propose the use of federated learning for COVID-19 data training and deploy experiments to verify the effectiveness.

Federated learning is a framework of learning across multiple institutions without sharing patient data. It has the potential to fundamentally solve the problems of data privacy and data silos. Applications of federated learning in medical big data are promising researches. Federated learning is capable of utilizing the non-shared data from different hospitals, enlarging the sample size of the model training, and improving the accuracy of the model. The core of federated learning is to use data sets distributed on multiple devices to jointly build a shared model and does not require local raw data sharing. This precisely protects patient data. In the case that COVID-19 medical imaging data is still distributed in various countries and hospitals, federated learning experiments for medical images of COVID-19 that conducted in this work are necessary (Fig. 1).

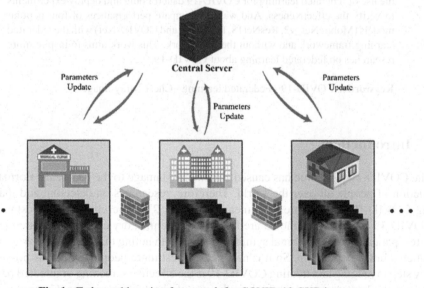

Fig. 1. Federated learning framework for COVID-19 CXR images

In this work, we conducted four individual experiments to present the performances in federated learning of four different networks for COVID-19 CXR images: COVID-Net [18], ResNeXt [14], MobileNet_v2 [13], and ResNet18 [1]. Further, we analyzed the results and proposed possible future improvements to inspire more research in federated learning for COVID-19.

2 Related Work

With the continuous development of the new coronavirus epidemic, more and more researchers are committed to joining the ranks of fighting the epidemic through AI-related technologies. Researchers use AI to make it play a role in the epidemic. A series of recent studies on COVID-19 medical imaging analysis and diagnosis have sprung up. These studies have completed the diagnosis of COVID-19 based on medical imaging technology. We use the current chest x-ray technology to complete the image generation of the special radiological features. After that, the researchers used machine learning methods to classify and recognize the images generated during the CT scan diagnosis process. This method greatly reduces the workload of medical staff, and at the same time plays a role in assisting doctors in diagnosing the pathological characteristics of patients. At present, many studies have targeted disease as a binary classification problem, that is, "normal", "pneumonia" and "COVID-19". Next, we introduce the application of COVID-Net in COVID-19 image classification and recognition and complete diagnosis of pathological features.

2.1 COVID-Net for COVID-19 Identification

COVID-Net specifically proposes a neural network that uses PEPX compression network structure to identify COVID-19 pneumonia CXR images. At the same time, it retains the performance of the network to a great extent and is highly sensitive to the pneumonia characteristics of COVID-19. Based on the advantages of CXR imaging for rapid triage of COVID-19 screening, availability, ubiquity, and portability, they make predictions through the COVID-Net interpretability method. This allows us to not only gain a deeper understanding of the key factors associated with COVID cases. This can help clinicians perform better screening. We can also review COVID-Net, a method based on CXR images to verify that it is making decisions.

2.2 Federated Learning

Federated learning is recent emerging research that has been extensively studied in the fields of financial security, artificial intelligence, and robotics [4, 10, 11].

The training data will be distributed on each mobile device, not all of them will be sent to the central server, and only the updated data on each device will be aggregated to the central server. After joint optimization, the central server returns to the global state of each device and continues to accept the updated data calculated by each client in the new global state. This method is Federated Learning [12]. Federated Learning or Federated

Machine Learning [9] can solve the problem of unprotected large-scale private data and complete updating learning of devices without exchanging large amounts of data.

This decentralized training model approach provides privacy, security, regulation, and economic benefits [22]. Federated Learning presents new statistical and system challenges when training models on distributed device networks [15]. Federated Learning, which relies on scattered data, brings many aspects of research: Fei Chen et al. identified the combination of Federated Learning and Meta-learning as a major advance in Federated Learning [3]. Konstantin Sozinov et al. have made some progress in applying Federated Learning to human activity identification [16].

3 Federated learning System for COVID-19 CXR Images

In this section, we provide a comprehensive overview of federated learning. Furthermore, the definition, architecture, training process and, parameters update method of the federated learning system [12] for COVID-19 CXR images are considered.

3.1 Basic Definition

In the work, we define N COVID-19 CXR images owners as $\{F_1, F_2, \cdots, F_N\}$. We assume that they are from different hospitals. Patient medical data is not allowed to be shared, including CXR images. Under this constraint, all of them want to train their own model by merging their respective data $\{D_1, D_2, \cdots, D_N\}$. A conventional method exists to put all the data together and use $D = D_1 \cup D_2 \cup \cdots \cup D_N$ to train to get a model M_{SUM}. Federated learning is a systematic learning process. In this process, the data owners jointly train the model M_{FED}. During this process, any data owner F_i will not disclose their own data D_i to others. In addition to this, the accuracy of M_{FED} represented as V_{FED} should be very close to the V_{SUM} performance of M_{SUM}. In the form of expression, let ε be a non-negative real number; If $|V_{FED} - V_{SUM}| < \varepsilon$, we can think that the federated learning algorithm has ε error accuracy.

3.2 Framework of the Federated Learning System

In this part, we will introduce the basic framework of federated learning, the training structure, and the way to update the parameters. Federated learning is a distributed learning method. The server is used to maintain the overall main model and distribute it to various agents. For privacy issues, agents train models locally. The server will set the score S, and select the agents according to the proportion to update the central model of the server. Then upload the agent-improved model parameters to the server to update the server model parameters. Subsequently, it is distributed to agents to improve their models. In this way, we continue to improve the central model of the server and the local model of the agents. This approach is capable of ensuring the accuracy and privacy of the agents, utilize the agents' computing power and a large amount of data to learn, and maintain an excellent central model.

In the FL training system, the owner of the data acts as a participant in the FL process. And they jointly train the machine learning model of the aggregation server center. In this system, we promise that the data owners are honest and the data they provide is real. This requires data owners to use their more and real private data for training and submit the trained local model to the FL server.

Generally, the FL training process includes the following three training steps. We first define that the local model refers to the model trained on each participating agent, and the global model refers to the model after the FL server has been aggregated.

- Step 1: Implements task initialization. The server determines the training task, which is to determine the target application and corresponding data requirements. At the same time, the server specifies the global model and establishes parameters during the training process, such as the learning rate. Afterward, the server allocates the initialized global model W_{t_G} and training tasks to the participating clients to complete the task allocation.
- Step 2: Implements the training and update of the local model. The training is carried out based on the global model W_{t_G}, where t represents the current iteration index, and each participating user uses local data and equipment to update the local model parameters W_{t_i}. The final goal of the participant i in the iteration t is to find the optimal parameter W_{t_i} that minimizes the loss function $L(W_{t_i})$.
- Step 3: Realizing the aggregation and update of the global model. The server aggregates the local models of the participating users and sends the updated global model parameters W_{t+1_G} to the users who hold the data.

4 Experiments

In this session, we will explain our experiments on the recognition of COVID-19 pneumonia CXR images using various models and federated learning frameworks.

4.1 Dataset

The dataset used to train and evaluate the model is the COVIDx dataset, which is one of the open-access datasets with the largest number of COVID-19 pneumonia CXR images. It contains covid chestxray dataset [5], COVID-19 Chest X-ray Dataset, Actualmed COVID-19 Chest X-ray Dataset, covid-19 radiography dataset which is public on Kaggle and RSNA Pneumonia Detection Challenge's dataset [8]. There are 15,282 images in this dataset, including 13,703 images for training and 1,579 images for testing. There are three kinds of labels in the dataset. They are normal (which is asymptomatic), pneumonia (which is non-COVID19 pneumonia), and COVID-19 (which is pneumonia caused by novel coronavirus). The various data distributions are shown in Fig. 2 below. It is assumed that the data in the training set is representative and can reflect the accuracy of the model.

4.2 Experimental Setting

Model. The main task in the experiment is image classification. There are already many classic neural networks in this field, and there are models specifically designed for the recognition of COVID-19 pneumonia CXR images. Four models are used in the experiments.

- COVID-Net: A neural network specifically proposed to identify COVID-19 pneumonia CXR images utilizes PEPX to compress the network structure while preserving the network's performance to a large extent. At the same time, it has a high sensitivity to the pneumonia characteristics of COVID-19.
- ResNet18: It is a residual neural network. An identity mapping layer is added to the ordinary neural network to make the network as deep as possible. To a certain extent, it can prevent the accuracy falling caused by overfitting due to the deepening of the network.
- ResNeXt: It is based on the residual neural network using a split-transform-merge strategy to convert single-core convolution into multi-core convolution, but the topology is the same as ResNet18.
- MobileNet_v2: It is a lightweight convolutional neural network. Unlike the residual neural network, the residual neural network uses a convolution kernel to first compress and extract features and then expand, but it expands and extracts more features and then compresses.

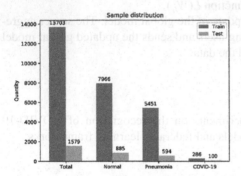
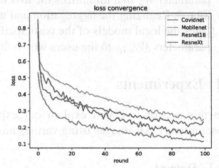

Fig. 2. Data distributions in COVIDx dataset   **Fig. 3.** Loss convergence with training rounds

4.3 Implementation and Training

Federated learning is a pseudo-distributed training completed on one machine in our experiment. For each agent, there is a separate model, which is reset to the updated central model after each central model update. The models are all implemented by PyTorch, and the training set and test set images are resized to (224,224) for model training. Each agent uses the Adam optimizer with learning rate = 2e-5 and weight decay = 1e-7. The framework for federated learning is trained under the GPU acceleration of NVIDIA Tesla V100 (32 GB) on Ubuntu 18.04 system. Other training-related parameters are shown in Table 1.

Table 1. Training-related parameters in the experiment

Parameter	Value	Description
Agents number	5	The number of agents
Frac	0.4	The proportion of agents participating in the central model update for each round
Local epoch	3	Epochs update per round
Local batch size	10	Local update batch size
Learning rate	2.00E-05	Learning rate of optimizer
Weight decay	1.00E-07	Decay of learning rate with training epoch

4.4 Experimental Results and Analysis

During the experiment, the loss of several models can converge, and the decline of loss during the training process is shown in Fig. 3.

After using the same parameter training four models for 100 rounds, the result is shown in Table 2. ResNet18 has the fastest convergence speed and the highest accuracy rate (96.15%, 91.26%) on both the training set and the testing set. The ResNeXt convergence rate is closely followed, but the accuracy rate is not as good as the second-ranked COVID-Net. Although MobileNet_v2 has a loss value similar to COVID-Net, the accuracy rate on the testing set is not satisfactory.

Table 2. Model sensitivity to data using federated learning framework

Model	Training set	Testing set
COVID-Net	92.40 ± 0.004%	89.17 ± 0.015%
MobileNet_v2	91.16 ± 0.005%	86.83 ± 0.017%
ResNet18	**96.15 ± 0.003%**	**91.26 ± 0.014%**
ResNeXt	94.66 ± 0.004%	90.37 ± 0.015%

To explore the sensitivity of the models to each label, we counted the accuracy of each model for each label, and the performance results of the models are shown in Fig. 4 and Table 3.

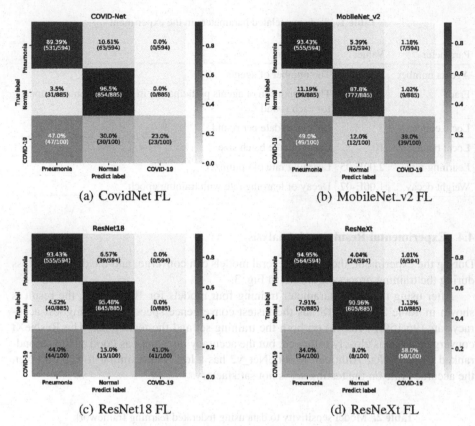

Fig. 4. Four models perplexity of each label

Table 3. Four models perplexity of each label

Model	Normal	Pneumonia	COVID-19
COVID-Net	96.47 ± 0.004%	88.24 ± 0.009%	51.04 ± 0.05%
MobileNet_v2	94.87 ± 0.005%	87.20 ± 0.009%	50.26 ± 0.05%
ResNet18	**98.16 ± 0.003%**	**93.91 ± 0.006%**	66.32 ± 0.047%
ResNeXt	96.18 ± 0.004%	92.66 ± 0.007%	**73.58 ± 0.044%**

We compared the training results without the federated learning framework with those using the federated learning framework. Because the round is 100 and local_epoch is 3 in the federated learning parameters, we set epoch to 300 when training the model separately, to compare with the loss convergence during the federated learning training process, as shown in Fig. 5. It was found that the loss convergence rate caused by the use of federated learning decreased slightly. The result of the training accuracy of a single network is shown in Table 4.

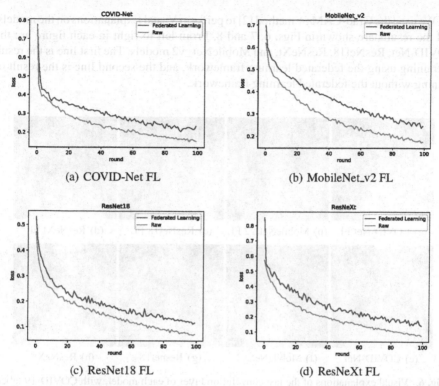

Fig. 5. Loss convergence speed comparison of whether to use the federated learning framework

Table 4. Loss convergence speed comparison of whether to use the federal learning framework

Model	Training set	Testing set
COVID-Net	94.50 ± 0.004%	90.06 ± 0.015%
MobileNet_v2	94.10 ± 0.004%	88.98 ± 0.015%
ResNet18	**98.06 ± 0.002%**	91.07 ± 0.014%
ResNeXt	97.66 ± 0.003%	**91.26 ± 0.01%**

As presented in Fig. 5, we compared the training procedure based on federated learning with the training procedure without federated learning. MobileNet_v2 has a larger accuracy gap between the FL based approach and the individual approach while ResNet18 has a smaller accuracy gap. If considering the number of parameters, MobileNet_v2 and ResNet18 have a higher performance. MobileNet_v2 has the fewest parameters and the lowest accuracy. ResNet18 has the second-fewest parameters and the highest accuracy.

We used the Grad-CAM++ method [2] to perform Visual Explanations on the models, and the results are shown in Figs. 6, 7 and 8. From left to right in each figure are the COVID-Net, ResNet18, ResNeXt, and MobileNet_v2 models. The first line is the result of training using the federated learning framework, and the second line is the result of training without the federated learning framework.

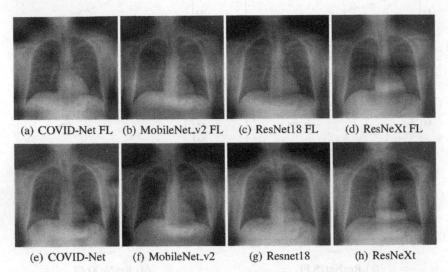

(a) COVID-Net FL   (b) MobileNet_v2 FL   (c) ResNet18 FL   (d) ResNeXt FL

(e) COVID-Net   (f) MobileNet_v2   (g) Resnet18   (h) ResNeXt

Fig. 6. Visual explanations of the last convolution layer of each model, with COVID-19 label

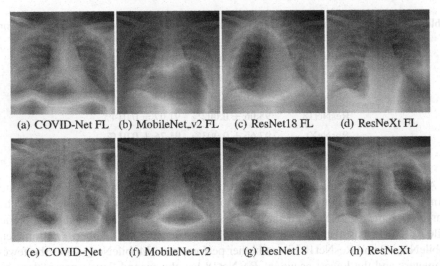

(a) COVID-Net FL   (b) MobileNet_v2 FL   (c) ResNet18 FL   (d) ResNeXt FL

(e) COVID-Net   (f) MobileNet_v2   (g) ResNet18   (h) ResNeXt

Fig. 7. Visual explanations of the last convolution layer of each model, with normal label

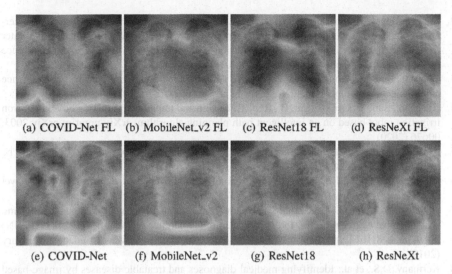

(a) COVID-Net FL   (b) MobileNet_v2 FL   (c) ResNet18 FL   (d) ResNeXt FL

(e) COVID-Net   (f) MobileNet_v2   (g) ResNet18   (h) ResNeXt

Fig. 8. Visual explanations of the last convolution layer of each model, with pneumonia label

5 Conclusion

In the work, we conducted experiments on COVID-19 identification with CXR images based on the federated learning framework. We conducted CXR images training with four different models: MobileNet_v2, ResNet18, ResNeXt, and COVID-Net, and the comparison experiment between training with federated learning framework and training without federated learning framework. The experimental results show that ResNet18 has the best performance both in training with FL and without FL. ResNeXt has the best performance in images with COVID-19 labels. MobileNet_v2 has the fewest number of parameters. Therefore, the work indicates that ResNeXt and ResNet18 are better chosen for COVID-19 identification among the four popular models.

Acknowledgement. This work was supported by the Hainan Provincial Natural Science Foundation of China (Grant No. 2019RC041 and 2019RC098), Research and Application Project of Key Technologies for Blockchain Cross-chain Collaborative Monitoring and Traceability for Large-scale Distributed Denial of Service Attacks, National Natural Science Foundation of China (Grant No. 61762033), Opening Project of Shanghai Trusted Industrial Control Platform (Grant No. TICPSH202003005-ZC), and Education and Teaching Reform Research Project of Hainan University (Grant No. hdjy1970).

References

1. Ayyachamy, S., Alex, V., Khened, M., Krishnamurthi, G.: Medical image retrieval using Resnet-18. In: Medical Imaging 2019, Imaging Informatics for Healthcare, Research, and Applications. vol. 10954, p. 1095410. Proceedings of SPIE (2019)

2. Chattopadhyay, A., Sarkar, A., Howlader, P., Balasubramanian, V.N.: Grad-CAM++: generalized gradient-based visual explanations for deep convolutional networks. In: IEEE Winter Conference on Applications of Computer Vision 2018, pp. 839–847. IEEE Winter Conference on Applications of Computer Vision, NV (2018)

3. Chen, F., Luo, M., Dong, Z., Li, Z., He, X.: Federated meta-learning with fast convergence and efficient communication. arXiv preprint arXiv:1802.07876 (2018)

4. Chen, M., Sun, Y., Cai, X., Liu, B., Ren, T.: Design and implementation of a novel precision irrigation robot based on an intelligent path planning algorithm. arXiv preprint arXiv:2003.00676 (2020)

5. COVID-19 image data collection. arXiv 2003.11597. https://github.com/ieee8023/covid-chestxray-dataset. Accessed 04 Dec 2020

6. Geyer, R.C., Klein, T., Nabi, M.: Differentially private federated learning: a client level perspective. arXiv preprint arXiv:1712.07557 (2017)

7. Ji, S., Pan, S., Long, G., Li, X., Jiang, J., Huang, Z.: Learning private neural language modeling with attentive aggregation. In: International Joint Conference on Neural Networks (IJCNN) 2019, pp. 1–8. IEEE International Joint Conference on Neural Networks, Budapest, Hungary (2019)

8. Kermany, D.S., et al.: Identifying medical diagnoses and treatable diseases by image-based deep learning. Cell **172**(5), 1122–1131 (2018)

9. Konečný, J., et al.: Federated learning: Strategies for improving communication efficiency. arXiv preprint arXiv:1610.05492 (2016)

10. Liu, B., Wang, L., Liu, M.: Lifelong federated reinforcement learning: a learning architecture for navigation in cloud robotic systems. IEEE Robot. Autom. Lett. **4**(4), 4555–4562 (2019)

11. Liu, B., Wang, L., Liu, M., Xu, C.Z.: Federated imitation learning: a novel framework for cloud robotic systems with heterogeneous sensor data. IEEE Robot. Autom. Lett. **5**(2), 3509–3516 (2020)

12. McMahan, B., Moore, E., Ramage, D., Hampson, S., Arcas, B.A.: Communication efficient learning of deep networks from decentralized data. In: International Conference on Artificial Intelligence and Statistic 2017, vol. 54, pp. 1273–1282. Proceedings of Machine Learning Research, Fort Lauderdale (2017)

13. Sandler, M., Howard, A., Zhu, M., Zhmoginov, A., Chen, L.C.: MobileNetV2: inverted residuals and linear bottlenecks. In: Proceedings of the IEEE Conference on Computer Vision and Pattern Recognition (CVPR) 2018, pp. 4510–4520, IEEE Conference on Computer Vision and Pattern Recognition, Salt Lake City (2018)

14. Sharma, A., Muttoo, S.K.: Spatial image steganalysis based on resnext. In: IEEE 18th International Conference on Communication Technology (ICCT) 2018, Chongqing, People's Republic of China, pp. 1213–1216. IEEE (2018)

15. Smith, V., Chiang, C.K., Sanjabi, M., Talwalkar, A.S.: Federated multi-task learning. In: Advances in Neural Information Processing Systems 2017, vol. 30, pp. 4424–4434. Advances in Neural Information Processing Systems, Long Beach, CA (2017)

16. Sozinov, K., Vlassov, V., Girdzijauskas, S.: Human activity recognition using federated learning. In: 16th IEEE ISPA/17th IEEE IUCC/8th IEEE BDCloud/11th IEEE SocialCom/8th IEEE SustainCom 2018, Melbourne, Australia, pp. 1103–1111. IEEE (2018)

17. Wang, G., Dang, C.X., Zhou, Z.: Measure contribution of participants in federated learning. In: IEEE International Conference on Big Data (Big Data) 2019, pp. 2597–2604. IEEE International Conference on Big Data, Los Angeles, CA (2019)

18. Wang, L., Wong, A.: COVID-Net: a tailored deep convolutional neural network design for detection of COVID-19 cases from chest x-ray images. Sci. Rep. **10**(1), 19549 (2020)

19. Xu, Z., Yang, Z., Xiong, J., Yang, J., Chen, X.: Elfish: resource-aware federated learning on heterogeneous edge devices. arXiv preprint arXiv:1912.01684 (2019)

20. Yan, B., et al.: An improved method for the fitting and prediction of the number of COVID-19 confirmed cases based on LSTM. CMC-Comput. Mater. Con. **64**(3), 1473–1490 (2020)
21. Zhang, Y., et al.: Covid-19 public opinion and emotion monitoring system based on time series thermal new word mining. CMC-Comput. Mater. Con. **64**(3), 1415–1434 (2020)
22. Zhao, Y., Li, M., Lai, L., Suda, N., Civin, D., Chandra, V.: Federated learning with non-IID data. arXiv preprint arXiv:1806.00582 (2018)

A Novel Network Covert Channel Model Based on Blockchain Transaction Parity

Jiaohua Qin[1,2] (iD), YuanJing Luo[2] (iD), Xuyu Xiang[2]([⊠]) (iD), and Yun Tan[2] (iD)

[1] Hunan Applied Technology University, Changde 415000, Hunan, China
[2] College of Computer Science and Information Technology, Central South University of Forestry and Technology, Changsha 410004, China

Abstract. As information security is constantly challenged, it is very necessary to construct a practical and secure new model of information hiding. The existing cover channel models often has the risk of being easily disturbed and destroyed, and the different characteristics of shared resources are needs to be utilized to guarantee its concealment. Due to the security and reliability, decentralization, robustness and other characteristics, Blockchain has been applied to information hiding field (steganography), however, its concealment and practicality are difficult to meet the actual demand. In order to overcome the defects of the covert storage channel and blockchain-based information hiding scheme, we propose a novel network covert channel model based on Blockchain transaction addresses parity and formalize this network covert channel under the blockchain environment. By modulating the parity of the transaction address, the sender can transmit the secret message to the receiver through adding addresses when processing the business without occupying additional block chain space. Meanwhile, the relevant technologies of Blockchain (cryptography, P2P, etc.) ensure that the scheme has good tamper-resistant, multi-line communication and receiver anonymity, guarantying the concealment of communication and the security of information.

Keywords: Network covert channel · Blockchain · Information hiding

1 Introduction

With the development of computer software and hardware, the common information encryption methods have been seriously challenged [1]. In order to enhance the concealment and security of communication, the information hiding technology is proposed, which hides the secret information in a specific way through the open carrier, making it difficult to be discovered [2]. Covert channel (CC) is a key technology of information hiding, it is a communication channel that violates communication restriction rules to transmit hidden information in network environment. It uses the carrier features (protocol field, time feature, etc.) of network information carrier (network protocol, network packet, etc.) to transmit covert information and prevent information from being discovered [3]. Cover channels is constantly developing in the new network environment, and the network covert channel methods also can be divided into covert storage channel

© Springer Nature Switzerland AG 2021
X. Sun et al. (Eds.): ICAIS 2021, CCIS 1423, pp. 54–63, 2021.
https://doi.org/10.1007/978-3-030-78618-2_5

and covert time channel according to the classification of traditional covert channels. However, most of the covert storage channel can be tampered with the communication content by the communication normalization method [4, 5] without reliability guarantee. The network covert storages channel is easy to be targeted detected without reliability guarantee; the capacity of network covert time channel is small and easy to be changed by network condition. Secure communication needs to not only hide the secret message, but also protect the anonymity of sender and receiver, so cover channels are facing great challenges.

Blockchain is essentially a distributed and non-tamper able database, it uses cryptography, consensus algorithm, timestamp and other technologies to ensure that the data on the chain will not be tampered with, and its P2P network, consensus mechanism and openness of blockchain can guarantee the safe transmission of information. Therefore, hiding information based on blockchain in decentralized network environment has lots of advantages. Coinbase and OP_RETURN scripts can be used to communicate, for example, Matzutt [6] et al. summarized several methods of embedding arbitrary information by bitcoin scripts, Juha [7] proposed a simple block chain covert communication method and proved the security of the method. However, these methods also face some problems: inserting additional information may make blockchain data redundant, reducing the concealment.

In order to overcome the defects of the covert storage channel and blockchain-based information hiding scheme, and further guarantee the security and concealment of communication, we proposed a novel network covert channel model based on Blockchain transaction addresses parity. In this scheme, we set "1" as the information expressed by odd transaction and "0" as the information expressed by even transaction. Before communication, the sender and the receiver share the transaction address, and during the transaction, the sender send the secret information to the receiver by modulating the sender address and additional address. The receiver can extract a binary sequence to recover the secret information by determining the parity of all transactions in the order in which they are received. In general, this proposed model has the following advantages:

1. The relevant technologies of Blockchain (cryptography, P2P, etc.) ensure that the Blockchain data will not be tampered with and can be safely transmitted. For the drawbacks of existing network covert channels, the network covert channel model under the Blockchain environment has good tamper-resistant, multi-line communication and receiver anonymity, guarantying the concealment of communication and the security of information, which greatly ensures the concealment and security of the scheme and lays a theoretical foundation for the new network covert channel based on Blockchain environment.

2. Blockchain contains large numbers of transactions and contracts, which are suitable for information hiding. For the drawbacks of existing Blockchain-based information hiding algorithm, the novel network covert channel model based on Blockchain transaction parity can transmit the secret message when processing the business without occupying additional block chain space, which greatly expands the practicability of this new network covert channel.

The rest of this paper is organized as follows: Sect. 2 introduces the related works. We introduce the proposed scheme in Sect. 3 and analyze its performance in Sect. 4. Finally, Sect. 5 summarizes it.

2 Related Works

2.1 Covert Channel

Information hiding technologies can be generally divided into four categories [8]: steganography [9], anonymous communication, copyright identification and covert channel. Compared with other three technologies, covert channel pays more attention to communication model, which greatly enhances the concealment of communication process. Lampson [10] first gave the definition of covert channel in 1973, and the prisoner problem presented by Simmons [11] in 1984 described the communication scenarios of covert channel. In general, covert channel methods include covert storage channel, covert timing channel, covert hybrid channel, covert behavior channel and air-gap covert channel [12]. With the development of network technology, the research of covert channel is extended to network environment, and the network covert channel methods also can be divided into covert storage channel and covert time channel according to the classification of traditional covert channels [3].

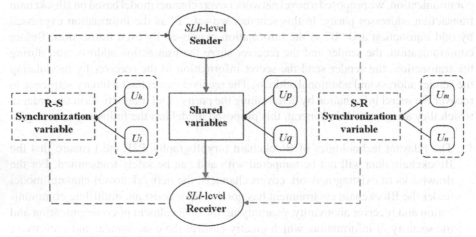

Fig. 1. The necessary conditions of covert channel.

As shown in Fig. 1, the construction of covert channel needs to meet certain conditions. The covert storage channel must fully satisfy: 1. the sender and receiver can access the same property of the shared variable; 2. the sender can change the shared variable state; 3. the receiver can detect the state change of the shared variable; 4. there must be a synchronization mechanism between the sender and receiver. The covert time channel must fully satisfy: 1. the sender and receiver can access the same property of the shared variable; 2. the sender and receiver can access time reference, such as a real-time clock;

3. the sender must be able to adjust the response time of the receiver to detect changes in the shared variable; 4. there must be some mechanism for the sender and receiver processes to initiate covert communication and order events correctly.

However, the existing network covert channels have the following disadvantages: the network covert storage channel is easy to be targeted detected without reliability guarantee; the capacity of network covert time channel is small and easy to be changed by network condition [13]. Besides, most of the existing network covert channel methods only support direct communication between communication parties, and the communication lines are static and single, which are easy to be targeted, detected, interfered and blocked [14]. Although the existing dynamic routing technology can realize the change of transmission line, the transmission process is still single, and lack of stubborn guarantee. Therefore, covert channel needs to utilize the different characteristics of shared resources to improve concealment.

2.2 Blockchain

Blockchain is first proposed by Satoshi Nakamoto in 2008 [15], which is a new application mode of distributed data storage, point-to-point transmission, consensus mechanism, encryption algorithm and other computer technologies. In simple terms, Blockchain is a data structure that combines data blocks in a sequential order according to timestamp, it ensures the non-tampering and non-forgery of the entire chain based on cryptography. In Blockchain, each block contains the hash value of the previous block, so that blocks are linked together to form a single chain in this way (see Fig. 2).

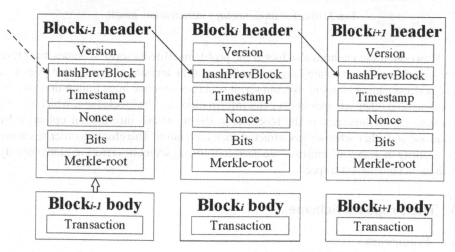

Fig. 2. Structure of blockchain.

Block chain is divided into data layer, network layer, consensus layer, actuator layer, contract layer and application layer. The stability of the bottom layer provides flexibility for the upper layer [16]. The structure of blockchain (see Fig. 3) combines distributed large-scale formula mechanism, consensus economic incentive and flexible intelligent contract, which are the biggest characteristics of blockchain [17]. When generating a transaction, additional information can be logged in an immutable distributed ledger using smart contract and cryptography techniques [18], which means the transaction data of blockchain are permanently stored and cannot be modified. This provides an idea for information hiding based on the blockchain, some schemes use Coinbase, OP_RETURN of blockchain for covert communication [19].

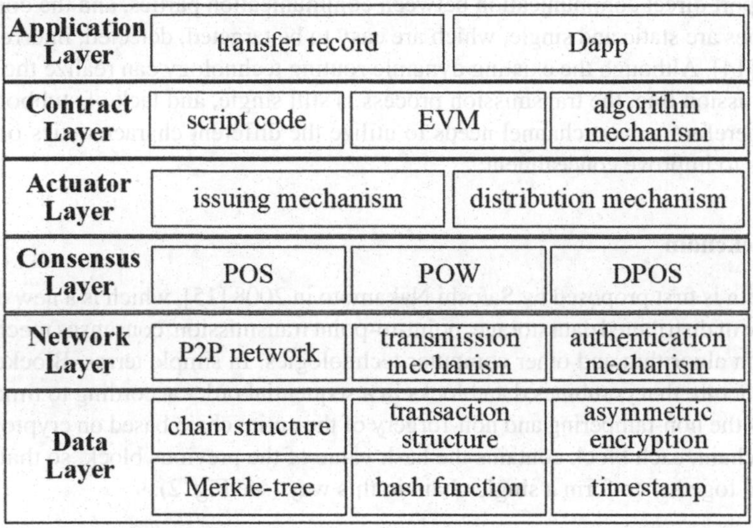

Application Layer	transfer record		Dapp	
Contract Layer	script code	EVM	algorithm mechanism	
Actuator Layer	issuing mechanism		distribution mechanism	
Consensus Layer	POS	POW	DPOS	
Network Layer	P2P network	transmission mechanism	authentication mechanism	
Data Layer	chain structure	transaction structure	asymmetric encryption	
	Merkle-tree	hash function	timestamp	

Fig. 3. Blockchain technology infrastructure model.

However, these methods also face some problems. Bitcoin script schemes need fake Bitcoin addresses, which are easy to identify, and the amount of money that goes to a fake address cannot be spent; Bitcoin script schemes generate huge transaction scripts; Coinbase and other schemes insert extra information into the blockchain, which is easy to cause data redundancy in the blockchain; the malicious information uploaded by Coinbase and other schemes has attracted social attention. Therefore, in order to ensure the security of secret information, we need to transmit secret information more secretly without occupying extra space.

3 The Proposed Scheme

3.1 Framework

In this system, before communication, the sender and the receiver need to share the transaction address, and during the transaction, additional transaction addresses can be added in addition to the sender address. After customizing the transaction parity, the sender can send the secret information to the receiver by modulating the sender address and additional address. The receiver can extract a binary sequence by determining the parity of all transactions sequentially to recover the secret information. In this scheme, we set "1" as the information expressed by odd transaction and "0" as the information expressed by even transaction. To sum up, the framework of network covert channel model based on Blockchain transaction parity is shown in Fig. 4.

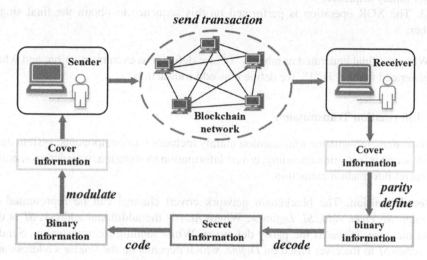

Fig. 4. Framework of proposed scheme.

3.2 Parity Definition

Before communication, we need to define the parity of the trading address, so that the secret information can be mapped into it for transmission. In this paper, we defined the parity of transactions through the following steps (see Fig. 5).

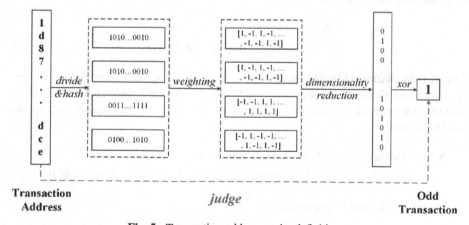

Fig. 5. Transaction address parity definition.

Step1. Divide the transaction address into four segments and obtain the binary sequence through hash operation;
Step2. Weight the generated binary sequence and reduce its dimensionality to obtain a shorter binary sequence;
Step3. The XOR operation is performed on this sequence to obtain the final single number.

When the final generated number is "0", we define it as even transaction, and when the generated number is "1", we define it as odd transaction.

3.3 Information Transmission

In this system, information transmission mainly includes four components: system definition, secret information encoding, covert information modulation, transaction sending and secret information extraction.

System Definition. The blockchain network covert channel can be represented as *<Sender, Receiver, Add, SI, Define>*. Where *Add* is the additional address, *SI* is the secret message, *Define* is the parity definition. While sending the transaction, Sender also sends *SI* to Receiver based on *Define*, which depends on the sender's address and *Add*.

$$Define(odd) = hash(Address(sender), Add) = 1 \tag{1}$$

$$Define(even) = hash(Address(sender), Add) = 0 \tag{2}$$

Secret Information Encoding. *SI* is divided and encoded into some binary sequences, their binary lengths are defined as *L* to record location information. Then these binary sequences are combined with L to obtain *SI'* (see Fig. 6) so that it can be transmitted by the communication network.

$$SI' = code(SI)$$
$$= combine\,(hash\,(divide\,(SI))) \tag{3}$$

Covert Information Modulation. Define is used as the symbol to modulate *SI'* into the cover information *SI''*, so that it can be transmitted secretly through the block chain network environment. Assuming *SI'* is the binary sequence of N-bit, then N transactions need to be sent:

$$SI' = \{Define1,\ Define2,\ Define3, \dots DefineN\}$$
$$= \{hash(Address(sender),\ Add1),\ \dots,\ hash(Address(sender), AddN)\} \tag{4}$$

Therefore, *SI''* can be expressed as:

$$SI'' = \{Add1,\ Add2,\ \dots,\ AddN\} \tag{5}$$

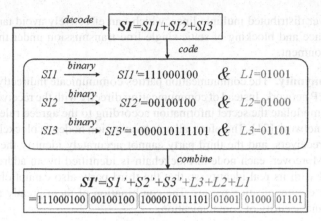

Fig. 6. The reversible coding rule.

Transaction Sending. Sender needs to set up *{Add1, Add2, ..., AddN}* in advance and copy them in order when sending the transaction.

Secret Information Extraction. When the transaction is received, Receiver can get *SI'* through Add, then can determine the parity of the transaction according to Define. Since Eq. 1 and Eq. 2, *SI'* can be get through Eq. 4, and *SI* can be obtained by decoding *SI'* (see Fig. 5).

4 Performance Evaluation

The core technology of Blockchain not only meets the demand of network covert channel, but also can overcome its existing disadvantages and realize highly robust covert communication. This paper builds a covert channel model based in blockchain network and achieves information transmission by defining the parity of blockchain transactions. The security of this scheme can be analyzed from the following three aspects:

Tamper-Resistant. Most of the network covert storage channel model can be eliminated by the communication normalization method [20], that is, tampering with the communication content. In blockchain network environment, the received information are stored by all nodes in a chain based on unified rules. When the attacker wants to tamper with data, he must compute a branch of the data chain and obtain recognition from other nodes. Since all data is stored iteratively, in order to achieve the same length as the legally stored data chain, the attacker needs to supplement the workload of all blocks after tampering, which is huge and difficult to achieve. Therefore, the transaction address under blockchain network can be stably saved and not affected by external technology.

Multi-line Communication. The blockchain P2P network communication technology can greatly alleviate the single point of failure and enables the secret information to be transmitted over distributed multiple-lines, which can effectively avoid targeted detection, interference and blocking of static single line transmission under the traditional network environment.

Receiver Anonymity. The communication parties communicate indirectly through the block chain P2P network. Instead of communicating directly with the receiver, the sender only needs to modulate the secret information according to the agreed rules and send it to blockchain network [21]. Therefore, all communication nodes in blockchain network are potential receivers, and the third party cannot accurately identify the recipient of information. Moreover, each node in blockchain is identified by an address, which is not associated with its real identity, so that the third party also cannot obtain the real identity of the communication parties. The combination of them greatly improves the concealment and security of communication.

5 Conclusion

In this paper, we propose a novel network covert channel model based on Blockchain transaction parity and formalize this network covert channel under the blockchain environment, which mainly builds covert channel model based on blockchain network and transmits secret information through defining the parity of blockchain transaction addresses. By combining blockchain related technologies, the disadvantages of covert channel models in traditional network environment are remedied. Compared with them, this scheme greatly improves the concealment and security of communication through tamper-resistant, multi-line communication and receiver anonymity of blockchain. Besides, this scheme directly transmits secret information while dealing with business without occupying additional block space and causing data redundancy, thus reducing the skepticism of the attacker. In general, this scheme further expands the practical scope of the new covert channel model in block chain network.

Acknowledgments. This work was supported in part by the National Natural Science Foundation of China under Grant 61772561; in part by the Key Research and Development Plan of Hunan Province under Grant 2019SK2022; in part by the Science Research Projects of Hunan Provincial Education Department under Grant 18A174 and Grant 19B584; in part by the Degree & Postgraduate Education Reform Project of Hunan Province under Grant 2019JGYB154; in part by the Postgraduate Excellent teaching team Project of Hunan Province under Grant [2019]370-133; in part by the Postgraduate Education and Teaching Reform Project of Central South University of Forestry & Technology under Grant 2019JG013; in part by the Natural Science Foundation of Hunan Province under Grant 2020JJ4140 and Grant 2020JJ4141.

References

1. Wang, W., Qin, J., Xiang, X., et al.: A privacy-preserving and traitor tracking content-based image retrieval scheme in cloud computing. Multimedia Syst. (2021). https://doi.org/10.1007/s00530-020-00734-w

2. Liu, Q., Xiang, X., Qin, J., et al.: Coverless steganography based on image retrieval of DenseNet features and DWT sequence mapping. Knowl.-Based Syst. **192**, 105375–105389 (2020)
3. Nakamoto, S.: Bitcoin: a peer-to-peer electronic cash system. Consulted **1**(2012), 28 (2008)
4. Handley, M., Paxson, V., Kreibich, C.: Network intrusion detection: evasion, traffic normalization, and end-to-end protocol semantics. In: Conference on Usenix Security Symposium, p. 9 (2001)
5. Lewandowski, G., Lucena, N.B., Chapin, S.J.: Analyzing network-aware active wardens in IPv6. In: Information Hiding, International Workshop, pp. 58–77 (2006)
6. Matzutt, R., Hiller, J., Henze, M.: A quantitative analysis of the impact of arbitrary blockchain content on bitcoin. In: 22nd International Conference on Financial Cryptography and Data Security (FC) (2018)
7. Partala, J.: Provably secure covert communication on blockchain. Cryptography **2**(3), 18 (2018)
8. Petitcolas, F.A.P., Anderson, R.J., Kuhn, M.G.: Information hiding-a survey. Proc. IEEE **87**(7), 1062–1078 (1999)
9. Luo, Y., Qin, J., Xiang, X., et al.: Coverless image steganography based on multi-object recognition. IEEE Trans. Circuits Syst. Video Technol. (2021). https://doi.org/10.1109/TCSVT.2020.3033945
10. Lampson, B.W.: A note on the confinement problem. Commun. ACM **16**(10), 613–615 (1973)
11. Simmons, G.J.: The prisoners' problem and the subliminal channel. In: Chaum, D. (ed.) Advances in Cryptology, pp. 51–67. Springer US, Boston (1984). https://doi.org/10.1007/978-1-4684-4730-9_5
12. Li, Y., Ding, L., Wu, J., et al.: Survey on key issues in networks covert channel. J. Softw. **30**(8), 2470–2490 (2019)
13. Wu, J., Wang, Y., Ding, L., et al.: Improving performance of network covert timing channel through Huffman coding. Math. Comput. Model. **55**(1–2), 69–79 (2012)
14. Li, Y., Ding, L., Wu, J., et al.: Research on a new network covert channel model in blockchain environment. J. Commun. **40**(5), 67 (2019)
15. Nakamoto, S.: Bitcoin: A Peer-to-Peer Electronic Cash System. Bitcoin (2008). https://bitcoin.org/en/bitcoin-paper
16. Crosby, M., Pattanayak, P., Verma, S., et al.: Blockchain technology: beyond bitcoin. Appl. Syst. Innov. **2**, 6–19 (2016)
17. Chowdhury, M.J.M., Colman, A., Kabir, M.A., et al.: Blockchain as a notarization service for data sharing with personal data store. In: 17th IEEE International Conference on Trust, Security and Privacy in Computing and Communications, pp. 1330–1335 (2018)
18. Truong, N.B., Sun, K., Lee, G.M., et al.: GDPR-compliant personal data management: a blockchain-based solution. IEEE Trans. Inf. Forensics Secur. **15**, 1746–1761 (2020)
19. Li, R., Song, T., Mei, B., et al.: Blockchain for large-scale internet of things data storage and protection. IEEE Trans. Serv. Comput. **12**(5), 762–771 (2019)
20. Hackius, N., Petersen, M.: Blockchain in logistics and supply chain: trick or treat? In: Hamburg International Conference of Logistics, pp. 3–18 (2017)
21. Wang, C., Wang, X., Lv, Y., et al.: Categorization of covert channels and its application in threat restriction techniques. J. Softw. **31**(1), 228–245 (2020)

An Improved CNN Model for Fast Salient Object Detection

Bin Zhang, Yang Wu, Jiaqiang Zhang, and Ming Ma[(⊠)]

Graduate Student of Computer Technology, Inner Mongolia University, Hohhot 010000, China
csmaming@imu.edu.cn

Abstract. In an image, how to quickly and effectively extract the useful regions named target regions in the scene according to the saliency features such as spatial domain, frequency domain etc. for further analysis of salient object detection is one of the challenging topics in the field of image segmentation. Most of the existing salient target detection methods use convolution network to extract high-order semantic features, combine pyramid pooling model to fuse high-order and low-order semantic features, and use Adam or SGD optimizer to optimize the model to obtain the salient object. However, the traditional convolution network model is not optimized for the model parameters, and finally redundant parameters will appear in the model, which will aggravate the training time and practical application detection time of the model. Although SGD is fast, it will fall into a large number of local suboptimal solutions or saddle points in the process of non-convex error function optimization. Adam has better performance, but the speed is slightly slower then t -> ∞ that will not have a good generalization performance. In order to solve the above problems, a new optimization strategy is proposed to compress the model. At the same time, AdaX, an optimizer with SGD speed and Adam performance, is used to optimize the model. Through the test on the open data set DUTS, ESSCD and etc., the proposed optimization model method reduces the parameters of the original model, and also improves the training speed and application detection speed of the model.

Keywords: Salient target detection · Optimization strategy · Deep learning

1 Introduction

With the continuous deepening and research in the field of deep learning, hardware performance has significantly improved the deep learning algorithm. Salient object detection [20] has become an important way of computer vision preprocessing. The research of saliency target detection model has gradually formed FCN [27], Pyramid Pooling Module [12], the following context we called PPM and other application methods from biological heuristic [1–3], frequency domain spectral residual [4], phase spectrum [5, 6], test background [7, 8], heuristic learning [9], multi-scale model detection [10, 11], and deep learning [19], which greatly promoted the development of saliency target detection. For example, Wang proposed a multi-stage enhanced model detection architecture on the

© Springer Nature Switzerland AG 2021
X. Sun et al. (Eds.): ICAIS 2021, CCIS 1423, pp. 64–74, 2021.
https://doi.org/10.1007/978-3-030-78618-2_6

basis of FCN, multi-stage fusion PPM is used to fuse high-order semantic information and low-order semantic information. Refining the network in different stages helps to separate the sharp and tailed edges in rough saliency mapping, and can segment salient objects with high resolution. The proposed network structure is designed in ECSSD, THUR15K, DUTOMRON datasets, good results have been achieved on HKU-IS and DUTS datasets; the real-time model architecture based on pooling design proposed by Cheng et al. [13] is inspired by the above structure, and proposes a structural design of PoolNet. The highlight of this model architecture design is that the global guidance module is introduced to fuse high-level and low-level semantic information of different scales, and a feature is also proposed. The new design of aggregation module, as the information after merging and merging, can better weight the composition of the input feature map. In terms of real-time performance, it can achieve a single NVDIA Titan XP for the input 300 * 400 size of image. At the same time, good results have been achieved on ECSSD, PASSCAL-S, DUTO, SOD, DUTS-TS datasets. However, compared with the size of the model, neither of the two methods has compressed the model and further processed it, nor optimized the control of loss function no further analysis is made on the model optimization measurement.

In view of the above analysis, although the research based on FCN and PPM level has made a significant breakthrough, but how to compress the existing model, optimize the loss, get the model parameters smaller, network more optimized and maintain the accuracy of the learning task is still a very challenging task. Inspired by SqueezeNet [14], we choose to optimize the traditional convolution network and compress it with expand and squeeze modules. The squeeze module contains three 1 * 1 convolution layers, and the expand module contains four 1 * 1 convolution layers and four 3 * 3 convolutions layers, using 1 * 1 convolution instead of 3 * 3 convolution, the parameter amount will be reduced to 1/6 of the original. The number of input channels is reduced by the squeeze layer, and the operation of down sampling is delayed. This not only provides the convolution with a larger feature map, but also retains more information at the same time, which improves the accuracy rate, thus maintaining the accuracy and greatly reducing the parameter amount. In terms of loss function, the traditional saliency model uses SGD loss optimization. In recent years, Adam [16] function has been used for loss optimization. However, although SGD is faster, it can't optimize the loss function of Nonconvex Optimization surface. Adam is also an optimizer proposed recently, but it is not easy to converge when t -> ∞ and the generalization performance is poor. We use a new full-scale model optimizer AdaX [15] acts on the optimizer of loss function. The optimizer is an improved version of Adam optimizer. It takes into account the accuracy of Adam and the speed of SGD. At the same time, it fixes the problem of Adam in the attenuation strategy. By using the above two methods, the model is compressed and the parameters of the model are reduced. At the same time, the problems caused by the traditional optimizer are solved less, less loss.

2 Related Work

2.1 Pyramid Pooling Module

Generally speaking, the receptive field can be roughly used to obtain the context information. In the traditional FCN, due to the lack of sufficient attention to the context information of the scene, the segmentation of some different scales of objects is not very ideal. PPM proposes a relatively good way to fully utilize the global information. The pooling pyramid first pools the input feature map of different sizes The size of traditional pooling layer is 1 * 1, 2 * 2, 3 * 3, 6 * 6, and then 1 * 1, 2 * 2, 3 * 3, 6 * 6 characteristic graphs are obtained by 1 * 1 convolution layer convolution, then the bilinear difference is filled to the original input feature map size. The multi size feature map is cascaded with the original feature map, and then the 1 * 1 convolution kernel is used to reduce the concatenated feature map channel to and finally, the prediction result of semantic segmentation which is consistent with the number of channels in the input feature map is obtained.

2.2 PoolNet

On the pyramid pooling model, PoolNet introduces the global guidance module called GGM module and feature aggregation Module called FAM module, GGM module, the high-order semantic information extracted from PPM is sampled and fused in different sizes. FAM looks at the spatial position of significant objects from different multi angle scales and enlarges the receptive field of the whole network and low-order semantic information of different stages to obtain the real-time detection of salient objects. The effect can reach 30fps.

2.3 Fire Module

Inspired by SqueezeNet, which uses several Fire Modules, where the fire module is composed of squeeze and expand. The squeeze is composed of several 1 * 1 convolution blocks, and then the expand part is composed of 1 * 1 and 3 * 3 convolution layers. If 1 * 1 convolution is used to replace 3 * 3 convolution layer, the parameter quantity will be reduced of the original value, and the channel number of 3 * 3 convolution layer will be reduced, so the parameter quantity will be correspondingly reduced due to the large characteristics since there is more information in the graph, the lower sampling layer is set back, which improves the network accuracy.

2.4 AdaX

AdaX optimizer is an improved version of Adam optimizer. For Adam, when $t \rightarrow \infty$, the training is unstable, because the gradient becomes smaller in the late training period, and the training itself tends to be stable. Therefore, the significance of correcting the learning rate is not significant and it is not easy to converge, It may converge to the suboptimal solution that Adam's denominator V_t is too sensitive to small gradients, resulting in Adam's step size being very large, even if the gradient decreases exponentially, Adam's step size is still larger than a constant. Therefore, although Adam converges very fast, it may not be worth the loss, converging to a suboptimal solution, and it is difficult to return to the optimal solution because the gradient at the suboptimal solution is too small. For AdaX, when t -> ∞, it satisfies the above ideal properties which changing the original exponential forgetting V_t to exponential superposition. Therefore, from this point of view, AdaX is an improvement of Adam.

3 Optimizer

3.1 Optimizer Introduction

We use fire to compress the model of feature extraction based on the existing U-shape saliency detection structure. The structure of module uses different convolution blocks to compress the model. On the premise of ensuring the accuracy approximation, the model is compressed to reduce the number of model parameters. At the same time, we introduce the use of AdaX optimizer, which is an improvement of Adam optimizer. With the increase of training time, the learning rate of the optimizer will degenerate to constant increases the generalization robustness of the model. See Fig. 1 for specific optimization introduction structure, and refer to PoolNet for architecture design.

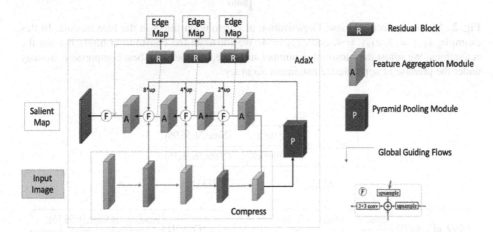

Fig. 1. The pipeline of our proposed saliency detection algorithm. In the feature extraction part, we use 1 * 1 and 3 * 3 convolution blocks to compress the model with different sizes. At the same time, AdaX optimizer is used to replace the traditional Adam and SGD optimizer to optimize the loss.

3.2 Compression Model

We change the structure of the model and use Fire Module in SqueezeNet to replace VggNet [17] model. The core idea of compression algorithm is to use small convolution kernel as far as possible to reduce the number of input channels that the number of layer I parameters = the number of input channels * the number of cores of output channels * the size of cores, and put the down sampling in the layer behind the network as much as possible, so that more semantic information can be obtained. We changed the number of the structure so that the model is proportional to the original size, but the number of parameters is greatly reduced. The original fire module structure as Fig. 2 and our details structure of Fire Module as Fig. 3.

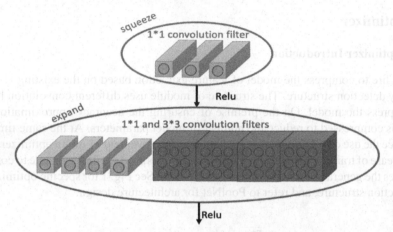

Fig. 2. Microarchitectural view: Organization of convolution filters in the Fire module. In this example, $s_{1x1} = 3$, $e_{1x1} = 4$, and $e_{3x3} = 4$. We illustrate the convolution filters but not the activations. We adjust the convolution number structure to achieve the best compression strategy under the premise of approximate maximum accuracy.

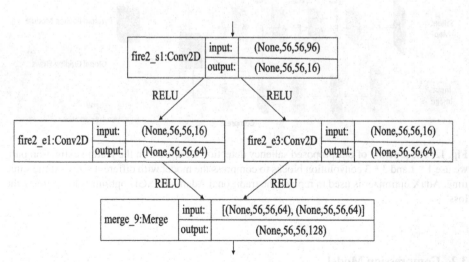

Fig. 3. The details of our Fire Module. In every module that we use the size of 1 * 1 kernels to Squeeze module parameters then use the size of 1 * 1 and the size of 3 * 3 respectively to get the different information of maps.

3.3   The Introduction of AdaX Optimizer for Adam Optimizer

The first-order momentum introduces inertia to the gradient descent that the steeper the slope, the faster you can run, and the second-order momentum introduces the adaptive learning rate and compared with SGD, which needs to adjust the learning rate manually, Adam optimizer can automatically adjust the learning rate. When t -> ∞, the training is unstable because the gradient becomes smaller in the late training period, and the training itself tends to be stable The significance of positive learning rate is not significant, and it is not easy to converge. It may converge to the suboptimal solution and at this time, the denominator V_t of Adam algorithm is too sensitive to small gradient, resulting in the step size of Adam algorithm is very large, even if the gradient is reduced at exponential level, the step size of Adam is still larger than a constant. Therefore, although Adam converges very fast, it may not be worth the loss, converging to a suboptimal solution, and it is difficult to return to the optimal solution because the gradient at the suboptimal solution is too small. Therefore, the correction force of learning rate should be reduced, and the learning rate should be constant and it is equivalent to degenerate to SGD optimizer at this time.

$$V_t = (\frac{1 - \beta_2}{1 - \beta_2^t})\text{diag}(\sum\nolimits_{i=1}^{t} \beta_2^{t-i} g_i^2) \tag{1}$$

For AdaX optimizer, when t -> ∞, the above ideal properties are satisfied which changing the original exponential forgetting V_t to exponential superposition.

$$V_t = (1 + \beta_2)V_{t-1} + \beta_2 g_t^2 \tag{2}$$

Therefore, from this point of view, AdaX optimizer is an improvement of Adam optimizer. With the increase of training time, AdaX optimizer gradually forms memory function, so it has better generalization ability. It is more suitable for the case of long training time and large data set. The introduction of gradient optimization algorithm makes the original loss optimization more stable, and the model generalization energy is obtained, the force is more robust.

4   Experimental Results

The proposed framework is implemented based on the python torch tools. All the experiments are performed using the Adam optimizer with a weight decay of 5e-4 and an initial learning rate of 5e-5 which is divided by 10 after 15 epochs and then we use the AdaX optimizer with the same initialization parameters to test and analyze the experimental results. Our network is trained for 24 epochs in total and was tested with 11 epochs. The backbone parameters of our network such as SqueezeNet and ResNet-50 [18] are initialized with the corresponding models pretrained on the ImageNet Dataset [31] and the rest ones are randomly initialized. By default, our ablation experiments are performed based on the SqueezeNet backbone and the union set of MSRA-B and HKU-IS datasets as done in [22] unless special explanations. On all training sets and test sets, the image size we used remains unchanged, as shown in [23]. The detailed experimental results are analyzed as follows.

4.1 Loss Functions and Datasets

We also used six public datasets, including HKU-IS [21], DUTOMRON [26], SOD [28], PASCAL-S [25], ECSSD [24] and DUTS [29]. We used standard cross entropy loss to detect salient objects and balanced binary cross entropy loss for edge detection [30] as Fig. 4.

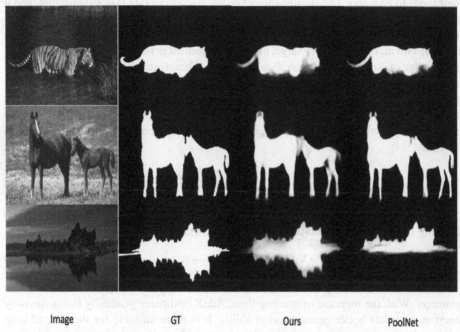

Image   GT   Ours   PoolNet

Fig. 4. Compared with the latest detection method PoolNet, although the edge accuracy of our proposed optimization method is reduced, but the detection range is improved. At the same time, it can also detect some edge details, and can highlight the overall saliency target. After the model fusion, the overall saliency information is significantly prominent.

4.2 Evaluation Criteria

We evaluate the performance of our approach and other methods using three widely-used metrics: precision-recall curves called PR, FPS, and mean absolute error called MAE. F-measure, denoted as F_β, is an overall performance measurement and is computed by the weighted harmonic mean of the precision and recall:

$$F_\beta = \frac{\left(1 + \beta^2\right) * \text{Precision} * \text{Recall}}{\beta^2 * \text{Precision} + \text{Recall}} \qquad (3)$$

where β^2 is set to 0.3 as done in previous work to weight precision more than recall. The MAE score indicates how similar a saliency map S is compared to the ground truth G:

$$MAE = \frac{1}{W * H} \sum_{x=1}^{W} \sum_{y=1}^{H} |S(x, y) - G(x, y)| \tag{4}$$

where W and H denote the width and height of S, respectively.

Precision Recall Curves. We use different networks on DUTS-TE and HKU-IS datasets for comparative analysis. We can find that our network which use dark purple curve is superior to some networks in precision and recall, but there is a certain gap compared with other networks (see Fig. 5 and Fig. 6).

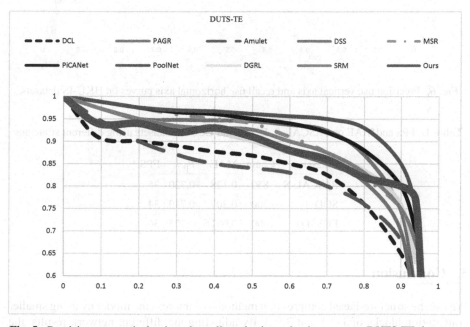

Fig. 5. Precision use vertical axis and recall use horizontal axis curves on DUTS-TE datasets.

Average Speed. Compared with the Average Speed that FPS of the original network that is not optimized, we use the same test data set for detection, and the input original image is still 400 * 300. The FPS of the original network can reach 32 on our devices, and the FPS after optimization can reach 34+ on our devices using different databases, which has an obvious speed improvement. And Table 1 shows the number of pictures named Count, MAE, F_β and FPS.

Parameters. The parameter is reduced from 68261057 to 52512705, about 1/6 less, and training speed from 37 h to cut down 22 h when we use the original datasets to train model.

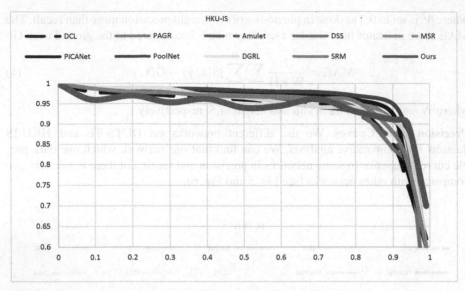

Fig. 6. Precision use vertical axis and recall use horizontal axis curves on HKU-IS datasets.

Table 1. FPS and MAE on PASCAL-S, DUTS and ECSSD datasets using different strategies

Dataset	Count	MAE	F_β	FPS
PASCAL-S	850	0.128	0.720	35
SOD	300	0.207	0.740	34
ECSSD	1000	0.0816	0.705	36

5 Conclusion

We use the structure-based compression method to compress the model by using smaller convolution blocks of 1 * 1 and 3 * 3. By adjusting the different network results, the parameters of the model are reduced, and the training speed and detection speed are improved. On the premise that the precision loss is almost constant, the AdaX optimizer with better generalization performance is used to pan the model on large data sets significant results have been obtained. Our experiments on the open datasets SOD, ECSSD and etc., as well as the pass rate, recall rate, F value, MAE evaluation index is basically the same as the current popular algorithms, but the model parameters and generalization performance are greatly enhanced.

Acknowledgement. This work is supported by CERNET Innovation Project (NGII20190625).

References

1. Koch, C., Poggio, T.: Predicting the visual world: silence is golden. Nat. Neurosci. $2(1)$, 9–10 (1999)
2. Yang, C., Zhang, L., Lu, H., Ruan, X., Yang, M.: Saliency detection via graph-based manifold ranking. In: IEEE Conference on Computer Vision and Pattern Recognition 2013. CVPR, pp. 3166–3173. IEEE Computer Society (2013)
3. Qin, Y., Lu, H.C., Xu, Y.Q.: Saliency detection via cellular automata. In: IEEE Conference on Computer Vision and Pattern Recognition 2015. CVPR, pp. 110–119. IEEE Computer Society (2015)
4. Hou,X.D., Zhang, L.Q.: Saliency detection: a spectral residual approach. In: IEEE Conference on Computer Vision and Pattern Recognition 2007. CVPR, pp. 17–22. IEEE Computer Society (2007)
5. Guo, C.L., Ma, Q., Zhang, L.M.: Spatio-temporal saliency detection using phase spectrum of quaternion fourier transform. In: IEEE Conference on Computer Vision and Pattern Recognition 2008. CVPR, pp. 23–28. IEEE Computer Society (2008)
6. Guo, C.L., Zhang, L.M.: A novel multiresolution spatiotemporal saliency detection model and its applications in image and video compression. IEEE Trans. Image Process. $19(1)$, 185–198 (2010)
7. Liu, T., Sun, J., Zheng, N.N.: Learning to detect a salient object. In: IEEE Conference on Computer Vision and Pattern Recognition 2007. CVPR, pp. 17–22. IEEE Computer Society (2007)
8. Liu, T., Zheng, N.N., Ding, W.: Video attention: learning to detect a salient object sequence. In: 19th International Conference on Pattern Recognition 2008. ICPR, pp. 1–4. IEEE Computer Society (2008)
9. Tong, N., Lu, H.C., Ruan, X.: Salient object detection via bootstrap learning. In: IEEE Conference on Computer Vision and Pattern Recognition 2015. CVPR, pp. 1884–1892. IEEE Computer Society (2015)
10. Xu, L., Cui, G.M., Zheng, C.P.: Fusion method of visible and infrared images based on multi-scale decomposition and saliency region extraction. Laser Optoelectron. Prog. $54(11)$, 1–3 (2017)
11. Zhu, W.J., Liang, S., Wei, Y.C.: Saliency optimization from robust background detection. In: IEEE Conference on Computer Vision and Pattern Recognition 2014. CVPR, pp. 2814–2821. IEEE Computer Society (2008)
12. Wang, T., Borji, A., Zhang, L.: A stagewise refinement model for detecting salient objects in images. In: IEEE Conference on Computer Vision and Pattern Recognition 2017. CVPR, pp. 4039–4048. IEEE Computer Society (2017)
13. Liu, J.J., Hou, Q., Cheng, M.M.: A simple pooling-based design for real-time salient object detection. In: IEEE Conference on Computer Vision and Pattern Recognition 2019. CVPR, pp. 3917–3926. Computer Vision Foundation/IEEE (2019)
14. Iandola, N.F., Moskewicz, M.W., Ashraf, K., Han, S., Dally, W.J., Keutzer, K.: SqueezeNet: AlexNet-level accuracy with 50x fewer parameters and <1 MB model size. CoRR abs/1602.07360 (2016)
15. Li, W., Zhang, Z., Wang, X.: AdaX: Adaptive Gradient Descent with Exponential Long-Term Memory. CoRR abs/2004.09740 (2020)
16. Kingma, D.P., Ba, J.: Adam: A Method for Stochastic Optimization. ICLR (Poster) (2015)
17. Simonyan, K., Zisserman, A.: Very deep convolutional networks for large-scale image recognition. In: ICLR (2015)
18. He, K.M., Zhang X.Y., Ren, S.Q., Sun, J.: Deep residual learning for image recognition. In: IEEE Conference on Computer Vision and Pattern Recognition 2016. CVPR, pp. 770–778. IEEE Computer Society (2016)

19. Lee, G., Tai, Y.W., Kim, J.: Deep saliency with encoded low-level distance map and high-level features. In: IEEE Conference on Computer Vision and Pattern Recognition 2016. CVPR, pp. 660–668. IEEE Computer Society (2016)
20. Liu, T., et al.: Learning to detect a salient object. IEEE Pattern Anal. Mach. Intell. **33**(2), 353–367 (2011)
21. Li, G.B., Yu, Y.Z.: Visual saliency based on multiscale deep features. In: IEEE Conference on Computer Vision and Pattern Recognition 2015. CVPR, pp. 5455–5463. IEEE Computer Society (2015)
22. Li, G., Xie, Y., Lin, L., Yu, Y.Z.: Instance-level salient object segmentation. In: IEEE Conference on Computer Vision and Pattern Recognition 2017. CVPR, pp. 247–256. IEEE Computer Society (2017)
23. Hou, Q.B., Cheng, M.M., Hu, X.W., Borji, A., Tu, Z.W., Torr, P.: Deeply supervised salient object detection with short connections. IEEE Trans. Pattern Anal. Mach. Intell. **41**(4), 815–828 (2019)
24. Yan, Q., Xu, L., Shi, J.P., Jia, J.Y.: Hierarchical saliency detection. In: IEEE Conference on Computer Vision and Pattern Recognition 2013. CVPR, pp. 1155–1162. IEEE Computer Society (2013)
25. Li, Y., Hou, X.D., Koch, C., Rehg, J.M., Yuille, A.L.: The secrets of salient object segmentation. In: IEEE Conference on Computer Vision and Pattern Recognition 2014. CVPR, pp. 280–287. IEEE Computer Society (2014)
26. Yang, C., Zhang, L.H., Lu, H.C., Ruan, X., Yang, M.H.: Saliency detection via graph-based manifold ranking. In: IEEE Conference on Computer Vision and Pattern Recognition 2013. CVPR, pp. 3166–3173. IEEE Computer Society (2013)
27. Shelhamer, E., Long, J., Darrell, T.: Fully convolutional networks for semantic segmentation. IEEE Trans. Pattern Anal. Mach. Intell. **39**(4), 640–651 (2015)
28. Movahedi, V., Elder, J.H.: Design and perceptual validation of performance measures for salient object segmentation. In: IEEE Conference on Computer Vision and Pattern Recognition 2010. CVPR, pp. 49–56. IEEE Computer Society (2010)
29. Wang, L.J., et al.: Learning to detect salient objects with image-level supervision. In: IEEE Conference on Computer Vision and Pattern Recognition 2017. CVPR, pp. 3796–3805. IEEE Computer Society (2017)
30. Xie, S.N., Tu, Z.W.: Holistically-nested edge detection. Int. J. Comput. Vision **125**(1–3), 3–18 (2015)
31. Deng, J., Dong, W., Socher, R., Li, L.J., Li, K., Li, F.F.: ImageNet: a large-scale hierarchical image database. In: IEEE Conference on Computer Vision and Pattern Recognition 2009. CVPR, pp. 248–255. IEEE Computer Society (2009)

Control System Design of Transport Robot Based on Multi-color Recognition

Long-fei Liu, Jie Kang[✉], Xiao-ying Chen, Jing-jia Wang, Xiao Ma,
and Cheng-han Yang

College of Mechanical and Electrical Engineering, Sanjiang University, Nanjing 210012, China

Abstract. According to the rules and requirements of the handling project of the China Engineering Robot Contest, an intelligent handling robot with Freescale KL25 chip as the core controller and capable of automatically identifying multiple colors was designed. Based on the completion of the hardware circuit and mechanical structure, the robot's trajectory on the field is planned through software programming. Establishing a handling strategy allows the robot to efficiently grasp, transport, and stack objects. The focus is on the infrared tracking module, the color recognition module software design and the robot path planning strategy research. After the completion of the robot construction, through experiments in various links, the total number of loops compared to the traditional handling scheme has increased by about 11.1%, and the running time has been reduced by about 41.5%. The effect is good.

Keywords: Handling robot · Multi-color recognition · Modular design

1 Research Status

With the rapid development of the logistics industry in recent years, the research and design of handling robots have become more and more diversified, and their functions have become more and more powerful. After consulting and researching relevant domestic and foreign documents in recent years, as shown in Table 1, it is found that logistics handling robots are developing towards intelligence, high efficiency, and large-scale development.

Table 1. Current research status of logistics handling robots at home and abroad

Robot name	Kiva robot	Transwheel robot	"Cao Cao" robot
Producing countries	The United States	Israesl	China
Research the company	Amazon	Shenkar Institute of Engineering and Design	Alibaba
Research initial time	In 2012	In 2015	In 2015
Characteristics	strong bearing capacity	It has facial recognition function	Fast speed and high efficiency
Application places	warehouse	Flat surface	warehouse

X. Sun et al. (Eds.): ICAIS 2021, CCIS 1423, pp. 75–88, 2021.
https://doi.org/10.1007/978-3-030-78618-2_7

2   Handling Robot Design Requirements and Overall Design Plan

According to the requirements of the competition rules, an intelligent robot that can complete tracking, color recognition, and handling tasks in accordance with established procedures is designed. It will move in the arena (as shown in Fig. 1), sort and transport blocks of different colors but the same shape to the corresponding area of the color. The closer to the center ring, the higher the score (1–10 ring), and the final score will be accumulated The team with the highest and shortest time wins.

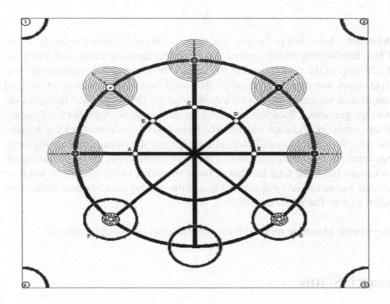

Fig. 1. Map of the robot handling competition

According to design requirements, KL25 is the core control module to control the color recognition module, infrared tracking module, motor drive module, and mechanical structure module. Subsequent software design is carried out in blocks according to the modular design concept. The system modular design framework is shown in Fig. 2. This article focuses on the software design of the tracking module and the color recognition module and the research on the robot handling planning strategy.

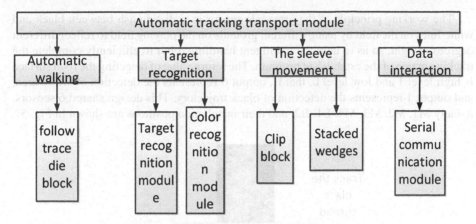

Fig. 2. Block diagram of system modular design

3 Tracking Module Software Design

The tracking sensor uses a digital grayscale sensor, which is mainly composed of a pair of photosensitive pairs, a voltage comparator and a potentiometer. The working voltage is 5V, and the detection distance is between 15 mm and 25 mm (Figs. 3 and 4).

Fig. 3. Physical image of tracking sensor side

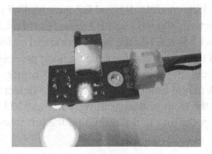

Fig. 4. The effect of tracking sensor operation

The working principle of the grayscale sensor is to distinguish between black and white lines on the field by using different grounds on the playing field to reflect different degrees of light, so as to help the intelligent handling robot to efficiently complete the tracking action of the established program. The return value of detecting the road surface is high level 1 and low level 0, that is, output 0 represents the detection of white area, and output 1 represents the detection of black trajectory. This design shared 6 sensors, namely M1, M2, M3, M4, B1, B2, and their installation positions are shown in Fig. 5:

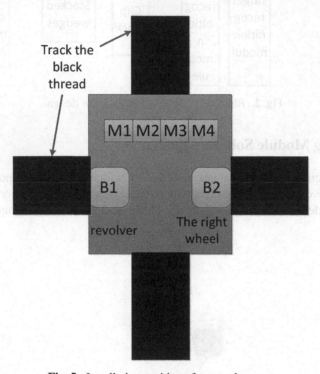

Fig. 5. Installation position of grayscale sensor

Among them, M1, M2, M3, and M4 are installed side by side in the middle of the car body as the main tracking module. B1 and B2 are installed under the steering gear. When passing the intersection, when B1 and B2 detect the black line at the same time, it is determined that the robot has reached the intersection and no longer tracks at this time. Figure 5 is a flow chart of the 6-way sensor in the tracking process. When the robot starts to track on the playing field, the four-way sensor in the center of the car body detects the black line of the track in real time. If only M2 and M3 detect the black line, it means There is no deflection in the front of the car. If only M1 and M2 detect the black line, it means that the car body is shifting to the right, and the left wheel is decelerated at this time. If only M3 and M4 detect the black line, it means that the car body is deviated to the left. At this time, the right wheel is slowed down, and this method is used to ensure the correct direction of travel. The specific programming process is shown in Fig. 6.

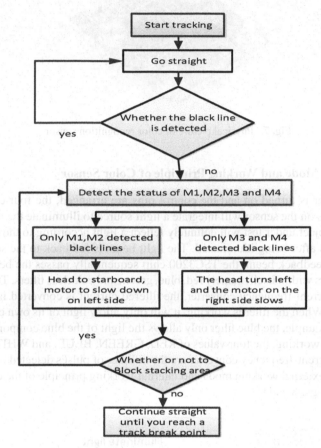

Fig. 6. Trace flow chart

4 Color Recognition Module

In order to accurately identify the color of the transported object, a sensor module with the TSC3200D chip as the core is used. Four light-emitting diodes are arranged at the four corners of the sensor, and the middle part is composed of the main chip and its peripheral circuits. Its appearance is shown in Fig. 7.

Fig. 7. Physical picture of color recognition sensor

4.1 Working Mode and Working Principle of Color Sensor

After the power is turned on and the control pins are arranged, the four-corner light-emitting diodes on the sensor will integrate a light source to illuminate the object under test, and the object under test will definitely reflect a light according to the principle of light refraction after being illuminated. The light beam is fed back to the sensor. After receiving the feedback beam, the TSC3200 chip sequentially passes the beam through four color filters within itself, namely red, blue, green, and colorless filters. Then through the internal current-frequency converter, the filtered current is converted into a digital output signal. When the filter is working, it will only allow light of its own color to pass through. For example, the blue filter only allows the light of the blue component to pass. By this way of working, the four values of RED, GREEN, BLUE, and WHITE obtained through the current-frequency converter are the number of pulses detected by each filter in 0.25S. The external working mode and internal working principle of the color sensor are shown in Figs. 8 and 9.

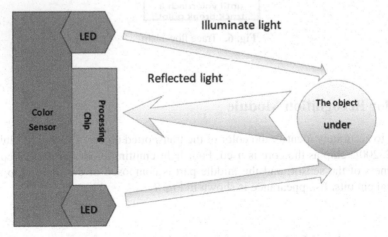

Fig. 8. A schematic diagram of the external working mode of the color sensor

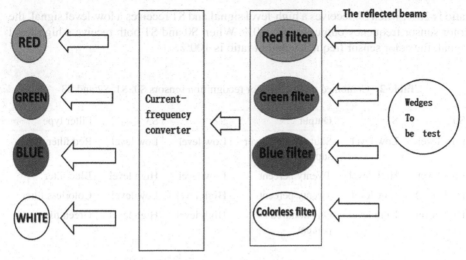

Fig. 9. Internal working principle of color sensor

4.2 Color Sensor Working Mode Software Configuration

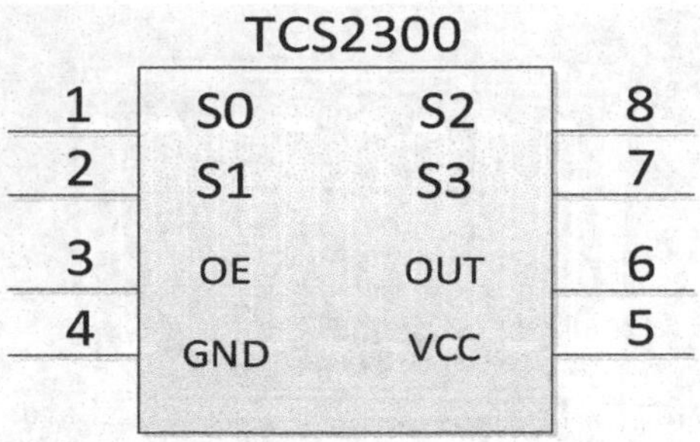

Fig. 10. Pins and functional block diagram of color recognition sensor

It can be seen from Fig. 10 that the required filter is selected through the dynamic combination of the two selectable pins on the sensor. The frequency range of the output to the processor after being converted from current to frequency is 2 Hz–500 Hz. You can also program the other two pins to control its output scale factor or power-off mode. The specific selection mode is shown in Table 2. When both S2 and S3 receive low-level signals, the color sensor is selected to work as the red filter. When S2 receives low-level signals and S3 receives high-level signals, the color sensor is selected as blue filters. When S2 receives a high-level signal and S3 receives a low-level signal, the color sensor is selected as a colorless filter. When both S2 and S3 receive a high-level signal, the color sensor is selected as a green filter the work. For the combination of S0 and S1, when both S0 and S1 receive a low-level signal, the color sensor stops working. When S0 receives a low-level signal and S1 receives a high-level signal, the color sensor frequency output ratio is 20%, when S0 receives a high-level signal and S1 receives a low-level signal, the color sensor frequency output ratio is 20%. When S0 and S1 both receive a high-level signal, the color sensor frequency output ratio is 100%.

Table 2. Combined modes of color recognition sensors S0, S1, S2 and S3

S0	S1	Output	S2	S3	Filter type
Low level	Low level	Shut off the power supply	Low level	Low level	Red filter
Low level	High level	Twenty percent	Low level	High level	Blue filter
High level	Low level	Twenty percent	High level	Low level	Colorless filter
High level	High level	One hundred percent	High level	High level	Green filter

Figure 11 (a) and (b) are screenshots of measuring the number of pulses output by connecting an oscilloscope to the OUT pin of the sensor when the color sensor detects a green object. From (b), it can be seen that the operating voltage of the color sensor is 3V, the pulse period is 154.0us, and the duty cycle is 50%.

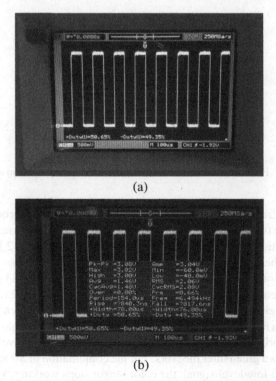

(a)

(b)

Fig. 11. (a) Color sensor pulse detected by oscilloscope. (b) Measurement of color sensor pulse output

In the hardware connection, let S0 and S1 of the color recognition sensor connect to the PTC6 and PTC7 interfaces of the single-chip microcomputer respectively. In the program, you only need to set the high and low level output of the PTC6 pin and PTC7 pin to select the filter mode of the color recognition sensor.

4.3 Software Algorithm of Color Sensor

As shown in Fig. 12, this figure is the debugging interface obtained by calling the add to watch debugging interface on the IAR compilation platform when the color sensor detects the green object. On the debugging interface of the platform, you can clearly see the four in the color sensor. The four kinds of pulse output numbers obtained by the filter when detecting the green object block. With the debugging function of the platform, this article prepared five different color blocks in the experiment according to the standards provided by the competition official. In a variety of different environments, the software was repeatedly tested and averaged, and the results were more accurate and stable. The pulse frequency output under the four kinds of filters is shown in Table 3.

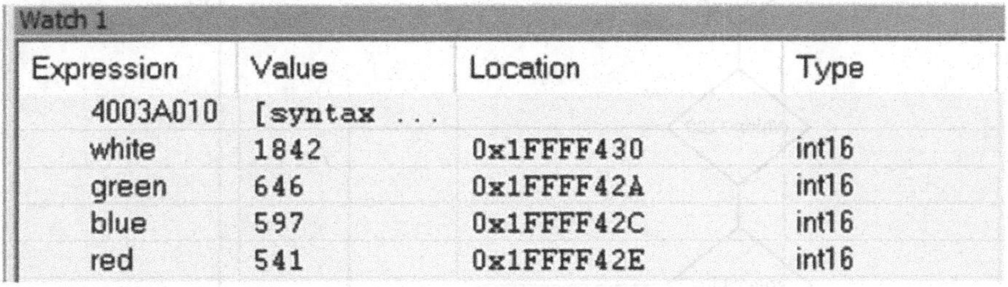

Watch 1			
Expression	Value	Location	Type
4003A010	[syntax ...		
white	1842	0x1FFFF430	int16
green	646	0x1FFFF42A	int16
blue	597	0x1FFFF42C	int16
red	541	0x1FFFF42E	int16

Fig. 12. Pulse output under four filters was tested on the debugging interface of IAR compilation platform

Table 3. Output frequencies of different block in each filter

S2	S3	Filter type	Red wedges	Green wedges	Blue wedges	White wedges	Black wedges
Low level	Low level	Red	836	268	300	1460	115
Low level	High level	Blue	589	406	497	1265	101
High level	Low level	Colorless	1695	1188	638	4122	333
High level	High level	Green	476	646	603	1161	103

It can be seen from Table 3 that the output frequency of the white object under the colorless filter is very large and can be easily distinguished, while the output frequency of the red object under the colorless filter is second only to the white object. The frequency of the black block is the smallest under all kinds of resolvers. The blue and green values under their respective filters are greater than each other. According to observing the value of the four filters, a simple color recognition algorithm is planned. The general idea is: first detect the measured object block to obtain the pulse value of the four filters, and first determine the value of white: if If it is greater than 2100, the block is a white block; if it is less than 2100 but greater than 1100, the block is a red block. If white is less than 1100, compare the size of green and blue. If the value of green is large, the block will be green. If the above conditions are not met, then the absolute value of the three primary color values is compared with each other to determine whether the block is blue or black. The above is the basic idea of the color recognition algorithm. Figure 13 is a flowchart of the algorithm.

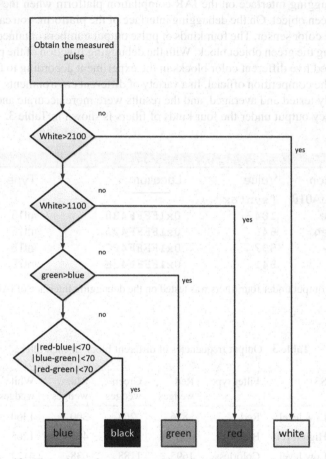

Fig. 13. Flow chart of color recognition algorithm (Color figure online)

5 Research and Experiment of Robot Handling Planning Strategy

The traditional robot handling planning strategy (clamping scheme) is to grab one block at a time, send it to the corresponding color area after identification, and then repeat until all the handling is completed. The flow chart is shown in Fig. 14. Place the physical

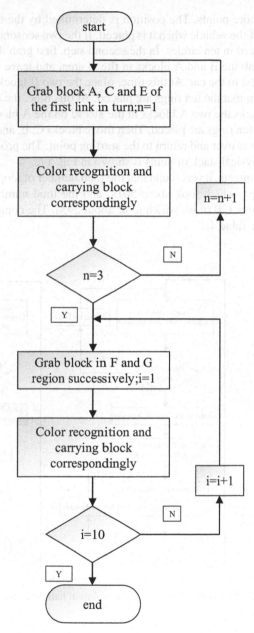

Fig. 14. Flow chart of the handling strategy of the clamp-on solution

objects as shown in Fig. 16. In order to better improve the robot handling score and operating efficiency, this paper proposes a new handling planning strategy (sleeve type scheme): the first step, the robot grabs objects A, C, and E on the arc through the sleeve in turn. Blocks, and then color recognition according to the order of the blocks in the sleeve, place the blocks to score points. The position is determined by the two line-following sensors on the front of the vehicle when it is placed. If the two sensors detect at the same time, the block is placed in ten circles. In the second step, first grab the A and B blocks in the F area, then grab the B and A blocks in the G area, and leave the A block in the G area in the hook next to the car. At this time, place the two B blocks at the bottom of the sleeve and confirm that the ten rings are placed. At this time, the sleeve grabs the A block in the hook, stacks the two A blocks in the sleeve on the A block in the first link, and confirms that the ten rings are placed. Then move blocks C, E, and D in this way. At this point, the mission is over and return to the starting point. The process plan is shown in Fig. 15, and the physical stack of items is shown in Fig. 17.

After many experiments, it was found that the total number of loops in the test clamp scheme was 117 rings, which took about 501s, and the total number of rings in the sleeve-type scheme was 130 rings, which took about 293s. The comparison of the two strategies is shown in Table 4:

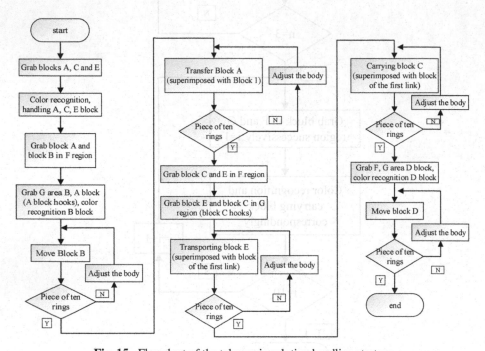

Fig. 15. Flowchart of the telescopic solution handling strategy

Fig. 16. The physical image of the clamp-type solution block placement

Fig. 17. The physical image of the sleeve-type solution block stacking

Table 4. Comparison of robot handling planning strategies

Strategy comparison	Maximum number of transports at a time	Maximum number of rings per block	Maximum number of loops in multiple blocks	Number of blocks moved	Total number of rings	carry out Time (seconds)
Clamp-on strategy	1	10	9	13	117	501s
Telescopic strategy	4	10	10	7	130	293s

6   In Conclusion

This article focuses on the software design of the handling robot for the tasks and requirements of the robot competition. According to the idea of modular design, the software programming of robot tracking, color recognition and other modules are designed respectively. On the basis of fully studying the principle of the use of the color sensor, the law of obtaining the corresponding total number of pulses for different colors under four filters was discovered and summarized, and then the control algorithm was designed for software programming. On this basis, a new handling planning strategy (sleeve type solution) is proposed. Compared with the traditional clamp type solution, the total number of robot loops has increased by about 11.1%, and the running time has been reduced by about 41.5%. After repeated tests and actual experiments verify that this method is stable and reliable. At present, the results have been used to participate in the national and provincial handling robot competitions and have won many championships with excellent results.

Funding Statement. This paper is sponsored by the "Qinglan Project" of Jiangsu universities, the General Natural Science Research Project of Jiangsu universities (19KJD510005) and the Industry-university cooperative education Project of the Ministry of Education (201902168015). Thank the anonymous reviewers and editors for their valuable comments and suggestions on improving the quality of the paper.

Conflicts of Interest. The authors declare that they have no conflicts of interest to report regarding the present study. The authors declare that they have no conflicts of interest to report regarding the present study.

References

1. Wang, W.D., Wang, N.: Design of intelligent handling robot based on STM32 microcontroller. China New Commun. **19**(14), 5 (2017)
2. Li, M.J., Zuo, K.J.: Material handling robot based on freescale microcontroller. J. Bin Zhou Univ. **33**(02), 77–82 (2017)
3. Zhang, L., Li, Y., Li, L.L.: Experimental teaching practice of single chip microcomputer based on "robot handling" competition. Exp. Teach. Instrum. **32**(Z1), 126–212 (2015)
4. Zhang, Y.Y., Li, Y.F.: Design of intelligent handling robot based on AT89S52 MICRO controller. Electron. World **13**, 46–47 (2013)
5. He, L.B.: Design and implementation of competitive handling robot. Nanjing University of Finance and Economics (2013)

SACache: Size-Aware Load Balancing for Large-Scale Storage Systems

Yihong Su[1], Hang Jin[1], Fang Liu[1(✉)], and Weijun Li[2]

[1] School of Computer Science and Engineering, Sun Yat-Sen University, Guangzhou, China
liufang25@mail.sysu.edu.cn
[2] Shenzhen Dapu Microelectronic Co., Ltd., Shenzhen, China

Abstract. The fast cache could be used in storage clusters to alleviate load imbalance caused by highly-skewed requests between storage nodes. In a smaller cluster, we can use a single cache node to solve the I/O bottleneck caused by load imbalance. However, in a Large-scale cluster, we may need more than one cache node to afford enough capacity, which brings a new load balance problem in cache nodes. DistCache successfully solved this problem by applying the power-of-two-choices. In the above storage clusters, cache nodes cache the hottest objects while ignoring the size of objects, which leads to poor performance when meeting objects with variable sizes. We present SACache, a size-aware mechanism for large-scale storage clusters, which can improve I/O performance by maximizing the benefit of the unit cache. In this mechanism, we set an object admission filter to filter out objects with lower caching benefit. To adapt to changing request patterns, we record recently requested objects and their size, then replay those requests periodically in a cache simulator to find the best cache admission parameter using a greedy algorithm and apply it to the object admission filter. We apply this mechanism in a prototype distributed storage system. Experimental results show that it can increase the system's overall bandwidth when the object's size is different.

Keywords: Load balancing · Size-aware · Large-scale storage · Caching

1 Introduction

Distributed object storage systems provide scalable storage for modern data-intensive applications where data is stored as key-value pairs, and applications can access values from a storage cluster that spans thousands of nodes with a unique key [1–4]. Key-value storages are already widely deployed in social networking, data analytics, Web search, download centers, and other applications. In the real world, the request loads are high-skewed, few popular objects may receive most of the requests, which brought challenges to the load balancing. However, skewed access leads to a spatial locality. Thus, we can load hot objects into the cache, improve the system bandwidth, and reduce latency, resulting in a better user experience and meet stricter service-level objectives (SLOs).

© Springer Nature Switzerland AG 2021
X. Sun et al. (Eds.): ICAIS 2021, CCIS 1423, pp. 89–105, 2021.
https://doi.org/10.1007/978-3-030-78618-2_8

In a typical object storage system, HDD is used as the storage medium with a large capacity with low cost; however, it has a high access latency. Due to disk seek time (about 10 ms), HDD is not friendly to random access. Besides, the access speed of HDD is slower than RAM. If we cache some objects into RAM, we can reduce disk I/O's performance overhead. Meanwhile, caching hot objects can also be used as a load balancing strategy for a storage cluster. For a cluster with n storage nodes, caching $O(n\log n)$ hottest objects can balance the system, regardless of the number of objects [5].

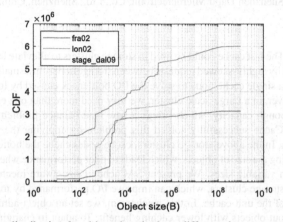

Fig. 1. Cumulative distribution for object sizes in three different data centers, traces are from an IBM Docker Registry.

In an object storage system, cache replacement algorithms (e.g., LRU and LFU) prioritize hot objects and evict objects in the cache. In real-world applications, there are also differences in size between objects besides differences in popularity. Figure 1 shows the object distribution of three traces from the IBM Docker Registry production [6]. We can find that the range of object size is vast, from KB magnitude to GB magnitude. In this case, if using the unmodified cache management algorithm, putting a large object into the cache can cause multiple small objects to be evicted. If we need to access these small objects once again, we need to access HDD storage nodes, resulting in a large number of HDD random access, which will decrease the system's overall bandwidth.

Because the object size range in an object storage system is wide, to maximize the value of the small but expensive RAM, we need a mechanism to evaluate the benefit of an object being cached and decide whether to be admitted by the cache. At the same time, this mechanism should be able to automatically adapt to different data load characteristics and dynamically adapt to the change of load characteristics over time. Therefore, it is necessary to analyze the benefits of storage systems based on HDD and RAM characteristics and design a cache admit mechanism to maximize the system performance with limited cache capacity.

We present SACache, an easy-to-understand cache management strategy suitable for storage systems with large size differences. Based on a lightweight cache node simulator (shadow cache), SACache searches for the current optimal caching parameters by replaying the recent trace of object request records (including object name and size) in the cache node. It can be used as both a cache management mechanism for stand-alone object storage systems and an optimization method for large distributed object storage.

SACache adds a cache admission mechanism based on the cache replacement algorithm, ensuring that small objects have a greater probability of being cached. Simultaneously, there is a caching parameter in the admission mechanism, which determines how much object size affects the probability of being admitted. The shadow cache is the key to finding the appropriate caching parameters, and there is a shadow cache in each cache node to simulate the node's performance under a specific caching parameter. When searching for caching parameters, we compare the shadow cache's performance under different caching parameters to select the optimal caching parameter. Fine-grained search interval can guarantee higher precision but may bring unacceptable time overhead. Based on empirical observation, we implement a fast search algorithm that achieves high precision through fewer search times so that the parameter search time is completely acceptable.

1. We implement an object storage prototype system integrating SACache, measure performance improvement and stability of SACache in the simulation environment (for both single-node and storage cluster). Our contribution can be summarized as follows:
2. We analyze and summarize a benefit formula of the object storage system with a caching mechanism.
3. We designed an efficient shadow cache to simulate the behavior of real cache nodes.
4. We implement a fast parameter search algorithm for searching the optimal caching parameters.
5. We evaluated the performance improvement of SACache under different loads in a simulation environment for both single-node and storage clusters.

2 Background and Motivation

2.1 Cache Based Load Balancing

Partitioning is frequently-used in the extensible object storage system, where each node independently provides the storage and query of partial objects. Uneven request loads can lead to performance differences between nodes, resulting in reduced cluster throughput and increased latency. A hash-based partitioning function is sufficient to partition the objects evenly in a cluster with constant storage nodes. For applications that require scalability, consistent hashing is used to ensure that objects can be partitioned evenly after adding or removing a server node. However, these schemes are insufficient for the load imbalance caused by the difference in popularity among objects.

Popularity differences between objects are usually highly skewed in real-world internet applications. Object access Popularity tends to follow Zipf distribution, and a small amount of hot object will be requested frequently. The skewed access makes small capacity high-speed caching system accepts many requests, which avoids many requests sent directly to the back-end storage nodes by taking full advantage of the cache characters of low latency and high bandwidth. Some researchers have used a small but fast enough cache node in a cluster as a front-end load balancer, and the lower bound of cache size depends only on the number of back-end storage nodes in the system but independent of the total number of objects in the cluster. Caching at least $O(n\log n)$ hottest objects can ensure load balancing among n storage nodes [5]. Based on this theory, SwitchKV [7] uses RAM cache to balance the SSD storage nodes, and NetCache [8] uses a faster in-switch cache to balance storage nodes based on RAM. Furthermore, DistCache [9] uses two independent hash functions to partition objects in two equivalent cache clusters.

2.2 Cache Systems with Variable Object Sizes

Existing caching algorithms mostly focus on eviction policies (i.e., LRU, LRU-K [10], SLRU [11], ARC [12]), which tend to have no admission policy and cache all accessed objects. At the same time, these studies are designed for caching similar object sizes. In recent years, researches on caching with variable object sizes have emerged. The size-based AdaptSize [13] caches an object with a probability of $e^{size/c}$, and adjusts the parameter c based on a Markov model. Rl-Cache [14] implements an admission policy based on reinforcement learning, and it uses more features to characterize objects in a request trace. However, the optimization goals of the above AdaptSize, RL-Cache are the object hit ratio, which is not consistent with load balancing.

In order to improve the performance of the load balancer when the object size is different, we add an admission filter to the front-end cache. The existing related work about cache admission policy is primarily for the CDN scenario and aims to maximize the object hit ratio. Unlike them, SACache is designed for optimizing load-balancing performance for storage systems with objects of different sizes.

2.3 Motivation

In cache systems, there are at least two kinds of storage media with different characteristics: one is a high speed, low latency but expensive medium, which is suitable for cache; the other is a medium with low speed, high latency but low price, it is suitable for storage. The above works do not consider the size of the object, however, in some Internet applications, for example, in a storage cluster of web resources, the size of objects (web pages, pictures, videos) varies greatly. Meanwhile, the storage medium's access characters determine that when objects have the same popularity, caching many small objects incurs a more significant overhead than caching one large object. For example, caching ten small objects of size one does not yield the same benefits as caching one big object of size ten, this is mainly due to the low latency nature of the cache media, which we will explain it in the following paragraphs (Table 1).

Table 1. Notation used for the analysis.

Symbol	Meaning
t_s	Latency of storage medium
t_c	Latency of cache medium
k_s	Inverse of the storage medium bandwidth
k_c	Inverse of the cache medium bandwidth
s	Object's size
v	Object's popularity
e	Benefit of unit cache capacity

Suppose that in a storage-cache system with a cache node and a storage node, HDD is used as the storage medium, and DRAM is used as the cache medium. Based on this system, we ignore the network overhead to analyze the benefits of caching an object. For HDD, each data Access Time can be divided into three parts: seek time (T_s), rotational time ($1/(2r)$), and transfer time ($B/(rN)$), where r is the rotation speed of the disk, N is the number of bytes on a track, and B is the number of bytes form an IO transfer. Seek time and rotational time determine the average access latency, while transfer time determines the transmission bandwidth. Typical access latency is about 10 ms, and the transfer bandwidth is about 200 MB/s. The time cost of an s bytes IO transfer can be formulated as $t_s + k_s * s$. For RAM with random access character, the time cost can also be formulated $t_c + k_c * s$, The current common two-channel DDR4 has about 50 GB/s bandwidth and 100 ns latency, so $t_s \gg t_c$ and $k_s > k_c$.

In the above object caching system with limited memory, it is important to fully utilize cache capacity to reduce the overall request wait time. We want to define a metric for objects in cache to evaluate the "cost performance." The *benefit* of caching an object comes from the wait time saved by requesting the object directly from the cache; if the object is requested v times over a period of time, the saved time is $v * (t_s - t_c + k_s * s - k_c * s)$; and the *cost* is s, the capacity occupied by the object. So we can define a $\frac{benefit}{cost}$ ratio (i.e., the benefit of unit cache) e for objects in the cache, and it is the ratio of the IO time divided by used space of caching an object, we have:

$$e = \frac{v * (t_s - t_c + k_s * s - k_c * s)}{s} \tag{1}$$

For a specific object storage system, t_s, t_c, k_s, and k_c are measurable constants. It is easy to see that when v is constant, e decreases as s increases; which indicate that for two objects with the same popularity, the smaller object has a higher $\frac{benefit}{cost}$ ratio.

To prevent low-value objects from occupying cache space, we want the e value of the objects kept in the cache to be higher than a lower bound $\underline{e}$. To find out the condition for different objects to reach this lower limit, we need to study the popularity condition for different objects of different sizes to have the same value of e. We describe popularity v as a function of object size s.

$$v(s) = \frac{e * s}{(t_s - t_c) + (k_s - k_c) * s} \tag{2}$$

If the latency and bandwidth of the storage system and the cache system is known, we can give an object of size s the popularity v needed to keep the unit cache benefit equal to $\underline{e}$. Figure 2 shows an equal e curve of a storage-cache system, where the X-axis is the size of the object, the Y-axis is the relative popularity, and the benefit is consistent at any point in the curve. And the background color on Fig. 2 corresponds to the unit cache benefit e under a coordinate $\langle s, v \rangle$, darker color indicate higher e.

We can design a cache admission policy based on the $v(s)$ function, the keynote is that only a object of size s reaches the popularity v, which makes benefit e higher than $\underline{e}$, the object can be admitted by cache. The key is to find an appropriate $\underline{e}$ that maximizes the storage node bandwidth under the current load characteristics (e.g., object size distribution and request skew). Too small $\underline{e}$ will disable the cache admission policy and too big $\underline{e}$ will make it almost impossible for an object to be cached. In Sect. 3, we will show the specific design of the cache admission mechanism which we call SACache.

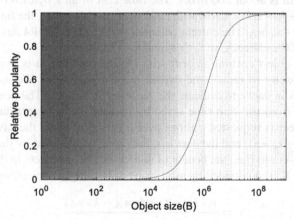

Fig. 2. An equal benefit curve, reflecting the popularity to ensure the same unit cache benefit as the object size increases. And the depth of the red color reflects the level of the unit cache benefit e. (Color figure online)

3 SACache System Design

The SACache mechanism is applied in all cache nodes, and the fundamental idea of this mechanism is to decrease the admission probability of big objects. In applications with different sizes of objects, accepting a large object when the cache space is insufficient will lead to the eviction of many small objects, which may be requested again soon. The cache admission policy is designed in cooperation with the load balancing mechanism to maximize the system's load balancing. In this section, we provide an overview of SACache's architectural design and implementation, as well as two use cases for SACache.

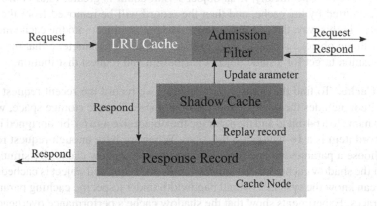

Fig. 3. Cache node architecture.

3.1 SACache Architecture

Figure 3 shows an overview of the SACache node's architecture. SACache adds an admission policy to LRU, called the admission filter, which intercepts PUT operations to LRU. The admission filter has a cache parameter c, which, together with the object's *size*, determines the request frequency for the object to be admitted. Finding the appropriate parameter c is the key to maximize load balancing performance. Cache node will record recent requests, replay them in the shadow cache, and use a greedy algorithm to search the best cache admission parameter to maximize the optimization object (i.e., bandwidth).

Object Admission Filter. In SACache, small size objects will have more chances to be admitted by the cache node. Based on the Eq. (2) in Sect. 2, we design an admission function. For an object of size *size* and popularity K, it will be admitted by the cache if $K > v(size)/v(c)$. The cache parameter c ranges between 1 and *cache_size*, and it is essential to find optimal parameter c_{opt}; we use an accelerated search method to search for c_{opt} in the logarithmic space with shadow cache, which we will describe later.

Another important thing is to find a method to sense the popularity of an object. To achieve this, we use a recent visit counter to provide a popularity reference for cache admission; The counter is essentially a FIFO queue of length N, and it will record at most N unique latest cache miss objects' visit count. For cache miss in the cache node, the visit counter will be refreshed after fetching the object from the storage node, then the visit count of the uncached object increased by one. If the uncached object does not exist in the FIFO queue, it will be pushed a new record to the queue; and of course, if the FIFO queue's length has reached N after the push, the last record entry will be deleted before push operation. The recent visit counter is equivalent to the popularity estimation of an object. An object in a recent visit counter will be decided to be admitted after it is refreshed. Specifically, if an object's visit count is greater than $v(size)/v(c)$, it will be admitted by the cache, and then the record will be removed from the recent visit counter. In this way, the popularity needed to put an object into the cache increases linearly with the object's size, and there is a static optimal parameter c that maximizes the optimization target for a static object distribution and request distribution.

Shadow Cache. To find the optimal parameter c, we record the recent request traces, and each item includes the object name and object size. To save storage space, we map the object name to a 64-bit id and then storage the object size as a 64-bit unsigned integer, so the record item is a 16-byte tuple $\langle id, size \rangle$. When we have enough request records, we can choose a parameter c and replay the traces in a shadow cache. By simulating a request in the shadow cache, we can know whether the requested object is cached or not. Then we can know the system's overall bandwidth under a specific caching parameter c in these traces. Experiments show that the shadow cache's performance overhead is not too large, and the simulation of 250k requests can be completed within 40 ms.

Greedy Search. In SACache, the caching parameter c is in the range of $[1, cache\_size]$. We take log-scale caching parameter $\log(c)$ as the x-axis and the optimization goal (e.g., hit ratio or bandwidth) as the y-axis. In order to get high precision results quickly, we designed a greedy search algorithm. The algorithm consists of multiple iterations: in each iteration, c is selected at equal log-scale intervals; the optimization goal under parameter c is obtained through the shadow cache, the c_{opt} that maximizes the optimization goal is the optimal parameter in this iteration. In the next iteration, the search range will change; the new search range is centered around $\log(c_{opt})$, and the range will be halved. In this way, each iteration's execution time is similar, but each iteration's accuracy is doubled than the previous iteration. We use the above search algorithm in our system, and we search 16 parameters in each iteration and have five iterations. So we run the simulator 50 times, but the search accuracy is equivalent to 256 times ($256 = 16 \times 2^{5-1}$). The pseudocode is shown in Appendix A.

3.2 Implementation

Cache Node. The cache node caches objects as key-value pairs (e.g., A: value and B: value). With a size-aware admission policy, small objects will be cached preferentially. To manage the cached objects in memory, we use a traditional LRU algorithm. Specifically, we implement an LRU cache using two containers (list and unordered_map) in C++ STL. The list in unordered_map is a doubly-linked list that is efficient at inserting and deleting when the address of the element is known. We use unordered_map to map the object name to the object address, so we can locate the object in constant time complexity. On a cache miss, the cache node visits the storage node and relays the object directly to the client, rather than having another access storage node on the client to request the object. At the same time, the object admission filter will decide whether to save the missed object. We use a single-consumer task queue to operate the cache, which ensures thread safety. The cache node will record information such as object requests, the number of cache hits, and the most recent hit ratio to measure SACache's performance.

Client. The client is implemented to test our storage system by requesting objects from the cache node through the HTTP API. The client can either replay the existing trace to generate requests or generate trace by configuring the object size distribution and access popularity distribution. Besides, we implement DistCache by storing the cache node's address on the client.

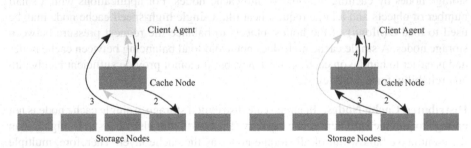

Fig. 4. Cache miss and object can't be cached.   **Fig. 5.** Cache miss and object can be cached.

3.3 Request Path

In SACache, we used a client agent to connect to numerous clients and the object storage cluster. In order to reduce the overhead caused by frequent network interactions within the system, long-lived connections are established between the agent and the cache nodes and storage nodes in the cluster. On a cache hit, the cache node returns the object kept in memory to the agent. For a cache miss, the cache node will update its visit counter and forwards the request to the storage node where the accessed object exists.

Due to the existence of the admission filter mechanism in SACache, an object returned directly to the cache node by the storage node in case of a cache miss could be refused by the cache admission filter, which causes additional transfer overhead. We want the storage node to have the ability to determine whether the current object needs to be cached or not. If it is not cached, returning the object directly to the client agent can save an object transfer overhead. In the prototype system implementation, the cache node will append the parameter c and the object's visit count K (from visit counter) to the request to the storage node. In this way, the storage node can judge the next network transmission direction by comparing the object access counts K and $v(size)/v(c)$. When $K < v(size)/v(c)$, the object can be directly returned to the client agent; Otherwise, the object needs to be returned to the cache node, which forwards the object to the client agent. Figure 4 and Fig. 5 show two types of routing processing for a cache miss; the pseudocode is shown in Appendix B.

3.4 Use Cases

SACache is a general mechanism for increasing system bandwidth in scenarios with varying object sizes. It can be used in both single cache nodes and distributed cache nodes, which we describe next.

Single Cache Node. Compared with storage nodes, storage media of cache nodes perform better in bandwidth and latency, which can be used to ensure load balancing between storage nodes by caching hot objects into cache nodes. For applications with a small number of objects and a large request heat tilt, a single high-speed cache node may be used to load $O(n\log n)$ of the hottest objects to balance the request pressure between storage nodes. A single cache node does not avoid load balancing between cache nodes and is easier to handle on cache consistency, but it cannot provide sufficient bandwidth and reliability for a larger cluster.

Distributed Cache Nodes. In large-scale distributed storage, a single cache node is not enough to provide sufficient cache capacity. The bandwidth also needs to be higher than the cumulative bandwidth of all storage nodes as the cache layer. Therefore, multiple cache nodes are needed to realize load balancing among storage nodes. Simply copying hot objects to all cache nodes does not take full advantage of expensive memory and incurs write time synchronization overhead; and if objects are divided into different cache nodes by a hash function, load imbalance will occur between cache nodes under a highly skewed load. We can refer to DistCache to implement a distributed cache system. Because there is no coupling between the cache nodes, SACache can be easily extended to a distributed cache without additional modifications.

4 Evaluation

4.1 Experimental Setup

Our testbed is a server machine equipped with an 8-core 16-thread CPU (AMD 3700x), 16 GB memory (Samsung 16 GB DDR4-3200 memory), and we use G++ 9.3.0 compiler and running the simulation program on ubuntu20.04. We conduct four experiments to show the characteristics of SACache in different aspects. In the following subsections, we explore the performance benefits of SACache and the costs of introducing the SACache mechanism. The experimental results show that our SACache can improve the load balancing performance within the accepted performance cost.

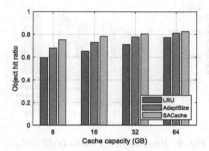
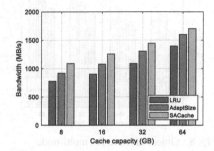

Fig. 6. Object hit ratio for single cache node.   **Fig. 7.** Bandwidth for single cache node.

4.2 Experimental Result

Performance on Single Cache Node. In this section, we evaluate the performance (including hit ratio and throughput) of SACache compared to AdaptSize and LRU cache on an object storage system with a single cache node and ten storage nodes. We generate random request trace with Zipf distribution; under this workload, a small number of objects are accessed frequently, and most objects are rarely accessed. Simultaneously, small objects account for more bytes and large objects for less, consistent with the trace from the IBM Docker registry. Traditionally, the hit ratio is an important indicator to evaluate cache replacement algorithms. In a cache system for objects of the same size, a higher hit ratio means a higher IOPS performance. Figure 6 shows the hit ratio performance of three different caching policies, with cache sizes ranging from 8 GB to 64 GB. We use a log-scale x-axis to present a wide range of cache capacities. We can observe from Fig. 6 that for the three different caching policies, as the cache's capacity increases, the cache can keep more objects, and less cache replacement occurs, which leads to a higher hit ratio. Simultaneously, with the increase of cache capacity, the hit rate will reach saturation and approach an upper bound. Considering the object size difference, both AdaptSize and SACache can achieve a higher hit ratio than LRU cache for different cache capacity. SACache improves the mean hit ratio and max hit ratio by 16.7%

and 26.2% over LRU cache, respectively. Moreover, compared to AdaptSize, SACache improves the mean hit ratio by 10.6% and improves the max hit ratio by 5.8%. However, in applications with different object sizes, the hit ratio is insufficient to indicate performance, so we also record the cache system's bandwidth with different policies. Figure 7 shows the bandwidth of the system under different cache capacities. As shown in the hit ratio experiment, SACache is superior to AdaptSize and LRU cache in bandwidth performance. Compared to LRU, SACache's bandwidth is 33.5% higher on average and 39.9% higher at most.

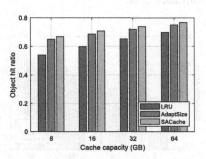

Fig. 8. Object hit ratio for multi-node cache.

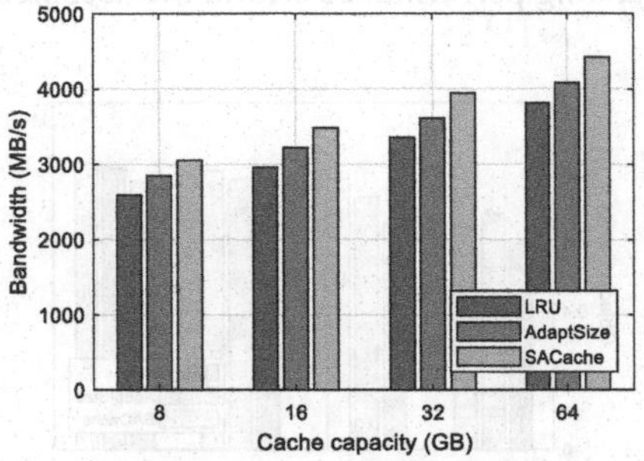

Fig. 9. Bandwidth for multi-node cache.

Performance on Distributed Cache Nodes. To verify the applicability of SACache in large-scale storage systems, we examine the performance of SACache for distributed cache nodes. The request mode of the generated trace is the same as that on a single cache node, but the scale of the dataset is larger, with both the number of unique objects and the length of the trace greater than the set in the single-node test. The cache nodes in SACache are not independent of each other, and there is no data interaction, which allows the multi-node cache to be extended without modifying the nodes. Referring to DistCache's design, we realize a load-balancing distributed cache system, which contains a total of 16 cache nodes in two layers. The client agent records the load of the cache node and chooses the node with a lower load adaptively according to power-of two-choices [15] when requesting objects. Figure 8 and Fig. 9 respectively show the bandwidth and hit ratio performance for distributed caches. Similar to the performance on a single node, SACache is superior to AdaptSize, suggesting that SACache can also be used as a new optimization approach in distributed cache systems.

Bandwidth Scalability of Different Policies. Figure 10 shows the system bandwidth scalability using cache as the load balancer. Different admission policies show good scalability under Zipf access popularity. This is because the front-end cache node absorbs most of the popular objects, making the remaining cold objects distributed evenly on the back-end storage node. However, SACache still performs better in scalability than the other two policies.

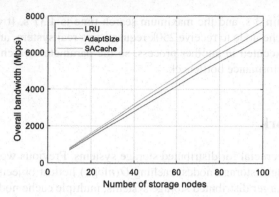

Fig. 10. Bandwidth for single cache node.

Parameter Updating Time Cost. Figure 11 and Fig. 12 show the cache admission parameter updating time cost of SACache, with parameter updated every specific number of requests to track changes in the load. In our prototype system tests, we have 100K requests per minute. Compared to a simple LRU-based cache system without object admission filter, SACache inevitably incurs additional time cost to handle requests and search for the best caching parameters. However, the added cost of handing requests itself is negligible, so we focus on the optimal parameter search time cost. We use the trace collected to generate requests to evaluate the elapsed time of the SACache parameter search. For each parameter search, the cache node will replay the last 250k requests (in about 150 s) recorded and calculate the hit rate; we use a greedy algorithm to speed up finding the best caching parameter c with the highest hit rate. The experimental result shows that 99.3% of 30369 parameter search tests based on different traces can

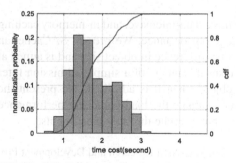

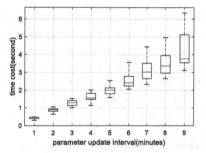

Fig. 11. The time cost of update the cache admission parameter every 150 s. We repeat the experiment and showed the distribution and cumulative probability sum of time consumption in the figure.

Fig. 12. As the interval between update parameters increases, the time cost of the parameter search increases linearly because longer records are used for parameter searches.

be completed within 3 s, and the maximum search time is 4.31 s. It will take several minutes for the cache node to receive 250k requests in a real system, and the parameter search could be executed in another process, so the parameter searching in SACache would not be a performance bottleneck.

5 Related Work

Load balancing is crucial for distributed storage systems. Previous work indicates that in a system owning n storage nodes, caching $O(n\log n)$ hottest objects can avoid load unbalancing. For larger distributed storage systems, multiple cache nodes are needed to provide sufficient capacity for the storage cluster. To achieve load balancing among cache nodes, DistCache proposes a two-layer caching architecture and uses independent hash functions for request routing. However, in object storage systems, the size of objects is often different. For storage systems with variable object sizes, the size-aware load balancing mechanisms can achieve higher performance or lower cost. AdaptSize is the first size-aware cache admission policy for hot object caching in CDN. To achieve a higher object hit ratio, it searches for the optimal caching parameters based on a novel Markov cache model and continuously adjusts the caching parameters according to the change of request patterns. FOO and PFOO [16] gave the theoretical upper bound hit ratio of caching with variable object sizes and reveal that the current caching system is still far from optimal. To achieve cost-friendly load balancing by caching hot objects, we design SACache with a focus on object size differences; the experimental results show that the performance of SACache is better than AdatpSize.

6 Conclusion

Modern internet applications are becoming more data-intensive, and in-memory caching is crucial for improving applications' storage performance. We present SACache, an efficient caching mechanism that considers the difference in object size and is aimed at maximizing system bandwidth. SACache takes advantage of a simple admission filter that evaluates the benefits of caching an object when it is admitted. We present the design and implementation of SACache and evaluate the load-balancing performance improvement of SACache in large scale distributed cache through experiments.

Acknowledgement. This work is supported by The Key-Area Research and Development Program of Guang Dong Province (2019B010107001), National Key Research and Development Program of China (2019YFB1804502), and National Natural Science Foundation of China (61832020, 61702569).

Appendix A

Algorithm 1 Search for c_{opt} (optimal parameter).

Input: The recent request trace

Output: The optimal cache admission parameter

1:     **function** SEARCHOPTIMALPARAMETER (R)
2:          $N \leftarrow$ number of iterations
3:          $M \leftarrow$ number of searches per iteration
4:          $c_{opt} \leftarrow 0$
5:          $c_{min} \leftarrow 0$
6:          $c_{max} \leftarrow cache\_size$
7:          **for** $it = 1$ to N **do**
8:              **for** c in   LOGSPACE (c_{min}, c_{max}, M) **do**
9:                  **if** SIMSCORE (R, c) > SIMSCORE (R, c_{opt}) **then**
10:                     $c_{opt} \leftarrow c$
11:                  **end if**
12:                  $c_{min} \leftarrow$ MAX $(0, c_{opt} - cache\_size/2^{it+1})$
13:                  $c_{max} \leftarrow$ MIN $(cache\_size, c_{opt} + cache\_size/2^{it+1})$
14:              **end for**
15:          **end for**
16:          **return** c_{opt}
17:     **end function**
18:
19:
20:     **function** SIMSCORE (R, c)
21:          $s \leftarrow 0$ ▷sum of object size
22:          $t \leftarrow 0$ ▷sum of access time
23:          SHADOWCACHE . SETPARAMETER (c)
24:          **for** $i = 1$ to N **do**
25:              $s \leftarrow s + R[i].size$
26:              **if** SHADOWCACHE . GET $(R[i].key, R[i].size)$ **then**
27:                  $t \leftarrow t +$ CACHEACESSTIME $(R[i].size)$
28:              **else**
29:                  $t \leftarrow t +$ STORAGEACESSTIME $(R[i].size)$
30:              **end if**
31:          **end for**
32:          **return** t/s
33:     **end function**

Appendix B

Algorithm 2 Path choosing for storage nodes.

1: $K \leftarrow$ visit count of *object*
2: **if** $K < v(size)/v(c)$ **then**
3:          SENDOBJECTTO(object, clientAgent)
4: **else**
5:          SENDOBJECTTO(object, cacheAgent)
6: **end if**

References

1. Ghemawat, S., Gobioff, H., Leung, S.-T.: The google file system. In: Proceedings of the Nineteenth ACM Symposium on Operating Systems Principles, pp. 29–43 (2003)
2. Hastorun, D., et al.: Dynamo: Amazon's highly available key-value store. In: Proceedings of SOSP. Citeseer (2007)
3. Beaver, D., Kumar, S., Li, H.C., Sobel, J., Vajgel, P., et al.: Finding a needle in haystack: Facebook's photo storage. In: OSDI, vol. 10, pp. 1–8 (2010)
4. Factor, M., Meth, K., Naor, D., Rodeh, O., Satran, J.: Object storage: the future building block for storage systems. In: 2005 IEEE International Symposium on Mass Storage Systems and Technology, pp. 119–123 (2005)
5. Fan, B., Lim, H., Andersen, D.G., Kaminsky, M.: Small cache, big effect: provable load balancing for randomly partitioned cluster services. In: Proceedings of the 2nd ACM Symposium on Cloud Computing, SOCC 2011. Association for Computing Machinery, New York (2011)
6. Anwar, A., et al.: Improving docker registry design based on production workload analysis. In: 16th USENIX Conference on File and Storage Technologies (FAST 2018), Oakland, CA, pp. 265–278. USENIX Association, February 2018
7. Li, X., Sethi, R., Kaminsky, M., Andersen, D.G., Freedman, M.J.: Be fast, cheap and in control with switchkv. In: 13th USENIX Symposium on Networked Systems Design and Implementation (NSDI 2016), Santa Clara, CA, pp. 31–44, USENIX Association, March 2016
8. Jin, X., et al.: Netcache: balancing key-value stores with fast in-network caching. In: Proceedings of the 26th Symposium on Operating Systems Principles, pp. 121–136 (2017)
9. Liu, Z., et al.: Distcache: provable load balancing for large-scale storage systems with distributed caching. In: 17th USENIX Conference on File and Storage Technologies (FAST 2019), Boston, MA, pp. 143–157. USENIX Association, February 2019
10. O'neil, E.J., O'Neil, P.E., Weikum, G.: An optimality proof of the LRU-K page replacement algorithm. J. ACM (JACM) **46**(1), 92–112 (1999)
11. Morales, K., Lee, B.K.: Fixed segmented LRU cache replacement scheme with selective caching. In: 2012 IEEE 31st International Performance Computing and Communications Conference (IPCCC), pp. 199–200 (2012)
12. Megiddo, N., Modha, D.S.: ARC: a self-tuning, low overhead replacement cache. Fast **3**, 115–130 (2003)
13. Berger, D.S., Sitaraman, R.K., Harchol-Balter, M.: Adaptsize: orchestrating the hot object memory cache in a content delivery network. In: 14th USENIX Symposium on Networked Systems Design and Implementation (NSDI 2017), Boston, MA, pp. 483–498. USENIX Association, March 2017

14. Kirilin, V., Sundarrajan, A., Gorinsky, S., Sitaraman, R.K.: RL-cache: learning-based cache admission for content delivery. IEEE J. Sel. Areas Commun. **38**(10), 2372–2385 (2020)
15. Mitzenmacher, M.: The power of two choices in randomized load balancing. IEEE Trans. Parallel Distrib. Syst. **12**(10), 1094–1104 (2001)
16. Berger, D.S., Beckmann, N., Harchol-Balter, M.: Practical bounds on optimal caching with variable object sizes. Proc. ACM Meas. Anal. Comput. Syst. **2**(2), 1–38 (2018)

Heterogeneous-ISA Application Migration in Edge Computing: Challenges, Techniques and Open Issues

Hang Jin[1], Yihong Su[1], Fengzhou Liang[1], and Fang Liu[1,2]($\boxtimes$)

[1] School of Computer Science and Engineering, Sun Yat-sen University,
Guangzhou 510006, China
{jinh26,suyh35,liangfzh}@mail2.sysu.edu.cn
[2] School of Design, Hunan University, Changsha 410082, China
fangl@hnu.edu.cn

Abstract. With the development of mobile edge computing, more and more services are moved to the edge of the network, and devices there are usually with low computational abilities and little storage resources. To make it lightweight and elastic, containers can be adopted in the edge environment when migrating a certain application. With the host OS kernel shared, applications can be deployed with the least computational resources they need, making it possible to deploy more of them on relatively low-end devices. Migration is also used in scenarios like maintenance or load balance, etc. We noticed that in edge environment, devices and servers are usually built with heterogeneous Instruction Set Architectures (ISAs) processors. X86 processors are widely used in desktop PCs, laptops and servers while smart-phones are built with an ARM processor, which leads to a serious problem that a container cannot be migrated to a heterogeneous machine to continue running directly. In this paper, we firstly give an overview of heterogeneous-ISA migration, and its applications and techniques. Then we discuss the existing heterogeneous execution solution from the perspective of applicable scenarios, latency, power consumption, requirements for computational resources, etc. Next, a comparison study is given on each of the characteristics to depict the details and differences in existing works. At last, challenges and open research issues which are waiting for further studies on container migration are listed.

Keywords: Heterogeneous migration · Edge computing · Container

1 Introduction

Edge Computing [1] is a novel computing paradigm in which computation are performed at the edge of the network. Data are processed closer to the user in both physical and in the topology of the network. Thanks for edge computing, instead of sending all data generated by mobile devices (e.g. smartphones and IoT devices) to the cloud, data can be processed at anywhere between the end user and the data center so the burden of backbone network bandwidth and data center is reduced and the request for a certain service can be responded faster than cloud computing.

© Springer Nature Switzerland AG 2021
X. Sun et al. (Eds.): ICAIS 2021, CCIS 1423, pp. 106–118, 2021.
https://doi.org/10.1007/978-3-030-78618-2_9

Virtualization technology is widely used nowadays to make full use of a physical server by dividing it into independent execution environments logically. The most commonly used virtualization technologies are Virtual Machines (VMs) and Containers. Normally, each VM represents a single full-system execution environment so it will provide user with a highly isolated environment by installing and running a full operating system inside which will occupies much computation and storage resources. In the age of cloud computing, VMs are deployed in data centers for isolation and they are transparent to users. With the development of edge computing, more and more relatively low-end devices, such as gateways, routers, wireless APs and mobile phones, are working at the edge of the network. Since these devices have little computation resources, it is not advisable to deploy VMs without a deeper consideration. In some circumstances, containers can be simply deployed and managed at the edge since they only require little computation and storage resources.

Migration is a technology commonly used by cloud service providers to migrate a VM from a certain physical server to another for maintenance or load balance propose in cloud computing while container migration is more likely to be used in edge computing to provide user with a certain service consistently though the mobile user is moving to a new place physically.

At the edge of the network, devices there are not always built in the same Instruction Set Architecture [2] which means that we cannot migrate a container built in a certain instruction set to another so heterogenous-ISA migration is proposed to provide a method for applications to migrate to any other edge nodes, regardless of what instruction set the source node and the destination node are.

However, after we studied the existing works which focus on heterogenous-ISA application migration, there is no public literature to make a comparative insight about this topic, especially container migration. In this paper, our research analyzes various solution in heterogenous-ISA migration problems and provide an overview of the existing challenges, techniques and open issue.

As we did our best to know, this paper is the first to provide a full overview of the heterogenous-ISA application migration, especially container migration. Contributions of this paper can be summarized as follows:

- Reviewing the solution of the existing works on application migration in mobile edge computing from the perspective of techniques.
- Analyzing the adaptive application scenarios and motivation of existing solution to migrate an application to a heterogenous-ISA platform.
- Helping to make a choice when selecting a solution or technique route to perform a heterogenous-ISA migration in production environment.
- Identifying the existing challenges and open issues of heterogenous-ISA migration which are worth more research conducted on.

The remaining part of this paper are organized as follows. In Sect. 2, we list and discuss several main solutions of running applications on heterogenous platforms. In Sect. 3, we classify this problem in detail from the perspective of different types of programming languages and their respective solution on this problem. In Sect. 4, we analyze some typical existing works from the perspective of main purposes. In Sect. 5, we make comparisons on the typical works, then list the challenges and open issues in heterogenous-ISA application migration. Finally, we summarize our conclusions in Sect. 6.

2 Virtualization and Migration

Execution isolation is essential for both cloud and edge applications, which can be realized by virtualization technology. We summarize this into measures below: simulation, VM and container. The rest of this section will discuss them in detail.

From the perspective of migration, there are two types of ways to migrate a VM or container: non-live migration and live migration. Non-live migration means the state of the runtime information is saved to a file for further use such as instance cloning, state backup and rolling back, etc. Live migration is used to provide consistent service, such as quick replication [3], load balancing [4], and keeping relatively closed to the user [2], etc.

2.1 Simulation

Simulation refers to migrating the application process to the destination platform and keeping running on a full-system simulator (e.g., QEMU [5]) on the destination site, and the simulator simulates the whole hardware of a computer. However, the simulated hardware is usually implemented by software which leads to a performance bottleneck compared with running on real hardware so it is not adaptable to be used in production environment in most circumstances.

2.2 Virtual Machine

Each virtual machine is an isolated execution environment on the host machine with its own guest operating system running inside. To deploy a VM, a hypervisor is necessary for management use. A virtual machine can be deployed right on the top of host hardware [6] or on the host operating system [7, 8]. Though VMs can provide relatively more independent execution environment for guest processes, the guest operating system installed will take much storages and memory spaces, regardless of whether a system component or service is utilized by the application.

In the age of cloud computing, VM is most popular virtualization solution utilized by data centers to divide an integrate server into small virtual machines logically while the hardware resources are shared physically. Cloud service providers (AWS, Aliyun, etc.) can also rent VMs to customers and provide them with a remote access to deploy their applications on these infrastructures, which is also known as Infrastructures as a Service (IaaS). As we described above, a virtual machine has a relatively isolated execution environment but it will occupy a great amount of physical resources.

VMs can be packed and exported to other physical servers by simply migrating the disk image and settings to achieve this. However, to migrate a VM lively, the whole state and data of the running VM should be all transferred to the destination site, including register state, memory, storage data and network connections. Existing method to lively migrate memory of a VM are summarized as pre-copy [9], post-copy [10] and hybrid-copy [11]. The storage data can be migrated by method similar to that of memory data migration. Though there is quite an amount of works on VM migration, it can be difficult to migrate them to a heterogenous-ISA platform since it is heavy and there are some OS-level limitation which is ISA-related. We will not make a further discussion about VM migration.

2.3 Containers

Container is a technology which is implemented by sharing the host OS kernel with the container's own file system. As containers can be generated and disposed easily and provide a relatively isolated lightweight execution environment for guest process, they are widely deployed in production for application packing, management and environment isolation. Since containers share the host OS kernel instead of executing processes in their own guest OS execution environment, the level of isolation is less than that of VMs.

Since containers are executed on the top of host OS, the migration of them are more similar to process migration. The usually used method of migrating a container/process lively is CRIU [12], an open source checkpointing tool for checkpointing and restoring an image of the migrated container/process. Similar with VM migration, container migration also consists of migration of register state, memory, storage data and network connections. In the rest of our paper, we will not differentiate container migration and process migration since they are basically similar to each other.

2.4 A Comparative Study

In this section, we summarize the advantages and disadvantages of the main ways of migration discussed above. Figure 1 shows the basic architecture of each specific measure of virtualization and Table 1 shows the comparative features of them.

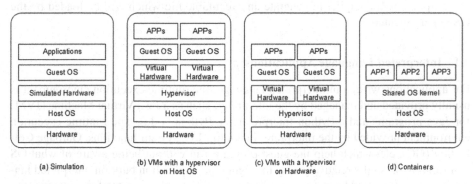

Fig. 1. Basic architecture of various measures of virtualization

Table 1. Features of various measures of migration

Method	Oriented scenarios	Performance	Volume of data	Migration velocity	Migration overhead	Support for heterogenous migration	Environment isolation
Simulation	Experimental	Very low	Large	Very slow	High	Fine	Fine
Virtual machines	Cloud	Normal	Large	Slow	Normal	Terrible	Fine
Containers	Cloud & edge	Normal	Little	Fast	Low	Acceptable	Acceptable

As we depicted above, simulation can lead to a serious performance bottleneck caused by its software simulation of electric hardware so it is more likely to be used in experiments rather than commercial use. There is a huge amount of works on VM migration, but that focuses on heterogenous migration can be rare since there are always an operating system running inside, which communicates with the virtual hardware and it's hard to migrate it to a heterogenous platform. As there are serval limitations for VM migration in the edge scenarios, containers can fit the edge computing environment better, since containers can be lightweight, and occupy less resources than VMs do.

3 Typical Works

In this section, we will discuss some typical works about container migration in detail. In the scope of container migration, applications nowadays are usually written in one or more high-level programming languages. These high-level programming languages can be classified as: interpreted languages (e.g. Java, Python, Perl, etc.), in which programs are written when going to be executed, an interpreter is indispensable to interpret the source code; compiled language (e.g. C, C++, etc.), in which programs are written should be complied by a compiler to generate an executable file which will be loaded by the OS when executed.

3.1 Interpreted Language Applications

For applications written in interpreted language, the runtime execution environment is usually provided and managed by the interpreter, such as a Java Virtual Machine (JVM) for Java programs and a Python Interpreter for Python codes. The runtime execution environment provided by the interpreter including I/O, system functions, Garbage Collection (GC), etc. which help the guest program run without being aware of what OS is it running on so it's relatively easy to migrate an application built on interpreted languages. As interpreted languages are usually provided with cross-platform interpreters, applications can run on the heterogenous-ISA platform [4] easily. Some optimization methods are also proposed to reduce the overhead of migrating an interpreted language application.

Chen et al. [13] proposed a programming framework COCA to offload computations in cloud computing. COCA utilized aspect-oriented programming (AOP) to offload Java applications in which computation can be offloaded to a destination site by inserting additional information into the application to be migrated.

Bruno and Ferreira [14] proposed ALMA, a solution for JVM live migration. The key idea of their work is to make a trade-off between the overhead of GC and the transmission of data that needed to be transferred to the destination site. ALMA check each heap memory periodically and estimate the time to be taken to collect each heap memory area. By comparing the estimated velocity to collect a certain memory area and the velocity of transmit this memory area to the destination site, the decision whether the garbage in this memory area should be collected to get a minimal time of the sum of the GC and transmission.

3.2 Compiled Language Applications

Compiled language applications can be loaded by the OS and executed directly and the code should be compiled to the instruction set of the target machine. So, when compared with interpreted language programs, it is much harder to make it compatible for a process to migrate across heterogenous platforms. There are some works proposed to extinct the boundaries of heterogenous-ISA platforms to migrate a process on a certain platform to another.

Barbalace et al. [4] focus on the energy consumption of a certain workload on an ARM and an x86 server. They implement a whole toolchain from the OS-level, including an extended OS based on Popcorn Linux [15], customized multi-ISA compilers to generate multi-ISA binaries and runtime support of migration to the heterogenous-ISA platform. The compilation toolchain in their proposed model finally link the program of heterogenous-ISA version of the source code, ensuring that symbol addresses of the program can be linked to the same address for alignment so that the related entry points of functions and variables can keep the same even running in heterogenous-ISA platforms for an easy state transformation.

Checkpoint/Restore In Userspace (CRIU) [12] is an open source project which can save the state of a container/process into an image file on the disk. And we can transfer the image files to the destination to restore the whole state of the migrated process. Note that since CRIU snaps the whole state of a certain process including code segment of the process, if the image were transferred to a heterogenous site with different instruction set, the process cannot be restored unless we exert extra operations to the image files. There are numerous works struggling to realize heterogenous-ISA migration based on CRIU.

Barbalace et al. proposed H-Container [2], which stands for Heterogenous-ISA Container, to migrate a container to the heterogenous-ISA platform. H-Container decompiles the executable of the migrated application into LLVM IR as the intermediate represent, and then insert some "migration points" for program to get paused at to trigger a migration operation. After this, the migrated application will be re-compiled to the destination instruction set. What's more, H-Container deals with the runtime state of the running application to transform the image file to fit the destination site then restore the execution of the container on the destination site.

Unikernel can be also used in cross-ISA migration. Oliver et al. proposed Heterogeneous EXecution Offloading (HEXO) [16], utilizing unikernel virtual machine which is an integrate OS-level application combined part of the kernel with user application to migrate workloads on embedded platforms to save energy in HPC data centers. HEXO requires migration points inserted into the application source code and compile it using a heterogeneous-ISA toolchain to generate images of multi-ISAs for offloading or migration.

Process migration has also been studied in heterogenous-ISA chip multiprocessors. DeVuyst et al. [17] studied how to migrate a process to a heterogenous-ISA core with little performance loss to make a full use of heterogeneous-ISA CMP. Their work includes identifying the program state, modifying the complier to compile a program with data properly placed in the memory when executed so that migration cost can be reduced and they also had a research on binary translation. The main idea of their work is to keep the form of a program running in the memory the same in both source core and the heterogenous destination core that the program can keep running natively to achieve an acceptable performance.

Bhat et al. [18] proposed an operating system with replicated kernels which is extended form Popcorn Linux and a customized compiler to migrate a process on an ARM-x86 heterogenous platform. Their work focuses on migration in the heterogenous platform which is composed of ARM and x86 architecture. There is a kernel on each architecture which is compiled natively and communicates with each other via Popcorn communication layer. Popcorn Single System Image runs on the both kernel and so does the application. The application is buillt with the customized compiler in which addresses of variables and function entry are placed to the same virtual address. The executable also contains codes of both ISAs, the OS will map the corresponding code in the executable to the same ISA. To migrate a process, the state on the source processor is going to be packed and sent to the destination ISA via the communication layer and restored after sending.

3.3 Hybrid Applications

Hybrid applications refers to applications that composed of one or more parts discussed above. Android, one of the most popular operating system for smartphones and smart SoCs, can be a great example for this. According to the official documentation [19], an Android application can run native binaries of libraries or modules that written in C codes for better performance. They are usually high-frequency or computation-intensive functions or codes, which is called NDK libraries and can boost the overall execution performance of the application.

Lee et al. [20] are the first to notice the migration of hybrid applications on Android platform. As they described, the most popular Android applications such as Firefox, VLC Player, etc., are built with C/C++ codes up to more than 50% of total codes to boost the performance of the APPs. Most of the smartphones with Android installed are equipped with ARM processors while servers and desktop PCs are usually x86. Noticing the performance gap of state-of-the-art smartphones and servers, this work proposed Native Offloader, to identify the heavy tasks of an application that are able to be migrated to a x86 server independently. The key of their work is the Native Offloader Compiler, which analyzes the native codes of the application, partitions the original code into client IR codes and server IR codes, then compiles IR codes for both platforms to enable migration. When the workload running, client submits related data including identifier, stack pointer and page table to the server and receives the dirty pages from the server via network connections.

4 Purpose of Migration

In this section, we studied the existing works and classify them from the perspective of main purpose and adaptable scenarios. We summaries this as several different aspects and we believe that it will be of great importance to get a better comprehension of these works.

4.1 Following User Mobility

Edge computing indicates offloading computation closer to the user to provide user with low-latency services, and this will leads to a problem of following the user. In this context, users are with great mobility, and so are the IoT devices.

The main purpose of H-Container [2] is to utilize as more potential target in the edge cloud as possible to migrate those services in need of low latency such as gaming and real-time calculation. There is a strong heterogeneity at the edge of the network that edge devices can be servers, PCs, laptops or any embedded SoC devices such as routers, gateways or wireless APs. These devices are built with x86, ARM and other CPU processors. By enabling migrating containers to heterogenous-ISA platforms, there can be more candidate places to migrate a container that is serving the current user onto. So the possibility to migrate an application to closest edge device to provide the user with a consistent low-latency service when the user is moving to another edge cloud is boosted.

4.2 Performance

The weak ability of computation can also be one of the serious problems that IoT devices at the edge of the network have, since these embedded devices are usually equipped with relatively low performance processors. When users are running some computation-intensive applications on their smartphone, they will be willing to migrate their workloads to an edge device with stronger computation ability to boost the performance of the application. This idea can be found in [20], which migrates partitioned computation-intensive code from heavy tasks of an application to the server to acquire better performance.

4.3 Energy Efficiency

Energy efficiency is now attracting more and more global attention to achieve the purpose of environment protection. And data centers are also trying to do so to cut down the electricity cost. Experimental evaluation of [4] indicates an average of 30% energy reduction by migrating applications to ARM platforms. The similar purpose can be found in HEXO [16] for HPC workloads migrating to embedded devices with the unikernel virtual machine discussed above. Works of [17, 18] are also intended to get a greater energy efficiency by migrating processes onto heterogenous-ISA multiprocessors. The migration studied in this work is about the migration between processor cores instead of that between heterogenous machines.

5   Discussions

In this section, we will give some discussions on the works we mentioned above, summarize the features of typical works and give an overview of them. Then we discuss how a decision can be made among these valuable works from the perspective of applicable scenarios, purpose and techniques, when a migration is required. At last, the existing challenges and open research issues in heterogenous-ISA application migrations are listed.

5.1   Comparative Study

We summarize the scenarios, techniques and advantages of some works discussed above, which are listed in Table 2. The timeline of these works is depicted in Fig. 2, which gives an explicit relation and the development of them.

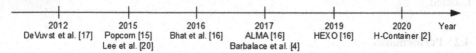

2012	2015	2016	2017	2019	2020	Year
DeVuyst et al. [17]	Popcorn [15]	Bhat et al. [16]	ALMA [16]	HEXO [16]	H-Container [2]	
	Lee et al. [20]		Barbalace et al. [4]			

Fig. 2. Timeline that typical works are proposed

Table 2. Comparison of existing typical works

Aspect	DeVuyst et al. [17]	Lee et al. [20]	Bhat et al. [18]	ALMA [14]	Barbalace et al. [4]	HEXO [16]	H-Container [2]
Virtualization Technology	Container	None	None	JVM	Container	Unikernel	Container
Year	2012	2015	2016	2017	2017	2019	2020
Platform	Heterogeneous multicore	Mobile	Heterogeneous multicore	Universal	Universal	Universal	Universal
Workload	Compiled	Hybrid	Compiled	Interpreted, Java APPs	Compiled	OS-level Application	Compiled
Scenario	Heterogeneous multicore	Native Android code	Heterogeneous multicore	Universal	Universal	HPC data center	Edge
Main purpose	EE, PF	EE, PF	EE	FT, LB, EE, FS, LU, etc	EE	EE, PF	UM
System component	CP, BT, ES, SP	CR, IR	CP, ES, SP	JVM, CRIU	CP, IR	CP, Unikernel	CP, IR, BT, CRIU
Limitation	Rare platform in edge environment	Lack of demonstration for real Android Apps	Rare platform in edge environment	For Java applications only	Source code is required	Not in real edge environment	Lack of demonstration for security
Mobile Device Support	No	Yes	No	No	Yes	No	Yes

Sorted by year the work is proposed from left to right. The abbreviation list: FT: Fault Tolerance. LB: Load Balance. EE: Energy Efficiency. FS: Fast Start. LU: Live Updates. UM: User Mobility. PF: PerFormance. CP: ComPiler. ES: Extended System. SP: Special Platform. IR: Intermediate Represent. BT: Binary Translation.

5.2 Scenarios and Selection

In this section, we will summarize typical works from the other view of user choice. Figure 3 shows the process to select one of existing techniques and solutions, which will help user decide when choosing to apply one of these solutions in the future. Note that the final decision is not always fitting to a requirement perfectly and some of that can be developed from the nearest solution, e.g. when migrating a Python application, it might be derived from ALMA [16] or other similar works which are not listed since Python applications are running in a similar way that Java applications do while both of the languages are interpreted ones.

5.3 Open Research Issues

Though some typical works about application migration are proposed, there are still some open issues remaining to be addressed. With the development of edge computing, there will be more importance and challenges in the field of application migration.

User Privacy and Migration Security. Privacy protection is now drawing more and more attention for mobile users and enterprises. As an important measure to migrate an application, more attention should be paid on the privacy and security protection. An application cannot run without data to be processed. In the circumstance of edge computing, when users are enjoying the convenience brought by application migration, how

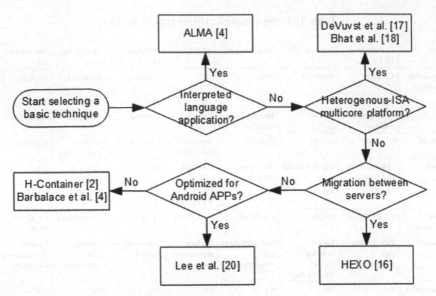

Fig. 3. A decision-making guide diagram

to ensure the safety of data generated or provided by users can be an essential problem to be studied. The protection includes not only the safety of VMs or containers user application running in, but also the communication between the source and destination site when executing a migration operation. More effective measures should be proposed to boost the security of the data and user privacy.

Flexible Heterogenous-ISA Application Migration. As typical works show, when applying a heterogenous-ISA migration solution, there are always modification to be applied to the source code of the application, which is not friendly for developers to develop or update their applications.

Optimization for Particular Edge Scenarios. Although techniques of heterogenous-ISA migration have been studied in various platforms and they are likely to be adopted by edge scenarios, there are still little works focus on real scenarios in edge computing, especially for users with smart devices. To adapt to the edge computing scenario, solutions should be optimized for the real edge environment and evaluated, while existing works commonly focus on the performance of proposed solution itself.

6 Conclusion

In this paper, we described some typical works and solutions dedicating to solve the problem of heterogenous-ISA application migration. They are all likely to be adopted to boost the edge computing for purpose of quality of user services, performance and energy saving, etc. We also give a comparative study on the existing techniques to summarize their applicable scenarios and benefits by applying corresponding solutions.

Then we presented a guidance for decisions on selecting migration solutions. At last, open research issues are listed.

Acknowledgement. This work is supported by the National Natural Science Foundation of China (62072465).

References

1. Shi, W., Cao, J., Zhang, Q., Li, Y., Xu, L.: Edge computing: vision and challenges. IEEE Internet Things J. **3**(5), 637–646 (2016)
2. Barbalace, A., Karaoui, M.L., Wang, W., Xing, T., Olivier, P., Ravindran, B.: Edge computing: the case for heterogeneous-ISA container migration. In: 16th ACM SIGPLAN/SIGOPS International Conference on Virtual Execution Environments (VEE) (2020)
3. Lertsinsrubtavee, A., Ali, A., Molina-Jimenez, C., Sathiaseelan, A., Crowcroft, J.: PiCasso: a lightweight edge computing platform. In: 2017 IEEE 6th International Conference on Cloud Networking (CloudNet) (2017)
4. Barbalace, A., et al.: Breaking the boundaries in heterogeneous-ISA datacenters. In: Twenty-Second International Conference on Architectural Support for Programming Languages and Operating Systems (ASPLOS) (2017)
5. QEMU. https://www.qemu.org/. Accessed 23 Dec 2020
6. What is ESXI? Bare Metal Hypervisor, ESX, VMware. https://www.vmware.com/products/esxi-and-esx.html. Accessed 23 Dec 2020
7. Oracle VM VirtualBox. https://www.virtualbox.org/. Accessed 23 Dec 2020
8. Windows VM, Workstation Pro, VMware. https://www.vmware.com/products/workstation-pro.html. Accessed 23 Dec 2020
9. Clark, C., et al.: Live migration of virtual machines. In: 2nd Symposium on Networked Systems Design and Implementation (NSDI) (2005)
10. Hines, M.R., Deshpande, U., Gopalan, K.: Post-copy live migration of virtual machines. ACM SIGOPS Oper. Syst. Rev. **43**(3), 14–26 (2009)
11. Hu, L., Zhao, J., Xu, G., Ding, Y., Chu, J.: HMDC: live virtual machine migration based on hybrid memory copy and delta compression. Appl. Math **7**(2L), 639–646 (2013)
12. CRIU. https://www.criu.org/Main_Page. Accessed 23 Dec 2020
13. Chen, H., Lin, Y., Cheng, C.: COCA: computation offload to clouds using AOP. In: 2012 12th IEEE/ACM International Symposium on Cluster, Cloud and Grid Computing (CCGRID) (2012)
14. Bruno, R., Ferreira, P.: ALMA: GC-assisted JVM live migration for java server applications. In: 17th International Middleware Conference (2016)
15. Barbalace, A., et al.: Popcorn: bridging the programmability gap in heterogeneous-ISA platforms. In: Tenth European Conference on Computer Systems (EuroSys) (2015)
16. Olivier, P., Mehrab, A.K.M.F., Lankes, S., Karaoui, M.L., Lyerly, R., Ravindran, B.: HEXO: offloading HPC compute-intensive workloads on low-cost, low-power embedded systems. In: 28th International Symposium on High-Performance Parallel and Distributed Computing (HPDC) (2019)
17. DeVuyst, M., Venkat, A., Tullsen, D.M.: Execution migration in a heterogeneous-ISA chip multiprocessor. In: The seventeenth international conference on Architectural Support for Programming Languages and Operating Systems (ASPLOS) (2012)
18. Bhat, S.K., Saya, A., Rawat, H.K., Barbalace, A., Ravindran, B.: Harnessing energy efficiency of heterogeneous-ISA platforms. ACM SIGOPS Oper. Syst. Rev. **49**(2), 65–69 (2016)

19. Concepts, Android NDK, Android Developers. https://developer.android.com/ndk/guides/concepts. Accessed 23 Dec 2020
20. Lee, G., Park, H., Heo, S., Chang, K.A., Lee, H., Kim, H.: Architecture-aware automatic computation offload for native applications. In: 48th International Symposium on Microarchitecture (MICRO) (2015)

The Interaction Between Probe and Cavity Field Assists Quantum Synchronization

Qing-Yu Meng[1], Yong Hu[1], Qing Yang[1], Qin-Sheng Zhu[1(✉)], and Xiao-Yu Li[2]

[1] School of Physics, University of Electronic Science and Technology of China, Chengdu 610054, China
zhuqinsheng@uestc.edu.cn
[2] School of Information and Software Engineering, University of Electronic Science and Technology of China, Chengdu 610054, China

Abstract. As an important technology of the quantum detection, the quantum synchronization detection is always used in the detection or measurement of some quantum systems. A detection schemes are key to the study of quantum system. The quantum synchronization detection which is presented between the probe and the quantum system is always used in detection application. A probing model is established to describe the probing a qubit system in the cavity field and to reveal the effect of the environment (cavity) on the quantum synchronization occurrence as well as the interactions among environment, a qubit system and probing equipment. By adjusting the frequency of the probe, the in-phase and out-of-phase synchronization can be achieved. So the information of the probe can be used to obtain the quantum system. Simultaneously, the effect of γ_3 which describes the interaction strength between the probe and environments for quantum synchronization is discussed under different the values of Ohmic dissipation index s. Finally, the machine learning method is applied to present an optimization for classification and regression of synchronization transition dependent on s and γ_3. This opens the way for studying the generalized form of quantum synchronization through machine learning algorithms (Artificial neural network) in the future.

Keywords: Quantum synchronization · Machine learning · Ohmic index

1 Introduction

With the development of automation program, it has become the main target of modern science and technology [1]. Automation program has brought a lot of convenience to people, and intelligent automation is the most important part of the research. Because the popularity of intelligent automation can fully save human resources, material resources and time resources, the machine learning is widely applied in nowadays society. It is a branch of computer science developed from the theory of pattern recognition and computational learning in artificial intelligence [2]. Recently, some theory and application of the machine learning have been extent to physical field. Generally, it is mainly divided into two important directions, one is quantum machine learning. The other is traditional machine learning to solve physical problems.

© Springer Nature Switzerland AG 2021
X. Sun et al. (Eds.): ICAIS 2021, CCIS 1423, pp. 119–129, 2021.
https://doi.org/10.1007/978-3-030-78618-2_10

Quantum machine learning [3], as a research hotspot of machine learning in the next decade, is very worthy of our in-depth study. When quantum computer encounters machine learning, it can be a mutually beneficial and complementary process. On the one hand, we can take advantage of quantum computing to improve the performance of classical machine learning algorithms, for example, the efficient implementation of machine learning algorithms on classical computers [4, 5]. On the other hand, we can also use machine learning algorithms on classical computers to study some problems of the quantum systems. Quantum reinforcement learning is an important branch of QML. In quantum reinforcement learning, a quantum agent interacts with the classical environment and receives rewards from the environment to adjust and improve its behavior strategy. In some cases, quantum acceleration is achieved due to the quantum processing power of the agent or due to the possibility of quantum superposition to detect the environment. To sum up, quantum machine learning is a useful and interesting area of research.

The other is that classical machine learning deals with physical problems. As a part of both artificial intelligence and statistics, machine learning comes from the computer science field in which the goal is to learn the potential patterns from previously given data sets, and make a decision or prediction for future unknown situation based on these learned patterns [6–8]. Recently, these learning tools have been used for dealing with some quantum problems, such as quantum synchronization, i.e., the adjustment of the rhythm of a self-sustained oscillation to a weak perturbation, is a universal feature of many complex dynamic systems [9]. Quantum synchronization has been used in some recent systems, especially in spin systems [10]. This phenomenon can emerge not only in the well-known case of systems exhibiting self-sustained oscillations [11], but also during transient dynamics [12–14]. In addition, quantum synchronization is also used in many systems, such as IBM [15], Bose-Einstein condensate [16] and so on [17, 18]. Therefore, it is vital to detect the conditions and related parameters that affect synchronization.

In this paper, the quantum synchronization of a model which consist of the probing equipment (it is also a qubit system) and one qubit quantum system in environment (cavity) is presented and studied by Machine Learning (ML). Different the model of Ref [19], the interaction between the probing equipment and cavity is considered. Firstly, the master equation is obtained based on this model. Secondly, we calculate and obtain the analytical solutions for the related physical quantity of the quantum synchronization, namely the mean value of $\sigma_p^x(t)$ (probing equipment) and $\sigma_q^x(t)$ (one qubit quantum system). Simultaneously, the influence of different parameters in the quantum synchronization are further studied, especially, the parameters for γ_3^+ (the coupling strength between probing equipment and environment) and γ_0 (the coupling strength between one qubit quantum system and environment). The artificial neural network (ANN) is used to classify the learned data and recognize the new patterns according to the previous knowledge, and applied to find out the transition between in-phase synchronization and out of synchronization. Not only that, ANN is used to understand the relationship among ohmic dissipation (Ohmic index s), probe frequency ω_p and the quantum synchronization in different environments.

2 Model

Let us consider a new model involving the interaction between the probe and the cavity field in the external dissipative environment (cavity). The total Hamiltonian is:

$$H = \sum_{j=p,q} \frac{\omega_j}{2}\sigma_j^z + \sum_k \Omega_k a_k^\dagger a_k + \sum_k g_k(a_k^\dagger + a_k)\sigma_q^x + \lambda\sigma_q^x\sigma_p^x + \sum_k \beta_k(a_k^\dagger + a_k)\sigma_p^z \quad (1)$$

Where σ_j^i $(i = x, y, z)$ are Pauli matrices and a_k $(a_k^\dagger)$ describe the bosonic eigenmodes of the bath with energies Ω_k. The dissipation process is completely determined by the spectral density of the environment $\mathcal{J}(\omega) = \sum_k g_k\delta(\omega - \Omega_k)$. In the external environment, the qubit q of the system is dissipated and coupled with the qubit p of the probe, which can be obtained from experiments as the external probe. The frequency of probe (ω_p) is adjustable, and ω_q is the frequency of system. Since it is not enough to talk only about coupling between the system and the environment, interaction between the probe and the environment is considered in the last term of Eq. 1 (Ref [19] doesn't consider this term). β_k describes the strength of coupling between probe and environment. Assuming weak dissipation and weak coupling, the dynamics of the density matrix $\rho(t)$ of the pair of qubits can be studied in the Born-Markov and secular approximations with Lindblad master equation

$$\dot{\rho}(t) = -i[H_s + H_{LS}, \rho(t)] + \mathcal{D}[\rho(t)] \quad (2)$$

where the small Lamb shift H_{LS} commutes with H_s and $\mathcal{D}[\rho(t)]$ is the standard dissipator. Among them, we have.

$$D(\rho) = \gamma_1^+[\eta_1\rho\eta_1^\dagger - \frac{1}{2}\{\eta_1\eta_1^\dagger, \rho\}] + \gamma_1^-[\eta_1^\dagger\rho\eta_1 - \frac{1}{2}\{\eta_1\eta_1^\dagger, \rho\}]$$

$$+\gamma_2^+[\eta_2^\dagger\rho\eta_2 - \frac{1}{2}\{\eta_2\eta_2^\dagger, \rho\}] + \gamma_2^-[\eta_2^\dagger\rho\eta_2 - \frac{1}{2}\{\eta_2\eta_2^\dagger, \rho\}] \quad (3)$$

$$+\gamma_3^+[AA^\dagger\rho - A\rho A^\dagger - A^\dagger\rho A + \rho A^\dagger A] + \gamma_3^-[A^\dagger A\rho - A^\dagger\rho A - A\rho A^\dagger + \rho AA^\dagger]$$

$$+\gamma_4^+[BB^\dagger\rho - B\rho B^\dagger - B^\dagger\rho B + \rho B^\dagger B] + \gamma_4^-[B^\dagger B\rho - B^\dagger\rho B - B\rho B^\dagger + \rho BB^\dagger]$$

where $\rho = \rho(t)$, $A = \eta_1^\dagger\eta_2$, $B = \eta_1^\dagger\eta_2^\dagger$.
It is useful to absorb the trigonometric factours in Eq. (3) and define the decay retes

$$\gamma_1^+ = cos^2(\theta_+ + \theta_-)\mathcal{J}(E_1)[1 + n(E_1)], \quad \gamma_1^- = cos^2(\theta_+ + \theta_-)\mathcal{J}(E_1)n(E_1)$$
$$\gamma_2^+ = sin^2(\theta_+ + \theta_-)\mathcal{J}(E_2)[1 + n(E_2)], \quad \gamma_2^- = sin^2(\theta_+ + \theta_-)\mathcal{J}(E_2)n(E_2),$$
$$\gamma_3^+ = \beta_k^2 sin^2(\theta_+ + \theta_-)[1 + n(E_1 - E_2)], \quad \gamma_3^- = \beta_k^2 sin^2(\theta_+ + \theta_-)n(E_1 - E_2)$$
$$\gamma_4^+ = \beta_k^2 sin2\theta_+ cos2\theta_-[1 + n(E_1 + E_2)] \quad \text{and} \quad \gamma_4^- = \beta_k^2 sin2\theta_+ cos2\theta_- n(E_1 + E_2).$$

Then, we can write a complete set of equations of motion for the density-matrix elements of the system in the fermionic basis. And we have the following blocks of equations relevant for master equation in interaction picture:

$$\frac{d\rho_{00,01}}{dt} = \gamma_1^+\rho_{10,11} - \frac{1}{2}(2\gamma_1^- + \gamma_2^+ + \gamma_2^-)\rho_{00,01} + \gamma_3^-\rho_{00,01} + \gamma_4^-\rho_{00,01} \quad (4)$$

$$\frac{d\rho_{10,11}}{dt} = \gamma_1^- \rho_{00,01} - \frac{1}{2}(2\gamma_1^+ + \gamma_2^+ + \gamma_2^-)\rho_{11,01} + \gamma_3^+ \rho_{10,11} + \gamma_4^- \rho_{10,11} \quad (5)$$

$$\frac{d\rho_{00,10}}{dt} = \gamma_2^+ \rho_{01,11} - \frac{1}{2}(2\gamma_2^- + \gamma_1^+ + \gamma_1^-)\rho_{00,10} + \gamma_3^+ \rho_{00,10} + \gamma_4^- \rho_{00,10} \quad (6)$$

$$\frac{d\rho_{01,11}}{dt} = \gamma_2^- \rho_{00,10} - \frac{1}{2}(2\gamma_2^+ + \gamma_1^+ + \gamma_1^-)\rho_{01,11} + \gamma_4^- \rho_{01,11} + \gamma_3^- \rho_{01,11} \quad (7)$$

The synchronization phenomenon caused by the dissipation of the quantum bit system, and the expressions of $<\sigma_p^x(t)>$ and $<\sigma_q^x(t)>$ in general have been given. In the presence of more oscillating modes decaying at rates, Synchronization is achieved whenever there is appreciable separation between the two largest decay times characterizing the dynamics. By comparing the trajectories of $<\sigma_p^x(t)>$ and $<\sigma_q^x(t)>$, we can find out the synchronization clearly. Then, slowly decaying local degrees of freedom experience monochromatic oscillations at the unique surviving frequency, while the relative phases among them are locked. This model introduces two new variables by γ_3, γ_4 adding bath and system interactions. When temperature T = 0, we have

$$<\sigma_p^x(t)> = 2\cos(\theta_+ - \theta_-)\frac{(\gamma_1^+ - \gamma_3^+)\rho_{00,01}(0) + \gamma_1^+ \rho_{10,11}(0)}{(\gamma_1^+ - \gamma_3^+)}e^{-\frac{\gamma_2^+ t}{2}}Re\left(e^{iE_2 t}\right)$$

$$+ 2\sin(\theta_+ - \theta_-)\frac{(\gamma_2^+ + \gamma_3^+)\rho_{00,10}(0) + \gamma_2^+ \rho_{01,11}(0)}{(\gamma_2^+ + \gamma_3^+)}e^{\frac{(\gamma_1^+ + 2\gamma_3^+)t}{2}}Re\left(e^{iE_1 t}\right)$$

$$(8)$$

$$<\sigma_q^x(t)> = 2\cos(\theta_+ + \theta_-)\frac{(\gamma_2^+ + \gamma_3^+)\rho_{00,10}(0) + \gamma_2^+ \rho_{01,11}(0)}{(\gamma_2^+ + \gamma_3^+)}e^{\frac{(\gamma_1^+ + 2\gamma_3^+)t}{2}}Re\left(e^{iE_1 t}\right)$$

$$+ 2\sin(\theta_+ + \theta_-)\frac{(\gamma_1^+ - \gamma_3^+)\rho_{00,01}(0) + \gamma_1^+ \rho_{10,11}(0)}{(\gamma_1^+ - \gamma_3^+)}e^{-\frac{\gamma_2^+ t}{2}}Re\left(e^{iE_2 t}\right) \quad (9)$$

Here, the two energies are $E_1 = \left(\sqrt{4\lambda^2 + \omega_-^2} + \sqrt{4\lambda^2 + \omega_+^2}\right)/2$ and $E_2 = \left(\sqrt{4\lambda^2 + \omega_-^2} - \sqrt{4\lambda^2 + \omega_+^2}\right)/2$, where $\omega_\pm = \omega_q \pm \omega_p$ and $\theta_\pm = \frac{1}{2}\arcsin\left(2\lambda/\sqrt{4\lambda^2 + \omega_\pm^2}\right)$.

As a result of such dynamical structure, in the long-time limit, the two qubits experience monochromatic, synchronous oscillations if either $\gamma_1 \ll \gamma_2$ or $\gamma_1 \gg \gamma_2$. The frequency of such synchronous oscillations is $\omega_{sync} \simeq E_1$ for $\gamma_1 \gg \gamma_2$ and $\omega_{sync} \simeq E_2$ for $\gamma_1 \ll \gamma_2$ [20]. The cases where the two decaying rates are of the same order of magnitude are characterized by the absence of synchronization, that can be quantified using the so-called Pearson correlation coefficient [10]. Let us now assume a power-law spectral density for the bath [21]:

$$\mathcal{J}(\omega) = 2\gamma_0\omega^s\omega_c^2/\left(\omega_c^2 + \omega^{2s}\right) \quad (10)$$

With $\omega_c = 20\omega_q$, $\gamma_0 = 0.01$ and $T = 0$. The condition for the absence of synchronization $\gamma_1 = \gamma_2$ is satisfied along a line in the $\omega_p - s$ diagram which corresponds to $s = log\overline{\frac{E_1}{E_2}} \, tan^2 \left(\overline{\theta_+} + \overline{\theta_-}\right)$, where the bar indicates that all the parameters must be calculated at a given probe frequency $\omega_p = \overline{\omega_p}$. Then, determining the value of ω_p at which the transition from in-phase to out-of-phase synchronization takes place amounts to estimating the value of s [20].

In Fig. 1, in-phase synchronization and lack of synchronization under different ω_p have been plotted, they correspond to the same ohmic dissipation s. As the result of the probe frequency ω_p is allowed to be tuned, leading to trajectories with different dynamical evolution as shown in Figs. 1a and 1b. We can see that Fig. 1a has the best synchronization and Fig. 1b has the worst. There are two important factors affecting attenuation are γ_3 and γ_0. In Fig. 1c, increasing γ_0 we can find that the attenuation generated by dissipation becomes larger and the oscillation in the figure disappears faster than Fig. 1a. And then, increase γ_3 tenfold and we find that it takes longer to generate synchronization (compare with Fig. 1a).

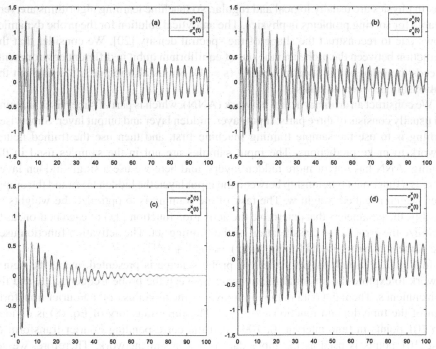

Fig. 1. Blue and red lines represent $<\sigma_p^x(t)>$ and $<\sigma_q^x(t)>$, Panels (a) and (b): evolution of qubit and probe exhibiting in-phase synchronization ((a) $\omega_p/\omega_q = 1.2$ and $s = 2$), no synchronization((b) $\omega_p/\omega_q = 1$ and $s = 2$). The other parameters: $\gamma_0 = 0.01$ and $\lambda = 0.2\omega_q$. Blue lines represent $<\sigma_p^x>$ and red lines $<\sigma_q^x>$. Panels (c): $\gamma_0 = 0.05$, $\omega_p/\omega_q = 1.2$ but other parameters remain the same as (a) and (b). And Panels (d): $\gamma_3 = 0.05$, $\omega_p/\omega_q = 1.2$ and other parameters remain the same as (a) and (b). (Color figure online)

3 Machine Learning Algorithms Classify the Environments(s)

With the efficient application of machine learning technology in image recognition, decision making and logical inference, the algorithm of machine learning has attracted more and more attention from physicists. Before using machine learning algorithm to solve quantum computing problem, it is necessary to understand an important method of machine learning – artificial neural network (ANN). An artificial neural network is similar to the human brain, and the whole process is divided into training, testing and results. Artificial neural network is divided into supervised learning and unsupervised learning. In most cases, we used supervised learning. Part of the data was used to train the neural network, and part of the data was used to test the learning results. The former datasets are called the training set, the ANN uses these labelled data to learn or approximate a proper solution to the problem at hand. During the learning process, the neural network classifies data according to different labels and calculates classification errors. Then the classification results were tested with the data from the training set. When new data is entered, the machine tries to give the correct label to the data, i.e. regression. Machine learning algorithms are good at finding internal laws between data, and problems in physics are usually logical and regular, so machine learning algorithms are very suitable for solving problems in physics. The analytical solution for the probe dynamics allows one to reconstruct the shape of the spectral density [20]. We consider that the interaction between the probe and the out of equilibrium qubit in different environments exceeds the usual ohmic spectral density ($s = 1$). So it's also important to find out the relationship between ω_p and s.

We construct an artificial neural network (ANN), which is part of supervised learning and usually consists of three parts: input layer, hidden layer and output layer. Supervised learning is to use the sample training machine first, and then use the trained neural network to make predictions. The input samples are not in the samples used in the training. ANN has one or more hidden layers, and here we use a single hidden layer. There is a functional relationship between the input layer, the hidden layer and the output layer, which is called weight w. The task of the training is to optimize the weights w, possibly, the parameters that determine the activation function $\varphi(x)$ of each neuron, as to minimize the error in the classification of the training set. The activation function used here is the standard sigmoid function $\varphi(x) = 1/\left(1 + e^{-x}\right)$.

In Fig. 2, a visual image of the ML probe scheme is presented, using the neural network to explore the potential relationship between the probe frequency ω_p and the environment s. The input data in the input layer is the modulus of the Fourier transform $\mathcal{F}(\omega)$ of the time domain function $<\sigma_p^x(t)>$. The time trajectory of Eq. (8) is divided into 101 points in time interval [0, 100], and the corresponding Fourier transform of these 101 points is used as the input data of the neural network. Therefore, we set the number of neurons in the input layer of the neural network as 101.The number of hidden layer neurons is also 101, including an activation function $\varphi(x)$. In this scenario, the output layer has a single neuron that contains the results we get. The connections between the layers are considered to be of feed-forward only type and the strength of these connections (weights) are optimized via back-propagation [22].

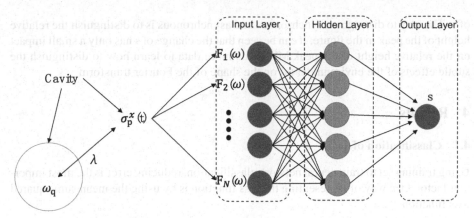

Fig. 2. Schematic view of the scheme. The Fourier transform $\mathcal{F}(\omega)$ of the measured data $<\sigma_p^x(t)>$ is used as input data to train the hidden layer, where the learning takes place. Then, the output layer projects the results.

The probe frequency is allowed to be tuned, because the ω_p changes with the corresponding $<\sigma_p^x(t)>$, as shown in Fig. 1. And different values of s correspond to different ohmic dissipation. In this case, three different values of s (s = 0.5, s = 1, s = 2) are selected to correspond to sub-Ohmic, Ohmic and super-Ohmic dissipation respectively. The purpose of the neural network is to teach it how to distinguish the trajectory of the Fourier transform, and to give the correct label in the training layer. When we give a new ω_p, the neural network will predict the value of the s corresponding to the ω_p correctly. The training set consisted of N spectra with three different labels, and the test set consisted of another 0.3N spectra with three different labels. Through these data, the neural network will learn how to divide the spectrum into three categories corresponding to different values of s. An example of a training set in Fig. 3 (note that only part of the spectrum is drawn), $\mathcal{F}(\omega)$ has been shown, each ω_p corresponds to three possible values

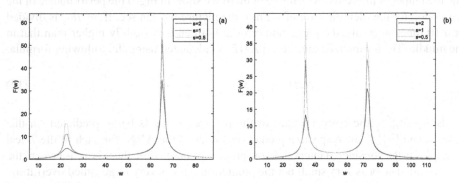

Fig. 3. Fourier transform of the probe dynamics for (a) $\omega_p = 1.2\omega_q$, (b) $\omega_p = \omega_q$. In all cases the yellow line corresponds to s = 0.5, the red line to s = 1 and the blue line to s = 2. The qubit-bath coupling coefficient is $\gamma_0 = 0.01$, in order to better visualize the differences between the trajectories for each value of s (Color figure online).

of s. The way to distinguish synchronous and asynchronous is to distinguish the relative height of the peak in the figure. It can be seen that the change of s has only a small impact on the relative height of the peak. ML needs more data to learn how to distinguish the subtle effects of the environment (s) on the shape of the Fourier transform.

4 Results

4.1 Classification of s

Using training set to train neural network classification, reducing error is the most important factor. One way of representing the loss function is by using the mean sum squared loss function:

$$MSE = \frac{1}{n} \sum_{i=1}^{m} (o - y)^2 \tag{11}$$

In this function, o is our predicted output, and y is our actual output. The mean sum squared loss function is the sum, over all the data points, of the square of the difference between the predicted and actual target variables, divided by the number of data points. The results for the classification of s are summarized in Fig. 4. The ANN trained 20,000 times with 30 sets of data. From the picture, it can be seen that MSE was very small at 3000 times. After 3000 training sessions, the training error decreased gradually. This shows that the neural network can classify the input data and the results are available.

4.2 Regression of s

As a further step, instead of asking the ML algorithm to identify the correct label among a family of discrete values, we can try to estimate the value of s itself through a continuous regression obtained in the limit of infinite labels. In this case, the performance of the algorithm can be tested by measuring the deviation between the true s of any tested data and the output of the ANN. As a figure of merit we show in Fig. 5 the performance of the regression for the identification of s. From the picture we can see, if ω_p / ω_q is divided into 10 times intervals, the regression error at both ends is slightly higher than that in the middle. The normalized mean error NME is calculated using the following formula:

$$NME = \frac{1}{T} \sum_{i=1}^{T} \frac{|-s_i - s_i|}{s_i} \tag{12}$$

Being $\{s_i\}_{i=1}^{T}$ the correct values of the parameter that is being predicted (in this case, s) and $\{\bar{s}_i\}_{i=1}^{T}$ the respective prediction values of the ANN, for each of the T test examples in the considered interval. In the process of prediction, there is a case where the classification error is very small but the prediction error is very large called overfitting. To solve this problem, the data amount of training set is usually increased. When ANN has learned each case, it can successfully predict the new case.

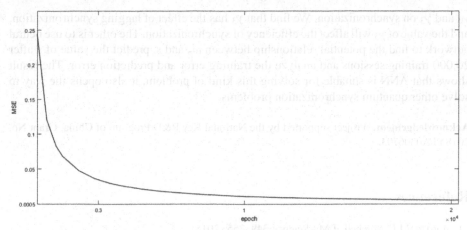

Fig. 4. The figure shows the training error (MSE) of the training set when training in the neural network. We selected 30 sets of data to train 200,000 times. MSE drops quickly before 3000 training sessions.

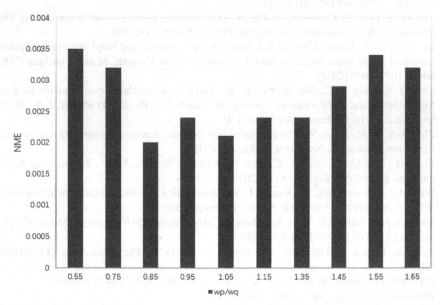

Fig. 5. The figure shows the regression of s for different intervals of the probe frequency. Using the modulus of the Fourier transform of $\omega_p/\omega_q = \{0.55\text{–}0.65\}$ as the input data, the neural network will automatically classify the corresponding s value.

5 Conclusion

In this article, we establish a quantum synchronization model and study the properties of synchronization. The main conclusions are as follows: one is to obtain the analytic solutions of $\sigma_p^x(t)$ and $\sigma_q^x(t)$ based on the master equation, and to show the influence of

γ_0 and γ_3 on synchronization. We find that γ_3 has the effect of lagging synchronization, and the value of γ_3 will affect the efficiency of synchronization. The other is to use neural network to find the potential relationship between ω_p and s, predict the value of s after 20,000 training sessions and analyze the training error and prediction error. The result shows that ANN is suitable for solving this kind of problem, it also opens the way to solve other quantum synchronization problems.

Acknowledgement. Project supported by the National Key R&D Program of China, Grant No. 2018YFA0306703.

References

1. Jordan, M.I., Mitchell, T.M.: Science **349**, 255 (2015)
2. Li, X.-Y., Zhu, Q.-S., Zhu, M.-Z., Huang, Y.-M., Hao, W., Shao-Yi, W.: Machine learning study of the relationship between t. EPL **127**, 20009 (2019)
3. Biamonte, J., Wittek, P., Pancotti, N., Rebentrost, P., Wiebe, N., Lloyd, S.: Quantum machine learning. Nature **549** 195–201 (2017)
4. Zhu, Q.-S., Ding, C.-C., Wu, S.-Y., Lai, W.: Geometric measure of quantum correlation: The influence of the asymmetry environments. Physica A **458**, 67 (2016)
5. Li, X.-Y., et al.: Researching the link between the geometric and rènyi discord for special canonical initial states based on neural network method. Comput. Mater. Continua CMC **60**(3), 1087–1095 (2019)
6. Zhu, Q.-S., Ding, C.-C., Wu, S.-Y., Lai, W.: The role of correlated environments on non-Markovianity and correlations of a two-qubit system. Eur. Phys. J. D **69**(10), 1–9 (2015). https://doi.org/10.1140/epjd/e2015-60223-4
7. Zhu, Q.-S., Fu, C.-J., Lai, W.: The correlated environments depress entanglement decoherence in the dimer system. Z. Naturforsch. **68a**, 272 (2013)
8. Li, X.-Y., Zhu, Q.-S., Zhu, M.-Z., Hao, W., Shao-Yi, W., Zhu, M.-C.: The freezing Rènyi quantum discord. Sci. Rep. **9**, 14739 (2019)
9. Pikovsky, A., Rosenblum, M., Kurths, J.: Synchronization A Universal Concept in Nonlinear Sciences. (Cambridge University Press, Cambridge (2001)
10. Osimani, M., Chillemi, C.: F. In: Knee Imaging. ANRPR, pp. 35–36. Springer, Milano (2017). https://doi.org/10.1007/978-88-470-3950-6_6
11. Mari, A., Farace, A., Didier, N., Giovannetti, V., Fazio, R.: Phys. Rev. Lett. **111**, 103605 (2013)
12. P. P. Orth, D. Roosen, W. Hofstetter, K. Le Hur, *Phys. Rev. B*, 82, 144423(2010).
13. Ameri, V., et al.: Phys. Rev. A **91**, 01230 (2015)
14. Militello, B., Nakazato, H., Napoli, A.: Phys. Rev. A **96**, 023862 (2017)
15. Koppenhöfer, M., Bruder, C., Roulet, A.: Quantum Synchronization on the IBM Q System arXiv:1910.12675(2019)
16. Li, W., Li, C., Song, H.: Quantum synchronization of chaotic oscillator behaviors among coupled BEC-optomechanical systems. Quantum Inf. Process. (2017)
17. Qu, Z.G., Chen, S.Y., Wang, X.J.: A secure controlled quantum image steganography algorithm. Quantum Inf. Process. **19**(380), 1–25 (2020)
18. Qu, Z.G., Wu, S.Y., Liu, W.J., Wang, X.J.: Analysis and improvement of steganography protocol based on bell states in noise environment. Comput. Mater. Continua **59**(2), 607–624 (2019)

19. GarauEstarellas, G., Giorgi, G.L., Soriano, M.C., Zambrini, R.: Adv. Quantum Technol. **2**, 1800085 (2019)
20. Giorgi, G.L., Galve, F., Zambrini, R.: Probing the spectral density of a dissipative qubit via quantum synchronization. Phys. Rev. A **94**, 052121 (2016)
21. Breuer, H.-P., Petruccione, F.: The Theory of Open Quantum Systems. Oxford University Press, Oxford, UK (2007)
22. Hinton, G.E.: Artif. Intell. **40**, 185–234 (1989)

Big Data

Big Data

W-Louvain: A Group Detection Algorithm Based on Synthetic Vectors

Xueming Qiao[1], Xiangkun Zhang[1], Ming Xu[2], Mingyuan Zhai[1], Mingrui Wu[3], and Dongjie Zhu[3(✉)]

[1] State Grid Weihai Power Supply Company, Weihai 264200, China
[2] State Grid Shandong Electric Power Company, Jinan 250000, China
[3] School of Computer Science and Technology, Harbin Institute of Technology, Weihai 264200, China
zhudongjie@hit.edu.cn

Abstract. Most of the hidden dangers of network system security are caused by group events. Group analysis and data mining for them are of great significance to ensure network security. Although the existing group detection algorithms have achieved a series of results, they can only be divided on one of the network structure and group attributes, but cannot combine them together, which has certain limitations. The comprehensive vector can be constructed by collecting and mining the group data which cause the hidden danger of security, which can analyze the hidden danger of security from the aspects of network structure and node attribute, so as to realize the guidance and control of group behavior. Therefore, in view of the above problems, this paper proposes a group detection algorithm based on synthesis vector, which can finally find a special group which is closely connected in structure and very similar in attribute. Firstly, the comprehensive similarity is calculated based on the fusion vector in the sharing layer of the comprehensive vector computing model. Then, reconstruct the weighted network diagram. Finally, based on Louvain algorithm, the improvement is carried out. The improved algorithm is referred to as the W-Louvain algorithm. The W-Louvain algorithm is used to divide the groups, and the closely connected vectors in the structure and the very similar vectors in the attributes are divided into the same group. Experiments show that on multiple datasets the evaluation indexes of W-Louvain algorithm, such as modularity Q, number k of community, density D of community and similarity degree S of comprehensive vector attribute, are better than the existing methods.

Keywords: Information security · Comprehensive vector · Group detection · Data mining

1 Introduction

With the development of information technology, the network becomes an indispensable part of the human society. People are more and more dependent on the network. However, the information network of our country starts late, the technology is relatively

© Springer Nature Switzerland AG 2021
X. Sun et al. (Eds.): ICAIS 2021, CCIS 1423, pp. 133–144, 2021.
https://doi.org/10.1007/978-3-030-78618-2_11

backward, and the shortage of technical talents makes the network information security of our country become a big deficiency. Network security and hidden dangers are increasingly prominent, always related to our vital interests [1]. A series of problems and hidden dangers, such as the diversification of cyber threats, the diversification of virus transmission, the endless emergence of cyber security vulnerabilities, the poor network order, and the weak awareness of cyber security among residents, are constantly affecting the long-term stability of the country [2]. Therefore, it is particularly important to ensure the security of the network. Taking Shandong electric power marketing business system as an example, there are a lot of security problems, such as the third-party outsourcing team using the intranet system to input data, system job number theft, borrowing, public, people's rights mismatch, business fee collection, project acceptance, etc. Group analysis [3–5] and data mining [6–8] for the groups with security risks above-mentioned are of great significance to ensure network security. The traditional group discovery algorithm, one is based on the network structure for group division, and the attribute of the comprehensive vector node itself is ignored. The other is the group division based on the group attribute similarity clustering, and the important feature of the structure is ignored, and the attribute of the group is not likely to be enumerated. Blondel et al. proposed the Louvain algorithm [9], which can find the high-modularity partition of a large network in a short time, and then merge the communities with the largest module increment. Through repeated iterations, the modularity Q value tends to be stable, thus giving the final community partition result. This algorithm is one of the fastest non-overlapping community discovery algorithms [10]. However, this kind of group discovery algorithm based on network structure has ignored the attribute of the node itself. The Spectral Clustering algorithm proposed by Shi and Malik maps the data vector of high dimensional space to the vector of low dimensional space by calculating similarity matrix, degree matrix and Laplace matrix, and then uses other clustering algorithms to cluster in low dimensional space. However, the clustering effect of this method is not good when there are many clustering categories, and the structural features are ignored. Therefore, it is of great significance to find an effective group discovery [5, 11, 12] algorithm to divide the synthesis vectors which are closely connected in structure and very similar in attributes into the same group. In this paper, the data of the above group security risks are collected and excavated to construct the comprehensive vector. Not only the network structure [13, 14], node attributes [15] and other aspects of the security hidden dangers can be deeply understood, but also from the group level to find and study, to achieve the guidance and control of group behavior [16]. The existing group Detection algorithms have achieved a series of successes in the fields of public security intelligence, location prediction, network public opinion prediction and so on [17], but there are still the following shortcomings:

(1) The interactive network data is huge, the network is complex, the information is very scattered. And it is difficult to extract and classify by means of an artificial method. The interaction network has many attributes and a wide variety of groups. When considering attributes, it is not possible to have all the attributes listed, or all the attributes of the nodes are similar.

(2) The group discovery algorithm based on network structure ignores the attributes of the node itself. The group discovery algorithm based on group attribute similarity

clustering ignores the important feature of structure. Therefore, there are some limitations in the process of dividing groups.

Therefore, the multi-source heterogeneous data will be fused, and feature-sharing can be used to improve the efficiency of feature extraction. According to the shortcomings of the current group discovery algorithm, this paper proposes a group discovery algorithm based on synthesis vector. Firstly, the comprehensive similarity is calculated based on the fusion vector in the sharing layer of the comprehensive vector computing model. Then, reconstruct the weighted network diagram. Finally, based on Louvain algorithm, the improvement is carried out. The improved algorithm is referred to as the W-Louvain algorithm. The W-Louvain algorithm is used to divide the groups, and the closely connected vectors in the structure and the very similar vectors in the attributes are divided into the same group.

2 The Design of the Group Detection Algorithm Based on Comprehensive Vector

The following is a flow chart of a group detection algorithm based on comprehensive vector (see Fig. 1).

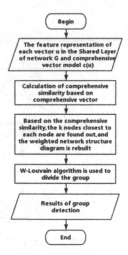

Fig. 1. Flow chart of population discovery algorithm based on comprehensive vector.

The overall design of the group detection algorithm based on comprehensive vector is as follows:

(1) Input network G and the feature of each of the integrated vectors u represents $c(u)$ in the shared layer of comprehensive vector model.
(2) Calculation of comprehensive similarity based on comprehensive vector.

(3) Based on the comprehensive similarity, the k nodes closest to each node are found out, and the weighted network structure diagram is rebuilt.
(4) The group partition is carried out by using the W-Louvain algorithm proposed in this paper, and the partition results are output.

In this algorithm, the calculation process of comprehensive similarity based on the comprehensive vector calculation model is detailed in Sect. 2.1, and the design of W-Louvain algorithm is detailed in Sect. 2.2.

2.1 Comprehensive Similarity Calculation Based on Comprehensive Vector Model

In this paper, through deep learning and fusion of multi-source heterogeneous interactive data information, based on comprehensive vector, comprehensive mining of effective features hidden in a variety of network information. Therefore, this paper proposes a group detection algorithm based on comprehensive vector. Firstly, a comprehensive vector computing model is designed. The multi-source data is then fused using the shared layer of the comprehensive vector calculation model (as shown in the Fig. 2). By integrating a plurality of different forms of data sources, a single identical representation is represented, providing a more reliable and more thorough description than a single data source.

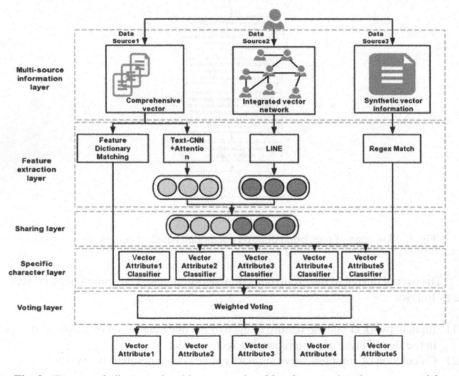

Fig. 2. Framework diagram of multi-source and multi-task comprehensive vector model.

By considering the correlation between different data sources, the sharing layer encodes different information sources after learning them through their respective models, encodes them as vectors, and takes vector connection as user characteristics $c(u)$, as shown in the following formula:

$$c(u) = m_u \oplus g_u \oplus R_u \tag{1}$$

Where represents the eigenvector learned in the multi-scale CNN Attention model, represents the eigenvectors learned in the network, represents the connection between the content and the IP eigenvectors that match probabilities of the respective categories based on the local feature dictionary table and the topographic dictionary table. After integration, the data sources can learn together, one data source can serve as additional information supplement of another data source, and different information sources can be fused to obtain better decision representation. The sharing layer not only integrates different information sources, but also connects the implicit relationship between each sub-task to achieve the goal of mutual benefit and win-win.

By using different similarity calculation methods, the division result may also be different, so we find a more suitable similarity calculation method. Because the fusion vector of the shared layer contains not only the basic attribute feature, but also the network structure characteristic of the first order and the second order neighbor degree of the comprehensive vector. And therefore, the comprehensive similarity of the comprehensive vector can be calculated by using the vector.

Firstly, the cosine similarity method is used to calculate the comprehensive vector similarity based on the fusion vector in the shared layer of the integrated vector model. To measure the magnitude of the difference between two different comprehensive vectors, the cosine value of the included angle between the two vectors in the vector space is calculated. The formula is as follows.

$$S_{uv} = \frac{c(u) \cdot c(v)}{\|c(u)\|^2 \times \|c(v)\|^2} \tag{2}$$

In formula (2), S_{uv} represents the comprehensive similarity between the comprehensive vector u and the comprehensive vector v based on the fusion vector in the comprehensive vector model. $c(u)$ represents the feature representation of the synthetic vector u in the Shared layer of the synthetic vector computing model in formula (1). Similarly, in formula (1) of $c(v)$, the feature representation of the integrated vector v in the Shared layer of the integrated vector computing model. $\|c(v)\|^2$ is the result of the square root of the sum of the squares of $c(u)$ elements. That is the L2 norm of $c(u)$. $\|c(v)\|^2$ is in the same way. The larger the value of S_{uv} and the smaller the angle of vector, the more similar the two comprehensive vectors are.

Then, Eq. (3) is proposed to calculate the synthesis vector and similarity.

$$M_{uv} = \alpha L_{uv} + (1 - \alpha) S_{uv} \tag{3}$$

Among them, M_{uv} is used to represent the comprehensive similarity of the comprehensive vector u and v. L_{uv} is used to judge whether there is a relation between the comprehensive vectors u and v. If there's a connection between u and v, L_{uv} is 1, otherwise it's 0. That is to determine whether there are edges between nodes in the network graph. S_{uv} is a comprehensive vector similarity calculated by formula (2) based on the fusion vector in the comprehensive vector model. α represents the weight of two similarity, $\alpha \in (0, 1)$. Different similarity weights will give different weights to attributes and structures, which will have different effects on group division.

2.2 Design of W-Louvain Algorithm

To accurately judge the closeness of the relationship between the synthesis vectors, the network graph G alone cannot achieve the desired effect, because the network graph G can only see whether there are edges connected between the synthesis vectors but cannot reflect the attributes of the synthesis vectors themselves. Therefore, this paper first calculates the comprehensive similarity based on the comprehensive vector model according to the algorithm introduced in Sect. 2.1. And take the comprehensive similarity as the weight of the edge. Then, k nodes closest to each node were found according to the comprehensive similarity, and the weighted network structure graph G_k was rebuilt to divide the group.

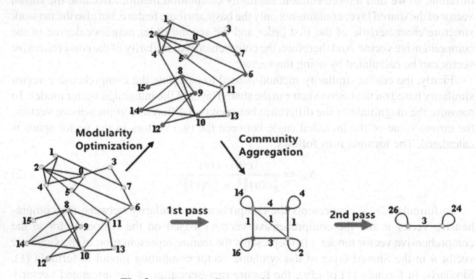

Fig. 3. Schematic diagram of Louvain algorithm.

As is known to all, Louvain algorithm (schematic diagram is shown in Fig. 3) can find the high-modular partition of a large network in a short time, and then merge the communities with the largest increase of modules. Through repeated iterations, the Q value tends to be stable, thus giving the result of community partition. However, this algorithm is not applicable to the weighted graph. Therefore, this paper is improved based on this algorithm. The improved algorithm is W-Louvain algorithm. The weighted module degree increment calculation formula is designed, as shown in formula (4):

$$
\Delta Q_W = \left[\frac{W_{in} + 2W_{i,in}}{2W} - \left(\frac{W_{tot} + w_i}{2W} \right)^2 \right] - \left[\frac{W_{in}}{2W} - \left(\frac{W_{tot}}{2W} \right)^2 - \left(\frac{w_i}{2W} \right)^2 \right]
$$
$$
= \frac{1}{2W} \left(w_{i,in} - \frac{W_{tot} w_i}{W} \right) \tag{4}
$$

In the formula, W represents the sum of the weights of all the edges in the network. w_i represents the sum of the weights of the edges connected to node i. $W_{i,in}$ represents the sum of the weights of all edges of a node from node I to community c. Win represents the sum of internal weights in community c. W_{tot} represents the sum of the weights of all edges connected by nodes in community c.

The iterative process of the W-Louvain algorithm is presented in this paper. In the first stage, each node of the weighted network graph is first set to a different community. Secondly, each node I is moved from its original community to the community of its neighbor node j, and the increment of modularity that will occur is evaluated by formula (4). When the value added is positive, the node I is placed in the community with the largest value added; if it is not positive, it will remain in the original community. All nodes are repeated in accordance with the procedure with the sequential application. when no node movement can improve the modularity, the first stage ends. at this time, the modularity q reaches the local maximum.

In the second stage, the community found in the first stage is regarded as a node to build a new network. The weight of the edge between the nodes in the two communities as the weight of the edge between the new nodes, links between nodes of the same community as the self-circulation of that community in the new network.

The weighted graph is obtained based on the comprehensive similarity of the comprehensive vector, and the re-constructed weighted network graph is divided by the W-Louvain algorithm, so that the integrated vector divided into the same group is both structurally and very similar in structure, and a more reasonable division result is obtained.

3 Experiment

3.1 Datasets

In this paper, three groups of real comprehensive vector data crawling from the network are used to carry out the experiment. The dataset comprehensive is shown in Table 1.

In this paper, the following methods are used to experiment with the above datasets:

Spectral Clustering. In the traditional attribute clustering algorithm, Spectral Clustering algorithm is more prominent for high-dimensional vector clustering. In this paper, spectral clustering algorithm is used to cluster through the fusion vector of the shared layer of the comprehensive vector model.

Louvain. The Louvain algorithm is used to divide the operation comprehensive vector network graph into groups.

W-Louvain. A group discovery algorithm based on comprehensive vectors is proposed in this paper.

Table 1. Specific description of population discovery datasets.

Data Set	GDD (Large-scale)	GDD (Medium-scale)	GDD (Small-scale)
Number of nodes	4,333	612	205
Number of edges	10,832	1,714	430
Node average	2.5	2.8	2.1

3.2 Experiment Process

To evaluate the quality of group division, four evaluation indexes are used in this paper. They are modularity Q, number of communities k, density of community D, and synthetic vector attribute similarity S. In this paper, the value of k is taken as the average degree of the network graph G. Experiments were conducted on the above three groups of experimental data according to different algorithms to find the best value of similarity weight in formula. The experimental images are as follows:

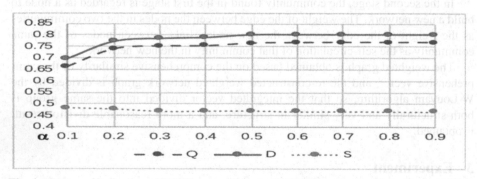

Fig. 4. Curves of indicators with different α values on GDD (Large-Scale). (Color figure online)

The horizontal axis represents the value of similarity weight α, and the vertical axis represents the different index values under different values. The index of modularity Q is represented by blue dotted line. The index of community density D is represented by red solid line. The index of group attribute similarity S is represented by green dotted line.

As shown in Fig. 4, in GDD (large-scale) Scale, modularity Q and community density D first increase with the increase of similarity weight value of α. When α is more than 0.5, it tends to be stable gradually. The similarity of synthetic vector attribute S decreases with the increase of α. When α is more than 0.5, the declining trend slows down and tends to be flat.

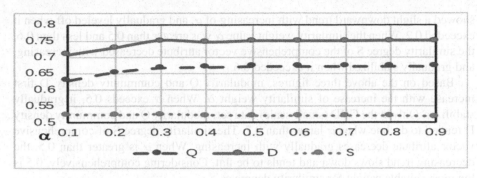

Fig. 5. Curves of indicators with different α values on GDD (Medium-Scale).

As shown in Fig. 5, in the size of GDD (Medium-Scale), modularity Q also first increases with the increase of similarity weight, when the value of α exceeds 0.5, it gradually stabilizes. The community density D first showed an upward trend with the increase of the weight value of similarity degree. When the weight value was 0.3, it reached the maximum value. When the weight value was greater than 0.5, it tended to be flat. The similarity degree S of the comprehensive vector attribute decreases gradually with increasing of α, but the decreasing trend is not obvious. When the weight value is greater than 0.5, it tends to be stable gradually.

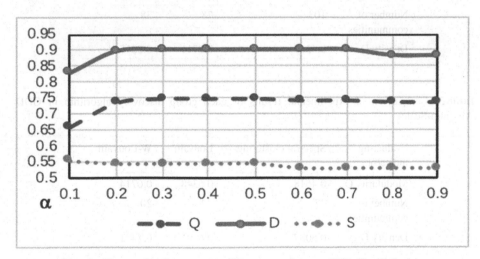

Fig. 6. Curves of indicators with different α values on GDD (Small-Scale).

As shown in Fig. 6, in the GDD (small-scale) Scale, the community density D also first increases with the increase of the value of similarity weight α. When the α is more than 0.2, it gradually becomes stable; when α is more than 0.7, it decreases; when α is more than 0.8, it gradually flattens. Modularity Q first shows an upward trend with the increase of the weight value of similarity, and then flattens out when the weight value is greater than 0.2. The similarity degree S of the comprehensive vector attribute showed a slight downward trend with increasing of α, and gradually leveled off when it exceeded 0.2. When the similarity weight value α was greater than 0.5 and less than 0.6, the similarity degree S of the comprehensive vector attribute decreased with increasing, and gradually stabilized when it exceeded 0.6.

Based on the above three figures, modularity Q and community density D first increase with the increase of similarity weight α. When α exceeds 0.5, it gradually stabilizes. Only in the GDD (small-scale) data set, modularity Q and community density D tended to decline when α larger than 0.7. The similarity degree S of comprehensive vector attribute decreases gradually with increasing. When α is greater than 0.5, the decreasing trend slows down and tends to be flat. Considering comprehensively, 0.5 is the most suitable weight for similarity degree α.

After determining the most suitable similarity weight, three different algorithms are used to divide the groups. The experimental results of three different algorithms on three different sets of data sets are as follows (Tables 2, 3 and 4):

Table 2. Comparison of experimental results of each group discovery algorithm in GDD (Large-Scale).

Evaluating indicator	Spectral clustering	Louvain	W-Louvain
Modularity Q	0.4208	0.7538	0.7655
Number of communities	103	78	38
Density D	0.4369	0.7711	0.8015

Table 3. Comparison of experimental results of each group discovery algorithm in GDD (Medium-Scale).

Evaluating indicator	Spectral clustering	Louvain	W-Louvain
Modularity Q	0.4618	0.6348	0.6714
Number of communities	37	32	20
Density D	0.5087	0.6791	0.7491

According to the comparison of the above three tables, the classification effect of Spectral Clustering algorithm is the worst in data sets of GDD (Large-Scale), GDD (Medium-Scale) and GDD (Small-Scale). The partition effect of Louvain algorithm is general. The W-Louvain algorithm proposed in this paper has the best partition effect on the three datasets. Therefore, group detection algorithm based on integrated vector is better than other two algorithms. The comprehensive vector, which is closely related in structure and very similar in attribute, is successfully divided into a group.

Table 4. Comparison of experimental results of each group discovery algorithm in GDD (Small-Scale).

Evaluating indicator	Spectral clustering	Louvain	W-Louvain
Modularity Q	0.3555	0.7398	0.7481
Number of communities	10	10	8
Density D	0.4821	0.8928	0.9017

4 Conclusion

In this paper, a group detection algorithm based on synthesis vector is proposed. The algorithm first calculates the comprehensive similarity based on the fusion vector in the multi-source multi-task integrated vector model sharing layer. Then, the most similar k nodes of each node are found based on the comprehensive similarity, and the structure diagram of the weighted network is reconstructed. In the end, the W-Louvain algorithm proposed in this paper is used for group division. And three groups of data sets with different sizes are compared with Spectral Clustering algorithm and Louvain algorithm. The experimental results show that the group discovery algorithm based on comprehensive vector proposed in this paper has achieved the best results in all the evaluation indexes. A comprehensive vector that is both structurally and functionally similar in structure can be divided into the same group. The experimental results show that the W-Louvain algorithm proposed in this paper has a relatively good division effect on a plurality of data sets.

However, in that algorithm experiment, the information source is single, and there may be some limitation. Therefore, we need to further study the feature extraction methods of different information sources to improve the accuracy and accuracy of comprehensive vectors. The group detection algorithm studied in this paper is an improvement based on non-overlapping community algorithm, but further research on overlapping community algorithm is still needed in order to have more room for development.

Acknowledgement. This work is supported by State Grid Shandong Electric Power Company Science and Technology Project Funding under Grant no.520613200001,520613180002, 62061318C002, Weihai Scientific Research and Innovation Fund (2020) and the Grant 19YG02, Sanming University.

References

1. You, C., Zhu, D., Sun, Y.: SNES: social-network-oriented public opinion monitoring platform based on elastic search. Comput. Mater. Continua **61**(3), 1271–1283 (2019)
2. Chuai, Y.: Security problems and countermeasures of network information construction. Electron. Technol. Softw. Eng. **22**, 202–203 (2019)

3. Pan, L., Wu, P., Huang , D.: Research advances in online social networking groups. J. Electron. Inf. Technol. **39**(9), 2097–2107 (2017)
4. Liu, Y., Zhang, J., Chen, J.: A method based on maximum frequent item set mining for weibo hype group discovery. Comput. Eng. Appl. **53**(04), 90–97 (2017)
5. Wang, Y., Han, T., Zhou, K.: Group discovery algorithm based on key map in public security intelligence. J. Zhejiang Univ. (Eng. Edn.) **51**(06), 1173–1180 (2017)
6. He, Z., Wu, M., Li, X.: Overview of data mining. Chinese Foreign Entrepr. **33**, 234 (2019)
7. Li, Y.: Research on the application of artificial intelligence in computer network technology in the era of big data. Sci. Technol. Innov. **31**, 90–91 (2019)
8. Wu, C.: Research on the application of data mining technology in the field of Internet. Comput. Knowl. Technol. **36** (2019)
9. Blondel, V.D., Guillaume, J.L., Lambiotte, R.: Fast unfolding of communities in large networks. J. Stat. Mech. Theory Exp. **2008**(10), 1–13 (2008)
10. Rungan, Z., Yu, W., Xin, C.: Discovery and visualization algorithm of large-scale social network community. Comput. Aided J. Des. Graph. **29**(02), 328–336 (2017)
11. Atzmueller, M., Doerfel, S., Mitzlaff, F.: Description-oriented community detection using exhaustive subgroup discovery. Inf. Sci. **329** (2016)
12. Zhang, B., Zhang, L., Mu, C.: A most influential node group discovery method for influence maximization in social networks: a trust-based perspective. Data Knowl. Eng. **121** (2019)
13. Zhu, D., Sun, Y., Li, X.: MINE: a method of multi-interaction heterogeneous information network embedding. Comput. Mater. Continua **63**(3), 1343–1356 (2020)
14. Zhu, D., Sun, Y., Cao, N.: BDNE: a method of bi-directional distance network embedding. In: 2019 International Conference on Cyber-Enabled Distributed Computing and Knowledge Discovery (CyberC), pp. 158–161. IEEE, Guilin (2019)
15. Zhu, D., Wang, Y., You, C., et al.: MMLUP: multi-source & multi-task learning for user profiles in social network. Comput. Mater. Continua **61**(3), 1105–1115 (2019)
16. Li, P., Peng, W., Danhua, H.: Research progress of online social network group discovery. J. Electron. Inf. Technol. **33**(09), 2097–2107 (2017)
17. Zhenglin, H.: Characteristics of social network crime. Netw. Secur. Technol. Appl. (06), 183–184 (2014)

Application of Non-negative Matrix Factorization in Fault Detection of Distribution Network

Shilin Wang[1]([⊠]), Huiyuan Cui[2], Xueyu Han[1], Nan Zhang[1], and Zhu Liu[1]

[1] State Grid Information and Telecommunication Group Co., Ltd., Xicheng District, Beijing 102211, China
[2] Daxing International Airport, Daxing District, Beijing 102600, China

Abstract. The application and promotion of smart distribution transformer terminal based on software definition has played a positive role in promoting the construction of distribution Internet of Things. This paper presents a new non-negative matrix factorization algorithm, generalized projection non-negative matrix factorization algorithm. Based on this algorithm, the statistical monitoring model is constructed, and the monitoring statistics suitable for the new monitoring model are designed. Then, the monitoring model is deployed in the form of a software APP to the smart distribution transformer terminal to realize the operation state monitoring and fault detection function of the distribution network. Finally, using the Simulink in MATLAB as the simulation plat-form to simulate the single-phase grounding fault of distribution network, the result shows that the fault monitoring model based on generalized projection non-negative matrix decomposition can better complete the detection task of single-phase grounding fault, and which detection effect is to meet the real-time requirements of fault detection in the field.

Keywords: Distribution network · Fault detection · Smart distribution transformer terminal · Generalized projection non-negative matrix factorization · Single-phase to ground fault

1 Introduction

The distribution network is located at the end of the power system and directly interacts with the majority of electricity customers [1, 2]. The quality of which operation would have a direct impact on the reliability of power supply and the customer's power experience. A statistical analysis of customers' average outage time data shows that 90% of outage time can be caused by a fault in the distribution network [3, 4]. Comparing with western developed countries, China has been promoting the construction of distribution network, however, its distribution network reliability level is still low [5, 6]. To this end, the National Energy Administration and the National Development and Reform Commission respectively issued the Notice of the National Energy Administration on Issuing the Action Plan for the Construction and Reconstruction of the Distribution Network

© Springer Nature Switzerland AG 2021
X. Sun et al. (Eds.): ICAIS 2021, CCIS 1423, pp. 145–157, 2021.
https://doi.org/10.1007/978-3-030-78618-2_12

(2015–2020) and the Guiding Opinions of the National Development and Reform Commission on Accelerating the Construction and Transformation of Distribution Networks. In order to improve the coverage of distribution automation, shorten the outage time and improve the reliability of distribution network, more funds should be invested in the construction and transformation of distribution network. By 2020, the power supply reliability rate of central cities (regions) will reach 99.99%, and that of urban areas will reach 99.88%. However, by the end of 2017, the coverage rate of distribution automation in China was only 35%, and it was planned to reach 60% in 2018. More efforts remain to be made in the construction and transformation of distribution network.

With the increasing importance of distribution network reliability, many experts, scholars and engineers develop relay protection algorithms and equipment by introducing a lot of mathematics and signal processing technology into the fault detection field of distribution network, which greatly promotes the development and progress of distribution network fault detection technology. The current distribution network fault detection technology can be classified into the following categories: methods based on fault current and voltage amplitude [7], methods based on low-frequency and high-frequency information [8], methods based on Kalman filter and pattern recognition [9], methods based on wavelet transform [10], methods based on artificial neural network [11, 12], methods based on fuzzy reasoning [13], methods based on multivariate statistical analysis [14]. Among them, the method based on multivariate statistical analysis cannot be widely used in the fault detection of distribution network, It is only used for signal extraction and feature dimensionality reduction, and there is no method that can realize the entire process of fault detection. This paper introduces a new improved algorithm of non-negative matrix factorization (NMF)—Generalized Projection Non-negative Matrix Factorization (GPNMF) [15] algorithm into the field of distribution network fault detection. Deploying the GPNMF-based fault detection model to the smart distribution transformer terminal of the station area could realize the monitoring of the operation status of the distribution network and online fault detection, that can also improve the level of lean management and active service in the distribution station area, and promote the application and promotion of software-defined terminals in the distribution of Internet of Things. As a new multivariate statistical analysis technology, NMF has attracted more and more attention. The authors of [16] have applied NMF and its improved algorithm to the fault detection of industrial process successfully. However, the above-mentioned literature can realize the off-line detection of system faults, which lacks real-time performance.

In this paper, the distribution network fault detection method is deployed in the smart distribution transformer terminal of the substation area in the form of software app, so as to realize the monitoring and fault detection function of the distribution network, boost the transformation of the distribution network from passive management to active management mode, improve the level of lean management and active service, and promote the application and promotion of software defined terminal in the distribution Internet of things.

2 Introduction to NMF Related Algorithms

2.1 NMF Basic Algorithm

The NMF algorithm was first proposed by Lee in the journal Nature [17]. Its construction idea of the algorithm is: the overall feature of a thing is composed of a non-negative linear combination of partial features [18]. And NMF algorithm requires the data matrix to be decomposed and the decomposition result to satisfy non-negative constraints. The definition of NMF can be described as:

Given an m-dimensional column vector $x(x \geq 0)$, n-times sampling is carried out, and the data sample matrix obtained is $X = [x_1, x_2, \cdots, x_n] \in R^{m \times n}$, where x_i ($i = 1, 2, \cdots, n$) is the sample vector. The purpose of NMF is to obtain non-negative matrices $W \in R^{m \times k}$ and $H \in R^{k \times n}$ such that.

$$X = WH \tag{1}$$

can be true. Where W is the base matrix and H is the coefficient matrix. Generally, the value of k should make $(m + n)k < mn$ hold [17].

The decomposition process of the matrix X by the NMF algorithm can be regarded as an optimization process of a nonlinear problem. The change of the objective function value is used to describe the closeness between the obtained result and X. Reference [19] chooses the square of Euclidean distance as the objective function, and its mathematical form is as follows:

$$\min_{W,H} F = \begin{cases} E(X \| WH) = \frac{1}{2} \|X - WH\|_F^2 \\ \text{s.t. } W \geq 0, \ H \geq 0 \end{cases} \tag{2}$$

In the process of researching the NMF algorithm, it is found that when W or H is used as a variable alone, the objective function in Eq. (2) is convex, but when W and H are used as variables, it is not. Therefore, the NMF algorithm established based on Eq. (2) can only obtain the local optimal solution but not for the global optimal solution. In reference [19], the objective function in Eq. (2) is optimized alternately in the way that similar to the optimization strategy in expectation maximization (EM) algorithm, and then a set of iterative rules can be obtained. From the theoretical point of view, the iterative rules are proved to be convergent, and the mathematical description form is as follows:

$$\begin{cases} H_{kj} \leftarrow H_{kj} \dfrac{(W^T X)_{kj}}{(W^T WH)_{kj}} \\ W_{ik} \leftarrow W_{ik} \dfrac{(XH^T)_{ik}}{(WHH^T)_{ik}} \end{cases} \tag{3}$$

The iterative rule in Eq. (3) is called multiplication iteration rule, which is the most widely used rule in NMF and its improved algorithm. Therefore, the iterative rule can be used as a benchmark algorithm to test the performance of the new algorithm.

2.2 Projection Non-negative Matrix Factorization Algorithm

Since the NMF algorithm was proposed, many improved algorithms have emerged. Most of them are based on the objective function of the NMF benchmark algorithm and improve the performance of the NMF algorithm by adding different constraints. Reference [20] provides a brand-new improvement idea. By embedding linear projection, the unknown variables in the basic NMF algorithm are reduced from two to one, which reduces the difficulty of solving the algorithm. The algorithm is named projective nonnegative matrix factorization (PNMF) algorithm, and its objective function is as follows:

$$\min_{W} F = \begin{cases} \frac{1}{2}\|X - WW^{T}X\|_{F}^{2} \\ \text{s.t. } W \geq 0 \end{cases} \tag{4}$$

Expand the objective function in Eq. (4) and remove the constant term, the following results can be obtained as follows:

$$F(W) = \frac{1}{2}Tr(-2XX^{T}WW^{T} + WW^{T}XX^{T}WW^{T}) \tag{5}$$

Where $Tr()$ is the trace of the matrix.

For Eq. (5), the first order differential of W is obtained as follows:

$$dF(W) = \frac{1}{2}d(Tr[-2XX^{T}WW^{T} + WW^{T}XX^{T}WW^{T}])$$
$$= Tr((-2W^{T}XX^{T} + W^{T}XX^{T}WW^{T} + W^{T}WW^{T}XX^{T})dW) \tag{6}$$

Then the gradient matrix of the objective function of the PNMF algorithm is:

$$\frac{\partial F(W)}{\partial W} = -2XX^{T}W + WW^{T}XX^{T}W + XX^{T}WW^{T}W \tag{7}$$

When solving the PNMF algorithm, the gradient descent method is used in reference [20], and the iterative rule form is as follows:

$$W_{ij} = W_{ij} - \delta_{ij}\frac{\partial F}{\partial W_{ij}} \tag{8}$$

Where δ_{ij} is the step size. Since NMF class algorithms require that the basis matrix W satisfy the nonnegative requirement, the value of δ_{ij} is:

$$\delta_{ij} = \frac{W_{ij}}{(WW^{T}XX^{T}W)_{ij} + (XX^{T}WW^{T}W)_{ij}} \tag{9}$$

The iterative rule of the PNMF algorithm obtained by introducing Eq. (9) into Eq. (8):

$$W_{ij} = W_{ij}\frac{2(XX^{T}W)_{ij}}{(WW^{T}XX^{T}W)_{ij} + (XX^{T}WW^{T}W)_{ij}} \tag{10}$$

Compared with the iterative rule of the basic NMF algorithm, only W is the unknown variable in Eq. (10), which reduces the difficulty of solving the PNMF algorithm. It also reduces the uncertainty of understanding and the influence of the initial iteration on the results.

3 GPNMF Algorithm

The significance of PNMF algorithm provides a new idea for further study of NMF algorithm. However, although the PNMF algorithm improves the performance of NMF algorithm to some extent, it is found that the algorithm still has the following shortcomings in the follow-up study: under the iteration rule of Eq. (10), it cannot guarantee that the value of the objective function in the PNMF algorithm is monotonically decreasing, and there may be shaking [20]. In addition, the operating data collected by various collectors in the power industry do not necessarily meet non-negative requirements. In order to make the NMF algorithm get better application in the power industry, this paper tries to relax the non-negative requirement of the decomposition matrix X. by referring to the improvement ideas of PNMF algorithm, this paper gives a new idea of NMF algorithm—GPNMF algorithm. The decomposition form in Eq. (1) of the new algorithm is rewritten as:

$$X_\pm = X_\pm H_+^T H_+ \tag{11}$$

Where "$\pm$" means that the matrix X contains both positive and negative numbers.

The objective function of GPNMF algorithm is constructed based on the square of Euclidean distance. As shown in Eq. (12).

$$\min_{W,H} F(W,H) = \begin{cases} \frac{1}{2}\|X - WH\|_F^2 \\ \text{s.t. } W = XH^T \end{cases} \tag{12}$$

In order to avoid the same defects as the PNMF algorithm, the GPNMF algorithm uses the Lagrange method to solve the optimization problem in Eq. (12). Assuming that the matrix X satisfies the non-negative condition, Lagrange multipliers Ψ and Λ are introduced, and the objective function in Eq. (12) is rewritten into the following form:

$$\tilde{F}(W,H) = \|X - WH\|_F^2 + Tr(\Psi^T(W - XH^T)) + Tr(\Lambda(H^TH - I)) \tag{13}$$

Define the Lagrangian function as follows:

$$\begin{aligned} L(H') &= \tilde{F}(W,H') \\ &= \|X - WH'\|_F^2 + Tr(\Psi^T(W - XH'^T)) + Tr(\Lambda(H'^TH' - I)) \\ &= Tr(-2X^TWH' - \Psi^TXH'^T) + Tr(H'H'^TW^TW) + Tr(H'^TH'\Lambda) \\ &\quad + Tr(X^TX + \Psi^TW - \Lambda) \end{aligned} \tag{14}$$

Auxiliary functions will be used in the following derivation process, and the definition of auxiliary functions is given here firstly.

Definition 2–1: We call $G(h, h')$ an auxiliary function of $F(h)$, if $G(h, h')$ and $F(h)$ make Eq. (15) hold [19].

$$G(h, h') \geq F(h), \quad G(h, h) = F(h) \tag{15}$$

To construct the auxiliary function of (14) accurately, it is not enough to rely on the definition of the auxiliary function. The following propositions need to be defined.

Proposition 2–1: The matrices $A \in R^{k \times k}$, $B \in R^{k \times k}$, $B' \in R^{m \times k}$ are arbitrary matrices, and A is a symmetric matrix, then Eq. (16) holds:

$$\sum_{ij} \frac{(BA)_{ij} B_{ij}'^2}{B_{ij}} \geq Tr(B'^{\mathsf{T}} B' A) \tag{16}$$

The detailed proof process of Proposition 2-1 is given in reference [21].

The auxiliary function of Eq. (14) is constructed according to Definition 2-1 and Proposition 2-1, and its mathematical form is defined as:

$$G(H, H') = Tr(-2X^{\mathsf{T}} WH' - \Psi^{\mathsf{T}} XH'^{\mathsf{T}}) + \sum_{ij} \frac{(H^{\mathsf{T}} W^{\mathsf{T}} W)_{ij} H_{ij}'^{\mathsf{T}2}}{H_{ij}^{\mathsf{T}}}$$

$$+ \sum_{ij} \frac{(H\Lambda)_{ij} H_{ij}'^2}{H_{ij}} + Tr(X^{\mathsf{T}} X + \Psi^{\mathsf{T}} W - \Lambda) \tag{17}$$

Find the first-order partial derivative of the variable H' for Eq. (17), and set $\partial G(H, H')/ H' = 0$. After finishing, the following results can be get:

$$H_{ij}' = H_{ij} \frac{(2W^{\mathsf{T}} X + \Psi^{\mathsf{T}} X)_{ij}}{(2W^{\mathsf{T}} WH + 2H\Lambda)_{ij}} \tag{18}$$

The values of Lagrange multipliers Ψ and Λ are determined by KKT conditions. The first partial derivative of Eq. (13) with respect to variable W is obtained as follows:

$$\frac{\partial \tilde{F}(W, H)}{\partial W} = -2XH^{\mathsf{T}} + 2WHH^{\mathsf{T}} + \Psi \tag{19}$$

Let $\frac{\partial \tilde{F}(W,H)}{\partial W} = 0$, the value of Ψ is obtained as follows:

$$\Psi = 2XH^{\mathsf{T}} - 2WHH^{\mathsf{T}} \tag{20}$$

It can be found from Eq. (11) that the closer the value of $H^{\mathsf{T}} H$ is to the identity matrix I, the closer the equal sign in Eq. (11) is true. Therefore, GPNMF implies an orthogonal constraint on H. Bring $W = XH^{\mathsf{T}}$ and $H^{\mathsf{T}} H = I$ into Eq. (20) and get $\Psi = 0$.

For Eq. (13), the first order partial derivative of variable H is obtained as follows:

$$\frac{\partial \tilde{F}(W, H)}{\partial H} = -2W^{\mathsf{T}} X + 2W^{\mathsf{T}} WH - \Psi^{\mathsf{T}} X + 2H\Lambda \tag{21}$$

Let $\frac{\partial \tilde{F}(W,H)}{\partial H} = 0$, and put $\Psi = 0$ into Eq. (21) to obtain Eq. (22):

$$H\Lambda = W^{\mathsf{T}} X - W^{\mathsf{T}} WH \tag{22}$$

Multiply H^{T} on both sides of Eq. (22), and put $W = XH^{\mathsf{T}}$ and $H^{\mathsf{T}} H = I$ into Eq. (22). After finishing, the value of Λ is 0.

Bring $W = XH^T$, $\Psi = 0$ and $\Lambda = 0$ into Eq. (18), the iteration rules are obtained as follows:

$$H_{ij} = H_{ij}\frac{(HX^TX)_{ij}}{(HX^TXH^TH)_{ij}} \tag{23}$$

It can be seen that the iterative rule in Eq. (23) is similar in form and structure to that of the PNMF algorithm, but the denominator of Eq. (23) is more concise. In the previous analysis, it is known that the iterative rules of the PNMF algorithm have certain flaws. In order to avoid similar situations in Eq. (23), this paper proposes a new iteration rule based on Eq. (23), as Eq. (24) shown.

$$H_{ij} = H_{ij}(\frac{(HX^TX)_{ij}}{(HX^TXH^TH)_{ij}})^{\frac{1}{4}} \tag{24}$$

Under the iterative rule of Eq. (24), if the equal sign is to be established, the value of $(HX^TX)_{ij}/(HX^TXH^TH)_{ij}$ should be 1.

The iterative rule in derivation (24) is carried out once the matrix X satisfies the non-negative condition. The following discusses the case of releasing the non-negative constraint on X. Define X_+ as the absolute value of all positive elements in X, and X_- as the absolute value of all negative elements in X. The calculation formula is:

$$\begin{cases} X_+ = \dfrac{1}{2}(|X| + X) \\ X_- = \dfrac{1}{2}(|X| - X) \end{cases} \tag{25}$$

Where $|X|$ is the absolute value of all elements in X, and $X_{\pm} = X_+ + X_-$ can be obtained from Eq. (25). Substituting formula (25) into $(HX^TX)_{ij}/(HX^TXH^TH)_{ij}$, the following results can be obtained:

$$\frac{(H[X^TX]_+ + H[X^TX]_-H^TH)_{ij}}{(H[X^TX]_- + H[X^TX]_+H^TH)_{ij}} = 1 \tag{26}$$

Then the mathematical description form of the iteration rule in Eq. (24) can be rewritten as follows:

$$H_{ij} = H_{ij}(\frac{(H[X^TX]_+ + H[X^TX]_-H^TH)_{ij}}{(H[X^TX]_- + H[X^TX]_+H^TH)_{ij}})^{\frac{1}{4}} \tag{27}$$

Equation (27) is the iterative rule of GPNMF algorithm.

4   Fault Detection Method Based on GPNMF

4.1   Monitoring Model Construction

According to the structure of Eq. (1) and Eq. (11), the monitoring model is defined as follows:

$$X = W\hat{H} + E \tag{28}$$

Where $\hat{H}$ is the reconstruction value of matrix H, and its calculation method is shown in Eq. (29):

$$\hat{H} = (W^T W)^{-1} W^T X \tag{29}$$

It can be seen that the new monitoring model decomposes the measurement space where the decomposition matrix X is located into two subspaces. Because the construction idea of NMF algorithm thinks that the overall characteristics of a thing are composed of some non-negative linear combinations of characteristics. The subspace formed by $W\hat{H}$ is named the characteristic subspace, and the subspace formed by E is named the residual subspace.

The monitoring statistics applicable to Eq. (28) are constructed below. In the fault detection method based on principal component analysis (PCA), the measurement space of process variables is decomposed into principal component subspace and residual subspace. The PCA method relies on the monitoring statistics T^2 and SPE to detect system failures [22]. Among them, T^2 mainly describes the fluctuation of the first a principal variable in the system, and SPE describes the gap between the current system operation and the monitoring model [23]. Based on the structure and connotation of the monitoring statistics T^2 and SPE, new monitoring statistics T_G^2 and SPE_G are constructed to describe the changes in the feature subspace and residual subspace in the GPNMF algorithm. The definition equation of T_G^2 and SPE_G are as follows:

$$T_G^2 = \hat{H}(i)^T \hat{H}(i) \tag{30}$$

$$SPE_G = (x(i) - \hat{x}(i))^T (x(i) - \hat{x}(i)) \tag{31}$$

Where: $\hat{H}(i)$ and $x(i)$ are the i-th column of matrix $\hat{H}$ and X respectively, and $\hat{x}(i)$ is the reconstruction values of $x(i)$. The calculation method is as follows:

$$\hat{x}(i) = WH(i) = WW^T x(i) \tag{32}$$

After defining the monitoring statistics, the control limitation problem should be solved. In this article, kernel density estimation (KDE) will be used to obtain the control limits of T_G^2 and SPE_G, and the value of the confidence interval θ is 99% during the calculation process.

5   Fault Detection Method Based on GPNMF

The fault detection method based on GPNMF mainly includes two parts, namely offline modeling and online detection.

Offline modeling:

1) Select the variable that needs to be monitored from the many acquisition variables, collect the operating data of the selected variable under the normal state to form the training sample matrix X of the GPNMF monitoring model, and normalize X;

2) The cumulative contribution rate method is used to determine the initial value of the coefficient k in the GPNMF algorithm, and the cumulative contribution rate can be set to 85% during the calculation process, and the value of k can be adjusted according to actual needs;

3) Initialize the GPNMF algorithm by random initialization method to obtain the initial value H_0 of the coefficient matrix H;

4) The GPNMF algorithm is used to decompose the training sample matrix X to obtain the corresponding coefficient matrix H;

5) The values of T_G^2 and SPE_G corresponding to each training sample are calculated by Eqs. (30) and (31);

6) The KDE method is used to calculate the actual distribution of T_G^2 and SPE_G, and the control limits $T_{G\theta}^2$ and $SPE_{G\theta}$ of T_G^2 and SPE_G are obtained under the condition of the confidence interval c of 99%.

Online detection:

1) The matrix X_{new} of the sample to be tested is normalized, and then $\hat{H}_{new}$ is calculated by Eq. (29);

2) The T_{Gnew}^2 and SPE_{Gnew} corresponding to each sample to be tested are calculated by Eqs. (30) and (31);

3) Compare the newly obtained T_{Gnew}^2 and SPE_{Gnew} with $T_{G\theta}^2$ and $SPE_{G\theta}$ respectively. If the values of T_{Gnew}^2 and SPE_{Gnew} are greater than the values of $T_{G\theta}^2$ and $SPE_{G\theta}$, it means that there is a fault in the system, otherwise it means that the system is operating normally.

6 Simulation Verification

According to statistics, single-phase grounding faults account for up to 80% of the total number of power distribution network faults. Therefore, this paper selects a single-phase ground fault as a simulation example to verify the performance of the proposed fault detection model based on the GPNMF algorithm. Simulink in MATLAB software is used to build a simulation system model. The system consists of three-phase power supply, main transformer, transmission line, distribution transformer, and user load. Among them, the three-phase power supply is used to generate 110kV three-phase alternating current; the relevant parameters of main transformer and distribution transformer are shown in Table 1; there are 6 transmission lines, including overhead and cable lines, whose parameters and length are shown in Table 2 and Table 3 respectively; the distribution transformer is connected with the user's load, and the load is three-phase symmetrical load.

In this example, 58 process variables are selected as monitoring variables: three-phase voltage on secondary side of main transformer, three-phase current of each transmission line, three-phase voltage and current at secondary side of each distribution transformer, and zero sequence current of fault line. The simulation time is set to 1s, the sampling time is 50 μs, and a single-phase ground fault occurs in the system at 0.8s. A total of 20 000 data samples were obtained in the simulation process, including 16

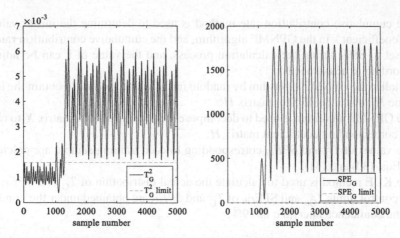

Fig. 1. Fault detection results for single-phase to ground fault

000 normal operation data samples and 4 000 fault operation data samples. Intercept 5000 sample points between 0–0.25 s to form the training set, and intercept 5000 sample points between 0.75–1 s to form the test set, that is, the single-phase ground fault in the system is taken from the 1001th sampling point in the test device occur. The training set and test set are input into the fault detection model based on the GPNMF algorithm to detect single-phase ground faults. The detection results are shown in Fig. 1.

Table 1. Parameters of main transformer and distribution transformer.

Parameter	Main transformer	Distribution transformer
Connection mode	YY_0	YY_0
Rated capacity	$31.5 \, MV \cdot A$	$1 \, MV \cdot A$
Primary voltage	110 kV	10 kV
Secondary voltage	10 kV	400 V

After a single-phase ground fault occurs, the voltage and current of the faulty phase will change from the normal state to the fault state. At the beginning of the process, the value of the voltage and current deviation from the normal state is small, which will bring no small challenge to the detection effect of the GPNMF monitoring model. It can be seen from reference [15] that when the GPNMF monitoring model is faced with a gradual fault, false detection will occur at the early stage of the fault, which is also confirmed by the detection results in Fig. 1. It can be seen from Fig. 1 that the T_G^2 and SPE_G statistics of GPNMF monitoring model detect most of the fault samples. At the beginning of the failure, T_G^2 and SPE_G have different degrees of error detection. After that, all the failure samples are detected. The detection result of T_G^2 statistic is slightly worse than that of SPE_G statistic. However, from the perspective of real-time detection, the difference between the occurrence of a fault and the complete detection of the fault

Table 2. Parameters of transmission line.

Parameter	Overhead line	Cable line
Positive sequence resistance $R_1/(\Omega/km)$	0.17	0.078
Positive sequence to ground inductance $L_1/(mH/km)$	1.21	0.270
Positive sequence admittance $C_1/(\mu F/km)$	9.70	695.000
Zero sequence resistance $R_0/(\Omega/km)$	0.23	0.106
Zero sequence to ground inductance $L_0/(mH/km)$	5.48	1.223
Zero sequence ground admittance $C_0/(\mu F/km)$	6.00	358.000

Table 3. Length of transmission line.

Line	1	2	3	4	5	6
overhead line/km	3	1	0	2	5	0
cable line/km	0	0.5	1	0	0	0.5

sample by the T_G^2 statistic is 0.025 s, and this lag time is very small. In conclusion, the fault monitoring model based on GPNMF algorithm can detect the fault timely and effectively when the single-phase ground fault occurs in the distribution network. And if the model is deployed to the smart distribution transformer terminal, the real-time monitoring of the operation status of the distribution network can be realized.

7 Conclusion

In the context of the State Grid Corporation of China vigorously promote the construction of the distribution Internet of Things, the large-scale deployment of smart distribution transformer terminal in distribution stations has been actively promoted. This paper proposes to introduce GPNMF algorithm, a new NMF improved algorithm, into the distribution network fault detection to realize the operation status monitoring and fault detection functions of the distribution network. The simulation results show that the new algorithm can effectively detect single-phase ground faults in the distribution network, and the use of this algorithm can make the smart distribution transformer terminal have a better real-time fault reporting function. The research work of this paper aims to improve the lean management and active service level of the distribution network, as well as the large-scale application and promotion of smart distribution transformer terminal in the distribution of Internet of Things.

References

1. Wang, S., Wang, C.: Analysis of modern distribution system. Higher Education Press, Beijing (2014)
2. Primadianto, A., Lu, C.N.: A review on distribution system state estimation. IEEE Trans. Power Syst. 32(5), 3875–3883 (2017)
3. Yu, Y., Luan, W.: Smart grid and its implementations. Proc. CSEE 29(34), 1–8 (2009)
4. Liu, J., Liu, C., Zhang, X.: Coordination of relay protection for power distribution systems. Power Syst. Protect. Control 43(9), 35–41 (2015)
5. Song, Y., Zhang, D., Wu, J.: Comparison and analysis on power supply reliability of urban power distribution network at home and abroad. Power Syst. Technol. 32(23), 13–18 (2008)
6. Jia, Y.: Assessment and Application of Distribution Network Reliability. North China Electric Power University, Hebei (2013)
7. Hanninen, S., Lehtonen, M.: Method for detection and location of very high resistive earth faults. Eur. Trans. Electr. Power 9(5), 285–291 (1999)
8. Uriarte, F.M.: Modeling, Detection, and Localization of High Impedance Faults in Low-Voltage Distribution Feeders. Virginia Polytechnic Institute and State University, Virginia (2003)
9. Girgis, A.A., Chang, W., Makram, E.B.: Analysis of high impedance fault generated signals using a kalman filtering approach. IEEE Trans. Power Delivery 5(4), 1714–1724 (1990)
10. Salim, R.H., Oliveira, K.R., Filomena, A.D., Resener, M., Bretas, A.S.: Hybrid fault diagnosis scheme implementation for power distribution systems automation. IEEE Trans. Power Delivery 23(4), 1846–1856 (2008)
11. Sun, P., Cao, Y., Liu, Y.: Fault classification technique for power distribution network using binary ant colony algorithm and fuzzy neural network. High Volt. Eng. 42(7), 2063–2072 (2016)
12. Samantaray, S.R., Dash, P.K., Upadhyay, S.K.: Adaptive Kalman filter and neural network based high impedance fault detection in power distribution networks. Int. J. Electr. Power Energy Syst. 31(4), 167–172 (2009)
13. Das, B.: Fuzzy logic-based fault-type identification in unbalanced radial power distribution system. IEEE Trans. Power Delivery 21(1), 278–285 (2006)
14. Guo, M., You, L., Hong, C.: Dentification method of distribution network faults based on singular value of LCD-Hilbert spectrums and multilevel SVM. High Vol. Eng. 43(4), 1239–1247 (2017)
15. Niu, Y., Wang, S., Lin, Z.: Fault detection based on GPNMF for industrial process. J. Syst. Simul. 30(2), 521–532 (2018)
16. Li, X., Yang, Y., Zhang, W.: Fault detection method for non-Gaussian processes based on non-negative matrix factorization. Asia Pac. J. Chem. Eng. 8(3), 362–370 (2013)
17. Lee, D.D., Seung, H.S.: Learning the parts of objects by non-negative matrix factorization. Nature 401(6755), 788–791 (1999)
18. Li, L., Zhang, Y.: A survey on algorithms of non-negative matrix factorization. Acta Electronica Sinica 36(4), 737–743 (2008)
19. Lee, D.D., Seung, H.S.: Algorithms for non-negative matrix factorization. In: 14th International Proceedings on Neural Information Processing Systems, pp. 556–562. MIT Press, Cambridge (2000)
20. Yuan, Z., Oja, E.: Projective nonnegative matrix factorization for image compression and feature extraction. In: Kalviainen, H. (ed.) Scandinavian Conference on Image Analysis, pp. 333–342. Springer, Heidelberg (2005)
21. Ding, C., Li, T., Peng, W.: Orthogonal nonnegative matrix t-factorizations for clustering. In: 12th ACM SIGKDD International Proceedings on Knowledge Discovery and Data Mining, pp. 126–135. Association for Computing Machinery, New York (2006)

22. Zhou, D., Li, G., Li, Y.: Data-Driven Industrial Process Fault Diagnosis Technology: Methods Based on Principal Component Analysis And Partial Least Squares. Science Press, Beijing (2010)
23. MacGregor, J.F., Kourti, T.: Statistical process control of multivariate processes. Control Eng. Pract. 3(3), 403–414 (1995)

Patent Citation Network Analysis Based on Improved Main Path Analysis: Mapping Key Technology Trajectory

Zikui Lu(iD), Yue Ma, and Luona Song(⊠)

University of Posts and Telecommunications, Beijing 10036, China

Abstract. Nowadays, more and more people realize the importance of patent for innovation activities. Patent citation network analysis is one of the most important methods for patent measurement, patent mining, and core patent identification. In nowadays, finding technology trajectories and analyzing major technologies in patent networks are intensively used in technological competition. Main path analysis (MPA) is a famous directed graph-based method to extract main paths in certain networks, such as a citation network. However, the accuracy of main path identification may be distracted due to a large volume of wrong references when using MPA in patent citation networks solely. To tackle this challenge and extract reasonable main paths from patent citation network, in this paper, we combined the classic MPA with the PageRank algorithm and we tested this new combined method on authorized patent datasets. The results show that the improved method achieved better performance in average cited frequency and other indicators of core patents comparing with traditional MPA.

Keywords: Citation network · Main path analysis · PageRank

1 Introduction

For any researchers who want to engage in researching and developing new innovative technologies in a scientific domain, the first step is to understand the evolution of core technologies and to find the key point. Therefore, we need to extract core technology among countless documents before we start to study. Patent documents, recording innovation completely and detailly, are regarded as the foundation of technology, products, and processes. According to the World Intellectual Property Organization, 90% of the world's technologies are registered in patent, so make use of patent information effectively will contribute greatly to master technology and creation. Additionally, analyzing core patents is the most efficient way to use patent information. Patent documents contain references and a large number of relationships of citation constitute a patent citation network, which can be analyzed to find core patents. In general, innovations are based on the existing research, as well as the citation network demonstrates an inheritance relationship according to the idea of technological evolution, thus, every patent can be regarded as a piece of a fragment of knowledge. The main paths in the network are the backbone of technological progress, which include more core patents.

© Springer Nature Switzerland AG 2021
X. Sun et al. (Eds.): ICAIS 2021, CCIS 1423, pp. 158–171, 2021.
https://doi.org/10.1007/978-3-030-78618-2_13

The study of references, as one of the means to trace patterns of technological advancements, has been growingly used among scientific publications. As a result, many methods have been proposed to exact and represent the evolution patterns of ideas, including algorithmic historiography, knowledgeflow, and influence trajectories [1].However, those means are considered too complex to understand. Thus, new ways have been designed to find critical subnetworks as a summary of core patens. Main path analysis (MPA), originally proposed by Hummon and Doreian [2], has been applied in various domains to extract main paths. Compared with historical and descriptive methods used before, it enriches the engineering perspective for technological research and makes a significant contribution to the identification of core patents and extraction of the mainstream [3].

Although applied by many studies of citation networks, MPA is not always a proper method to exploit the main paths of patent citation networks. Through experiments, we have discovered the number of patent references can reach hundreds or even thousands incredibly, which will cause the main paths to concentrate on those patents because MPA includes a greedy algorithm. Once the citation network contains nodes with large references, the result will be not accurate enough through MPA.

PageRank, an algorithm proposed by Google to rank webpages, can evaluate the quality of webpages. It assigns relative importance and authority scores to each webpage through hyperlinks, which can be regarded as the basis for webpage ranking. Absolutely, the algorithm is still applied in most search engines. Inspired by that, we use the idea of PageRank to calculate the importance of the patents, then traverse paths of citation network to extract main paths. The results show obvious improvements in the average cited frequency and coverage ability of core patents founded by our methods.

2 Related Work

2.1 Main Path Analysis

The goal of the MPA is to find main paths. A main path of citation network is a connected subnetwork of important citation arcs connecting a number of origin nodes (typically, historical files) to destination nodes (typically, recent publications) [4]. Citation arcs, if the arcs sit on many paths between origin nodes and destination nodes, are considered as have evolutionary importance to a certain filed, thus it is appended to the main paths of the corresponding citation network. Briefly speaking, main paths approximately demonstrate development trajectories among the major ideas.

First step of the MPA is to weight citation arcs based on some distinctive features. In terms of knowledge transfer, the weight of citation arc (u, v) is measured by the number of search paths passing through (u, v) between a set of sources and destinations. Regularly, Search Path Count (SPC) and Search Path Node Pair (SPNP) are used to weight citation arcs [5].

SPC measures the importance of the arcs in the network by counting the number of times the connection between two adjacent nodes traversed by all paths of the corresponding network. Let $N^-(m)$ denotes the path from the source point s to the point m, and $N^+(n)$ denotes path from node n to destination t, then for any path from s to t passes arc (m, n), the value of the arc π is [6]:

$$\pi = \sigma \cdot (m, n) \cdot \tau, \tag{1}$$

where σ denotes all paths from s to m, τ denotes all paths from n to t. The mathematical expression of the weight N (m, n) of the citation arc is shown in Eq. 2:

$$N(m, n) = N^-(m) \times N^+(n) \tag{2}$$

$$N^-(m) = \begin{cases} 1 & m = s \\ \sum_{n:nRm} N^-(m) \ others \end{cases} \tag{3}$$

$$N^+(m) = \begin{cases} 1 & m = t \\ \sum_{n:nRm} N^+(v) \ others \end{cases} \tag{4}$$

where nRm denotes m cites n.

After obtaining the weighting directed graph, for extracting main paths, MPA then use deep first method and greedy algorithm to get paths consisting of arcs with highest traversal weight from sources and destinations.

Since SPC is the most typical algorithm for weighting network, in the comparative experiment we also use SPC to weight arcs.

2.2 PageRank

The reason why a page has a link to another one is because the later has more authoritative and reliable content. The basic idea of PageRank to rank webpages is to calculate number of links to the webpages. [7] They proposed a concept of PR value represent importance of one page. Furthermore, the value of each page is related to the number of external links that link to its own and their PR value. Therefore, the method reduces impact of link number on weight. For example, webpage $w1$ is linked by a meaningful webpage and webpage $w2$ is linked by many webpages with poor information, because of the different PR value among webpages link to w1 and $w2$, the PR value of $w1$ may large than $w2$. Formula for PageRank is as follow:

$$PR(u) = d \sum_{v \in B_u} \frac{PR(v)}{L(v)} + \frac{1 - d}{n}, \tag{5}$$

where B_u denotes a collection of all webpages link to webpage u, v denotes a webpage belonging to B_u, $L(v)$ denotes the number of external links of webpage v, d denotes damping factor, n denotes the number of all the webpage in this network.

3   Datasets

In this paper, we use "Etching the Insulating Layers" and "Encapsulations" in chip manufacturing as keywords to draw the core patent technology trajectories [8] for two patent sets respectively.

3.1 Datasets

As a first step, we build patent datasets respectively. The datasets are extracted from USPTO(United States Patent and Trademark Office) [9], which including all the US patents from July 31,1790 to present as well as full searchable text. When searching related patents, USPTO allows patents to be retrieved by International Patent Classification (IPC). The IPC strategy selects patents by consulting a broad range of secondary sources and searching in International Patent Classification Table [10]. Then, we can confirm query statements "ICL/H01L21/311" and "ICL/H01L21/02 AND ICL/H01L21/56" to retrieval related patents. The partial table of IPC is shown in Table 1.

Table 1. Internet patent classification table

IPC	Description
H01L21/00	Processes or apparatus specially adapted for the manufacture or treatment of semiconductor or solid-state devices or of parts thereof
H01L21/02	Manufacture or treatment of semiconductor devices or of parts thereof
H01L21/311	Etching the insulating layers
H01L21/56	Encapsulations, e.g. encapsulating layers, coatings

Then, we analyze the number of patent references, and remove the patents with unreasonable citations from datasets. When it comes to patents related to "Etching the Insulating Layers", we obtain 5496 patents with application time span from 1975 to 2020. By exploiting distribution of patent references we remove patents with number of citations more than 300, the citations of those patents are incredible, which can cause unnecessary calculations. Figure 1 shows the distribution of the patent citations, after removing patents with unreasonable references, there are 5448 patents left. In same way, there are 2921 patents build dataset of patents related to "Encapsulations".

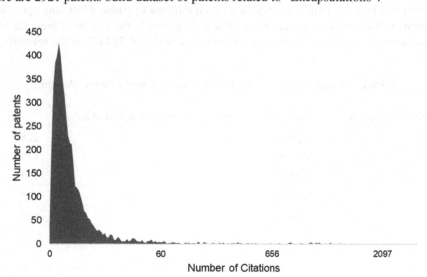

Fig. 1. Distribution of the citations of patents related to "Etching the Insulating Layers"

3.2 Improved Method

In the present article, we use PageRank [10] to improve weighting algorithm for MPA and give patent nodes value directly, instead of using the method of giving value of arcs, which helps to reduce the effects of unreasonable references to main paths.

Supposing there are two citation networks like Fig. 2. Left network shows relationship of single reference, node A references node B (knowledge flow from B to A) and node B references node C. According to SPC, it's obvious that weight of arcs BA and CB are both 1. Comparingly, right network demonstrates node B cites many other nodes. Although relationship of BA in both networks are same, with the number of node B references increases the value of BA will raise correspondingly according to MPA. The number of paths from source nodes to the destination nodes pass BA are increasing. So, if node B has unreasonable references, the mistake references can amplify the weight of arc BA. Due to the main paths is the path consist of largest citation arcs, the arc BA in later network has greater probability be selected to the main path and node B be regarded as core patent.

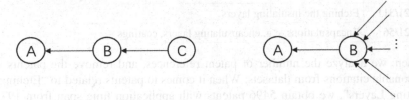

Fig. 2. Two cases of patent citation

In fact, a network composed of thousands of nodes is much more complicated than the case of graph with only two or three nodes. Normally, about five thousand patents and their citations can build a network with even millions of paths, while, any operation for nodes will cause huge effect on the network, especially for weight of arcs. Table 2 shows the impact of changes of references in patent node '3951843' on the network.

Table 2. Changes in network when the number of patent citations changes

Number of citations	Number of paths in network	Weight of related arc
8	3125682	225
6	3125464	175
5	3125355	150
3	3125028	75
1	3124810	25

Therefore, to prevent unreasonable references from distracting the main paths, weighting algorithm should be improved. In order to weighting more reasonable, before we calculate value of patents, we assume each node that not be referenced has same initial value I, and the other nodes has initial value i in the network [11]. When a patent has N citations, it divides its value into N parts, and gives a piece of part to every patent it references. In this way, patent will give lower values to other nodes cited once it has many references, comparingly, patent will transfer all value itself to the node cited if it has just one citation. Then we can calculate the real value of each patent in the network, which we call PR value. The expression of calculating PR value is as follow:

$$\text{PR}(\text{patent}) = \begin{cases} \sum_{v \in U} \frac{h(v)}{L(v)} & \textit{indegree of the patent not equals to } 0 \\ I & \textit{indegree of the patent equals to } 0 \end{cases}, \quad (6)$$

where PR denotes PR value of current patent, v denotes patent that cites current patent, U denotes a collection of patents, $h(v)$ refers to the initial value of a patent. While, in our method, we no longer assign weight to arc between nodes, but give value to patent nodes directly, which means that, when calculating the weight of the patents in the network, we have to build network according to relationship of reference. When extracting main paths according to direction of knowledge flow. The Algorithm of SPC and improved weighting algorithm is shown in Table 3 and Table 4 respectively.

Table 3. Algorithm of SPC

Algorithmic 1 Method of Search Path Count
Input: *oldGraph, startNodes[], paths[]*
Output: *newGraph*
Function WeightingGraph(*oldGraph,startNodes[],paths[]*)
1:    for each *path* ∈ *paths[]* do
2:      for each *i,j* ∈ *path[]* do
3:          *OldGraph*[*i*][*j*]['weight'] ← *oldGraph*[*i*][*j*]['weight']+1
4:      end for
5:    end for
6:end function

Table 4. Algorithm of improved method

Algorithmic 2 Improved Weighting Method
Input: *oldGraph* , *startNodes*[], *endNodes*[],*n*[],*noded*[],*I*,*i*
Output: *newGraph*
1: **function** CoPagerank(*oldGraph*,*startNodes*[],*endNodes*[],*noded*[],*n*[])
2:　　**for** each *node* ∈ *n*[] **do**
3:　　　**if** *node* ∈ *startNodes*[] **then**
4:　　　　*oldGraph*[*node*]['pr']← *I*
5:　　　**end if**
6:　　　*NAL*←len(list(*oldGraph*[*node*]))
7:　　　*nodeA* ← list(*oldGraph*[*node*])
8:　　　**for** *nextnode* in [*nodeA*] **do**
9:　　　　**if** (*node*,*nextnode*) ∈*noded* **then**
10:　　　　　do nothing
11:　　　　**else**
12:　　　　　*oldGraph*[*nextnode*]['pr']←*oldGraph*[*nextnode*]['pr']+*i*/*NAL*
13:　　　　　*noded*.append(*node*,*nextnode*)
14:　　　　**end if**
15:　　　**end for**
16:　　　**for** *nextnode* in *nodeA* **do**
17:　　　　**if** *nextnode* not in *endNodes*[] **then**
18:　　　　　CoPagerank(*oldGraph*,*startNodes*[],*endNodes*[],*noded*[],*n*[])
19:　　　　**end if**
20:　　　**end for**
21:　　**end for**
22: **end function**

After getting directed graph, we follow the idea of MPA and traverse all paths to find the paths with largest PR value, that is main paths.

3.3 Evaluation

For better measure importance of the main paths, we propose some indicators. A patent citation network often contains more subnetworks, which reflect different branches in the development of this domain. When the degree values of all nodes of a subnet are greater than or equal to K value, the subnet is called K-core graph. Because the cited frequency of patents is equal to out-degree value of corresponding nodes in citation network, the K value here is considered as out-degree value. The larger the K value is, the larger the average out-degree value of the subnet is, and the more nodes the subnet can affect, so the subnet is more important to the citation network. Consequently, for a collection of nodes, calculating the number of nodes in different K-core graphs of a network can reflect the importance of the collection to it. We can measure importance of main paths that extracted by MPA and method we improved respectively through this way. Since out-degree value can reflect cited situation of node in network, so average out-degree value of main paths also reasonable indicator for measure importance of main paths.

K-core decomposition is regular method help find core subgraph (the largest connected subgraph) in network [12]. In K-core graph, all the edges including nodes whose degree value less than k also been removed from network. 1-core net represents original graph, and $(K + 1)$-core net is subgraph of K-core graph. We can also observe changes by measuring graph density, average degree, number of connected blocks, average clustering coefficient and other indicators besides number of nodes and edges.

Graph density of a simple graph is defined as the ratio of the number of edges with the maximum possible edges. Since patent citation network has no mutual references, the more nodes the network has, the lower density of the net will have. Because the new node cannot refer to all previous nodes in citation network. For directed simple graphs, the density is:

$$D = \frac{|E|}{2\binom{|V|}{2}} = \frac{|E|}{|V||V-1|},$$ (7)

where E is the number of edges, V is number of nodes.

Six Degrees of Separation is a conjecture in the field of mathematics, which point out that it spends only 6 steps to connect any two people in the world on average. In other words, if each individual build link to their friends, link relationship will cover all the individuals after 6 times traversal. Based on the Six Degrees of Separation, we can measure the coverage ability of core patents to judge the importance. In patent citation network, if node A refers to node B, then node B has an impact on node A. We can consider that node B connects to node A. Because core patents have more influence than other patents, so they can connect to most patent nodes faster than others. Under the same conditions, we can measure importance of two sets of core patents by comparing the number of other patent nodes the core patents node can connect to in citation network.

4 Experiment Result

First of all, we build patent citation networks according to the related patents of "Etching the Insulating Layers" and "encapsulation" technologies. Among them, the former graph has 40605 nodes and 77426 edges; the later graph has 21344 nodes and 45865 edges. "Etching the Insulating Layers" related patent references network is shown in Fig. 3. Different color nodes denote different out-degree value.

Secondly, we calculate main paths through our method and MPA respectively and we will analyze those patents below.

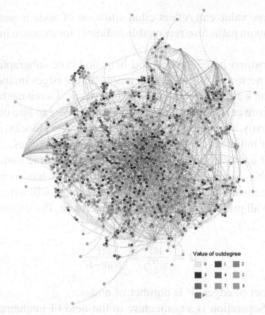

Fig. 3. Citation network of patents related to "Etching the Insulating Layers" (part)

Figure 4 shows the main paths of patents related to "Etching the Insulating Layers" found by our method and MPA.

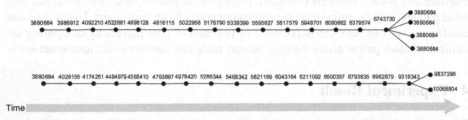

Fig. 4. Main path calculated by MPA and our method, the above is extracted by our method, the below is extracted by MPA. The patent on the left is granted before the patent on right

4.1 K-core Graph

We decompose graph through K-core decomposition according to set k = 10, 15, 20, 25, 30, and then analyze connected subgraphs by calculating features mentioned above, preparing for the experiment of counting number of patents existing in k-core graph. Table 5 shows the relevant data of the k-core graph of the patents related to "Etching the Insulating Layers".

Obviously, the numbers of nodes and edges are decreasing sharply as the *K* value of the network increases, which shows scale of net is becoming smaller and smaller.

Table 5. Data of k-core graph of the patents related to "Etching the Insulating Layers"

K	Nodes	Edges	Density	Connect blocks
K10	2626	13303	0.002	50
K15	1264	5442	0.003	49
K20	720	2780	0.005	37
K25	468	1439	0.007	31
K30	321	679	0.008	27

Additionally, when K value of the network increases, the density of graph becomes greater, which means that nodes remaining in K-core graph with high average cited frequency-cy, so they have higher reference value than nodes being removed. With the K value increasing, the number of connect blocks is decreasing, which means that the technologies represented by remaining connect blocks have more reference value than others.

In next experiment, we set k = 1, 5, 10, 15, 20, 25, 30 to decompose patent citation networks of two technologies respectively. Then we calculate number of core patents that existing in different K-core graphs of citation network for two technologies, the core patents were extracted by our method and MPA respectively. The result demonstrates our method has superior performance than MPA. The result as is shown in Fig. 5. In the experiment of patents related to "Etching the Insulating Layers", the number of core patents that remaining in different subgraphs through our method is greater than that through MPA, and all of the subgraphs with high average cited frequency. In the experiment of patents related to "Encapsulation", our method also performs better than MPA.

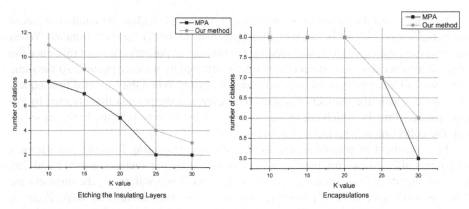

Fig. 5. Situations of core patents in different k-core graphs of two citation networks

4.2 Average Cited Frequency and Coverage

In the following experiments, the results show core patents found by our method are worthier.

We calculate the average cited frequency of core patent sets extracted by the two methods. Result of experiment of patents related to "Etching the Insulating Layers" shows that the value of average cited frequency (average out-degree value) of core patents extracted by our method and MPA are 17.66 and 11.61, as well as, the number in experiment of patents related to "Encapsulations" are 30.9 and 20.61 respectively. A patent with high cited frequency shows this patent is worthy of references [12]. So, a set of patents with high value of average cited frequency is more valuable than the set with lower number. The results prove main paths founded by our method show better performance. The detailed data is shown in Table 6.

Table 6. The results of experiments of two patent citations

feature \\ method	Etching the Insulating Layers		Encapsulations	
	MPA	our method	MPA	our method
Average cited frequency	11.61	17.66	20.61	30.90
2-cluster	251	319	688	748
3-cluster	544	795	882	894
K20	5	7	8	8
K30	2	3	5	6

In order to test the influence of core patent nodes, we calculate the number of patent nodes that can be affected by two sets of core patent nodes under the same situation. When the traversal time equals to 1, we calculate the number of patent nodes that reference the core patents, because these patents are directly affected by the core patents. At the same time, we call the collection of affected nodes 1-cluster. When the traversal time equals to 2, we calculate the number of patents that reference the patents that affected by the core patents directly, which are indirectly affected by the core patents. In this case, we call the collection of affected nodes 2-cluster, and so on [13].

In experiment of patents related to "Etching the Insulating Layers", the numbers of patents affected by core patents, which extracted by our method, are 319 and 795 respectively. In the experiment of patents related to "Encapsulation", the numbers are 748 and 894 respectively. All of the results are greater than number in MPA. Figure 6 shows the situation of nodes affected by core patents when traversal time equals to 3, core patents in left figure are extracted by MPA and core patents in right figure are extracted by our method. Affected nodes are marked with red color, unaffected nodes are marked with black color. Obviously, the core patents in the right figure have stronger influence[14].

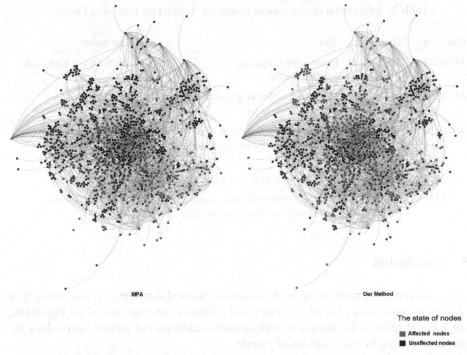

Fig. 6. Situation of 3-cluster of MPA and our method (Color figure online)

4.3 Discussion Main Paths and Related Domains

In main paths of patents related to "Etching the Insulating Layers", the result contains 18 patents extracted from 5448 patents, whose time span is from 1975 to 2018. And technologies of core patents include "semiconductor preparation method", "thin film etching process", "high-density plasms etching" and other methods. In the result of patents related to "encapsulation", main paths contain 12 patents extracted from 2921 patents and the time span is from 1970 to 2019. Those patents include technologies of "Solder interconnection structure on organic substrates", "Semiconductor device and method of forming micro interconnect structures", "BAG packaging" and so on. After consulting relevant literature, those patents can better descript development of the domain respectively. Table 7 demonstrates part of the information of core patents in "Etching the Insulating Layers".

Table 7. Information of core patents related to "Etching the Insulating Layers"

Patent. no	Issue year	Title	Assignee name
3880684	1975	Process for preparing semiconductor	Mitsubishi Denki Kabushiki Kaisha
4174251	1979	Method of selective gas etching on a silicon nitride layer	ITT Industries, Inc
4568410	1986	Selective plasma etching of silicon nitride in the presence of silicon oxide	Motorola, Inc
4793897	1988	Selective thin film etch process	Applied Materials, Inc.
9318343	2016	Method to improve etch selectivity during silicon nitride spacer etch	Tokyo Electron Limited

5   Conclusion

After experiments, patents extracted by improved method show better performance than MPA in average value of cited frequency and ability of coverage. Based on PageRank, our method reduces the impact of unreasonable references of patents and solves the problems caused by over citations of patents.

Certainly, there are still defect in our method, for example, our method doesn't take damping factor into consideration. Researchers cannot consult information endlessly during they creation, and the factor can help us approach the real situation. So, there should be another parameter in the algorithm to represent this constraint. In the following research, we plan to conduct more experiments in more fields to find reasonable damping factor, and improve our method further.

Acknowledgement. I would like to thank professor Mei Song for her important comments on several drafts of this work. I thank associate professor Xiaojuang Wang for the stimulating and meaningful guidance she made as a reviewer. I gratefully acknowledge help from my parents, they always encourage me when I am frustrated, so I can finish this work.

Funding Statement. This work was supported by the National Natural Science Foundation of China (61601053).

References

1. Yi-Ning, T., Shu-Lan, H.: Constructing conceptual trajectory maps to trace the development of research fields. J. Assoc. Inf. Sci. Technol. **67**(8), 2016–2031 (2015)
2. Hummon, N.P., Dereian, P.: Connectivity in a citation network: the development of DNA theory. Soc. Netw. **11**(1), 39–63 (1989)
3. Kumar, A., Mishra, S., et al.: Link prediction in complex networks based on significance of Higher-Order Path Index (SHOPI). Phys. A **545**(1), 1–17 (2020)

4. Xiao-Rui, J., Xiao-Hao, Z., et al.: Main path analysis on cyclic citation networks. J. Assoc. Inf. Sci. Technol. **71**(5), 578–595 (2020)
5. Jiang, X., Hai, Z.H.: Forward search path count as an alternative indirect citation impact indicator. J. Informetr. **13**(1), 1–28 (2019)
6. Liu, J.S., Lu, L.Y.Y., Ho, M.-C.: A few notes on main path analysis. Scientometrics **119**(1), 379–391 (2019). https://doi.org/10.1007/s11192-019-03034-x
7. Reinstaller, A., Reschenhofer, P.: Using PageRank in the analysis of technological progress through patents: an illustration for biotechnological inventions. Scientometrics **113**(3), 1407–1438 (2017). https://doi.org/10.1007/s11192-017-2549-x
8. Mina, A., Ramlogan, R., et al.: Mapping evolutionary trajectories: applications to the growth and transformation of medical knowledge. Res. Policy **36**(1), 789–806 (2007)
9. Batagelj, V., Ferligoj, A., Squazzoni, F.: The emergence of a field: a network analysis of research on peer review. Scientometrics **113**(1), 503–532 (2017). https://doi.org/10.1007/s11192-017-2522-8
10. Epicoco, M.: Knowledge patterns and sources of leadership: mapping the semiconductor miniaturization trajectory. Res. Policy **42**(1), 180–195 (2013)
11. Ruas, P., Lamurias, A., Couto, F.M.: Linking chemical and disease entities to ontologies by integrating PageRank with extracted relations from literature. J. Cheminform. **12**(1), 1–11 (2020). https://doi.org/10.1186/s13321-020-00461-4
12. Su-Fen, Z., Peng, R., et al.: HeteroRWR: a novel algorithm for top- k co-author. IEICE Trans. Inf. Syst. **103**(1), 71–84 (2020)
13. Hamed, A.Y., et al.: A genetic algorithm to solve capacity assignment problem in a flow network. Comput. Mater. Continua **64**(3), 1579–1586 (2020)
14. Cai, C., Xu, H., et al.: An attention-based friend recommendation model in social network. Comput. Mater. Continua **65**(3), 2475–2488 (2020)

On-Chain and Off-Chain Collaborative Management System Based on Consortium Blockchain

Kete Wang[1](✉), Yong Yan[2], Shaoyong Guo[1], Xin Wei[1], and Sujie Shao[1]

[1] Beijing University of Posts and Telecommunications, Beijing 100000, China
wangkete@bupt.edu.cn
[2] State Grid Zhejiang Electric Power Co., Ltd., Electric Power Research Institute, Zhejiang 310000, China

Abstract. The blockchain system can provide a trust infrastructure for sharing data among untrusted parties. However, storing the original shared data directly on the blockchain is not suitable for large-scale data sharing scenarios. Therefore, we designed a data sharing system architecture in which data hashing and response records are stored on the blockchain and the original data is stored in the off-chain database. This architecture can alleviate the system overload and protect privacy problems to a certain extent. This paper proposes a three-tier system structure to ensure the function of the network. Subsequently, formulate request rules, deploy smart contracts, and build a platform based on the alliance chain. Finally, the system functions and performance are analyzed and compared through experiments. The results show that the system can realize efficient and transparent information sharing while satisfying on-chain and off-chain collaborative management, and the system has certain advantages in function, overall performance and throughput performance.

Keywords: Consortium blockchain · Collaborative management · Data share

1 Introduction

With the development of society, the use of identification is more and more frequent, and different types of identification are formed in different ways, but they all have security problems such as easy tampering and poor credibility. Compared with traditional physical storage evidence, review and certification is more complicated. When the identification is stored in a centralized manner, once the center is attacked or tampered with externally or internally, the credibility will decrease. In addition, to ensure the security of storage, the electronic storage of evidence often needs to use multiple backup methods, which will cause problems such as high storage costs. The identification has a strong relevance to the data, but it is difficult to support the data because of the difficulty of authentication, the large quantity, and the high cost of storage [1].

With the development of Internet technology, centralized architecture can no longer meet the requirements of security and performance. The researchers then turned to distributed storage and cloud computing, but the platform was vulnerable to DDos attacks

© Springer Nature Switzerland AG 2021
X. Sun et al. (Eds.): ICAIS 2021, CCIS 1423, pp. 172–187, 2021.
https://doi.org/10.1007/978-3-030-78618-2_14

and ignored issues such as authentication. The emergence of blockchain provides a feasible solution to the problems of traditional electronic storage of evidence [2]. Blockchain technology [3, 4] has a unique block-chain structure to store data, as well as timestamps, cryptography, consensus mechanisms, peer-to-peer communication, and distributed storage, which are jointly maintained by multiple parties to achieve decentralization and trusted data, hard-to-tamper target. Blockchain can build trust and centralization, and distributed storage protects electronic evidence. Electronic evidence includes transaction information and time stamp storage in summary form. Multiple parties jointly maintain consistency, reducing the possibility of tampering and making it more secure.In terms of data sharing, due to the lack of mutual trust between different companies or different government departments, the risks of data leakage and improper use, and the differences in administrative interests between companies or government departments, many data owners are unwilling to share. In terms of data privacy, literature [5] et al. proposed an EHR sharing protocol based on the security and privacy protection of the blockchain by using the decentralization, anonymity, unforgeability and verifiability of the blockchain. In the solution, the data requester can search for the required keywords from the data provider, find the relevant HER on the blockchain, and obtain the re-encrypted ciphertext from the cloud server after obtaining the authorization of the data owner. This solution mainly Use searchable encryption and conditional proxy re-encryption to achieve data security, privacy protection and access control.

In terms of data access control and security, literature [6] according to most database systems and enterprise information systems are role-based access control technology, but due to the simple role access control, its flexibility and control granularity sometimes cannot meet the actual access control. Therefore, a security access control model based on RBACV1 and ABAC is proposed to solve this problem.

In terms of credible deposits, literature [7] proposes an Ethereum trusted deposit framework based on smart contracts for the data management problems of the Ethereum platform, and then through centralized data unified processing, certified data distributed storage and efficient dynamics Forensic mechanism to achieve. Finally, the system development scheme design based on smart contract shows the feasibility of the mechanism. Hou Yibin et al. [8] tried and studied the combination of blockchain technology and electronic evidence technology to highlight the digitalization of electronic evidence and the security and reliability of blockchain technology. The electronic evidence storage system architecture in the form of batch packaging of evidence improves the efficiency of evidence storage.

Therefore, the main technical contributions of this paper are summarized as follows:

- This article proposes a fabric-based on-chain and off-chain data collaborative management mechanism based on the problems of easy tampering, low data trust, unguaranteed security, data islands, and large storage capacity in traditional storage methods.
- Through the designed on-chain smart contract for certification and virtualized resource pool as an off-chain database, this article uses blockchain technology to make the certification data safe and reliable, and at the same time alleviate the storage pressure on the chain. Consortium chain nodes are jointly maintained by multiple institutions,

and each consortium block chain node (CBN) is executed by a private server belonging to a trusted authority.

- The system establishes a two-way communication between organization A and organization B. After data collection or addition, the identification is stored in the blockchain through a smart contract, and the data is added to the shared database. The blockchain will serve as a depository. Including the hash of the verification data and the organization to which the recorded data belongs.

2 Related Work

2.1 Hyperledger Fabric

HyperLedger Fabric [9, 10] is a modularized distributed ledger solution platform and the underlying basic framework of a permission blockchain. It has the advantages of convenient expansion and pluggability, and is suitable for enterprise-level applications. In the ledger, the data blocks are linked in sequence in the order of generation time, and cryptography [11], consensus algorithm [12] and other methods are used to ensure the uniformity, non-tampering and unforgeability of the data of the ledger. Compared with other public chains, HyperLedger Fabric's differences are mainly reflected in the two aspects of privateness and permission. Members of its organization can register through membership services to ensure the security of platform access. The main structure of Hyperledger is shown in Fig. 1.

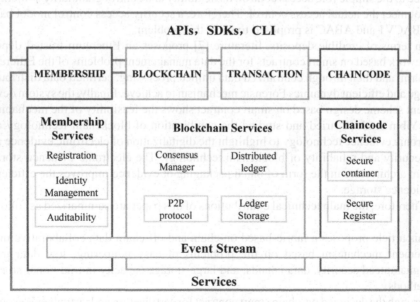

Fig. 1. Hyperledger architecture

Member management services ensure the security of Fabric platform access and provide system members with registration, management and audit functions. The blockchain service is the core part, which provides support for the main functions of the blockchain, including consensus mechanism management, implementation of distributed ledgers, storage of ledgers, and communication between nodes. The chain code service part provides an environment for the deployment and operation of smart contracts.

2.2 Transaction Process

In the Fabric network environment, its nodes can be divided into Endorsing peer, Committing peer, Orderer peer, Anchor peer and Leading peer according to different functions. Among them, the Endorsing peer will endorse the transaction according to the called smart contract and return it to the client. Committing peer is responsible for verifying transaction data and saving it in the ledger. The Orderer node is responsible for sorting transactions and creating blocks. Anchor peer is responsible for cross-organization communication. Leading peer is the representative of all members in the organization, responsible for connecting to the Orderer node and broadcasting the received messages. The specific transaction process is described in Fig. 2 below.

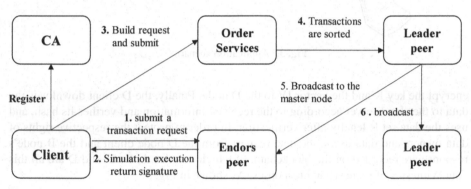

Fig. 2. Description of the transaction process

3 Requirements Analysis

3.1 Application Scenario

It shows an application scenario of on-chain storage of certificates and off-chain data transmission. In this scenario, there are 4 participants A, B, C, and D. Each participant has its own data. The original data is in ciphertext. The form is stored on the cloud server. The identification of the original data (that is, the data catalog information, including the basic description, category, owner, etc. of the data) and its hash digest are stored on the blockchain. Suppose that due to certain services, node D needs to obtain data set R, and the client of node D finds that node B has data set R by querying the catalog information on the chain. Therefore, the client of the D node initiates a data acquisition request to the B node, and the B node uses the public key of the D node client to symmetrically

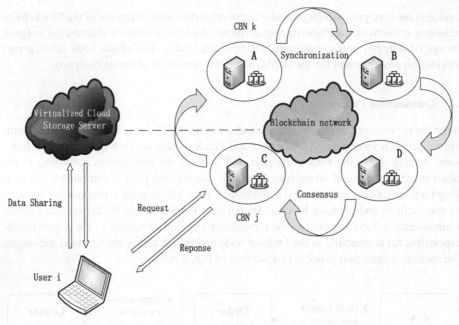

Fig. 3. Application scenario

encrypt the key K and the vector IV to the D node. Finally, the D client downloads the data to the cloud server according to the received information and verifies its hash, and uses the data set R legally after verification. In order to protect the respective rights of data owners and data users, the data request from the D node client and the B node's response are recorded on the blockchain, of which 4 nodes A, B, C, and D are all this data Witnesses of requests and responses. As shown in Fig. 3.

3.2 Functional Module

The user registration module mainly means that the user must submit a request and perform authentication registration first to participate in the system, and only after passing the system audit can the user participate in the system, which ensures that the identity of the system participant is clear. The system will also record the user's operating behavior to ensure that the responsibility of the electronic deposit data can be traced.

The original data storage module is mainly responsible for passing the user's original data to the logic layer through the front end, and to the cloud storage server through the call interface. After obtaining the hash value of the file, it is encrypted by the access control module for the next step of identification On the chain. In the same way, the original data storage module needs to call the interface through access permission control to download the original data from the cloud server.

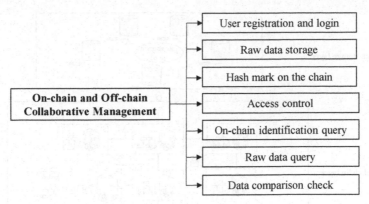

Fig. 4. System module

The hash mark on-chain module is mainly responsible for storing the summary of the user's data information in the ledger. The user submits an application to the system before the data is uploaded, and after the application is approved, the unique identification ID assigned by the system will be obtained to identify user information. The chain can handle different service requirements and control the participation of nodes through different channels. In the process of chaining, smart contracts approved by judicial review are used for chaining to avoid uncertain factors caused by human intervention. In the same way, the identification query module on the chain uses the unique identification ID to request the corresponding node to perform the identification query on the blockchain.

The main purpose of the access control module is to enhance the privacy of data uploaded by users in the system. When user A does not want other users in the same channel to query the hash value of the electronic evidence file uploaded by him, and then query the file he uploaded, he can use symmetric encryption for the hash value of the file before the data is uploaded to the chain encrypt it in the method, and then use the public key of user B who is authorized to access the encrypted key and initial vector to asymmetrically encrypt, and then send the encrypted data to user B who is authorized to access through the service layer, and the user who is authorized to access B can use its private key to decrypt the encryption key and initial vector of user A, and then decrypt the hash value of the file.

The data comparison verification module mainly verifies the correctness and traceability of data or files. Check the hash results of the blockchain and the cloud database, and return the two results to the client if they are correct. As shown in Fig. 4.

4 Design and Implementation

4.1 Architecture Design

This paper establishes a system model that can realize encrypted data transmission, identity verification and secure data storage. The entire system architecture is divided into three layers, namely the user layer, the blockchain layer and the data storage layer. As shown in Fig. 5.

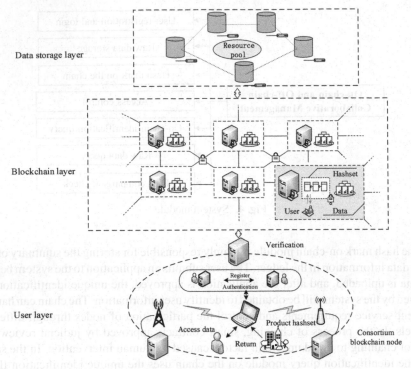

Fig. 5. System architecture

A. **User layer**

The user layer, including the process of data collection, encryption, and transmission, interacts with the storage layer and the blockchain layer through visual interfaces such as the web. In addition, including user registration and authentication. This layer implements data storage, query, and credibility verification, provides access interfaces, and automatically executes after triggering smart contracts. For example, trusted verification, by querying database data and blockchain authentication information, the hash is compared and displayed on the web. The user interacts with the system through the interface.

B. **Blockchain layer**

The node maintains the consistency of the Consortium blockchain according to the preset consensus mechanism, and verifies the integrity of the data and the identity of the corresponding user by checking identity information through signatures and certificates. The blockchain layer uses existing access points to access the CBN server for triggering. After identity authentication, the data is packaged and hashed into the blockchain through the smart contract, and the original data is packaged and stored in the database. In other words, the node packs the transactions generated within a specific time window into the data block of the Merkle tree structure. In addition, the client accesses the blockchain through the smart contract, parses the required data through the smart contract, performs privacy protection processing on the original data owner, and performs credibility verification through hash comparison to ensure that the data is true and credible and returned to the requester. In short, due to the consensus-based distributed data verification mechanism, the system brings an immutable, anonymous, irrevocable and traceable blockchain distributed ledger for the auditable data in the system verification.

C. *Data storage layer*

Since the blockchain is not designed for large-scale database storage, a collaborative management mechanism for verification on the off-chain storage chain should be required. Instead, only data identifiers such as identity verification information, hash values, and data signs are stored on the alliance chain nodes. Store a large amount of user data in a virtualized resource pool.

4.2 Smart Contract Design

Smart contracts in the Fabric network are also called chain codes. They run in Docker containers and are mainly written in Golang. All peers in the system can call the contract to access data hash transaction information after adding the chain code. The core smart contract part of this system is mainly for hash mark on-chain and on-chain query. The created transaction includes user number, transaction number, timestamp, hash, type, description, and attribution. The structure is expressed as Hd = (User, ID, Timestamp, Hash, Type, Describe, Belong). When operating, use the system package provided by Fabric to communicate with the blockchain network, namely Shim package and Peer package. The Shim package contains the interface method for the interaction between the smart contract and the Hyperledger, which provides the context of the Hyperledger network for the operation of the chaincode.

Table 1. Hash related attributes

Method	Request	Input	Output	Description
Init	GET	N/A	Boolean	Initialize the chaincode and return a boolean
Invoke	GET	N/A	Boolean	Forward parameters to the corresponding method
Regist	POST	HASH, ID	TxID	Register hash, mark return transaction ID
SetHash	GET	ID	HASH	Set hash mark
QueryHash	GET	ID	Data	Query hash mark
Indentify	GET	Data, HASH	Boolean	Verify the credibility and correctness of data

To call the chain code in Fabric to query the ledger information, the system must implement the ChaincodeStubInterface interface under the shim package in the chaincode chainCode. The chain code provides a hash service for users and mainly defines the related functions of Table 1. According to different request types of chaincode calling methods, transactions are divided into query and invoke. For example, simple query of ledger information will directly send query; if it involves update and increase, etc., the invoke transaction will be sent, waiting for other nodes to endorse to complete the transaction (Table 2).

Table 2. Chaincode related functions

Property	Type	Description
User	String	User ID
ID	Int	Transaction ID
Timestamp	Date	Time to record data
Hash	String	File or data hash
Type	String	Data type
Describe	String	Data description
Belong	String	Data Ownership Organization

The hash on the chain is mainly stored in the ledger through the PutState method in the shim package in Fabric. First, you need to define a suitable JSON data structure to store the data that needs to be on the chain. Get the parameters through the ChaincodeStubInterface in Shim, and then you need to check Whether the format and content of the upload parameters meet the requirements, in addition, the GetState method needs to be used to verify whether the data already exists in the ledger. When the data is verified to meet the requirements, it is converted into a JSON string and stored and the PutState method is called to store the data on the chain. If successful, the result of the chain is returned. The specific algorithm flow is summarized as follows (Table 3).

Table 3. Chaining and storage

Algorithm 1
Input: Hd (User, ID, Timestamp, Hash, Type, Describe, Belong)
Output: (Putstate Result, Event, TxID)
1:     Get parameters Hd through ChaincodeStubInterface
2:     If the number of Hd is not 7, then return an error message
3:     Check whether the number ID already exists by GetState(ID)
4:     If number exist ,then return error
5:     If the number does not exist, convert the information in Hd into a JSON string
6:     Through Putstate function of shim to storage into hyperledger
7:     Return Result

Table 4. Query and verification

Algorithm 2	
Input:	T(ID)
Output:	(Getstate result, Query result)
1:	Get parameters Hd through ChaincodeStubInterface
2:	If the number of Hd is not 1, then return an error message
3:	Read the data content of Number ID through GetState(ID)
4:	Determine whether the read data is empty, if so, return an error message
5:	Return the query result.

The smart contracts queried on the chain are mainly used to obtain data from the ledger through the GetState method of the shim package in Fabric. The user can use the ID when hashed on the chain as the query condition, first check whether the input parameters meet the requirements, and then query the data information numbered ID according to the GetState method, and judge whether the retrieved data is null or whether there is an error. Finally, the query result is returned. The specific algorithm flow is summarized as follows (Table 4).

Table 5. Permission access control

Algorithm 3	
Input:	(Hash, K, IV, PK_B)
Output:	(E_Hash, E_K, E_IV)
1:	The hash value of the input data
2:	XOR hash to initial vector, temp ← hash to IV XOR
3:	The results of step 2 are encrypted symmetrically_ Hash ← AES_ E (K, Temp)
4:	Using PK_B to encrypt K and IV asymmetrically, E_ K, E_ IV ← ECC_ E (PK_B, K, IV)
5:	Returns the encrypted hash E_ Hash and ciphertext e_ K and ciphertext e_ IV

The design scheme of system privacy protection mainly realizes data privacy protection by encrypting the data submission link. When user A does not want the hash value of the uploaded file to be seen by all users in the channel, he can use the AES encryption algorithm to encrypt the hash value of the file before uploading the data to the chain. The process is described as follows: User A uses the key K and the initial vector IV to encrypt the data. The encryption function is defined as AES_E(K, Hash), where K is the key and Hash is the hash of the data returned by the database sql. When user B is expected to view the data, user B's public key PK_B can be used to perform ECC asymmetric encryption on the key K and the initial vector IV. The encryption function is defined as ECC_E(PK_B K, IV), and the encrypted text is ciphertext E_K and ciphertext E_IV are sent to user B through the business layer after encryption (Table 5).

5   Evaluation

The first part introduces the required hardware configuration and basic software environment. The second part introduces the construction of Hyperledger fabric and node introduction. The third part introduces the function of data storage query on the system chain and the system access control. The fourth part tests and compares the system throughput.

5.1   Environment Configuration

This article installs a virtual machine in the host and deploys the Hyperledger to run in the virtual machine. The required software environment is shown in Table 6 below.

Table 6. Software environment

Software environment	Detailed information
OS	Ubuntu 20.04.1 LTS
Docker	v19.03.12
Docker-compose	v1.26.0
Go	go1.13.8
Hyperledger Fabric	v1.2.0

5.2   Operating Environment

Set up four different types of nodes in the fabric operating environment. As shown in the following Table 7.

The setup process of Hyperledger's operating environment is as follows:

1. Generate the peer node and orderer node to generate the certificate and key. In this article, two peer organizations are set up, each organization contains two nodes, and an orderer node is set.
2. Use the encryption tool configtxgen to read the configuration information in the configtx.yaml file:

Table 7. Fabric node types

Node name	Node type
Leveldb	Database node
Peer	Bookkeeping node
Orderer	Sort node
CA	CA node

3. Create a channel and read information. Finally, create a container according to the docker compose startup image, add each node to the created channel, and build it. After the network operating environment of Hyperledger is built, the chain code needs to be installed and instantiated before the chain code can be used normally. The chain code installation process is shown in the Fig. 6.

Fig. 6. Fabric successfully built

5.3 System Functions

To verify the add function of the system, the user uploads the file through the database provided by the web to get the hash value. After the members of the organization encrypt the hash, the ID, user identity, and timestamp assigned by the system are uploaded to the blockchain through the SDK. When UserA adds data to the system, the page is shown in the Fig. 7, and the terminal is Fig. 9.

To verify the query function of the system, user UserA initiates a request to UserD. UserD uses A's public key to encrypt the password and sends it to A. After a series of

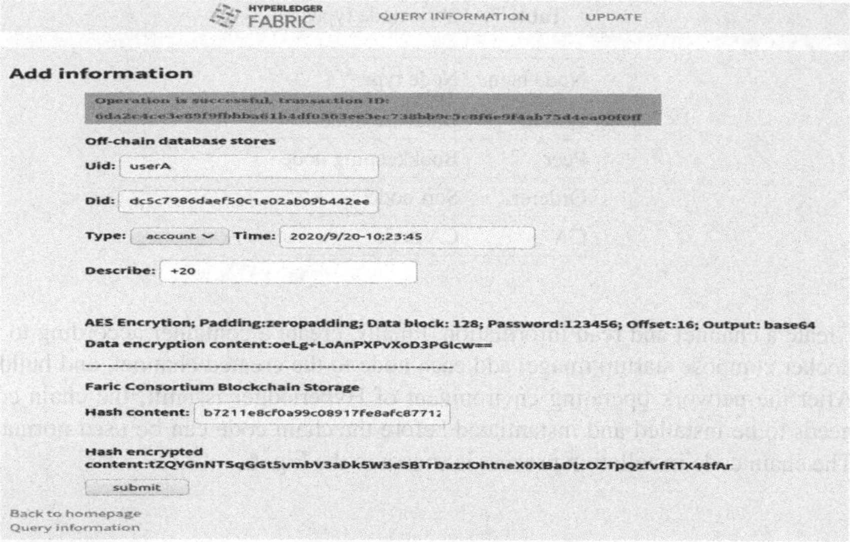

Fig. 7. Data Insertion page

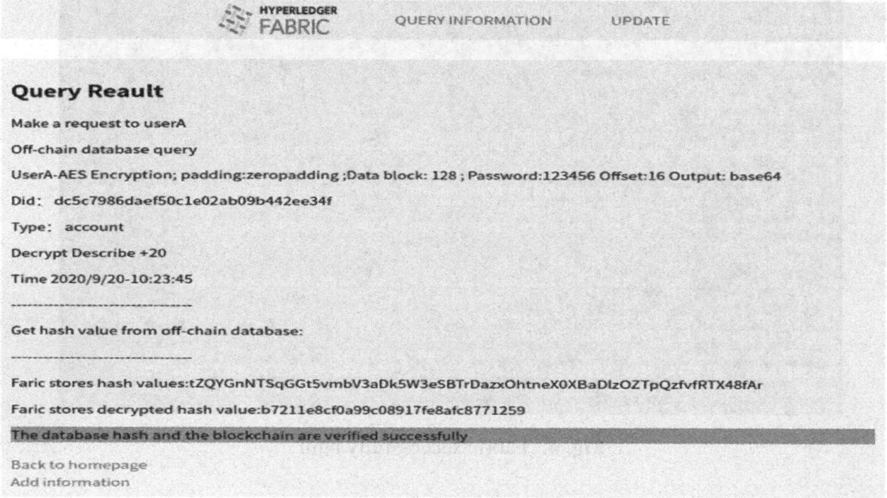

Fig. 8. Query and verify records page

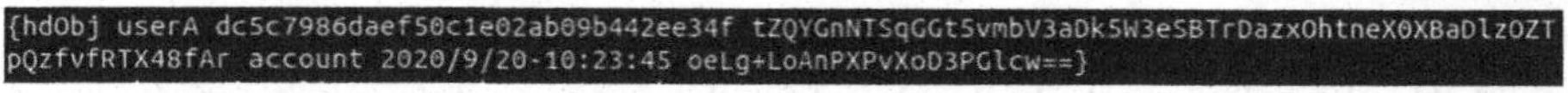

{hdObj userA dc5c7986daef50c1e02ab09b442ee34f tZQYGnNTSqGGt5vmbV3aDk5W3eSBTrDazxOhtneX0XBaDlzOZT
pQzfvfRTX48fAr account 2020/9/20-10:23:45 oeLg+LoAnPXPvXoD3PGlcw==}

Fig. 9. Inserted terminal

decryptions, A obtains the hash, and then requests the database to get the data decrypted through the web and verify it. After the verification is successful, it is displayed on the

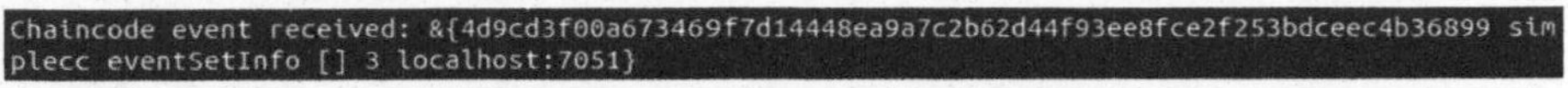

Chaincode event received: &{4d9cd3f00a673469f7d14448ea9a7c2b62d44f93ee8fce2f253bdceec4b36899 sim
plecc eventSetInfo [] 3 localhost:7051}

Fig. 10. Query and verify terminal

screen, the query result is shown in Fig. 8, and the query background record is shown in Fig. 10.

5.4 System Performance

This performance test mainly uses the Caliper tool for testing, which is a blockchain performance benchmark framework and allows users to use predefined use cases to test different blockchain design solutions and obtain performance test results. The system tested the throughput of different numbers of nodes, and the throughput and latency of different read and write times.

When the number of nodes is an experimental variable, the nodes grow from 0 to 35 with a step size of 5. Repeat the experiment under different nodes to take the average value, and the experimental results are shown in Fig. 11.

TPS
Throughputs
Number of nodes
0
10
20
30
40
0
5
10
15
20
25
30
35

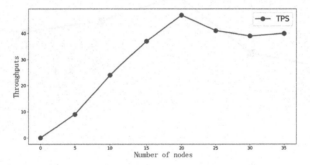

Fig. 11. The effect of nodes on throughput

The throughput of the write function reaches its peak at 20 requests, decreases slightly with the increase in the number of accesses, then increases slightly, and finally stabilizes. The throughput of the read function shows an upward trend as the number of requests increases, indicating that the system can withstand a certain scale of access requests.

By comparison, in the Hyperledger fabric, the system reads without submitting new transactions, and does not interact with the ordering node and the submitting node. Therefore, the system read throughput is better than the write throughput. The specific data is shown in Fig. 12.

The delay of the write function is basically 0.3 or less, reaching a peak at 100 times. As the number of accesses increases, the average delay decreases and tends to stabilize. The delay of reading the function is basically lower than 0.1, and the average delay decreases with the increase of the number of visits, reaching the lowest at 1000 times. The specific data is shown in Fig. 13.

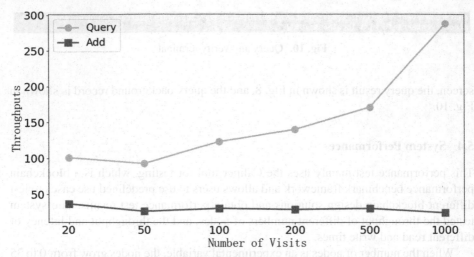

Fig. 12. Throughput test

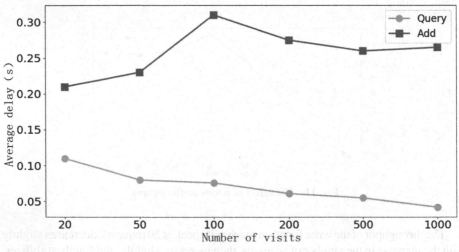

Fig. 13. Latency test

6 Conclusion

The rapid development of blockchain technology and the high level of social attention have made blockchain applications in various fields. This paper proposes a fabric-based on-chain and off-chain data collaborative management mechanism based on the problems of easy tampering, low data trust, unguaranteed security, and large storage capacity in traditional storage methods. Through the designed on-chain smart contract for certification and virtualized resource pool as an off-chain database, this article uses blockchain technology to make the certification data safe and reliable, and at the same time alleviate the storage pressure on the chain. The nodes of the alliance chain are jointly maintained by multiple institutions, etc., which solves the problems of information opacity, sharing, and security to a certain extent. The system establishes channels in different organizations, nodes can access each other, and the encryption algorithm is used to solve the privacy problem, but the security problems and throughput problems in complex environments need to be further improved in follow-up research.

Acknowledgement. This work has supported by State Grid Corporation of China science and technology projected "Key Technologies Research and Application of High Elastic Power Grid based on blockchain" (5700-202019374A-0–0-00).

References

1. Shangang, Z., Chao, W.: Review and judgment on the evidence ability of electronic data. People's Procur. Semimon. **8**, 34–36 (2018)
2. Xin, Z., Tao, L.: Research on the judicial deposit system of blockchain. Cyberspace Secur. **10**(7), 44–47+72 (2019)
3. Junfei, H., Jie, L.: Survey on blockchain Research. J. Beijing Univ. Posts Telecommun. **41**(2), 5–12 (2018)
4. Yong, Y., Feiyue, W.: Blockchain: the state of the art and future trends. Acta Automatica Sinica **42**(4), 481–494 (2016)
5. Wang, Y., Zhang, A., Zhang, P., et al.: Cloud-assisted EHR sharing with security and privacy preservation viaconsortium blockchain. IEEE Access **7**, 136704–136719 (2019)
6. Ding, X., Yang, J.: An access control model and its application in blockchain. In: 2019 International Conference (2019)
7. Didi, C., Wei, C.: Mechanism of trusted storage in Ethereum based on smart contract. J. Comput. Appl. **39**(4), 145–152
8. Hou, Y., Liang, X., Zhan, X.: Block chain based architecture model of electronic evidence system. Comput. Sci. **45**(S1), 361–364 (2018)
9. Cachin, C.: Architecture of the hyperledger blockchainfabric [EB/OL]. http://bytacoin.io/main/Hyperledger.pdf. Accessed 12 July 2016
10. Stallings, W.: Cryptography and network security: principles and practice. Int. Annals Criminol. **46**(4), 121–136 (1999)
11. Ruffing, T., Moreno-Sanchez, P., Kate, A.: Coinshuffle: practical decentralized coin mixing for bitcoin. In: Kuty łowski, M., Vaidya, J. (eds.) ESORICS 2014. LNCS, vol. 8713, pp. 345–364. Springer, Cham (2014). https://doi.org/10.1007/978-3-319-11212-1_20
12. Androulaki, E., Barger, A., Bortnikov, V., et al.: Hyperledgerfabric: a distributed operating system for permissioned blockchains. In: Proceedings of the Thirteenth EuroSys Conference. Association for Computing Machinery, New York, NY, United States

The Implementation of Aeronautical Information Exchange Model in SWIM

Bingjie Ren[✉] and Yuanchun Jiang

Civil Aeronautical University of China, Tianjin 300300, China
2019022081@cauc.edu.cn

Abstract. System Wide Information Management (SWIM), as an advanced civil aeronautical information management method, aims to solve the problems of global civil aeronautical information systems such as difficulty in obtaining common data in a timely manner and high information exchange costs. SWIM was first proposed by Europe and the United States and was recognized and valued by the International Civil Aviation Organization. It is to ensure the correct information transmission at the correct time. In order for the consistent information in the "virtual information pool" to be efficiently, accurately and securely transmitted, the information and data in the SWIM environment need to be defined in detail and standardized, so the two sides of data interaction can maintain the consistency in syntax and semantics. The Aeronautical Information Exchange Model (AIXM) is a core standard model for data transmission and format conversion, which mainly involves information in the aeronautical intelligence field. It covers multiple thematic elements such as airspace, airports and air routes, and provides a standardized description for data conversion and transmission in this field. The article analyzes the model composition of AIXM in the SWIM information exchange model, the modeling process, and the key technologies involved in model establishment, and preliminary design and implementation of AIXM.

Keywords: SWIM · Information exchange model · AIXM

1 Introduction

The continuous development of the civil aeronautical industry has optimized the civil aeronautical information network to a certain extent, but the current global civil aeronautical information system is still unable to communicate flexibly and conveniently. When data is exchanged between different or a large number of civil aeronautical systems, many complicated problems such as data interface independence will arise. The phenomenon of "information islands" [1] will become a great obstacle to information sharing between systems. SWIM, as the basis of flight coordinated operation control, is a standard and flexible civil aeronautical information sharing strategy. It can not only make the standardized interaction of information a reality, but also ensure that the information is used securely and efficiently, and thus play a role in promoting the realization of a new generation of air traffic management operational concept and mode.

© Springer Nature Switzerland AG 2021
X. Sun et al. (Eds.): ICAIS 2021, CCIS 1423, pp. 188–199, 2021.
https://doi.org/10.1007/978-3-030-78618-2_15

The SWIM global interoperability framework has a clear division of labor for the functions of each layer. The information exchange model layer [2] can set standards for the content and format of the information to be exchanged between service providers and consumers. The information exchange model layer includes the three main standards: AIXM, FIXM, WXXM and other information exchange standards. They are models formed after categorizing and modeling different aeronautical business data and representing them in a unified manner. It is the basis and core of data conversion from multi-source heterogeneous to unified format.

AIXM is a data exchange specification, which is led by Europe and the United States and vigorously promoted, mainly involving relevant data in the aeronautical information domain. Unified Modeling Language (UML) modeling standards and XML Schema specifications are used in the process of model building.

In this paper, the concept and components of AIXM are introduced in detail by analyzing the deficiencies of existing aeronautical information systems in data interaction. At the same time, the main technologies involved in AIXM are analyzed. Finally, the model building method of AIXM is given.

2 Aeronautical Information Exchange Model

2.1 AIXM Overview

AIXM is an important member of the SWIM data model family. It is an exchange model designed for aeronautical data. It describes the entities, attributes and relationships between aeronautical elements such as airports, runways, and airspace, and performs modeling. The goal of AIXM is to ensure that the complete and accurate aeronautical data contained in the Aeronautical Information Services (AIS) can have a uniform format on a global scale, while enabling digital interaction and management in the SWIM system.

AIS will gradually transition to Aeronautical Information Management (AIM), and gradually realize the dynamic management of AIS. While AIXM improves the AIS system, it can also promote the information circulation of the AIS systems of various countries. Finally, it provides good and reliable data support for the entire flight process, aircraft operation monitoring and flow management.

2.2 AIXM Composition

The AIXM model mainly consists of two parts [3]. One part is the Aeronautical Information Concept Model (AICM), which can describe various concepts involved in the aeronautical information field in the form of a collection of Feature, Attribute and Association. The other part is the aeronautical data exchange model AIXM XML Schema. It is derived from AICM and uses XML Schema to encode aeronautical data in a certain format, thereby realizing electronic data transfer between computer systems [4], also known as AIXM's XML architecture.

Unlike FIXM, AIXM data sources have greater requirements for time and geospatial description. Therefore, the AIXM model needs to be based on certain geospatial description specifications and meet the time description requirements. In the latest version of the AIXM5 modeling standard officially released by the SWIM working group, AIXM needs to comply with the ISO19100 series of spatial information standards.

2.3 Time Slice Model

AIXM must have a detailed time model to meet the time-critical requirements of the aerospace system. Through out the life cycle of aeronautical elements, their attributes may change. Therefore, AIXM specifically sets a time model mechanism when modeling, that is, a time slice model. The time slice model encapsulates the time-varying attributes of dynamically changing elements.

AIXM uses a time model when describing characteristic events and states. The GML standard mentions that an event is an action that occurs instantaneously or within a period of time, and its essence is that one or more functional attributes have changed. The state is a set of feature attributes that are valid for a period of time, which can be captured by instances through the function of time stamps.

It can be seen intuitively in Fig. 1 that the vertical lines represent events, and the part of the feature attribute set between events is the state. Among them, P1, P2, … P5 are the element attribute values along the time axis, and the reference time slice is the value of all time-varying element attributes defined by the effective time of the time slice; for example, TS2 in Fig. 1 contains P1, P2, P4 and the value of P5. Temporary time slices are only those that contain temporarily changed attribute values. Regarding the UML model, because the temporary incremental time slice needs to be distinguished from the baseline time slice, an additional attribute called "interpretation" is required in the AIXM FeatureTimeSlice class.

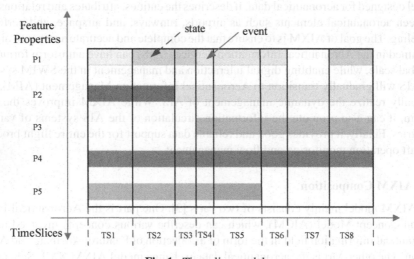

Fig. 1. Time slice model.

Encapsulating the time change attributes of the AIXM dynamic change elements as "AIXM TimeSlice" can better describe the characteristic attributes of the state and the event during this period. Each "status" time slice contains the time change attribute value of the event between two consecutive changes and has a specified validity period and a constant which reflects the information of each attribute.

3   Method of Establishing AIXM

3.1   AIXM Modeling Process

The data modeling process is the basis for the establishment of the SWIM data model and a prerequisite to ensure the success of data conversion. The model of AIXM can be categorized and structured from an object-oriented perspective. Therefore, the entire AIXM model needs to be established in the order of conceptual model, logical model and physical model. The modeling sequence is shown in Fig. 2.

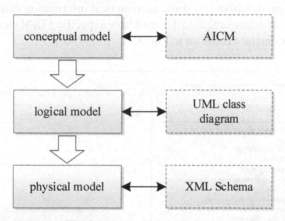

Fig. 2. Level of model building.

AICM extracts and categorizes the required data from the level of aeronautical business requirements, thereby forming the concept of entities. It is used to describe the specific meaning of the aeronautical information domain and is a model of an organization or an industry's interest area. AICM is not only a conceptual model, but also a logical basis for database design. The logical model can consider the association between entities on the basis of the conceptual model. It can be used to describe the structure of the aeronautical information domain and use UML class diagrams to describe it. The AIXM physical exchange model further forms a structured data description on the basis of the logical model, which is used to provide a physical method of storing data. Using XML Schema for data description, the characteristics, attributes and business rules in AICM can be mapped to XML to realize the conceptual model.

XML Schema is a concept in the Extensible Markup Language XML, which can describe the structure of XML language documents [5] and defines the elements that can appear in an XML instance and its type specifications. The current physical model that AIXM can support is AIXM XML Schema, that is, XML Schema is used to represent AIXM.

On the basis of meeting the basic rules of AIXM modeling, the basic structure can be defined for extension and other operations, and the brakes can be adapted to the needs of various aviation. Establishing various aviation data models can better integrate with international standards.

3.2   AIXM UML Class Diagram Example (Airport/Heliport Class Diagram)

As a standardized modeling language, UML is a modeling tool for object-oriented design. Among them, the Class Diagram provides a graphical representation for modeling objects and their relationships [6], representing a class of objects with the same attributes and the relationships between classes, and the Package diagram divide the related classes into a package to organize the related relationships of the class diagram more structured.

The definition of aeronautical elements in AICM is based on ICAO Annex 15 concerning aeronautical information necessary to support international navigation. Each aeronautical element describes a realistic aeronautical information entity. Take the airport/heliport element as an example to illustrate how a specific AIXM element is modeled in AICM. Its class diagram is shown in Fig. 3.

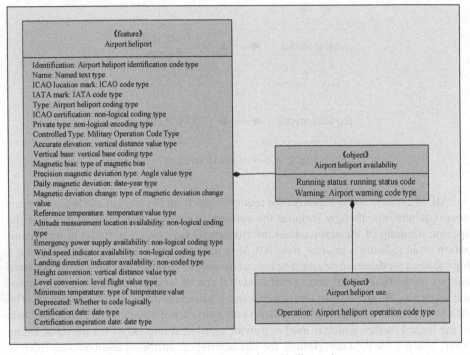

Fig. 3.   UML class diagram of airport heliport elements.

It can be seen from Fig. 3 that the airport heliport (AirportHeliport) element has the stereotype <<feature>> and several attributes and the types of these attributes, and the element has the availability of the airport heliport with the stereotype <<object>> (AirportHeliportAvailability) object. In AICM, object is used to describe the abstraction of a thing entity and is often used to represent the attributes of an entity. In this example, the availability object of an airport heliport is an associated combination object of the elements of an airport heliport (AirportHeliport). Its life cycle and elements are closely related, and elements and objects cannot exist separately.

According to the AICM model's description of the data set, the following mapping method is used to derive the AIXM XML Schema physical model. First, according to ICAO's AICM and AIXM XML Schema mapping specification, the UML class name is directly mapped to the XML Schema.

Then according to the time slice model of AIXM, the corresponding rule model is created in the process of element mapping. For each AIXM element in AICM, create XML schema elements in the order of the arrows in Fig. 4.

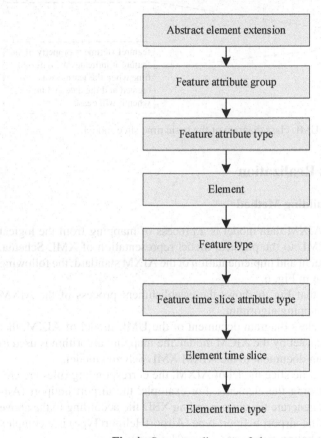

Fig. 4. Sequence diagram of element mapping.

Because of the time requirements of elements, the creation of elements is based on and precedes the feature time slice (FeatureTimeSlice). For AIXM objects, since the object cannot exist independently of the element, the TimeSlice object entity will not be created. The airport heliport element can create XML Schema elements according to the above mapping sequence.

The UML class diagram of the basic time slice model is shown in Fig. 5. There are several possible TimeSlice types for the complete AIXM Feature Time Slice model. AIXM TimeSlice cannot be deleted or modified, and its model is based on the "append only" principle.

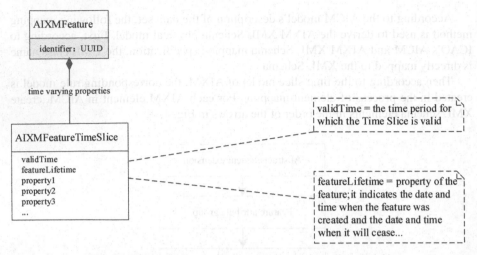

Fig. 5. The UML class diagram of the basic time slice model.

4   Modeling Process Realization

4.1   Process of Model Building Method

The establishment of the AIXM data model is a process of mapping from the logical model representation of UML to the physical model representation of XML Schema. Therefore, in the establishment and implementation of the AIXM standard, the following methods are used, as shown in Fig. 6.

It can be clearly seen that Fig. 6 shows the establishment process of the AIXM standard, which uses the mapping algorithm.

First, according to the class diagram document of the UML model of AIXM, that is, the description of the data set by the AICM model, the mapping algorithm is used to map the UML class diagram document to the AIXM XML Schema model.

Then, according to the time slice model of AIXM, the corresponding rules are created in the process of mapping the elements. For example, the airport heliport (Airport/Heliport) element can generate the corresponding XSD file according to the above mapping sequence, where the airport heliport type (AirportHeliportType) is a complex type mapped by the airport heliport element (AirportHeliport).

Finally, use the JAXB Referennce Implementation (JAXB RI) tool to generate the Java class with the corresponding data structure from the obtained XSD document conforming to the XML Schema specification. Java class is used as the basic data structure in the development of data conversion module to realize the data conversion function.

After obtaining the XSD document conforming to the XML Schema specification, the XML can be instantiated according to the aeronautical data of the actual system. Figure 7 describes this process.

Marshal is a process of converting java objects into xml objects, and unmarshal is its reverse process. Fill the real data in the infrastructure layer into the JAVA class, which can be instantiated by this method.

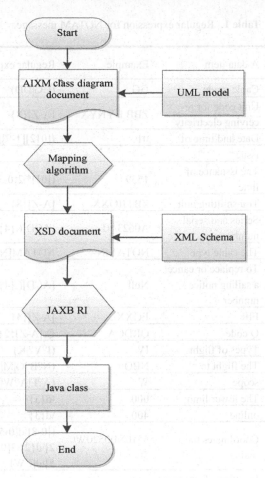

Fig. 6. AIXM standard establishment process.

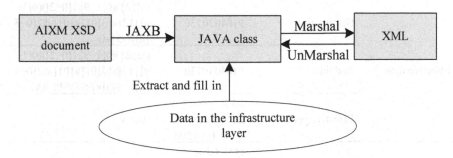

Fig. 7. Instantiation process.

Table 1. Regular expression for NOTAM message.

NOTAM components	A data item	Example	Regular expression
	Cable grade	GG	(GG|DD)
Header	Unit code for receiving electricity	ZBB BYNYX	[A-Z]{8}
	Date and time of issue	01	([012][1-9]|3[01])
	The issuance of time	1539	([01]*|2[0-3])([0-5]*)
	Transmitting unit	ZBTJIOXX	[A-Z]{8}
	Series and serial number/year	A0623/91	[ACD](.{4})/(.{2})
Telegram serial number and code	The cable type	NOTAMN	NOTAM[NCR]
	To replace or cancel a sailing notice number	Null	[ACD](.{4})/(.{2})
	FIR	EGXX	[A-Z]{4}
	Q code	QRDCA	Q([A-Z]{2})([A-Z]{2})
	Types of flight	IV	(I?V?|K)
	The flight to	NBO	(N?B?O|M|K)
	scope	W	(A?E|A?W|K|A)
Restricted line	The lower limit	000	\d{3}
	online	400	\d{3}
	Coordinates the radius	5510N00520W050	([0-8]\d[0-5]\d[NS])([0-2]\d{2}|3[0-5]\d)[0-5]\d[EW]
	Location of situation	EGTT EGPX	([A-Z]{4}){1,7}
	Starting time	9104030730	(\d{2})(0[1−9]|1[0−2])(0[1−9]|[12]\d|3[01])([01]\d|2[0−3])([0−5]\d)
Effective time	End time	9104030730	(\d{2})(0[1−9]|1[0−2])(0[1−9]|[12]\d|3[01])([01]\d|2[0−3])([0−5]\d)(EST)?|PERM
	Effective period	APR 03 07 12 21 24 AND 28 0730 TO 1500	\D.*\s
Plain language		DANGER AREA DXX IS ACTIVE	\E.*\s
Upper and lower limits	Lower limit	GND	SFC|GND|\d{6}M\s(AGL|AMSL)|FL\d{3}
	Upper limit	12200AMSL	UNL|\d{6}(AGL|AMSL)|FL\d{3}

4.2 Source Data Processing

The Notice To Airmen (NOTAM) message is an important business message in the integrated aeronautical information series delivered by AIS in the current aeronautical information business. It is a typical carrier of dynamic aeronautical information. NOTAM and the static data Aeronautical Information Publication (AIP) jointly serve the information business in the aeronautical domain. The specifications provided by AIXM support dynamic air navigation information including NOTAM. While ensuring the consistency and accuracy of aeronautical information required by pilots and airlines, AIXM's digital interaction provides the best choice for the efficient transmission of aeronautical service data, and it supports future ATC systems.

NOTAM is a notice to pilots distributed by means of a communications network and notifying aviation of facilities, services, procedures, or dangerous beginnings or changes, and states. According to the NOTAM dispatch procedure [7], The NOTAM message is mainly composed of header, telegraph number, qualified line, and the body part of a-G item.

The parse of NOTAM message using regular expression is shown in Table 1.

Table 1 lists the data items and corresponding regular expressions of the NOTAM message. Therefore, any regular expression can be matched and the corresponding data item can be extracted as the aeronautical information data source.

4.3 Model Test Results

The test uses the black box test method, which refers to testing whether the module can correctly accept input and get the correct output. Select the NOTAMN in the NOTAM message as the test case for the AIXM input data subset. The message test case and test results are as follows and the test case is shown in Table 2.

Table 2. NOTAM test case.

A0046/13 NOTAMN
Q) ZABB/QFALC/IV/NBO/A
/000/999/5353N02802E005
A) ZABB B) 1309012100 C) 1309020200
E) AERODROME CLOSED

Based on the corresponding airport AIP data, the XML data about airport elements obtained from the above test cases are shown in Table 3.

In Table 3, the information data item about airport closure in NOTAM message was superimposed on the aviation information compilation of Beijing Airport, and XML was instantiated with AirportHeliport as the main element.

Table 3. NOTAM test case results.

```
    <aixm:AirportHeliport xmlns:gco= "http://www.isotc211.org/2005/gco " xmlns:aixm=
"http://www.aixm.aero/schema/5.1 " xmlns:gmd= "http://www.isotc211.org/2005/gmd "
xmlns:gts= "http://www.isotc211.org/2005/gts " xmlns:gsr= "
http://www.isotc211.org/2005/gsr " xmlns:gss= "http://www.isotc211.org/2005/gss "
xmlns:message= "http://www.aixm.aero/schema/5.1/message " xmlns:event= "
http://www.aixm.aero/schema/5.1/event " xmlns:gml= "http://www.opengis.net/gml/3.2 "
xmlns:ns10= "http://www.w3.org/1999/xlink ">
    <gml:boundedBy   xmlns:xsi=  "  http://www.w3.org/2001/XMLSchema-instance "
xsi:nil= "true "/>
    <aixm:timeSlice>
      <aixm:AirportHeliportTimeSlice>
      <aixm:designator >ZABB</aixm:designator>
      <aixm:name >Beijing International Airport</aixm:name>
      <aixm:locationIndicatorICAO >ZABB</aixm:locationIndicatorICAO>
      <aixm:designatorIATA >PEK</aixm:designatorIATA>
      <aixm:type>aerodrome only</aixm:type>
      <aixm:certifiedICAO >YES</aixm:certifiedICAO>
      <aixm:privateUse >NO</aixm:privateUse>
      <aixm:controlType>civil control</aixm:controlType>
      <aixm:fieldElevation uom= "ft ">15.2</aixm:fieldElevation>
      <aixm:verticalDatum nilReason= "12 ">12</aixm:verticalDatum>
      <aixm:magneticVariation >121.666</aixm:magneticVariation>
      <gml:validTime>
          <gml:TimePeriod gml:id= "CY01_TS02_TP01 ">
          <gml:beginPostion>2013-09-01T21:00:00<gml:beginPostion>
          <gml:endPostion>2013-09-02T02:00:00<gml:endPostion>
    <gml:TimePeriod>
    <gml:validTime>
  <aixm:interpretation>TEMPDELTA</aixm:interpretation>
  <aixm:sequenceNumber>46</aixm:sequenceNumber>
  <aixm:availability>
  <aixm:AirportHeliportAvailability>
      <aixm:operationalStatus>
              AERODROME CLOSED
      </aixm:operationalStatus>
      </aixm:AirportHeliportAvailability>
  </aixm:availability>
  </aixm:AirportHeliportTimeSlice>
  </aixm:timeSlice>
</aixm:AirportHeliport>
```

5 Conclusion

This article mainly introduces AIXM in the SWIM platform information exchange model. At the same time, combined with the modeling process and related technologies, the model mapping algorithm is used to build a model that conforms to the AIXM data standard. The preliminary modeling and experiments are performed to complete the conversion from XSD to XML documents.

In future research, efforts can also be made from the following aspects: First, based on the analysis of the basic rules of the information exchange model, the extensibility of the data model can be used to expand the corresponding data structure and definition from the elements, entity attributes and data types according to the characteristics of different national air traffic control systems according to the special business requirements, so as to adapt to the requirements of aviation elements of different countries. In addition, the designed AIXM can be connected to the actual system for testing and optimization. After the model is established and tested, the AIXM is tried to be deployed.

The establishment of AIXM can not only standardize and structure data, reduce the cost of information exchange, but also provide a reference for the construction of other information standards in the future.

References

1. Bian, B.: On the information island problem in enterprise informationization. China Manag. Inf. Technol. **4**, 22–25 (2007)
2. SWIM Concept – DRAFT Version 0.9 ICAO Air Traffic Management Requirements and Performance Panel (ATMRPP)
3. EUROCONTROL and Federal Aviation Administratio. Aeronautical Information Exchange Model (AIXM) Exchange Model goals, requirements and design (2006). http://aixm.aero/sites/aixm.aero/files/imce/AIXM50/aixm_5_proposal_20060620_whitepaper_pdf
4. Liu, B.: Research and design of aeronautical information dynamic information processing system. M.S. dissertation, University of Electronic Science and Technology of China, China (2014)
5. W3C.XMLSchema [EB/OL]. https://www.w3.org/standards/xml/schema
6. Unified Modeling Language. What is UML [EB/OL]. https://www.uml.org/index.htm. Accessed 25 Jan 2020
7. CAAC Air Traffic Control Bureau.Guidance Manual for issuance of Notices to Mariners, pp. 4–17 (2008)

CCTL: Cascade Classifier Text Localization Algorithm in Natural Scene Image

Xueming Qiao[1], Mingli Yin[1], Liang Kong[1], Bin Wang[1], Xiuli Chang[2], Qi Ma[3], Dongjie Zhu[4(✉)], and Ning Cao[5]

[1] State Grid Weihai Power Supply Company, Weihai 264200, China
[2] Shandong Institute of Shipbuilding Technology, Weihai 264209, China
[3] School of Computer Science and Cyberspace Security, Hainan University, Haikou 570228, China
[4] School of Computer Science and Technology, Harbin Institute of Technology, Weihai 264209, China
zhudongjie@hit.edu.cn
[5] College of Information Engineering, Sanming University, Sanming 365000, China

Abstract. Natural scene images often contain a lot of important texts, which carry the information we need, so it has important practical value to locate text information. This paper proposes a Cascade Classifier Text Localization (CCTL) algorithm. Firstly, a cascade classification algorithm based on Real AdaBoost is proposed to improve the accuracy of text localization. Secondly, a perceptual-based grouping algorithm is proposed to establish a perceptual organization framework. The use of adjacency and similar rules to group texts can improve the effect of text grouping. The proposed algorithm is verified and evaluated on the ICDAR dataset. At the same time, it is compared with other algorithms. The experimental results show that the proposed method has superiority in natural scene text detection.

Keywords: Scene text detection · Cascade classifier · Real AdaBoost · Perceptual organizational framework

1 Introduction

With the rapid development of mobile Internet and the popularity of wearable devices, a large amount of digital image and video information is generated all the time. These digital images and video information are mostly recorded natural scenes describing people's daily life. Natural scene detection has important significance and value in the fields of content-based multimedia retrieval, automatic driving, intelligent transportation [1–4]. These natural scenes contain a large amount of text information. The detection and localization of text areas is an important step in natural scene detection. Text area detection in natural scene images belongs to the category of image recognition, but it is more complicated than traditional text OCR. Firstly, the natural scene image has a higher proportion of non-text content. Secondly, there are cluttered backgrounds, lighting conditions, perspectives, fonts, and their colors. At present, there are already many research results in

© Springer Nature Switzerland AG 2021
X. Sun et al. (Eds.): ICAIS 2021, CCIS 1423, pp. 200–210, 2021.
https://doi.org/10.1007/978-3-030-78618-2_16

this field. Chen [5], Basavanna [6] and Nirmala [7] proposed methods based on neural net-works, grayscale contrast and Gabor filters. The detection results and accuracy have been greatly improved, and the text localization function has been effectively completed, but such algorithms include complex classifiers or convolution operations, which makes the computational complexity higher. Zhang [8], Sun [9] and Zhao [10] proposed edge-based approaches that took less time and achieved better positioning result. However, the error rate of such methods is higher if the edge of the detected background is complex. This paper proposes a Cascade Classifier Text Localization (CCTL) algorithm. Firstly, in the image feature classification layer, the ER region classification algorithm based on cascaded classifier with Real AdaBoost is proposed to improve the anti-interference ability; Secondly, in the text grouping layer, a perceptual-based grouping algorithm is proposed to establish a perceptual organization framework, and the use of adjacency and similarity rules to group texts can improve the accuracy of text recognition. The actual experiment proves that the proposed method is superior to the existing method in accuracy and recall rate, it can be well applied to natural scene text detection.

2 Related Work

The existing methods can be roughly divided into three types, namely texture-based methods, edge-based methods, and composite methods.

The texture-based method distinguishes the text as a texture different from the background, and uses discrete cosine, wavelet transform, and Fourier to identify the texture features. Chen [5], Basavanna [6] and Nirmala [7] proposed methods based on neural networks, grayscale contrast and Gabor filters. The detection results and accuracy have been greatly improved, and the text localization task has been effectively completed. Although these methods can largely exclude the influence of background on text localization, the application of this algorithm will require some more convolution operations and complicated classifiers, which increased the complexity.

The principle of the edge-based method is based on the contrast between the text and the background, and the edge of the text itself is very different from the background. The general steps are as follows: in the first step, an edge detection operator is selected to be able to detect the edge information we need; in the second step, a morphological operator is selected to be able to connect the edges at the boundary of the text; in three steps, heuristics are used to filter to filter out non-text areas and detect text areas. Zhang [8], Sun [9] and Zhao [10] simplified the pulse neural network and described the edge characteristics of the image according to the gradient to locate the text and extract clearer text edges with shorter time and better result. But if the edge of the detected background is very complex, then there are more detection errors in the edge-based approach.

Each algorithm has its advantages, and its advantages often show in scenes with certain characteristics. Therefore, in the face of changing scenes, multiple algorithms can be selected simultaneously by judging the characteristics of the scene. In recent years, many scholars have used this method to identify texts. For example, Pan [11] and Minetto [12] use composite methods for text recognition. This method has higher accuracy and requires less time, but how to choose the appropriate method according to the specific scenario and make a reasonable combination is a challenge.

3   Cascade Classifier Text Localization Algorithm

This paper proposes a text localization algorithm based on cascaded classifier. The algorithm flow is shown in Fig. 1. The algorithm mainly includes three parts: image feature extraction, image feature classification and text grouping algorithm.

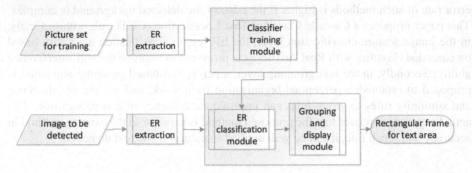

Fig. 1.   The flow diagram of CCTL.

3.1   Cascade Classification Algorithm Based on Real AdaBoost

In this paper, we designed the two-level Real AdaBoost classifier, whose structure is shown in Fig. 2. The first-level classifier adopts some feature values with low resolution but small calculation, and firstly filters the extreme value region ER, and use them as the input of the second-level classifier. In the second-level classifier, we use the eigenvalues with more accurate resolving but more computational complexity to accurately classify the filtered results of the first-level classifier to extract the text region.

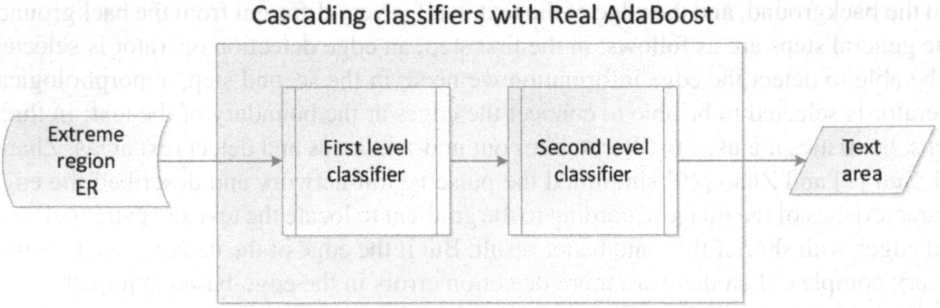

Fig. 2.   The structure of two-level classifier structure.

In the first-level classifier, we use five features with small computational and incremental calculations to extract features from extreme regions.

1.   Area (a): The number of pixels in the extreme value area.

2. Regional coordinates ($x_{\min}, y_{\min}, x_{\max}, y_{\max}$): The coordinates of the lower left vertex and upper right vertex pixel of the region.
3. Perimeter (p): Area boundary length. The calculation method is shown in Fig. 4-a. Initialization function $\Psi(p)$ depending on whether the pixel p at the threshold changes the boundary length of the region, the operator $\oplus$ is an addition operator.
4. Euler number (η): It is a topological feature of a binary image and is used to represent the difference between the connected area and the hole in the area. The Euler number of a region is calculated as shown in Eq. (1). C_1, C_2, C_3 respectively represent the number of pixel templates included in the area as shown in Fig. 3. Initialization function shown in Fig. 4-b represents the number of contained in the pixel p at the threshold. is an addition operator.

$$\eta = \frac{1}{4}(C_1 - C_2 + 2C_3) \tag{1}$$

$$Q_1 = \left\{ \begin{matrix} 1 & 0 \\ 0 & 0 \end{matrix}, \begin{matrix} 0 & 1 \\ 0 & 0 \end{matrix}, \begin{matrix} 0 & 0 \\ 1 & 0 \end{matrix}, \begin{matrix} 0 & 0 \\ 0 & 1 \end{matrix} \right\}, Q_2 = \left\{ \begin{matrix} 0 & 1 \\ 1 & 1 \end{matrix}, \begin{matrix} 1 & 0 \\ 1 & 1 \end{matrix}, \begin{matrix} 1 & 1 \\ 1 & 0 \end{matrix}, \begin{matrix} 1 & 1 \\ 0 & 1 \end{matrix} \right\}, Q_3 = \left\{ \begin{matrix} 0 & 1 \\ 1 & 0 \end{matrix}, \begin{matrix} 1 & 0 \\ 0 & 1 \end{matrix} \right\}$$

Fig. 3. Pixel template of 2 × 2.

5. Horizontal crossing number (C_i): a vector whose length is h, it is used to indicate the change in the number of pixels belonging to ($p \in r$) and not belonging to ($p \notin r$) regions on the specified row i in the region r. The calculation method is shown in Fig. 4-c. The initialization function $\Psi(p)$ depends on whether the pixel adjacent to the pixel p at the threshold exists. The operator $\oplus$ is calculated on the same row (i)where both pixel (p) and region (r) exist.

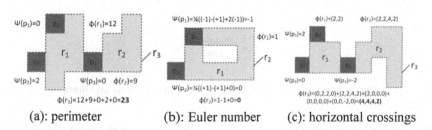

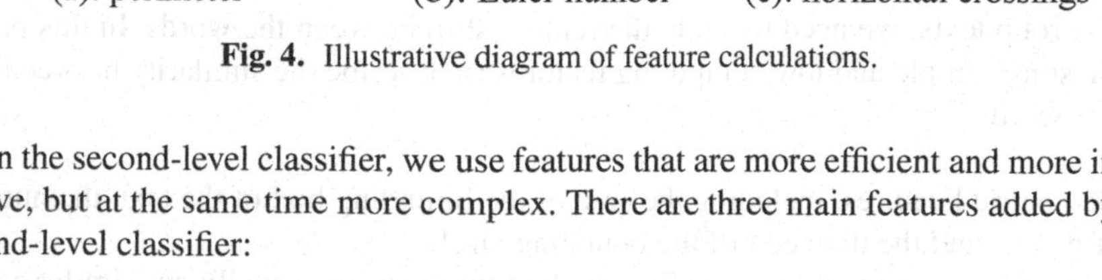

(a): perimeter (b): Euler number (c): horizontal crossings

Fig. 4. Illustrative diagram of feature calculations.

In the second-level classifier, we use features that are more efficient and more informative, but at the same time more complex. There are three main features added by the second-level classifier:

1. Hole area ratio (a_h/a): where a is the area of the area (as described in the first-level classifier), and a_h is the area of all the holes in the area, which is the number of pixels.

The hole area ratio has a more accurate resolution than the feature of the number of holes in the first-stage classifier. Because in a large extreme region, the effect of a small hole on the area is significantly smaller than that of a large area, the hole area ratio is an important feature.

2. Convex area ratio (a_c/a): where b is the area of the convex shell in the area. The convex part of the area is a very important feature in the text, and the convex area ratio can be used to classify the text better.

3. Number of inflection points on the outer boundary (k): The number of changes in convex and concave surfaces at the outer boundary pixels of the representative region. Usually, the number of inflection points of a character is a limited number. It is obvious that the number of inflection points of the outer boundary of the English alphabet does not exceed 10. There are many spikes on the border of some non-text areas, such as trees or weeds, so there will be a lot of inflection points on the outer boundary.

3.2 Perceptual-Based Text Grouping Algorithm

To perform further operations on the text area, such as text recognition, then we need to group the texts and merge the texts with similar characteristics. We propose a perceptual-based grouping algorithm which establishes a perceptual organization framework that is grouped by performing three steps on the text area. First some possible grouping hypotheses is created by detecting different feature subspaces; Then the most meaningful areas are reserved after the analysis process, thus providing a holistic cluster; Finally, these meaningful clusters are integrated through evidence accumulation. The structure of the algorithm is shown in Fig. 5.

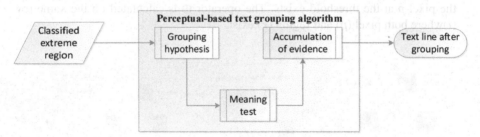

Fig. 5. The structure of perceptual-based text grouping algorithm.

To group texts, we need to study the relationship between the words. In this paper, we use some simple and low computing features to describe the similarity between text lines or words.

1. Geometric Features, including the area of the bounding box of the text, the number of pixels, and the diameter of the bounding circle.

2. Area intensity and color mean. Text in the same text line usually has similar colors and intensities, therefore, we calculate the intensity mean and color mean of the pixels in the text area in the color space as a feature of similarity between words.

3. Strength and color mean of the outer boundary, we just calculate the intensity and color mean of the pixels on the outer boundary of the text area.
4. Stroke width, there is generally a similar stroke width between a word or a line of text.
5. Average gradient magnitude of the boundary, we calculate the average gradient magnitude at the boundary of the text area.

To capture the distance between the regions and the similarity between the regions, all these features are added to the spatial information, that is, the coordinates of the center of the region. Therefore, we limit the areas in the same group to only spatially adjacent areas.

Suppose that n extreme regions are extracted from the image, where k extreme regions have a common feature. The k extreme regions form a group G. We call the group G a group hypothesis. In each of the above feature subspaces, grouping hypotheses are performed, and clustering analysis is performed according to the inclusion relationship between the grouping hypotheses, and a corresponding tree diagram is constructed. Each node in the tree represents a grouping hypothesis that will be evaluated in a perceptual sense in the next phase. If the common feature does not happen by chance, then this common feature is an important attribute of group G. Here we assume that the observation quality of all extreme regions is random and evenly distributed, then the distribution probability observed for G is also random and consistent with the binomial distribution. Therefore, in the N extreme regions, the probability distribution of the G group with common features in the extreme regions is shown in Eq. (2), which we use as the meaning of the group hypothesis.

$$B_G(k, n, p) = \binom{n}{k} p^k (1 - p)^{n-k} \tag{2}$$

Where p is the probability that a single extremum region has the above characteristics. If each node A, subsequent node B and each ancestor node C satisfy Eq. (3), then we mark node A as the most meaningful.

$$B_B(k, n, p) > B_A(k, n, p) \quad and \quad B_C(k, n, p) \geq B_A(k, n, p) \tag{3}$$

The largest meaningful cluster is detected in each feature subspace, and these clusters are combined to form a cluster set. We use the clustering set P to calculate the evidence belonging to the same group of each pair of extreme regions, and generate a symmetric matrix D:

$$D(i, j) = \frac{m_{ij}}{N} \tag{4}$$

Where m denotes the number of times the extreme value region i and the extreme value region j are assigned to the same maximum meaningful cluster in the cluster set P. The matrix D will be used as a dissimilarity matrix for the final cluster analysis of all extreme regions using hierarchical clustering.

4 Experimental Results and Analysis

4.1 Experiments and Results of the First Level Classifier

Figure 6 is a part of an image, which is taken as the extreme value region of the detection image, and then input into the classifier for classification. The red arrow represents the initial pixel when extracting the extreme value region. When the threshold value changes from 0 to 255, the corresponding extremum region is classified in the first-level classifier. Only when the voting rate of the final decision classifier is greater than the extremum region of the prescribed threshold, will it be input into the second-level classifier. As shown in Fig. 7, the extreme value region of the red point meets the condition and can enter the second level classifier.

Fig. 6. The sample picture.

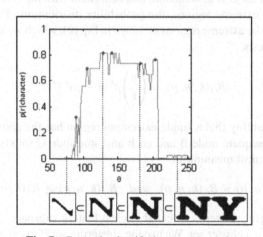

Fig. 7. Correctly classified extremum region.

4.2 Experiments and Results of the Second Level Classifier

Then, we input the extremum region filtered by the first-level classifier into the second-level classifier, extract all classification features (including the first-level and second-level classification features), and conduct classification operation. The extremum region is divided into text and non-text regions.

Figure 8 is the detection image. We extracted the extremum region and classified it by the first-level classifier to obtain the filtered extremum region under four channels. Then we used the second classifier to further filter these extremum regions. Figure 9 shows the classification results of detection images in the second level classifier.

Fig. 8. Image to be tested.

Fig. 9. The results of the classification of all channels in the second level classifier.

4.3 Comparative Experiment and Analysis

The proposed in this paper is tested on the ICDAR 2011 dataset [10] which contains 255 images with 1189 words and 6,393 letters. According to the evaluation algorithm, the corresponding recall, accuracy, and mean F1-score are obtained, and then compared with other text localization algorithms.

It can be seen from Table 1 that the recall rate (63.5%) of is higher than that of the 2011 ICDAR champion Kim (62.5%), whose accuracy rate (83%) and the mean value

F1-score (71.3%) are better. However, compared with the algorithms of runners Yi, H. Liu [13] and Neumann [14], it is found that the algorithm has advantages in both the recall rate and the accuracy and mean F1-score. Figures 10 and 11 show an example of positioning results. It can be seen that the algorithm can accurately locate the target text from complex scenes.

Table 1. Experimental results of CCTL on the ICDAR 2011 dataset

Algorithm	Recall	Accuracy	Mean F1-score
Kim (ICDAR 2011 champion)	62.5%	83.0%	71.3%
CCTL	**64.7%**	**73.1%**	**68.7%**
Yi (ICDAR 2011 run-up)	58.1%	67.2%	62.3%
H. Liu	57.7%	67.0%	62.0%
Neumann	52.5%	68.9%	59.6%

Fig. 10. An example of CCTL positioning on ICDAR.

Fig. 11. An example of CCTL positioning results on ICDAR.

5 Conclusion

This paper proposes the Cascade Classifier Text Localization (CCTL) algorithm. Firstly, in the image feature classification part, we propose a cascade classification algorithm based on Real AdaBoost, which improves the accuracy of text area recognition and recall rate; Secondly, in the text grouping section, according to the process of human perception of objects, we propose a perceptual-based grouping algorithm, which can improve the effect of text grouping. Of course, in the image feature classification module, whether it can be combined with other features to further improve the accuracy of text positioning; in the text group module, whether there is a more efficient and accurate classifier is our next research.

Funding Statement. This work is supported by State Grid Shandong Electric Power Company Science and Technology Project Funding under Grant no. 520613200001, 520613180002, 62061318C002, Weihai Scientific Research and Innovation Fund (2020) and the Grant 19YG02, Sanming University.

Conflicts of Interest. The authors declare that they have no conflicts of interest to report regarding the present study.

References

1. Rong, X., Yi, C., Tian, Y.: Recognizing text-based traffic guide panels with cascaded localization network. In: Hua, G., Jégou, H. (eds.) ECCV 2016. LNCS, vol. 9913, pp. 109–121. Springer, Cham (2016). https://doi.org/10.1007/978-3-319-46604-0_8
2. Zhu, Y.F., Liao, M.S., Yang, M.T.: Cascaded segmentation-detection networks for text-based traffic sign detection. IEEE Trans. Intell. Transp. Syst. **19**(1), 209–219 (2017)
3. Dey, N., Ashour, A.S.: Applied examples and applications of localization and tracking problem of multiple speech sources. In: Direction of Arrival Estimation and Localization of Multispeech Sources Springer Briefs in Electrical and Computer Engineering SECE. Springer Cham (2018). https://doi.org/10.1007/978-3-319-73059-2_4
4. Paul, S.F., Saha, S.S., Basu, S.T.: Text localization in camera captured images using fuzzy distance transform based adaptive stroke filter. Multimedia Tools Appl. **78**(13), 18017–18036 (2019)
5. Chen, X., Zhang, H.: Text area detection from video frames. In: Shum, H.-Y., Liao, M., Chang, S.-F. (eds.) PCM 2001. LNCS, vol. 2195, pp. 222–228. Springer, Heidelberg (2001). https://doi.org/10.1007/3-540-45453-5_29
6. Basavanna, M.F., Shivakumara, P.S., Srivatsa, S.K.T.: Multi-oriented text detection in scene images. Int. J. Pattern Recogn. Artif. Intell. **26**(07), 1255010 (2012)
7. Nirmala, S.F., Nagabhushan, P.S.: Foreground text segmentation in complex color document images using Gabor filters. Signal Image Video Process. **6**(4), 669–678 (2012)
8. Zhang, X.F., Sun, F.S.: Pulse coupled neural network edge-based algorithm for image text locating. Tsinghua Sci. Technol. **16**(1), 22–30 (2011)
9. Sun, Q.Y.F., Lu, Y.S.: Text location in scene images using visual attention model. Int. J. Pattern Recognit Artif Intell. **26**(04), 1255008 (2012)
10. Zhao, X.F., Lin, K.H.S., Fu, Y.T.: Text from corners: a novel approach to detect text and caption in videos. IEEE Trans. Image Process. **20**(3), 790–799 (2010)

11. Pan, Y.F.F., Hou, X.S., Liu, C.L.T.: A hybrid approach to detect and localize texts in natural scene images. IEEE Trans. Image Process. **20**(3), 800–813 (2010)
12. Minetto, R.F., Thome, N.S., Cord, M.T.: Text detection and recognition in urban scenes. In: 2011 IEEE International Conference on Computer Vision Workshops (ICCV Workshops), Barcelona, pp. 227–234. IEEE (2011)
13. Liu, H.F., Ding, X.S.: Handwritten character recognition using gradient feature and quadratic classifier with multiple discrimination schemes. In: Eighth International Conference on Document Analysis and Recognition (ICDAR 2005), Seoul, pp. 19–23. IEEE (2005).
14. Neumann, L.F., Matas, J.S.: Text localization in real-world images using efficiently pruned exhaustive search. In: 2011 International Conference on Document Analysis and Recognition, Beijing, pp. 687–691. IEEE (2011)

Research on the Application of Big Data Analysis in University Library

Juan Hu, Shunhang Xu, Yuhui Hu, Wenhao Shi, and Yangfei Xiao(✉)

Hunan University of Finance and Economics, Changsha 410205, China

Abstract. Big data is built on the foundation of today's horse racing technology. The rise and development of big data has become one of the most typical features of the industry's Internetization in the new IT era. The data stored in the world has overflowed every database, and industry big data has become the focus of attention of all walks of life. Governments at all levels and all enterprises and institutions hope to dig out high-quality, high-value-added data from big data. Information, and use it to improve their profit and service model, and enhance their status in the public and industry. In the era of big data, for libraries that provide teaching and scientific research services to the teachers and students of the school, they can use efficient and fast information technology, such as big data analysis, to conduct in-depth analysis and analysis of various data in university libraries. Digging, effectively understanding the reading situation of the whole school, and analyzing their reading hobbies and reading habits, the library can effectively use this information to improve the types of books purchased by the library, which can more effectively increase resource utilization.

Keywords: Big data · Big data analysis · University library

1 First Section

In this era, humans on the entire planet basically lie on the Internet like a spider every day. In fact, this situation is equivalent to that everyone has become a source of manufacturing data invisibly, and an unimaginable amount of data is generated from all over the world every day. According to calculations by some people concerned, when the clock hands of this century point to 20, the number of data storage contributed by the entire world can even touch the figure of 40EB. These signs are always present as we show that the upsurge of the big data wave is actually an inevitable event held by the torrent of the times. When the Internet is driven by fast-paced technology to throw fishing nets into the world, data presents characteristics such as diversity and complexity. Big data analysis, the term represents the ability to predict from a large amount of data through data collection and data mining. Related laws [1] can provide strong decision support for management.

In terms of urban planning, through the mining and analysis of urban geography, weather and other natural information and economic, social, cultural, and demographic and other humanistic and social information, it can provide strong decision-making

X. Sun et al. (Eds.): ICAIS 2021, CCIS 1423, pp. 211–223, 2021.
https://doi.org/10.1007/978-3-030-78618-2_17

support for urban planning and strengthen the forward-looking and scientific nature of urban management services. Sex. In terms of traffic management, real-time mining and analysis of road traffic information can effectively alleviate traffic congestion, and quickly respond to emergencies, providing a scientific decision-making basis for the sound operation of urban traffic. In the security field, through big data mining, man-made or natural disasters and terrorist incidents can be discovered in time, and emergency response capabilities and security prevention capabilities can be improved.

More than half of the universities in my country have completed the first round of digital campus construction, laying a solid foundation for the research of campus big data [2]. Colleges and universities play an important social role, and their main service targets are mainly teachers and students on campus. Using big data analysis technology to improve the service quality of university libraries and make them better serve teachers and students is an inevitable development in the future. Trend [3]. Libraries have been using the document information service system for many years and have accumulated a large amount of data. These data were completely useless in the past, but now these dormant data are beginning to be used as a good piece of steel. The application of big data analysis can use the data that readers keep on the library system as a basis, and obtain information about their hobbies and hobbies from it, which can provide reference for the work of managers.

At present, some colleges and universities have seized the favorable opportunity to develop big data services and achieved some results. For example, the big data management software developed by Wuhan Library can analyze readers' habits and push personalized reading bibliographies [4]. This is the most reasonable use of university library resources. It uses big data analysis to mine and analyze readers' borrowing information, predict readers' needs, and provide corresponding services for their needs. This is the traditional library's personalization A major step in the transformation of the library.

2 Related Works

Big data, the word "The Third Wave", its creator is a sociologist in the United States. This person tells the world through this book that if IBM's computer raises the curtain of the information age, then big data will be the star actor of this show [5]. However, due to the size of the decibel, the cry this time was quickly submerged in the noise of the times. Until the clock of this century reached the number 9, "Nature" impressively posted the three big characters of big data on its own. On the cover, the word finally got people's attention after years of lurking [6]. After strenuous exploration by people of insight from all walks of life, people's understanding of big data has reached a higher level. So under the meaning of big data itself, people began to have a lot of gloom on them. The tide of big data was set off by the big hands of the times, and big data officially took to the stage and started a lively performance.

Big data is a trend sweeping the world. Since its inception, major countries in China and the West have invested a lot of resources to study it. So what exactly is big data? Big data means the results of people who are alert and open up a new path to explore in this era when data is generated like a fishing net. In fact, it is more like a logical method than an actual technology. Its formation idea revolves around compiling a fishing net that is more convenient for collecting data [7]. For people from all walks of life in different situations, it can interpret different meanings in the eyes of these people. With the growing popularity of big data, its definition usually refers to data with 4V characteristics such as huge volume (Volume), faster processing speed (Velocity), diverse data types (Variety), and high commercial value (Value) [8].

The intensive action on big data abroad was initiated by the first black president of the United States. He not only led the country to throw a huge amount of funds into this field, but even organized more than a dozen campaigns on this strategy at the government level. Department, and drawn several plans on the desk of the White House to assist in the research work. This scene seems to remind people of the time when the research and development of nuclear weapons was proposed [9]. Such bold and resolute handwork is very clear to the world that the United States has pulled the exploration in this field to the height of the country. At the same time, with the state taking the lead as an example, every nongovernmental organization is also suddenly alert and squeezing into the big data road in an endless stream. For the United States, it is well known that it has the world's most abundant talents and technology reserves, so starting from the government's focus on big data, they have broken the way in developing this road [10].

After the United States took the lead in entering the field of big data, countries around the world gradually woke up, using the routes developed by the United States as a reference, and began scrambling to plant their own flags on this territory. Big data is gradually being used in all walks of life, and the government uses this tool as a piece of sweet pastry in several government tasks such as monitoring and crime prevention. The use of data comparison and analysis to discover potential terrorists has made it difficult for many violent groups to hide, and at the same time, it has indeed greatly reduced the crime of the entire country. As a pioneer in this field, the United States has even applied this skill to presidential elections. Through observing people's various data to determine their general political orientation, voters use this method to explore their own Supporters, so that they can get as many votes as possible [11].

As for the commercial sector in the United States, it is even more handy to use big data. According to research, Coca-Cola uses big data to study people's living habits, and obtains certain results in their habitual research. Afterwards, relying on this advantage, it maximizes its turnover. At the same time, there is also a well-known business giant Wal-Mart [12]. They use big data to update their business strategies, and they have obtained the result that beer and diapers are sold in one place, which can increase the sales of both [13]. They tried to implement this plan with suspicion, and the final outcome was as expected by Big Data. This incident is still widely circulated in the business scope, making people start to be convinced of the capabilities of big data.

My country started to step into the field of big data in recent years. At first, a simple working group was organized to explore the value of big data. Later, after discovering the resolute and resolute measures taken by the United States on this road, the government finally focused its vision on big data, and began to officially drag it to the height of the country when the clock hand of this century pointed to the number 16.

When the long river of time flows to the bank of 16 years, our country has drawn a pointer called the "13th Five-Year Plan" on the road of big data. The value that big data can provide to a country is unimaginable, and it can even be regarded as a strategic resource in the new era. Nowadays, my country's big data industry has reached the scale of a towering tree under the frantic expansion and expansion. According to research, it can be understood that the industries associated with big data in recent years have touched the extremes of hundreds of billions per year.

Big data is a trend sweeping the world. This trend has different development directions in different countries. After all, the national conditions of each country are different. In China, big data is not as popular as foreign countries, which is why China is not as bold as foreign countries. For pioneers in this industry in our country, there is an urgent shortage of peers, and people's impression of "big data" is basically still at a very basic level. Someone used Google to conduct a simple test. The principle of the test is to investigate the search volume of the term big data at home and abroad. Finally, according to the number of statistics, it is found that the number of foreign searches on this far exceeds that of our country, although it may also be because there are few people using Google in China. But basically it's not a blind person who can find it, but you can find some clues in everyone's environment. For example, how many people around you who only know the term big data? Although the government of our country has taken the lead in setting an example by including big data in the form of the national strategy, it is clear that the civilian population has not even reached the standard of hindsight. Similarly, this also means that at this level, there is still a lot of room for my country to continue to strive for expansion, so this paper's research on big data can bring very rich returns.

3   Big Data Analysis Method

From the analysis of the internal structure of big data, when the scalpel separates its heart, it can be seen that the essence is actually the act of analyzing the data. And the value that it can make people crazy is also precisely the result we need after completing the analysis of the massive data. From this we can basically understand that the exploratory behavior in the field of big data is actually to study the behavior of sorting and summarizing the data, how can this action more quickly and accurately hit the bullseye set by the researcher. Therefore, the expansion of the field of big data, in the absence of data analysis, is simply empty talk of building a castle in the sky. We need to use some analytical methods to obtain useful information from big data.

3.1   Correlation Analysis

Association analysis is one of the current main analysis techniques, and association rules themselves are an important technology in the field of data mining. The most classic application of association analysis is shopping basket analysis in the retail field. In the process of transforming a university library into a personalized service library, association rules can be used to discover the relationship between users' use of documents and find documents that are frequently used at the same time, so as to help the system to inform users when they browse, download, and borrow. Recommend relevant literature. The recommendation algorithm based on association rules first generates association rules based on the literature usage data of all users, and then makes recommendations based on the current user's browsing and consulting behavior. When the user's literature usage data in the system becomes big data, it needs to use big data analysis-oriented Association rule mining algorithm [14].

3.2 Cluster Analysis

Clustering analysis technology reasonably classifies several objects according to certain rules, so that similar objects have a higher similarity, which is of great significance for deviation analysis and classification of clusters. Carry out reasoning based on case, rule and sequence pattern calculation on the structured data of library database. Through data mining and in-depth data processing, the hidden information can be obtained by analyzing the relevance of information, the commonality and characteristics of related data, and can automatically summarize important data models, reveal the system of information resource associations, and deeply analyze readers' needs and potential Knowledge needs, providing precise knowledge needs discovery services.

3.3 Recommendation Algorithm Based on Matrix Factorization

Matrix decomposition refers to decomposing a matrix into the product of two matrices. For the student-book matrix (borrowing matrix) in this article, denoted as R m × n, it can be decomposed into the product of two or more matrices. Assuming that it is decomposed into two matrices Pm × k and Q k × n, we need to make The product of the matrix Pm × k and Q k × n can restore the original matrix R m × n.

$$R^{m \times n} = P_{m \times k} \times Q_{k \times n} \tag{1}$$

Among them, the matrix Pm × k represents the relationship between m types of students and k attributes, and the matrix Q k × n represents the relationship between k attributes and n types of books.

Matrix Factorization Method. 1. The Square of the error between the original borrowing matrix R M × n and the reconstructed borrowing matrix R ^ M × n can be used as the loss function, namely.

$$e_{i,j}^2 = \left(r_{i,j} - r^{i,j} \right)^2 = \left(r_{i,j} - \sum_{k=1}^{k} p_{i,k} q_{k,j} \right)^2 \tag{2}$$

Finally, the minimum value of the sum of the losses of all missing items needs to be solved.

$$Min = \sum_{r_{i,j \neq -}} e_{i,j}^2 \tag{3}$$

2. For the above-mentioned square loss function, it can be solved by gradient descent method. The core steps of gradient descent method are. Step1: Solve the negative gradient of the loss function.

$$\frac{\partial}{\partial p_{i,k}} e_{i,j}^2 = -2 \left(r_{i,j} - \sum_{k=1}^{k} p_{i,k} q_{k,j} \right) q_{k,j} = -2 e_{i,j} q_{k,j} \tag{4}$$

$$\frac{\partial}{\partial p_{i,k}} e_{i,j}^2 = -2 \left(r_{i,j} - \sum_{k=1}^{k} p_{i,k} q_{k,j} \right) p_{i,k} = -2 e_{i,j} p_{i,k} \tag{5}$$

Step2: Update the variable according to the direction of the negative gradient.

$$p_{i,k}' = p_{i,k} - \alpha \frac{\partial}{\partial p_{i,k}} e_{i,j}^2 = p_{i,k} + 2\alpha e_{i,j} q_{k,j} \tag{6}$$

$$q_{k,j}' = q_{k,j} - \alpha \frac{\partial}{\partial q_{k,j}} e_{i,j}^2 = q_{k,j} + 2\alpha e_{i,j} p_{i,k} \tag{7}$$

3. Through continuous iteration, until the algorithm finally converges.

Prediction. Using the above process, we can get the value of each element in the matrix P m × k and Q k × n, so that we can predict the book category j for the Student i.

$$\sum_{k=1}^{k} p_{i,k} q_{k,j} \tag{8}$$

4 Application of Big Data Analysis in University Library

American academic libraries began to use big data analysis technology to guide students' learning and improve library services. Purdue University Library in the United States launched the "Signal Project". Through the analysis and comparison of the information in the student information system and the library management system, it provides special services to those students who use the library for less time. Resources are reclassified and arranged to improve data utilization efficiency. In order to improve the quality of service, Northwestern University Library has also specially developed the "University Library Personalized Service Assistant" system [15], which records in detail each student's study time, study arrangement, study status and study effectiveness and other personal information, And through the analysis of student information, put forward suggestions to improve the library's opening hours and resource allocation, to provide support and help for students' learning progress.

4.1 Data Collection

In the application of big data analysis in university libraries, the collection of readers' borrowing data is a very important part. These data can be unstructured and structured (data expressed and realized logically by a two-dimensional table structure, strictly following the data Format and length specification, mainly through relational database for storage and management). The specific content of the data includes readers' use of library resources, such as electronic resources, paper resources, etc., information retrieval records, Internet browsing records, and interaction records with the library. The collected data must meet the requirements of authenticity, objectivity, etc., because it is the basis for data mining and analysis. Big data data collection can be obtained through real-time data, non-real-time data, and other methods. The current common collection methods mainly include four types of network data collection, database collection, system log collection and other data collection. In this article, we mainly use database collection to collect the corresponding data.

This article mainly uses database collection to collect the corresponding data. This article collects the data of the borrowing records of 36 students in a class in a semester in the database. Among the 36 students, there are 24 females and 12 males. According to their academic performance, they are divided into 3 types of students. Student 1 means 12 students with excellent grades, student 2 means 12 students with medium grades, and student 3 means not grades. How good 12 students. Literary books include novels, essays, classics, literature and history books include biographies of historical figures, academics refer to books related to this professional course, popular books include bestsellers, online novels, etc., and life books include health, health, Books on tourism, education, etc. The 36 students' borrowing of different types of books in a semester is shown in Table 1.

Table 1. Different types of students' borrowing status of different types of books

	Literature	Literature and History	Academic	Popular	Newspapers and magazines	Lifestyle
Student 1	47	23	95	22	0	2
Student 2	24	0	74	23	0	16
Student 3	1	0	22	70	3	0

4.2 Data Processing and Analysis

We have collected data using database collection, but the collected data has the characteristics of massive quantification, repeatability, and high dimensionality. In order to ensure the effectiveness of data mining and in-depth processing, certain technologies and methods need to be used to analyze the collected data. Perform pretreatment. For example, noise data can be smoothed, missing data can be filled, outlier data can be cleaned, etc., which can effectively save later analysis and processing costs and improve processing efficiency. In order to turn complex data into a structure that is easy to process, you can also use a highly reliable, distributed massive log collection, aggregation transmission system such as Flume to achieve the purpose of rapid analysis and processing in the later stage. After processing the data, we can use cluster analysis to classify the data according to certain rules, integrate the same type of data, and clean up some outlier data for the next step, Table 2 It is the result of processing the outlier data.

This article uses a recommendation algorithm based on matrix decomposition as the prediction method. In order to facilitate the calculation, the collected data should be made into a student-book matrix, and the value of each element in the matrix is between 0 and 5. We use some data processing methods to process the collected data and make the results into Table 3, ('-' indicates that the borrowing record is 0).

Table 2. Result of processing outlier data

	Literature	Literature and History	Academic	Popular	Newspapers and magazines	Lifestyle
Student 1	47	23	95	22	0	0
Student 2	24	0	74	23	0	16
Student 3	0	0	22	70	0	0

Table 3. Data processing result table

	Literature	Literature and History	Academic	Popular	Newspapers and magazines	Lifestyle
Student 1	2	1	4	1	–	–
Student 2	1	–	3	1	–	1
Student 3	–	–	1	3	–	–

4.3 Forecast of Data Processing and Analysis Results

Big data analysis can provide effective decision support for managers, so the accuracy must be guaranteed. An effective forecasting method is very necessary. In the above, we have made a student-book matrix from the data processing results, and the matrix decomposition method can effectively make forecasts. The prediction results are shown in Table 4.

Table 4. Forecast results table

	Literature	Literature and History	Academic	Popular	Newspapers and magazines	Lifestyle
Computer science and Technology	1.9973	1.0035	3.9825	1.1230	0.5764	0.0008
Linguistics	0.9940	0.3524	2.7876	0.9923	0.0950	0.9737
E-commerce	0.0895	0.1460	1.1362	3.0047	0.0036	0.1383

As shown in Table 4, we used the matrix factorization algorithm to predict the borrowing value of various types of books by various students. According to the data in the table, we can make such a prediction result: In colleges and universities, most students still use the library as the first way to acquire knowledge. Most students go to the library to borrow books related to their own courses of study, such as academic books. After all, in the university, students still value their own learning very much. They will actively go to the library to find some books related to the professional courses to recharge themselves. Many students will also borrow popular books to spend their free time outside of class and make themselves happy. Some students will also borrow some books of literature and history and literature to cultivate their sentiment and increase their historical knowledge, so that they can become more cultural. Only a few students go to borrow newspapers, magazines and life-related books, such as travel and health books. Due to the rapid popularization of the modern Internet, the knowledge of life is updated very quickly. The speed of acquiring knowledge from the Internet is much faster than from books, and the accuracy rate is also high. Students are accustomed to obtaining this information from the Internet. Therefore, very few students will borrow these kinds of books, because the library resources are updated slowly, and when students see the information from the library, it may be out of date.

4.4 Experimental Verification of Big Data Analysis

In order to judge the accuracy of the prediction made by the matrix factorization algorithm, we sampled a survey of 60 students from 3 majors. Divide 60 students into two groups, one experimental group and one control group. In the experimental group. We recommended to 30 students the literature, popular and academic books with higher scores in the results predicted by the matrix factorization algorithm. In the control group, we recommended books with low scores in the results predicted by the matrix factorization algorithm to 30 students, such as literature and history, newspapers and magazines, and life books. According to the obtained data, the following Tables 5, 6 and 7 are drawn.

Table 5. General list of borrowing survey

	Literature	Popular	Academic	Literature and History	Newspapers and magazines	Lifestyle
Computer science and Technology	12	17	29	7	1	0
linguistics	10	15	22	5	0	0
E-commerce	14	11	20	2	3	2

Table 6. The proportion of borrowing in the experimental group

	Literature	Popular	Academic
Computer science and Technology	18.18%	25.75%	43.93%
Linguistics	19.23%	28.84%	42.30%
E-commerce	26.92%	21.15%	38.46%

From the above table, we can clearly see the result: in the matrix factorization algorithm, the number of times that books with high scores are predicted to be borrowed is

Table 7. Control group borrowing proportion table

	Literature and History	Newspapers and magazines	Lifestyle
Computer science and Technology	10.60%	1.54%	0
Linguistics	9.63%	0	0
E-commerce	3.84%	5.76%	3.84%

much higher than that of books with low scores. In the matrix factorization algorithm, books with low scores are predicted to be borrowed. Very few times, and even many types of books have not been borrowed. From the results of this experiment, we can realize that the prediction of the matrix factorization algorithm is basically accurate, which means that the application of big data analysis in university libraries is feasible.

5   In Conclusion

Data can't speak, we can use some tools to make it "speak". In the final analysis, the meaning or function of big data is to support decision-making through data. Using big data analysis, you can summarize experience, discover patterns, and predict trends. These data can provide auxiliary services for our decision-making through the corresponding data prediction model. The more data and information we have, the more accurate the calculation model, and the more scientific, accurate, and reasonable prediction results generated. On the other hand, although data itself has its meaning and expression, data itself does not generate value. Big data must be combined with other specific fields and industries to have value. There is a large amount of data sleeping in university libraries. We don't usually care about these data, but it contains a lot of valuable information. The application of big data analysis in university libraries can bring great benefits. In the era of big data University libraries should make certain innovations to improve the service quality and efficiency of libraries.

5.1   Personalized Recommendation

For academic libraries, recommendation is a technology that provides students with suggestions to help them select books, papers, patents and other literature and make final decisions. Taking book recommendation as an example, the technical difficulty of recommending popular books is not high, and the user conversion rate is not necessarily ideal, so personalized recommendations are needed. There are many researches on personalized recommendation, and accuracy is an important indicator to measure the recommendation system, and it has received wide attention. But in fact, just considering accuracy is not enough, good recommendation results should also be novel and surprising. For example, a student is ready to borrow "Data Structure", and he will borrow it regardless of whether it is recommended to him or not. The result of recommending "Data Structure" is only to facilitate the student to borrow a book that he originally intended to borrow. Students will find this recommendation result is not new and cannot surprise him. The application of big data analysis in university libraries can analyze the student's reading interest and reading preference based on the student's borrowing information in the library, and even predict the student's reading interest from the trend of the student's borrowing books. Offset, recommending books to students on this basis can effectively make students feel surprised and attract more students to the library. A good personalized recommendation service for university libraries should not only accurately predict student behavior, but also expand users' horizons and help students discover documents that they might be interested in but not so easy to find.

5.2 Personalized Search

Retrieval has precise retrieval and fuzzy retrieval. Take book retrieval as an example. In precise retrieval, users clearly know the book information they need. However, this is not the case in fuzzy search. The user does not know exactly the name of the book and other information, and may just want to find out some useful information for him. Retrieval, like recommendation, is a tool for users to find information. This determines that the data to be processed for retrieval and recommendation and the information returned to users are often homogeneous, but they also have obvious differences. If it is said that a recommendation needs to satisfy the user's desire for "novelty" to some extent, the search requires precision. For example, if you enter "computer" when searching, you need to determine whether the user needs computer professional books or non-computer professional books about computer applications and operations. In addition to the accuracy requirements, the search also needs to consider optimizing the ranking of search results. For example, "data structure" is the core course of computer science, and there are many teaching materials. Enter "data structure" when searching, and the returned search results can be sorted differently for different users. For teachers, you can put advanced textbooks and English textbooks in front; for students who are just starting to learn the course, put introductory textbooks in front. The advanced retrieval applications of university digital libraries under the big data environment also need to be personalized to further improve the accuracy of retrieval results and the rationality of retrieval results ranking. Since retrieval requires more precision than recommendation, retrieval requires more accurate personalization.

5.3 Decision Support

Many fields can use big data to improve management and decision-making. The rapid development of big data affects all walks of life. In the era of big data, the application of big data analysis in university libraries can effectively use library data to analyze the reading hobbies and reading habits of students of different majors, and then use diagrams or text to make it clear to managers See what types of books are borrowed the most, what types of books are borrowed less, and what types of books are rarely borrowed. Library administrators can use these data to effectively understand the reading habits and reading hobbies of most students, and then plan to adjust the types of books purchased according to the reading hobbies of students. For example, you can buy more books related to courses. Introduce some, and those books that almost no one borrows, such as newspapers, magazines and life books, can be bought less or not. The application of big data analysis in the library can realize the reasonable distribution of library resources, reduce unnecessary waste of resources, optimize the types of books in the library, realize the sustainable development of the library, and further improve the library's big data service Quality, provide students with efficient, personalized and convenient services, and realize the transformation and upgrading from a traditional library to a smart library.

Acknowledgement. This work was supported in part by the National Natural Science Foundation of China, grant number 72073041. Open Foundation for the University Innovation Platform in the Hunan Province, grant number 18K103.2011 Collaborative Innovation Center for Development and Utilization of Finance and Economics Big Data Property.

Hunan Provincial Key Laboratory of Finance&Economics Big Data Science and Technology.2020 Hunan Provincial Higher Education Teaching Reform Research Project under Grant HNJG-2020–1130, HNJG-2020–1124. 2020 General Project of Hunan Social Science Fund under Grant 20B16.

Scientific Research Project of Education Department of Hunan Province (Grand No. 20K021), Social Science Foundation of Hunan Province (Grant No. 17YBA049).

References

1. Li, Y., Yu, P., Li, L.: Research on the knowledge service system of university libraries under the "big data + micro service" model. Library Theory and Practice **3**, 99–103 (2017)
2. Song, Y.: Research on the smart service of general engineering college libraries under the big data environment. J. Agricult. Libr. Inf. Sci. **1**, 55–158 (2017)
3. He, F., He, K.Q.: Discussion on big data and its scientific problems and methods. J. Wuhan Univ. (Sci. Ed.) **1**, 1–12 (2014)
4. Dong, Y.: Design of big data analysis system for readers' demand information in university library. Libr. Work Res. **2**, 56–59 (2017)
5. Yang, Z., Xu, L.: Research on my country's personal information protection legislation in the big data era. J. Nanjing Univ. Posts Telecommun. (Nat. Sci. Ed.) **36**(2), 1–9 (2016)
6. Bi, W.J.: Talking about data mining in the era of big data. Consum. Electr. **8**, 163 (2014)
7. Shu, P.: "More wins, less wins"——Speaking from the big data engine released by Baidu. Shanghai Quality, 5 (2014)
8. He, T.: Big data and university library innovation service. Anhui Xinhua Univ. Libr. **029**, 006 (2017)
9. Tom, K.: Big Data Is a Big Deal[EB /OL].2014. http://www.whitehouse.gov/blog/2012/03/29/big-data-big-deal
10. Executive O OTP. Big Data Across the Fedral Government [EB/OL] (2014). http://www.whitehouse.gov/sites/default/files/microsites/ostp/big_data_fact_sheet_final_1.pdf
11. Liu, Q.: American experience and inspiration in the era of big data. People's Forum **15**, 30–31 (2013)
12. Jin, Y.P.: Internet + era: cultural and technological innovation-new features of creativity. Jiangsu Soc. Sci. **2**, 250–256 (2016)
13. Ding, J.F.: Opportunities and challenges in the big data era. China Econ. Trade **6**, 53–54 (2013)
14. Liu, Y.J., He, S., Feng, X.L., Wu, Q.H., Xiong, T.C., et al.: Research on the application of big data mining in the personalized service of university library. Library Work Res. **5**, 23–29 (2017)

15. Siemens, G., Long, P.: Penetrating the fog: analytics inlearning and education. Educause Rev. **5**, 30–32 (2011)
16. Xiang, L., Yang, S., Liu, Y., Li, Q., Zhu, C.: Novel linguistic steganography based on character-level text generation. Mathematics **8**, 1558 (2020)
17. Xiang, L., Guo, G., Li, Q., Zhu, C., Chen, J., et al.: Spam detection in reviews using lstm-based multientity temporal features. Intell. Autom. Soft Comput. **26**(6), 1375–1390 (2020)
18. Yang, Z., Zhang, S., Hu, Y., Hu, Z., Huang, Y.: VAE-Stega: linguistic steganography based on variational auto-encoder. IEEE Trans. Inf. Forensics Secur. **16**, 880–895 (2021)

Research on Support Vector Machine in Traffic Detection Algorithm

Renjie Zhang[1], JinYang Huang[2], YaXin Yan[2], and Ying Gao[2(✉)]

[1] Hunan Post and Telecommunication College Network Center, Changsha 410015, China
[2] Hunan University of Finance and Economics, Changsha 410205, China

Abstract. In order to reduce the impact of traffic incidents on traffic operation, an Automated Traffic Incidents Detection (SVM-AID) algorithm based on Support Vector Machine (SVM) is proposed. This algorithm is of great significance for improving the efficiency of traffic management and improving the effect of traffic management. This article first introduces the background of the topic selection of the Traffic Incidents Detection algorithm, the research status at home and abroad. Then it focuses on the Optimal Separating Hyperplane, linear separable SVM, linear inseparable SVM, nonlinear separable SVM, and commonly used kernel functions. Then, the design flow chart based on the SVM-AID algorithm is given, and the principle component analysis method, Normalization Method and the selection method of Support Vector Machine parameters are introduced. Finally, using the processed data, 4 experiments were designed to test the classification performance of the SVM-AID algorithm, and the influence of each parameter in the SVM on the classification effect was analyzed. The results of the final experiment also showed us the design The effectiveness of the SVM-AID algorithm.

Keywords: Traffic Incidents Detection · Support Vector Machine · Kernel Function

1 Introduction

Since the world's first highway was completed and opened to traffic in the 1930s, countries around the world have vigorously implemented highway planning and construction. By the end of 2006, the total journey of highways in my country had reached 45,300 km [1]. Expressways can not only promote economic growth and social development, but also bring huge economic and social benefits [2]. However, with the rapid development of expressways, some problems have emerged in traffic operation and handling. With the continuous increase of traffic flow, the frequency of congestion and traffic accidents is also increasing, and the impact of the composition is also increasing [3]. In order to reduce the negative impact of traffic accidents on the operation of expressways, research on Traffic Incidents Detection algorithms, rapid detection of traffic incidents, recognition and recognition of the scene, and the use of traffic flow guidance, can effectively reduce the impact of traffic incidents on traffic incidents [4].

© Springer Nature Switzerland AG 2021
X. Sun et al. (Eds.): ICAIS 2021, CCIS 1423, pp. 224–237, 2021.
https://doi.org/10.1007/978-3-030-78618-2_18

2   Related Works

Expressway incident detection is the key and center of the expressway traffic processing system, so the research on incident detection has impressive results [3, 5, 6]. First, we compare the traffic parameter data between neighboring stations to identify possible sudden traffic accidents [6].

In 1990, based on the catastrophe theory Prasuet et al. developed the McMeST algorithm. The algorithm uses multiple non-crowded and congested traffic data to establish a template of the distribution relationship between traffic and occupancy [6].

In 1995, CHEU and others developed an algorithm based on a multi-layer feedforward network (MLF), which is composed of three layers of input layer, center layer and output layer [6].

In recent years, with the increase in scientific research funds invested in this area, some experts and scholars in the transportation field have proposed Traffic Incidents Detection algorithms. The domestic research on the AID algorithm mainly converges on the application of new theories and new technologies, including wavelet transformation, BP network, SVM, etc. [7, 8].

Li Wenjiang and Jing Bian proposed an incident detection algorithm based on wavelet analysis: logic judgment to determine whether there is a traffic incident is the basic idea of this method [9].

Lv Qi and Wang Hui proposed a traffic detection algorithm based on dynamic BP network. The algorithm learns the training algorithm of the static BP network, and improves the shortcomings of the static BP network training algorithm that the convergence speed is slow [10].

Liang Xinrong and Liu Zhiyong proposed a SVM algorithm based on the principle of structural risk minimization. According to the different reasons for the traffic flow parameters of traffic operation and non-traffic work, the input samples of the whole algorithm added to the algorithm [11].

3   First Section

In 1993, Vapnik et al. developed a new trainable machine learning method-Support Vector Machine (SVM) theory. It is a model based on statistical learning theory, maximum classification principle and structural risk minimization principle. Support Vector Machine algorithm has good generalization ability and is very suitable for dealing with limited small sample problems in pattern recognition and regression analysis [1–5].

3.1   Description of Classification Problem

Consider such a classification problem: The set of sample sets contain l sample points is:

$$T = \{(x1, y1), \ldots (xl, yl)\} \in (X \times Y)^l \tag{1}$$

Where the input index vector is $x_i \in X = R^n$. The output is $y_i \in Y = \{+1, -1\}$, i = 1, 2, ..., l. The training sample is a collection of these l sample points. So for a given new input x, how to infer whether its output is +1 or −1 according to the training set.

The classification problem is described in mathematical language as follows:

For a given training sample, where T = {(x1, y1), ... (xl, yl)} ∈ $(X \times Y)^l$, among them $x_i \in X = R^n$, $y_i \in Y = \{+1, -1\}$, $i = 1, 2, ..., l$. Find a real-valued function g(x) on X = Rn. It can be seen from the above that finding a rule that can divide the point of Rn into two parts is the essence of solving the classification problem.

The above two types of classification problems are called classification learning machines. Because when g(x) is different, the decision function f(x) = Sgn((x)) will also be different.

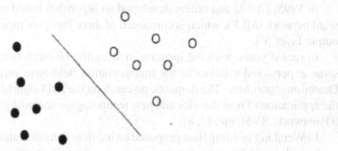

Fig. 1. Linearly separable problem.

As shown in Fig. 1, the linearly separable problem is a classification problem that can easily separate two types of training samples with a straight line.

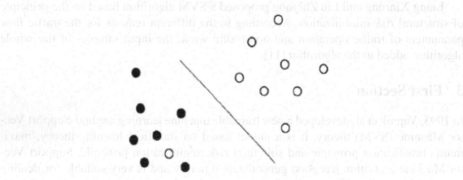

Fig. 2. Linear inseparable problem

As shown in Fig. 2, the linear inseparability problem is a classification problem that roughly separates the training samples with a straight line.

As shown in Fig. 3, the non-linear separable problem is a classification problem that will produce large errors when divided by a straight line. The Support Vector Machines corresponding to the above three classification problems are linear separable Support Vector Machines, linear inseparable Support Vector Machines and nonlinear separable Support Vector Machines.

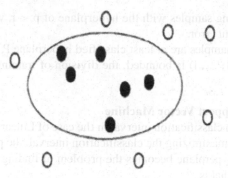

Fig. 3. Nonlinear separable problem

3.2 Linear Separable Support Vector Machine

Optimal Separating Hyperplane

In the two-dimensional linear separable situation shown in Fig. 4, the solid point and the hollow point are used to represent the two types of training samples. The classification line that completely separates the two types of samples is H_0, the normal vector of the classification line for w. First, suppose that the normal direction w of the optimal classification line H_0 has been determined. At this time, the optimal classification line H_0 is moved up and down in parallel until it touches a certain type of sample. The line between H1 and H−1 is the best classification line among these candidate classification lines.(W • X) + b = −1 is the normalized representation of the line H1; (W · X) + b = −1 is the normalized representation of the line H−1. The distance between the two classification boundary lines is $2/\|w\|$. as mentioned above, the normal direction w with the largest distance between H1 and H−1 is obtained.

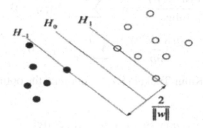

Fig. 4. The best classification surface

It can be seen from Fig. 4 that individual samples determine the maximum classification interval. The samples that happen to fall on the two classification boundary lines H_1 and H_{-1} are called support vectors. Next, analyze why Support Vector Machines use the principle of maximizing classification interval:

For any training sample (x, y), the form of the test sample is $(x + \Delta_{x}, y)$, where the norm of perturbation $\Delta_x \in H$ is upper bounded by a positive number. If we use an interval as To divide the training samples with the hyperplane of p < r, we should separate all the test samples without error.

Since all training samples are at least classified hyperplane P, and the length of any input sample xi (i = 1, ..., l) is bounded, the division of training samples will not be changed.

Linear Separable Support Vector Machine

$2/\|w\|$ is the maximum classification interval in the case of Linear Separability. According to the principle of maximizing the classification interval, the problem of finding the Optimal Separating Hyperplane becomes the problem of finding the minimum normal direction w. $1/2 \|w\|^2$, that is:

$$\begin{cases} (w \cdot X_i) + b \leq -1 y_i = -1 \\ (w \cdot X_i) + b \geq 1 y_i = 1 \end{cases} \tag{2}$$

Combining the (2), we can get $y_i(w \bullet x) + b) \geq 1$. The Optimal Separating Hyperplane constructed in the case of Linear Separability is transformed into the following quadratic programming problem:

$$\begin{cases} s.t. y_i((w \cdot x) + b) \geq -1 \\ \min_{w,b} \frac{1}{2}(w \cdot w) \end{cases} \tag{3}$$

The original problem of solving the Optimal Separating Hyperplane. Duality theory converts the original problem of solving the Optimal Separating Hyperplane into a dual space into a dual problem solution. Define the Lagrange function as:

$$L(w, b, a) = \frac{1}{2}(w \cdot w) - \sum_{i=1}^{l} a_i [y_i(w \cdot x_i) + b) - 1], a_i \geq 0 \tag{4}$$

$$\frac{\partial(w, b, a)}{\partial w} = w - \sum_{i=1}^{l} a_i y_i x_i = 0 \tag{5}$$

$$\frac{\partial(w, b, a)}{\partial b} = \sum_{i=1}^{l} a_i y_i = 0 \tag{6}$$

According to the Karush-Kuhn-Tucker (KKT) theorem, the optimal solution should also satisfy:

$$a_i(y_i(w \cdot x + b) - 1) \geq 0 \forall i \tag{7}$$

From Eq. (7) can see that the coefficient a_i is required to be non-zero, so w can be expressed as:

$$w = \sum_{SV} a_i y_i x_i \tag{8}$$

Substituting Eqs. (6) and (5) into Eq. (4), we get:

$$L(w*, b*, a) = \sum_{i=1}^{l} a_i - \frac{1}{2}\|w*\|^2 = \sum_{i=1}^{l} a_i - \frac{1}{2}\sum_{i=1}^{l}\sum_{j=1}^{l} a_i a_j y_i y_i (x_i \cdot x_j) \tag{9}$$

The optimization problem of Eq. (3) is transformed into a dual space, becomes a dual problem.

$$\max L(a) = \sum_{i=1}^{l} a_i - \frac{1}{2} \sum_{i=1}^{l} \sum_{j=1}^{l} a_i a_j y_i y_i (x_i \cdot x_j)$$

$$\text{s.t. } a_i \geq 0, i = 1, 2, \ldots, l$$

$$\sum_{i=1}^{l} a_i y_i = 0 \tag{10}$$

If the coefficient a_i* of the support vector is the optimal solution, then

$$w^* = \sum_{i=1}^{l} a_i * y_i x_i \tag{11}$$

For any given test sample x, select the non-zero support vector coefficient ai*, substitute it into Eq. (7) to obtain b*, and then use the obtained ai*, b*, training sample xi, training result y_i and The test sample x is put into the Eq. (12).

$$f(x) = \text{sgn}[\sum a_i * y_i (x_i \cdot x) + b^*] \tag{12}$$

3.3 Linear Inseparable Support Vector Machine

The basic idea of the Linear Non-Separability Support Vector Machine problem is to introduce a non-linear transformation $\phi(x)$, so that the input space Rn can be mapped to a high-dimensional feature space: $\tilde{z}: X \subseteq Rn \xrightarrow{\phi(X)} Z \subseteq \tilde{z}$. Then find the high-dimensional feature space as shown in Fig. 5.

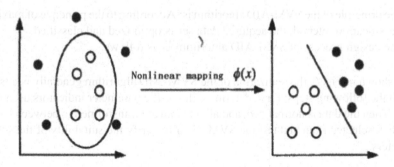

Fig. 5. Shows the nonlinear mapping

The method of obtaining the Optimal Separating Hyperplane of nonlinear separable Support Vector Machine. The Kernel functions mainly used for classification problem processing are:

(1) Polynomial function Kernel function

$$K(x, x_i) = [< x \cdot x_i > +1]^q \tag{13}$$

(2) Gaussian Radial Basis Kernel function

$$K(x, x_i) = \exp(-\frac{||x - x_i||}{6^2}) \tag{14}$$

(3) Tangent Hyperbolic Kernell function

$$K(x, x_i) = \tanh[v < x \cdot x_i > +c] \tag{15}$$

Because the final result is determined by a small number of support vectors, we can "reject" a large number of redundant samples by grabbing these key samples. It has better "robustness" [6].

4 Design of Event Detection Algorithm Based on SVM

Based on the principle of traffic accident detection and support vector machine theory introduced in the previous chapter, the event detection algorithm based on SVM is designed to detect the occurrence of traffic events.

4.1 The Principle and Design Process of SVM-AID Algorithm

(1) The principle of the SVM-AID algorithm is: According to the principle of maximum classification interval, the acquired data set is optimized and classified.
(2) The design process of SVM-AID algorithm is as follows:

As shown in Fig. 6, the realization of the SVM-AID algorithm generally needs to go through the following steps: First, determine the traffic parameter indicators used in this design. Then the data is normalized, and all the data are transformed to between $[-1, 1]$. After that, selected train and test the SVM. Finally verify the suitability of the selected parameters.

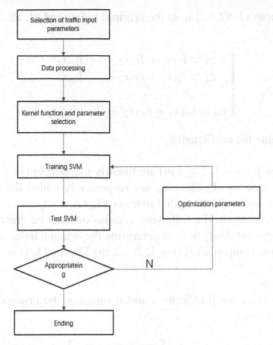

Fig. 6. Design steps of SVM-based event detection algorithm

4.2 Traffic Parameter Selection

Because if you choose all the multiple related indicators of each traffic sample, it will greatly increase the complexity of the analysis problem. Consider whether you can use a few new indicators to replace the original indicators based on this relationship between the variable indicators.

Principal Component Analysis

(1) Basic concepts: The Principal Component Analysis method replaces the original indicators with a few independent indicators to reflect the information to be presented.
(2) Basic principles: Suppose there are p indicators and n samples to construct an n × p order matrix.

$$X = \begin{bmatrix} x_{11} & x_{12} & \cdots & x_{1p} \\ x_{21} & x_{22} & \cdots & x_{2p} \\ \vdots & \vdots & \vdots & \vdots \\ x_{n1} & x_{n2} & \cdots & x_{np} \end{bmatrix} \qquad (16)$$

Definition: denote $x1, x2, \ldots, x_p$ as the original index, and $z1, z2, \ldots, z_m$ ($m \le p$) as the new index.

$$\begin{cases} z_1 = l_{11}x_1 + l_{12}x_2 + \cdots l_{1p}x_p \\ z_2 = l_{21}x_1 + l_{22}x_2 + \cdots l_{2p}x_p \\ \quad\quad \ldots\ldots \\ z_m = l_{m1}x_1 + l_{m2}x_2 + \cdots + l_{mp}x_p \end{cases} \tag{17}$$

How to determine the coefficient l_{ij}:

1) 1) z_i and z_j ($i \ne j$; $i, j = 1, 2, \ldots, m$) are linearly independent of each other;
   Then the new indexes $z1, z2\ldots, z_m$ are respectively called the first, second, ..., principal components of the original indexes $x1, x2, \ldots, x_p$.
   From the above analysis, the following conclusions can be drawn: the essence of Principal Component Analysis is to determine the original index x_j ($j = 1, 2, \ldots, p$) on each principal component z_i ($i = 1, 2, \ldots, m$) The load l_{ij} ($i = 1, 2, \ldots, m; j = 1, 2, \ldots, p$).
2) Calculation steps.
   Assuming that there are p indicators and n samples, the original data becomes a matrix of n × p order.

$$X = \begin{bmatrix} x_{11} & x_{12} & \cdots & x_{1p} \\ x_{21} & x_{22} & \cdots & x_{2p} \\ \vdots & \vdots & \vdots & \vdots \\ x_{n1} & x_{n2} & \cdots & x_{np} \end{bmatrix} \tag{18}$$

3) Standardize raw data. Use the standardized matrix to find the correlation coefficient matrix.

$$r_{ij} = \frac{\sum_{k=1}^{n}(X_{ki} - \bar{X}_i)(X_k - \bar{X}_j)}{\sqrt{\sum_{k=1}^{n}(X_{ki} - \bar{X}_i)^2}\sqrt{\sum_{k=1}^{n}(X_{kj} - \bar{X}_j)^2}} \tag{19}$$

$$R = (r_{ij})_{p \times p} \tag{20}$$

4) Use the correlation coefficient matrix to obtain the characteristic root and the corresponding characteristic vector.

$$\lambda_1 \ge \lambda_2 \ge \cdots \ge \lambda_p > 0 \tag{21}$$

$$a_1 = \begin{bmatrix} a_{11} \\ \vdots \\ a_{p1} \end{bmatrix}, a_2 = \begin{bmatrix} a_{12} \\ \vdots \\ a_{p2} \end{bmatrix}, \ldots, a_p = \begin{bmatrix} a_{1p} \\ \vdots \\ a_{pp} \end{bmatrix} \tag{22}$$

5) Calculate the contribution rate and cumulative contribution rate of the principal components.

Contribution rate.

$$\frac{\lambda_i}{\sum_{i=1}^{p} \lambda_k} i = 1, 2, \ldots, p \tag{23}$$

Cumulative contribution rate

$$\frac{\sum_{k=1}^{i} \lambda_k}{\sum_{i=1}^{p} \lambda_k} i = 1, 2, \ldots, p \tag{24}$$

The index corresponding to the characteristic value whose cumulative contribution rate exceeds 85% is the 1..., mth (m ≤ p) principal components.

Acquisition and Discrimination of Traffic Input Data
This paper is determined by analyzing the experimental results. After that, the samples are divided based on the critical crowding density km.

Selection of Training Samples and Test Samples
The downstream the flow and density measured at the detection station t, t−1, t−2 are compared with the flow and density measured at the upstream detection station t−2, t−3, t−4. When selecting training samples, several sets of data can be selected from the data as the design test samples [7].

4.3 Choice of Model and Kernel Function

Selection of Kernel Function. The most commonly used Kernel functions for SVM are Polynomial kernel functions and The Radial Basis Kernel function is selected in the SVM-AID experiment, and its form is as follows:

$$K(x, x_i) = \exp(-\frac{\|x - x_i\|}{\sigma^2}) \tag{25}$$

Selection of Penalty Coefficient C and δ core width. In the SVM algorithm, We use one of the fixed Penalty Coefficient C or the kernel δ width and change the other to detect the same set of data.

4.4 Algorithm Simulation and Result Analysis

Simulation experiment 1-Use Principal Component Analysis to Select Input Traffic Flow Parameters. In the traffic database, 350 sets of samples whose attributes are density, flow, and speed are selected. The experimental results are as follows:

Table 1. Results of simulation experiment 1.

Main ingredient	Contribution rate	Cumulative contribution rate
1	0.74828	0.74828
2	0.24927	0.99755
3	0.0024474	0.9999974

He principal components 1, 2, and 3 in Table 1 above correspond to the three variable indicators of density, flow, and speed respectively. In the following simulation experiments, two indicators of density and flow are used to detect traffic incidents.

Simulation Experiment 2-With or Without Normalization Control Experiment.
The Normalization Method is used to process them to reduce the data span. Two sets of data are selected, one set of data is normalized, and the other set of data is not processed. Results are as follows:

Table 2. Results of simulation experiment 2.

Category	Event detection rate	False picking rate	Classification accuracy	Detection time (s)
Normalized	100%	7.2%	92.8%	1.031
No normalization	5.6%	12.7%	87.3%	1.141

By analyzing Table 2, the following conclusions can be drawn:(1) Normalization is faster than no normalization, processing data faster and saving time. (2) By adjusting the non-uniform data scale to $[-1, 1]$. (3) Normalization speeds up the convergence when the program is running.

Simulation Experiment 3-Choice of Penalty Coefficient C and δ Core Width.
Because of the selection of different Penalty Coefficients or core widths, the performance indicators of the algorithm will all be affected. Therefore, the following two experiments are designed to select the Penalty Coefficient and the kernel width. The experimental results are as follows:

It can be analyzed from Table 3 and Fig. 6, so C = 300 is selected in SVM-AID. The experimental results are as follows:

Table 3. Experimental results of fixed δ transformation C.

C value	Classification accuracy	Detection time (s)
0	100%	0.7298
100	95%	0.329
150	94.4%	0.345
200	93.5%	0.356
300	93.2%	0.361
400	93.2%	0.367
500	93.2%	0.372

Table 4. Experimental results of fixed C transformation $\delta.\delta$ value

δ value	Classification accuracy	Detection time (s)
0.5	15%	0.312
1	38%	0.313
2	59%	0.328
3	71%	0.339
4	85%	0.348
5	93.2%	0.355
6	95%	0.336
7	95.2	0.36

It can be analyzed from Table 4, as the kernel δ width increases, the average detection time will continue to grow. When the δ value reaches 6, the classification accuracy rate does not increase significantly, and the detection time is still increasing. Therefore, select $\delta = 6$ in SVM-AID.

Simulation Experiment 4–4 Road Sections Are Tested with Selected Parameters.
Choose 4 sets of data from different road sections, each set of data consists of 30 sets of training data and 361 sets of test data. The experimental results are as follows:

Table 5. Results of simulation experiment 4.

Road section	Event detection rate	False detection rate	Classification accuracy
N_1	100%	6.8%	93.18%
N_2	98.68%	2.5%	97.5%
S_1	100%	15.2%	84.8%
S_2	100%	0	100%

It can be seen from Table 5 that the event detection rate is as high as 98%. By comparing the results of 4 road sections, it can be seen that the classification accuracy rate is slightly less than the event detection rate.

5 Summary

This article first analyzes the digs deep into the characteristics of expressway traffic flow under traffic incident conditions. Afterwards, using Support Vector Machine theory, a Traffic Incidents Detection algorithm based on Support Vector Machine was proposed. Then the traffic flow parameters, Penalty Coefficients and kernel width of the SVM-AID algorithm are determined through multiple experiments, and the influence of each parameter in the SVM algorithm on the identification of traffic incidents is analyzed, and the suitability of the selected parameters is verified.

Acknowledgements. This work was supported in part by the National Natural Science Foundation of China, grant number 72073041. Open Foundation for the University Innovation Platform in the Hunan Province, grant number 18K103.2011 Collaborative Innovation Center for Development and Utilization of Finance and Economics Big Data Property.

Hunan Provincial Key Laboratory of Finance & Economics Big Data Science and Technology. 2020 Hunan Provincial Higher Education Teaching Reform Research Project under Grant HNJG-2020–1130, HNJG-2020–1124.2020 General Project of Hunan Social Science Fund under Grant 20B16.

Scientific Research Project of Education Department of Hunan Province (Grand No. 20K021), Social Science Foundation of Hunan Province (Grant No. 17YBA049).

References

1. Jiang, D.Y.: Freeway incident automatic detection system and algorithm design. J. Transp. Eng. **1**(1), 77–81 (2001)
2. Liu, W.M.: Highway System Control Method. China Communications Press, Beijing (1998)
3. Zhang, L.C., Xia, L.M., Shi, H.W.: Highway event detection based on fuzzy clustering support vector machine. Comput. Eng. Appl. **243**(17), 208–229 (2006)
4. Dai, L.L., Han, G.H., Jiang, J.Y.: An Overview of road detection event algorithms. Int. Intell. Transpo. (2005)
5. Tan, G.L., Jiang, Z.F.: Discussion on automatic detection algorithm for expressway accidents. J. Xi'an Jiao Tong Univ,**19**(3),55–57.70 (1990)

6. Jiang, G.Y.: Road Traffic State Discrimination technology and Application. China Communications Press, Beijing (2004)
7. Jiang, Z.F., Jiang, B.S., Han, X.L.: Simulation study on on-ramp control of expressway. China Journal of Highway and Transport, Beijing, pp.83–89 (1997)
8. Teng, Z.S: Intelligent detection System and data Fusion. China Machine Press, Beijing (2000)
9. Li, W.J., Jing, F.S.: Event detection algorithm based on wavelet analysis. J. Xi'an Highway Univ. **17**(28), 134–138 (1997)
10. Lu, Q., Wang, H.: Traffic event detection algorithm based on dynamic neural network model. J. Xi'an Highway Univ. **20**(6), 105–108 (2003)
11. Zhou, L.Y.: Expressway event Detection Algorithm based on Support Vector Machine. Master's Thesis of Chang' a University (2009)
12. Wen, H.M., Yang, Z.S.: Research on the progress of traffic incident detection technology. Traffic Transp. Syst. Eng. Inf. **5**(1), 25–28 (2006)
13. Zhao, X.M., Jin, Y.L., Zhang, Y.: Theory and Application of Highway Monitoring System. Publishing House of Electronics Industry Press, Beijing (2003)
14. Shi, Z.K., Huang, H.X., Qu, S.R., Chen, X.F.: Introduction to Traffic Control System. Science Press, Beijing (2003)
15. Tian, Q.F.: Research on intelligent Algorithm for Traffic Incident Detection on Urban Expressway. Master's Thesis of Beijing University of Technology (2010)

Application Research on Crop Straw Biomass Waste in Logistics Packaging System

P. H. Wei[1], R. H. Xie[1], L. Fu[1], Y. J. Zheng[1,2], and H. Zhao[1,2(✉)]

[1] School of Light Industry and Textile, Qiqihar University, Qiqihar 161006, China
[2] Flax Processing Technology Engineering Center of Ministry of Education,
Qiqihar 161006, China

Abstract. A lightweight buffer protection material was prepared by compounding crop straw biomass waste with secondary fiber, which was used for transportation and packaging applications. By selecting different kinds of crop straws and changing the proportion, the material performance test results show that the system has good buffer performance. Under the same content, the mechanical properties of straw and secondary fiber composite buffer material are better than that of industrial hemp stalk core material. Under the same filling conditions, crop straw/secondary fiber composites have good cushioning and protection performance. This study is of great significance for exploring the application of crop straw/secondary fiber buffer protection materials in logistics and transportation, and developing new environmental protection packaging materials for replacing foam plastic products with biomass wastes, providing reference for the application of logistics and transportation industry.

Keywords: Resources · Environment · Biomass · Crops · Packing for transport

1 Introduction

With people's attention to the environment, new eco-environmental materials have become the focus of the world's attention [1–3]. It is of great significance to make use of waste renewable biological resources to prepare high-performance new materials and gradually reduce the consumption of non-renewable resources. Biomass waste is an important way to solve the shortage of energy, materials and chemicals in the post-fossil era [4]. Biomass-based fiber has good natural degradability, resource regeneration and environmental coordination, and China is a big agricultural country with abundant biomass resources and poor utilization effect. For example, corn, rice, wheat straw, soybean and other straws are burned, pineapple leaves, banana fruit shafts and other biomass by-products rot, which not only wastes biomass resources, but also causes great damage to the environment [5–8]. There is a huge amount of lignocellulosic biomass in China, and the annual output of straw biomass alone exceeds several hundred million tons, which is the main raw material in papermaking, chemical industry, textile and bioenergy industries [9–11]. Traditional biomass single component is directly converted and

X. Sun et al. (Eds.): ICAIS 2021, CCIS 1423, pp. 238–250, 2021.
https://doi.org/10.1007/978-3-030-78618-2_19

utilized, which has the disadvantages of serious waste of resources, low added value of products and severe environmental pollution [12].

At present, the cushioning packaging materials used at home and abroad are mainly foamed plastics, corrugated cardboard, honeycomb cardboard, molded products, bubble films, fibers, crumb materials, rubber and so on [13–15]. In terms of choosing cushioning packaging materials, a green environmental protection revolution is emerging, and taking degradable materials as the main packaging materials has become the mainstream of sustainable development of packaging in the world [16]. In this paper, crop straw/secondary fiber was used to prepare composite materials with buffer protection performance to solve the technical problems such as single resource utilization of biomass, serious waste of raw materials, serious environmental pollution and so on.

2 Experimental Part

2.1 Experimental Materials

Waste paper pulp, gelatin (biochemical reagent), corn starch (in accordance with GB/T8885-1988), carboxymethyl cellulose (industrial grade), foaming agent (ether, chemically pure), release agent (talcum powder, chemically pure); corn straw and hemp stalk core.

2.2 Instruments and Equipment

Dutch beating machine, electronic balance, GBJ-A fiber standard dissociator, ZT6-00 sheet reader, rat glass reactor, 101-0A electric blast drying oven, DV - II rotary viscometer, DB-KY50 carton compression testing machine, screen, self-made mold. HITACHI S-4300 scanning electron microscope, SmartLab X-ray diffractometer, differential scanning calorimeter, Spotlight 400 infrared/near-infrared chemical imaging system of PE company in the United States, STA 449 F3 Jupiter synchronous thermal analyzer.

2.3 Experimental Pretreatment

Raw material pretreatment Soak the waste paper for swelling, pour it into the blender, add water to the pulp consistency (mass fraction) of 5%–8%, and dissolve. Before the test, the waste pulp was treated with fiber according to GB/t10336–2002.

Pretreatment of Fillers Pretreatment of Hemp Stalk Core. The hemp stalk core is roughly crushed with a special crusher, the core part is transferred to 15% acetic acid solution for 24 h, washed and dried in the oven for 6h, and then finely crushed by the crusher. The hemp stalk core fiber of 40–60 mesh is screened out by screen mesh for standby.

Corn Straw Pretreatment. The corn straw is crushed with a crusher, and 40–60 mesh corn straw fiber is screened through the screen, and then decomposed and fermented with biological agents. After the fermentation is completed, it is washed with tap water and dried in the oven for standby.

Adhesive Pretreatment. Weigh a certain amount of corn starch, dissolve it in warm water solution with mass ratio of 1:2, and mix evenly. Transfer it into a round bottom flask, put it on a heat collecting magnetic stirrer, add magnetite, control the temperature at 75 °C and control the speed of 10 rad/s, and heat until the starch solution is sticky and transparent.

Weigh a certain mass of carboxymethyl cellulose, add water solution with mass ratio of 1:15, mix evenly, and let stand for 20 min.

The CMC solution and the paste starch were mixed evenly, the additives were added, and the mixture was kept at a constant temperature.

Sample environment pretreatment before the experiment, the sample environment was treated with temperature and humidity according to GB/t4857.2-2005, and the sample quality was basically constant [17–19].

2.4 Preparation of Buffer Material

Take a certain amount of size, in the pulp concentration (mass fraction) of 5–8% for 20 min, and in the physical turbulence, mechanical stirring conditions, successively add adhesives (carboxymethyl cellulose, gelatinized starch, gelatin), foaming agent (SDS), biomass filler, release agent, test AIDS. After mixing evenly, it was transferred to the self-made mold, put into the 120 °C electric constant temperature blast drying oven, dried for 6–8 h, and then the foam body was obtained(Fig. 1).

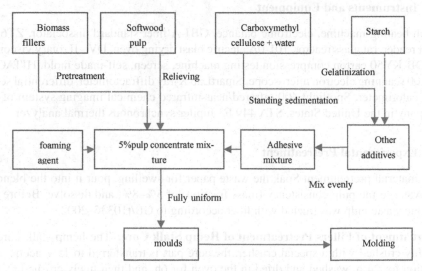

Fig. 1. Flow chart of molding process of foaming buffer material

2.5 Experimental Design of Different Fillers

The results showed that the total amount of waste pulp and filler was 30 g, the mass fraction of foaming agent was 0.05%, the mass fraction of adhesive was 2%, and the mass fraction of release agent was 1.5%. The comparative experimental method was used to analyze the effects of different fillers and proportions on the properties of foam cushioning materials with the buffer coefficient maximum stress curve, resilience and density as the optimization objective parameters.

3 Determination of Foam Properties

3.1 Determination of Buffer Coefficient

According to GB/t8168-2008 standard, the static compression test was carried out on the prepared buffer material, and the corresponding stress-strain curve, buffer coefficient maximum stress curve were obtained, and the influence of waste pulp, different proportion and different fillers on the compressive properties of cushioning materials was discussed.

3.2 Determination of Resilience

A certain amount of load was applied to the thickness direction of the foam body. When the strain reached half of the value, the shape remained unchanged and the loading lasted for 5 min. After unloading for 30 s, the thickness of the sample was measured, and the test was repeated for three times, and the rebound rate was measured.

$$\varepsilon_H = \frac{T_a - T_b}{T_a} \times 100\%$$

$$\bar{\varepsilon}_H = \frac{\varepsilon_{H1} + \varepsilon_{H2} + \varepsilon_{H3}}{3} \times 100\%$$

Where: ε_H-rebound rate; T_a-the thickness of initial specimen after single deformation (cm); T_b-the thickness of specimen after single deformation (cm).

3.3 Density Measurement

Place a flat and rigid plate on the test sample to make the sample subject to compression load of (0.20 ± 0.02) kPa. After 30 s, measure the thickness of four corners and the length of each side of the test sample (the accuracy shall not be less than 0.005 cm). The average value was calculated and accurate to 0.01 cm. The weight of the experimental sample was weighed with a balance of 0.01 g and the density was calculated.

4 Results and Discussion

4.1 Properties of Foams with Different Fillers

Corn Straw Filling. As shown in Fig. 2, when corn straw was used as filler, with the increase of corn straw proportion, the surface color of foam became lighter, the formability decreased, and the surface roughness increased. The physical properties are shown in Table 1 (Table 2).

(a)Macro-   (b)300x

Fig. 2. Macroscopic & microscopic morphology of corn foam

Table 1. Physical properties of foams with corn as filler

Fill ratio/%	25	30	35	40	45	50
Density/g.cm^{-3}	0.0482	0.0453	0.0441	0.0406	0.0389	0.0386
Rebound rate/%	33	39	42	43	45	45

Table 2. σ-c curve according to σ-ε curve of corn straw.

ε	σ_1/MPa	U_1(J/cm^3)	c_1
0	0	0	∞
0.2	1.5	0.15	10.0000
0.4	1.5	0.45	3.3333
0.6	1.8	0.78	2.3077
0.8	1.8	1.14	1.5789
1.0	2.0	1.52	1.3158
1.2	2.2	1.94	1.1340
1.4	2.5	2.41	1.0373

It can be seen from Table 1 that when corn straw is used as filler, with the increase of filling proportion, the rebound rate shows an upward trend, while the density shows a downward trend. The reason is that the density of corn straw is small, and the hydrogen bonding ability with waste pulp fiber is weaker than that of waste pulp fiber itself, which leads to the decrease of fiber adhesion [20–23]. When the content of corn straw accounts for 40–50% of the total amount, the change of foam density is not obvious, which indicates that the binding capacity between fibers is not the most important factor affecting the density at this stage, which may be due to the surface of foam body During the molding process, the gas escaped with the pores, and there was bubble structure in the foam body. However, the gas content had a great influence on the density of the foam body, so the change was not obvious.

Hemp Stalk Core Filling. When hemp stalk core was used as filler, the surface roughness of foam increased, the resilience decreased, the density increased and the cushioning performance increased with the increase of core content. See Fig. 3, Tables 3 and 4.

(a)Macro-   (b)300x

Fig.3. Macroscopic & microscopic morphology of hemp stalk core foam

Table 3. Physical properties of foams with hemp stalk core as filler

Fill ratio / %	25	30	35	40	45	50
density /g.cm^{-3}	0.0284	0.0342	0.0357	0.0372	0.0356	0.0328
Rebound rate / %	48	40	37	33	40	42

As shown in Table 3, when hemp stem core is a filler, the density of foam body is much higher than that of other foams with the same proportion of fillers. The reason is that hemp stalk core has water retention property [24–26]. Under the same drying conditions, hemp stalk core foam has large moisture content and high density. When the filling ratio is more than 40%, the density of the foam decreases. The reason may be that the moisture factor has reached the upper limit of the foam density. The reason is that the springback decreases first and then increases. In a certain range, the water content increases, and the shape of the foam increases, and the rebound rate decreases. When the filling ratio is greater than 40%, the moisture factor has reached the upper limit of the impact of the foam resilience rate.

Hemp Stalk Core/Corn Stalk Filling. When the fixed ratio of hemp stalk core and corn straw was 1:1.5, with the increase of filling ratio, the density of foam decreased, and the resilience first decreased and then increased, as shown in Fig. 4.

According to the analysis in Table 5 and 6, when hemp stalk core/corn straw was used as filler, the density showed a downward trend with the increase of filling ratio, and the rebound rate showed a trend of first decreasing and then increasing. The reason is

Table 4. σ-c curve according to σ-ε curve of hemp straw.

ε	σ_1/MPa	σ_2/MPa	U_1(J/cm³)	U_2(J/cm³)	c_1	c_2
0	0	0	0	0	∞	∞
0.2	1.8	2.2	0.18	0.22	10.000	10.000
0.4	2.2	3.2	0.58	0.76	3.7931	4.2105
0.6	2.5	3.4	1.05	1.42	2.3810	2.3944
0.8	2.7	3.6	1.57	2.12	1.7191	1.6981
1.0	2.9	5.0	2.13	2.98	1.3615	1.6779
1.2	3.4	5.2	2.76	4.00	1.2319	1.3000
1.4	3.6	5.4	3.41	5.06	1.0405	1.0671
1.6	4.1	5.9	4.23	6.19	0.9693	0.9531
1.8	4.8	6.8	5.12	7.46	0.9375	0.9115
2.0	–	7.7	–	8.91	–	0.8642

(a)Macro-   (b)300x

Fig. 4. Macroscopic & microscopic morphology of corn foam hemp stalk core foam

Table 5. Physical properties of Hemp straw core/corn straw filled foam

Fill ratio/%	25	30	35	40	45	50
Density/.cm⁻³	0.0421	0.0407	0.0388	0.0382	0.0367	0.0351
Rebound rate/%	43	40	39	37	41	43

that corn straw fiber has a greater influence on the foam density than hemp stalk core fiber, and hemp stalk core fiber has a greater influence on the foam volume density when the two kinds of biomass materials are combined [27, 28]. The possible reason is that when the two fillers are mixed as fillers, the bonding mode between fibers is complex: the binding capacity of different fillers, the binding capacity with other fillers and the binding capacity with waste pulp fiber are not the same, so it is difficult to achieve the ideal fiber bonding mode. Therefore, when the two fillers are mixed as fillers, the apparent

Table 6. σ-c curve according to σ-ε curve of Hemp straw core/corn straw filled foam

E	σ_1/MPa	U_1(J/cm^3)	c_1
0	0	0	∞
0.2	1.666	0.17	9.8000
0.4	3.332	0.33	10.0969
0.6	4.686	0.47	9.9702
0.8	5.935	0.59	10.593
1.0	6.664	0.67	9.9462
1.2	7.280	0.71	9.9718
1.4	7.809	0.78	9.1870
1.6	8.538	0.85	10.0447
1.8	9.475	0.95	9.9736

morphology of foams is obviously different, the physical properties will fluctuate in a certain range, and the linear change is not obvious, as shown in Fig. 5.

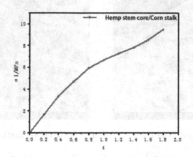

Fig. 5. Stress-strain curve of hemp stalk core/corn stalk mixed filling

4.2 Cushioning Properties of Foams with Different Fillers

As shown in Fig. 6(a), taking hemp stalk core as an example, with the increase of filling ratio, the cushioning coefficient of foamed body increases, the buffering efficiency decreases, and the cushioning performance decreases. The results show that the binding capacity between hemp stalk core fiber and waste pulp fiber is not strong, the resilience of foam decreases with the increase of filling ratio, and the cushioning performance of foam decreases.

Take 30% corn stalk foam and 30% hemp stalk core foam as examples. Under the same filling ratio, the buffer coefficient of hemp stalk core foam is greater than that of corn straw foam, that is, the buffer performance of corn straw foam is greater than that of hemp stalk core foam, as shown in Fig. 6.

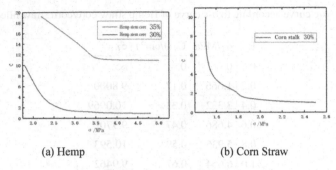

(a) Hemp   (b) Corn Straw

Fig. 6. Stress - strain curve

4.3   Morphology of Foams with Different Fillers

Taking corn straw foams and hemp stalk core foams as examples, under the same magnification, the fiber bonding degree of corn straw foams is better than that of hemp stalk core foams, and the gap between fibers of hemp stalk core foams is larger than that of hemp stalk core foams, as shown in Fig. 7.

(a) 500x Corn Foam   (b) 500x Hemp stalk core Foam

Fig. 7. Microscopic morphology of corn foam and hemp stalk core foam

As shown in Fig. 7(a), the corn straw foam has strong fiber bonding degree, large interlacing degree, large proportion of slender fiber components, and good tensile and cushioning properties. The density and resilience of the foamed body are affected by the less space between the fibers and less bubble structure per unit volume.

As shown in Fig. 7(b), the fibers in hemp stem core foam are mostly coarse and short fibers, and the binding capacity between fibers is weaker than that of corn straw foam; there are many gaps between fibers, and there are more pore structures per unit volume than corn straw foam, and the foam body has good resilience; there are cristae on the surface of the foam body, which is the adhesive.

4.4   Infrared Spectrum Analysis of Hemp Stalk Core/Corn Stalk Foam

Figure 8 shows the infrared spectrum of hemp stalk core/corn straw foam. The characteristic absorption peaks at 1157 cm^{-1} and 3220 cm^{-1} correspond to the - CHO and C-H stretching vibrations of cellulose phosphate, respectively. With the increase of filling ratio, the peak height increased, indicating that the cellulose content of filler was higher than that of waste pulp. The density of foam decreases with the increase of cellulose content.

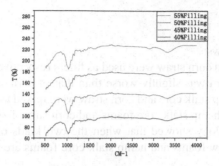

Fig. 8. Infrared spectrum analysis of hemp straw core/corn straw foam

4.5 DSC Analysis of Hemp Stalk Core/Corn Straw Foam

Figures 9 show the DSC and TG curves of hemp stalk core/corn straw foam, respectively. It can be seen from Fig. 9 that the endothermic peak of hemp stalk core/corn straw foam at 60 °C is caused by water evaporation in hemp stalk core/corn straw foam body during molding, and the water evaporation temperature of hemp stalk core/corn straw foam is greatly reduced, which is due to the reduction of hydrogen bonding between hemp stalk core/corn straw foam and the composite hemp stalk core/corn straw foam The moisture absorption of straw foams decreased, resulting in the increase of water evaporation endothermic peak amplitude, and the peak moved to the high temperature side [29, 30], so the hydrophobicity of hemp stalk core/corn straw foam increased. There was an obvious exothermic peak of hemp stalk core/corn straw foam at 360 °C, which was caused by the degradation of hemicellulose macromolecular chain, while there was no obvious exothermic peak near the foaming body of hemp stalk core/corn straw. The

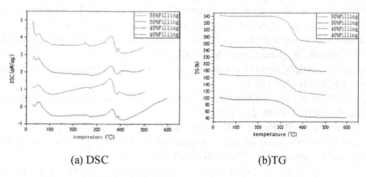

(a) DSC   (b)TG

Fig. 9. DSC and TG of hemp straw core/corn straw foam

results showed that hemp stalk core/corn straw foam had protective effect, cellulose and lignin of hemp stalk core/corn straw foam began to decompose at a higher temperature, which also showed that hemp stalk core/corn straw foam had good flame retardant performance, which was consistent with the TG experimental results mentioned above.

5 Conclusion

The results are as follows:

Hemp stalk core and corn straw were used as fillers respectively, and the formability of hemp stalk core foam was slightly worse than that of corn straw foam at the same filling ratio. When hemp stalk core and corn straw were mixed as fillers, the formability of foams was between hemp stalk core foams and corn straw foams.

The micro morphology showed that when the two kinds of fillers are fillers, the filler fibers in corn straw foams and hemp stalk core foams are mostly combined with themselves.

The ratio of fillers has great influence on the density and resilience of foams. When corn straw was used as filler, the change of foam density was negatively correlated with the increase of filling ratio, and the rebound rate was positively correlated; when hemp stalk core was used as filler, the density change first increased and then decreased with the increase of filling proportion, and the rebound rate was opposite. In the two kinds of fillers, one is filler and the other is mixture of two kinds of fillers, the cushioning performance of corn straw foam is the best.

Acknowledgements. The authors thank for the financial supports by the Heilongjiang Province advantageous characteristic discipline special project YSTSXK201857; Heilongjiang Province Education Department basic business expense scientific research project(135309513, 135309109, 135409505, 135409415) support.

References

1. Rong, L., et al.: Yield gap and resource utilization efficiency of three major food crops in the world-a review. J. Integrat. Agricult. **20**(02), 349–362 (2021)
2. Sun, Y., Yuan, Y., Wang, Q., Ji, S., Wang, L., et al.: Impact force magnitude and location recognition of composite materials. Comput. Mat. Continua **64**(3), 1647–1656 (2020)
3. Ren, Z., et al.: Multiple roles of dissolved organic matter released from decomposing rice straw at different times in organic pollutant photodegradation. J. Hazardous Mat. **401** (2021)
4. Shiah, Y., Huang, S., Hematiyan, M.R.: Efficient 2d analysis of interfacial thermoelastic stresses in multiply bonded anisotropic composites with thin adhesives. Comput. Mat. Continua **64**(2), 701–727 (2020)
5. Zonneveld, M., et al.: Diversity and conservation of traditional African vegetables: Priorities for action. Diversity Distrib. **27**(2) (2020)
6. Noori, H., Mortazavi, B., Pierro, A.D., Jomehzadeh, E., Zhuang, X., et al.: A systematic molecular dynamics investigation on the graphene polymer nanocomposites for bulletproofing. Comput. Mat. Continua **65**(3), 2009–2032 (2020)
7. (Alex) Koh,C.H., Kraniotis, D.: A review of material properties and performance of straw bale as building material. Constr. Build. Mat. **259** (2020)

8. Yan, B.: Improvement of the economic management system based on the publicity of railway transportation products. Intell. Autom. Soft Comput. **26**(3), 539–547 (2020)
9. Liuzzi, S., et al.: Characterization of biomass-based materials for building applications: the case of straw and olive tree waste. Ind. Crops Prod. **147** (2020)
10. Karami, B., Janghorban, M., Rabczuk, T.: Forced vibration analysis of functionally graded anisotropic nanoplates resting on winkler/pasternak-foundation. Comput. Mat. Continua **62**(2), 607–629 (2020)
11. Wang, D., et al.: Preparation and characterization of foamed wheat straw fiber/polypropylene composites based on modified nano-TiO 2 particles. Composites Part A **128** (2020)
12. Khatri,K., et al.: Sugar contents and oligosaccharide mass profiling of selected red seaweeds to assess the possible utilization of biomasses for third-generation biofuel production. Biomass Bioenergy **130** (2019)
13. Schaffasz, A., et al.: Sorghum as a novel crop for central Europe: using a broad diversity set to dissect temperate-adaptation. Agronomy **9**(9) (2019)
14. Dominguez, J., Rubio, G.: Agriculture. In: Rubio, G., Lavado, R.S., Pereyra, F.X. (eds.) The soils of Argentina. WSBS, pp. 209–238. Springer, Cham (2019). https://doi.org/10.1007/978-3-319-76853-3_16
15. Witherup, C., et al.: Genetic diversity of Bangladeshi jackfruit (Artocarpus Heterophyllus) over time and across seedling sources. Econ. Botany **73**(2) (2019)
16. Jamla, M., Archak, S.: Genomic resources of plant abiotic stress tolerance: an overview of functional and regulatory proteins. Indian J. Plant Genetic Resour. **32**(1) (2019)
17. Durante, M., Formisano, A., Boccarusso, L., Langella, A., Carrino, L.: Creep behaviour of polylactic acid reinforced by woven hemp fabric. Composites Part B, **124** (2017)
18. Wu, S., Chen, S., Zhao, Y.: Evaluation and optimization of old magzines deinking process of a modified lignin sulfonates deinking agent. Paper Biomat. **4**(01), 31–39 (2019)
19. Rasool,G., et al.: The interactive responses of fertigation levels under buried straw layer on growth, physiological traits and fruit yield in tomato plant. J. Plant Interact. **14**(1) (2019)
20. Harouna, D.V., et al.: Under-exploited wild Vigna species potentials in human and animal nutrition: a review. Global Food Secur. **18** (2018)
21. Xie, Y.L., et al.: An inexact stochastic-fuzzy optimization model for agricultural water allocation and land resources utilization management under considering effective rainfall. Ecol. Indicat. **92** (2018)
22. Hua, K., Zhu, B.: Dissolved organic nitrogen fluxes and crop yield after long-term crop straw incorporation. Nutrient Cycling in Agroecosystems **112**(1) (2018)
23. Cheng, N., et al.: Comparisons of two serious air pollution episodes in winter and summer in Beijing. J. Environ. Sci. **69** (2018)
24. Wang, Z.-W., Wang, L.-J.: Accelerated random vibration testing of transport packaging system based on acceleration PSD. Packaging Technol. Sci. **30**(10) (2017)
25. Robichaud, P.R., et al.: Evaluating the effectiveness of agricultural mulches for reducing post-wildfire wind erosion. Aeolian Res. **27** (2017)
26. Ammenberg, J., Feiz, R.: Assessment of feedstocks for biogas production, Part II—results for strategic decision making. Resour. Conserv. Recycl. **122** (2017)
27. Guo, D.: Effect of electron beam radiation processing on mechanical and thermal properties of fully biodegradable crops straw/poly (vinyl alcohol) biocomposites. Rad. Phys. Chem. **130** (2017)
28. Vávrová, K., et al.: Short-term boosting of biomass energy sources – determination of biomass potential for prevention of regional crisis situations. Renew. Sustain. Energy Rev. **67** (2017)

29. Yang, Y., et al.: Spatial and temporal dynamics of agricultural residue resources in the last 30 years in China. Waste Manage. Res. **34**(12) (2016)

30. Kaya,A.I., Sahin, H.T.: The effects of boric acid on fiberboard made from wood/secondary fiber mixtures: Part 3. utilization of recycled waste office paper fibers. Chem. Sci. Int. J. (2016)

Research on Data Analysis to Improve English Vocabulary Learning Performance

YingLin Liu, YuanMeng Yi, ZiZhen Qin, and Songlin Cao[✉]

Hunan University of Finance and Economics, Changsha 410205, China

Abstract. As data analysis technology becomes more mature and data applications become more and more extensive, people have accumulated a large amount of data. Data analysis technology has had a positive impact in the education field. In English learning, English vocabulary is the key to learning English and the basis for learning English. But the main obstacle to learning English is the memory of English words. Therefore, this research attempts to combine the ten-day recitation method with Ebbing Haus' forgetting curve to assist the memory of English words. Through the grey relational analysis of data analysis, the feasibility and effectiveness of this method are studied. The data used are recorded data in the memory word test, word familiarity rate, fuzzy rate, forgetting rate, test word score data and final word learning score data. Store English word learning records in a database or data warehouse in the form of data. Using these data to reasonably analyze the ten-day recitation method is very helpful for improving English vocabulary learning performance.

Keywords: Data analysis · Grey relational analysis · Word learning · Ten-day recitation method

1 Introduction

With the rapid development of globalization, the scope of application of English has become larger and larger in our real life. Nowadays, we may involve English in every field.

To learn English, there must be an accumulation of vocabulary, and students must memorize English words through continuous recitation and dictation. However, improper memory methods may affect our grasp of words. Therefore, we must propose an efficient and long-lasting memory method. In recent years, data analysis technology has developed more and more mature, and people will use data analysis technology to find valuable information from the accumulated large amount of data. For example, a lot of information will be recorded in our English word learning software, such as learner registration, login information, browsing path information, word test information, word learning records, etc. We can use data analysis technology combined with memory methods to help the learning of English words. Students' English vocabulary learning scores are one of the important basis for measuring students' English learning, but the correlation of word learning scores is difficult to quantify using traditional methods,

© Springer Nature Switzerland AG 2021
X. Sun et al. (Eds.): ICAIS 2021, CCIS 1423, pp. 251–264, 2021.
https://doi.org/10.1007/978-3-030-78618-2_20

and it is difficult to provide accurate guidance and early warning for students' English learning. Therefore, using grey relational analysis method to carry out relational analysis on English vocabulary learning to quantify the degree of relevance between each word learning, and to provide a scientific basis for improving the English vocabulary curriculum system. Now is the era of big data, and the knowledge and patterns we have discovered from large amounts of data are very meaningful.

2 Related Works

The application of data mining is very extensive, because it is a multidisciplinary field that integrates the latest research results of machine learning, database technology, artificial intelligence, knowledge engineering, statistics, information retrieval and other technologies. The latest development of data mining abroad is mainly the further study of knowledge discovery methods, such as the improvement of Boosting method and Bayesian method; the close integration of KDD and database; the application of statistical traditional regression methods in KDD [6]. The domestic research on data mining started later than abroad and is still immature. Our research technology is only in the developing stage. The domestic research direction is mainly in the theoretical aspects of data mining, learning algorithms and practical applications. The researched product has not yet been recognized by the international market, let alone used in the international market. In the field of education, data mining is currently not as extensive as telecommunications, retail and other industries. It is just a new information processing technology. In the education field, it mainly extracts, transforms, analyzes, and model-processes data in a large number of educational databases, and then extracts key data from educational decision-making; data mining is mainly to provide truly valuable information for educational decision-making. In order to obtain better educational benefits; therefore, it is necessary to obtain value information that is conducive to educational decision-making and promotes educational development through in-depth analysis from a large amount of educational data.

Data mining technology has been developed for more than ten years, and the research field of data mining has obtained rich experience and obvious results abroad. For example, Han, J. and Fu, Y (1995), etc., research on the discovery of quantitative association rules and other types of association rules, Mehta, M. (1996), et al. Research on fast classification algorithms for large databases, Owen, AB (1999) Research on the tubular neighborhood of classification and regression, Friedman, JH (1997) improved the nearest neighbor classification method, and research on clustering rules, data generalization, reduction and feature extraction [8]. In foreign countries, they will not only bring research in various fields closer to the field of data mining, but also develop a lot of product software about data mining. These results are very influential internationally.

Data mining technology is mainly used in telecommunications, retail, insurance, finance and other industries in China. But more and more domestic entrepreneurs have gradually realized the importance of data mining. The research and application of data mining technology will be more extensive in the future. But we still have many problems and challenges that we still need to face, such as improving the efficiency of data mining, the problem of dynamic data mining in heterogeneous data sets and the problem of data mining in a distributed environment. In addition, the multimedia database has developed rapidly in the past few years, so the main point of research and development in the future will be the software and mining technology of the multimedia database. In the domestic academia, business and government departments, the research and application of data mining has begun to receive more and more attention, but its practical application is still in the initial stage, mainly based on academic research.

3 Data Analysis Related Technologies

Data mining has six modes, which are deviation pattern, clustering mode, regression mode, association mode, sequence mode and classification mode. The research on English vocabulary learning performance here mainly uses relational analysis.

3.1 Data Analysis Concept

Data analysis is to use the laws and patterns discovered from historical data to make predictions. That is to extract potential value from a large amount of fuzzy data. The data amount information obtained by data analysis requires careful search of the data source to ensure the accuracy of the information value. Rather than predicting discovery by intuition. And the useful data for data analysis should be information obtained from random and fuzzy data. The collected data should also be collected under unclear premises. Such data will be available and effective.

3.2 Data Analysis Process

The steps of data analysis will vary according to the application in different fields, but generally speaking, people will have 6 basic steps when analyzing data: Task Definition, Data Collecting, Data Preparation, Modeling, E-valuation, and Development. As shown in Fig. 1.

(1) Problem definition and data collection: First, determine the object of mining. This article studies the English word learning performance. This must have a large amount of data. The data can be collected from many mobile phone English word recitation apps, or from New Oriental's English word test Get it in the exam. Data collection needs to be collected in practice in various ways, and the workload is large and time is long.

(2) Data preparation: Students will inevitably have some interfering data in the entry of English word learning scores. Therefore, the score data should be cleaned before data mining to eliminate inconsistent data and interfering data. Therefore, the data must be preprocessed first, so that more effective and rich information can be obtained, which is conducive to the subsequent processing of the data analysis process.

(3) Build a model: use grey correlation method and some data analysis tools to analyze the preprocessed and collected data and information. Before analysis, we must first determine the relevant algorithms used in data analysis and how to evaluate

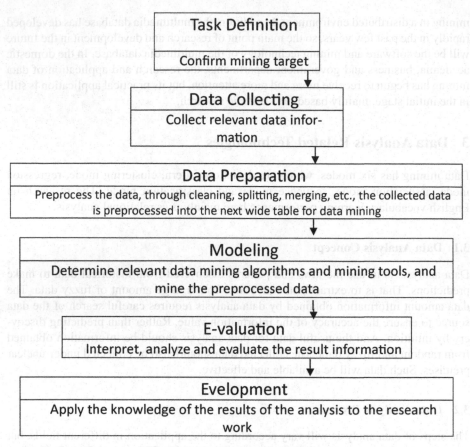

Task Definition

Confirm mining target

Data Collecting

Collect relevant data information

Data Preparation

Preprocess the data, through cleaning, splitting, merging, etc., the collected data
is preprocessed into the next wide table for data mining

Modeling

Determine relevant data mining algorithms and mining tools, and
mine the preprocessed data

E-valuation

Interpret, analyze and evaluate the result information

Evelopment

Apply the knowledge of the results of the analysis to the research
work

Fig. 1. Data analysis process diagram

the results of these algorithms. Therefore, the effectiveness of the algorithm, the interpretability of the results and the complexity of the algorithm must be evaluated. The effective improvement of the improvement of English vocabulary learning performance can be effectively applied by combining the information obtained through data analysis and processing into the practice of English learning.

(4) Finally, the results are interpreted and evaluated and knowledge is applied.

3.3 Grey Relational Analysis

Grey relational analysis is a method of quantitative description and comparison of the development and change of a system. It judges the closeness between things according to the similarity of things. Its purpose is to seek the main relationship between various factors in the system and find out the factors that affect the target value. Important factors, so as to grasp the main characteristics of things, promote and guide the rapid and effective development of the system. The development time is not long, but in economic, social and other fields, gray theory has become a powerful tool for forecasting, decision-making, analysis and control. To learn English, the foundation lies in vocabulary, learning vocabulary well, the difficulty lies in memory, and the key to memorizing words lies in the method. Therefore, this article uses gray correlation analysis to compare the degree of relevance by studying different word learning methods, and finds the most effective way to improve English word learning performance. We mainly explore the ten-day recitation method of Wang Jiangtao.

Introduction to Analysis Algorithms. Reference series and comparison series: a data series that reflects the characteristics of the system's behavior is called a reference series. a data sequence composed of factors affecting system behavior is called a comparative sequence. The reference sequence (also called the parent sequence) and the comparison sequence (also called the sub sequence) are expressed as

$$X_0 = \{X_0(k)|k = 1, 2, 3, \ldots, n\} \tag{1}$$

$$X_i = \{X_i(k)|k = 1, 2, 3, \ldots, n\} \tag{2}$$

Dimensionless processing of reference series and comparison series: Because each factor in the system may have different meanings, the dimensions of the data will not be the same. In order to facilitate the comparison and get the correct conclusion in the comparison, the data should be processed in a dimensionless manner during the gray correlation analysis. The processing process is as follows:

$$X_i(k) = \left\{ \frac{X_i(k) - minX_0(l)}{maxX_0(l) - min(l)}, k = 1, 2, 3, \ldots, n \right\} \tag{3}$$

Where is the initial value, $maxX_0(l)$ is the largest number in the initial value, and $min(l)$ is the smallest number.

Difference sequence: The difference sequence is to subtract the comparison sequence from the reference sequence, and then take their absolute value. The formula is as follows:

$$X_i(k) = |X_0(k) - X_i(k)|, k = 1, 2, 3, \ldots, n \tag{4}$$

The gray correlation coefficient of the reference series and the comparison series: The degree of difference in the geometric shape of the curve of the gray correlation degree is the degree of correlation. Therefore, the degree of association can be the size of the difference between the curves. For a reference series X_0, there are several comparison series $X_1, X_2, \ldots, X_i$ ($i = 1, 2, 3, \ldots, n$). The correlation coefficient between each comparison series and the reference series at each time (that is, each point in the curve) $\varepsilon_i(k)$ ($k = 1, 2, 3, \ldots, n$) can be calculated by the following formula:

$$\varepsilon_i(k) = \frac{min\ i\ mink|X_0(k) - X_i(k)| + \rho \times max\ i\ maxk\ |X_0(k) - X_i(k)|}{|X_0(k) - X_i(k)| + \rho \times max\ i\ maxk\ |X_0(k) - X_i(k)|} \tag{5}$$

In the formula, ρ is the resolution coefficient, and the value range of ρ is between 0 and 1. When ≤ 0.563, the resolution is the best. The smaller the ρ is, the greater the resolution is. Here, $\rho = 0.5$ is taken; $min\ i\ mink\ |X_0(k) - X_i(k)|$ in the formula is the minimum difference between the two levels. $min\ i\ mink\ |X_0(k) - X_i(k)|$ is the maximum difference between the two levels; $|X_0(k) - X_i(k)|$ is the absolute value of each point on the curve of each comparison series X_i and each point on the curve of the reference series X_0, which is the difference series.

Relevance: There is more than one relevance coefficient. It is the relevance value of the reference sequence X_0 and the comparison sequence X_i at each moment. It can also be said to be the value of the degree of association between the points in the curve. But it is not conducive to overall comparison, because the data obtained is too scattered. So we need to take their average value. This value is the degree of association. The average value of the total value of the correlation coefficient at each moment (each point in the curve) can be expressed as the degree of correlation (degree of correlation) between the reference sequence X_0 and the comparison sequence X_i. The formula is as follows:

$$\gamma_i = \frac{1}{n} \sum_{k=1}^{n} \varepsilon_i(k) \tag{6}$$

Compare the gray correlation degree between the series and the reference series γ_i. If the correlation is better, the value of γ_i is closer to 1.

4 Application of Data Analysis in Improving English Vocabulary Learning Performance

4.1 Research on English Word Learning

Although we have always received English learning education, there are still many people who do not have a thorough understanding of the original text and feel vague. The reason is that the number of words is too small. Generally speaking, our students learn English vocabulary to deal with exams and obtain certificates. Therefore, many English software uses a system of one, a fast learning method, divided into learning stages (junior high school, high school, level four, level six, postgraduate entrance examination, TOEFL, etc.) to provide word learning. For the community, there will also be software suitable for their own situation to learn English words. For example, pay attention to the learning of daily spoken language and the learning of business terms. An important reason for the low efficiency of our Chinese students in remembering words is that when we recite words, we generally only pay attention to the spelling and interpretation of words, and often ignore the pronunciation of words. In fact, the pronunciation of English is closely related to the spelling of English. If you can accurately remember the pronunciation of English, sometimes you don't need to memorize the spelling of English by rote, and you can spell it naturally. Similarly, if you just memorize the spelling when you recite a word, you will easily get mixed and wrong. Generally, when learning software, Chinese explanations are provided, but Chinese explanations have great limitations. Because of the differences between Chinese and Western cultures, there will be great differences in application, so it is more appropriate to provide English explanations. In summary, when building an English word learning model, we should choose words and word pronunciation together to learn, so that we can mobilize the learning of words through vision, hearing, and language, which will help improve the efficiency of word learning. In the interpretation of words, English explanations should also be added to facilitate the application and understanding of word learning.

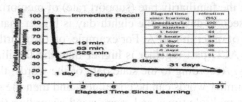

Fig. 2. Ebbing House's forgetting curve

Therefore, observing the trend of the curve on the way, it is found that the memory retention declines faster than the display, and then slowly declines. Therefore, if the vocabulary can be reviewed in time, the memory retention will be longer. In response to this memory law, most of today's recitation software uses the Ebbinghaus cycle memory process to remind learners to review, and to allow unfamiliar words to appear repeatedly to minimize the forgetting rate. There are many software for memorizing words. Generally, when you start to recite, it will let you choose your study time, study amount, and study time length. Other software can set the reminder time for learning words, and then the software will remind you at the corresponding time. Some software, such as Happy Cichang, is mainly characterized by a mode to memorize vocabulary. Generally speaking, each kind of word software has its own characteristics to memorize words, and sticking to a certain kind of software can achieve good results. The English word learning of data analysis can better help these software to improve its functions, and it is more scientific and more valuable.

Case Analysis. We can apply data analysis methods to better improve our English vocabulary learning performance. According to New Oriental's Wang Jiangtao's ten-day recitation method, there are two methods for this method. The task of memorizing words will be allocated in 10 or 20 days to complete. Because 10-day recitation is more difficult for students with weak English words, so according to this same method Method (ten-day recitation method) can be divided into 20 days to recite words. In a survey of 500 people in New Oriental, 30% of the students who recited the words in ten days could complete it, and 50% of the students who recited the words in 20 days could complete it. After completing the recitation in 10 or 20 days, every 15 days thereafter. Will repeat the review, and basically 95% of them are very familiar with words when they are applied to the test. It shows that the ten-day recitation method is very effective, and the study of this method is very practical.

Take the ten-day memorization of words as an example, as shown in Table 1, divide the words to be recited into ten parts, A ~ J parts. On the tenth day, you can recite the J part, which is the last part. Repeat the recited words every 5 min, half an hour, 1 day, 2 days, 4 days, 7 days, and 14 days. So the association analysis will associate your recitation record with this strategy. For example, on the second day you have to repeat A and recite B, on the third day you have to repeat B and recite C... Repeat A on the eighth day.

Then the situation of reciting words every day will be recorded, familiarity, forgetting, fuzzy three states, the word is successfully remembered once to be familiar, repeated twice, the memory error is fuzzy, and three or more times are forgotten. Association rules can be used for data analysis based on the state of each part of memory. According to the memory curve, the familiarity rate (support rate) of memorizing words in Part A on the first day, the second day, and the eighth day is higher than the familiarity rate of reciting words out of order in Part A. For example, on the fourth day, the familiarity rate of repeating the ACD part together is higher than the familiarity rate of reciting each part individually. According to the state data of the words, the forget rate caused by the confusion of similar words can be correlated, and then the data can be retrieved from the database for multiple times and memorized according to the memory curve. Data analysis will allow us to learn more accurately and greatly improve our learning efficiency.

Table 1. Memory table of ten-day recitation method

	1	2	3	4	5	6	7	8	9	10
Am	A	B	C	D	E	F	G	AH	BI	CJ
Pm	A	AB	BC	ACD	BDE	CEF	DFG	EGH	FHI	GIJ
	11	12	13	14	15	16	17	18	19	20
Am	D	E	F	G	AH	BI	CJ	D	E	F
Pm	HJ	I	J							
	21	22	23	24	25	26	27	28	29	30
Am	G	H	I	J					A	B
	31	32	33	34	35	36	37	38	39	40
Am ara>	C	D	E	F	G	H	I	J		

The test of English words is also very important. We can also use the data to analyze the learners' correlations between the words they have learned and their test scores, and analyze the patterns implicit in the learners' learning behavior records, so as to provide references for the number of word reviews.

4.2 Build a Module for Improving English Vocabulary Learning Performance

After studying New Oriental's ten-day recitation method, this article builds a module to improve English vocabulary learning performance. The data source of New Oriental's English word test scores is obtained based on this designed module. English word learning module mainly includes word memory module, word interpretation checking module, word spelling checking module and word testing module. The specific process is shown in Fig. 2 and 3.

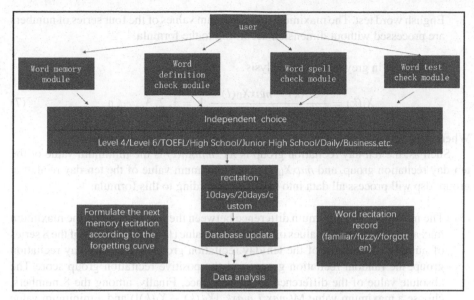

Fig. 3. Flow chart of improving English vocabulary learning performance

4.3 Application of Relevance Analysis in English Vocabulary Learning Performance

Before data mining, word learning can be divided into 3 levels: familiar, fuzzy and forget. The higher the familiarity rate, the better the score. The English word learning score is divided into four levels: excellent, good, pass, and fail. Divide the ways of reciting English words into four groups: ten-day recitation group, twenty-day recitation group, random order recitation group and positive order recitation group. When Wang Jiangtao studied the ten-day recitation method, he collected statistics. Therefore, the data uses the test data of New Oriental University students' recitation of words as an example. Use dsp tool to realize grey relation analysis. Import the data into it, use the tools correctly, and get the correlation size.

Applying Grey Relational Analysis to Analyze English Words Learning Performance

(1) Reference sequence and comparison sequence: this analysis takes the final unified vocabulary test scores of all new oriental students as reference sequence X_0, taking the score of the ten-day recitation group, the score of the twenty-day recitation group, the score of the out-of-order recitation group, and the score of the positive recitation group as compare series X_i (X_1, X_2, X_3, X_4)

(2) Dimensionless processing of reference series and comparison series: filter out the results of the ten-day recitation group, the twenty-day recitation group, the out-of-order recitation group, the positive-order recitation group, and the average final

English word test. The maximum and minimum values of the four series of numbers are processed without dimension according to the formula.

The formula in grey relational analysis

$$X_i(k) = \frac{X_i(k) - maxX_0(l)}{maxX_0(l) - minX_0(l)}, k = 1, 2, 3, \ldots, n \tag{7}$$

Where $X_0(l)$ is the initial value.

Such as: the ten-day recitation group is X_1, $minX_0(l)$ is the minimum value of the ten-day recitation group, and $maxX_0(l)$ is the maximum value of the ten-day recitation group. dsp will process all data into new data according to this formula.

(3) The maximum and minimum difference between the two levels: find the maximum max and minimum min values of the absolute value ($|X_0(k) - X_i(k)|$) of the 8 series of numbers, the scores of the ten-day recitation group, the twenty-day recitation group, the random recitation group, and the positive recitation group score The absolute value of the difference of the sequence. Finally, among the 8 numbers, choose a maximum value M($max\ i\ maxk\ |X_0(k) - X_i(k)|$) and a minimum value N($min\ i\ mink\ |X_0(k) - X_i(k)|$). As shown in Table 2.

$$M = 0.8255, N = 0.0001.$$

Table 2. Two-level maximum and minimum difference table

Test team Grades	Recite group results for ten days	Recite group results in 20 days	Out-of-order recitation group Grades	Recite group results in positive order
min	0.0001	0.0002	0.0004	0.0002
max	0.6866	0.6871	0.8255	0.6222

(4) According to the correlation coefficient formula.
(5) Calculate the correlation coefficient between the results of the ten-day recitation group, the twenty-day recitation group, the out-of-order recitation group, the positive-order recitation group, and the final English word average score.
(6) Relevance: According to the relevance formula Calculate the correlation between the score of the ten-day recitation group, the score of the twenty-day recitation group, the score of the out-of-order recitation group, the score of the positive-order recitation group, and the average English word score at the end of the term. As shown in Table 3.

Table 3. Relevance table

	Recite group results for ten days	Recite group results in 20 days	Recite group results out of order	Positive order recitation group Grades
Correlation	0.7941	0.7715	0.7673	0.7629

(7) Relevance ranking: Finally, it is necessary to sort the relevance. The relevance between them is mainly sorted according to the size in the relevance table. The association sequence can reflect the association relationship between the parent sequence and the child sequence. The relevance of the 4 subsequences to the average score of the final English word test is sorted according to their relevance to form a set of relevance sequences. The data in Table 3 shows that the scores of the ten-day recitation group, the score of the twenty-day recitation group, the score of the out-of-order recitation group, the score of the positive-order recitation group, and the average final English word score are related to 0.7941, 0.7715, 0.7673, 0.7629, respectively., According to the degree of relevance, the order from largest to smallest is the score of the ten-day recitation group, the score of the twenty-day recitation group, the score of the out-of-order recitation group, and the score of the normal recitation group.

5 Analysis and Discussion

Using the grey correlation analysis method, the results of the ten-day recitation group, the twenty-day recitation group, the out-of-order recitation group, the positive-order recitation group, and the end-of-term English word average score are quantitatively studied, and the results can be analyzed. It shows that the ten-day recitation method is very helpful for learning English words, and the memorization of words is more profound and firm.

5.1 Analysis of the Validity of English Vocabulary Learning Results and Analysis of the Differences

Through the research of this article, we can understand that the key to learning English words is how to use short time and memory rules to effectively solve the key aspects of English word recitation problems. Using data analysis to get the ranking of relevance, the 10-day recitation method has the best effect on English vocabulary learning, and the positive sequence recitation has the weakest effect.

In the future vocabulary learning, you can use the ten-day recitation method to learn. This method is difficult to adhere to, because the amount of words recited every day is relatively large and the time is relatively long. But as long as you can persist this effect will not be a short-term memory, and you will forget it after the exam. Because it uses the forgetting curve to learn and memorize, it is repeated and repeated memory. If you persist, it will become your permanent memory. The twenty-day recitation method is suitable for those who are not so strong in English ability. If the ten-day memory is more difficult for them, they can use the twenty-day recitation. The principle is the same, but the time will be relatively longer. The best way to learn words is out-of-order learning. According to data analysis results, out-of-order learning has a greater impact on word learning performance than positive-order learning. Learning words in positive order, you will subconsciously sort and memorize English words. You can connect to the next word when you see the previous word. This kind of memory is a false memory. In formal applications and examinations, the words will not follow you The order of recitation of the English word list appears. Once the order is disturbed, the words will not be remembered, so it is not recommended to use the positive order recitation method to learn English words, it is not very useful for improving English word learning performance.

5.2 Suggestions for Improving English Vocabulary Learning Performance Based on Data Analysis

Through this research, first when reciting English words, we not only need to remember the shape and meaning of the words, but also pay special attention to the sounds of the words. We can learn its pronunciation in many ways, such as: listening to the sound in software and mobile phones, or seeing the English standard in books or the Internet, and spelling it out by ourselves. There are also many ways to remember form and meaning, such as directly looking at its form and interpretation, or associating to remember its form and meaning. The memory after imagination and thinking is stronger than the direct memory. As mentioned above, the recognition of an English word whether you fully remember and understand it means that as long as you see the word, you know what it is, instead of seeing the word, you must first think of its Chinese translation to associate it with what it is. So sometimes you think you have memorized a word, but you don't actually remember it, or you're not impressed. This is because what we may emphasize when reciting words is only the effects of repeated recitations, while ignoring that the memorized words also have a "cognitive level". The cognitive level is the processing of information, generally understanding, distinguishing, Imagine, compare, etc. Constantly stimulate the brain to truly recognize and remember this word. According to the grey relational analysis of data analysis, although ten-day recitation is more effective than other memory methods using forgetting curves, we still need to emphasize the "cognitive level" of words.

In building a module to improve the learning performance of English words, the designed English word learning module mainly includes a word memory module, a word definition checking module, a word spelling checking module and a word testing module. The paraphrase check module and the word test module can be used to improve the cognition of English words. The paraphrase can use English to explain the meaning of words and add sentences to understand the meaning better, which is better and flexible to understand than Chinese paraphrases. The English word test can be tested with English scenarios, which is more practical.

6 Summary and Outlook

Association rules in data analysis have always been used in business fields, such as web pages, video apps, Alibaba sales, chat software, etc. everywhere. Nowadays, association rules are also beginning to try to apply to the field of education. Using educational data mining technology and learning analysis technology to build related models in the education field, explore the correlation between educational variables, and provide effective support for education and teaching decisions will become the future of education. development trend.

This research is to use data analysis to study the learning methods of English words. It mainly introduces the concepts of the main analysis and algorithms used in the research to improve the learning performance of English words, and what are the current word learning methods. Analyze and compare which learning method is more effective for English word learning, and the research under data analysis is accurate and efficient. The main method to improve English vocabulary performance is the memorization of English words. This study is the 10-day recitation method of New Oriental teacher Wang Jiangtao. Although the method is short, the memorization time is long and it is very efficient. In English learning, vocabulary and vocabulary are very critical factors, so this research is of great help and significance to the majority of English learning troubled people. And this method can be used not only in the learning of English words, but also in any learning that needs to be memorized, such as: mathematical formula memory, medical knowledge memory, legal learning memory, etc.

However, in practical application, the research method requires people with perseverance, and only perseverance can get its maximum use value.

Acknowledgement. This work was supported in part by the National Natural Science Foundation of China, grant number 72073041. Open Foundation for the University Innovation Platform in the Hunan Province, grant number 18K103. 2011 Collaborative Innovation Center for Development and Utilization of Finance and Economics Big Data Property.

Hunan Provincial Key Laboratory of Finance&Economics Big Data Science and Technology. 2020 Hunan Provincial Higher Education Teaching Reform Research Project under Grant HNJG-2020–1130, HNJG-2020–1124. 2020 General Project of Hunan Social Science Fund under Grant 20B16.

Scientific Research Project of Education Department of Hunan Province (Grand No. 20K021), Social Science Foundation of Hunan Province (Grant No. 17YBA049).

References

1. You, H.: A study on english word memory strategies of middle school students based on scallop effect [J/OL]. Modern Commun. 1 (2008)
2. Tang, X.: Research and application of association rules data mining. J. Yancheng Inst. Technol. (Nat. Sci. Ed.) (02), 44–46+57 (2008)
3. Liu, M.: Research on Personalized Learning System Based on Data Mining Technology. Yangzhou University (2009)
4. Yuan, L.: Li Feng's improved association rule Apriori algorithm in the course score analysis. China Education Inf. (17), 62–65 (2017)

5. Chen, C.: Big data mining and analysis. Software **35**(04), 130–131 (2014)
6. Huizhong, W., Anqun, P.: Research status and development trend of data mining. Ind. Mine Autom. **37**(02), 29–32 (2011)
7. Hu, T.: Application of Data Mining Technology in Educational Decision Support System. Zhejiang Normal University (2015)
8. Wu, X.: Analysis of College Students' Academic Performance Based on Association Rule Data Mining Technology. Southwest Jiaotong University (2010)
9. Wroblewski, J., Stawicki, S.: SQL-based KDD with Infobright's RDBMS: attributes, reducts, trees. In: Kryszkiewicz, M., Cornelis, C., Ciucci, D., Medina-Moreno, J., Motoda, H., Ras, Z.W. (eds.) RSEISP 2014. LNCS (LNAI), vol. 8537, pp. 28–41. Springer, Cham (2014). https://doi.org/10.1007/978-3-319-08729-0_3
10. Li, W.: Using the rules of memory to improve the memory efficiency of English words. J. Mudanjiang Educ. Colle. (03), 155+159 (2017)
11. Zheng, J., Zhang, J.: The research about data mining of network intrusion based on Apriori algorithm. In: 2016 7th International Conference on Education, Management, Computer and Medicine (EMCM 2016) (2017)
12. Li, L.: Grey Relational analysis of factors affecting students' inquiry learning. Sci. Technol. Inf. **16**, 486–487 (2009)
13. Gu, E., Zheng, B., Liu, M., Lin, Y.: Relational analysis of student performance with grey theory. J. Zhengzhou Coll. Animal Husbandry Eng. (04), 34–36+50 (2014)
14. Li, S.: Grey association analysis of college english learning——taking ningxia university English learning as an example. J. Ningxia Univ. (Nat. Sci. Edition), **32**(04), 426–427 (2011)
15. Yi, W., Teng, F., Xu, J.: Noval stream data mining framework under the background of big data. Cybern. Inf. Technol. **16**(5) (2016)
16. Wu, Y., Zheng, W., Sun, F., Zhang, L., Xu, Y.: Gray correlation analysis of the influencing factors of college students' math performance. Math. Learn. Res. (15), 4–5 (2017)
17. Liu, Y.: Research on mathematics learning based on data analysis technology. Modern Teach. (21), 39–41 (2017)
18. Li, H.: Research on Mining Method of University Teaching Evaluation Data. Hebei Normal University (2017)
19. Xiang, L., Yang, S., Liu, Y., Li, Q., Zhu, C.: Novel linguistic steganography based on character-level text generation. Mathematics **8**, 1558 (2020)
20. Xiang, L., Guo, G., Li, Q., Zhu, C., Chen, J., et al.: Spam detection in reviews usinglstm based multientity temporal features. Intell. Autom. Soft Comput. **26**(6), 1375–1390 (2020)
21. Yang, Z., Zhang, S., Hu, Y., Hu, Z., Huang, Y.: VAE stega: linguistic steganography based on variational auto encoder. IEEE Trans. Inf. Forensics Secur. **16**, 880–895 (2021)

Hungarian Method in a Car-Sharing System Application Research

Duohui Li, Sisi Tan, Jianzhi Zhang, and Wangdong Jiang[✉]

Hunan University of Finance and Economics, Changsha 410205, China

Abstract. Since the rapid growth of China's population at the beginning of the 21st century, a phenomenon has emerged in most cities: "It is difficult to take a taxi". Most citizens go to and from work every day, and it is difficult to get a taxi in time, especially when it is rainy or snowy, or when it is a holiday. "Taxi difficulty" has become an issue that needs urgent attention in a city. Following the sustainable development concept advocated by the state, how to improve the utilization efficiency of cars in cities has become a big problem that the relevant departments need to consider. First of all, we think of using dynamic car sharing to optimize the utilization rate of cars, so as to complete the improvement of urban traffic, improve the efficiency of urban transportation system, reduce traffic congestion, fuel consumption and pollution, etc. Secondly we believe that with the implementation of dynamic car sharing with Hungarian Method the efficiency is maximized.

Keywords: Improve the efficiency of transportation system · Hungarian method · Dynamic carpool

1 Introduction

Since the rapid growth of China's population at the beginning of the 21st century, a phenomenon has emerged in most cities: "It is difficult to get a taxi". Most citizens go to and from work every day and find it difficult to get a taxi in time, especially when it is raining or snowing, or when it is a holiday. "Taxi difficulty" has become a city and its relevant departments urgently need to pay attention to the problem. Following the sustainable development concept advocated by the state, how to improve the utilization efficiency of cars in cities has become an increasingly considerate issue for the authorities and people. The utilization rate of carpooling provides a good opportunity for the improvement of urban traffic [1], improving the efficiency of urban transportation system, reducing traffic congestion, fuel consumption and pollution, etc. Moreover, ride-sharing can reduce costs for participants by sharing costs, which has positive social and economic benefits.

In our daily life, we often encounter such a problem: an organization needs to complete N tasks, and M people happen to be able to undertake these tasks. The efficiency of each individual to accomplish different tasks varies due to his or her expertise, thus raising the question of who should be assigned to accomplish which tasks to maximize the

X. Sun et al. (Eds.): ICAIS 2021, CCIS 1423, pp. 265–275, 2021.
https://doi.org/10.1007/978-3-030-78618-2_21

total benefit (or the total cost) of completing N tasks. Such problems are called assignment problems or assignment problems. Now we use the classical Hungarian Method in the assignment problem to solve the bus problem.

2 Related Works

In 2004, Chang TingMao, Han ZhongGeng "Using the Hungarian Method" to solve a class of optimization problems" [1] gave the Hungarian Method MATLAB to achieve the general program, and used to solve the typical assignment problems such as marriage.

In 2011, Notes on Hungarian Method [2] by Chen Yuanming improved The Hungarian Method on the basis of analyzing the Hungarian Method, and proposed the "incremental zero method" to solve the incomplete assignment problem. In 2013, Qiu Yong studied the scheduling problem of multiple maintenance activities under bad environment by using the improved Hungarian Method in His research on Scheduling Algorithm of Multiple maintenance activities under bad environment [3].

In 2014, Ma Xiaona proposed the balance method to solve the non-standard assignment problem in "A New Computing Spell with Fewer People and More Tasks" [4], which is more concise and intuitive compared with the traditional algorithm. In 2014, Zhao Wanlin's Model and Algorithm of Abnormal Flight Emergency Scheduling [5] solved the problem of abnormal flight emergency scheduling with the Hungarian Method, and achieved good results. 2014, He Fujiang, Ren Jinxia fast order reduction Hungarian Method model of cloud computing task distribution [6] in order to improve the efficiency of the distribution of the cloud computing tasks, on the basis of the standard Hungarian Method is put forward a fast order reduction optimization algorithm, this algorithm through continuous established in eliminating the matrix elements, quickly reduce the order of the matrix, improve the computational efficiency of Hungarian Method.

In 2014, Li established a study on Weapon-Target Dynamic Firepower Allocation and War Effectiveness Evaluation [7] to transform the firepower allocation problem into the assignment problem, and studied the weapon-target dynamic firepower allocation by using the Hungarian Method. Although the Hungarian Method has been applied in practice, and achieved good results. However, the traditional Hungarian Method can only solve the problem of "the total cost is the sum of the costs of each task", but in practical engineering, many cases do not meet this condition. Therefore, it is necessary to improve the algorithm so that it can better solve practical problems.

3 Hungarian Method Model

3.1 Model Definitions and Overview

Hungarian Method is put forward in 1965 by Hungarian mathematician Edmonds, thus its name [8]. It is a combinatorial optimization algorithm to solve the task assignment problem in polynomial time and promotes the original dual method later.

Hungarian Method is the idea of using the sufficient proof in Hall theorem, and is the most common algorithm in bipartite graph matching. The core idea of this algorithm is to find the augmented path, which is an algorithm that USES the augmented path to find the maximum matching of bipartite graphs [9].

Suppose an undirected graph $G = (V, E)$. If vertex set V could be divided into two disjoint subsets V1 and V2, the choice of the subset with the largest number of edges in such sub-set was called the maximal matching problem of graph. If in a match, $|V1| \leq |V2|$ and the number of matches is equal to V1, the match is said to be a perfect match or a complete match. In particular when V1 is equal to V2 it's called a perfect match.

3.2 Model Basic Concept

Alternate path: start from an unmatched point, then go through an unmatched edge, a matched edge, and an unmatched edge in turn... The paths formed in this way are called alternate paths.

Augmentation path: Start from one unmatched point and alternate paths. If you proceed to another unmatched point (excluding your starting point), we call this alternate path Augmented paths.

Maximum Matching and Optimal Matching. In a subgraph G M, M any two of the concentrated while are not attached to the same vertices, says that M is a match. Choose such the number of edges of a subset of the largest known as figure maximum matching problem of maximum matching the number of edges is called maximum matching number. If every vertex in a graph is associated with an edge in the graph, the match is called a perfect match, also known as a complete match. If the source sink is added to the left and right sides and graph G is equivalent to a network flow, the maximum matching problem can be turned into the maximum flow problem. The essence of Hungarian Method to solve this problem is to find the most popular augmented path. The maximum matching of Fig. 1 is shown in the thick edge of Fig. 2:

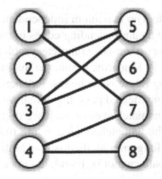

Fig. 1. Example diagram of dichotomy

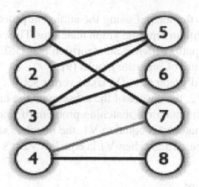

Fig. 2. Example diagram of dichotomy

The optimal match is also called the maximum weighted match, which means that in a bipartite graph with weighted edges, a match is made to make the weight of the matching edge and the maximum [11]. In general, X and Y sets have the same number of vertices, and the optimal match is also a complete match, that is, every vertex is matched. If the Numbers are not equal, you can convert them by adding 0 edges to the complement. KM algorithm is generally used to solve this problem [12].

Minimum Coverage. The minimum coverage of a bipartite graph is divided into minimum vertex coverage and minimum path coverage:

Minimum vertex coverage refers to the minimum number of vertices so that every edge in a bipartite graph G is associated with at least one of the points. The minimum vertex coverage of a bipartite graph = the maximum matching number of the bipartite graph;

Minimum path coverage, also known as minimum edge coverage, means to cover all vertices in a binary graph with as few nonintersecting simple paths as possible. The minimum path coverage number of a bipartite graph = the maximum matching number of a bipartite graph of |V|.

Maximum Independent Set. The maximum independent set is to find a set of points in which any two points have no corresponding edges in the graph. For general graphs, the maximum independent set is an NP complete problem; for bipartite graphs, the maximum independent set = |V |-bipartite graph, the maximum matching number [13]. The black dot in the following figure is the largest independent set:

Due to the nature of the augmented path, the matching edge in the augmented path is always one more than the unmatched edge, so if we discard the matching edge in an augmented path and select the unmatched edge as the matching edge, the number of matches will increase. The Hungarian Method is constantly looking for an augmented path [14]. If the augmented path cannot be found, the maximum matching is achieved.

For example:

1. No initial match (Fig. 3):

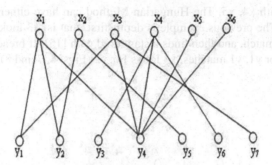

Fig. 3. Bipartite graph

2. Selected the first x point to find the first with the attachment (Fig. 4)

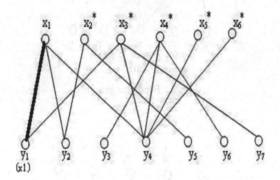

Fig. 4. Bipartite graph

3. Select the second point and find the second line (Fig. 5)

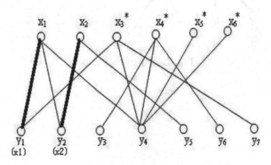

Fig. 5. Bipartite graph

4. Find out that the first edge x3y1 of X3 has been occupied, find out the staggered path x3—y1—x1—y4 from which x3 starts, remove the edge x1y1 that has been matched in the staggered path from the match, and add the remaining edge x3y1 x1y4 to the match

5. Same thing with x4, x5. The Hungarian Method can have either limited depth or breadth first. The previous example is depth-first, that is, x3 looks for Y1, and Y1 already has a match, and then finds a staggered path [15]. If breadth first, it should be: x3 looks for y1, y1 matches, x3 looks for y2 (Figs. 6, 7 and 8).

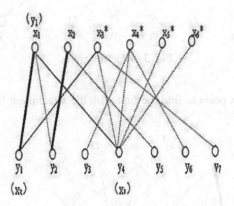

Fig. 6. Bipartite graph

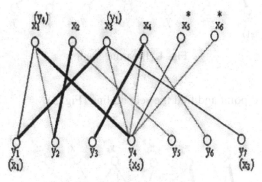

Fig. 7. Bipartite graph

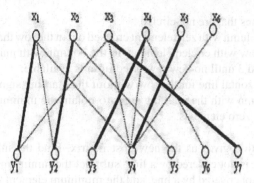

Fig. 8. Bipartite graph

3.3 Data Model

1. The cost matrix of the assignment problem is transformed so that zero elements appear in every row and column. Subtract the smallest element of the row from each element of the cost matrix; The minimum element of the column is subtracted from each column element of the resulting cost matrix.

2. To try to assign and seek for the optimal solution, follow the following steps:

After the first step transformation, there are zero elements in each row and column of the cost matrix. But we have to find n individual zero elements. If it can be found out, the elements in the corresponding solution matrix (XI_j) of these independent zero elements are 1 and the rest are 0 to obtain the optimal solution. When n is small, observation and temptation can be used to find out N independent zero elements. If n is large, it needs to be searched in a certain order. The common steps are as follows:

Start with a row (column) with only one zero element and circle the zero element. This means that only one task can be assigned to the person represented in the line. Then cross out the other zero elements in the circled column (row). This means that the delegate's tasks have been assigned and there is no need to consider others.

Circle a zero element with only one column (row), and then cross out the zero element in the row (column) where the circled element is located. Repeat steps (1) and (2) until all zero elements are circled or crossed out.

If there are still zero elements drawn in circles, and there are at least two zero elements in the same row (column), different schemes can be used to test. Start with the row (column) that has the fewest zero elements left, compare the number of zero elements in the column in which the row has the fewest zero elements, select the zero element in the column with the fewest zero elements and circle, then cross out the other zero elements in the same row. Repeat until all zero elements are circled or crossed out.

If the number of zero elements in the circle m is equal to the dimension of the matrix N, then the optimal solution of the assignment problem has been obtained; If m < n, go to the next step.

3. In order to find the maximum number of independent zero elements in the cost matrix, the minimum line covers all zero elements. Follow these steps:

1) Mark the lines that are not circled
2) Check the column with zero element crossed out in the row that has been checked;
3) Match the row with circled elements in the column with matching sign;
4) Repeat 2 and 3 until no new row or column is available;
6) Draw a horizontal line for the row without the marking sign, and a vertical line for the column with the marking sign, to obtain the minimum number of lines covering all zero elements.

4. The transformation gives us the new cost matrix. Find the minimum element in the element that is not covered by a line, subtract the minimum element from each element that is not covered by a line, add the minimum element to each element that is not covered by a line, and get the new matrix. Turn step (2).

3.4 Hungarian Method to Optimize Taxi System Experiment

Assuming that there are ABCDEF6 cars, six people with order Numbers from 1 to 6 need to ride separately, and the time taken by each car to pick up each person (unit min) is shown in Table 1.

Table 1. The time it takes each car to pick up each passenger

People Car	A	B	C	D	E	F
1	30	19	18	25	31	45
2	11	61	25	23	30	6
3	29	47	19	24	20	14
4	43	28	40	15	17	33
5	41	59	16	11	38	20
6	35	41	40	37	29	30

So get the cost matrix

$$\begin{bmatrix} 30 & 19 & 18 & 25 & 31 & 45 \\ 11 & 61 & 25 & 23 & 30 & 6 \\ 29 & 47 & 19 & 24 & 20 & 14 \\ 43 & 28 & 40 & 15 & 17 & 33 \\ 41 & 59 & 16 & 11 & 38 & 20 \\ 35 & 41 & 40 & 37 & 29 & 30 \end{bmatrix}$$

After the first step transformation we get this

$$
\begin{bmatrix}
7 & 0 & 0 & 7 & 13 & 27 \\
0 & 54 & 19 & 17 & 24 & 0 \\
10 & 32 & 5 & 10 & 6 & 0 \\
23 & 12 & 25 & 0 & 2 & 18 \\
25 & 47 & 15 & 0 & 27 & 9 \\
1 & 11 & 11 & 8 & 0 & 1
\end{bmatrix}
$$

After step two transformation, we can get this

$$
\begin{bmatrix}
7 & \otimes & \emptyset & 7 & 13 & 27 \\
\oplus & 54 & 19 & 17 & 24 & \emptyset \\
10 & 32 & 5 & 10 & 6 & \otimes \\
23 & 12 & 25 & \otimes & 2 & 18 \\
25 & 47 & 15 & \emptyset & 27 & 9 \\
1 & 11 & 11 & 8 & \otimes & 1
\end{bmatrix}
$$

Use $\otimes$ to represent the circled zero element, and after the transformation of step three, we can get this.

$$
\begin{bmatrix}
7 & \otimes & \emptyset & 7 & 13 & 27 \\
\otimes & 54 & 19 & 17 & 24 & \emptyset \\
10 & 32 & 5 & 10 & 6 & \otimes \\
23 & 12 & 25 & \otimes & 2 & 18 \\
25 & 47 & 15 & \emptyset & 27 & 9 \\
1 & 11 & 11 & 8 & \otimes & 1
\end{bmatrix}
$$

According to step four, find the smallest element of 2 among the unlined elements, get a new matrix and then go to step two, and finally get it.

$$
\begin{bmatrix}
0 & 1 & 0 & 0 & 0 & 0 \\
1 & 0 & 0 & 0 & 0 & 0 \\
0 & 0 & 0 & 0 & 0 & 1 \\
0 & 0 & 0 & 1 & 0 & 0 \\
0 & 0 & 1 & 0 & 0 & 0 \\
0 & 0 & 0 & 0 & 1 & 0
\end{bmatrix}
$$

It is the optimal solution, namely B1 + A2 + F3 + D4 + C5 + E6.

4 Summary

As a classical algorithm to solve the assignment problem, the Hungarian Method has the advantage that the precise global optimal solution of the assignment problem can be obtained without the program falling into an infinite loop [16]. However, with the increase of the dimension of the cost matrix, the time cost of the algorithm becomes longer, mainly because in most cases, the algorithm cannot obtain the optimal solution through a single allocation, which requires iterative solution through multiple transformation of the cost matrix, so that the operation time of the program becomes longer. It is effective to apply the Hungarian Method in the ride system to obtain the optimal allocation, but the time cost needs to be optimized. In the future research, it can be optimized to optimize the time complexity and add dynamic carpooling and other functions.

Acknowledgments. This work was supported in part by the National Natural Science Foundation of China, grant number 72073041. Open Foundation for the University Innovation Platform in the Hunan Province, grant number 18K103.2011 Collaborative Innovation Center for Development and Utilization of Finance and Economics Big Data Property.

Hunan Provincial Key Laboratory of Finance&Economics Big Data Science and Technology.2020 Hunan Provincial Higher Education Teaching Reform Research Project under Grant HNJG-2020–1130, HNJG-2020–1124. 2020 General Project of Hunan Social Science Fund under Grant 20B16.

Scientific Research Project of Education Department of Hunan Province (Grand No. 20K021), Social Science Foundation of Hunan Province (Grant No. 17YBA049).

Statement of Financial Aid and Conflict of Interest. The authors did not receive specific funding for this study. And the author states that we have no conflict of interest with respect to this study report.

References

1. Chang, T.M., Han, Z.G.: Solving a class of optimization problems with "Hungarian Method." J. Inf. Eng. Univ. **01**, 60–62 (2004)
2. Chen, Y.M.: Notes on the Hungarian method. J. Lishui Univ. **33**(05), 78–81 (2011)
3. Qiu, Y.: Research on scheduling algorithm with multiple maintenance activities in deteriorating environment, Zhejiang University of Commerce and Industry (2013)
4. Shen, B.L., Zhao, Y., Huang, Y., Zheng, W.M.: Research progress of dynamic ride-sharing in the context of big data. Comput. Res. Dev. **54**(01), 34–49 (2017)
5. Zhao, W.L.: Model and Algorithm of Abnormal Flight Emergency Scheduling, Civil Aviation University of China (2014)
6. Tian, M.Z.: Research and Application of Auction Algorithm, Qingdao University (2015.)
7. Li, J.L.: Research on Weapon-target Dynamic Firepower Allocation and combat effectiveness Evaluation, Nanchang Hangkong University (2014)
8. Liu, P., Gao, J., Liu, Y.: Optimization of target allocation problem based on auction algorithm, Ordnance Ind. Autom. (09), 22–24 (2008)
9. Yu, W.T., Peng, J., Wu, M., Zhang, X.Y.: Multi-agent task allocation algorithm based on auction. Comput. Simul. **25**(12), 184–188 (2008)
10. Men, R., Guo, T., Cao, J.Y.: Design and implementation of taxi sharing system based on intelligent terminal. J. Longdong Univ. **26**(05), 5–8 (2015)
11. Ding, P.: Research and Application of Grid Pricing Algorithm Based on Combinatorial Bidirectional Auction, Beijing University of Posts and Telecommunications (2011)

12. Ding, X.A.: Design of Mobile Car sharing System on Android Platform based on intelligent Search function. In: Signal Processing Expert Committee of China High-Tech Industrialization Research Association, Special Issue of the Fifth National Conference on Signal and Intelligent Information Processing and Application (Volume One), vol. 4, Signal Processing Expert Committee of China High-Tech Industrialization Research Association (2011)
13. Wu,J.C., Zhou, R., Ran, H.M., Ding, Q.X.: Performance comparison between Genetic algorithm and Auction algorithm in Task assignment. Electro-Optics and Control **23**(02), 11–15+82 (2016)
14. Richardson, A.J., Young, W.: Spatial Relationships between Carpool Members's Trip Ends, TRR 823 (2012)
15. Pearlstein, A.: A Study of Staff and Faculty Commuters at The University of California, Los Angeles, TRR 1082 (2015)
16. Yan, J.: Research on Cloud Resource Allocation Based on Combinatorial Bidirectional Auction, North China University of Water Resources and Electric Power (2016)
17. Xiang, L., Yang, S., Liu, Y., Li, Q., Zhu, C.: Novel linguistic steganography based on character-level text generation. Mathematics **8**, 1558 (2020)
18. Xiang, L., Guo, G., Li, Q., Zhu, C., Chen, J., et al.: Spam detection in reviews usinglstm based multientity temporal features. Intell. Autom. Soft Comput. **26**(6), 1375–1390 (2020)
19. Yang, Z., Zhang, S., Hu, Y., Hu, Z., Huang, Y.: VAE stega: linguistic steganography based on variational auto encoder. IEEE Trans. Inf. Forensics Secur. **16**, 880–895 (2021)

Network Topology Discovery Based on Classification Algorithm

Chongyang Xu[✉], Yi Man[✉], Luona Song[✉], and Yinglei Teng[✉]

Beijing University of Posts and Telecommunications, Beijing 100876, China
manyi@bupt.com, lilytengtt@bupt.edu.cn

Abstract. Due to the complexity of the situation in real life, the network topology may be missing, which will cause great obstacles to troubleshooting persons. Because of the complexity of network topology, there are some relations between the alarms of network elements with topology. In response to this problem, a classification algorithm to predict the topological relationship between network elements by alarms is proposed in this paper. Firstly, extract the data features, then perform correlation item mining on the original alarm data, and then use the alarm correlation items of the mined network element pairs as the input set of the classification algorithm to obtain the classification result of whether there is a topological relationship between the two network elements. The result of the maximum correct rate in the test set is 91.16%, and the maximum AUC is 0.95. It can be seen that the classification model established by this method has excellent performance and provides a good idea for completing the network topology.

Keywords: Network topology · Data mining · Classify algorithm

1 Introduction

Network topology is a method used to express the logical and physical connections of the network [1–3]. Through the network topology, network administrators can intuitively understand the current network operating conditions, and accurately locate network faults for isolation. In addition, network administrators can accurately analyze the bottlenecks that exist in the entire network to specifically reshape the network and improve the overall performance of the network. In the network topology, once a network element fails, it will lead to lots of alarms. If the topology relationship is missing, it is difficult to find out the real wrong network element [4]. The automatic network topology discovery technology has become the key to the construction of network topology [5]. In the existing research, the network topology discovery is based on the network layer, and the specific description is in the related work part; in [6], in order to ensure the safe operation of the telecommunication network, the method using device alarm is proposed, which has higher accuracy than using traffic information. Inspired by this, this paper proposes a classification algorithm to predict the topological relationship between the two network elements. If there is a topological relationship between two wireless network elements, there may be associated alarms, or there are some rules between the alarms. In [7], it is

© Springer Nature Switzerland AG 2021
X. Sun et al. (Eds.): ICAIS 2021, CCIS 1423, pp. 276–286, 2021.
https://doi.org/10.1007/978-3-030-78618-2_22

revealed that there will be some valuable information among a large number of alarms generated by the network elements. Data mining is used to find the alarm rules.

Combining the above two aspects of research, firstly, mine the association item set of the original alarm data to get the rules of alarm association items between network element pairs with topological relationship or not, and then use the two classification algorithm to establish the model, and apply the model to the alarm of unknown network element pair to predict the relationship between the two network elements. In the second part of this paper, the current research methods will be explained for discovering topological relationships between network elements. The third part introduces the specific algorithm of this method, the fourth part analyzes the results obtained by this method.

2 Related Work

In order to solve the problem of network topology automatic discovery, many related methods have been proposed. In [8], the Research and Computing Center of Lomonosov Moscow State University is developing the Octotron software suite. This work describes the proposed method for automatically discovering the Ethernet communication network topology in a supercomputer, and conducts an Octotron model. In [9], Flathagen and Bentstuen proposed a method for discovering the topology between switches through which an software defined network (SDN) controller transfers data. It uses the OpenFlow Discovery Protocol (OFDP) customized the Link Layer Discovery Protocol (LLDP) for an SDN.

In [10], several heuristic algorithms are designed to find the network topology, And an algorithm has been implemented and extensive experiments have been conducted on the Kent State University Computer Science Network. In [11], it is proposed that the current IPv6 network topology discovery technology is considered to be inefficient. So it introduces how to expand the detection space, analyzes the reasons for the expansion of the detection space. In [12], a new topology discovery algorithm is proposed for mobile ad hoc networks, it is developed on Linux system. By mixing mobile agents and data collection, the algorithm aims to solve the topology discovery problem in hierarchical Ad Hoc network scenarios.

In [13], an algorithm for identifying the types of network devices and discovering the connectivity between them was proposed, and the connectivity of the devices with the final host and management information base (MIB) enabled and switches and routers was discussed and evaluated.

In [14], a network topology discovery algorithm based on OSPF protocol is proposed and its implementation method is introduced. It is different from most traditional topology discovery algorithms based on SNMP and ICMP protocols. Through the above research, it can be seen that no classification algorithm has been proposed to predict the topological relationship between network elements. Therefore, a new method is proposed, which uses the alarms generated by topologically related network elements to establish a classification model. The alarms generated by the network elements of unknown topology are input to this model to predict whether the two network elements have a topology relationship.

3 Algorithm

3.1 Overall Description of the Method

This method is divided into four steps: (1) Simply process the original alarm data, count the number of occurrences of each type of alarm in each time window, and use the associated item mining algorithm to obtain the corresponding associated item set, including binomial sets and polynomial sets; (2) It is only necessary to judge whether there is a topological relationship between the two network elements,so it is necessary to mine the item set data that comes out is processed into the form of "A ==> B" (A and B respectively represent a type of alarm); (3) Find the A and B alarms that meet the time window range in the original alarm file, and to check whether there is a topological relationship between the two alarm network elements by the resource file. We can get the alarm information of the two network elements with topological relationship and the alarm summary of the two network elements without topological relationship; (4) Sort the obtained data set into two parts: training set and test set, then judge the quality of this classifier by the correct rate and ROC Area.

3.2 Introduction to the Original Alarm Data and Its Simple Processing

There are 32543 alarms in total. The data sample is shown in Table 1. The alarm fingerprint is the unique identifier for the alarm entry; the alarm location object ID is the network element where the alarm occurs, which is the most fine-grained location information; the home device network element ID is the upper level of the positioning object,which may also be the same as the positioning object; the alarm occurrence time and clearing time are accurate to the minute, there are basically a large number of alarm entries in every minute; the alarm title determines the alarm type; the city ID is the same. There are 7 different districts and counties in total; the network management alarm level corresponds to the alarm title; the alarm target equipment type, equipment type, and equipment room are descriptions of the alarm equipment, just select one of them is enough; the profession distinguishes the alarm network to which it belongs, and this article uses wireless network alarm data.

Table 1. Original alarm data.

Alarm finger print	Alarm location object ID	Home device network element ID	Alarm occurrence time	Clearing time	Alarm title	City ID	District ID	The network manaerent alarm level	Alarm target equipment type	Equipment type	Equipment room	Profession
25252 39599	−7899 91960	15584 5823	2016/3/25 0:03:00	2016/3/25 0:05:00	Cell faul -ty	20032 19373	21402 66616	1	8105	9201	−12246 2328	Wirel -ess
221040 8821	−14641 58348	−15981 31537	2016/3/25 0:02:00	2016/3/25 0:02:00	State change to enable degraded	20032 19373	−16584 48670	2	9300	9201	−17044 02691	Wirel -ess

From a comprehensive perspective, an alarm can be uniquely identified by "alarm location object ID (id) + alarm occurrence time (time) + alarm title (title) + alarm object equipment type (type)". Firstly, filter out these four columns, and then arrange them in the positive order of time and store them in the id_time_title_type.csv file. Part of the data is shown in Table 2.

Table 2. Part of Id_time_title_type.csv.

Alarm location object ID	Alarm occurrence time	Alarm title	Alarm target equipment type
−1266589937	2016/3/25 0:00:00	IP RAN/0 HEARTBEAT FAILURE	9201
1418969938	2016/3/25 0:00:00	RRH/31 CCM-SLAVE LINK	9201
−723530600	2016/3/25 0:00:00	RRH VSWR MAIN/11 VSWR LEVEL 2	9201

3.3 Selection of Associated Item Mining Algorithm

Apriori and FP-Growth are commonly used to mine association items. The Apriori algorithm scans the transaction database multiple times, and uses candidate frequent sets to generate frequent sets each time. Candidate set statistics is very time-consuming. The pruning step also needs to detect the k−1 subset of each k-candidate item set, which is also time-consuming.FP-growth uses a tree structure to directly obtain frequent sets without generating candidate frequent sets, which greatly reduces the number of scanning transaction databases, thereby improving the efficiency of the algorithm. In this paper, considering the huge amount of alarm data, the FP-Growth algorithm is used to mine the alarm related items in order to improve mining efficiency.

3.4 Selection of Classification Algorithm

The classification algorithm is a kind of supervised learning. Common classification algorithms are NBC algorithm, LR algorithm, ZeroR, C4.5 decision tree algorithm, Bayesian algorithm, SVM algorithm, random forest algorithm, ANN algorithm, etc. In this paper, it is a two-category problem. The topological relationship between two network elements can only be presence and absence. To get the best model, the best way is to test each algorithm one by one through cross-validation, compare them, then adjust the parameters to ensure that each algorithm reaches the optimal solution, and finally choose the best one. In this article, considering that the C4.5 decision tree is simple to calculate, easy to understand, and highly interpretable, it can be selected as one of the classification algorithms; the random forest is composed of multiple decision trees, which can be selected as the second classification algorithm. In addition, Bayes, Naive Bayes, and ZeroR are also selected as contrast classification algorithms. As an open data mining platform, Weka has assembled a large number of machine learning algorithms that can undertake data mining tasks, including data preprocessing, classification, regression, clustering, association rules, and visualization on a new interactive interface. Therefore, the data mining algorithm and classification algorithm in this paper are implemented by weka.

3.5 Analysis of Specific Steps

Process the Original Alarm Data for Mining. From Sect. 3.1, the time range is from 0:00 on March 25th to 24:00 on the 26th, and the time span is 48 h. However, the network element can generate up to 10 alarms within 1min sometimes, but if the network element A has a topological relationship with the network element B, then after a certain type of alarm occurs in A, a certain type of alarm will occur in B, but this time interval will definitely not exceed a certain time range. In this article, the time window is set to 10 min and the step size is set to 1min. On the one hand, this is more in line with the actual situation, and on the other hand, it can ensure that there are enough data items for mining algorithms. That is, the time range of the first time window is 00:00-25th 00:10 on the 25th; the time range of the second time window is 00:01-25th 00:11 on the 25th...and so on. Note that the start time point of the second time window is not 0:11, this may happen that the two network elements corresponding to the alarms of the mined alarm correlation items M and N in the time window range cannot be found at the same time in the same cluster in the cluster file wifi.json. In order to avoid the occurrence of "the number of topologically related alarm entries is zero", the step size is set to 1 min. The specific processing algorithm is shown in Fig. 1:

```
#Get the alarm of each time window
1: Import the original data set to the list；
2: Set the initial time window：start_time=day25 00:00 , end_time=day25 00:10；
3: For items in original data list：
4:    If (item1.time between start_time and end_time) && (item2.time between
start_time and end_time):
5:       Result[i].append(item1).append(item2);
6:    Else:
7:       start_time=start_time+1min;
8:       end_time=start_time+10min;
9:       i++;
#Extract the total alarm attributes category
10:create table attr (select distinct title from table id_time_title_type)
#Count the number of occurrences of each type of alarm in each time window
11:For i in Result:
12:   For t in attr:
13:      If(Result[i][j]==attr[t]):
14:      nums[t]++;
```

Fig. 1. Process the original data for mining Algorithm.

In summary, the number of time windows = total time span/time window = 48 × 60/1 = 2880 time windows, firstly list the alarms that occur in each time window. Part of the data is shown in Table 3. The serial numbers 1–4 correspond to the first to fourth time windows, and the second column is all the alarms that occurred in this time window. Because there are too many alarms, all the alarms that occurred in each time window are not fully displayed.

Table 3. Alarms in each time window.

1	[' CELL OPERATION DEGRADED', 'CELL FAULTY', 'RRH VSWR MAIN/11 VSWR LEVEL 2', 'RRH VSWR MAIN/41 VSWR LEVEL 2',......]
2	['CELL OPERATION DEGRADED', 'RRH VSWR MAIN/11 VSWR LEVEL 2', 'RRH VSWR MAIN/11 VSWR LEVEL 2', 'RRH VSWR MAIN/11 VSWR LEVEL 2',......]
3	['CELL OPERATION DEGRADED', 'State change to Enable Degraded', 'State change to Enable Degraded', 'RRH VSWR MAIN/11 VSWR LEVEL 2', ...]
4	['CELL FAULTY', 'CELL FAULTY', 'CELL FAULTY', 'CELL FAULTY', 'CELL FAULTY', 'CELL FAULTY', 'RRH VSWR MAIN/11 VSWR LEVEL 2', ...]

In addition, we also need to count the total number of alarm categories. According to statistics, there are 216 different alarm categories, so you can process how many times each alarm type has occurred in each time window, but the data input to weka can only be discrete variables, so the number is described as whether occurs or not. That is, in this time window, when the number > 0, then set to "t"; the number = 0, then set to "?". Part of the data is shown in Table 4.

Table 4. Data set for mining.

CELL OPERATION DEGRADE	CELL FAULTY	RRH VSWR MAIN/11 VSWR LEVEL 2	RRH VSWR MAIN/41 VSWR LEVEL 2	IP RAN/0 HEARTBEAT FAILURE	RRH/31 CCM-SLAVE LINK	State change To Disable Failed
t	t	t	t	t	t	t
t	t	t	t	t	t	t
t	t	t	t	t	t	t
t	t	t	t	t	?	?
t	t	t	t	t	?	?

Association item Mining Algorithm. The associated items mined by the FP-Growth algorithm include binomial sets and multinomial sets, as shown in Table 5. As shown in the first item, it means that within a time window after the "CELL OPERATION DEGRADE" alarm and the "RRH VSWR MAIN/41 VSWR LEVEL 2" alarm occurred together, "RRH VSWR MAIN/11 VSWR LEVEL 2" also occurred and repeated 2800 times.

Table 5. Part of original alarm related items.

CELL OPERATION DEGRADE = t RRH VSWR MAIN/41 VSWR LEVEL 2 = t 2800 ==> RRH VSWR MAIN/11 VSWR LEVEL 2 = t 2800
CELL OPERATION DEGRADE = t RRH VSWR MAIN/11 VSWR LEVEL 2 = t 2800 ==> RRH VSWR MAIN/41 VSWR LEVEL 2 = t 2800
CELL OPERATION DEGRADED = t 2800 ==> RRH VSWR MAIN/11 VSWR LEVEL 2 = t RRH VSWR MAIN/41 VSWR LEVEL 2 = t 2800

However, in this paper, only the relationship between two network elements is discussed, so the multinomial set is divided into binomial sets, and duplicates are deleted, so "=t" and the specific number of occurrences should be removed. The specific mining algorithm is as follows (Fig. 2):

```
#split
1: For items in result:
2:   item.split by("=").split by("==>");
3:   return new_result;
#Remove num
4: For items in new_result:
5:   For t in attr:
6:     if item.strip() ==t;
7:     Result.append(item);
#Pairwise
8:For items in Result:
9:   item[0]+"==>"+item[1]
```

Fig. 2. Process multinomial sets Algorithm.

After processing, part of the binomial set is shown in Table 6, and the entire data is saved in the correlation_result.csv file:

Put the Final Data Set to Classification Algorithm. Classification algorithms are important, but good data sets are better than good algorithms. The alarm data feature

Table 6. Part of Binomial sets.

First warning	Second warning
IP RAN/0 HEARTBEAT FAILURE	TPU's CHP DSP0 initialization failed
RRH VSWR MAIN/41 VSWR LEVEL 2	RRH VSWR MAIN/11 VSWR LEVEL 2
RRH/31 LOW RSSI	CELL OPERATION DEGRADED
Relay alarm indication signal	State change to Enable Degraded
RRH VSWR MAIN/11 VSWR LEVEL 2	State change to Enable Degraded
Relay alarm indication signal	TPU's CHP DSP0 initialization failed

selected in this paper is {alarm location object ID, alarm occurrence time, alarm title, alarm device object type}, abbreviated as {ID, time, title, type}. Since the result of classification is whether there is a topological relationship between two network elements, there should be two pairs of features. That is, the final data set organization form should be {ID1, time 1, title1, type1, ID2, time 2, title2, type2, link}. Link = 1 or 0, respectively indicates whether there is a topological relationship between the two network elements.

In order to get such a data set, firstly we need to find the alarm items with the network element IDs title1 and title2 in the original alarm file, and pay attention to whether they meet the following two conditions: (1) The interval between time 1 and time 2 needs to be in one time window, that is, within 10 min, if it is not met, it cannot be paired; (2) For the two alarms that can be paired, pay attention to whether ID1 and ID2 are in the same cluster of the cluster file. If so, then link = 1, otherwise link = 0. And the specific algorithm is as follows (Fig. 3):

```
1: For items in correlation_result:
2: For i in id_time_title_type.csv:
3:     If abs(i[item1].time-i[item2].time)<10min;
4:     For w in wifi.json:
4:         If i[items1].ID1 in w and  i[item2].ID2 in w;
5:             link=1;
6:         Else:
7:             link=0;
8:     Else:
9:         Break;
```

Fig. 3. Topo_link items Algorithm.

After performing this processing on all alarm related items, data set classfierResult.arff file that can be classified is obtained. Part of the data is shown in Table 7. Among them, the number of alarm items with a topological relationship: the number of alarm items without a topological relationship = 1:4.

Table 7. Data set for classify.

ID1	Time1	Title1	Type1	ID2	Time2	Title2	Type2	link
−1266589937	2016/3/25 0:00:00	IP RAN/0 HEARTBEAT FAILURE	9201	188179815	2016/3/25 0:00:00	CELL OPERATION DEGRADED	8105	0
−1266589937	2016/3/25 0:00:00	IP RAN/0 HEARTBEAT FAILURE	9201	−1006855543	2016/3/25 0:00:00	CELL FAULTY	8105	0
−1266589937	2016/3/25 0:00:00	IP RAN/0 HEARTBEAT FAILURE	9201	−1447458579	2016/3/25 0:04:00	RRH VSWR MAIN/41 VSWR LEVEL 2	9201	0

As mentioned in Sect. 3.3, the classification algorithms selected in this paper are J48, random forest, ZeroR, Bayes algorithm, and Naive Bayes algorithm. Two methods are also adopted for the division of training set and test set: (1) 66% of the training set and 34% of the validation set; (2) 10-fold cross-validation. There are a total of 10 methods in this combination, and the correct rate and AUC are shown in Table 8.

Table 8. Final correct rate and AUC.

Algorithm	Correct rate	AUC
J48 + 66%	91.10%	0.95
J48 + 10-fold	91.15%	0.95
ZeroR + 66%	81.22%	0.5
ZeroR + 10-fold	81.15%	0.5
Bayes + 66%	89.18%	0.931
Bayes + 10-fold	89.23%	0.931
Naive Bayes + 66%	87.03%	0.915
Naive Bayes + 10-fold	87.05%	0.916
Random Forest + 66%	91.11%	0.949
Random Forest + 10-fold	91.16%	0.948

3.6 Result Analysis

As shown in Table 8, from the perspective of correctness, random forest classification is the best, followed by J48, with a difference of only 0.06%; from the AUC point of view, the ZeroR classification algorithm has AUC = 0.5, which means that random guessing is used, the model is of little significance and can be discarded; the AUC of other classification algorithms are all in the [0.85, 0.95] interval, indicating that the classification model is effective. On the one hand, this shows that the characteristics of the data set adopted in this paper are good;on the other hand, it also shows that the correlation item of the alarm is used to judge whether there is a topology relationship between two network elements is reliable.

4 Summary

Because the topological relationship between network elements in real life is missing, which brings obstacles to troubleshooting persons, a classification algorithm is proposed to predict whether there is a topological relationship between two network elements. After experimental verification, the data extracted by this method have good features, and the model prediction effect after classification is excellent, which can be applied in practice.

Acknowledgement. The research of this article is supported by National Key R&D Program of China(No. 2018YFB1201500).

References

1. Lu, H.-M.: An algorithm of network topology analysis based on SNMP. Sci. Technol. Inf. (2012)
2. LAN MAN Standards Committee of the IEEE Computer Society (2005) IEEE Std 802.ID-2004 [S/OL]. [S.l.]: The United States of America: The Institute of Electrical and Electronics Engineers, Inc. (2004). [2005–07–07].
3. ElMoukaddem, F., Torng, E., Xing, G.: Maximizing network topology lifetime using mobile node rotation. IEEE Trans. Parallel Distrib. Syst. **26**, 1958–1970 (2015). https://doi.org/10.1109/TPDS.2014.2329851
4. Hatonen, K., Klemettinen, M., Mannila, H., et al.: Knowledge discovery from telecommunication network alarm databases. In: Proceedings of the Twelfth International Conference on Data Engineering, 1996. IEEE (1995)
5. Zhang, X.: An optimization algorithm of network topology discovery based on SNMP protocol. **6**(1), 104–111 (2018)
6. Takada, A., Hayashi, N., Nakamura, M., Seki, T., Yamagoe, K.: Topology discovery method using network equipment alarms. In: 2020 16th International Conference on Network and Service Management (CNSM), Izmir, Turkey, pp. 1–5 (2020). https://doi.org/10.23919/CNSM50824.2020.9269090
7. Bellec, J.H., Kechadi, M.T., Carthy, J.: A new efficient clustering algorithm for network alarm analysis. In: International Conference on Parallel & Distributed Computing Systems. DBLP (2005)
8. Sobolev, S., Stefanov, K., Voevodin, V.: Automatic discovery of the communication network topology for building a supercomputer model. In: Numerical Computations: Theory & Algorithms: International Conference Numerical Computations: Theory & Algorithms. AIP Publishing LLC (2016)
9. Flathagen, J., Bentstuen, O.I.: Proxy-based optimization of topology discovery in software defined networks. In: 2019 International Conference on Military Communications and Information Systems (ICMCIS). IEEE (2019)

10. Gobjuka, H., Breitbart, Y.J.: Ethernet topology discovery for networks with incomplete information. IEEE/ACM Trans. Networking **18**(4), 1220–1233 (2010)
11. Mingming, Z., Junyong, L.: An improved solution for IPv6 network topology discovery based on source routing mechanism. 279–282 (2009)
12. Chen, P., Su, J., Guo, W.: The implementation of a new topology discovery algorithm in mobile ad hoc network. In: International Conference on Multimedia Technology. IEEE (2010)
13. Pandey, S., Choi, M.J., Won, Y.J., et al.: SNMP-based enterprise IP network topology discovery. Int. J. Network Manage. **21**(3), 169–184 (2011)
14. Wang, J., Chen, B., Tan, C.X.: Design and implementation of network topology discovery system based on OSPF. Adv. Mat. Res. **760–762**, 2100–2103 (2013)

Research on Feature Words for IoT Device Recognition Based on Word2vec

Zi-Xiao Xu[1], Xiu-Bo Chen[1,3(✉)], Gang Xu[2], Kai-Guo Yuan[3], Jun Cui[1,2,3], and Yi-Xian Yang[1,3]

[1] Information Security Center, State Key Laboratory of Networking and Switching Technology, Beijing University of Posts and Telecommunications, Beijing 100876, China
xb_chen@bupt.edu.cn
[2] School of Information Science and Technology, North China University of Technology, Beijing 100144, China
[3] State Key Laboratory of Public Big Data, Guizhou University, Guiyang 550025, Guizhou, China

Abstract. With the advent of the IoT era, more and more IoT device has begun to integrate into our daily life. Effective recognition of all kinds of IoT device is the premise to ensure the safety of IoT devices. Furthermore, if a certain device can be identified more finely, such as brand and model information. Then it can be associated with the device vulnerability library to obtain more detailed device security information. According to the existing research, the richer the feature lexicon of IoT devices, the finer the granularity of device recognition will be. The paper is based on word2vec technology to expand the IoT device recognition feature vocabulary. Firstly, the keywords carried by the device information are used as the input of the search engine, and the corpus of keywords is constructed. Secondly, we use word2vec to model the corpus, and then extract the known IoT device feature words related to keywords from the model. Finally, based on the binary correlation judgment algorithm proposed in this paper, we judge the correlation between keywords and feature words in turn. If the correlation is consistent, keywords will be added to the corresponding feature lexicon.

Keywords: Internet of things security · Word2vec · Fine-grained

1 Introduction

With the rapid popularization of mobile Internet, more kinds of IoT devices have joined the daily network. Today, the number of IoT devices in the world has exceeded 20 billion, whereas ARM predicts that by the year 2035 the world will be connected with more than one trillion IoT devices [1]. A large number of a wide variety of network devices will expose more network security problems and bring severe challenges to network maintenance personnel. Many historical security incidents have shown that IoT devices are extremely easy for hackers to launch large-scale network attacks as broilers. Here is a typical case [2]: A high-risk vulnerability in remote code execution was exposed

© Springer Nature Switzerland AG 2021
X. Sun et al. (Eds.): ICAIS 2021, CCIS 1423, pp. 287–298, 2021.
https://doi.org/10.1007/978-3-030-78618-2_23

288 Z.-X. Xu et al.

in 2017. An attacker remotely executes arbitrary code by sending a malicious packet to port 37215 of the router. In just 24 h, hackers used the vulnerability to create a bot net containing 18000 Huawei routers, followed by a list of IP address. It is worth noting that the attacker only used a known vulnerability to complete such a large-scale attack. Then it can be seen that the security of IoT devices still needs to be greatly improved.

Some scholars' research [3] found that IoT devices with similar product attributes may have the same vulnerability. If IoT devices can be identified quickly and accurately, corresponding security policies can be formulated. This provides basic security guarantee for the IoT environment. Therefore, the effective identification of IoT devices in the network space is of great significance to grasp the security situation of physical devices in the network space.

Table 1. Common IoT device vulnerabilities and exposures

CVE-ID	Type	Brand	Model	Risk
CVE-2016-10277	Mobile	Motorola	All Series	Critical
CVE-2017-17215	Router	Huawei	HG532	Critical
CVE-2019-16288	Router	Tenda	N301	High
CVE-2019-17507	Router	D-Link	DIR-816	High
CVE-2019-17508	Router	D-Link	DIR-859	Critical
CVE-2019-9677	IPC	DAHUA	IPC-HDW1X2X	High
CVE-2020-9502	IPC	DAHUA	SD6AL Series	High
CVE-2020-14100	Router	Xiaomi	R3600	Critical
CVE-2020-9958	Mobile	Apple	IPHONE6s	High

More and more scholars have been involved in the subject of how to effectively identify the device of IoT. At present, the existing device identification methods of IoT are mainly divided into two categories: one is to construct the classification fingerprint of the device [4], and the other is to construct the device identification model through machine learning [5]. Nmap [6], a well-known network scanning tool, scans device information and then matches it with the existing fingerprint database to obtain the scanned device type. Although the artificial fingerprint database constructed by the hardware information of the device can be used to accurately identify the IoT device. However, the fingerprint in the fingerprint database is easy to degenerate, which does not have good distinguishing ability for relatively new and similar devices. Although machine learning recognition method can reduce the logical flow of recognition and judgment, it can only recognize the existing equipment. For the newly added equipment, not only the training set needs to be reconstructed, but also the classifier needs to be trained for a long time. And due to the constant change of the model, the historical data needs to be re-examined. This is not efficient in a scenario where new devices are constantly being added. In addition, machine learning's recognition granularity is relatively low and can only give device type or device brand. If fine-grained identification can be made, then the type, brand,

and model of the device can be further given. The information about the security risks of the device can then be matched. Table 1 lists the typical vulnerability information of IoT devices in recent years.

If we can get fine-grained attribute information for the device, such as type, brand, and model. Then the specific existing security vulnerability number can be matched according to the CVE (Common Vulnerabilities and Exposures) website, and then the risk coefficient and security defect of the device can be understood. This is very important to reinforce the safety of the IoT devices and develop an effective safety policy.

The core structure of this paper is mainly divided into two parts: The first part is the main idea of this paper, including the introduction of the IoT device recognition feature words, word2vec tool introduction and binary relationship judgment algorithm, the results of this part mainly rely on the related ideas of word vectors [7, 8]. The second part is the experimental part. The main ideas of the first part are demonstrated in practice according to the equipment environment. From the devices information processing to the IoT devices feature word analysis, and finally gives the IoT device recognition results.

2 Related Work

In order to obtain as much information as possible from IoT devices, the methods of detection, scanning and traffic monitoring are generally adopted to obtain the information of IoT devices. However, for some devices, there are very few effective keywords that can be extracted, which is not enough to give complete information of the IoT device. Zou [3] found that the known model can help to infer the type and brand, and the known type and model can infer the brand. As long as the automatic IoT devices information database is constructed in advance, the device can be identified finely according to the semantic information in the message header. Xu [9] did not build the IoT devices information database, but put the agreement keywords into the search bar of the third-party e-commerce website, and extracted the type, brand and model information of the device from the returned result page.

Although the above two ways of matching device information are different, they are essentially related to more information through a single information. Through this way of search, we can get more device information as much as possible when the device information is not enough. The above process is also the core idea to support the fine-grained identification of IoT device. However, there are still some problems in the existing fine-grained schemes:

The method of Zou [3] requires continuous crawling of data, otherwise, new device cannot be identified. Xu's [9] method needs to be compared and judged in several third-party websites, which will send more query requests and the device data of the third-party websites may not be complete enough. Through the actual observation, it is found that the IoT device information slogans generated by detection or traffic protocol are often mixed with other characters or confused by device manufacturers. If direct matching is used, there will be a large rate of missing reports. If fuzzy matching is used, there will be a large false alarm rate.

This paper mainly analyzes the second problem mentioned above. In order to solve this problem, it is necessary to verify and accumulate some confused information slogans of IoT devices. An effective way is to give keyword information through search engine. For example, we collected the keyword tencent _tingting from a smart speaker of Tencent. Figure 1 shows the results of Bing search engine. The key words in the red boxes are the identification result information: the device type is smart speaker, the device brand is Tencent, and the device model is tinging.

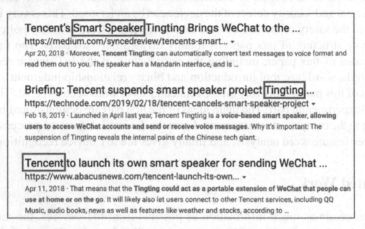

Fig. 1. The results of Bing search engine (Color figure online)

Although the above method is intuitive and easy to understand, it has the following two problems:

1) IoT devices carry too much irrelevant information, and the workload of human screening is too large.
2) The method based on human observation is prone to false positives and omissions.

In the following sections, this article describes how to use word2vec to solve this problem. The main ideas are written in the next section.

3   Main Idea

3.1   IoT Device Recognition Feature Words

According to the information returned by the device, Li [10] found that the word camera appears mostly in the web camera and the firewall is concentrated in the firewall. This kind of words contribute a lot to the identification of the type of IoT devices. This paper defines this kind of words as type feature words. For more fine-grained identification, in addition to type feature words, brand feature words and model feature words are also required. In this paper, IoT device recognition feature words are divided into the following six categories:

A. **device type feature words**: Words that are more relevant to the type of device, such as camera, indicate that they are related to web camera.

B. **device brand feature words**: Words that are more relevant to the brand of device, such as *MI*, which are related to Xiaomi company.

C. **device model feature words**: Words that are more relevant to the model of device, for example, *myna* stands for the model of a smart speaker of Huawei.

D. **combined feature words**: Words related to a variety of features may include a variety of relationships such as type and brand, type and model, and brand and model. For example, *miwifi* is both a type feature word and a brand feature word.

E. **common feature words**: Words that most IoT devices will carry, such as *server*, *http* and so on.

F. **irrelevant model feature words**: some feature words without recognition meaning, as well as some random code, string.

Table 2 lists some common feature words of IoT devices, in which Label is the serial letter of the features marked above.

Table 2. Some IoT device recognition feature words

Label	Feature words	Type	Brand	Model
A	ipcam, cam, webcam	IPC	–	–
A	routers, ipp, routing	Router	HG532	–
B	gimitv, gimi	–	Xgimi	–
C	DH-IPC-HFW2235M	–	–	DH-IPC-HFW2235M
D	miwif	Router	Xiaomi	–
D	L655	Printer	Epson	L655
E	http, server, dns	–	–	–
F	443, 8080, SECF10222	–	–	–

If the first four words in Table 2 can be obtained, the IoT devices can be identified intuitively. The question is, how to complete the conversion between feature words and give the final result? The next section gives the answer.

3.2 IoT Device Recognition Feature Words

Before fine-grained device recognition, we first constructed three database tables, which are device type feature words table, device brand feature words table and IoT device information table. Among them, the first two tables are used to accumulate device feature words in the process of IoT device recognition, and the latter table stores the relevant IoT devices. The data storage and acquisition of this table refer to the web crawler processing ideas of Zou [4]. When we get some IoT device feature words in the information obtained from the device, we can obtain the device result based on the following steps:

1. The query words are matched with the type feature words table and the brand feature words table. According to the feature words table, the corresponding device type and device brand are obtained.
2. According to the type and brand obtained in the first step, the matching result will be the model list. At this point, the fine-grained device recognition results can be output. In order to effectively match and accumulate the IoT device identification words, this paper establishes the device type attribute library, the device brand attribute library, and the device model attribute library. Among them, the table represents the IoT device type feature vocabulary, represents the IoT brand feature vocabulary. Figure 2 shows how the string "webcam dahuap2p dh-ipc-hfw2125m" gives the final recognition result through the IoT device feature lexicon.

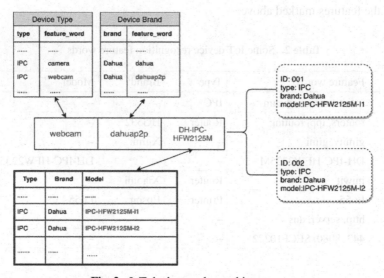

Fig. 2. IoT device result matching process

3.3 Binary Correlation Judgment Algorithm Based on Word2vec

Human language can not be directly recognized in the computer, and can only be recognized by the computer by converting into machine language composed of binary code. Therefore, in order to realize the language text processing, it is necessary to establish a model for the text so that the machine can recognize and process. In 1986, Hinton [11] first proposed the concept of distributed expression, namely Word Embedding. The purpose of word vector is to quantify and classify the semantic similarity between linguistic items based on the distribution attributes in large sample of language data.

Word2vec. In 2013, Tomas mikolov and others [7, 8] from Google team designed and developed a program called word2vec. Word2vec is a tool that uses deep learning to train word vectors. Its main idea is that there are hidden relations between words in massive texts. After training a large number of texts, word vectors with high quality and similar semantics can be obtained. Word2vec has two bag models: Skip-Gram and CBOW. Mikolovet [7] states that while CBOW models are often slightly faster, skip-gram models tend to perform better on smaller data sets. Since the data set we use is small, we will choose Skip -Gram as the model.

Construction of IoT Device Feature Words Corpus. Corpus is a kind of semantic material specially used to store the problems that need to be analyzed. How large a corpus is and whether it is better or not has always been a controversial issue. Considering that the IoT device feature words are extremely irregular. Theoretically, there is no absolute large corpus containing all the IoT device feature words. Generally speaking, our corpus can be divided into two types: one is the online corpus, which contains the most common device feature words. The corpus of this part is from Shodan, which is the world's first search engine for Internet-connected devices, and the major third-party e-commerce websites. The second is a small corpus built by the search engine, which can capture relatively new and special IoT device feature words.

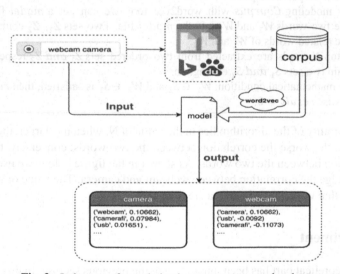

Fig. 3. Judgment of correlation between camera and webcam

We choose Baidu and Bing as corpus. Baidu is friendly to Chinese and Bing is friendly to English. Different from the traditional corpus which has been constructed in advance, the search engine can query almost any IoT device feature words. In this paper, the keyword pages obtained by search engines are used as corpus. The corpus contains 50 titles and their corresponding web page summary information for each keyword. Here we choose Baidu and Bing as the corpus, which is different from the traditional corpus which has been constructed in advance. Baidu has a good friendliness to Chinese, while Bing has a good friendliness to English. Here, if the corpus is searched, as shown in the figure, four Web links will be displayed. The search engine contains the largest corpus in the world, and can display the search results in seconds. Figure 3 shows the judgment of correlation between camera and webcam.

The judgment idea of the algorithm mainly refers to how to prove that two sets are equal. If it is necessary to prove whether two sets are equal, it is enough to prove that two sets are each other subsets. Similarly, if it is necessary to determine the correlation between two words, it is only necessary to prove that the two words are semantically related to each other. The following is a similar description of the algorithm.

Algorithm 1: Binary Correlation Judgment.

Input: The binary to compare the correlation is (W_1, W_2), the size of the set is N.

Output: The result of binary correlation is $result$, $result = 1$ indicates that binary group (W_1, W_2) is correlated and $result = 0$ indicates that binary group (W_1, W_2) is uncorrelated.

1. Construct query string s = "$W_1 W_2$", put it into Baidu and Bing search engines. Then we'll get the page results after filtering and word segmentation. The result is the specific corpus $Courpus$.

2. After modeling $Courpus$ with word2vec tool, we can get a $model$ file. We input the two words W_1 and W_2 into the $model$ file. Two sets Z_1, Z_2 contains the semantic related words of W_1 and W_2.

3. The top N words are extracted from two ordered sets Z_1 and Z_2 respectively. We obtain two sets S_1 and S_2 of length n.

4. If the mathematical condition: $W_1 \in S_2$ and $W_2 \in S_1$ is satisfied, then $result = 1$, otherwise $result = 0$.

The flexibility of the algorithm lies in the value of N. when n is larger, the longer the set length is, the worse the correlation between the two words; conversely, the stronger the correlation between the two words. As shown in the figure below, we use the search engine to judge the correlation between webcam and camera. The value of n is set to 3. We can see that webcam and camera are related.

4 Experiment

The core theoretical part has been introduced in the previous section. In this section, six devices that are difficult to identify are selected for analysis. See Table 3 for details of the six devices. Each device is given a model.

Table 3. The Information of six IoT devices

	IP	Type	Brand	Model
1	192.168.1.1	Speaker	Huawei	AIS-BW50-00
2	192.168.1.2	Air Cleaner	Xiaomi	Third generation
3	192.168.1.3	Speaker	Lenovo	Smart Assistant
4	192.168.1.4	Gateway	Xiaomi	Second generation
5	192.168.1.5	Router	Dlink	DIR-850L
6	192.168.1.6	Router	Netgear	WNR3500U

4.1 Filter the Data from IoT Devices

In this experiment, the methods to obtain effective data of equipment are tool scanning and traffic protocol parsing [9]. Scanning tool (Nmap) [6], bro [12] used for traffic protocol analysis. Set up a folder for each IP address, and there will be several protocol files under each folder. At the same time, a large amount of protocol data is stored under each file. In order to extract valid keywords from the protocol, we divided each document equally into 10 parts. According to the TF-IDF [13] algorithm, the effective keywords in the top ranking are extracted from each document. Table 4 shows the protocol keywords extracted from the massive information generated by the six devices.

Table 4. Filtered device data

	IP	Data
1	192.168.1.1	speaker-drcn myhwclouds logservice1 cn-north-2 hicloud metrics1
2	192.168.1.2	Sc5 zhimi-airpurifier-v6 tz miio78721060
3	192.168.1.3	LenovoSmartAssistant lenove Sc5 chnshp com cn
4	192.168.1.4	dns unmatched reply dhcp line mismatch single miio131974673 Sc5 lumi-gateway-v3
5	192.168.1.5	dlinkroute7 gsp10-ssl-cn SHA imtt ECDHE weixin gspe11-ssl ocsp gspe DIR-850L mydlink
6	192.168.1.6	reply anonymous updates1 stream WNR3500U txt recv no OOPSp fileinfo netgear

From the last column of Table 3, we can find that the data carried by each device contains some IoT device feature words. The next part of the work is to extract and verify these feature words.

4.2   Extraction and Verification of Feature Words for IoT Device

Figure 4 shows the process of feature word extraction and verification of IoT devices. The main steps are divided into two steps: extraction and verification. The following figure shows all the processes in this section.

Extraction of Feature Words. The data obtained in Table 4 is spaced by spaces to generate a list with checked keywords. Put the words in the list into the search engine as query statements in turn, and use the query results as a corpus. Based on this corpus, a model is built using Word2vec and the top 10 related feature words are extracted. Extract the known Internet of Things device feature words from 10 feature words. At this point, a binary (KeyWord, Feature Word) is formed, in which KeyWord is the key word extracted in Table 4, and Feature Word is the feature word recognized by known IoT devices.

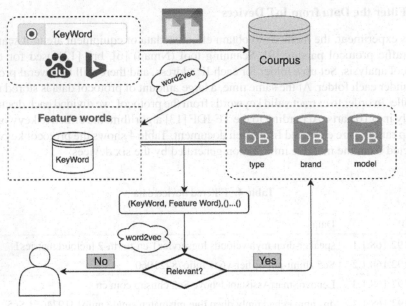

Fig. 4. Extraction and verification of feature words for IoT device

Verification of Feature Words. Referring to the binary relation verification judgment algorithm in 3.4.2, we make a correlation judgment for (KeyWord, Feature Word). In this algorithm, the size of N is inversely proportional to the correlation. We set the value of N to 5, indicating strong correlation. All binaries (KeyWord, Feature Word) are validated in turn according to the algorithm flow. If the binary correlation is determined, KeyWord has the same characterisics as Feature Word, that is, KeyWord is added to the feature lexicon to which Feature Word belongs. Table 5 shows the binary from Table 4.

4.3 IoT Deivce Recognition Results

After steps 4.2.1 and 4.2.2, we have added valid Internet of Things device feature words to the corressponding database. At this time, according to the device identification process in Sect. 3.2, we get the device identification results in Table 6.

Table 5. Binary group data

	IP	Binary data
1	192.168.1.1	(speaker-drcn, speaker), (myhwclouds, huawei)
2	192.168.1.2	(zhimi-airpurifier-v6, air purifier), (zhimi-airpurifier-v6,xiaomi)
3	192.168.1.3	(LenovoSmartAssistant, speaker), (LenovoSmartAssistant, Smart Assistant)
4	192.168.1.4	(lumi-gateway-v3, gateway), (lumi-gateway-v3,xiaomi)
5	192.168.1.5	(dlinkroute7, dlink), (dlinkroute7, router)
6	192.168.1.6	(WNR3500U, router)

Table 6. Recognition results

	IP	Device type	Device brand	Device model
1	192.168.1.1	Speaker	Huawei	–
2	192.168.1.2	Air Cleaner	Xiaomi	–
3	192.168.1.3	Speaker	Lenovo	Smart Assistant
4	192.168.1.4	Gateway	Xiaomi	–
5	192.168.1.5	Router	Dlink	DIR-850L
6	192.168.1.6	Router	Netgear	WNR3500U

From the results, we can identify more novel types of IoT devices, such as air purifiers and smart gateways. There are three types of device models that can be identified. There are many reasons why a device model cannot be identified. It may be related to data acquisition or the Internet of Things device itself. Further research is needed in the future on devices that fail to obtain models.

5 Conclusion

Aiming at the problem of fine-grained identification of IoT devices, this paper studies the feature words of IoT device identification. Because the IoT devices contain a lot of information, it is hardly advisable to use manual observation. How to effectively identify and verify the features of physical networking devices is an urgent problem to be solved. In this paper, firstly, the search engine is used to build the corpus of feature words; secondly, the skip-gram model of word2vec is used to model the corpus; finally, the self-created algorithm is used to test the correlation between keywords and feature words. The verified keywords are added to the corresponding feature words. Through the experiment, we set up 6 devices that are difficult to recognize or relatively novel. We have successfully extracted effective feature words from the device data and added them to the feature word library. Owing to the addition of feature words, we can obtain the identification results of IoT devices with fine granularity.

From the existing experimental results, this paper cannot extract complete information of IoT devices. The information obtained from the device not enough. On the other hand, the data filtering phase may filter out keywords. In future work, we will conduct further research on data acquisition and data filtering.

References

1. ARM predicts 1 trillion IoT devices by 2035 with new end-to-end platform. https://news.itu.int/arm-pelion-iot-end-to-end-platform/
2. Security Notice - Statement on Remote Code Execution Vulnerability in Huawei HG532 Product. https://www.huawei.com/en/psirt/security-notices/huawei-sn20171130-01-hg532-en
3. Zou, Y., Liu, S., Yu, N.: IoT device recognition framework based on web search. J. Cyber Secur. 3(4), 25–40 (2018)
4. Cui, A., Stolfo, S.J.: A quantitative analysis of the insecurity of embedded network devices: results of a wide-area scan. In: Proceedings of the 26th Annual Computer Security Applications Conference, pp. 97–106 (2010)
5. Miettinen, M., et al.: IoT sentinel: automated device-type identification for security enforcement in IoT. In: 2017 IEEE 37th International Conference on Distributed Computing Systems (ICDCS), pp. 2177–2184. IEEE (2017)
6. Nmap Security Scanner. https://nmap.org/
7. Mikolov, T., Chen, K., Corrado, G., Dean, J.: Efficient estimation of word representations in vector space, arXiv preprint, arXiv:1301.3781 (2013)
8. Mikolov, T., et al.: Distributed representations of words and phrases and their compositionality. In: Advances in Neural Information Processing Systems, pp. 3111–3119 (2013)
9. Xu, Z.-X., Dai, Q.-Y., Xu, G., Huang, H., Chen, X.-B., Yang, Y.-X.: IoT device recognition framework based on network protocol keyword query. In: Sun, X., Wang, J., Bertino, E. (eds.) ICAIS 2020. LNCS, vol. 12239, pp. 219–231. Springer, Cham (2020). https://doi.org/10.1007/978-3-030-57884-8_20
10. Li, F.H.: The Design and Implementation of Network Equipment Identification System. Diss (2017)
11. Rumelhart, D.E., Hinton, G.E., Williams, R.J.: Learning representations by back-propagating errors. Nature 323(6088), 533–536 (1986)
12. The world's leading platform for network security monitoring. https://zeek.org/
13. Ramos, J., et al.: Using TF-IDF to determine word relevance in document queries. In: Proceedings of the First Instructional Conference on Machine Learning, pp. 133–142 (2013)

Coverless Information Hiding Method Based on Combination Morse Code and Double Cycle Application of Starter

Ya Wen[1], Jianjun Zhang[1(✉)], Yan Xia[1], Haijun Lin[1], and Guang Sun[2]

[1] College of Engineering and Design, Hunan Normal University, Changsha 410081, China
[2] Big Data Institute, Hunan University of Finance and Economics, Changsha 410205, China

Abstract. With the continuous development of modern network technology and data informatization, information security has been paid more and more attention by the society, and coverless information hiding has been becoming a new and important research field of information security. At present, the capacity of text coverless information hiding is very limited, generally 3–4 words per text. In order to increase the capacity of text coverless information hiding, this paper proposed a novel method of text coverless information hiding. In this method, the punctuation combination modified by Morse code is combined with the use of starter, list and loop statement to realize the hiding of a number of words in a normal text without modified. The experiments' results show that this new method can hide more words and express all the words composed of representable characters.

Keywords: Text coverless information hiding · Morse code · Information security

1 Introduction

With the continuous development of modern network technology and data informatization, information security has attracted more and more attention, and information hiding without carrier is a new and important research field of information security. Text-based information hiding technology has become a research hotspot in the field of information security [1]. Today, the rapid development of science and technology has brought about explosive growth in information quantity, followed by problems such as how to ensure the security and integrity of important information and how to protect intellectual property rights. Information hiding technology has emerged to solve these problems, and plays a very important role in modern society [2–4]. After years of research, Chinese researchers first proposed the method of coverless information hiding in 2015. Coverless information hiding method does not need to modify the carrier. It hides the information through the existing natural carrier without changing the statistical characteristics of the text information of the carrier, and can resist the existing steganalysis and other attack methods. The application of Tibetan poetry in ancient China is the most complete and primitive application of this method. Information hiding technology, which

© Springer Nature Switzerland AG 2021
X. Sun et al. (Eds.): ICAIS 2021, CCIS 1423, pp. 299–311, 2021.
https://doi.org/10.1007/978-3-030-78618-2_24

has been widely used in secret communication and copyright protection, has become a hot research direction in the field of information security.

At present, some people have studied the using of big data technology and artificial intelligence to the text coverless information hiding, and made great progress. Xianxi Chen proposed a novel text coverless information hiding method based on Chinese character encoding and Zhili Zhou proposed a novel coverless information hiding method based on multi-keyword [5, 6]. Zhangjie Fu proposed an improved, label-based coverless information hiding method [7]. Yuling Liu proposed a coverless information hiding method by using Chinese Pinyin. This method uses phonetic combinations as hidden labels and POS (Part of Speech) to represent the number of keywords [8]. In order to improve the retrieval efficiency, Xianyin Chen proposed a text coverless information hiding method using double labels. This method designed two labels by odd-even judgment and converts characters to binary numbers as positioning labels for secret information, and improved the retrieval efficiency of carrier text by establishing inverted indexes [9]. Lingyun Xiang proposes a character-level linguistic steganographic method (CLLS) to embed the secret information into characters instead of words by employing a long short-term memory (LSTM) based language model [10]. Jianjun Zhang proposed a coverless text information hiding method based on the word rank map [11].

Compared with image or other steganography, text steganography is the most difficult steganography due to the lack of redundancy. However, it needs less memory and provides simpler communication, so it is widely used. At present, the number of characters that can be hidden by coverless information hiding technology is very limited, generally 3–4 words per text. For example, for 200,000 texts in [12], the appropriate hiding capacity is 15 bits per text. Therefore, the information that can be transmitted is relatively small. The main goal of this new method is to increase the number of hidden characters by leaps and bounds, and at the same time, make the technology realize the hidden meaning more effectively. In this method, the list is used for cyclic operation, and six modules are used to extract punctuation, count combination frequency, count character frequency, convert ciphertext to digital information, convert digital information to ciphertext, and encrypt representative numbers to achieve the effect of hiding information as much as possible in a text. The use of starters can make a text express more combinations and thus more characters. Through experiments, this method can hide at least hundreds of words and cover all kinds of words.

2 Related Works

2.1 Morse Code

American Morse invented Morse code in 1837, which is composed of two symbols, ■ and ● Morse code must be mastered by every radio communicator, and it played a very important role in early radio. With the continuous development of communication technology, many countries stopped using Morse code in 1999. However, because it occupies the least bandwidth and has a technical and artistic characteristic, it is very popular in real life. Morse code was first represented by some dots and dashes representing numbers. The numbers correspond to words, that is, you need to look up a code table to know the numbers corresponding to each word. You can tap points, strokes and pauses in the middle with one key. However, the telegraph was invented by Moss, but he didn't have the relevant expertise, so he asked someone to make the equipment and set the corresponding rules. Later, these rules were put into Moss's patent, which is now known as the American Morse code, through which the world's first telegraph was transmitted. Inspired by Morse code, this method takes commas and periods in English text as ● and ■, and sets rules to represent characters. However, in order to find specific combinations more conveniently, this method limits the scale of combinations to be consistent, which makes the method more efficient.

2.2 Start Character

In the method of combining corresponding characters inspired by Morse code, the combination consists of five punctuation marks. Even if the combination is divided from scratch to the maximum extent, the types and quantities of combinations that can be divided are very limited. In order to make a single text express more kinds and quantities of combinations, this method defines a starter. In this paper, the initial characters are composed of 1–4 punctuation combinations (more digits can be set if necessary), with a total of 30 kinds, such as:, ., .,. ..,,. When the hiding module operates, the first character of the ciphertext is taken out first. For this character, a single text first circulates 30 initial characters, and after finding the initial characters, it will be grouped into five groups. If there is a combination corresponding to this character, the representative numbers of this text will be stored in the list. After that, the second character does the same thing, but only needs to loop the text in the list. This process goes round and round, and eventually all texts that can represent ciphertext will be obtained. Take out the first text in the list, cycle the starter again, repeat the previous operation to find the corresponding combination of each character, store the corresponding starter representative number and group number in the list respectively, and finally output the text representative number and these two lists. When extracting information, you will input the text representative number, the initial character string and the group number string. You can find the text directly, group it according to the initial character string, and then look at the group number string to easily get the specific combination, so as to get the corresponding characters. After outputting the characters one by one, you will get the required ciphertext string.

Table 1. Comparison table with or without starter

	There is no starter type (pieces)	There are starter types (pieces)	Number of groups without starter (pieces)	Number of groups with starters (pieces)
1366	2	11	2	32
4056	6	18	6	127
3364	4	16	4	63
735	7	17	7	98
3598	2	8	2	22
1715	3	15	5	82
3936	12	21	13	281
4687	2	9	2	24

As shown in Table 1, we randomly selected 8 texts whose ID are 1366, 4056, 3364, and so on, and counted the types and groups of characters that they can express with and without the starter. As shown in the table, it is obvious that both the types of characters that can be expressed and the number of groups that can be differentiated have been greatly increased by multiples. With the increase of the types of characters that can be expressed, it can greatly reduce the difficulty of finding text and make a single text express as many words as possible. With the increase of the number of differentiated groups, there are not only more kinds of expressions, but also the same character can be expressed with different starters and groups, thus greatly increasing the security of the method.

2.3   Construction of the Text Data Set

Large text data set is an important guarantee for coverless information hiding. This method uses crawler to crawl 5076 English texts from the Internet. This text set includes texts with different text contents such as politics, economy, military affairs, science and technology, life, etc. The specific distribution is shown in Table 2.

Table 2. Text type distribution

Text content	Number of texts (pieces)
Politics	1015
Economics	1269
Military	532
Science and technology	658
Life	1116
Entertainment	486

3   Proposed Method

The combination of commas and periods in English punctuation marks is used to indicate the initial character and specific combination. The initial character is formed by 1–4 punctuation marks, while the specific combination is formed by 5 fixed punctuation marks. After counting the frequency of specific combinations and characters, a character correspondence table is obtained and the results are input into the module. When hiding, after entering ciphertext, the module will find all texts that can express all characters of ciphertext under the double cycle of starter and specific combination, and take out the first one. According to this text, it will output the starter and group number corresponding to all characters of ciphertext. When extracting, the input text represents numbers, initial character strings and group number strings, and the module will directly find the corresponding text, and find the corresponding specific combination according to the initial character and group number, thus outputting one character of ciphertext. When encrypting, the module will randomly put the numbers represented by the text into any generated number list, then use 1 in another list containing 0 and 1 to represent the positions of the numbers represented by the text, then express the 0 and 1 list as binary numbers, and then convert them into decimal numbers and output them together with the number list.

3.1 Preprocess

The overall process is shown in Fig. 1, in which the character correspondence table is obtained, which is the basis of this technology. Character correspondence table makes the combination of punctuation and characters correspond one by one, and programs the corresponding information, which can effectively represent various characters in English text. The use of commas and periods, which are commonly used in English punctuation, can increase the possibility of finding texts on the one hand, and increase the relevance between texts on the other hand. At the same time, inspired by Morse code, it is thought that using punctuation combination to represent characters can represent 26 letters (not case sensitive) +1 space character (used to separate words to avoid confusion) +5 numbers with high frequency, so 5 punctuation marks are used as a combination to represent these characters. The combination with high frequency in the text set corresponds to the characters with high frequency, in order to increase the search possibility. In order to get the character correspondence table satisfying the above functions, there are some preprocessing work and three program modules are used.

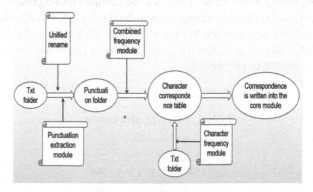

Fig. 1. Pretreatment work.

Get the Folder Composed of Txt File Set. First of all, a large number of English documents are obtained. This is available by writing Python crawler and crawling the website. A total of 5076 English texts have been used to test this method, and their topics are news, involving quality, international, life, war, diplomacy, economy and other aspects. Secondly, the English literature collection of txt is obtained. In case of docx file set, it can be converted in small batches by ready-made docx-txt conversion software for many times or by compiling relevant programs. The txt text set of 5076 English documents used in this paper is obtained by several small batch conversions by conversion software. Then the English text can be represented by numbers. This is to make it more convenient to generate random numbers when randomly selecting texts. This is achieved by selecting all English texts and renaming them to the same name. At this time, although the files have the same file name, they will be distinguished by numbers in brackets, for example: wen (1).

Get Punctuation Folder. It is necessary to extract commas and periods from English documents and save them in other files to obtain a document set of English punctuation. This is to make grouping easier later. This step will use the first module: filter out commas and periods from all files in the text set folder in a loop, and save them in another folder. The files in this folder also have the same name, and the numbers in brackets are used to distinguish the files.

Get a Specific Combination Frequency. For the 5076 English texts, count the number of each specific combination under different initial characters and store the corresponding information in Excel. This is to verify whether there are specific combinations that cannot be expressed and to get the frequency of each specific combination. In this step, the second module will be used: first, cycle the starter, which is represented by a punctuation mark, such as:, or. There are also two punctuation marks or a combination of three punctuation marks or even four punctuation marks, such as:,, ,., ,,.,. These situations constitute a total of 30 kinds of starters (starters are not taken from scratch to increase confidentiality), and a total of 32 kinds of specific combinations are recycled (5 punctuation marks can be transformed into 32 kinds of combinations). After the text is read from the beginning to the starter, it starts to be grouped into 5 groups (the last group is less than 5 neglected), which combination is judged to be +1. Finally, these 5076 texts are counted under different starters, as shown in Table 3. Operate and calculate the total number and probability of each specific combination in Excel and arrange them from top to bottom according to probability.

Table 3. Text type distribution

	,	,	,.,	...,
,.,,	1547	1523	1265	555
,,.,,	1484	1499	1318	482
,,,.,	1432	1390	1173	589
.,,.,	1405	1277	1098	522
,,,.,	1168	1222	1139	384

Get the Character Frequency. Get character arrangement with high frequency. This is to get the character correspondence table by corresponding to the specific combination with high frequency. This step will use the third module: loop txt text set to record the number of letters and save them in Excel. Calculate the probability of characters and rank them in Excel, and copy this part to Excel which has been operated before, then get the character correspondence table which makes the characters with high frequency correspond to the specific combinations with high frequency.

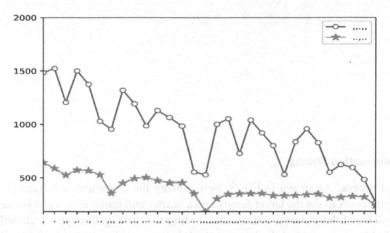

Fig. 2. Number of groups under different starters.

In Fig. 2, two specific combinations of high frequency and low frequency are selected, and the number of groups differentiated by them in the case of 30 kinds of starters is plotted. For a specific combination with high frequency, the number of groups with a small number of starter components is relatively more. For a specific combination with low frequency, the number of initial symbols is a little less than the number of initial symbols, but there is little difference. Table 4 is a character correspondence table obtained after preprocessing, and its correspondence results will be written into the hiding module and the extracting module.

Table 4. Character correspondence table

Particular combination	Character	Particular combination	Character
,··,,	e	,··,,	f
,,··,,	t	·,··,	y
,·,·,	a	··,,	w
·,,,·,	n	··,,,,	b
,,,,·,	i	···,	v
,,··,	o	·,,···	k
,·,,,,	s	··,·	Spaces
·,·,	r	,····,	0

(continued)

Table 4. (*continued*)

Particular combination	Character	Particular combination	Character
·,··,,	h	,,,·	1
·,,,,	l	,,,,,	2
,··,,	d	··,,,	x
,·,,·	c	·...	j
··,·,,	u	,,·...	z
,,··,,	m	,·...	5
·,,,·	p	·..·,,	3
,,,,,	g	··.,,	q

3.2 Information Hiding

Hiding Process. As shown in Fig. 3, by inputting the ciphertext, the function of the hiding process is to get the target English text, starter and group number. It is one of the core modules of this coverless information hiding technology, through which ciphertext can be hidden in a text and the key to unlock it later can be obtained. Hidden module adding the information of the character correspondence table operates as follows: after inputting the ciphertext string, first take out the first character of the ciphertext. For this character, a single text first circulates 30 initial characters, and after finding the initial characters, it will be grouped into five groups. If there is a combination corresponding to this character, the representative number of this text will be stored in the list. After that, the second character does the same thing, but only needs to loop the text in the list. This process goes round and round, and eventually all texts that can represent ciphertext will be obtained. Take out the first text in the list (because it is necessary to represent as many words as possible on one text), cycle the starter again, repeat the previous operation to find the corresponding combination of each character, store the corresponding starter representative number and group number in the list respectively, and finally output the text representative number and these two lists. This method can input infinite characters, depending on computer performance and program efficiency, so long as it can represent corresponding characters, it can represent any word composed of these characters.

Encryption Process. Encrypt the numbers representing the text to a certain extent, which will further strengthen the encryption of this technology. Encryption module is as follows: input the representative numbers of the text, randomly generate 4 numbers, and store them in the list together with the representative numbers, where the representative numbers are stored is determined by a random number. Set another list, which is 1 when it represents the corresponding position of numbers and 0 at other positions, then convert this binary number into a decimal number, and finally output this digital list and decimal number.

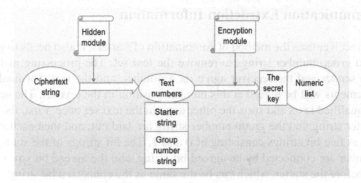

Fig. 3. Information hiding process.

3.3 Information Extraction

Extraction Process. It is another core of this coverless information hiding technology whose function is to get ciphertext after inputting representative number, starter and group number. Extraction module after writing is like this. It needs to input the text representative number, the initial character string and the group number string. After reading the text content, it will be grouped into five groups according to the initial character, and then the specific combination will be determined by the corresponding group number. After that, there will be a judgment statement to get the secret characters and output them in turn as shown in Fig. 4.

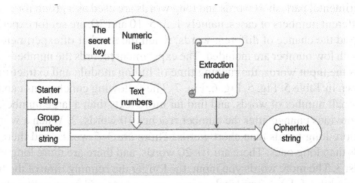

Fig. 4. Information extraction process.

Decryption Process. With basic mathematical knowledge, decimal numbers can be converted into binary numbers. The maximum decimal number obtained by this method is 8, so the corresponding binary numbers can be easily obtained. After that, the representative numbers of the text can be obtained by looking at the position where 1 is located corresponding to the corresponding position of the number list.

4 Communication Extraction Information

When the receiver uses the method of combination of starters, it also needs to get starter strings and group number strings to remove the text set. The processing method here is that the sender and the receiver agree on a number, and the text that finally meets the requirements will be placed at this number position in the text set. The sender sets aside the qualified texts and sorts the other texts in the text set once. First, the numbers of the starter string and the group number string are laid out, and then each number is expressed as five bit strings consisting of 0 and 1. The bit strings of the starter and the group number are connected by an agreed bit string, and the agreed bit string needs to be added before the starter, which can be the same as the connected bit string. Thus, the core bit string is completed. After that, the core bit string is put into a long bit string, but it should be noted that the bit string in front of the core bit string cannot have the agreed bit string. Next, according to the order of placing the text sets in the bit string, according to the publishing time, the latter text indicates 0 earlier than the previous text publishing time, otherwise it indicates 1. Finally, the qualified text is inserted into the text set to form the text set to be sent. After receiving the text set, the receiver can get the qualified text, starter string and group number string according to the rules. In this way, there is no need to send additional digital strings, and the information security can be guaranteed more.

5 Discussion

5.1 Efficiency Testing

In the experimental part, short words and long words are used as a group for comparison, and five different numbers of cases, namely 1, 3, 5, 10 and 20, are set for experiments. In order to avoid the chance of different words, when the number of experiments is large, all words with low number are included. The experiment records the number of texts that can express the input words, the running time of hiding module and extracting module.

As shown in Table 5, Fig. 5, Fig. 6, Fig. 7. The following conclusions can be drawn. 1. Enter a small number of words, and find far more texts than a large number, but there will be no obvious change after the number reaches 10 words. 2. When a word is used, there are more long words than short words. There are 3–5 words, and there are more short words than long ones. There are 10–20 words, and there are more long words than short words. 3. The more words you input, the longer the running time of the hiding and extracting module. 4. Long words take more time to hide and extract than short words. Regardless of the length of words, the number of texts generally decreases sharply, turns to decrease slowly, and finally tends to be stable. Analysis is that the frequency difference of characters is large, which leads to sharp decrease, slow decrease and final stable state. Whether it is hiding or extracting time, there are more long words than short words, and as the number of words increases, the analysis shows that there are more characters in long words than short words, so it takes more time, and the number of words increases in the same way.

Table 5. Efficiency experimental results

	Number of texts (pieces)	Hide time(second)	Extraction time(second)
1 Short words	476	4.774725899998884	0.0005117000000005589
1 Long words	560	5.4195459	0.0012040000000013151
3 Short words	202	5.134456199999999	0.0028684000000112064
3 Long words	100	6.035466800000002	0.003884400000000454
5 Short words	181	5.341586999999999	0.0018780999999989945
5 Long words	55	6.2760763	0.0066940999999971496
10 Short words	13	5.569208799999999	0.0034412000000010323
10 Long words	38	6.729200000000002	0.017087300000000027
20 Short words	12	5.615020399999999	0.006754100000009089
20 Long words	38	7.257971999999995	0.016603800000002167

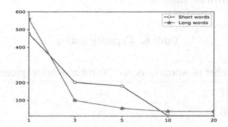

Fig. 5. Number of texts corresponding to long and short words

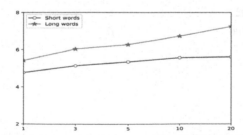

Fig. 6. Long and short words correspond to hidden time

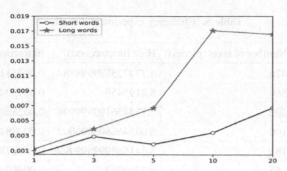

Fig. 7. Long and short words correspond to extraction time

5.2 Capacity Testing

As the number of words continues to grow, the number of texts continues to decline. However, the number of texts stabilizes at 6 after falling to a certain number when the number of words is 300. The reason is that 300 words roughly cover most characters. The testing result is shown in Table 6.

Table 6. Capacity testing

Number of words (pieces)	Number of texts (pieces)
147	14
330	6
479	6
658	6
794	6
927	6
1100	6

6 Conclusion

In this paper, we proposed a new text coverless information hiding method. The use of lists and loops realizes the purpose of methods, and initiators and groupings make methods meaningful and valuable. Through the cooperation of the six programs, a character correspondence table based on text set can be obtained. According to the principle that high-frequency punctuation corresponds to high-frequency letters, a text can represent more high-frequency words. Through experiments, it can be known that this coverless information hiding technology can theoretically represent unlimited words, provided that the text can express the letters owned by these words under the double search of 30 starters and 32 specific combinations. Punctuation adds relevance, the combination reduces the difficulty of finding corresponding text, the initiator increases the confidentiality and makes the text search rate higher, and the key further enhances the confidentiality performance. During the research, it is found that the relevance can be further studied to make the texts more relevant under the condition of multi-texts, the number and form of initiators can be further studied, and the key can be expressed in a more complex way to achieve confidentiality.

Acknowledgments. This research was funded by the National Natural Science Foundation of China (No. 61304208), Scientific Research Fund of Hunan Province Education Department (18C0003), Research project on teaching reform in colleges and universities of Hunan Province Education Department (20190147), Changsha City Science and Technology Plan Program (K1501013-11), Hunan Normal University University-Industry Cooperation. This work is implemented at the 2011 Collaborative Innovation Center for Development and Utilization of Finance and Economics Big Data Property, Universities of Hunan Province, Open project, grant number 20181901CRP04.

References

1. Luo, Y., Huang, Y.: Text steganography with high embedding rate: using recurrent neural networks to generate Chinese classic poetry. In: Proceedings of the 5th ACM Workshop on Information Hiding and Multimedia Security, pp. 99–104. Association for Computing Machinery, New York (2017)
2. Huang, Y., Tang, S., Yuan, J.: Steganography in inactive frames of VoIP streams en-coded by source code. IEEE Trans. Inf. Forensics Secur. **6**(2), 296–306 (2011)
3. Huang, Y., Liu, C., Tang, S., Bai, S.: Steganography integration into a low-bit rate speech codec. IEEE Trans. Inf. Forensics Secur. **7**(6), 1865–1875 (2012)
4. Xiao, B., Huang, Y.: Modeling and optimizing of the information hiding communication system over streaming media. J. Xidian Univ. **35**(3), 554–558 (2008)
5. Chen, X., Chen, S., Wu, Y.: Coverless information hiding method based on the Chinese character encoding. J. Internet Technol. **18**(2), 313–320 (2017)
6. Zhou, Z., Mu, Y., Zhao, N., Wu, Q.M.J., Yang, C.-N.: Coverless information hiding method based on multi-keywords. In: Sun, X., Liu, A., Chao, H.-C., Bertino, E. (eds.) ICCCS 2016. LNCS, vol. 10039, pp. 39–47. Springer, Cham (2016). https://doi.org/10.1007/978-3-319-48671-0_4
7. Fu, Z., Ji, H., Ding, Y.: Label model based coverless information hiding method. J. Internet Technol. **19**(5), 1509–1514 (2018)
8. Liu, Y., Wu, J., Xin, G.: Multi-keywords carrier-free text steganography method based on Chinese Pinyin. Int. J. Comput. Sci. Eng. **21**(2), 202 (2020)
9. Zhou, X., Chen, X., Zhang, F., Zheng, N.: A novel coverless text information hiding method based on double-tags and twice-send. Int. J. Comput. Sci. Eng. **21**(1), 116–124 (2020)
10. Xiang, L., Yang, S., Liu, Y., Li, Q., Zhu, C.: Novel linguistic steganography based on character-level text generation. Mathematics **8**, 1558 (2020)
11. Zhang, J., Shen, J., Wang, L., Lin, H.: Coverless text information hiding method based on the word rank map. J. Internet Technol. **18**(2), 427–434 (2017)
12. Xia, Z., Li, X.: Coverless information hiding method based on LSB of the character's unicode. J. Internet Technol. **18**(6), 1353–1360 (2017)

Application of Grey Forecasting Model to CPI Index Forecast

Yifu Sheng[1], Jianjun Zhang[1]($\boxtimes$), Wenwu Tan[1], Jiang Wu[1], Haijun Lin[1], and Guang Sun[2]

[1] College of Engineering and Design, Hunan Normal University, Changsha 410081, China
[2] Hunan Finance and Economics College, Changsha 410205, China

Abstract. The CPI index is the final price of social products and services. It is an important indicator for economic analysis and decision-making, monitoring and control of the overall price level, and national economic accounting. Because the CPI index is originally a univariate data indicator, in order to better predict the economic impact of the new coronavirus pneumonia by analyzing the CPI index, in this paper we chose the gray prediction model that has an excellent predictive effect on univariate data. Firstly, we got all CPI data from 2015 to 2019 from the Oriental Wealth Data Center. Secondly we predicted the CPI index for January, February, and March 2020 by using the gray prediction model. Thirdly, the trend of the forecast data was visualized with Python. Finally, the predicting result was compared with the real data, and the reason for the difference was analyzed.

Keywords: CPI index · Data forecasting · Grey forecasting model · Python visualization

1 Introduction

CPI is an important indicator to measure inflation. The level of CPI can indicate the severity of inflation to a certain level. In recent years, a country's inflation problem is very worthy of attention [1]. On the one hand, a country's strong impulse for investment in fixed assets over the years has made the actual economic growth rate higher than the potential growth rate. Excessive growth demand will inevitably be accompanied by excessive issuance of credit currency, which constitutes inflationary pressure; On the other hand, data shows that China's total currency was 1.53 trillion yuan in 1990, and it reached 89.56 trillion yuan in 2011, which was 58.5 times billion yuan in 1990. In recent years, the central bank of the People's Republic of China has to put a large amount of RMB to hedge in order to alleviate the economic problems caused by the excessive pressure of RMB appreciation. At this stage, the inflationary pressure facing my country still cannot be underestimated [2, 3]. Since the constituent elements and influencing factors of CPI will be affected by time and space differences, and its internal changes will be affected accordingly. Therefore, the research on CPI is a process of continuous

© Springer Nature Switzerland AG 2021
X. Sun et al. (Eds.): ICAIS 2021, CCIS 1423, pp. 312–321, 2021.
https://doi.org/10.1007/978-3-030-78618-2_25

exploration and one of the hot issues that scholars from all walks of life have been paying attention to. Different scholars use different research models and research perspectives, but the basic direction is to predict the future development trend and influencing factors of CPI.

In 2008, Huang Yimin used support vector machines to analyze the CPI trends, and used the significance of coefficients to evaluate various economic indicators and the degree of influence on price fluctuations [4]. Long Shaobo pointed out that the increase in labor costs is an important reason for the increase in CPI, and the decline in the price of industrial production materials is an important reason for the decline in PPI, which explains the changes in PPI and CPI separately [5]. Zhang Xiaolin used monetary policy shocks, short-term demand shocks and long-term supply shocks to explain the many deviations between CPI and PPI since 2000 [6]. Tan Zhihui established a CPI influencing factor model using principal component analysis [7]. ARIMA is the most classic prediction model for CPI prediction, and Guo Xiaofeng used the ARIMA model to analyze and predict the CPI trends and give corresponding policy recommendations [8]. With the continuous development of big data technology, more and more studies begin to use big data technology for analysis. Guang Sun used Gephi, which is an efficient tool for data analysis and visualization in the era of big data, to visualization analysis for Business Performance of Chinese Listed Companies [9]. GM(1,1) is also a kind of time series model and is widely used in energy supply system and singular phenomenon prediction [10, 11], so we chose the GM(1,1) model to predict the CPI index for January, February, and March 2020.

Because the CPI index is originally a univariate data indicator, in order to better predict the economic impact of the new coronavirus pneumonia by analyzing the CPI index, we chose the gray prediction model that has an excellent predictive effect on univariate data, and introduced how to use the excellent characteristics of the gray model to make univariate forecasts in this paper. The CPI data used in the experiment are all from the Oriental Wealth Data Center (http://data.eastmoney.com/cjsj/cpi.html). We directly used the actual CPI data of China Statistics Network for modeling and forecasting, and visualized the trend in the coming months. In order to ensure the accuracy of the gray model prediction, we use the gray model to fit the existing data and observe the gap between the fitted data and the actual real data to evaluate the practicality of the model in real life.

2 Prediction Model

2.1 The Grey Forecasting Model

Grey theory is an emerging edge science theory that is initiated by the famous Chinese scholar Deng Julong, which is aimed at "poor information" or "small sample" systems with incomplete information. That is, when the gray system theory reflects reality, it conducts reasonable analysis and in-depth mining of incomplete information and obtains unknown information from it, and then makes a more accurate description of the overall development law and trend. Grey system prediction theory has the characteristics of large cross-section and strong permeability. Even if the system contains uncertain factors, it can be predicted. The ability to predict even when the sample size is small is a prominent advantage of gray theory. Researchers use three colors of "black", "white" and "gray" to indicate the degree of information transparency. "Pure black" means that the information is completely unknown, "pure white" means that the information is completely transparent, and "gray" means that part of the information is opaque or Part of the information is transparent [12]. From different angles and occasions, the content of "gray" can also be expanded into Table 1.

Table 1. Extension of the concept of 'gray'.

Perspective	Black	Grey	White
Information	Unknown	Incomplete	Complete
Performance	Dark	Light and dark	Light
Process	NEW	Alternate old	Old
Nature	Mess	Multiple ingredients	Pure
Method	Negative	Sublate	Positive
Attitude	Indulgence	Tolerant	Severe
Result	NO solution	Non-unique solution	Only solution

2.2 Grey Prediction Model GM(1,1)

The GM(1,1) model is widely regarded and applied as the core content of gray theory. The model flow chart is shown in Fig. 1

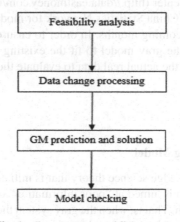

Fig. 1. Gray system establishment steps.

The model is built as follows:

(1) Let the original sequence $X^{(0)} = \left(x_{(1)}^{(0)}, x_{(2)}^{(0)}, \ldots, x_{(n)}^{(0)}\right)$, where: $x_{(1)}^{(0)} \geq 0, k = 1, 2, \ldots, n$, after one accumulation, the following sequence is obtained $X^{(1)} = \left(x_{(1)}^{(1)}, x_{(2)}^{(1)}, \ldots, x_{(n)}^{(1)}\right)$, where:

$$x_{(k)}^{(1)} = \sum_{i=1}^{k} x_{(i)}^{(0)}, k = 1, 2, \ldots, n \tag{1}$$

(2) Generate the full sequence of $x^{(1)}$ adjacent mean values $Z^{(1)} = \left(z_{(2)}^{(1)}, z_{(3)}^{(1)}, \ldots, z_{(n)}^{(1)}\right), k = 2, 3, \ldots, n$, where:

$$z_{(k)}^{(1)} = \frac{1}{2}(x_{(k)}^{(1)} + x_{(k-1)}^{(1)}) \tag{2}$$

(3) According to the grey system theory, the whitening differential equation about time t is established for $x^{(1)}$, that is, the GM(1,1) model $\frac{dx^{(1)}}{dt} + ax^{(1)} = b$. Among them: a, b are undetermined parameters, using the least square method to solve the problem can be obtained $(a, b)^T = (B^T B)^{-1} B^T Y_N$, and

$$B = \begin{pmatrix} -Z_{(2)}^{(1)} & 1 \\ -Z_{(3)}^{(1)} & 1 \\ \cdots & \cdots \\ -Z_{(n)}^{(1)} & 1 \end{pmatrix} \quad Y_N = \begin{pmatrix} x_{(2)}^{(0)} \\ x_{(3)}^{(0)} \\ \cdots \\ x_{(n)}^{(0)} \end{pmatrix} \tag{3}$$

(4) After solving a and b, the time response equation of Eq. (1) is obtained:

$$\hat{x}_{(k+1)}^{(1)} = \left[x_{(1)}^{(0)} - \frac{b}{a}\right]e^{-ak} + \frac{b}{a}(k = 0, 1, \ldots n) \tag{4}$$

(5) Cumulative reduction:

$$\hat{x}_{(k+1)}^{(0)} = \hat{x}_{(k+1)}^{(1)} - \hat{x}_{(k)}^{(1)} = \left(1 - e^{-a}\right)\left[x_{(1)}^{(0)} - \frac{b}{a}\right]e^{-ak}(k = 0, 1, \ldots, n-1) \tag{5}$$

(6) Absolute error:

$$\varepsilon_{(i)}^{(0)} = x_{(i)}^{(0)} - \hat{x}_{(i)}^{(0)} \tag{6}$$

(7) Relative error:

$$\omega_{(i)}^{(0)} = \left| \frac{x_{(i)}^{(0)} - \hat{x}_{(i)}^{(0)}}{x_{(i)}^{(0)}} \right| \tag{7}$$

Model test uses posterior error test, the steps are as follows:

(1) Calculate the average value of the original series:

$$\bar{x}^{(0)} = \frac{1}{n} \sum_{i=1}^{n} x_{(i)}^{(0)} \qquad (8)$$

(2) Calculate the mean square error of the original series:

$$S_1 = \left[\frac{\sum_{i=1}^{n} \left[x_{(i)}^{(0)} - x^{-(0)} \right]^2}{n-1} \right]^{\frac{1}{2}} \qquad (9)$$

(3) Calculate the mean of the residuals:

$$\bar{\Delta} = \frac{1}{n} \sum_{i=1}^{n} \Delta_{(i)}^{(0)} \qquad (10)$$

(4) Calculate the variance of the residual:

$$S_2 = \left[\frac{\sum_{i=1}^{n} \left[\Delta_{(i)}^{(0)} - \bar{\Delta}^{(0)} \right]^2}{n-1} \right]^{\frac{1}{2}} \qquad (11)$$

(5) Calculate the variance ratio:

$$C = S_1/S_2 \qquad (12)$$

(6) Calculate the probability of small residuals:

$$p = P\left\{ \left| \Delta_{(i)}^{(0)} - \bar{\Delta} \right| < 0.6745S_1 \right\} \qquad (13)$$

The model accuracy grade is shown in Table 2.

Table 2. The model accuracy grade.

Accuracy class	C	P
1 (Excellent)	C < 0.35	0.95 < P < 1
2 (Good)	0.35 < C < 0.5	0.8 < P < 0.95
3 (Qualified)	0.5 < C < 0.65	0.7 < P < 0.8
4 (Unqualified)	0.65 < C	P < 0.7

According to the calculated C and P values, the accuracy of the model is judged, and the optimal model is selected for prediction.

3   Data Modeling and Model Realization

3.1   Data Acquisition

The research data samples in this paper are all sourced from the Oriental Wealth Data Center. The actual monthly data of China's consumer price index from January 2015 to December 2019 is selected for a total of 60 periods, and some of the data are shown in Table 3.

Table 3. Partial data display.

Years	Values	Year-on-year	Month-on-month
2018-5	101.8	1.8%	−0.2%
2018-6	101.9	1.9%	−0.1%
2018-7	102.1	2.1%	0.3%
2018-8	102.3	2.3%	0.7%
2018-9	102.5	2.5%	0.7%
2018-10	102.5	2.5%	0.2%
2018-11	102.2	2.2%	−0.3%
2018-12	101.9	1.9%	0%
2019-1	101.7	1.7%	0.5%

Since the data of the Eastern Fortune Data Center is presented in the form of pictures, it is needed to convert the data into EXCEL files to facilitate subsequent data reading. After the conversion was complete, the Jupyter Notebook was used to read the CPI data. This tool can save the running results for easy visualization. Table 4 shows the complete data of CPI.

Table 4. Complete data read by Jupyter Notebook.

Years	Values
2015-01	100.8
2015-02	101.4
2015-03	101.4
2015-04	101.5
2015-05	101.2
...	...
2019-11	104.5
2019-12	104.5

We firstly carried out a comprehensive statistical description of the data and got a comprehensive grasp of the existing data. Usually the analysis of data statistics uses the maximum value, minimum value, average value, and standard deviation to make the overall description. We used python's built-in functions to directly find these four quantities, and then used the Pandas library to convert the data to Dataframe type. The output is shown in the Table 5.

Table 5. Descriptive statistics of CPI data

Data characteristics	Font size and style
Min	100.80
Max	104.50
Mean	102.04
Std	0.74

It can be seen from the descriptive statistics table that from January 2015 to December 2019, the consumer price index reached the highest 104.5 and the lowest 100.8 during such a long period of time. The difference between the highest and the lowest was not too large. It can be seen that the price fluctuations in the past five years are relatively small, which shows that the country's macro-control is in place. Now the per capita income is rising rapidly, but the CPI has not risen sharply, indicating that the national living standard has been greatly improved. With the improvement in performance, happiness is getting stronger.

3.2 Realization and Comparison of Data Prediction

The GM(1,1) model was chosen for the prediction because the grey model is suitable for small samples. We selected the data of the last 20 periods for modeling, and predicted the data of the latter three periods, namely the CPI 2020 data from January to March. We used the prepared GM(1,1) program as a class object and directly imported it into the main program to predict CPI data. The predicted result is shown in the Fig. 2.

It can be seen from the figure that the prediction effect is not good, and even the trend is opposite. The actual CPI value is significantly higher than the predicted data, but the predicted value and the actual value tend to close in the third month. In order to find out whether this difference is caused by the accuracy of the GM(1,1) model itself or the difference is caused by some special realization in reality that cannot be predicted, we randomly selected 20 cycles of data, then predicted the CPI values of the 20 cycles in the next three months, and finally compared the predicted results with the actual results to observe the effect of the forecast. If the prediction accuracy is better with the data of other periods, it proves to be caused by social factors outside the model. In order to ensure generality, 20 consecutive periods of data are randomly selected. This paper intercepts 20 periods of data from July 2017 to March 2019 for model construction. The data from

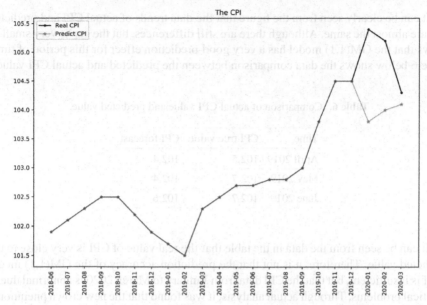

Fig. 2. Comparison of CPI forecast value and actual value.

April to June 2019 is predicted. Because these forecast months are randomly selected, and their actual values can be obtained, a good comparison effect can be achieved. The forecast results from April to June 2019 are shown in Fig. 3.

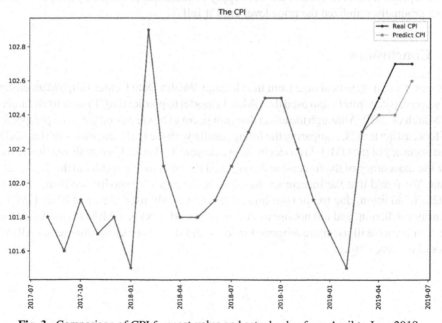

Fig. 3. Comparison of CPI forecast value and actual value from April to June 2019.

It can be clearly seen from the figure that the data trends of actual CPI and predicted CPI are almost the same. Although there are still differences, but the gap is very small. It shows that the GM(1,1) model has a very good prediction effect for this period of time. Table 6 below shows the data comparison between the predicted and actual CPI values.

Table 6. Comparison of actual CPI value and predicted value.

Time	CPI true value	CPI forecast
April 2019	102.5	102.4
May 2019	102.7	102.4
June 2019	102.7	102.6

It can be seen from the data in the table that the real value of CPI is very close to the predicted value. Therefore, it is not that the prediction accuracy of the GM(1,1) model itself is insufficient, but that the CPI data from January to March 2020 is abnormal due to practical problems. Through actual analysis, it was found that the new crown pneumonia epidemic occurred in January-March. When it was in the early stage of the epidemic, people across the country were required to quarantine themselves and set up quarantine checkpoints everywhere, which caused traffic inconvenience and factory shutdown. The prices of daily necessities for residents generally increased significantly. The increase was most obvious in January, reaching the maximum CPI in February. The decline in March was due to the rapid increase caused by closed management in the initial stage of the epidemic. Macro-control and the supply of materials provided by the government have gradually stabilized the price level until it fell.

4   Conclusions

We got the real statistical data from the Oriental Wealth Data Center (http://data.eastmo ney.com/cjsj/cpi.html), and used the GM(1,1) model to predict the CPI data from January to March of 2020. Although the effect does not seem to be very good from the perspective of forecasting trends, comparing the fitting results with the real data proves the feasibility and accuracy of the GM(1,1) model in the prediction. To this end, we analyzed the reasons for the inaccuracy of the forecast and compared the forecasting results to the 2019 actual data. We found that the inaccuracy was due to the new Coronavirus epidemic in early 2020. In addition, due to our own limited level, we only used the most basic GM(1,1) in gray prediction, and did not use more complex GM(1,N) or GM(M,N) models. In the next work, we will use more advanced models and the most classic time series ARIMA model for forecasting.

Acknowledgments. This research was funded by the National Natural Science Foundation of China (No. 61304208), Scientific Research Fund of Hunan Province Education Department (18C0003), Research project on teaching reform in colleges and universities of Hunan Province Education Department (20190147), Changsha City Science and Technology Plan Program (K1501013-11), Hunan Normal University University-Industry Cooperation. This work is implemented at the 2011 Collaborative Innovation Center for Development and Utilization of Finance and Economics Big Data Property, Universities of Hunan Province, Open project, grant number 20181901CRP04.

References

1. Liu, Y., Li, M., Wang, H.: Analysis of influencing factors of Chinese CPI. Bus. Res. **902**(17), 25–26 (2019)
2. Wu, L., Zhao, F., Liu, Y.: The departure of PPI and CPI revisited: from the view of staple commodity price and labor market friction. J. Central Univ. Fin. Econ. **2**(9), 80–90 (2020)
3. He, L., Fan, G., Hu, J.: Consumer price index and producer price index: which drives which? Econ. Res. **43**(11), 16–26 (1993)
4. Huang, Y.: The analysis of CPI trend and its influencing factors in China based on SVR. Zhejiang Gongshang University (2008)
5. Long, S., Yuan, D.: Analysis of the "positive and negative deviation" phenomenon between china's CPI and PPI under the new economic normal—based on the perspective of the difference in price transmission mechanism between departments. Fin. Trade Res. **27**(4), 1–8 (2016)
6. Zhang, X., Yang, Y., Zhang, Y.: A structural explanation of the continuous 'divergence' between CPI and PPI. China Econ. Stud. **1**(2), 15–26 (2018)
7. Tan, Z.: Influencing factors analysis of CPI based of functional data analysis. Tianjing University (2012)
8. Guo, X.: Forecast and analysis of China's CPI trend based on ARIMA model. Stat. Dec. **11**, 29–32 (2012)
9. Sun, G., Lv, H., Wang, D., Fan, X., Zuo, Y., Xiao, Y.: Visualization analysis for business performance of chinese listed companies based on gephi. Comput. Mat. Continua **63**(2), 959–977 (2020)
10. Liu, S., Dang, Y., Fang, Z., Xie, N.: Grey System Theory and Application, 2nd edn. China: Science Press, Beijing (2010)
11. Wang, Z., Dang, Y., Liu, S., Lian, Z.: Solution of GM(1,1) power model and its properties. Syst. Eng. Electron. **31**(10), 2380–2383 (2009)
12. Qian, W., Dang Y., Liu, S.: Grey GM(1,1,) model with time power and its application. Syst. Eng. Theory Pract. **32**(10), 2247–2252 (2012)

A Preliminary Study About Star Image Processing Method in Harsh Environment

Jianming Zhang⑩, Shuwang Yang, Junxiang Lian⁽✉⁾, Zhaoxiang Yi, and Jiaheng Liu

Tian Qin Research Center for Gravitational Physics and Astronomy, Sun Yat-Sen University,
Zhuhai 519082, People's Republic of China
lianjx3@mail.sysu.edu.cn

Abstract. The star sensor is a high precise attitude measurement equipment for the spacecraft, and star identification is one of the key techniques of star sensor's attitude determination. Star tracking mode is the main working mode of the star sensor. However, during star tracking, when the star sensor is in the harsh environment, the star imaging is seriously affected, which leads to the decline of star attitude determination accuracy and even the failure of star identification. The star sensor re-enters the "lost in space" mode, resulting in navigation interruption. In this paper, the pure digital simulation method is adopted. Firstly, the SAO guide star catalogue is properly processed, and then we used it to generate star maps. On this basis, a comprehensive noise model of harsh environment is established by analyzing the generation mechanism of the transient effect, plume effect and the false stars which like star. At the same time, Gaussian noise and salt noise are used to pollute the star image. Finally, the joint denoising algorithms such as threshold segmentation, inter frame star image comparison are used to process the star images. The experimental results show that Gaussian noise and salt noise can simulate the influence of space harsh environment on star sensor imaging well. The proposed joint denoising algorithm can restore the star image to the pure mode as much as possible.

Keywords: Star sensor · Harsh environment · False star · Image processing

1 Introduction

After half a century's development, star sensor has become the most important attitude measurement instrument in aerospace field. Star sensors use highly sensitive imaging devices to conduct sensitive imaging of stellar photons, and con- duct attitude calculation in the integrated circuit. Compared with other attitude measurement devices, like sun sensor, earth sensor magnetometer, horizon sensor et al., star sensor is of the higher measurement precision. However, the star sensor is easily affected by space radiation [1, 2], plumes [3], stray lights etc., which damages the performance of star sensor. And a large of number of false stars, may appear in the FOV (field of view) of the star sensor together with the true stars, some false stars which are very similar to the true stars, which seriously interferes with star identification, causing the failure in attitude determination

[4]. Then the star sensor will lose the star tracking mode and turns back to "lost-in-space" status, which will interrupt the navigation and affect the normal operation of spacecraft [5].

Because these harsh conditions seriously affect the reliability of star sensor, the robustness of star sensor to false stars has recently become a research hotspot, many researches have been devoted to improving the robustness of star sensors in harsh environment. According to the generating mechanism and motion characteristics, false stars can be divided into three categories [6], and the methods of improving the robustness of star sensor are as follows:

The first class is the false stars caused by the transient effect of electron ionization. Different from the radiation forms on earth (such as X-ray, Gamma ray, etc.), space radiation is ionizing radiation. When the atom accelerates to the speed of light in space, the electrons in the atom are stripped and only the nucleus is left. There are three kinds of radiation sources in space environment: first, particles captured by the earth's magnetic field, mainly the earth's radiation belts (also known as Van Allen belts); second, particles shot into space during solar flares (solar particle events); third, galactic cosmic rays (galactic cosmic rays) from high-energy protons and heavy ions outside the solar system All these types of space radiation are ionizing radiation [7, 8].

The influence of space radiation on star sensor can be divided into: one is the effect on the life and function of star sensor; the other is the appearance of false star points on the star map, resulting in the loss of satellite attitude. The main reason for these two effects is that the space radiation environment interacts with materials, resulting in atomic displacement and ionization. For specific photodetectors, the effects of space radiation mainly include cumulative effect and transient effect. The former affects the lifetime and accuracy of star sensor, while the latter generates noise and false star points, resulting in attitude loss [1, 7]. The transient effect of high-energy particles cannot be eliminated by shielding, and the secondary particle radiation may aggravate the radiation effect. The influence of transient effect can be reduced or eliminated by improving process and adopting special hardware, but it is not easy to realize. Therefore, image processing is generally used to eliminate the influence of transient effect.

The second category is the stationary false stars. Different from the transient effect, those false object have the same characteristics with the true stars in guide star catalogue. That is, after the defocusing of star sensor, both have the same point spread function (PSF) and do not move over time on the image, making them hard to identify. Delabie et al. [18] divided false stars into two simulation modes, one is that the magnitude of the false star is higher than the three brightest stars follows the most common case; the other is that the brightness of the false star is greater than the brightest star, the proposed distance-transform algorithm can guarantee 98% of the images correctly, when there are 650 false stars. For only a few of these false stars, the star identification algorithms, such as pyramid [19] and grid algorithm [20] can handle it well, as the number of false stars increase, the performance of the algorithms decrease significantly. Schiattarella et al. [21] proposed the Multi-Poles algorithm and Wang et al. [22] proposed the based Hash Map star identification algorithm, both are effective when the number of false stars in several times the number of true stars. Jiang et al. [25] proposed three techniques to speed up the tracking, and can guarantee the false star rejection during this period.

While, when the false star is close to guide star, it has a poor performance. Zhang et al. [23] introduced chi-square tests into the false star detection and isolation. Combined with the Kalman filter, the false star detection is realized by a global test, and the false star isolation is realized by a local test, the algorithm has an excellent performance in the robustness of star sensor.

The third category is the drift false stars. This kind of false star mainly refers to the false star caused by the plume effect, which shares the same characteristics (PSF) with the true stars. However, it is different from the true star and stationary false star, the false objects are close to the star sensor, and the false stars generated by these objects drift randomly. Randomness is similar to transient effect, causing their inconsistent positions in two consecutive star images. The number of drifting stars caused by the plume effect can be up to dozens of times the number of true stars, which makes almost all star identification methods invalid or the identification accuracy is too low. Schiattarella et al. [21] also considered the drift stars, as mentioned above, the proposed Multi-Poles algorithm has excellent performance. Drifting stars still cannot be effectively processed as transient false stars and motionless false stars, Wang et al. [6] proposed an algorithm utilizing the difference between the motion of false stars and true stars, by using the star voting and angular distance tracking which achieved the false star filtering, and experiment shows that even if there are 700 false stars in the star images, the algorithm can find all the real stars in 10 frames. Fan et al. [26] used the principle of constant angular distance between real stars and variable angular distances of false stars to complete the rapid elimination of false stars, Experiments on real star images show that the algorithm can meet the requirements of spacecraft even if there are a large number of false stars in the star image.

In summary, there have been methods which can cope with transient false stars, drifting stars and stationary false stars. However, when the number of false stars is very large, the false stars cannot be effectively processed. And the stars which are similar to the true stars are difficult to identify. The most studies just consider one of the three kinds of false stars. However, in the extreme harsh environment, the spacecraft is under the comprehensive influence of the three, which is more accord with the real environment. Therefore, this paper uses pure digital simulation to simulate this kind of noise environment, and considers the relationship between Gaussian noise, salt noise and this kind of noise environment. The remainder of this paper is organized as follows: in Sect. 2, the Van Allen belts, plume interference and some stationary false stars are introduction in detail; in Sect. 3, the simulation of star images and the comprehensive noise model of those effects are introduced; in Sect. 4, the denoising experiments on star images are carried out; in Sect. 5, conclusions of the proposed noise model and algorithm are drawn.

2 Van Allen Belts, Plumes Effect and False Stars

The introduction introduces the three main hostile environments that affect the robustness of star sensors, and the algorithms to deal with them. In this chapter, the corresponding concepts and mechanisms of three kinds of false stars are briefly described.

2.1 Van Allen Belts

In 1958, space scientist James Van Allen discovered two particle radiation bands in the plasma layer in the upper part of the earth's atmosphere, and named them the "Van Allen" radiation belt. In the later research and observation, it was found that the size of these two bands can be changed, and sometimes they will be separated into three bands [9].

Usually, the radiation band exists in the form of two bands, and it is in the form of a ring, which is similar to a "doughnut". The inner zone extends from 600 km to 10000 km from the earth's surface, and its inner boundary drops to about 200 km away from the earth's surface when solar activity is intense or the SAA occurs. The inner band contains a high concentration of electrons in the range of hundreds of keV. The energy of high-energy protons is more than 100 MeV. Protons are the main component of the inner band, and there are a few particles.

The outer zone extends from 14000 km to 60000 km above the surface. The data from Van Allen probes launched by NASA in August 2012 show that the inner edge of the outer band is obvious, and even the fastest and most energetic electrons cannot penetrate this "boundary" [9]. The outer layer is mainly composed of electrons with energy in the range of 0.1–10 MeV. Compared with the inner zone, the outer zone is more variable and vulnerable to solar activity. Secondly, the dose effect of star sensors has been studied deeply, and the corresponding measures and theories are relatively mature, so it is no longer an important factor affecting star sensors.

Transient effect, as the name suggests, is only a short-term effect, the efficiency of the action is only one cycle. The charged particles pass through the pixel and shoot into the sensitive layer of the imaging element. The energy is absorbed in its track. The electrons on neutral molecules or atoms interact with each other in Coulomb. The electrons break away and become free electrons. The molecules or atoms that lose the electrons carry positive charges, that is, ionization effect occurs, forming electron hole pairs.

The transient effect is mainly due to the ionization effect of particles passing through the detector. One of the main functions of ionization energy transfer is to increase the density of states at the $Si/SiO2$ interface. The induced state is the dark current center produced by the depletion region. Therefore, the transfer of ionization energy mainly affects the increase of dark current on the detector surface. For low ionization dose (Krad (Si)), the increase of average dark current is proportional to the received ionizing dose.

Like the electron hole pairs generated by photon collection in imaging de- vices, the electron hole pairs generated by ionization are also read out together. Therefore, the main influence of the transient effect on the star sensor is the noise and pseudo star points in the star map, and affects the attitude determination. At present, most star sensors use CCD or CMOS silicon-based detectors, so the linear energy transfer (let) can be used to describe the amount of charge generated by the interaction between proton and detector (Fig. 1).

The amount of charge generated in the pixel caused by the transient effect is obtained c the effective trajectory of high-energy proton, the energy loss calculated by the energy transmission line density and the charge collection efficiency. The charge collection under the sensor pixel is mainly divided into two layers. The sensitive layer is the part of sensitive photon imaging. It contains several depletion layers, which occupy different

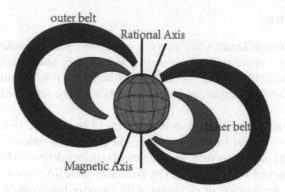

Fig. 1. Van Allen radiation belts sketch.

regions and are smaller than the pixel size. At the same time, it has a strong electric field and can collect 100% carriers. The electric field of the free layer is very small, and the charge in the free layer can only diffuse, so the depletion layer can only absorb the charge diffused from the free layer and collect it into the corresponding pixels. The charge collected in the free layer can be calculated according to Kirkpatrick's model.

2.2 Plume Effects

In hydrodynamic, a plume or a column is a vertical body of one fluid moving through another. For a spacecraft, the gas or particles emitted by the jets can reflect sunlight and form a large number of false stars in the FOV of a star sensor. Especially, the drift slowly false stars are harmful to the star identification performance. This phenomenon is called plume interference. The most of the plume effect occur in orbit, spacecraft require on-board or secondary propulsion system to perform orbit transfer, orbit maintenance, and attitude control maneuvers.

The plume effect cannot be described by one mathematical model alone, cause of the Vacuum plume covers all the continuum, transition, and free molecular flow regions. There are three kinds of methods to study the plume and its effects, including semi-experimental and analytical methods, numerical simulation method and Ground simulation and flight experiments. The Gaussian plume models also can be used in several fluid scenarios, as a simplified model.

2.3 Stationary False Star

For a star sensor, the stationary false stars are the space objects which reflect sunlight and image on the FOV. They do not move over time, and hard to distinguish. Star target is a point light source for star sensor, and the positioning accuracy of single pixel cannot meet the requirements of attitude measurement. Therefore, defocusing method is often used to make the star image spread to multiple pixels, and then sub-pixel positioning accuracy is obtained by subdivision positioning method [5]. Hence, the stationary false star has the same PSF as the true stars, and has the same simulation method in this paper.

The space objects mainly include: the man-made object (satellites and space debris), according to paper [18], the probability of having a man-made object in the $20 \times 20°$ FOV of a star sensor is around 1.44%; a planet or our solar system, such as Venus, Mars, Jupiter, Mercury, and Saturn, however, those can be filtered out by the magnitude threshold; comets, and other objects [24].

3 Establishment of Noise Models

This chapter introduces the three kinds of noise modeling methods, including the transient effect, drift objects and stationary false stars. The star images are generated by the SAO guide star catalogue, the specific implementation is as follows.

3.1 Star Map Simulation

Star image simulation is to project the star on the celestial sphere to the image plane of a star sensor, in which celestial sphere coordinate system, star sensor coordinate and star sensor image coordinate are needed. For a star that can be imaged on the image plane, the right ascension and declination (α, δ) of the star should meet the following conditions:

$$\begin{cases} \alpha_i \in (\alpha_0 - R/\cos \delta_0, \ \alpha_0 + R/\cos \delta_0) \\ \delta_i \in (\delta_0 - R, \ \delta_0 + R) \end{cases} \tag{1}$$

where, the R is the radius of the circular field of view. Different gray values are used to simulate stars with different brightness, which is ranging from 0 to 255. The smaller the star magnitude, the greater the corresponding brightness, and the larger the corresponding gray value:

$$G_i = 10 \times (m_{\max} - m_i) + G_{\min} \tag{2}$$

where, G_i is the gray value of the i-th star; $m_{\max}$ is the detection sensitivity of the star sensor, which is 8; and the $G_{\min}$ is the gray value corresponding to 8 magnitude, taking 180.

In star sensor imaging, the star can be regarded as a point light source, and the defocusing method is generally used to promote the accuracy of the star centroiding. In this paper, the two-dimensional Gaussian distribution function is used to approximate the diffusion function to spread the star image from a single pixel to 9 pixels. The expression of two-dimensional Gaussian function is as follows:

$$\mu_i = \frac{G_i}{2\pi\sigma^2} \exp(-\frac{(x - x_i)^2 + (y - y_i)^2}{2\sigma^2}) \tag{3}$$

where, (x_i, y_i) is the point source; σ represents the degree of dispersion of the gray value distribution, and the most of the energy is concentrated in 3×3 pixels. Then, the simulated star image is as follows (Fig. 2):

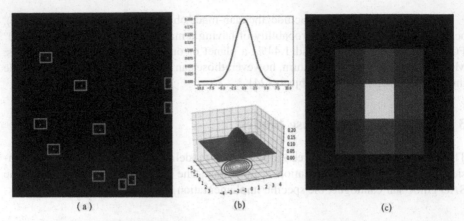

Fig. 2. (a). The simulated star image, simulated stars are in the green windows (b). The two-dimensional Gaussian energy distribution ($\sigma = 2$) of a star with magnitude 3 (c). The 3×3 pixels of the star imaging with Gaussian diffusion.

3.2 Van Allen Belts, Plume Effect and Stationary False Stars Model

This section introduces the establishment of the combined noise in detail. According to Kirkpatrick [29], [37], the star sensor's main devices used are CCD (charge-coupled devices) and CMOS APS (active pixel sens In essence, both of them are semiconductor integrated devices using photoelectric effect, but the way to collect and read out photo-generated charge is different. The star sensor can be described by CCD array which is the most commonly used, and is modeled as a stack of depletion layers and one diffusion layer. The charge is complete collected in the depletion, while, the charge in the diffusion layer can only be collected when they are diffused into the depletion.

The model of the interaction between high energy proton and detector can be described by the amount of charge produced by protons in silicon, this is the LET (linear energy transfer). According to quantum theory, the approximate energy loss of a heavy charged particle in the target material is given by:

$$\frac{dE}{dx} = 4\pi r_e^2 mc^2 \left(\frac{Z_i}{\beta}\right)^2 n_e \left[\ln\left(\frac{2mc^2\beta^2\gamma^2}{I}\right) - \beta^2\right]$$

$$\beta = \frac{v}{c}; \quad \gamma = \left(1 - \beta^2\right)^{-1/2}$$

(4)

According to Einstein's theory of Relativity and energy-mass function, and after the parameter is brought in, it is simplified:

$$\frac{dE}{dx} = 0.3565\text{MeV} \cdot \text{cm} \times \left(\frac{\psi}{\psi - 1}\right)\left[\ln(\Psi - 1) - \left(\frac{\Psi - 1}{\psi}\right) + 8.71\right]$$

(5)

For silicon at room temperature, it takes 3.65 eV to ionize an electron hole pair (EHP), then we get the relationship between the energy of the incident particle and the energy loss rate, and the relationship between the energy of the incident particle and the electron numbers in the Fig. 3.

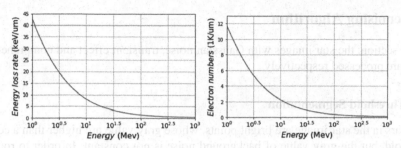

Fig. 3. The LET and the generated electron numbers per *um* of the proton energy

To compute the charge collected from the diffusion layer, shown as the dimension $Z_{diffusion}$ in Fig. 3, the Kirkpatrick model is applied. The Azimuth and Incidence are θ and Φ.

The plume effect can be described as some drift stars and the stationary false stars can be described as PSF, which are similar to the true stars.

The parameters of the noise model, see Table 1.

Table 1. The parameters of the Noise Models.

Impact factor	Parameter	Range	Illustration
Azimuth/($°$)	θ	0–90	Uniformly Distributed
Incidence/($°$)	ϕ	0–360	Uniformly Distributed
Position	x, y	N_{row}, N_{col}	Uniformly Distributed
Trajectory	l		Isotropic
Energy (Mev)	E	0–300	AP-8/9
Pixel size	s	7–15	12
Depletion/um	d_{dep}	4–10	6
Diffusion/um	d_{dif}	5–13	10
Drift number	m	10–500	Random PSF
Stationary number	n	10–100	Random

4 Denoising Algorithm

In this section, the star images with Gaussian noise, transient effect and comprehensive noise are processed respectively.

4.1 Threshold Segmentation

The stars in the star image are bright points, whose gray value are higher than a certain threshold, but the gray value of background noise is not constant. In order to roughly segment the two, we use multi window sampling method to determine the segmentation threshold. The calculation process is as follows:

$$T_s = \frac{1}{N} \sum_{i=1}^{N} (\mu_i + a \times \sigma_i) \tag{6}$$

Where, T_s is the segmentation threshold, N is the number of the sampling window, μ_i and σ_i are the mean and standard deviation of gray values in the i-th window, respectively, a is a constant, here it is 5. The star image is segmented by segmentation threshold:

$$I_1(x, y) = \begin{cases} I(x, y) & I(x, y) \geqslant T_s \\ 0 & I(x, y) < T_s \end{cases} \tag{7}$$

$I_1(x, y)$ is the gray value of pixels at (x, y) after threshold segmentation, and $I(x, y)$ is the gray value of pixels at (x, y) of the original star image. The effect of the threshold segmentation is as follows:

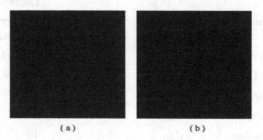

(a)   (b)

Fig. 4. (a). The simulated star image with Gaussian noise (b). The star image which is processed by the threshold segmentation.

4.2 Inter Star Image Frame Contrast

As we can see from the Fig. 4, the threshold segmentation method can remove most of the background noise, while the false stars which are similar to the true stars are still cannot be removed by the method. In star tracking mode, there are usually several frames to determine the output attitude. Unlike true stars, most of the false stars are randomly distributed. Therefore, the positions of most of the false stars, except for the real stars, are inconsistent between adjacent frames. Using this feature, we compare the images of adjacent frames and delete the images with different positions to achieve the goal of denoising. The inter frame comparison can be expressed as:

$$I'(x, y) = \begin{cases} \frac{I_1(x,y)+I_2(x,y)}{2} & I_1(x, y) > 0 \, \& \, I_2(x, y) > 0 \\ 0 & (I_1(x, y) = 0 \, \& \, I_2(x,)! = 0) \| (I_1(x, y)! = 0 \, \& \, I_2(x, y) = 0) \end{cases}$$

$$(8)$$

For the noise image generated by the transient effect, due to the large range of proton energy distribution, the corresponding pixels of the star image are also different. Therefore, the threshold segmentation method is not suitable for this kind of noise, only through a simple global threshold to remove non stellar brightness noise. And then, the frame comparison is carried out, and the result is as Fig. 5 shows:

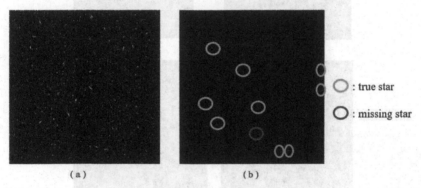

(a)   (b)

Fig. 5. (a). Star image with transient effect noise (b). Star image after the processing of the frame comparison.

4.3 Comprehensive Noise in the Star Image

In the comprehensive noise star image, we add 30 drift false stars and 5 stationary stars, respectively.

The transient effect of the star image can obtain a better denoising effect by using the method of inter frame comparison, and the drift false stars are also can be removed by this method. While the stationary false stars cannot be removed by the frame comparison method, cause of the two frames have the same position of the stationary false stars. This problem needs further discussion and study (Fig. 6).

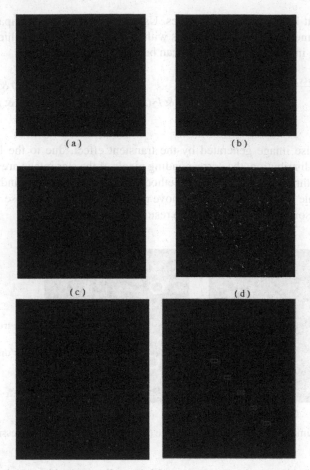

Fig. 6. (a). Star image with plume effect, 50 false stars (b). Star image with 5 stationary stars (c). Star image with 50 plume effect false stars and 5 stationary stars (d). The star image in harsh environment, transient effect plume effect and stationary false stars (e). The original star image (f). The processed star image which is in harsh environment.

5 Conclusion

In this paper, the influence of harsh environment on the imaging of star sensor is summarized, and the methods and measures taken at home and abroad are also discussed, the harsh environment including transient effects, plume effects and stationary false stars. The adverse effects on star sensor attitude determination in star tracking phase are described in detail. Furthermore, the generation mechanism and noise model of three types of false stars are discussed in detail, in which the transient effect is the most common, and a reasonable mathematical model is established. The simulated star image is generated by using the Sao navigation star catalogue. And then Gaussian random noise, salt noise and transient noise are added to it respectively. Finally, the noise is filtered out by threshold segmentation and inter frame comparison. The results show that the algorithm can effectively filter out most of the noise and retain most of the real stars. The noise filtering effect is excellent. At the same time, it is proved that Gaussian noise can simulate the influence of transient effect on star image. However, this method is not effective for stationary false stars and slow-moving drift false stars, which need further discussion.

References

1. Jorgensen, J.L., Riis, T., Betto, M.: Star tracker and vision systems performance in a high radiation environment. In: IEEE Aerospace Conference, vol. 2, pp. 95-103 (1999)
2. Howe, C.L., Weller, R.A., Reed, R.A., et al.: Distribution of proton-induced tran- sients in silicon focal plane arrays. IEEE Trans. Nucl. Sci. **54**(6), 2444–2449 (2007)
3. Scase, M.M., Caulfield, C.P., Dalziel, S.B., Hunt, J.C.R.: Time dependent plumes and jets with decreasing source strengths. J. Fluid Mech. **563**(563), 443–461 (2006)
4. Berrighi, G., Procopio, D.: Star sensors and harsh environment. In: Proceedings International ESA Conference Spacecraft Guidance, Navigation Control System, pp. 19–25 (2003)
5. Liebe, C.C.: Accuracy performance of star trackers-A tutorial. IEEE Trans. Aerosp. Electron. Syst. **38**(2), 587–599 (2002)
6. Wang, G.Y., Lv, W.C., Li, J., et al.: False star filtering for star sensor based on angular distance tracking. IEEE Access (2019)
7. Green, M.L., Hamman, D.J.: Radiation Effects Design Handbook, Section 5: The Radiations in Space and Their Interactions with Matter. 1971: NASA Lyndon B. Understanding Space Radiation. NASA, October 2002
8. Zell, H.: Van Allen Probe Spot an Impenetrable Barrier in Space. NASA, June 2017
9. Flynn, D.J., Fowski, W.J., Kai, T.: Flight performance of TOPEX/POSEIDON star trackers. Space Guidance, Control Tracking **1949**, 149–163 (1993)
10. Miller, S., Son, J.: On-orbit resolution of radiation induced loss-of-track anoma- lies for CT601 star tracker. In: AIAA Space 2001-Conference and Exposition. Wash- ington D. C. (2001)
11. Pochard, M., Blarre, L., Vilaired, D., et al.: New in-flight results of SED 16 au- tonomous star sensor (2003)
12. Blarre, L., Piot, D., Jacob, P., et al.: SED16 autonomous star sensor product line in flight results new developments and improvements in progress. In: AIAA Guidance Navigation and Control Conference and Exhibit (2005)
13. Minec-Dube, J., Jacob, P., Guillon, D.: Protons robustness improvement for the SED 26 STAR tracker (2006)
14. Jerebets, S: Star tracker focal plane evaluation for the JIMO mission. In: IEEE Aerospace Conference (2006)
15. Boldrini, F., Procopio, D., Airy, S.P., Giulicchi, L.: Miniaturised star tracker (AA-STR) ready to fly. In: Proceedings 4S Symposium Small Satellite Systems Services, vol. 571, p. 571, November 2004
16. Lauer, M., Jauregui, L., Kielbassa, S.: Operational experience with autonomous star trackers on ESA interplanetary spacecraft. In: Proceedings 20th International Symposium Space Flight Dynamics, pp. 1–6, September 2007
17. Delabie, T., Durt, T., Vandersteen, J.: Highly robust lost-in-space algorithm based on the shortest distance transform. J. Guid. Control Dyn. **36**(2), 476–484 (2013)
18. Mortari, D., Samaan, M.A., Bruccoleri, C., Junkins, J.L.: The pyramid star identification technique. Navigation **51**(3), 171–183 (2004)

19. Padgett, C., Kreutz-Delgado, K.: A grid algorithm for autonomous star iden- tification. IEEE Trans. Aerosp. Electron. Syst. **33**(1), 202–213 (1997)
20. Schiattarella, V., Spiller, D., Curti, F.: A novel star identification technique robust to high presence of false objects: the multi-poles algorithm. Adv. Space Res. **59**(8), 2133–2147 (2017)
21. Wang, G., Li, J., Wei, X.G.: Star identification based on hash map. IEEE Sensors J. **18**(4), 1591–1599 (2018)
22. Zhang, H., et al.: False star detection and isolation during star tracking based on improved chi-square tests. Rev. Sci. Instrum. **88**(8), 085004 (2017)
23. Nakajima, A., Yanagisawa, T., Kurosaki, H.: Optical observation facilities for space debris and moving objects. In: 56th International Astronautical Congress (International Academy Astronaut Space Debris and Space Traffic Management, 2005), pp. 33–42 (2005)
24. Jiang, J., Zhang, G.J., Wei, X., Li, X.: Rapid star tracking algorithm for star sensor. Aerosp. Electron. Syst. Mag. IEEE **24**, 23–33 (2009)
25. Fan, Q., Cai, Z., Wang, G.: Plume noise suppression algorithm for missile-borne star sensor based on star point shape and angular distance between stars. Sensors **19**, 3838 (2019)
26. He, B.J., Zhang, J.H., Cai, G.B.: Research on vacuum plume and its effects. Chin. J. Aeronaut. **26**(1), 27–36 (2013)
27. Connolly, P.: Gaussian plume model. personalpages.manchester.ac.uk. Re- trieved 25 April 2017.
28. Yan, B., Tang, X., Wang, J., Zhou, Y., Zheng, G.: An improved method for the fitting and prediction of the number of Covid-19 confirmed cases based on LSTM. Comput. Mater. Continua **64**(3), 1473–1490 (2020)
29. Liu, C., Yang, S.: Research on agent-based economic decision model systems. Intell. Autom. Soft Comput. **26**(5), 1035–1046 (2020)

Combining Turning Point Detection with Grid Transformation for Road Intersection Detection

Rutian Qing(✉), Yizhi Liu, Yijiang Zhao, Zhihou Guo, Zhuhua Liao, and Min Liu

Key Laboratory of Knowledge Processing and Networked Manufacturing in Hunan Province,
Hunan University of Science and Technology, Xiangtan 411201, China
rutianqing@mail.hnust.edu.cn

Abstract. Road intersection is one of the crucial elements in a road network. How to accurately detect road intersection is a vital process in road network construction. The traditional approach finds the turning point in trajectory by computing the trajectory point's turning angle and uses a clustering algorithm to cluster the turning point to yield the cluster point representing road intersection. However, the approach will detect some fake road intersection points. We propose an approach combining turning point detection with grid transformation for road intersection detection to address this issue. The process of grid transformation can filter the point in low-density area. So, the fake intersection point can be filtered by the process as far as possible. We use a real-world trajectory data set to conduct the experiment and receive a good result. The precision of our approach's experimental result is 14% more than the traditional approach's result, and the recall and the F-score are also higher than the traditional approach.

Keywords: Trajectory data mining · Road intersection detection · Network topology structure · Turning point detection · Grid transformation

1 Introduction

Digital map plays a key role in the fields of geographic data updating, intelligent transport, and smart city [1–3]. Traditional map-making approach is laborious and time-consuming [4, 5]. In the past few decades, automatic road extraction from satellite image has been extensively studied [6, 7]. By sampling and analyzing remote sensing image, the road information can be separated from the image [8]. But this approach is prone to be affected by surrounding objects (such as shadows, trees, or clouds) blocking the road, resulting in the discontinuity of the extracted road [9]. Remote sensing image is expensive to obtain, and the transmission and processing of them cannot keep pace with the changing frequency of roads in the real world. In recent years, some Internet companies, such as Google and Baidu, use expensive driverless car and intricate technical mean to collect highly accurate road data [10]. Due to the rapid change in real-world road network, newly generated road map can quickly become obsolete.

With the development of the Global Positioning System (GPS) technology, most urban public transportation tools (for instance, buses and taxis) are equipped with GPS

© Springer Nature Switzerland AG 2021
X. Sun et al. (Eds.): ICAIS 2021, CCIS 1423, pp. 335–347, 2021.
https://doi.org/10.1007/978-3-030-78618-2_27

devices [11–13]. GPS point can be collected from GPS device [14]. These data contain rich semantic information on an urban road, come from a wide range of sources [15–17]. The ubiquitous GPS data provide a new opportunity for the production and updating of road network [18]. Road intersection is quite vital to the construction of a road network. Therefore, the detection of road intersection can be used as the premise of constructing road network topology.

The study of road intersection detection has been carried out at home and abroad. Karagiorgou [19] finds turning point through the angle of trajectory point and performs clustering on these turning points. The clustering result represent the road intersection. However, some false intersections are detected in some non-intersection areas. It has some negative effects on the quality of the overall traffic network.

To solve this issue, we propose an intersection detection approach combining turning point detection and grid transformation. Similar to Karagiorgou's approach [19], we first find the turning point in the trajectory. Then, the intersection point is calculated. Generally, the intersection point is closer to the real road intersection center than a turning point. Even so, turning point is detected when vehicle turns illegally. So, we introduce grid transformation to deal with this issue. We divide the experimental area into several grids of the same size and use grid to represent the experimental area abstractly. By deciding the distribution of intersection point in the grid, the grid set conforms to the shape of the intersection point is found. After this treatment, the turning point left by illegal turning is largely filtered out. Finally, a clustering algorithm is used to cluster the intersection point in the grid. The clustering point generated by this algorithm represents the road intersection we detect.

Our contribution mainly lies in: a novel approach, combining turning point detection and grid transformation of road intersection detection, is proposed. In the proposed approach, the features of suspected road intersections are refined through grid transformation. And the experimental result shows its effectiveness and better than the traditional approach.

2   Related Work

There are two main approaches used in road intersection detection based on GPS trajectory: detecting road intersection by clustering and classification. Clustering-based is a classical approach. In this approach, redundant trajectory point is removed, and the remaining points are clustered. The cluster point represents the road intersection. In the classify-based approach, every region in an area is classified. In other words, the classification algorithm is used to confirm whether there is a road intersection in an area. The classify-based approach transforms the problem of road intersection detection into the problem of binary classification.

Clustering algorithms can extract valuable information from massive amounts of data [20]. In the clustering-based approach, the point close to the real road intersection is detected, and the clustering algorithm is applied to obtain the road intersection. Karagiorgou [19] used the change of turning angle between trajectory points to calculate the turning point. Then, these turning points are clustered to obtain the road intersection point of the overall traffic network. However, the experimental result of this approach contains many errors. Based on this approach, Wu [21] adopted a quite strict angle threshold on choosing turning point. Deng [22] introduced local G* statistics and selected candidate point at road intersection by considering the nearby point's direction. Zhang [23] used the topological features of road intersection to detect road intersection. By analyzing the features of node pixel, the road intersection can be found. Tang [24] used two turning points to form a turning-point pair and used a clustering algorithm to cluster the turning point-pair. Then, the clustering algorithm of local connectivity was used to detect the road intersection. After detecting the candidate point at the road intersection, the above algorithms cluster these points to obtain the road intersection.

The classify-based approach classifies test sample by analyzing the characteristics of road intersection. Gao [25] used the GeoHash algorithm to encode and partition the original trajectory and the region where the trajectory appeared. The road intersection feature set is constructed by mapping the coding trajectory and the active region coding matrix to a Boolean fusion matrix. Finally, a K-neighbor classification algorithm with a sliding window is used to realize intersection detection. Chen [10] used low-frequency GPS trajectory data to detect road intersection. This approach detects the stop point to eliminate the false turning point. Then, the trajectory point near the road intersection is compensated. Finally, the classification algorithm is used to deduce the structure of the region.

The clustering-based approach generally yields a point representing road intersection, while the classify-based approach yields a region contain road intersection. These approaches detect road intersection on a macro level and show the different scales on a micro-level. In the clustering-based approach, there are some fake road intersections detected sometimes. Therefore, based on Karagiorgou's approach [19], we propose a novel approach to detect road intersection. The approach first detects two turning points and uses grid transformation to find the region of high-density intersection point. Then, the intersection point in the high-density grid is judged. Finally, the intersection point is clustered by the clustering algorithm. The clustering result represents the road intersection detected by the approach. Our approach performs well and effectively alleviates the issue of error detection caused by a vehicle turning in non-intersection area.

3   The Proposed Approach

Our approach is consisting of four steps. These steps are data preprocessing, turning point detection, grid transformation, and road intersection detection. The framework of the proposed approach is shown in Fig. 1.

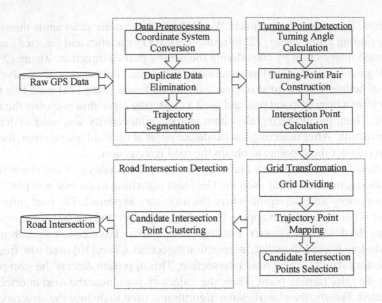

Fig. 1. The framework of the approach.

3.1 Definition

Definition 1: Trajectory Point. A trajectory point, including longitude, latitude, and time, represents an object's location at a certain moment.

Definition 2: Trajectory. A trajectory is consisting of several consecutive trajectory points.

Definition 3: Turning Point. Given three consecutive trajectory points A, B and C, let the extension line between A and B be $L1$, and the line segment between B and C be $L2$. Then, B's angle is defined as the angle between $L1$ and $L2$. If a trajectory point's angle is in the interval of the threshold, the point is a turning point. It is calculated in Sect. 3.3.

Definition 4: Turning-point Pair. Two consecutive turning points form a turning-point pair. In Fig. 2, P1 and P2 are the elements of a turning-point pair in the red circle.

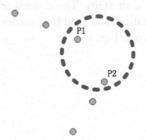

Fig. 2. A turning-point pair. (Color figure online)

3.2 Data Preprocessing

Coordinate system conversion. The raw GPS data is the data in the GCJ-02 coordinate system. For subsequent experiment, they need to be transformed into trajectory point in the WGS84 coordinate system.

Duplicate data elimination. When a vehicle is waiting for the traffic signal, the GPS device may yield many trajectory points with uniform coordinate value. These points should be eliminated. In Fig. 3(a), the file generated by the GPS device is showing many rows with uniform coordinate values. Nevertheless, we only keep one of them (Fig. 3(b)).

```
c,30.66278,104.0812,1477969621
c,30.66279,104.08121,1477969624
c,30.66279,104.08121,1477969627
c,30.66279,104.08121,1477969630
c,30.66279,104.08121,1477969633
c,30.66279,104.08121,1477969636
c,30.66279,104.08121,1477969639
c,30.66279,104.08121,1477969642
```

```
30.66272,104.08116,1477969618,0
30.66278,104.0812,1477969621,0
30.66279,104.08121,1477969624,1477969696
30.66281,104.08122,1477969699,0
30.66293,104.08129,1477969702,0
30.66304,104.08135,1477969705,0
30.66321,104.08146,1477969708,0
```

(a) Points with duplicate value.   (b) Eliminated duplicate point.

Fig. 3. GPS point with duplicate coordinate.

Trajectory segmentation. The trajectory is the input of our next work. Therefore, we use the gap of timestamp to segment GPS data into different trajectories. The principle of segmentation is: if the time interval between two trajectory points before and after exceeds a certain threshold, these points are divided into different trajectories. As shown in Fig. 4(a), we segment the trajectory points represented by two timestamps with certain differences selected by the red rectangle into different trajectories. Figure 4(b) is a visualization of these trajectories.

```
30.67037,104.07547,1477969951,0
30.67053,104.07511,1477969954,0
30.67064,104.07488,1477969957,0
30.67283,104.07822,1477970740,0
30.67276,104.07838,1477970743,0
30.67269,104.07856,1477970746,0
```

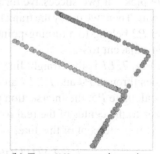

(a) Segmenting trajectories by timestamp.   (b) Two different trajectories.

Fig. 4. Trajectory segmentation. (Color figure online)

3.3 Turning Point Detection

When a vehicle makes a left turn or a right turn at an intersection, the vehicle's GPS device typically records no fewer than two trajectory points that fall within the intersection, known as turning point. The turning point indicates that the vehicle has a change of driving direction during the driving process, which may occur at the road intersection of the road.

The turning point can be calculated by calculating the turning angle of the trajectory point. In Fig. 5, a triangle is constructed with continuous trajectory points A, B, and C as vertices. The opposite edges of the vertices are a, b and c, respectively. α is one of the triangle's inner angles, and θ is the angle of the trajectory point B. Both α and θ can be calculated by Eq. 1.

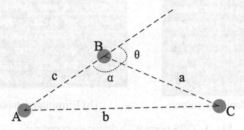

Fig. 5. Turning angle calculating.

$$\alpha = arccos\left(\frac{a^2 + b^2 - c^2}{2 * a * b}\right)$$
$$\theta = |180 - \alpha| \tag{1}$$

If a trajectory point has a turning angle bigger than a certain threshold, it is marked as a turning point. Although turning point is within the road intersection, it is still some distances from the center. Therefore, we use these turning points to calculate the point closer to the center of a road intersection.

We pick out two successive turning points in trajectories and make them a turning-point pair. Then, we query the trajectory point adjacent to the turning-point pair. In Fig. 6, P1 and P2 belong to a turning-point pair, and P3 is the trajectory point adjacent to P1, and P4 adjacent to P2.

In Fig. 7, L1 is the straight line that goes through P3 and P1, L2 is the straight line that goes through P4 and P2. L1 and L2 can be calculated by Eq. 2. We combine L1 and L2 to calculate P5, the intersection point of L1 and L2. Comparing with P1 and P2, P5 is closer to the center of the real road intersection. In Eq. 2, K is the slope of this line, and b is the intercept of this line.

$$LATITUDE = K * LONGITUDE + b \tag{2}$$

So far, we obtain many intersection points like P5. Nevertheless, two situations can impact the results of the detection. One is that vehicle does U-shape turning on the straight road in Fig. 8(a). Another is that the red intersection is not in the right area in Fig. 8(b). The red point in Fig. 8 is the wrong intersection point, and it should be filtered out.

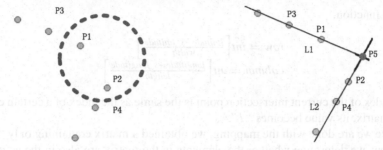

Fig. 6. A turning-point pair and its adjacent point.

Fig. 7. P5 is a crossing point.

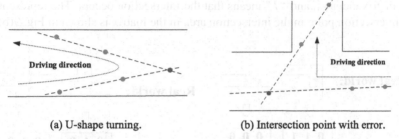

(a) U-shape turning.   (b) Intersection point with error.

Fig. 8. Intersection point in the wrong position. (Color figure online)

3.4 Grid Transformation

After the processing in Sect. 3.3, we obtained a large number of intersection points. However, some intersection points are not near the road intersection (see Fig. 8). When calculating the intersection position of two lines, it may appear that the position is not in the area of the road intersection. However, it is found that the intersection point around these false intersections is relatively sparse after many experiments. Therefore, we introduce the grid and use it to filter out the low-density intersections around.

The main idea of grid transformation is to use the grid as an abstract representation of an experimental area. Processing the data in the grid is to process the real data indirectly. We use the grid to filter out the surrounding low-density intersection points, and the remaining fall within the actual road intersection.

Grid division. The experimental area is divided into several grids of equal size. We use a matrix with the same size and number of grids to represent the grid. All of the elements in this matrix start at *"0"*.

Then, we map the intersection point to the matrix. Each intersection point's index in the matrix can be calculated by using Eq. 3. In Eq. 3, *"(row, column)"* is the index of the current intersection point in the matrix, *"(s_longitude, s_latitude)"* is the starting coordinate of the experimental area, *"(width, length)"* is the size of a grid, *"int[]"* is an integral function.

$$row = int\left[\frac{latitude - s\_latitude}{width}\right]$$
$$column = int\left[\frac{longitude - s\_longitude}{length}\right] \tag{3}$$

If the index of the current intersection point is the same as the index of a certain element in the matrix, its value becomes "*1*".

Once we are done with the mapping, we obtained a matrix containing only "*0*" and "*1*". Now, we determine whether the elements in the matrix are also in the actual road intersection.

Through analysis, we know that road intersections and non-intersections have different shapes. In Fig. 9, "*0*" means that no intersection occurs in the grid represented by the matrix element, and "*1*" means that the intersection occurs. The representation of the intersection point in the intersection area in the matrix is shown in Fig. 9(b).

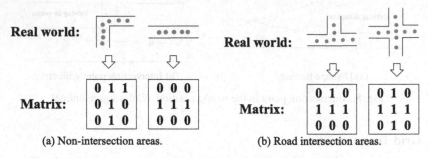

Fig. 9. The representation results of the intersection point in different media.

To filter out the situation in Fig. 9(a), we analyzed the elements with a value of "*1*" in the matrix. We take the current matrix element as the center to count the values of its surrounding elements. In a matrix, the surrounding elements of an element include the top, bottom, left, and right elements closest to it, as shown in Fig. 10. If the sum of the element values around the current element is greater than 2, the point in the grid that it represents is a candidate intersection point.

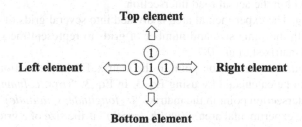

Fig. 10. Current element in center and its surrounding elements.

3.5 Clustering Candidate Intersection Point

After filtering, a large number of candidate intersection points are left. To uniquely represent road intersections, we use a clustering algorithm to cluster them. The steps of the algorithm are shown in Algorithm 1.

Algorithm 1. Clustering algorithm.

Input:	P; /*Point set */;
	eps; /* a point's surrounding area. */
	min_pts; /* the minimum number of points in the surrounding area. */
Output:	C, /* clustered point. */
1	For each p in P:
2	calculate the *distance* with q; /* q is one of the other points in P. */
3	if *distance* <= *eps*:
4	tmp_list.append(q)
5	if *len(tmp_list)* >= *min_pts*:
6	the tag of every points in *tmp_list* is set to *Visited*
7	yield a cluster point, c, its coordinate is decided by the point in the area.
8	C.append(c)

After the clustering, we obtained several clustering points representing the road intersections we detected.

4 Experiments and Analysis

4.1 Data Set

We use the GPS data of Chengdu provided by Didi to verify the proposed approach. The data set contains five elements shown in Table 1. Trajectory point in the data set is recorded at a frequency of 2 to 6 s per time. The attributes, *Latitude*, *Longitude*, and *Timestamp* are used in the experiment.

Table 1. Attributes of each GPS point.

Attributes	Example values
Order ID	glox.jrrlltB…
Driver ID	jkkt8kxn…
Latitude	30.66703
Longitude	104.04392
Timestamp	1501584540

We carried out the experiments in the area shown in Fig. 11 and downloaded the SHP format map of this area from OpenStreetMap, and marked the intersections of this area with green circles as the ground truth.

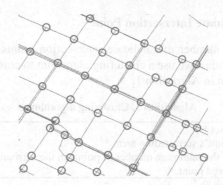

Fig. 11. Ground truth. (Color figure online)

4.2 Evaluation

Precision, *Recall* and F_{score} are used to evaluate the experimental results [10]. In Eq. 4, *Precision* represents the ratio of correctly matched intersections, *Recall* represents the ratio of correctly detected intersections, and F_{score} is the comprehensive weight value combining precision and recall.

$$Precision = \frac{matched\ intersections}{detected\ intersections}$$

$$Recall = \frac{matched\ intersections}{ground\ truth\ intersections} \qquad (4)$$

$$F_{score} = 2 * \frac{precision * recall}{precision + recall}$$

4.3 Experimental Result

The experiment results show in Fig. 12. To verify our approach's validity, we reproduce the experiment of the traditional approach [19].

As shown in Fig. 12, the green circle represents the road intersections successfully detected. The blue circles are the road intersections that have not been correctly detected; The red circle is the road intersections of error detection; The orange circle is the road intersections on OSM that was not updated in time.

We set a buffer radius of 40 m for each road intersection of the ground truth [10]. When the detection results fall within the range, it is deemed that the experimental result matches the real road intersections successfully. Based on this principle, the indicators of the experimental results are shown in Table 2.

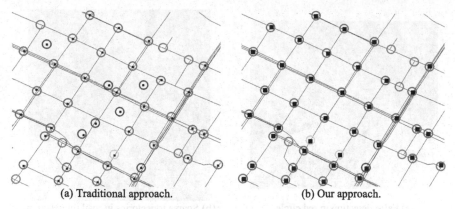

(a) Traditional approach.   (b) Our approach.

Fig. 12. Experimental results. (Color figure online)

Table 2. Comparison with the related work of road intersection detection.

Approaches	Precision	Recall	F_{score}	Containing the detection results in the orange circles?
Traditional approach	0.80	0.78	0.79	No
Our approach	0.92	0.88	0.90	
Traditional approach	0.83	0.81	0.82	Yes
Our approach	0.97	0.88	0.92	

4.4 Analysis

Generally, the traditional approach detects many turning points. However, some points are also detected when the vehicle makes an illegal turn. The approach is not able to process these points effectively. Therefore, this approach will detect many false intersections, as shown in the red circles in Fig. 12(a). Therefore, we use the grid transformation to filter most of the false road intersections and raise the precision of detection.

Our approach also detects a few numbers of false road intersections shown in Fig. 12(b). After analysis, the reason is that the area has high-density intersection point. In Fig. 13(a), many green intersection points around the red circle led to false detection.

After further analysis, some of the trajectories are very sparse (Fig. 13(b)) and lead some road intersections undetected. However, our approach detected intersections that were not timely updated to OSM (The orange circles in Fig. 12(b)).

(a) False detection in red circle.   (b) Sparse trajectories in road intersection.

Fig. 13. Analysis of some wrong result. (Color figure online)

5   Conclusions

We propose the approach of combining turning point detection with grid transformation for road intersection detection. This approach has two contributions. The first is that it can calculate the intersection point closer to the road intersection center, which improves the accuracy of intersection detection. Another is that it filters the intersection point of low-density areas through the grid, which reduces the number of misidentified intersections. In a word, the effectiveness is better than only using turning point to detect road intersection.

However, the proposed approach has some deficiencies. If a GPS device's sampling frequency is too low, the device may not be able to record enough trajectory point at road intersections. This approach may be difficult to detect the turning point of such a trajectory. Another disadvantage is that the approach is limited when the road intersection has a complex shape (such as an O-shaped intersection). Our further work has two directions. The first is how to obtain accurate turning point from low-frequency trajectory data. The other is how to get the shape of the road intersection through the trajectory data.

Acknowledgement. Vehicle trajectory data were acquired from the GAIA open data initiative (https://gaia.didichuxing.com) of Didi Chuxing.

Funding Statement. This project was funded by the National Natural Science Foundation of China (41871320, 61872139), Provincial and Municipal Joint Fund of Hunan Provincial Natural Science Foundation of China (2018JJ4052), Hunan Provincial Natural Science Foundation of China (2017JJ2081), the Key Project of Hunan Provincial Education Department (19A172), the Scientific Research Fund of Hunan Provincial Education Department (18K060).

Conflicts of Interest. The authors declare no conflicts of interest.

References

1. Li, L.: Extraction of road intersections from GPS traces based on the dominant orientations of roads. ISPRS Int. J. Geo-Inf. **6**(12), 403 (2017)
2. Cai, H.Y.: Auto-extraction of road intersection from high resolution remote sensing image. Remote Sens. Land Res. **28**(1), 63–71 (2016)
3. Liu, Y.: Extracting campus' road network from walking GPS trajectories. J. Cyber Secur. **2**(3), 131–140 (2020)
4. Hu, H.: Road extraction based on taxi trajectory data. Bull. Surv. Mapp. (7), 53–57 (2018)
5. Liu, J.P.: An incremental construction method of road network considering road complexity. Acta Geodaetica et Cartographica Sin. **48**(4), 480–488 (2019)
6. Wang, W.X.: A review of road extraction from remote sensing images. J. Traffic Transp. Eng. **3**(3), 271–282 (2016)
7. Guo, F.C.: A new method for automatic extracting road junctions from high resolution SAR images. J. Geo. Sci. Technol. **34**(2), 199–203 (2017)
8. Chen, G.: Extraction method of road network based on adaptive clustering learning. Bull. Surv. Mapp. (11), 30–35 (2018)
9. Li, W.D.: Research status of road network extraction from remote sensing images at home and abroad. Image Technol. **28**(2), 44–45 (2016)
10. Chen, B.Q.: Extended classification course improves road intersection detection from low-frequency GPS trajectory data. ISPRS Int. J. Geo-Inf. **9**(3), 181 (2020)
11. Wu, Q.Y.: GPS trajectory agglomeration and refined road network extraction. Acta Geodaetica et Cartographica Sin. **48**(4), 502–511 (2019)
12. Chen, H.: A differential privacy based (k-ψ)-anonymity method for trajectory data publishing. Comput. Mater. Continua, **65**(3), 2665–2685 (2020)
13. Mao, Y.: Application of wireless network positioning technology based on GPS in geographic information measurement. J. New Media **2**(3), 131–135 (2020)
14. Zhang, Y.: An algorithm for mining gradual moving object clusters pattern from trajectory streams. Comput. Mater. Continua **59**(3), 885–901 (2019)
15. Luo, T.: An improved DBSCAN algorithm to detect stops in individual trajectories. ISPRS Int. J. Geo-Inf. **6**(3), 181 (2017)
16. Tang, J.B.: An automatic method for detection and update of additive changes in road network with GPS trajectory data. ISPRS Int. J. Geo-Inf. **8**(9), 411 (2019)
17. Wu, H.Y.: Recent progress in taxi trajectory data mining. Acta Geodaetica et Cartographica Sin. **48**(11), 1341–1356 (2019)
18. Liu, C.Y.: A progressive buffering method for road map update using OpenStreetMap data. Int. J. Geo-Inf. **4**(3), 1246–1264 (2015)
19. Karagiorgou, S.: On vehicle tracking data-based road network generation. In: 20th ACM SIGSPATIAL GIS Conference, New York, USA, pp. 89–98 (2012)
20. Cu, G.R.: Weighted particle swarm clustering algorithm for self-organizing maps. J. Quant. Comput. **2**(2), 85–95 (2020)
21. Wu, J.W.: Detecting road intersections from coarse-gained GPS traces based on clustering. J. Comput. **8**(11), 2959–2965 (2013)
22. Deng, M.: Generating urban road intersection models from low-frequency GPS trajectory data. Int. J. Geogr. Inf. Sci. **32**(12), 2337–2361 (2018)
23. Zhang, C.L.: An intersection-first approach for road network generation from crowd-sourced vehicle trajectories. ISPRS Int. J. Geo-Inf. **8**(11), 473 (2019)
24. Tang, L.L.: Urban intersection recognition and construction based on big trace data. Acta Geodaetica et Cartographica Sin. **46**(6), 770–779 (2017)
25. Gao, Y.: Identifying urban intersections with GPS trajectories. Data Analy. Knowl. Discov. **3**(11), 24–34 (2019)

Evaluation of Training Effect of New Professional Farmers Based on BP Neural Network

Shangsheng Li and Chaosheng Tang(✉)

Hainan University, Haikou 570228, China
tcsjk@hainanu.edu.cn

Abstract. In order to promote the structural reform of agricultural supply sides, speed up agricultural modernization and improve the cultivation of new professional farmers, it is necessary to comprehensively evaluate the effect of this new professional farmer training. In view of the problem that the traditional evaluation method has great artificial influence when determining the weight in the evaluation process, the nonlinear mapping ability of BP neural network is used to reduce the subjective influence of people giving weight in the evaluation process, and the error is distributed to all units of each layer through gradient descent to complete the weight update. A classification model was created for this experiment, and 156 groups of data were used for training and 40 groups were used for testing. The classification accuracy on the test set reached 94.87%, so the training effect can be effectively evaluated by BP network. By averaging the weights of individual evaluation results obtained by the classification model, the comprehensive evaluation of this training are obtained finally. According to the comprehensive evaluation results, we can promote training institutions to improve relevant measures and promote the education and training of new professional farmers.

Keywords: New professional farmers · BP neural network · Comprehensive evaluation

1 Background

At present, China is in a critical period of transition from traditional agriculture to modern agriculture, and a large number of advanced agricultural sciences and technology and efficient facilities have been introduced into various fields of agricultural production, thus urgently need high-quality new-type professional farmers. However, China's farmers have a large population base and generally low academic qualifications: According to the survey statistics, primary and junior high school education accounts for 30% and high school accounts for 36% and junior college accounts for 23% and bachelor degree or above accounts for 9% [1]. In addition, due to regional differences and urban-rural differences, a large number of young and middle-aged rural laborers have flowed out, and rural hollowing has become an indisputable fact [2]. So much so that when people mention farmers, they will think of such terms as poverty and backwardness.

© Springer Nature Switzerland AG 2021
X. Sun et al. (Eds.): ICAIS 2021, CCIS 1423, pp. 348–357, 2021.
https://doi.org/10.1007/978-3-030-78618-2_28

For many years, the No. 1 Document of the Central Committee has always paid attention to the issues concerning agriculture, rural areas and farmers, and has repeatedly emphasized the great significance of modern agricultural development and rural revitalization strategy. In March this year, the Ministry of Agriculture and Rural Affairs issued the "High-quality Development Plan for New Agricultural Business Subjects and Service Subjects (2020–2022)", which pointed out that by 2022, the training of new professional farmers will be widely carried out, and online and offline training will develop together.

Cultivating new professional farmers is in line with the inevitable trend and inherent requirement of the implementation of the strategy of agricultural modernization and rural revitalization at present [3]. At present, all parts of the country are carrying out research and practice on new-type professional farmers, vigorously carrying out education and training activities for professional farmers, and achieving certain results [4–6].

In order to get a comprehensive evaluation of the training effect, it is often necessary to analyze various factors (the samples collected this time include 10 dimensions of evaluation). This also brings some problems. For example, when the amount of data is large, the increased number of evaluation factors will lead to excessive calculation. In addition, the weight design of the traditional evaluation method is very vague, and human factors have great influence when determining the weight. And with the passage of time and space, the influence degree of each dimension on the problem may also change, and the initial weight determined may not conform to the actual situation. Considering that comprehensive evaluation is a complex nonlinear model, it is necessary to establish a learning mechanism of weights, which is the advantage of artificial neural network [7–9]. In view of the uncertainty of the weights in the process of modeling the evaluation model, a BP neural network models is established to analyze the input and output, and the weights that meet the actual requirements are obtained through self-learning and self-adaptive ability to avoid the interference of subjective factors on the weights.

2 BP Neural Network

2.1 BP Network Definition

Back propagation (BP) neural network is a concept put forward by scientists led by Rumelhart and McClelland in 1986, It is a multilayer feed-forward neural network trained according to the error Back-Propagation (BP) algorithm. BP algorithm is an outstanding representative of many learning algorithms, and it is the most successful neural network learning algorithm so far [10]. At present, BP network has become a widely used neural network, especially in pattern recognition and classification, intelligent fault detection, image processing, function fitting, optimal prediction and so on [11–14].

The basic idea of BP algorithm is to divide the learning process into forward propagation and error backward propagation: 1. In forward propagation, the sample X is input from the input layer and transmitted to the output layer after being processed by the hidden layer. If the loss value between the actual output O and the expected output y of the output layer does not meet the requirements, the error back propagation stage will be entered. 2. Error back propagation is to transmit the output to the input layer by layer through the hidden layer in some forms, and distribute the error to all the units in each layer, so as to obtain the error signal of each layer as the basis for correcting each unit. The training of BP neural network is a process in which forward propagation and error back propagation are carried out repeatedly, and the weights of each layer are constantly adjusted, and the training ends when the preset learning times or other conditions are reached.

2.2 Important Parameters

Before the establishment of BP network model, it is necessary to initialize some important parameters and select relevant functions.

Weight W, Offset Term b. In BP neural network, weight w and offset b are set to fit the data better. Execute forward propagation in BP network through $f(W*X + b)$, and get the actual output result. Before the neural network is constructed, we can use the function to generate a set of numerical matrices with standard normal distribution as the initial weight w, and initialize the zero matrix with corresponding size as the offset item b. After initialization, W and B are constantly updated and adjusted during the fitting training of the BP neural network, and an accurate BP networks model are obtained finally.

Activate the Function. Nonlinear activation function is used to add nonlinear factors, so as to improve the ability of neural network to express the model and solve the problems that linear model cannot solve. In this experiment, the hidden layer uses tanh function, and the output layer uses sigmoid function.

Learning Rate. The selection of learning rate η is very important, and it is an important factor that affects the speed and performance of network training. If the learning rate is too large, the system will be unstable; if it is too small, the training period will be too long and the training requirements will not be met. In practical experiments, we tend to choose a smaller learning rate to keep the system stable, which can be judged by observing the error decline curve. The rapid decline indicates that the learning rate is appropriate, and if there is a large oscillation, it indicates that the learning rate is too large. We can set the initial learning rate in advance and adjust the learning rate according to the results after the model training. The learning rate of this paper is adjusted during training, and the whole model has the best training effect when the learning rate is 0.04.

2.3 BP Model

The BP neural network is composed of input layer, hidden layer and output layer. Three-layer neural network can solve the most nonlinear problems by selecting appropriate number of neurons. The input layer of this neural network model contains 10 neurons, corresponding to the 10 evaluation dimensions of the questionnaire. The number of neurons in the hidden layer is determined according to the empirical formula $J = 2*M + 1$ (M is the number of neurons in the input layer), which contains 21 neurons. The output layer contains three neurons, which correspond to three personal evaluation results. The structure diagram of BP neural network is shown in Fig. 1:

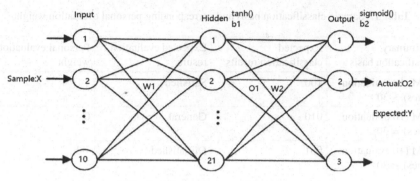

Fig. 1. BP neural network structure

3 Experiment and Result Analysis

3.1 Data Sources

In order to promote the education and training of new professional farmers more effectively and improve the quality and effect of training, questionnaires are distributed among farmers who have completed the training. This questionnaire designed a satisfaction questionnaire for ten aspects of this training, and divided the evaluation of farmers participating in training into five levels, which were named 'very dissatisfied', 'relatively dissatisfied', 'fair', 'relatively satisfied' and 'very satisfied', and the scores of each level were 5 points from low to high. Finally, 196 valid training evaluation data were obtained. Before training the model, the sample data is shuffled, 80% of the data is randomly selected as the training set, and the remaining 20% is used for testing.

3.2 Evaluation Criteria

In this paper, the training evaluation data are obtained through questionnaires. In order to build a personal evaluation classification model using BP neural network, the training set data are preliminarily classified to obtain the desired output results. Taking the sum of the 5-point evaluation values of 10 dimensions of sample data as the preliminary classification basis, the fuzzy classification process and the corresponding individual evaluation weights are shown in Table 1.

It can be seen from Table 1 that the sum of 10 evaluation values of training samples is taken as the fuzzy classification basis, and the expected classification results are divided into three categories as output to reduce the ambiguity of the five-point evaluation system, and the corresponding individual evaluation weights is given to prepare for the comprehensive evaluation of training. BP network is used to fit the input and output of the training set to obtain an accurate personal evaluation classification model, and the test set is used to verify the accuracy of the model. After verification, the personal evaluation weights of all samples are obtained by using the personal evaluation classification model, and the average value is taken as the comprehensive evaluation result of this training.

Table 1. Sample classification basis and corresponding personal evaluation weight

Preliminary classification basis	Expected classification results	Expected evaluation results	Personal evaluation weight
SUM (10 evaluation values) > 30	100	Satisfied	1
SUM (10 evaluation values) = 30	010	General	0
SUM (10 evaluation values) < 30	001	Dissatisfied	−1

3.3 Experimental Process

In this paper, BP neural network is used to analyze the training effect. Firstly, the evaluation data of ten dimensions of training samples are input, and the actual personal evaluation results are output by forward propagation. If the actual personal evaluation results are inconsistent with the expected evaluation results, the error back propagation is performed to fit the data, and the error is distributed to all units of each layer through cost function and gradient descent. A relatively accurate personal evaluation classification model is obtained by repeated training with the training set, and finally the comprehensive evaluation of the training effect are obtained through this model. The experimental process is as follows:

Forward Propagation. Forward propagation propagates from the input layer to the output layer. Before executing forward propagation, it is necessary to initialize the weight matrices (W1, W2) and bias term vectors (b1, b2) of the hidden layer and the output layer, and pay attention to the transformation of row and column coefficients during matrix operation in the propagation process. Take the evaluation data of ten dimensions as input, and carry out forward propagation to get the actual personal evaluation result O2 of BP model.

In the hidden layer, a training sample x is input from the input layer, and the weight W1 and the offset term b1 are operated by formula (1) to complete the preliminary division of data, and the nonlinear relationship is added by using the activation function tanh of hidden neurons (as shown in Fig. 2), and finally the output O1 of the hidden layer is obtained (as shown in formula 2).

$$Z_1 = W_1 * X + b_1 \tag{1}$$

$$O_1 = \tanh(Z_1) \tag{2}$$

$$O_1' = 1 - O_1^2 \tag{3}$$

Operation of the output layer is similar to that of the hidden layer, but it should be noted that the input of the output layer is the output O1 of the hidden layer, and the

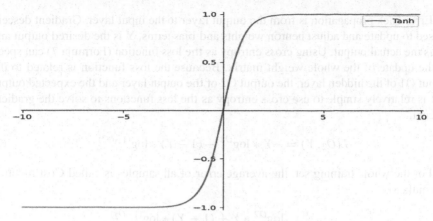

Fig. 2. Tanh function curve

weight and offset items become W2 and b2, finally, the actual personal evaluation result O2 of sample X is output by using the activation function sigmoid (as shown in Fig. 3).

$$Z_2 = W_2 * O_1 + b_2 \tag{4}$$

$$O_2 = sigmoid(Z_2) \tag{5}$$

$$O_2' = O_2 * (1 - O_2) \tag{6}$$

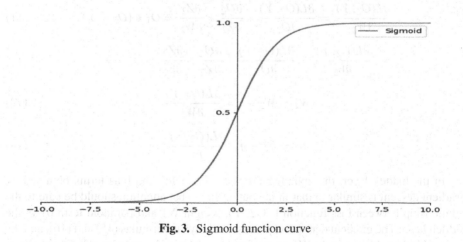

Fig. 3. Sigmoid function curve

Error Back Propagation. After the actual personal evaluation result O2 is obtained by forward propagation, if it is inconsistent with the expected personal evaluation result Y, in order to better fit the data, the error back propagation operation is performed to correct the weights and offsets of the neural network.

Error back propagation is from the output layer to the input layer. Gradient descent is used to update and adjust neuron weights and bias terms. Y is the desired output and O2 is the actual output. Using cross entropy as the loss function (Formula 7) can speed up the update of the whole weight matrix, Because the loss function is related to the output O1 of the hidden layer, the output O2 of the output layer and the expected output Y, it is relatively simple to use cross entropy as the loss functions to solve the gradient descent.

$$L(O_2, Y) = -Y * \log^{O2} - (1 - Y) * \log^{(1-O2)} \tag{7}$$

For the whole training set, the average error of all samples is called Cost function (Formula 8).

$$\text{Cost} = -\frac{\log^{O2} * Y + (1 - Y) * \log^{(1-O_2)}}{m} \tag{8}$$

In the output layer, the gradient descent formulas of weight and bias terms are shown in (9) and (10), and η is the learning rate. The derivative result of the loss function by the existing formula are shown in (11) and (12), and the updated weight W2 and offset b2 of the output layer are shown in (13) and (14).

$$\Delta W_2 = -\eta \frac{\partial L(O_2, Y)}{\partial W_2} \tag{9}$$

$$\Delta b_2 = -\eta \frac{\partial L(O_2, Y)}{\partial b_2} \tag{10}$$

$$\frac{\partial L(O_2, Y)}{\partial W_2} = \frac{\partial L(O_2, Y)}{\partial O_2} * \frac{\partial O_2}{\partial Z_2} * \frac{\partial Z_2}{\partial W_2} = O_1 * (O_2 - Y) \tag{11}$$

$$\frac{\partial L(O_2, Y)}{\partial b_2} = \frac{\partial L(O_2, Y)}{\partial O_2} * \frac{\partial O_2}{\partial Z_2} * \frac{\partial Z_2}{\partial b_2} = O_2 - Y \tag{12}$$

$$W_2 = W_2 - \eta * \frac{\partial L(O_2, Y)}{\partial W_2} \tag{13}$$

$$b_2 = b_2 - \eta * \frac{\partial L(O_2, Y)}{\partial b_2} \tag{14}$$

In the hidden layer, the updating process of weights and bias terms obtained by gradient descent is similar to that in the output layer, but attention should be paid to the relationship between loss function L(O2, Y), weight W1 and paranoid term b1 in the hidden layer. The gradient derivation process is shown in formulas (15) and (16), and the updated hidden layer weight W1 and offset term b1 are obtained by substituting them into formulas (17) and (18).

$$\frac{\partial L(O_2, Y)}{\partial W_1} = \frac{\partial L(O_2, Y)}{\partial O_2} * \frac{\partial O_2}{\partial O_1} * \frac{\partial O_1}{\partial Z_1} * \frac{\partial Z_1}{\partial W_1} = (O_2 - Y) * W_2 * (1 - O_1^2) * X \tag{15}$$

$$\frac{\partial L(O_2, Y)}{\partial b_1} = \frac{\partial L(O_2, Y)}{\partial O_1} * \frac{\partial O_1}{\partial Z_1} * \frac{\partial Z_1}{\partial b_1} = (O_2 - Y) * W_2 * (1 - O_1^2) \quad (16)$$

$$W_1 = W_1 - \eta * \frac{\partial L(O_2, Y)}{\partial W_1} \quad (17)$$

$$b_1 = b_1 - \eta * \frac{\partial L(O_2, Y)}{\partial b_1} \quad (18)$$

After the error back propagation is completed, the weights and offset terms of the neural network are updated once.

3.4 Analysis of Results

The training process of BP neural network is a process in which the forward propagation and error back propagation are carried out repeatedly and the weights of each layer are constantly adjusted until the preset learning times or other conditions are reached. Finally, the trained weight matrix and paranoid items are obtained (weight matrix w1 is 21 * 10 order, b1 is 10 * 1 order; W2 is of order 3 * 21 and b2 is of order 3 * 1. The weight matrix is too large, so it is not shown in this paper.) The trained personal evaluation classification model is tested by using the test set, and the average value of the personal evaluation weights of all samples are the comprehensive evaluation result of the training effect. The experimental results are as follows:

The relationship between the cost function value obtained by BP model and the training times is shown in Fig. 4. It can be seen from the figure that the error between the actual output O2 and the expected output Y gradually decreases during the repeated training of the model, and the curve converges after training for about 10,000 times, indicating that the fitting degree of training samples is getting higher and higher.

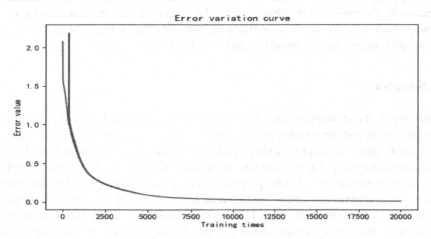

Fig. 4. Cost function diagram

According to the standards in Table 1, the results obtained by the individual evaluation classification model are given corresponding weights and averaged, and finally the comprehensive evaluation results of the training effect are obtained. The classification accuracy, expected training effect and predicted training effect calculated by personal evaluation classification model are shown in Table 2.

Table 2. Sample Classification accuracy and training effect

The data set	Classification accuracy	Expected training effect	Forecast the training effect
The training set	100%	0.187	0.187
The test set	94.87%	NONE	0.385
Total data set	98.46%	NONE	0.225

From the results in Table 2, it can be seen that after the training, the classification accuracy obtained by using the test set to verify the model is as high as 94.87%, which proves that the classification effect of the personal evaluation classification model is relatively good. The predicted training effect of the test set is higher than that of the training set, which is because the random distribution of all samples after shuffling leads to a higher proportion of satisfied people in the test set than in training set.After inputting all samples into the personal evaluation classification model, the comprehensive evaluation of training effect is 0.225, which lies between the training set and the test set, which shows the accuracy of the personal evaluation classification model from the side.

In this paper, the comprehensive evaluation of training effect are defined as the average value of evaluation weights of all samples. It can be seen from Table 1 that when the overall training effect value is close to 0, it means that the training effect is average, and when it is close to −1 or 1, it means dissatisfaction and satisfaction respectively. According to the above results, the comprehensive evaluation value of the training effect is 0.225, so it is judged that the training effect is higher than average and the overall training effect is biased towards satisfaction.

4 Summary

In this paper, the evaluation data obtained from the questionnaire are used to build a network model, and the weights and bias terms are automatically updated by using the self-learning and self-adapting ability of BP neural network, so as to give an objective evaluation to the multi-index comprehensive evaluation problem, which is very beneficial to weaken the human factors in the process of determining the weights. The constructed personal evaluation classification model has high accuracy, and the final comprehensive evaluation results are more accurate. Training institutions can improve relevant measures according to the comprehensive evaluation results, and promote the training of high-quality new-type professional farmers. BP network belongs to supervised learning, and a 5-point satisfaction survey should be added to the questionnaire design: 'Are you satisfied with this training?' The collected results are taken as the expected output of the model, which can reduce the subjective influence of the author on the preliminary classification of the training set. In addition, the uncertainty of the network structure and randomness of the initial weights lead to poor stability of the evaluation results. In future experiments, optimization methods such as genetic operator and particle swarm optimization operator should be considered to combine with the BP network to enhance the robustness of the network model and the accuracy of the evaluation results.

Acknowledgments. This work was supported by the Hainan Provincial Natural Science Foundation (618ms025); the Hainan Higher Education and Teaching Reform Research (hnjg2020–12).

References

1. Ning, D.: Research on the training of new professional farmers. Agric. Sci. Technol. Equip. **04**, 82–83 (2020)
2. Yang, G.: On the cultivation of new professional farmers under the background of rural revitalization. Anhui Agronomy Bull. **26**(19), 8–9 (2020)
3. Qin, Y., Wu, Z.: Research on perfecting the guarantee mechanism of vocational education and training for new vocational farmers. Educ. Vocation. (20), 75–79 (2020)
4. Song, H., Zhao, H.: Theoretical analysis and empirical research on the cultivation of new professional farmers. China Agric. Educ. (04), 51–56+86 (2017)
5. Xie, S.: Research on the application of distance network education in the training of new professional farmers—based on the background of rural revitalization. Reform Open. Up **12**, 72–74 (2020)
6. Shen, H., Huo, Y., Zhang, G.: Research on the cultivation mechanism of new professional farmers—based on the visual threshold of agricultural modernization. Modern Econ. Discuss. **01**, 65–69 (2014)
7. Han, L.: Theory, Design and Application of Artificial Neural Network. Chemical Industry Press, Beijing (2004)
8. Xia, P., Xu, A.H., Lian, T.: Analysis and prediction of regional electricity consumption based on BP neural network. J. Quantum Comput. **2**(1), 25–32 (2020)
9. Yuan, G.Z., Wang, J., Chen, B., Guo, W.: Assessing the forecasting of comprehensive loss incurred by typhoons: a combined PCA and BP neural network model. Jo. Artif. Intell. **1**(2), 69–88 (2019)
10. Yuan, B., Chen, G., Zheng, L.: Basic principle of BP neural network. Digit. Commun. World **08**, 28–29 (2018)
11. Alhussain, H.K., Altoaimy, L.: A neural network-based trust management system for edge devices in peer-to-peer networks. Comput. Mater. Continua **59**(3), 805–815 (2019)
12. Pan, J., Qin, H., Chen, X.X., Li, C., et al.: Image augmentation-based food recognition with convolutional neural networks. Comput. Mater. Continua **59**(1), 297–313 (2019)
13. Li, W., Zeng, G.X., Wang, H.: The instance-aware automatic image colorization based on deep convolutional neural network. Intell. Autom. Soft Comput. **26**(4), 841–846 (2020)
14. Oh, H.S., Kim, J., Park, C., Kim, Y.: Predicting concentration of PM10 using optimal parameters of deep neural network. Intell. Autom. Soft Comput. **25**(2), 343–350 (2019)

Evaluation of Training Effect of New-Type Professional Farmer Based on Cloud Model

Aite Wang⬚ and Chaosheng Tang(✉)⬚

Hainan University, Haikou 570228, Hainan, China
tcsjk@hainanu.edu.cn

Abstract. In order to make a comprehensive evaluation of the training effect of the new professional farmers from the training organization and management, training time, training cost and other aspects, and make an accurate judgment on the current situation and development direction of the new professional farmers training in China. Based on the cloud model theory, this paper realizes the transformation of qualitative index and quantitative evaluation, and organically combines fuzziness, randomness and discretization. After the characteristic data of the normal cloud generator is obtained by the reverse cloud generator and the information weight method, the normal cloud image is generated, and the training effect is evaluated according to the cloud image. The evaluation based on cloud model not only takes into account the fuzziness and randomness in the evaluation, but also takes into account the scientific nature of the data and the intuitiveness of the evaluation results. To a certain extent, it overcomes the shortcomings of the traditional evaluation methods, such as unstable evaluation conclusions and complex calculation. The evaluation conclusion is helpful for researchers to make an accurate judgment on the current situation and development direction of the training of new professional farmers in China.

Keywords: Cloud model · Forward normal cloud generator · Comprehensive evaluation · Information weight method · Normal distribution

1 Introductions

In order to reach a more objective and comprehensive conclusion, many factors should be evaluated separately before the final result can be reached. This also brings some problems. For example, when the amount of data is large, the overall amount of data will increase exponentially to the increase in the number of evaluation factors considered, resulting in a huge amount of calculation. Traditional evaluation methods are also subjective, not intuitive, and often use an accurate membership values as the evaluation conclusion [1]. For example, conventional fuzzy comprehensive evaluation is a transformation process of fuzzy to accurate, and its evaluation result is a fixed evaluation result from N evaluation units, so the fuzziness cannot be well reflected [2]. However, any prediction is inherently uncertain [3]. In addition, membership function is often used in the process of solving conventional fuzzy comprehensive evaluation. The idea is to quantify the fuzziness in the evaluation of things, and then to deal with it by using precise

© Springer Nature Switzerland AG 2021
X. Sun et al. (Eds.): ICAIS 2021, CCIS 1423, pp. 358–369, 2021.
https://doi.org/10.1007/978-3-030-78618-2_29

mathematics. This idea was questioned in academician Li Deyi's article [4], and then he proposed the concept of cloud model, providing a new idea of solving these problems.

The cloud model can better reflect the fuzziness and randomness of decision makers' evaluation information [5]. It is an uncertain transformation model of qualitative concept and quantitative description, so it can be used to describe the randomness, fuzziness and the relationship between them. Cloud theory can organically integrate the fuzziness and randomness of qualitative concepts in natural language and realize the conversion to qualitative language values and quantitative values, which is an important tool for studying uncertainty [6]. In this paper, the cloud model is used to comprehensively evaluate the effect of the new type of vocational farmer training, and the conversion to qualitative concept and quantitative value of natural language is realized.

2   The Cloud Model

2.1   Definition of Cloud

Cloud model was first proposed by Chinese academician Li Deyi in 1995, which is an uncertainty conversion model between a qualitative concept described by linguistic value and its numerical representation [7]. Based on fuzzy mathematics and probability theory, it can deal with the mutual transformation of uncertainty of qualitative concept and quantitative description by constructing a specified operator model [8].

U are a precise numerical said in the domain of quantitative theory, and C is the qualitative concept on U, if $x \in U$ quantitative values, and x is a random implementation of qualitative concept C, the certainty of x with respect to C: $\mu(x) \in [0, 1]$ is a steady tendency of random Numbers, $\mu: U \rightarrow [0, 1] \Pi\ x \in U\ x \rightarrow \mu(x)$, x on the theory of domain U called Cloud, the distribution of each x is called a Cloud droplets [9].

From the basic definition of cloud, it can be seen that the mapping of the concept T on the theoretical domain U from the theoretical domain U to the interval [0, 1] is an one-to-many relationship. In other words, the mapping between a certain element in the domain and its membership degree to the concept T is an one-to-many transformation, rather than the one-to-one relationship in the traditional fuzzy membership function. The cloud expressing the concept T is composed of many clouds droplets, each of which is a point where the qualitative concept maps to the numerical domain space, namely a concrete sample realization of the linguistic value of the qualitative concept quantitatively. This implementation is uncertain, and the model also shows that this point can represent the degree of certainty of the qualitative concept. Each cloud droplet is random, and each cloud droplet represents the degree of uncertainty of the qualitative concept, always changing slightly [10].

Such a quantitative value is an uncertain change in a qualitative conceptual language, and may not dramatically affect the overall characteristics of the cloud as each cloud droplet manifests itself. That a particular cloud droplet may not matter. However, the overall distribution characteristics of a certain number of clouding droplets reflects the fuzziness and randomness of cloud mapping, that is, the overall shape of the cloud reflects the uncertainty characteristics when qualitative concepts are expressed by quantitative values. Therefore, cloud effectively and completely integrates fuzziness and randomness to study the universal law of uncertainty contained in the most basic linguistic values in natural language, making it possible to obtain the scope and distribution law of quantitative data from the qualitative information expressed by linguistic values. It is also possible to effectively convert precise values of appropriate qualitative linguistic values.

Cloud method cannot be simply described as probabilistic method or fuzzy method. It is a very strict mathematical method to realize the conversion between qualitative concepts and quantitative data through cloud model, which makes the conversion between qualitative and quantitative become very clear, concrete and operable, and at the same time reflects the uncertainty of the conversion process.

2.2 Digital Characteristics of the Cloud

Cloud has three digital characteristics: The expected: Ex, The entropy: En and The super entropy: He [11].

1) Expected Ex:
   The expectation of cloud droplet spatial distribution of the theoretical domain is the central value of the concept in the theoretical domain, which is the most representative point of the qualitative concept, or the most typical sample of the quantization of the concept.

2) Entropy En:
   It is a measure of the uncertainty of qualitative concepts, which is determined by the randomness and fuzziness of qualitative concepts. It reflects the dispersion degree of the cloud droplet which represents the qualitative concept. At the same time, En reflects the margin of qualitative concepts as well as this and that, reflects the value range of clouding droplets acceptable to qualitative concepts in the field space, and is a measure of the fuzziness of qualitative concepts. The larger En is, the greater the range of clouding droplets accepted by the qualitative concept will be, and the vaguer the qualitative concept will be. Using the same number feature to reflect the randomness and fuzziness must also reflect the correlation between them. In other words, entropy reflects the uncertainty of qualitative concepts, which is manifested in three aspects. On the one hand, entropy reflects the size of the range of cloud droplet groups that can be accepted by linguistic values of the numerical domain space, namely, the degree of ambiguity, which is a measure of qualitative concepts as well as this and that. On the other hand, entropy also reflects the probability density that the cloud droplet group of the number domain space can represent the language value, and represents the randomness that the cloud droplet that represents the qualitative concept appears. In addition, entropy also reveals the correlation between fuzziness and randomness. Entropy can also be used to represent the granularity of a qualitative concept. Generally, the higher entropy is, the more macroscopic the concept is, the greater the fuzziness and randomness are, and the more difficult the deterministic quantization is.

3) Superentropy He:
   It is a measure of the uncertainty of entropy, and it is the entropy of entropy. It reflects the condensation of the uncertainty of all the points representing the value of the language in the theoretic space, and its size indirectly reflects the thickness of the cloud.

The following figure reflects the impact of the above three feature data on the cloud model (Figs. 1 and 2).

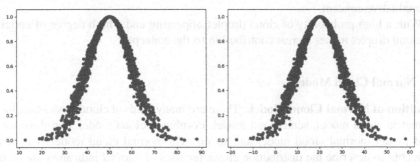

Fig. 1. Ex = 50, En = 10, He = 1, Ex = 20, En = 10, He = 1

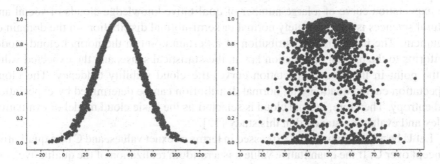

Fig. 2. Ex = 50, En = 20, He = 1, Ex = 50, En = 10, He = 10

According to the comparison of the above four figures, it can be seen that expected Ex determines the center position of the cloud map, entropy En determines the width of the cloud map, and superentropy He determines the thickness of the cloud map.

The unique feature of the numerical characteristics of cloud is that the entire cloud composed of thousands of clouding droplets can be delineated with only three numerical values, which fully integrates the fuzziness and randomness of the qualitatively expressed linguistic values. This method can greatly save storage resources and computing resources.

2.3 The Nature of Clouds

1) The field U can be one-dimensional or multidimensional.
2) The random implementation mentioned in the definition is the implementation in the sense of probability. The definiteness mentioned in the definition is the membership degree in the sense of fuzzy set and the distribution of the sense of probability. All of these reflect the relevance to fuzziness and randomness.
3) For any x ∈ U, the mapping from x to [0, 1] is a one-to-many transformation, and the certainty of x to C is a probability distribution rather than a fixed value.

4) Clouds are composed of clouding droplets, and there is no order for them. A cloud droplet is an one-time realization of qualitative concept in terms of quantity. The more cloud droplets there is, the more it can reflect the overall characteristics of this qualitative concept.

5) With a high probability of cloud droplet appearing and a high degree of certainty, cloud droplet makes a great contribution to the concept.

2.4   Normal Cloud Model

Definition of Normal Cloud Model. There are many kinds of cloud models, including symmetric cloud model, semi-cloud model, combined cloud model, two-dimensional cloud model, normal cloud model and so on. The normal cloud model is generally applicable to describe the distribution characteristics of various indicators and data in the field of natural science [12]. As a basic cloud model, normal cloud model is one of the powerful tools to represent language atoms. Normal distribution is universal, and the expectation curve of a large number of qualitative knowledge clouds of social and natural sciences is approximately normal or semi-normal distribution. In the domain of argument. The membership distribution of a certain point in the normal cloud model conforms to the normal distribution law in the statistical sense, and the expected value is the point in the cloud expectation curve, the cloud stability tendency. The cloud expectation curve equation with normal distribution can be determined by expectation and entropy. Therefore, normal cloud is selected as the basic cloud model of evaluation index and evaluation standard in this study [13].

Let U be a quantitative field expressed in terms of exact values, and C be a qualitative concept over U. If the quantitative value x is a random realization of the qualitative concept C, and if x satisfies x ~ N(Ex, En$'^2$), where En ~ N(En, He^2), and the determination of x to C satisfies the equation:

$$\mu = e^{-\frac{(x-Ex)^2}{2(En')^2}}$$

Then the distribution of x over the domain U is called a normal cloud.

Normal Cloud Models Algorithm. Forward cloud generator:

Given three digital characteristics of the cloud (Ex, En, He), a number of two-dimensional points that produce a normal cloud model – cloud droplet drop (x_i, μ_i) are called forward cloud generators. Input: digital eigenvalue (Ex, En, He), number of clouding droplets n. Output: N droplet and its determination degree. Diagram of forward normal cloud generator is shown in Fig. 3:

Fig. 3. Forward normal cloud generator

Reverse generator:

The reverse cloud generator is a transformation model to realize the transformation from quantitative values of qualitative concepts, which can transform a certain amount of accurate data onto qualitative concepts represented by digital features (Ex, En, He).Input: sample point xi, where I = 1, 2... n. Output: Numerical characteristics that reflect qualitative concepts (Ex, En, He).Schematic diagram of reverse cloud generator is shown in Fig. 4:

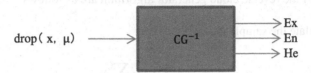

Fig. 4. Reverse cloud generator

3 Determination of Weights

Weight is a relative concept, is to a certain index. The weight of a certain index refers to its relative importance of the overall evaluation. There are many methods to determine the weight, the whole can be divided into two categories, namely subjective weighting method and objective weighting method. It includes expert consultation weighting method (Delphi method), factor analysis weighting method, information weighting method, independent weighting method, principal component analysis method, analytic hierarchy process (AHP method), optimal sequence diagram method, entropy weight method, standard deviation method and so on [14].

This study uses information weight method to determine the weight of each indicator. This method is based on the information contained in the index data to determine the weight of the index. The coefficient of variation method is adopted. The greater the coefficient of variation, the greater the weight will be. The weight calculation process of this method is as follows:

Suppose that a certain evaluation system has m indicators, assuming that the indicator Xi has N samples, and Xi is the mean value of the indicator Xi and Si is the standard deviation of Xi, then the coefficient of variation on the indicator is CV = Si/Xi. Taking CV as the weight score of each indicator, after normalization processing, the weight coefficient of information can be obtained.

4 Experiment and Result Analysis

4.1 Data Sources

The experimental data are from the grading papers issued on the spot after the training of new professional farmers, which cover the training population of a comprehensive way and are supervised by the staff, with high credibility, and are suitable for the evaluation of the training results.

4.2 Experimental Process

In this paper, the normal cloud model is used to analyze the training effect. The experimental process is as follows:

1) Based on the existing survey data, three characteristic data onto the normal cloud model for each evaluation factor are obtained by using the reverse cloud generator: expected Ex, entropy En, and super entropy He.

   The steps of the reverse cloud generator algorithm are as follows:

   I.   Calculate the sample mean of the data:

$$\overline{X} = \frac{1}{n} \sum_{i=1}^{n} x_i$$

   II. Calculate the absolute central moment of a first-order sample:

$$\overline{\beta} = \frac{1}{n} \sum_{i=1}^{n} |x_i - \overline{X}|$$

   III. Calculation of sample variance:

$$S^2 = \frac{1}{n-1} \sum_{i=1}^{n} (x_i - \overline{X})^2$$

   IV. Calculation of expectation Ex:

$$Ex = \overline{X}$$

   V.   Calculated entropy:

$$En = \sqrt{\frac{\pi}{2}} * \frac{1}{n} \sum_{i=1}^{n} |x_i - Ex|$$

   VI. Calculation of super entropy:

$$He = \sqrt{S^2 - E_n^2}$$

   The characteristic data of the ten evaluation factors obtained according to the above steps are shown in Table 1:

Table 1. Characteristic data of each evaluation factor

	manage age- ment	duration	cost	way	Content	Evaluation of teach- ers	Professional knowledge of teachers	Whether or not to under- stand	Teacher's attention to students	Whether the teacher answers the questions in time
Ex	3.443	3.255	3.417	3.634	3.619	3.721	3.762	3.691	3.453	3.600
$\bar{\beta}$	0.652	0.702	0.663	0.537	0.511	0.527	0.555	0.467	0.620	0.528
S^2	0.714	0.725	0.708	0.560	0.564	0.477	0.512	0.428	0.635	0.529
En	0.817	0.880	0.831	0.673	0.640	0.660	0.696	0.585	0.777	0.661
He	0.215	0.221	0.135	0.327	0.393	0.202	0.166	0.292	0.179	0.303

The feature data of Ex, En and He of ten evaluation factors were stored in a 10 * 3 two-dimensional matrix R, as shown below:

$$R = \begin{bmatrix} 3.443 & 0.817 & 0.215 \\ 3.255 & 0.880 & 0.221 \\ 3.417 & 0.831 & 0.135 \\ 3.634 & 0.673 & 0.327 \\ 3.619 & 0.640 & 0.393 \\ 3.721 & 0.660 & 0.202 \\ 3.762 & 0.696 & 0.166 \\ 3.691 & 0.585 & 0.292 \\ 3.453 & 0.777 & 0.179 \\ 3.600 & 0.661 & 0.303 \end{bmatrix}$$

2) The information weight method is used to determine the weight of each evaluation factor on the scoring data, and the calculation process is as follows:

I.   The expectation of calculating n score data for each evaluation factor:

$$\overline{X} = \frac{1}{n} \sum_{i=1}^{n} x_i$$

II. Calculate the standard deviation of n score data for each evaluation factor:

$$S = \sqrt{S^2}$$

III. Calculate the coefficient of variation of n score data for each evaluation factor:

$$CV = \frac{S}{\overline{X}}$$

IV. The coefficient of variation is taken as the weight score of each evaluation factor, and the weight coefficient of each factor is obtained through normalization:

$$a_i = CV_i \bigg/ \sum_{i=1}^{10} CV_i$$

The results are shown in Table 2:

Table 2. Weight coefficients of each factor

	Management	Duration	Cost	Way	Content	Evaluation of teachers	Professional knowledge of teachers	Whether or not to understand	Teacher's attention to students	Whether the teacher answers the questions in time
a_i	0.114	0.122	0.114	0.096	0.096	0.086	0.088	0.082	0.107	0.094

Store the above weight coefficients in a 1 * 10 matrix A, as shown below:

$$A = \left[\, 0.114\ 0.122\ 0.114\ 0.096\ 0.096\ 0.086\ 0.088\ 0.082\ 0.107\ 0.094 \,\right]$$

3) Multiply A matrix and R matrix to obtain the characteristic data of the comprehensive evaluation based on the normal cloud model determined according to the weight of each evaluation factor: [Ex, En, He] = [3.541, 0.733, 0.240].

Taking the above three characteristic data as parameters, the forward normal cloud generator is used to generate normal cloud map.

The algorithm steps of forward cloud generator are as follows:

I.   Generate a normal random number with En as expected value and He^2 as variance

$$Eni' = NORM\ (En,\ He^2);$$

II.   Generate a normal random number with Ex as expected value and $E_{ni}'^2$ as variance

$$x_i = NORM\ (Ex, E_{ni}'^2)$$

III.   According to the formula:

$$\mu = e^{-\frac{(x-Ex)^2}{2\left(E_n'\right)^2}}$$

Calculate the value of μ_i for each x_i in the normal graph.

IV.   Make (x_i, μ_i) as a cloud droplet in the number domain;

V.   Repeat the above steps until n desired cloud droplets are produced.

4.3 Result Analysis

The algorithm execution results are as follows:

Characteristic data of normal cloud map:

[Ex, En, He] = [3.540863982349558, 0.7331480509168373, 0.2397634024002 1485]

The generated normal cloud map is shown in Fig. 5:

In this training effect score, 0–1 points means very bad, 1–2 points means poor, 2–3 points means average, 3–4 points means good, 4–5 points means very good. According to the above results, the expected value Ex of the comprehensive evaluation is 3.541, the entropy is 0.733, and the super entropy is 0.240. The membership degree is the highest at the expected value Ex, that is, the score of 3.5 is the closest to the comprehensive evaluation made by the evaluator. The cloud chart of the comprehensive evaluation of this training is a normal cloud of an expectation of about 3.5, so the training effect is judged to be good. It can be found from the normal cloud chart that the fluctuation near the expected Ex is small and the membership degree is close to 1. The analysis result is highly reliable.

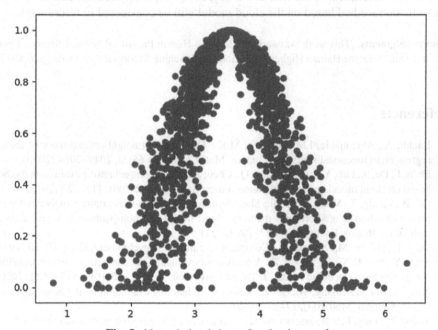

Fig. 5. Normal cloud chart of evaluation results

5 Conclusion

Cloud model overcomes the shortcoming of fuzzy mathematics that fuzzy concepts are strictly represented by precise and unique membership functions. Compared with fuzzy logic its advantages are the first of the cloud model to determine the precise value of degree is not a single, but a set of uniforms distributed random sample values, reflecting the distribution law of uncertainty reflects the fuzziness and randomness of relevance, and in the fuzzy set, membership degree to depict this essential sex, also often accurate determination of membership degree with subjective color; Secondly, the nature of the reasoning process using rules is the uncertainty reasoning process [15]. The cloud-based uncertainty reasoning and control rules is clear and intuitive, so there is no need for tedious reasoning calculation [16].

In the case of the same homologous data and grading standard division, the evaluation results obtained by using cloud model are consistent with those obtained by other evaluation methods such as AHP hierarchy analysis and BP neural network, which indicates that this method is feasible. In view of the ambiguity and uncertainty in the division of evaluation criteria, cloud model evaluation has better robustness than other evaluation methods. In addition, the cloud model evaluation method can present the scoring data in a more intuitive form and take into account a variety of evaluation factors. Therefore, it is of higher reference value to use the cloud model to evaluate various problems. The basic objective of this experiment has been completed. The weight determination method used in this experiment is the traditional objective weighting method, and the weight determination method based on the cloud model will be considered in future work.

Acknowledgments. This work was supported by the Hainan Provincial Natural Science Foundation (618ms025); the Hainan Higher Education and Teaching Reform Research (hnjg2020-12).

References

1. Bachir, A., Almanjahie, I.M., Attouch, M.K.: The k nearest neighbors estimator of the m-regression in functional statistics. Comput. Mater. Continua **65**(3), 2049–2064 (2020)
2. Shen, J., Du, S., Luo, Y., Luo, J., Yang, Q., Chen, Z.: Fuzzy comprehensive evaluation method based on cloud model and its application. Fuzzy Syst. Math. **26**(06), 115–123 (2012)
3. Gu, B., Zhang, T., Meng, H., et al.: Short-term forecasting and uncertainty analysis of wind power based on long short-term memory, cloud model and non-parametric kernel density estimation. Renew. Energy **164**, 687–708 (2021)
4. Deyi, L., Haijun, M., Xuemei, S.: Computer research and development **32**(6), 15–20 (1995)
5. Shao, Y., You, J., Xu, T., Zhong, Z.: A method for evaluating the competitiveness of securities companies based on cloud model. J. Tongji Univ. (Nat. Sci. Ed.) **48**(10), 1515–1522 (2020)
6. Jiang, J., Liang, J., Jiang, W., Gu, Z.: Research on learning evaluation model based on cloud theory. Comput. Mod. (03), 17–19 (2008)
7. Zhang, L., Yang, J.: State assessment of power transformers based on multidimensional normal cloud model. Electr. Meas. Instrum. **57**(04), 129–135 (2020)
8. Li, D., Meng, H., Shi, X.: Comput. Res. Dev. (06), 15–20 (1995)
9. Tang, X., Zheng, Q., Cheng, J., Sheng, V.S., Cao, R., et al.: A ddos attack situation assessment method via optimized cloud model based on influence function. Comput. Mater. Continua **60**(3), 1263–1281 (2019)
10. Wu, X., Du, X., Wu, Z., Wang, H.: Research on performance evaluation of rural drinking water safety engineering based on cloud model. Proj. Manag. Technol. **12**(06), 42–45 (2014)
11. Wang, G., Xu, C., Li, D.: Generic normal cloud mode. Inf. Sci. **280**(1), 1–15 (2014)
12. Liang, L., Xing, G., Wu, F.: Evaluation model and method based on cloud theory. J. Northeast. Univ. (Nat. Sci.) **40**(06), 881–885 (2019)
13. Kumar, C.R., Jayanthi, V.: A novel fuzzy rough sets theory based CF recommendation system. Comput. Syst. Sci. Eng. **34**(3), 123–129 (2019)

14. Zuo, J., Lu, Y., Gao, H., Cao, R., Guo, Z., et al.: Comprehensive information security evaluation model based on multi-level decomposition feedback for IoT. Comput. Mater. Continua **65**(1), 683–704 (2020)
15. Tang, J., Cao, K.: Map matching algorithm based on uncertainty reasoning of cloud model. Comput. Simul. (10), 220–224 (2007)
16. Zhu, H.: Research on maximum return evaluation of human resource allocation based on multi-objective optimization. Intell. Autom. Soft Comput. **26**(4), 741–748 (2020)

A Study on the Characteristics of College Students' Consumption Behavior Based on Clustering and Association Rules

Jie Wang[✉], XiWen Chen, KaiRui Cheng, YanLi Cao, and Bin Pan

Hunan University of Finance and Economics, Changsha 410205, China

Abstract. In 21st century, the development of information technology has led to an overall improvement in people's material level. Especially the big consumer group of college students. Campus information technology has now become a trend, which means that there is a large amount of consumer data accumulation. Behind the huge amount of behavioral data, there is potentially valuable information. By analyzing the data, we can understand the characteristics and needs of the consumption behavior of college students, so that we can better promote the process of campus informationization and help campus management.

Keywords: Clustering algorithm · Association rule algorithm · College students' consumption behavior

1 Introduction

The rapid development of computer technology, especially the rapid development and widespread application of database technology and computer network technology, the amount of data consumed by the campus has increased dramatically, accumulating a large amount of data, and is still showing an upward trend. The use of these data to mine valuable knowledge is of great significance to the promotion of campus information construction. Plus, in today's rapidly expanding consumption, campus consumption has become a major research focus. Analyze the consumption characteristics and consumption rules of college students, and reveal whether there is an intrinsic relationship with students' grades; as well as the research and application of algorithms for students' campus card flow consumption data, and thus mine valuable and effective information.

2 Related Works

College students' consumption behavior has now become a topic of great concern at home and abroad, college students are in a transitional period from natural persons to social persons, and it is representative to study their consumption behavior.

Clustering and association rules are more commonly used methods in mining data. They are widely used in finance, e-commerce, marketing, entertainment and so on. The

© Springer Nature Switzerland AG 2021
X. Sun et al. (Eds.): ICAIS 2021, CCIS 1423, pp. 370–380, 2021.
https://doi.org/10.1007/978-3-030-78618-2_30

current push messages and personalized recommendations in mobile apps are realized by these algorithms. Clustering analysis is mainly applied to find similar consumer groups, clustering and paving the way for later research. The main work of association rules is to find connections. Such as beer and diapers bundle sales, online personalized recommendations and so on.

3 Relevant Theories and Methods

3.1 Data Mining

Data mining is a hot topic of research and application in today's technology field. Various fields can be made smarter through data mining techniques. Data mining is also considered as a process of discovery of potential knowledge. Specifically, it refers to an important process of algorithmically searching for information hidden in massive amounts of data and discovering useful, understandable knowledge. 1 From a macro perspective, data mining can be seen as a hybrid of three types of people, namely computer scientists, software engineers, and statisticians. 2 It is an emerging academic field that spans multiple fields and is a key component of databases, machine learning and the intersection between the three components of statistics.

3.2 Cluster Analysis

Introduction to Cluster Analysis. Cluster analysis is a process of classifying a large amount of data. Therefore, data that is in the same group after classification will have many similarities, and there will be a great deal of variability between different groups. Cluster analysis extends this classification criterion even further. The principle of classification is to maximize the similarity within groups and maximize the differences between groups. 4 In short, data in the same group are maximally likely to be the same, and data in different groups are maximally likely to be different. Cluster analysis is fundamentally different from classification in that cluster analysis is exploratory and is unknown as to what is to be analyzed. In the process of classification, one does not need to develop a pre-defined classification criterion, it can start from the data itself, discover how to classify, and classify autonomously. The different methods used in the analysis often give very different results.

Classification of Clustering Algorithms. Currently, the widely used clustering algorithms that we apply to our research can be divided into the following six categories.

(1) K-means (K-means) clustering
    The K-means clustering algorithm must first select some classes and randomly initialize the centroids of each class. This requires a prediction of the number of classes, i.e. the number of centroids. This method is fast and easy to compute, but you have to anticipate the number of classes. The cluster analysis method is shown in the Fig. 1.

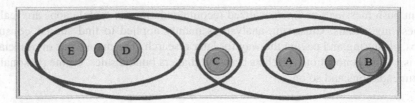

Fig. 1. K-means (K-means) clustering

(2) Mean Drift Clustering

Mean drift clustering is an algorithm based on mass centers and sliding windows in order to find the dense region where the data points are located. To locate the centroid of each class, this clustering method is implemented using the mean value of the points within the update window. The update is implemented using the candidate points of the centroids. Afterwards, the candidate windows are removed and the final set of centroids and their corresponding groupings are formed. The Mean Drift Clustering is shown in the Fig. 2.

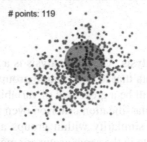

Fig. 2. Mean drift clustering

(3) Density-based clustering algorithm

Find any point in the database, and based on the number of points contained within the specified range found at that point, and assuming that the number of points calculated exceeds a predetermined limit, expand the range by that number.

Rationale for the Application of Cluster Analysis. Cluster analysis is based on the classification of different groups from the data characteristics found in the collected data. Specifically, it is to group the "same" college students into the same group and to classify the "different" college students into different groups, while maximizing the differences between the different groups of college consumers. 7 So using this principle, this paper groups consumers with similar characteristics into groups based on a comparison of attribute variables in the data, while maximizing the differences between the different groups.

3.3 Algorithm of Association Rules

Introduction to Association Rules. Association rules are an unsupervised machine learning method used for knowledge discovery. 8 It reveals interrelationships between data that are not directly represented in the data.

Correlation Rule Algorithm Classification

(1) Rule-based classification of variables
  For the class of variables dealt with in the rule, they can be divided into boolean logical and numeric types. Boolean logical variables are scattered fields that are easy to represent. For mining the association between such variables, they are generally used to discover common label attributes.
(2) Classification based on data abstraction levels in rules
  The different levels of data abstraction result in rules that can be classified into association at a single level and at multiple levels. There are high and low levels of data, i.e. qualitative data (e.g. gender) and quantitative data (e.g. height).
(3) Classification based on the number of dimensions in the rule

  According to the dimensionality, they can be classified as one-dimensional and multi-dimensional. One-dimensional association rules only need to consider the relationship of a single attribute in association mining, instead of having to deal with multiple attributes as in the case of multidimensional rules.

Rationale for the Application of Association Rules. An association rule is a potential interrelationship between two and more data objects. Discovering those strong rules from the database is the first task of identifying association rules, i.e., strong rules with both Confidence and Support greater than a given value. 10 The support of the association rule A -> B support = P(AB), which is the probability of both events occurring at the same time when probability is sought, and the confidence = P(B|A) = P(AB)/P(A), which is the probability that event B will also occur if event A occurs. Discovery rules are generally divided into two parts: generating frequent item sets and generating rules that satisfy the minimum confidence level on the basis of extrapolating the set of all items whose support satisfies the minimum support level, which produces rules that are strong 11.

Improvement of the A-Priori Algorithm. The A-priori algorithm is an association rule algorithm widely used to reduce the time to generate the set of frequent items. 12 In it, the A-priori algorithm has the property that all non-empty subsets of any frequent item set must also be frequent. 13 The A-priori algorithm is used to reduce the time to generate the set of frequent items by using both a join step and a pruning step. The core algorithm generates the current set of frequent items by preceding the current frequent items found. The A-priori algorithm generates candidate item sets based on connections and pruning, which reduces the size of the frequent item set and increases the speed of generating frequent item sets to some extent, but the frequent I/O accesses of the algorithm will reduce the performance 15. Therefore, the A-priori algorithm is improved in order to reduce the number of database accesses and thus reduce the I/O accesses. The central idea of this improved algorithm is to convert the data into a Boolean matrix when the database is accessed for the first time and to generate a final frequent item set based on the largest frequent item set.

The database shown, with Min support of 3, is shown in Table 1.

Table 1. Example database

TID	Project portfolio
T1	A, B, D, E, F, H
T2	B, C, F
T3	A, B, C, D, E
T4	C, D, H
T5	A, B, D, E, F

The data in the sample database is represented by a Boolean matrix, with the set of items in the vertical row and the instances in the horizontal row, and if the items appear in the instances, they are represented by the Arabic numeral 1 and vice versa. The following table can be obtained.

Table 2. Example database for Boolean matrix representation

	T1	T2	T3	T4	T5
A	1	0	1	0	1
B	1	1	1	0	1
C	0	1	1	1	0
D	1	0	1	1	1
E	1	0	1	0	1
F	1	1	0	0	1
H	1	0	0	1	0

As can be seen from Table 2, item A appears in T1, T3, and T5, the number of 1's represents the degree of support, and exactly satisfies the minimum support, so it can be left, and the item H that does not satisfy the minimum support is discarded by filling in the flag bit with 1 (1 is the initial value of the flag bit, 0 means it is the largest set of frequent items).

4 Clustering and Association Rules in the Consumer Behavior of College Students

It is important to grasp the content and characteristics of the consumption behavior of college students to help them establish a rational consumption concept. The study of college students' consumption behavior can be carried out from the characteristics of its consumption content and consumption mode. Currently, the most efficient way to do this is through data mining techniques. Data mining techniques can identify different groups of college students based on the characteristics of the data, which enables the analysis of the data and the study of the consumer behavior of college students. It is possible to find out whether the consumption behavior of college students is related to specific aspects such as the merit of grades, to discover the relevance of studying this topic.

4.1 Data Pre-processing

Nowadays, all universities have opened campus card service, students can use the campus card to make purchases on campus. By fully mining the data, the public can have a better understanding of the economic activities of the campus and the students' consumption behavior. However, large amounts of data must be preemptively weeded out of some discrete data in order to be mined more efficiently.

4.2 Case Studies of Cluster Analysis

In this paper, we will analyze the massive consumption data stored in the campus card in order to understand the consumption behavior characteristics of college students. In order to find a more concentrated and representative data, this study decided to use the data of students' dining in canteens as the data sample, which is more general. It can also be more comprehensive and accurate to measure the consumption behavior and habits of college students at school. In this paper, we analyze part of the dining patterns of college students through their breakfast consumption. We can do the following analysis.

Students who eat breakfast before class time are regular and have good consumption habits;

When there are fewer than 15 days in a month where breakfast is eaten before 7:50 a.m. (perhaps one or two days a week with one or two no classes), the student's consumption habits can be considered irregular (Table 3).

Table 3. Number of breakfasts eaten by some students in a single month

ID	AMOUNT
10570210707	24
10570210709	12
10570210708	15
10570210703	18
10570210704	22

Based on the patterns mentioned in the above-mentioned text, classes are divided according to the number of times students eat breakfast in a single month, and the consumption habits of students are summarized through two categories, regular and irregular, as shown in Table 4.

Table 4. Patterns of consumption habits of selected students

ID	ISNATURE
10572105074	Irregular
10572105075	Irregular
10572105076	Regular
10572105077	Regular
10572105078	Irregular
10572105079	Regular

In general, students' consumption levels are divided into three categories: high, medium, and low. In this paper, the k-means algorithm is used to process the consumption data and to understand the consumption level of current university students. In order to avoid the random selection of the initial central values of the three clusters, the following method is used: the initial value of the largest consumption group is the largest consumption value, the initial value of the medium consumption group is the average value, and the initial value of the low consumption group is the smallest consumption value. After the above treatment, the cluster analysis is performed using this algorithm.

The data sample shows that the results can be divided into three levels: high, medium and low. The levels of consumption are classified according to the criteria shown in Table 5 below.

Table 5. Criteria for classification of consumption levels

Consumption level	Clustering center
High	400
Medium	300
Lower	200

A clustering of students' monthly meal consumption reveals that the majority of students are in the mid to high range of consumption, with only a very small percentage of students in the low range.

4.3 Rules for Correlating College Students' Consumption Behavior and Grades

Data Processing of Achievements. The student performance data in this paper comes from sophomore students at a college with 200 males and 200 females. The scores of students at this stage are comparable and at the same time representative. In this paper, the method of calculating the scholarship scores is used to classify the achievement levels, and finally the proposed method is based on the data pre-processing process: x > 90 excellent, 90 < x < 80 good, 80 < x < 70 moderate, 70 < x < 60 pass, 60 > x fail. Finally, student performance was classified into five categories, as shown in Table 6.

Table 6. Student learning achievement grades

ID	GRADE
10571105097	Favorable
10571105098	Moderate
10571105099	Pass
10571105100	Moderate
10571105101	Moderate
10571105102	Pass

Analysis of consumption habits in relation to performance. In this paper, some of the results are as follows, based on the data collected on students' breakfast consumption and thus whether the consumption habits of students are regular or not, and correlated with their performance (Table 7).

Table 7. Data table linking consumption habits and student performance

ISNATURE	GRADE
Regular	Excellence
Irregular	Pass
Irregular	Favorable
Irregular	Moderate

With the data, the resulting Boolean matrix plots were further correlated and the following rule was found (set at 70% confidence level).

ISNATURE = Irregular -> GRADE = Pass conf (75%)

In this paper, the students with irregular consumption habits may stay up late at night, sleep lazily in the morning or even skip classes, which is not good for the long-term development of the students, so the relevant school departments should make corresponding measures to promote the formation of good habits to help students to really live up to the four years of university time.

Analysis of consumption levels in relation to achievements. The purpose of this paper is to explore the correlation between consumption levels and performance. Specific partial data tables are shown below (Table 8).

Table 8. Selected consumption levels and student performance tables

LEVEL	GRADE
Medium	Pass
Medium	Excellence
Lower	Fail
Lower	Favorable
High	Moderate

The following patterns can be derived from the correlation analysis.

Students with low consumption levels, i.e., those who spend around $300 per month on meals, generally have upper-middle grades. These students are highly motivated to learn and are more capable of suffering. Schools should give more attention and encouragement to these students so that they can improve their quality of life and thus enable them to learn better.

Analysis of consumption habits, levels of consumption and performance correlations. The three attribute fields are analyzed together in this paper with respect to the amount of money spent and the consumption habits developed that are affected by student consumption behavior, respectively, which are associated with achievement. The following figure presents some of the data tables for spending habits, spending levels, and student achievement, as shown in Table 9.

Table 9. Table of selected student achievements, consumption habits, consumption levels

ISNATURE	LEVEL	GRADE
Irregular	Medium	Favorable
Irregular	High	Moderate
Regular	Lower	Pass
Regular	Medium	Moderate
Irregular	Lower	Moderate

The modified A-priori algorithm is used to discover the association rules, and the data in the above figure is transformed into a Boolean matrix, as in Table 10.

Table 10.

	T1	T2	T3	T4	T5
Regular	1	0	1	1	0
Irregular	0	1	0	0	1
High	0	1	0	0	0
Medium	1	0	0	1	1
Lower	0	0	1	0	0
Excellence	1	0	0	0	0
Favorable	0	1	1	0	0
Moderate	0	0	0	1	0
Pass	0	0	0	0	1
Fail	0	0	0	0	1

A minimum support level of 10% and a confidence level of 70%, resulting in two rules as follows.

(1) LEVEL = Medium, GRADE = Pass → ISNATURE = Regulation conf: (0.8)

(2) GRADE = Failing → ISNATURE = Irregularity
   conf: (0.85)

(3) LEVEL = low → GRADE = medium.
   conf: (0.75)

From the rules derived, it is clear that student performance is inextricably linked to student spending habits, so effectively guiding students' spending habits and behaviors, such as requiring students to leave their dorm rooms before 8:00 a.m. and developing the spending habit of eating breakfast, etc., will affect students' long-term development.

5 Conclusion and Outlook

In this paper, a study on the consumption behavior of current college students based on clustering and association rules is conducted. The detailed work is summarized as follows: (1) collection and pre-processing of data from campus cards; (2) clustering of pre-processed consumption data to analyze the consumption levels and habits of college students; and (3) correlating students' grades with the consumption factors influenced by their consumption behavior, resulting in recommendations that are informative for school management. This study has helped me to gain a better understanding of data mining techniques. The unfortunate aspect of this study is that this paper does not go far enough in analyzing students' consumption behavior, and I had hoped that this study would provide some insight into the identification of poor students in schools, but this did not happen due to lack of capacity.

Acknowledgement. This work was supported in part by the National Natural Science Foundation of China, grant number 72073041. Open Foundation for the University Innovation Platform in the Hunan Province, grant number 18K103.2011 Collaborative Innovation Center for Development and Utilization of Finance and Economics Big Data Property.

Hunan Provincial Key Laboratory of Finance & Economics Big Data Science and Technology. 2020 Hunan Provincial Higher Education Teaching Reform Research Project under Grant HNJG-2020-1130, HNJG-2020-1124. 2020 General Project of Hunan Social Science Fund under Grant 20B16.

Scientific Research Project of Education Department of Hunan Province (Grand No. 20K021), Social Science Foundation of Hunan Province (Grant No. 17YBA049).

References

1. Wang, P.: Research on Consumer Behavior based on Data Mining Techniques. Jilin University, Jilin (2004)
2. Fayyad, U., Piatetsky Shapiro, G., Smyth, P.: From data mining to knowledge discovery in databases. AI Mag. **17**(3), 37 (1996)
3. Xu, J.: An Analysis of the Correlation Between Consumption Behavior and Performance based on Card Data. Nanchang University, Nanchang (2010)
4. Sheng, O.: Application of Data Mining in Consumer Behavior Analysis. Hunan University, Hunan (2011)
5. Zhang, C.: Research on Energy Saving of Campus Air Conditioning based on A-Priori Algorithm. Hangzhou University of Electronic Science and Technology, Hangzhou (2014)
6. Hua, X.: Design and Implementation of a Student Achievement Analysis-Oriented Data Mining System. Soochow University, Suzhou (2016)
7. Han, J., Kamber, M.: Data Mining Concept and Techniques. Machinery Industry Press, Beijing (2001)
8. Srikant, R., Agrawal, R.: Mining quantitative association rules in large relational tables. In: Proceedings of the 1995 Very Large Database Conference (1996)
9. Agrawal, R., Srikant, R.: Fast algorithms for mining association rules. In: Proceedings of 1994 International Conference on Very Large Data Bases (VLDB 94), Santiago, Chile (1994)
10. Wang, D.C.: Research and Application of Data Mining in Campus Card Consumption Behavior Analysis. Harbin Engineering University, Harbin (2010)
11. Zhang, H.: Research and Application of Data Mining in Campus Card Spending. Lanzhou Jiaotong University, Lanzhou (2016)
12. Zhou, W.: Study of Customer Group Consumption Behavior Based on Clustering and Association Rules. Chengdu University of Technology, Chengdu (2015)
13. Huang, J.: Research on the characteristics of college students' consumption behavior based on the big data environment. Fujian Comput. **33**(04), 75–76+94 (2017)
14. Wu, S., Yu, X., Ni, Y., et al.: The application of clustering technology in data mining for student achievement analysis. China Manag. Informatiz. (15) (2009)
15. Wu, L., Meng, Q.: Research and implementation of student achievement data mining. China Manag. Informatiz. (01) (2011)
16. Xiang, L., Yang, S., Liu, Y., Li, Q., Zhu, C.: Novel linguistic steganography based on character-level text generation. Mathematics **8**, 1558 (2020)
17. Xiang, L., Guo, G., Li, Q., Zhu, C., Chen, J., et al.: Spam detection in reviews using LSTM based multi entity temporal features. Intell. Autom. Soft Comput. **26**(6), 1375–1390 (2020)
18. Yang, Z., Zhang, S., Hu, Y., Hu, Z., Huang, Y.: VAE stega: linguistic steganography based on variational auto encoder. IEEE Trans. Inf. Forensics Secur. **16**, 880–895 (2021)

Research and Application of Nuclear Reactor Computational Data Framework Based on HDF5

Wei Lu[1], Jintao Feng[1], Hao Yang[2,3]([✉]), Hui Zeng[1], and Junjie Pan[1]

[1] Science and Technology on Reactor System Design Technology Laboratory,
Nuclear Power Institute of China, Chengdu 610213, China
[2] School of Computer Science, Chengdu University of Information Technology,
Chengdu 610225, China
haoyang@cuit.edu.cn
[3] School of Information and Software Engineering, University of Electronic
Science and Technology of China, Chengdu 610054, China

Abstract. Nuclear reactor computing software need to process and maintain complex and massive data sets. In order to meet the requirement of mass data storage and processing in software, the data storage model and I/O method and programming interface of HDF5 (Hierarchical Data Format v5) are deeply studied. According to the data storage and processing requirement of typical nuclear reactor computing data such as assembly or core neutronics computing data and core thermal-hydraulic computing data, RCDF-H5 (Reactor Compute Data Framework based on HDF5) is proposed. KYMRES (KYlin-2 Main RESults databank) and COMRES (COre Main RESults databank) are designed and implemented based on RCDF-H5. The performance tests show that RCDF-H5 has a higher I/O efficiency than conventional storage solutions. A new data storage and management solution for nuclear reactor computing software is provided.

Keywords: Data technology · HDF5 · Reactor compute data framework

1 Introduction

High-quality design tools is a prerequisite for conducting scientific research and engineering design tasks. The special scientific research and design calculation software for nuclear reactors brings together people's theoretical methods, design, construction and operation experience of nuclear reactors. It is an essential tool for nuclear reactor research and design. With the development and improvement of computer technology and performance, the application of various high-performance computing servers, the computing scale of nuclear reactor computing software continues to increase, the number and fineness of grids continue to increase, and the computing data becomes larger and larger. The demand for massive data storage management and input/output (I/O) capabilities has increased dramatically. Therefore, new requirements have been put forward for input/output technology and data storage management technology.

© Springer Nature Switzerland AG 2021
X. Sun et al. (Eds.): ICAIS 2021, CCIS 1423, pp. 381–394, 2021.
https://doi.org/10.1007/978-3-030-78618-2_31

With the advancement and development of data technology, various advanced data storage forms and standard formats continue to appear [1–3]. Among them, HDF is a self-descriptive, multi-object file format used to store and distribute scientific data. It was created by NCSA (National Center for Supercomputing Applications) to meet the needs of different groups of scientists in different engineering projects [4]. The latest version HDF5 has been deeply applied in meteorology, remote sensing and other fields. This article is aimed at the requirements of reactor core data management and storage, including various neutronics parameters of the assembly, various neutronics parameters of the core, and various thermal and hydraulic parameters of the core. Through research of the HDF5 data format and its programming technology, the Reactor Compute Data Framework based on HDF5 (RCDF-H5) is proposed, and successfully applied it to the advanced neutronics grid calculation software KYLIN-2, and advanced nodal method core three-dimensional small group neutronics calculation software CORCA-3D, and core thermal hydraulic sub-channel analysis software CORTH independently developed by Nuclear Power Institute of China, solutions for data storage management and efficient I/O problems in the field of reactor core numerical calculation are provided.

2   Characteristics of HDF5 Data Format

2.1   HDF5 File Organization

The HDF5 file is a container for storing various data by two basic data objects (HDF5 group and HDF5 dataset). The HDF5 group contains 0 or more HDF5 objects and supporting metadata. The HDF5 dataset is a multi-dimensional array of data elements and supporting metadata [5].

The use of groups and datasets is similar in many ways to using Linux directories and files. Objects in HDF5 files are often referenced by their absolute path. Through groups and datasets, arbitrarily complex data can be stored. In a hierarchical manner, the HDF5 file effectively establishes the organization and logical inclusion relationship between the various objects in the file, as shown in Fig. 1 [6].

When creating an HDF5 file, you need to create a "group + dataset". When creating a group, you need to specify the location and name of the group in the application. When creating a dataset, you need to specify the location, name, and Information such as data type, dataspace, and creation property lists.

(1) Data type: HDF5 dataset contains two data types: atomic data types and composite data types. Atomic data types cannot be decomposed into smaller data type units at the API level. They include integer, floating, date and time, string, and bitfield, opaque and other data types. Composite data type is a collection of one or more atomic data types (and/or arrays of these data types) [7]. As shown in Fig. 2.

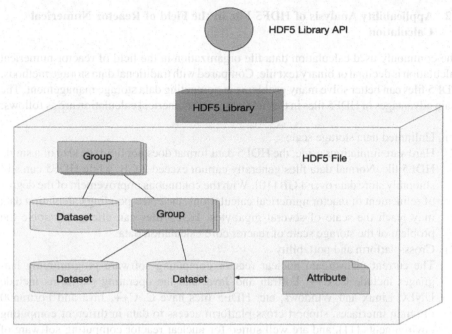

Fig. 1. File hierarchy of HDF5

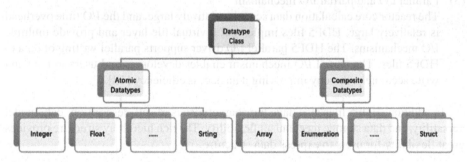

Fig. 2. Data type class of HDF5 dataset

(2) Dataspace: HDF5 dataspace describes the dimension of the data array. The dataspace is either a regular N-dimensional array of data points (called a simple dataspace), or a more general data collection composed of other methods (called a complex dataspace) [8]. The dimension of the dataset can be fixed or expandable. The dataspace can also describe a part of a dataset, which makes it possible to perform partial I/O operations on the selected dataset.

(3) Creation property lists: When creating a dataset, HDF5 allows users to specify how the original data is organized and compressed on disk [9]. This information is stored in the dataset creation property list and passed to the dataset interface. The original dataset on the disk can be stored continuously (the same as the linear method in memory management), divided into chunks, stored externally, etc.

2.2 Applicability Analysis of HDF5 File in the Field of Reactor Numerical Calculation

The commonly used calculation data file organization in the field of reactor numerical calculation is decimal or binary text file. Compared with traditional data storage methods, HDF5 files can better solve many problems in computing data storage management. The main advantages of HDF5 files in the field of reactor numerical calculation are as follows:

(1) Unlimited data storage scale
    Hardware limitations aside, the HDF5 data format does not limit the size of a single HDF5 file. Normal data files generally cannot exceed 2 GB, while HDF5 can still smoothly store data over 4 GB [10]. With the continuous improvement of the degree of refinement of reactor numerical calculations, the corresponding calculation data may reach the scale of several gigabytes. HDF5 files can effectively solve the problem of the storage scale of reactor core calculation data.
(2) Cross-platform and portability
    The current mainstream nuclear reactor computing software programming languages include C, C++, Fortran and Java, and the operating platforms include UNIX, Linux and Windows, etc. HDF5 files have C, C++, Java and Fortran90 program interfaces, support cross-platform access to data in different computing environments [11], and are well suited for nuclear reactor computing software of different programming languages and different operating platforms.
(3) Parallel I/O and partial I/O mechanism
    The reactor core calculation data scale is relatively large, and the I/O time overhead is relatively large. HDF5 files implement a virtual file layer and provide multiple I/O mechanisms. The HDF5 parallel I/O driver supports parallel writing of data to HDF5 files. The partial I/O mechanism enables developers and users to read and write accurately, thereby improving data access efficiency [12].

In addition, HDF5 files also have the characteristics of self-description, data model versatility, and data storage mechanism flexibility. The rich hierarchy structure provides great flexibility for users to express data structure.

2.3 HDF5 File Programming Realization

HDF5 Library provides a series of application program interfaces (API) [13]. These APIs provide routines for creating, accessing, and processing HDF5 files and objects. The HDF5 function library is implemented in C language, including shell functions written in Fortran90 and Java. The HDF5 files can be read and written in the reactor numerical calculation software through the above three programming languages [14].

The process of data writing using HDF5 library is shown in Fig. 3.

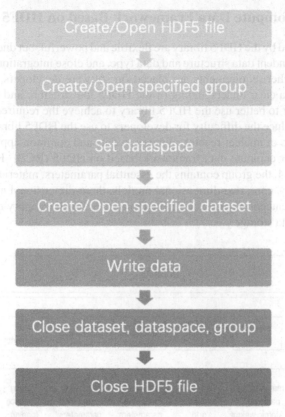

Fig. 3. The process of data writing using HDF5 library

The structures used to store data and positioning data in HDF5 are Dataset and hyperslab, and they are used as follows:

(1) Before defining dataset, the default value of data type, dataspace, storage layout, uninitialized data need to be specified. The dataset is scalable, and the size of the dataspace can be expanded in real time as needed, thereby changing the capacity of the dataset.

(2) Read or write data needs to locate in the dataspace to be read or written firstly, and then call the write or read function for access.

In the hierarchical data structure, accessing the content of HDF5 files is similar to accessing Windows folders: first specify the file name, and then use "/" to indicate the level. For example, "/Data/FEMData" represents a group or data set named FEMData under the group named Data in a file. HDF5 supports partial I/O, and can selectively read and write part of the data in the dataset [15]. This mechanism is implemented by Hyperslab. Partial I/O avoids redundant memory data copying and ensures data storage efficiency.

3 Reactor Compute Data Framework Based on HDF5 (RCDF-H5)

The APIs provided by the HDF5 library are flexible and powerful, but due to its numerous functions, independent data structure and data type, and close integration with the HDF5 file structure, higher requirements are placed on software developers. Developers are required to have a clear understanding of the HDF5 file structure and the functions of each API in order to better use the HDF5 library to achieve the required features.

In order to reduce the difficulty for developers to use the HDF5 library, according to the characteristics of nuclear reactor calculation data and common application requirements, the reactor compute data framework based on HDF5 (RCDF-H5) is proposed. As shown in Fig. 4, the group contains the essential parameters, material libraries, components, assembly, core, two-dimensional models, three-dimensional models and other commonly used categories of reactor calculation data. Each category contains a series of datasets for data storage.

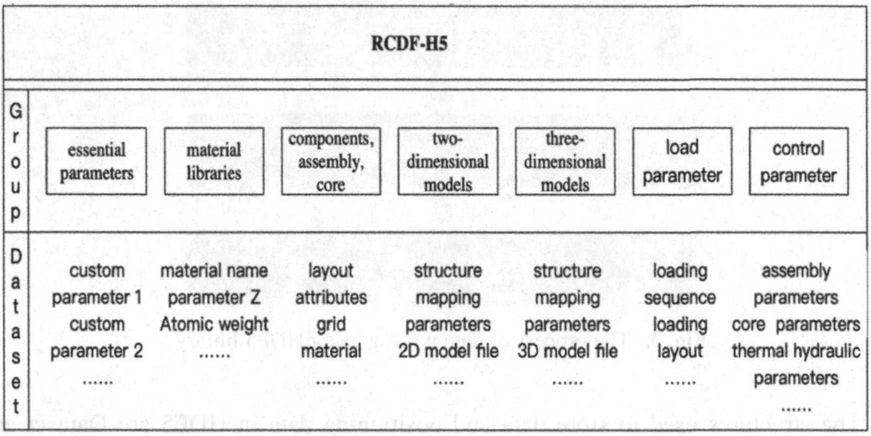

Fig. 4. Reactor compute data framework based on HDF5

The APIs of the HDF5 function library are recombined and encapsulated to form a set of programming interfaces for RCDF-H5. The main classes and functions are shown in Table 1, including the commonly used read and write operations for reactor calculation data.

Table 1. The main classes and functions of programming interfaces of RCDF-H5

Class	Function	Description
H5Out	CreatH5File	Create HDF5 file
	OpenH5File	Open HDF5 file
	CreatH5Group	Create group
	CreatH51DDataset	Create a one-dimensional dataset and write data

(*continued*)

Table 1. (*continued*)

Class	Function	Description
	CreatH52DDataset	Create a two-dimensional dataset and write data
	CreatH53DDataset	Create a three-dimensional dataset and write data
	CreatH54DDataset	Create a four-dimensional dataset and write data
	CreatH55DDataset	Create a five-dimensional dataset and write data
	CreatH5VLen2DDataset	Create an irregular two-dimensional dataset and write data
	CreatH5VLen3DDataset	Create an irregular three-dimensional dataset and write data
	CreatH5String1DDataset	Create a one-dimensional string dataset and write data
	CreatH5String2DDataset	Create a two-dimensional string dataset and write data
	CreatH5String3DDataset	Create a three-dimensional string dataset and write data
	CreatH5ExtendDataset	Create a scalable dataset and write data
	OpenH5ExtendDataset	Open a scalable dataset and write data
	CloseH5File	Close HDF5 file
H5In	OpenH5File	Open HDF5 file
	ReadH5Dataset	Read a dataset
	ReadH5StringDataset	Read a string dataset
	GetDatasetDims	Get the size of each dimension of the dataset
	CloseH5File	Close HDF5 file

RCDF-H5 uses the data types of the C++ language itself. The data types and structures defined by the HDF5 library are encapsulated in the framework. Developers can easily use RCDF-H5 to complete the design, management and I/O operation of the software data structure.

4   Application of RCDF-H5

Aiming at the two-dimensional grid data and three-dimensional grid data that are most commonly used in the reactor calculation process, the two-dimensional assembly neutronics data and the three-dimensional core neutronics and thermal-hydraulic data are taken as examples, the two-dimensional assembly parameter library KYMRES (KYlin-2 Main RESults databank) and the three-dimensional core parameter library COMRES (COre Main RESults databank) are designed and implemented based on RCDF-H5.

One of the advantages of RCDF-H5 is that it can manage the data in layers and groups. The design of the above parameter library is based on this idea.

4.1   Two-Dimensional Assembly Parameter Library

The two-dimensional assembly parameter library KYMRES contains essential data and state point data. The essential data can be divided into geometric data, option data, etc., and the state point data includes two-dimensional distribution fields: neutron flux, power, cross section, nuclear density, etc. [16, 17].

In order to enhance the usability and retrieval efficiency of KYMRES, the software data structure is directly mapped to the structure of KYMRES during design. The data of the same software module is designed as a group, and the subgroups are designed in units of the struct. The variables in the struct are designed as datasets in subgroups. The advantage of this design is that data can be exchanged between the software data structure and KYMRES very conveniently and efficiently.

The structure of KYMRES is shown in Fig. 5. Taking geometric data as an example, the geometric data is divided into groups such as boundary conditions according to its corresponding struct, and each group forms a dataset according to the member variables of each struct.

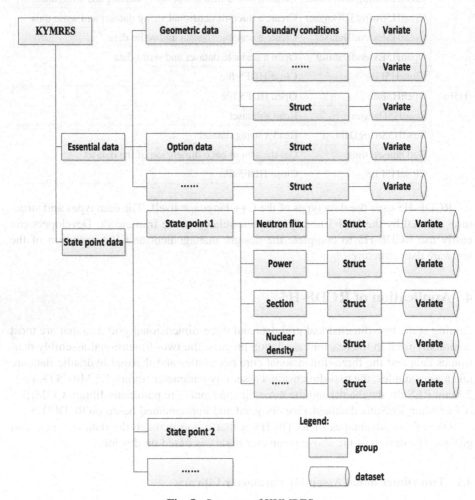

Fig. 5. Structure of KYMRES

KYMRES has been successfully applied to the advanced neutronics grid (assembly) calculation software KYLIN-2, which can be used for the software's own restart calculation and downstream core calculation [18–20].

4.2 Three-Dimensional Core Parameter Library

The three-dimensional core parameter library COMRES contains three-dimensional neutronics data and three-dimensional thermal-hydraulic data. Neutronics includes essential data and burnup step data. The essential data refers to the core geometric model and assembly information that do not change with burnup or core state. The burnup step data includes various parameters that change with the burnup or core state, such as three-dimensional distribution fields of neutron flux, power, cross section, nuclear density and other parameters [21, 22]. Thermal-hydraulic data is used to store various thermal-hydraulic parameters of the reactor core. The data is stored in the order of time step, sub-channel number, and axial section number. The stored data mainly includes fluid characteristic, core thermal hydraulic parameters, constitutive relationship parameters DNBR, etc. [23, 24]. The structure of COMRES is shown in Fig. 6.

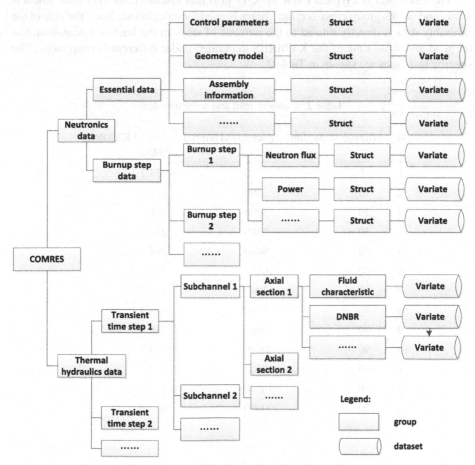

Fig. 6. Structure of COMRES

COMRES is a core three-dimensional neutronics parameter and thermal-hydraulic parameter library with complete information, which is provided for subsequent calculations of the core, such as first cycle loading calculation, refueling cycle loading calculation, core burnup calculation, core temperature field and flow field calculation, etc.

COMRES has been successfully applied to the advanced nodal method core three-dimensional small group neutronics calculation software CORCA-3D, the core thermal hydraulic sub-channel analysis software CORTH and other software.

5   Performance Test of RCDF-H5

Use the fstream class, a typical text file access method provided by the C++ language standard library, and the KYMRES based on RCDF-H5 to perform a comparison test of read and write performance. The test hardware is a Windows PC, the CPU is an Intel Core i5-2300 2.80 GHz quad-core processor, the memory capacity is 3 GB, and the operating system is Windows XP SP3 32-bit.

The test object is a typical PWR 17×17 grid fuel assembly, the fuel enrichment is 1.8%, and the 45-group cross-section library is used for calculation. Since the size of the assembly data is directly related to the number of steps in the burnup calculation, test the read and write time of the KYMRES generated under different burnup steps. The specific test cases are shown in Table 2.

Table 2. Cases of read and write time test

No.	Burnup steps num	Burnup (MWd/tU)	Size of KYMRES (MB)
1	0	0	73.2
2	10	500	131.1
3	20	3000	188.9
4	30	5500	246.8
5	40	8000	304.7
6	50	10500	362.6
7	60	13000	420.5
8	70	15500	478.4
9	80	18000	536.3
10	90	30000	594.2
11	100	50000	652.1
12	110	70000	709.9
13	120	90000	767.9

The time of reading data includes the time of file opening, reading, and closing, and the time of writing data includes the time of opening, writing, and closing. The test results are shown in Table 3, Table 4, Fig. 7, and Fig. 8.

Table 3. Results of write time comparison

Burnup steps num	Write time (s)		Writing efficiency improvement (%)
	RCDF-H5	C++ fstream	
0	2.743	11.97	436
10	5.091	21.925	431
20	7.541	32.001	424
30	9.193	42.099	458
40	12.068	52.155	432
50	13.759	61.779	449
60	16.139	71.932	446
70	17.104	82.024	480
80	18.595	91.962	495
90	22.656	101.857	450
100	24.515	111.783	456
110	26.642	122.072	458
120	28.288	132.053	467

Table 4. Results of read time comparison

Burnup steps num	Read time (s)		Reading efficiency improvement (%)
	RCDF-H5	C++ fstream	
0	0.642	1.509	235
10	2.026	4.700	232
20	3.446	7.960	231
30	4.941	11.661	236
40	6.257	14.954	239
50	7.66	18.078	236
60	9.023	20.933	231
70	10.494	25.081	239
80	11.884	28.522	240
90	13.388	30.792	230
100	14.618	34.352	235
110	16.145	37.618	233
120	17.541	41.572	237

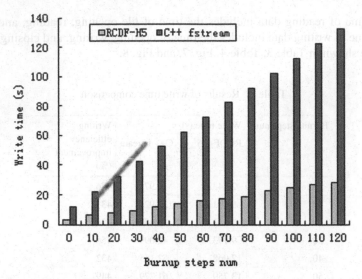

Fig. 7. Results of write time comparison

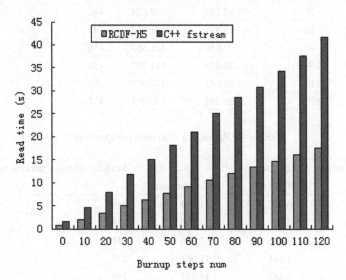

Fig. 8. Results of read time comparison

The test results show that KYMRES based on RCDF-H5 has high performance in reading and writing. Compared with C++ fstream, its writing efficiency is improved by nearly 5 times, and the reading efficiency is improved by more than 2.3 times. After parallel I/O, its read and write efficiency will be further improved. In actual engineering calculations, the reactor calculation data will reach as many as 10GB. Using RCDF-H5 can effectively solve the bottleneck problem of nuclear reactor calculation software data reading and writing.

6 Conclusion

In response to the requirements of nuclear reactor computing software for data storage and processing, the reactor computing data framework based on HDF5 (RCDF-H5) was proposed. Based on RCDF-H5, the two-dimensional assembly parameter library KYMRES and the three-dimensional core parameter library COMRES were designed and implemented.

KYMRES and COMRES manage and store data in hierarchical groups. The designated groups or datasets can be easily accessed without reading the library as a whole. Memory overhead is saved and multiple groups or datasets can be accessed at the same time. The support for partial I/O and parallel I/O has greatly improved the I/O efficiency. Reading and writing tests on KYMRES under different burnup steps show that the RCDF-H5 has high I/O performance, and the requirements of data storage management and efficient I/O of the reactor core numerical calculation software are meted.

Acknowledgements. This work was sponsored by the Sichuan Science and Technology Program (2020YFS0355 and 2020YFG0479).

References

1. Liu, Y.B., Wang, F., Ji, K.F., et al.: Research on metadata storage and querying of FITS file based on NoSQL. J. Comput. Appl. **32**(02), 461–465 (2015)
2. Liu, J., Huang, X.Y., Zhou, H.G., et al.: Unified coding for domestic new weather radar data based on NetCDF. Meteorol. Sci. Technol. **44**(02), 171–176 (2016)
3. Wang, S.J., Cui, P., Zheng, X.D., et al.: Representing atmospheric motion vectors of meteorological satellites in BUFR. Meteorol. Sci. Technol. **39**(03), 339–343 (2011)
4. HDF5 User's Guide Release 1.10.0 [EB/OL], Hierarchical Data Fomlat (HDF) Group. https://support.hdfgroup.org/HDF5/doc/UG/HDF5_Users_Guide.pdf. Accessed Mar 2016
5. HDF5 Reference Manual Release 1.8.8 [EB/OL], Hierarchical Data Fomlat (HDF) Group. https://support.hdfgroup.org/HDF5/doc/PSandPDF/HDF5_RefManual.PDF. Accessed Nov 2011
6. Mu, J., Soumagne, J., Byna, S., Koziol, Q., Tang, H., Warren, R.: Interfacing HDF5 with a scalable object-centric storage system on hierarchical storage. Concurr. Comput.: Pract. Exp. **32**(20), e5715 (2020)
7. Krijnen, T., Beetz, J.: An efficient binary storage format for IFC building models using HDF5 hierarchical data format. Autom. Constr. **113**, 103134 (2020)
8. Cabeleira, M., Ercole, A., Smielewski, P.: HDF5-based data format for archiving complex neuro-monitoring data in traumatic brain injury patients. Acta Neurochir. Suppl. **126**, 121–125 (2018)
9. Yang, L.P., Che, Y.G.: HDF5 based parallel I/O techniques for multi-zone structured grids CFD applications. J. Comput. Res. Dev. **52**(4), 861–868 (2015)
10. Feng, J.H., Chen, J.Z., Zhang, X.J.: System of data management based on the file of HDF. Comput. Digit. Eng. **39**(2), 102–1122011
11. Cai, Z.Q., Wu, W.Z., Lu, Q.W., et al.: An effective data analysis system of foreign exchange using HDF5 and Esper. Comput. Eng. Sci. **33**(04), 159–163 (2011)
12. Yang, L.P., Che, Y.G.: HDF5 based parallel I/O technology for structure grid CFD applications. J. Comput. Appl. **33**(09), 2423–2427 (2013)

13. Zhong, L., Li, H., Zhu, M.: Data redistribution strategy of FAST telescope based on HDF5 format. Comput. Mod. (06), 60–64 (2019)
14. Tong, D.Y., Qin, Z.G., Wei, Y.L., Li, Q.H.: Applying HDF5 in large-scale finite element software data management. Comput. Appl. Softw. **31**(02), 58–61 (2014)
15. Chai, X.M., Tu, X.L., Guo, F.C., et al.: Development and preliminary V&V for advanced neutron transport lattice code KYLIN-2. High Power Laser Part. Beams **29**(01), 94–100 (2017)
16. Feng, J.T., Lu, W., Chai, X.M., Tu, X.L., et al.: The KYLIN-2 assembly databank based on HDF5 file format. J. Comput. Appl. **38**(04), 1012–1016 (2018)
17. Chai, X.M., Tu, X.L., Lu, W., et al.: Development and verification and validation of MOC module in advanced neutronics lattice code KYLIN-2. Nucl. Power Eng. **37**(04), 154–159 (2016)
18. Lu, W., Yin, Q., Chen, D.Y., et al.: Numerical verification of KYLIN-II code based on IAEA plate fuel benchmark. Nucl. Power Eng. **38**(04), 168–171 (2017)
19. Tu, X.L., Pan, J.J., Chai, X.M., et al.: Research and development of visual graphic modeling for advanced neutron transport lattice code KYLIN-II. Nucl. Power Eng. **38**(03), 126–131 (2017)
20. An, P., Ma, Y.Q., Xiao, P., et al.: Development and validation of reactor nuclear design code CORCA-3D. Nucl. Power Eng. **51**(7), 1721–1728 (2019)
21. An, P., Ma, Y.Q., Guo, F.C., et al.: Development and validation of critical boron concentration and burnup calculation of software CORCA-3D. Nucl. Power Eng. **40**(04), 161–165 (2019)
22. Liu, Y., Tan, C.L., Pan, J.J., et al.: Development of self-reliant subchannel analysis code CORTH. Nucl. Power Eng. **38**(06), 157–162 (2017)
23. Ming, P.Z., Chen, D.Y., Wu, B., Lu, W., Liu, D., Yu, H.X.: Parallel analysis of linear systems in CORTH and KYLIN2. J. Nucl. Eng. Radiat. Sci. **4**(3), 031010 (2018)
24. Liu, W., Peng, S., Jiang, G., et al.: Development and assessment of a new rod-bundle CHF correlation for China fuel assemblies. Ann. Nucl. Energy **138**, 107175 (2020)

Exploiting API Description Information to Improve Code Comment Generation

Guang Yang, Qian Zhang, Yufei Wu, Tianxing Zhou, Huan Liu, and Wenting Feng[✉]

School of Computer and Electronic Information,
Nanjing Normal University, Nanjing 210023, China

Abstract. Code comments can improve the readability of program and help the programmer to efficiently promote the maintenance of the software. Therefore, the code comment generation task has important research significance. However, generating high-quality code comments is very challenging, because the function methods called in the code hide a lot of functional information, which is often related to the functionality of the source code. Therefore, we propose to use the function description information to improve the code comment generation model. In the paper, we have designed two models that combine code sequences and API description information to implement the code comment generation task, and conducted experiments on two open source data sets. The experimental results demonstrate the effectiveness of API function description information for code comment generation task.

Keywords: Annotation generation · API function description · Pointer generator network

1 Introduction

The basic task of code comment generation is to automatically convert code written in a programming language into textual comments written in natural language by analyzing the source code. High-quality code comments can effectively improve the efficiency of software maintenance. Therefore, the code comment generation technology has attracted more and more scholars' attention.

The study of code comment based on template and information retrieval used to dominate the field [1–3]. The disadvantage of these methods is that they rely too much on the terminology in the source code and ignore the connection between the data. Compared with traditional methods, deep learning methods have powerful feature representation and learning capabilities, which can automatically learn the connections between data from massive codes through multi-layer neural networks. [4] first used deep learning methods to generate annotated words. [5] was inspired by the machine translation model and applied the Neural Machine Translation (NMT) model to the code comment generation task. [5] also added an API encoder to capture semantics from source code with the help of API sequences, which improved the performance of code annotation generation model.

© Springer Nature Switzerland AG 2021
X. Sun et al. (Eds.): ICAIS 2021, CCIS 1423, pp. 395–406, 2021.
https://doi.org/10.1007/978-3-030-78618-2_32

Although their experimental results prove the effectiveness of deep learning methods for code comment generation task, these methods are limited to the apparent meaning of the code text and ignore some important information related to the code function. When programmers write code, they will call some encapsulated function methods to achieve specific functions. When the model generates comments, the generated comments may be inaccurate and incomplete because they cannot capture the meaning of these functions. Although the work of Hu et al. considered the relationship between api and code comments, it did not make full use of the actual meaning of api functions in the function library, so the model performance was limited.

In order to solve the problem of code comprehension, programmers usually take the method of understanding the meaning of the function first, and then continuing to read the code snippets. They often use the Internet to retrieve uncommon functions and deepen their understanding of code snippets by understanding the detailed description of the functions and specific usage scenarios. We analyzed several examples in the data set and found that the description information of the function called in the code fragment can provide useful information for understanding the code to a large extent. Therefore, we consider using the function description information to assist the code comment generation task.

In order to effectively utilize the description information of the function, we use sequence-to sequence (seq2seq) framework, the most widely used baseline model, as the fundamental architecture and propose two different methods to use the function description information: One is to integrate the vector of the function description information into the representation of the corresponding function name in the code fragment by concatenating the two vectors; the other is based on the pointer generator network. This method calculates the attention score of each word in the function description information at every time step. The decoder can selectively copy the words in the function description information to generate natural language comments. The result generated by the decoder can be derived from the natural language annotation vocabulary or function description information.

To evaluate our model, we experiment with the open source data sets Conala and Django. Experimental results show that our model can effectively utilize the description information of the function to improve the performance of the code comment generation task. The main contributions of this article are as follows: 1. We propose to use the description information of the function called in the code fragment to assist the code comment generation task. 2. We demonstrate the effectiveness of the API function description information for the code comment generation task through experiments.

2   Baseline Model

At present, the most widely used structure in the research of code comment generation task based on deep learning methods is the seq2seq framework [5, 6, 13, 14, 17]. These studies focused on changing the encoding method, or improving the decoding algorithm and they all achieved good experimental results. Therefore, we implement a baseline model based on the seq2seq framework.

Seq2Seq is an encoder-decoder structure model. The encoder converts a variable-length input sequence into a fixed-length vector, and the decoder decodes the fixed-length vector into a variable-length output sequence. Let $x = \{x_1, x_2, \ldots, x_m\}$ denote input sentence and $y = \{y_1, y_2, \ldots, y_m\}$ represent output sentence.

During the encoding process, in order to allow the hidden layer state vectors h_i to summarize the input words before time step i and after time step i, we use BiLSTM to encode the source code.

$$\mathrm{h}_t = f_{BiLSTM}(x_t, h_{t-1}) \tag{1}$$

During the decoding process, attention mechanism is introduced so that each time step can focus on the current encoding result. The output of time step i is determined by three factors: hidden state s_i of time step i, context vector c_i calculated by attention and output y_{i-1} of last time step $i - 1$. The calculations are as follows:

$$p(y_i|y_1, \ldots, y_{i-1}, x) = g_{LSTM}(y_{i-1}, s_i, c_i) \tag{2}$$

$$s_i = f_{LSTM}(s_{i-1}, y_{i-1}, c_i) \tag{3}$$

Context vector is calculated by weighted sum of all hidden state vectors. The calculations are as follows:

$$c_i = \sum_{j=1}^{T} a_{ij} h_j \tag{4}$$

$$\alpha_{ij} = \frac{\exp(e_{ij})}{\sum_{k=1}^{T} \exp(e_{ik})} \tag{5}$$

$$e_{ij} = a(s_{i-1}, h_j) \tag{6}$$

e_{ij} calculates the degree of matching between the information near the j-th word of the input sequence and the i-th word of the output sequence. During the test process, we use beam-search to select top k words with the highest prediction probability as the output at the current time step. To prevent the search process from biasing to shorter sentences, length normalization is performed:

$$P(y|x) = \frac{1}{n} \log(\prod_{k=1}^{n} p(y_k|x, y_1, y_1, \ldots, y_{k-1})) \tag{7}$$

n is the maximum step size for decoding.

3   Two Ways of Using API Function Description Information

3.1   Motivation

The description information of the function called by the code fragment can help us better understand the code. As shown in Fig. 1, several functions are called in the code snippet. According to the description information retrieved from the function called

Code:	for i in range(4): s = random.choice(some_dict.keys()) some_dict.pop(s)
Annotation:	remove random elements from a dictionary
Api:	*dict. pop* *random.choice*
Api description:	retrieve the item and remove it from the dictionary return a random element from the non-empty sequence.

Fig. 1. Annotation can be inferred from API description

from the code, the actual meaning of the code fragment can be easily inferred. We analyzed the examples in several data sets, finding that the code fragments containing the function name accounted for up to 70% of the data set. The description information of the functions and the comments of the code fragments contained in a large number of code fragments can provide useful information for programmers to understand the code.

Based on the above analysis, this paper proposes to use the function description information to improve the code comment generation model. Based on the baseline model, we propose two different methods to utilize function description information: One is to integrate the vector of function description information into the representation of the corresponding function name in the code fragment by concatenating two vectors; the other is based on the pointer generation network. This method generates natural language comments through model selectively copying function description information or the decoder outputting new comments words.

3.2 Vectors Concatenation

If we can somehow inform our model the actual meaning of the function in the code, then the model may produce a more accurate code representation. With this motivation, the most direct approach is to combine the function name and its description information into a new vector to replace the function name itself.

As shown in Fig. 2, the overall architecture is the encoder-decoder framework. On this basis, we have established a new LSTM-based function description information encoder *encoder_desc*, which encodes the description information corresponding to the function contained in each code snippet, and obtains the representation vector w^{des}. Then concatenate w^{des} with the vector w_i^{api} of the function name in the corresponding code fragment as the new vector representation of the function name:

$$w_i = f([w_i^{api}; w^{dex}]) \tag{8}$$

i is the position of the function name in the code. Its determination is based on the abstract syntax tree structure of the code and some heuristic rules.

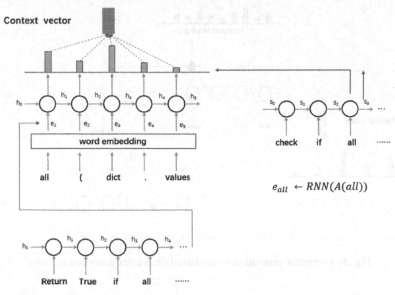

Fig. 2. Using API function description information by concatenating vectors

3.3 Pointer Generator Network

Since the sequence of function description information is often too long, the model lacks information during encoding. It results that the generated vector cannot fully represent the meaning of the function API, and that the performance of the model cannot continue to improve. Through the analysis of the code and function description information in the data set, we found that the content of the function description information and the code comment have a certain repetition rate. Therefore, in order to utilize the function description information more comprehensively, this paper proposes a method of using the function description information based on the pointer generator network.

Our model is based on a dual encoder structure. One of the dual encoders is a sequence encoder, which is used to encode a sequence of code fragments; the other is to construct a pointer network for function description information. The results generated by the decoder at each time step may have two sources: natural language annotation vocabulary and function description information. By calculating the score of each word in the function description information, the decoder selectively copies the words in the information which may be outputted. Finally, natural language comments corresponding to the code fragments are generated. The overall architecture of the model is shown in Fig. 3.

The encoder encodes input sequence $x^s = (x_1^s, \ldots, x_T^s)$ and function description information $x^d = (x_1^d, \ldots, x_K^d)$. We use BiLSTM network as the encoder part. The calculations are as follows:

$$h_t^s = f_{BiLSTM}(x_t^s, h_{t-1}^s) \tag{9}$$

$$h_k^d = g_{BiLSTM}(x_k^d, h_{k-1}^d) \tag{10}$$

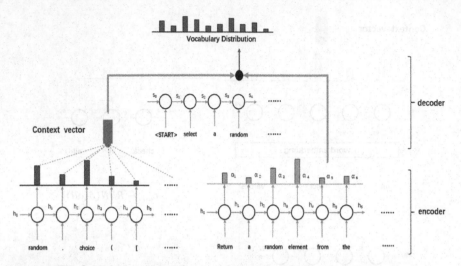

Fig. 3. Comment generation model based on pointer generator network

The decoding part uses the pointer-generator network [7]. The network mixes the seq2seq model and the pointer network [16]. It has the generation ability of seq2seq model and the copy ability of the pointer network, so that the model can accurately copy the function description information while retaining the ability of generating new comment words.

The final probability $P(w)$ of the word generated by the decoder is determined by the probability of natural language annotation vocabulary and attention distribution of function description information from source end:

$$P(w) = P_{predictor} * P_{vocab} + (1 - P_{predictor}) * P_{copy} \tag{11}$$

$P_{predictor}$ is the probability that the word is generated from natural language annotation vocabulary; P_{vocab} is the distribution of all the words from natural language annotation vocabulary; P_{copy} is the copy probability of each token in function description information. The calculations are as follows:

$$P_{predictor} = \sigma(g(y_{i-1}, s_i, c_i)) \tag{12}$$

$$P_{vocab} = soft \max(v[c_t, s_t] + b) \tag{13}$$

$$P_{copy} = \sum_{j:w_j=w} \alpha_{ij}^* \tag{14}$$

$$\alpha_{ij}^* = soft \max(e_{ij}^*) \tag{15}$$

$$e_{ij}^* = a(s_{i-1}, h_j^*) \tag{16}$$

σ is softmax function, v and b are trainable parameters.

During the training process, we use KL divergence as the loss function. KL divergence calculates the distance between two distributions. The loss function is defined as follows:

$$loss = -\frac{1}{n} \sum_{i=1}^{N} y_i(\log \hat{y}_i - \log y_i) \tag{17}$$

N is the maximum step size, $\hat{y}_i$ is the predicted probability, y_i is the gold result.

During the test, the model determines whether the function description information token is in the natural language vocabulary. As shown in Fig. 4, if the function description information token is in the natural language vocabulary, the predicted probability of the token at the current time step will be the sum of the vocabulary probability and the copy probability; if the function description information token is not in the natural language vocabulary, the probability of the token with the highest copy probability among all tokens in the function description information will replace the probability of UNK in the natural language vocabulary, and the word UNK is also replaced by this token. That means, the word with the highest copy probability is used as the candidate of the seq2seq decoder instead of the word UNK.

We observed that repeated words often appear in the comments generated by the model. Due to the attention mechanism, when the attention token first appears, the attention score of the token may still be very high at the next time step. If the model chooses to use the same token twice, it will cause the problem of word duplication.

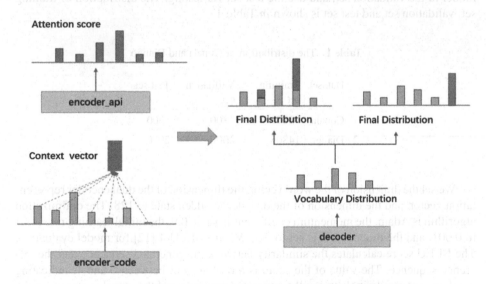

Fig. 4. Utilization of function description information

In order to avoid over-focusing on a certain part of the input sequence during the decoding process, we introduced an intra-temporal attention mechanism [9]. Ordinary attention is to sequentially calculate the current decoder state and the score of each hidden layer state of the encoder, and then normalize them to get the weight, and then get the context vector through the weighted sum. The intra-temporal attention mechanism modifies by first normalizing of all time steps t to obtain the normalized score at the corresponding time step, then normalizing to obtain the weight, and then obtaining the context vector through weighted sum of the hidden state of the encoder, which is a penalty for tokens that have received high attention scores in the past.

4   Experiments

4.1   Experiment Setup

We use public data sets Conala and Django as experimental data. The Conala data set was created by [10]. They extracted the problem code pairs from the Stack Overflow website, filtered them using heuristic rules, and after manual proofreading, they finally created a corpus containing 2879 pairs of python code and corresponding comments. There are 2016 code snippets containing functions in the Conala data set. The Django data set was created by [11], where the code was from the open source python application framework Django, and the comments were written by several professional engineers hired by the authors, and finally a corpus containing 18805 pairs of Python code and corresponding comments was obtained. There are 4662 code fragments containing functions in the Django data set. We divide the data set by the ratio of 8:1:1. We use the training set to train the model and the validation set to verify the model, save the best performing model in the validation set, and use the test set for testing. The distribution of training set, validation set and test set is shown in Table 1.

Table 1. The distribution of Conala and Django

	Dataset	Training set	Validation set	Test set
1	Conala	2279	300	300
2	Django	14805	2000	2000

We set the dimension of the word vector, the dimension of the dual encoder representation vector, and the dimension of the decoder's hidden state to 128. The optimization algorithm is Adam, the momentum coefficient is set to 0.9, the initial learning rate is set to 0.001, and the dropout rate is set to 0.5. We use BLEU-4 [12] for model evaluation. The BLEU score calculates the similarity between the generated sequence and the reference sequence. The value of the score is a real number between 0 and 1, indicating the degree of similarity between the generated sentence and the actual sentence. In the experiment, we multiply the BLEU score by 100 for presentation.

4.2   Obtaining API Function Documentation

API function documentation is a collection of description information of functions in the source code. For its acquisition, we take python as an example. Python's standard library provides a lot of functions, including built-in modules and other modules written in python. In addition, there are many third-party libraries available for program development using python, including functional modules from data processing to artificial intelligence, from web analysis to cyberspace. Through the analysis of the data set, in addition to the python standard library, this paper also selects the 10 most used third-party libraries in the data set including django, numpy, requests, matplotlib, beautifulsoup4, pandas, selenium, scipy, nltk, gensim.

We write a crawler to obtain the function names and their corresponding function description information from the official website of the above python libraries, and use the function names and their corresponding description information to build the api-desc library. As a result, more than 14,000 pairs of api-desc are obtained.

4.3 Experimental Results

Table 2 shows the results of the two models that API description information is used to improve the code comment generation task under the BLEU-4 index. The experimental results show that the performance of the code comment generation model based on vector concatenation and the code comment generation model based on the pointer generator network is better than the baseline. Although the baseline method uses the BiLSTM network to solve the long-distance dependency problem, it does not consider the functional information of the function in the code snippet which can hinder code comprehension. Our first model concatenates the function vector and the description information vector to transfer knowledge that could not be displayed to the model, which enriches the semantics of the code to a certain extent, but the model performance is limited. Compared with the model based on vector concatenation, the code comment generation model based on the pointer generator network can more effectively use the description information of the functions in the code. The model can accurately copy the function description information while retaining the ability of generating new comment words. As a result, the model can maximize the use of function description information to make the generated comments more complete and accurate. Although the size of the Conala data set is much smaller than the Django data set, the API content rate of the former is much higher than that of the latter, so the experimental results of the two are not much different. The improvement of the model performance proves the effectiveness of using API function description information when generating comments.

Table 2. Experimental results

	Models	BLEU-4	
		Conala	Django
1	Baseline	20.6	46.9
2	API_concat	21.0	47.3
3	Pointer generator network	**23.5**	**50.1**

4.4 Ablation Study

The generation model based on the pointer generator network improves the overall performance of the model by adding pointer network, intra-temporal attention and other modules. To verify the impact of each module on the model, we set up an ablation experiment to compare each module. The experimental results are shown in Table 3.

Table 3. Ablation experimental results

	Models	BLEU-4	
		Conala	Django
1	Baseline	20.6	46.9
2	Baseline + intra-temporal attention	20.9	47.1
3	Baseline + pointer network	23.1	49.5
4	Baseline + pointer network + intra-temporal attention	**23.5**	**50.1**

From the results of the ablation experiment in Table 3, it can be concluded that both pointer network and intra-temporal attention have a certain impact on the model. The benchmark model uses the BiLSTM network to encode the code sequence. The model only uses the information of the coding sequence, ignoring the richer function information, which limits the performance of the model. Intra-temporal attention mechanism is added for model modification. The improvement of experimental results shows that this mechanism avoids the model from paying too much attention to a certain part of the input sequence during the decoding process, making the generated comments more reasonable. The addition of the pointer network has greatly improved the experimental results, which shows that the pointer network gives different weights to the words in the function description information, so that the model effectively captures the words related to the comments, and successfully utilizes the function description information. The knowledge gained finally leads to more comprehensive and accurate results.

5   Related Work

The seq2seq framework is the most widely used method for implementing code comment generation tasks based on deep learning. [4] used deep learning methods for the first time to generate annotated words, using LSTM network combined with attention mechanism to generate natural language comments for C# code segments and SQL query statements. [5] applied the seq2seq model to the code comment generation task for the first time, and converted the abstract syntax tree structure of the code into a sequence as the input of the encoder, taking into account the structural information of the code sequence. In order to capture the code structure more effectively, [13] merged the sequence information and structure information of the code through a hybrid attention mechanism, and proposed a new code comment generation model based on reinforcement learning framework to deal with the exposure bias problem existed in traditional code comment generation framework. [14] tried to use the set of compositional paths in the code abstract syntax tree instead of code sequence or structure as the input of the encoder, and generated code comments based on the seq2seq framework. The experimental results showed the importance of code structure encoding. [18] also considered the structural information of the code, and proposed a new attention module, which uses the specific characteristics of the code fragments, such as identifiers and symbols, to explicitly model the structure of the code, and generates comments which are consistent with the functional semantics of the program to a certain degree.

Although these methods have achieved some success, they ignore some important information that relates to the intent of the code. Some uncommon functions called in the code will hinder the understanding of the code to a certain extent, and the meaning of these functions is often related to the functionality of the code, so some scholars have carried out research on the API. [15] used natural language comments to generate API sequences related to comments, and learned the potential association between words in the comments and related API sequences. [5] combined the API sequence summarization task and the code summarization task to establish the mapping between the API sequence and code comments through the API sequence summarization task, and then applied the learned API knowledge to the code summarization task to help generate summarization. Although their research considered the relationship between API function sequences and code comments, they did not make full use of the actual meaning of API functions in standard libraries and third-party libraries, so their performance was limited. In contrast, our method considers the function description information of the function called in the code, and combines the code sequence information with the description information of the function in it, so that the generated comments are more comprehensive and accurate.

6 Conclusion

This paper focuses on the utilization of function description information, which can enrich the semantics of the code, and proposes a framework for generating code comments by combining function description information and code sequence information. The pointer generator network model is used to integrate the function description information into the model and improves the performance of code comments generation task. We successfully demonstrate the effectiveness of API function description information for python code comment generation task. Nevertheless, there is still room for improvement in our experiments. The extraction rules of function description information need to be improved, and the extracted description information is not standard. In the official website of the third-party library, some function description information is missing, and we will use other channels to search for it in the future.

References

1. Sridhara, G., Hill, E., Muppaneni, D., et al.: Towards automatically generating summary comments for java methods. In: Proceedings of the IEEE/ACM International Conference on Automated Software Engineering, pp. 43–52 (2010)

2. Mcburney, P.W., Mcmillan, C.: Automatic documentation generation via source code summarization of method context. In: Proceedings of the 22nd International Conference on Program Comprehension, pp. 279–290 (2014)
3. Mcburney, P.W., Mcmillan, C.: Automatic source code summarization of context for java methods. IEEE Trans. Software Eng. **42**(2), 103–119 (2016)
4. Iyer, S., Konstas, I., Cheung, A., et al.: Summarizing source code using a neural attention model. In: Proceedings of the 54th Annual Meeting of the Association for Computational Linguistics (Volume 1: Long Papers), pp. 2073–2083 (2016)
5. Hu, X., Li, G., Xia, X. et al.: Deep code comment generation. In: Proceedings of the 26th Conference on Program Comprehension, pp. 200–210 (2018)
6. Hu, X., Li, G., Xia, X., et al.: Summarizing source code with transferred API knowledge. In: Proceedings of the International Joint Conference on Artificial Intelligence, pp. 2269–2275 (2018)
7. See, A., Liu, P.J., Manning, C.D., et al.: Get to the point: summarization with pointer-generator networks. In: Proceedings of the Association for Computational Linguistics, pp. 1073–1083 (2017)
8. Sun, F., Jiang, P., Sun, H., et al.: Multi-source pointer network for product title summarization. In: Proceedings of the Conference on Information and Knowledge Management, pp. 7–16 (2018)
9. Paulus, R., Xiong, C., Socher, R., et al.: A deep reinforced model for abstractive summarization. In: Proceedings of the International Conference on Learning Representations (2018)
10. Yin, P., Deng, B., Chen, E., et al.: Learning to mine aligned code and natural language pairs from stack overflow. In: Proceedings of the IEEE/ACM 15th International Conference on Mining Software Repositories (MSR), pp. 476–486 (2018)
11. Oda, Y., Fudaba, H., Neubig, G., et al.: Learning to generate pseudo-code from source code using statistical machine translation. In: Proceedings of the IEEE/ACM International Conference on Automated Software Engineering, pp. 574–584 (2015)
12. Papineni, K., Roukos, S., Ward, T., et al.: Bleu: a method for automatic evaluation of machine translation. In: Proceedings of the Association for Computational Linguistics, pp. 311–318 (2002)
13. Wan, Y., Zhao, Z., Yang, M., et al.: Improving automatic source code summarization via deep reinforcement learning. In: Proceedings of the 33rd ACM/IEEE International Conference on Automated Software Engineering, pp. 397–407 (2018)
14. Alon, U., Brody, S., Levy, O., et al.: code2seq: generating sequences from structured representations of code. In: Proceedings of the International Conference on Learning Representations (2019)
15. Gu, X., Zhang, H., Zhang, D., et al.: Deep API learning. In: Proceedings of the 2016 24th ACM SIGSOFT International Symposium on Foundations of Software Engineering, pp. 631–642 (2016)
16. Vinyals, O., Fortunato, M., Jaitly, N.: Pointer networks. In: Proceedings of the International Conference on Neural Information Processing Systems, pp. 2692–2700 (2015)
17. Allamanis, M., Peng, H., Sutton, C.: A convolutional attention network for extreme summarization of source code. In: Proceedings of the International Conference on Machine Learning, pp. 2091–2100 (2016)
18. Zheng, W., Zhou, H., Li, M., Wu, J.: CodeAttention: translating source code to comments by exploiting the code constructs. Front. Comp. Sci. **13**(3), 565–578 (2018). https://doi.org/10.1007/s11704-018-7457-6

A Tag Recommendation Method
for OpenStreetMap Based on FP-Growth
and Improved Markov Process

Yijiang Zhao[✉], Xicheng Guo, Yizhi Liu, Zhuhua Liao, and Min Liu

Key Laboratory of Knowledge Processing and Networked Manufacturing in Hunan Province,
Hunan University of Science and Technology, Xiangtan 411201, China

Abstract. Volunteer geographic information (VGI), as a new geographic information source, has gradually become an important complement for authoritative data sources. Yet, due to the non-professionalism and spontaneity of most volunteers, and the lack of effective contribution constraints, the issues of attribute quality of OpenStreetMap (OSM) objects, such as semantic inconsistency and incompleteness, have received many attentions. However, there are few methods for effectively improving OSM's semantic quality. In this paper, we proposed a tag recommendation method based on the combination of FP-Growth and the Markov process. The aim of our algorithm is to improve the quality of OSM objects by recommending some tags when volunteers contribute to the platform. The results show that the method based on FP-Growth and Improved Markov Process can effectively recommend tag-keys for different feature classes.

Keywords: Tag recommendation · Attribute quality · FP-Growth · Improved Markov process · OpenStreetMap

1 Introduction

Goodchild coined the term volunteered geographic information (VGI) to describe "the widespread engagement of large numbers of private citizens, often with little in the way of formal qualifications, in the creation of geographic information" [1]. At the same time, it has also been identified as a new source of information because of its characteristics of large volume, up-to-date, and accessibility. OpenStreetMap (OSM), as one of the most successful VGI platforms, now has been applied to many domains.

In OSM, the locations of features are represented by latitude and longitude, and their attributes are expressed by tags (i.e., key/value pairs). The majority of geographical features are represented as geographic elements (i.e., node/way/relation), with either one or more tags, in OSM. A tag is a key-value pair that is used to describe attribute features of map elements. Both key and value are free format text fields and often used to represent numeric or other structured items. For example, a residential road can be illustrated by way element with some tags ('highway = residential', 'lanes = 2', 'surface = asphalt', etc.). Any contributors can freely add new tags or edit existing tags

© Springer Nature Switzerland AG 2021
X. Sun et al. (Eds.): ICAIS 2021, CCIS 1423, pp. 407–419, 2021.
https://doi.org/10.1007/978-3-030-78618-2_33

of any OSM objects, even if these objects are created by others [2]. Due to its easy-to-use, OSM attracts many volunteers to contribute geographic objects. However, this mechanism also brings issues of semantic quality. For example, an inaccuracy tag, i.e., 'building = apartments', is used to describe a student dormitory ('building = dormitory' is more accurate according to the definition from the official website), which results in semantic inaccuracy (Fig. 1(a)). And an object is described only by one tag (Fig. 1(b)), which lacks some other pivotal information (lanes, surface, name, etc.) so that it leads to information incompleteness. Those quality issues of OSM will essentially affect the usability of the datasets. Therefore, the purpose of this paper is to address semantic accuracy and semantic completeness in OSM-liked systems.

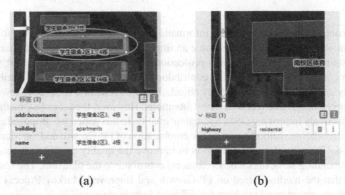

(a)   (b)

Fig. 1. Example of semantic quality. (a) Semantic inaccuracy: 'building = apartments' is used to describe a student's dormitory. (b) Semantic incompleteness: the user only uses one tag ('highway = residential') to describe a road object.

According to the research, different geographic objects are described by certain tags, which are associated with each other [3]. So, tag recommendation is a promising method proposed by some researchers. Many recommendations are performed by calculating the semantic similarity between tags. For example, Vandecasteele and Devillers automatically suggested relevant tags to contributors during the editing process [4]. Majic et al. detected equivalent existing attribute tags for the new tags [3]. The methods by calculating tag similarity are utilizing external data, files, or websites, which improve the complexity of data acquisition and processing. Another method is to construct a classifier. Karagiannakis et al. recommended OSM categories for newly inserted spatial entities [5]. However, it needed researchers to identify the ambiguous tag semantics, existing relatively subjective interference factors. Some researchers are developed only depend on the tag information. These researches applied association rules mining (ARM) to OSM data and achieved good experimental results [15, 16], which shows that ARM could reduce subjective bias in the data processing. Afterward, Ludwig et al. analyzed tags of multiple parks under different context requirements by association rule algorithm and discovered objects relationship of parks [6]. Therefore, the idea of our research is how to identify the relationships between tags by ARM and to recommend proper tags for volunteers when they contribute in the OSM platform. With our method, the semantic accuracy and completeness of attribute features of OSM objects will be improved. Then, the quality of the whole dataset will also be improved.

The remainder of the article is structured as follows. Section 2 gives a summary of studies related to quality assessment of VGI data. Section 3 gives a more detailed description of the OSM data and introduces the work of data preprocessing. Section 4 describes the underlying and proposed methods, as well as their corresponding experimental steps and results. A discussion follows in Sect. 5 and Sect. 6 concludes.

2   Related Works

As the VGI dataset lacks meta information on data quality, researchers question the reliability and fitness for use of VGI data. How to assess and guarantee its data quality is a hot issue and obtain much attention from academia and industry.

Many studies have explored the quality assessment and assurance methods of OSM data. Jacobs and Mitchell divide quality assessment methods into two categories [7]. The first category is an extrinsic quality assessment method comparing OSM data with authoritative reference datasets from different countries [8, 9]. They all came to a similar conclusion that in some areas the VGI data have a high quality. With the rapid development of OSM, OSM soon had richer data than many authoritative datasets in some fields. However, many authoritative datasets are difficult to acquire and their quality may not better than OSM data, which makes these assessment methods are limited usage in practical applications [10]. The other category is named internal quality assessment, which is to reflect data quality by analyzing information only from OSM data themselves. Troung et al. analyzed users' contribution behavior in the OSM platform to determine the reliability of users' contribution data [11]. However, when Mooney et al. studied the OSM annotation process, they found that most of the errors were caused by participants manually editing tags to objects with inaccurate values or spelling errors, so the lack of checking attributes in the annotation process of OSM was an important reason for the inaccurate data [2]. To address this issue, Ballatore et al. developed the OSM Semantic Network which obtained semantic relationships between geographic concepts from the description of OSM Wiki. And then they calculated the semantic similarity between OSM tags by co-citation algorithm P-Rank. Through assessing the rationality of their approach by comparing the results with an assessment dataset containing human judgments of geographic concepts, the approach could mimic the human similarity ranking of geographic concepts and could be applied in geographic recommendation systems [12]. Meanwhile, they came up with another method of computing semantic similarity which bases on lexical definitions of geographic terms, drawing from natural language processing techniques [13]. Afterward, Vandecasteele and Devillers utilized semantic similarity [12] and tag frequency proposed an OSMantic tool, which could automatically suggest tags, and give warnings when the similarity between the tags of a selected OSM object was too low [4]. Nevertheless, the above calculation methods of semantic similarity need to refer to external resources. And these resources are sometimes unobtainable. Thus, Majic et al. proposed an approach for computing the semantic similarity of OSM tags that has no need for external data or explicit definitions of tags but needed to obtain information from the TagInfo website to define the document key [3].

The increasing amount of VGI data allows the application of machine learning algorithms as one of the possible methodologies to analyze and improve its data quality [14]. Therefore, in addition to computing similarity, some research proposes machine learning models based on the properties of OSM objects to address this problem [2]. Karagiannakis et al. proposed an OSMRec tool, which extracts seven features from geometrical and textual aspects and trained an SVM classifier to recommend a set of tags for new objects [5]. Ali et al. identified the four ambiguous classes of green-area objects in OSM, by extracting topological rules between geographical objects and using an association rule algorithm [15]. Kashian et al. proposed a recommendation tool that uses the spatial association rule to extract spatial co-existence patterns between different points of interest (POI) in OSM [16]. In [15, 16], the authors skillfully combined the association rule algorithm with OSM data. The difference was that they analyzed the topological relationship of the object classes [15] and the spatial relationship of POI [16] respectively. Recently, Ludwig et al. used a similar algorithm to analyze the tags relationship of multiple parks under different context requirements and discovered many tag rules with referenced value and practical significance [6].

3 Data Description and Preprocessing

In this section, we briefly introduce the detail of the dataset and explain the work of data preprocessing.

3.1 Data Description

The data used for our experiments are provided by the OpenStreetMap community (http://download.openstreetmap.fr/extracts/asia/china/), which generates daily OSM data, and can be gotten freely, from OpenStreetMap.org. Beijing, China is selected as our study area, because it is the political, economic, and cultural center of China. And the development of Beijing is extremely fast in almost every field of China and OSM data in this area has good coverage, which makes it an ideal place for exploring the relationships between OSM tags.

OSM dataset consists of three types of basic geographic elements, i.e., node, way, and relation. To describe a particular element, all of them can have either zero, one, or more associated tags. A tag consists of two parts, 'key' and 'value'. For example, a motorway can be described by way element with some tags ('highway = motorway', 'lanes = 3', 'oneway = yes', etc.). In this example, 'highway' and 'motorway' represent 'key' and 'value' of tag, respectively. In this paper, our research mainly focuses on the 'key' of the OSM tag ('highway = motorway'). In order not to be confused, we use Tag-key represents the 'key' of tag in the following paragraphs. The number of the three kinds of elements in our experimental dataset is 1,351,555 (Node), 182,710 (Way), 6,712 (Relation).

3.2 Data Preprocessing

In order to perform subsequent experiments, the downloaded OSM dataset needs to be preprocessed. Therefore, the steps of data preprocessing will be introduced in this section.

Processing of Tag-Key. The aim of this study is to exploit the relationship between tags. Therefore, those objects in OSM dataset only have one tag will be filtered, because the one-tag object will not contribute tag relationship in our experiment. To enhance the processing efficiency, then, tag-key will be extracted from tags in the dataset.

Data Classification. Different kinds of geographic objects have different thematic attributes. Here, we use road and building as two examples. Road objects often have attributes like name, oneway, maxspeed, and lanes, while building objects has different another series of attributes like name, height, floors, etc. These two kinds of objects have different tags in OSM, which makes it to discover useful association patterns if we deal with all the data directly. Because the support and confidence degree of the association tags of different categories will vary greatly. The classification regulations we used refers to the standard proposed by the OSM Community (OpenStreetMap Data in Layered GIS Format) and feature-wiki in OSM. Part of the classification regulations is shown in Table 1. Geographic objects are managed by dividing into three levels, called layer1, layer2, layer3, respectively. Layer2 is selected for further processing according to our primary experiment results. OSM_tag in Table 1 is the tags used to classify OSM objects. For example, the object with the tag 'highway = motorway', is classified into Motorway (Layer3), Major road (Layer2), and Road (Layer1).

Table 1. Classification regulations of the tags (about road)

Layer1	Layer2	Layer3	Description	OSM_tag
Road	Major road	Motorway	Motorway/freeway	Highway = motorway
Road	Major road	Trunk	Important roads, typically divided	Highway = trunk
Road	Minor road	Residential	Roads in residential areas	Highway = residential
Road	Minor road	Pedestrian	Pedestrian only streets	Highway = pedestrian

Association rules algorithm (FP-Growth) is used to process the original data and classified data, respectively. The comparing result is shown in Fig. 2. The rules extracted from classified data extremely improve even with the same minimum support, e.g., 1 rule from the original data and 365 rules from classified data with minimum support 0.09 (Fig. 2). Agrawal proposed the Apriori algorithm for the first time [17]. Subsequently, the FP-Growth algorithm was proposed [18] by Han, which is more efficient than Apriori. Apriori and FP-Growth are the most popular and classical association rules algorithms. So many valid association rule algorithms are based on these two methods. Our experiment is concerned with mining from OSM tags. The FP-Growth algorithm is selected because its efficiency can meet our needs.

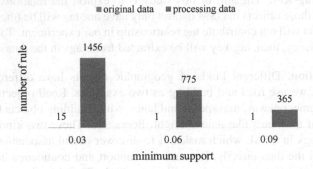

Fig. 2. The number of association rules (minimum confidence is 0.4 with different minimum support)

4 Method

In this section, we first show how to obtain recommendation rules using the FP-Growth in Sect. 4.1. And then in Sect. 4.2 and 4.3, it introduces how to utilize the Markov process and improved Markov process respectively to obtain the recommended Tag-key based on association rules of OSM data.

4.1 Mining Frequency Item-Sets Using the FP-Growth Algorithm

In this section, we will discuss how to mine recommendation rules by the FP-Growth algorithm. The basic process is shown in Fig. 3.

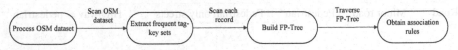

Fig. 3. Mining processing based on experimental data

The experimental data are selected from the major road category which has the most data in the level of Layer2. The experimental data include 19467 objects which contain 131 non-duplicate Tag-key.

Association rule mining (ARM) is a process to discover implicit relationships between objects from large-scale data [18]. An association rule of $X \rightarrow Y$, where X and Y are item attributes. X and Y are defined as the antecedent and the consequent item respectively. Support and confidence indicate how frequently items are in the database and how many times the item sets are presented, respectively. The following includes some important definitions in ARM.

- Definition 1. Support(X) means the proportion of transactions that include X in the database.

- Definition 2. Confidence(X → Y) is the proportion of transactions that include item X which also includes item Y in transactions of including X. If Support(X → Y) ≥ Min_Support and Confidence(X → Y) ≥ Min_Confidence, X → Y the rule is called strong rules.

Minimum support and minimum confidence were set to 0.2 and 0.5, respectively. A Tag-key should only be contributed once to a certain object. Each category can contain multiple objects so that a Tag-key in a category can be contributed multiple times. Figure 4 shows the Tag-keys ranking for the major road category. According to the amounts of Tag-keys repeatedly contributed, we can find that the top seven Tag-keys account for 80.92% of the total amounts of objects and it also means that these seven Tag-keys are frequently used. Therefore, we firstly explore implicit relationships among the seven Tag-keys.

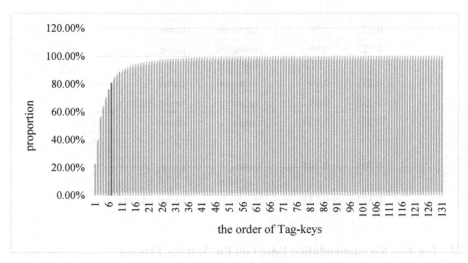

Fig. 4. Cumulative distribution of Tag-keys

After 19467 objects and 131 kinds of Tag-keys are processed by association rule mining algorithm, 57 rules are obtained, part of which is shown in Table 2. It is easy to see that four Tag-keys, i.e., 'oneway', 'highway', 'lanes', and 'name', often occur together when users contribute major road objects. It means that these four keys are the attributes volunteers pay attention to most. However, there are many redundant rules in the total 57 ones. And they look a little unordered. Obviously, it is difficult to recommend directly proper tags by using these unprocessed rules. For this reason, the Markov process is utilized to process these mined rules.

Table 2. The part of mining rules with minimum support = 0.2, minimum confidence = 0.5

Support	Confidence	Antecedent items	Consequent items
0.752	1	name	highway
0.742	1	oneway	highway
0.207	1	bridge	highway
0.334	1	ref	highway
0.211	1	layer	highway
0.572	1	oneway, name	highway
0.222	1	lanes, name	highway
⋮	⋮	⋮	⋮
0.222	0.99	name:en	name
0.222	0.99	name:en, highway	name
0.222	0.99	name:en	name
0.222	0.99	name:en	name, highway
0.264	0.938	lanes	oneway
⋮	⋮	⋮	⋮
0.209	0.741	lanes, highway	name, oneway
0.572	0.572	highway	name, oneway

4.2 Tag-Key Recommendation Based on the Markov Process

In this section, we will show how to use the Markov process to get a recommended sequence using the generated mining rules. Markov process is a random process that goes through the transition from one state to another. It has characteristics of 'no memory', which means the probability distribution of the next state only is determined by the current state. The following includes some important definitions in the Markov process.

- Definition 3. The state space consists of random variables $X_1, X_2, X_3 \cdots$. Each variable X_i has several different possible values, the set of all their possible values is denoted by $SS(X_1, X_2, \cdots, X_i)$.
- Definition 4. The probability of moving from one state to another is called the transition probability, and TP_{ij} represents the probability of state X_i going to state X_j.

- Definition 5. All the transition probabilities will form a matrix, and this matrix is called the transition probability matrix, and TPR$_{ss}$ represents the transition probability matrix in the SS($X_1, X_2, \cdots, X_i$).

$$TRP_{SS} = \begin{bmatrix} T_{11} & T_{12} & \cdots & T_{1i} \\ T_{21} & T_{22} & \cdots & T_{2i} \\ T_{31} & T_{32} & \cdots & T_{3i} \\ \vdots & \vdots & \ddots & \vdots \\ T_{i1} & T_{i2} & \cdots & T_{ii} \end{bmatrix} \tag{1}$$

In the process, the frequent 1-item sets of Tag-keys mined by FP-Growth are considered as Markov random variables, to construct the state space. The Tag-key selected by the user is regarded as the current state, and the next state is the random variable with the highest probability. The following is a brief description of the Markov model construction process.

1. Determining the state space of the Markov process. The state space consists of the Tag-keys involving in frequent 1-item sets mined by the FP-Growth algorithm.
2. Constructing the state transition matrix. There is no transition probability among Tag-keys. However, the confidence among Tag-keys is very similar to the probability when it comes to tag recommendation. Therefore, we use confidence to build the state transition matrix for the Tag-keys. Then, the matrix is normalized.
3. Defining the current state vector. The vector consists of the recommended Tag-key set. If the Tag-keys have been contributed, vector set 1, otherwise 0. And the vector is normalized.

After the pivotal concepts are set, the recommended probabilities of the Tag-key are calculated by the formula of the Markov process. Table 3 shows the results of Tag-keys being recommended for the current state, named ['highway', 'lanes']. The probability of the Tag-key represents the degree to which the user adds the corresponding Tag-key in the next step. So, 'oneway' and 'name' are the first two recommended Tag-keys.

Table 3. Recommendation probability of Tag-keys

Tag-key	Probability
oneway	24.1%
name	22.7%
ref	13.3%
highway	11.4%
layer	8.1%
bridge	7.8%
name:en	7.1%
lanes	5.1%

4.3 Tag-Key Recommendation Based on an Improved Markov Process

To address the issue of repeating recommendation caused by our first recommendation method and improve the convergence speed of Tag-key recommendation, the Markov process is improved. In this section, we will briefly describe our second proposed method. The main difference between the two methods is that the state transition matrix of the latter one will be changed when the state vector is updated. The transition probability of Tag-key that exists in the current state vector is set to 0 in the next state transition matrix. For example, the recommended Tag-key set is ['highway', 'name', 'oneway', 'ref', 'lanes'] and the user has selected the tag ['highway', 'lanes'], the state transition matrix should be updated as Table 4. The improved Markov process's results are presented and discussed in Sect. 5.

Table 4. The state transition matrix under ['highway', 'lanes'], conf is the confidence

	highway	name	oneway	ref	lanes
highway	0	conf	conf	conf	0
name	0	conf	conf	conf	0
One-way	0	conf	conf	conf	0
ref	0	conf	conf	conf	0
lanes	0	conf	conf	conf	0

5 Results and Analysis

In this section, we first compare the correctness and applicability of the two recommended results respectively. All results are based on the same situation that the user's contributing Tag-keys are ['highway', 'lanes']. The minimum support and minimum confidence values are 0.2, 0.5, respectively.

To explore the performance of the recommendation algorithm, we analyze by combining our recommended results with official statistics from the Taginfo (https://taginfo. openstreetmap.org/). Taginfo is a dataset for aggregating and analyzing information about OSM tags, from which the top 10 tag statistical results are shown in Table 5. The statistics from Taginfo are based on global OSM data. Table 3 indicates the result of the first method. Each of the frequent 1-item Tag-keys has its own recommended probability. Figure 5 shows the result of class 'highway = motorway' of the second method. When the first recommendation, 'oneway' (light blue) has the highest probability at all Tag-keys, and then the second recommendation is 'name' (red). It can be discovered that the results of the two proposed methods are generally consistent with the official statistics results (Table 5).

Table 5. The official results from the Taginfo website. (Other keys probability represent the probability of objects with 'highway = motorway' that also have other tags/keys. 'highway = motorway' probability represent the probability of objects with other tags/keys that also have 'highway = motorway')

Rank	Other keys probability	Other keys*	highway = motorway probability
1	99.67	oneway = *	5.78
2	98.16	oneway = yes	7.23
3	84.48	ref = *	6.69
4	85.70	lanes = *	7.33
5	66.18	name = *	0.80
6	60.41	maxspeed = *	4.56
7	39.78	surface = *	1.12
8	37.25	layer = *	4.26
9	33.89	bridge = *	6.87
10	32.66	bridge = yes	6.79

Although with high similarity, there are still subtle differences between the recommended lists with official data. First, with our two recommended methods, some tags, have a high rank in the official results ('maxspeed', 'surface'), are missing. This phenomenon reflects the distinction between Chinese users with other countries' contributors about road cognition and editing habits. When it comes to a motorway, Chinese users pay more attributes to one-way and lanes than maximum speed, surface material, etc. Second, compared with the official data, our recommended methods have an especial Tag-key 'name:en', which is caused by different languages cultures. Some Tag-keys may have different meanings around the world due to different languages and customs. For example, attribute 'name' often be described using Chinese name in China, however English name in the US and other English-speaking countries. So 'name:en' means the English name of the objects. It is only needed by countries where English is not the official language.

It can be seen in Fig. 5 that 'highway' (brown) and 'lanes' (black) are the zero-probability events in the first-round recommendation because ['highway', 'lanes'] is chosen as the initial state at this experiment and they should not be recommended as the current state. Afterwards, when 'oneway' is selected as a candidate, the current state update to ['highway', 'lanes', 'oneway'], so ['highway'], ['lanes'], ['oneway'] are the zero-probability events in the second-round recommendation. By contrast, it can be drawn from Table 3 that 'highway' can be recommended in our first recommendation algorithm, even the current state is ['highway', 'lanes']. Therefore, the improved method can address the problem of repeat recommendations of the first method and improve the recommendation speed. It has better applicability than the first proposed method in OSM tags recommendation.

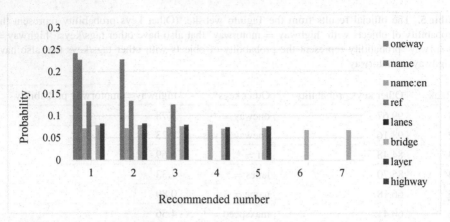

Fig. 5. Automatic recommendation results of our methods (Color figure online)

6 Discussions and Conclusions

To address the issue of OSM quality due to the lack of valid tag constraints when OSM users contribute tags, we propose two methods that utilize FP-Growth and Markov process. Although the first method can recommend Tag-keys, it has drawbacks as repeating recommendation and convergence. The latter one with the improved Markov process effectively addresses these issues by changing its state transition matrix. Finally, by combining our experiment with the official data, the correctness and applicability of our proposed methods are verified. At the same time, it is also discovered that there are some differences in the perception of objects and the meaning of Tag-key between users in different regions.

However, the proposed method has an issue that we only consider the frequency factors when recommending Tag-keys. In fact, not only the high-frequency Tag-keys worthy of recommendation but the ones that low frequency, especially contributed by professional users also have reference value. Meanwhile, multi-modal data will open countless opportunities for research [19]. Hence, taking other metrics, such as the contributor's trust level, into account will be researched in the next step.

Acknowledgment. This project was funded by the National Natural Science Foundation of China (41871320, 61872139), Provincial and Municipal Joint Fund of Hunan Provincial Natural Science Foundation of China (2018JJ4052), Hunan Provincial Natural Science Foundation of China (2017JJ2081), the Key Project of Hunan Provincial Education Department (17A070, 19A172), the Project Supported by Scientific Research Fund of Hunan Provincial Education Department (No. 18K060).

References

1. Goodchild, M.F.: Citizens as sensors: the world of volunteered geography. GeoJournal **69**(4), 211–221 (2007)

2. Mooney, P., Corcoran, P.: The annotation process in OpenStreetMap. Trans. GIS **16**(4), 561–579 (2012)
3. Majic, I., Winter, S., Tomko, M.: Finding equivalent keys in OpenStreetMap: semantic similarity computation based on extensional definitions. In: Geoal17: ACM Sigspatial Workshop on Artificial Intelligence & Deep Learning for Geographic Knowledge Discovery (2017)
4. Vandecasteele, A., Devillers, R.: Improving volunteered geographic information quality using a tag recommender system: the case of OpenStreetMap. In: Jokar Arsanjani, J., Zipf, A., Mooney, P., Helbich, M. (eds.) OpenStreetMap in GIScience. LNGC, pp. 59–80. Springer, Cham (2015). https://doi.org/10.1007/978-3-319-14280-7_4
5. Karagiannakis, N., Giannopoulos, G., Skoutas, D., Athanasiou, S.: OSMRec tool for automatic recommendation of categories on spatial entities in OpenStreetMap. In: Proceedings of 9th ACM Conference on Recommender Systems, pp. 337–338 (2015)
6. Ludwig, C., Fendrich, S., Zipf, A.: Regional variations of context-based association rules in OpenStreetMap. Trans. GIS **25**, 602–621 (2020)
7. Jacobs, K., Mitchell, S.W.: OpenStreetMap quality assessment using unsupervised machine learning methods. Trans. GIS **24**(5), 1280–1298 (2020)
8. Girres, J.F., Touya, G.: Quality assessment of the French OpenStreetMap dataset. Trans. GIS **14**(4), 435–459 (2010)
9. Zielstra, D., Hochmair, H.H., Neis, P.: Assessing the effect of data imports on the completeness of OpenStreetMap – a United States case study. Trans. GIS **17**(3), 315–334 (2013)
10. Tian, Y.J., Zhou, Q., Fu, X.: An analysis of the evolution, completeness and spatial patterns of OpenStreetMap building data in China. Int. J. Geo Inf. **8**(1), 35 (2019)
11. Truong, Q.T., De. Runz, C., Touya, G.: Analysis of collaboration networks in OpenStreetMap through weighted social multigraph mining. Int. J. Geogr. Inf. Sci. **33**(8), 1651–1682 (2018)
12. Ballatore, A., Bertolotto, M., Wilson, D.C.: Geographic knowledge extraction and semantic similarity in OpenStreetMap. Knowl. Inf. Syst. **37**(1), 61–81 (2012). https://doi.org/10.1007/s10115-012-0571-0
13. Ballatore, A., Wilson, D.C., Bertolotto, M.: Computing the semantic similarity of geographic terms using volunteered lexical definitions. Int. J. Geogr. Inf. Sci. **27**(10), 2099–2118 (2013)
14. Ali, A.L., Schmid, F., Al-Salman, R., Kauppinen, T.: Ambiguity and plausibility. In: ACM Sigspatial International Conference, pp.143–152 (2014)
15. Ali, A.L., Falomir, Z., Schmid, F., Freksa, C.: Rule-guided human classification of volunteered geographic information. ISPRS J. Photogramm. Remote Sens. **127**, 3–15 (2017)
16. Kashian, A., Rajabifard, A., Richter, K.F., Chen, Y.: Automatic analysis of positional plausibility for points of interest in OpenStreetMap using coexistence patterns. Int. J. Geogr. Inf. Sci. **33**(7), 1420–1443 (2019)
17. Agrawal, R., Srikant, R.: Fast algorithms for mining association rules in large databases. In: Very Large Data Bases, pp. 487–499 (1994)
18. Han, J., Pei, J.: Mining frequent patterns without candidate generation. ACM SIGMOD Rec. **29**(2), 1–12 (2000)
19. Vargas, J., Srivastava, S., Tuia, D., Falcao, A.: OpenStreetMap: challenges and opportunities in machine learning and remote sensing. IEEE Geosci. Remote Sens. Mag. **9**, 184–199 (2020)

Data Processing and Development of Big Data System: A Survey

Shuyan Yu(✉)

Shaoxing University Yuanpei College, Shaoxing 312000, China

Abstract. At present, data are generated all the time in the world, and these data contain great value. However, these data have problems such as huge scale, complex type, fast flow rate and low value density. Therefore, the research of big data analysis means and tools has increasingly become a research hotspot. On the basis of research at home and abroad, this paper attempts to analyze the definition, framework and typical big data processing systems of big data, especially focuses on the analysis and comparison of batch data processing system, stream data processing system, hybrid processing system and graph processing system, and obtains the characteristics, processing mechanism and applicable occasions of each system. The paper hopes to provide some references for understanding big data systems, solving problems in the process of big data processing and developing big data applications, and provide reference for improving the effectiveness and efficiency of data processing.

Keywords: Big data · Big data processing system · Batch processing · Stream processing

1 Introduction

With the continuous integration of multimedia, Internet of Things, social networking and other technologies into people's lives, the number and types of data have exploded. These data come from mobile devices, German transmitters, wearable devices and so on. For example, Internet search engines support billions of Web searches every day and process tens of thousands of terabytes of data which are transmitted every day in communication networks all over the world [1–4]. The application of information technology in the fields of science, technology and engineering has also produced huge amounts of data, such as optical monitoring and monitoring, which are generating data all the time. According to the research and analysis of data company Internet Data Center (IDC), 2025, the global data circle will mount to 175ZB [5] (Fig. 1).

People see great opportunities and value through these huge data. A large number of big data processing technologies and systems have been applied. At the same time, people are faced with many more challenges in the process of data processing. On the basis of research at home and abroad, this paper attempts to analyze the definition of big data, big data system framework, and typical big data processing systems, hoping to provide some reference for further understanding of big data platform and developing big data applications.

© Springer Nature Switzerland AG 2021
X. Sun et al. (Eds.): ICAIS 2021, CCIS 1423, pp. 420–431, 2021.
https://doi.org/10.1007/978-3-030-78618-2_34

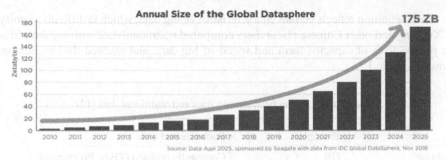

Fig. 1. Annual size of the global datasphere [5]

2   Big Data Definition

Regarding the definition of big data, the industry and academia have not yet reached a consensus.

The "4Vs feature model" is a definition method widely used by researchers. The 4 V model describes that big data has four characteristics: huge data capacity, diverse data types, fast change speed and low value density from four dimensions: Volume, Variety, Velocity and Veracity. As early as 2001, Laney Douglas an analyst at IDCMETA Group, the international data center of IT analysis company, put forward the "3Vs" model of data [10]. He pointed out that the growth of data is three-dimensional, that is, the growth of capacity, diversity and speed [6]. Then in 2011, IDC, the international data center, proposed: "Big data technology describes a new era of technology and system, which is designed to extract the value of data from large-scale and diversified data through high-speed capture, discovery and analysis technology [7]." Some scholars also put forward the "5Vs" model, and put forward the Veracity based on the first 4 V [8].

In addition, there are two definitions that are of great significance in the field of big data research:

First, from the perspective of comparison, it expresses the process of data evolution. In the report of McKinsey Company in 2011, big data was defined as a data set whose size exceeded the acquisition, storage, management and analysis capabilities of conventional database tools [6]. Wikipedia points out that big data are a large and complex data set which is difficult to deal with by using existing database management tools or traditional data processing techniques.

The second puts forward the concept of big data from the level of system and framework. Typical is the concept of big data proposed by NIST, National Institute of Standards and Technology [11]: "Big data means that the capacity of data, the speed of data acquisition or the representation of data limit the ability to analyze and process data using traditional relational methods, and it is necessary to use a horizontal expansion mechanism to improve processing efficiency." In addition, big data can be further subdivided into big data science and big data frameworks. Big data science is a research covering big data acquisition, regulation and evaluation technology; Big data framework is a software library and algorithm for distributed processing and analysis of big data problems among computing unit clusters. The instantiation of one or more big data frameworks is the big data infrastructure.

Each definition reflects certain characteristics of big data, which is difficult to unify. Li Xuelong and other Chinese researchers compared traditional data with big data from the perspectives of capacity, form and speed of big data, and reached the conclusions shown in Table 1:

Table 1. Comparison between big data and traditional data [12].

	Example	Font size and style
Volume	GB	Constantly updated (TB or PB currently)
Generated rate	Per hour, day,…	More rapid
Structure	Structured	Semi-structured or un-structured
Data source	Centralized	Fully distributed
Data integration	Easy	Difficult
Data store	RDBMS	HDFS, NoSQL
Access	Interactive	Batch or near real-time

3   Research Status at Home and Abroad

In September, 2008, Science published an article "Big Data: Science in the Petabyte Era", and the word big data was widely spread. The development and application of big data has attracted great attention from government departments all over the world. Since 2009, the US government has opened 400,000 original government data sets. In March 2012, the "Big Data Research and Development Initiative" was put forward, and the global open government data campaign was launched, with an investment of 200 million US dollars to promote the research and application of big data core technologies, involving six government departments and institutions including NSF and DARPA. Big data has become the cross-cutting and core field of American national innovation strategy, national security strategy and national information network security strategy [9]. Most research projects in the United States focus on the technical challenges brought by big data, mainly considering big data analysis algorithms and system efficiency. In November 2010, the Communication Commission of the European Union submitted the report "Open Data: Engine of Innovation, Growth and Transparent Governance" to the European Parliament, which focused on open data and formulated strategies to deal with the challenges of big data. In November 2011, the report was adopted by the EU Digital Agenda, and this strategy was officially promoted on December 12. Britain, France, Japan and other developed countries have also introduced policies to promote the research and application of big data.

Academia and industry have also acted one after another and cooperated to a certain extent. For example, the Massachusetts Institute of Technology established the Big Data Science and Technology Center (ISTC), which unites many universities and many international industrial giants such as Intel, Microsoft and EMC to explore solutions for sharing, storing and operating big data. IBM has reached agreements with thousands of universities around the world to cooperate in joint research, teaching and industry application case development of big data.

The research and application of big data has also been carried out earlier in China. In March 2012, the Ministry of Science and Technology issued the "Guidelines for the Collection of Alternative Projects in the Information Technology Field of the 12th Five-Year National Science and Technology Plan in 2013", which clearly stated "Advanced Storage Structure and Key Technologies for Big Data". In 2013, Shanghai put forward the Three-Year Action Plan for Promoting Big Data Research and Development in Shanghai, and Chongqing put forward the Notice of Chongqing Municipal People's Government on Printing and Distributing Chongqing Big Data Action Plan. In 2014, Guangdong Province established the Big Data Administration, which is responsible for researching, formulating and organizing the implementation of big data strategies, plans and policies, and guiding and promoting the research and application of big data. Guizhou, Henan, Chengde and other provinces and cities have also launched their own big data development plans, and then all provinces and cities have gradually set up big data management institutions. In August 2015, the State Council issued the "Action Plan for Promoting Big Data Development" with Guofa [2015] No. 50. The outline pointed out that data has become a national basic strategic resource [13]. In October 2017, Comrade Xi Jinping emphasized in the report of the 19th National Congress of the Communist Party of China that it is necessary to promote the deep integration of big data and the real economy. On November 3, 2020, the Proposal of the Central Committee of the Communist Party of China on Formulating the Fourteenth Five-Year Plan for National Economic and Social Development and the Long-term Goals for 2035 proposed to speed up digital development, develop digital economy, promote digital industrialization and industrial digitalization, promote the deep integration of digital economy and real economy, and build a digital industrial cluster with international competitiveness. With the continuous popularization of information infrastructure, China's data volume is expected to increase by an average of 30% in the next seven years, and will become the region with the largest data volume by 2025 [5].

Many Chinese universities and research institutions have set up big data research institutions. Academic organizations and activities related to big data have also been established and carried out. Actively carry out activities in academic research and technological innovation of big data. In 2012, china computer federation and china institute of communications established the Big Data Expert Committee, and the Ministry of Education established the "Sashi Big Data Analysis and Management International Research Center" at Renmin University; In June 2016, China Communications Enterprise Association Communication Network Special Committee, Beijing University of Posts and Telecommunications, Huawei and many other enterprises, universities, scientific research institutions and investment institutions established China Big Data Technology and Application Alliance; All provinces and cities have also established associations and organizations related to big data.

4 Big Data Dystem Framework

For different applications, big data systems usually involve many different stages. According to the life cycle of big data, a typical big data system can be divided into four stages, including data generation, data acquisition, data storage, data analysis and use.

4.1 Data Generation

Li Xuelong and other researchers divide the data generation model into three stages [12]: (1) In the 1990s, a large number of structured data were stored in the management systems of enterprises and institutions; (2) At the end of 1990s, web1.0 system produced a lot of semi-structured and unstructured data. After that, web2.0 applications generated user-created content from online social networks; (3) Mobile-centered networks produce highly mobile, location-aware, personal-centered and context-related data.

According to the characteristics of data, we usually divide data into batch data, stream data, interactive data and graph data. Batch data refers to the data which is stored in the hard disk in static form, with high accuracy, but seldom updated, long storage time, reusable, but low data value density. For example, data accumulated for a long time after enterprise informationization; In the field of Internet, multimedia data, user data and so on generated by social networks. Stream data usually refers to data collected in real time, such as server logs, intelligent monitoring, stock and futures trading markets, etc., Interactive data is the data generated by the system and users in the way of man-machine conversation, such as man-machine interactive data in online transaction processing and online analysis processing, data generated by various question-and-answer platforms such as search engines, instant messaging tools, Baidu Know, and so on. Many big data are presented in the form of large-scale graphs or networks, Graph data structure can well express the correlation between data, so it has a good performance in social networks, transportation and science. Data generated by man-machine conversation, such as man-machine interaction data in online transaction processing and online analytical processing, data generated by various question-and-answer platforms such as search engines, instant messaging tools and Baidu Know, etc. Many big data are presented in the form of large-scale graphs or networks. Graph data structure can well express the correlation between data, so it has a good performance in social networks, transportation and science.

4.2 Acquisition of Data

The raw data is collected by sensors, log files, Web crawlers, ETL tools, and some real-time collection tools like Flume, and then stored in the data center. Data centers usually have a certain mechanism to store and allocate data. The original data is pre-processed by integration, cleaning, redundancy elimination, etc., and the data set for specific requirements is obtained.

4.3 Storage of Data

After data is acquired, it is stored in a specific medium for downstream system analysis. The research on big data storage began in 2005, and technologies such as Direct attached storage (DAS), Network attached storage (NAS) and Storage area network (SAN) were deeply studied. Distributed file system is the main technology to deal with big data storage at present. The mainstream distributed file systems are GFS (Google File System), HDFS (Hadoop Distributed File System), Ceph (Open Source Distributed Storage Project), Lustre (Cluster File System developed by SUM Company), TFS (Taobao File System). IDC predicts that by 2025, 49% of the global stored data will reside in the public cloud environment [5]. Storage virtualization proposed in the field of cloud computing will become a hot spot of big data storage technology.

4.4 Analysis and Use of Data

Data analysis is the most valuable stage in the whole system, and its goal is to extract the hidden data in the data, and provide meaningful suggestions and help decision-making for users. According to the depth of data analysis, Blackett and others divide data analysis into descriptive analysis, predictive analysis and prescriptive analysis [14]. Descriptive analysis describes what happened according to the data, and derives and summarizes the potential patterns of the data, which are displayed by visual technology The depth of predictive analysis is deeper than descriptive analysis, which is used to predict the future data trends through data and give a certain forecast. Rule analysis has the deepest depth, which is used to analyze the rules between data, make decisions and optimize strategies.

Commonly used data analysis methods include statistical analysis, data mining, data visualization and so on. Statistical analysis is usually based on a certain goal, and statistical theory is applied to descriptive analysis and predictive analysis of data. Regression, factor analysis, clustering and discriminant analysis are commonly used statistical analysis methods. Data mining is to mine hidden rules, namely data patterns, from big data. The research on data mining is mature, including association, classification, clustering and so on. In December 2006, The IEEE International Conference on Data Mining (ICDM), an international authoritative academic organization, selected ten classic algorithms in the field of data mining: C4.5, k-Means, SVM, Apriori, EM, PageRank, AdaBoost, kNN, Naïve Bayes and CART. Although more than ten years have passed, these algorithms still have deep influence in the field of data mining. Data visualization is the hottest analysis method nowadays. Different from the traditional visualization of data, the data of big data is large in scale, complex in structure and dynamic, Therefore, the visualization of big data requires that large-scale, multi-source and dynamic information can be analyzed and presented to users in the form of charts.

5   Typical Big Data Processing System

With the explosive growth of big data, the improvement of minicomputer performance and the development of Internet technology, distributed computing platform has become the mainstream of big data processing system. According to different application scenarios, the typical distributed big data processing systems can be divided into the following categories.

5.1 Batch Data Processing System

Batch data processing system is suitable for the processing of massive pre-stored data, which requires less real-time processing, but higher data throughput, accuracy and comprehensiveness. The research of Digital World-From Edge to Core predicts that by 2025, the amount of data stored by enterprises will exceed 80% of the total global data. These data provide more useful information for decision makers. Enterprises are rapidly becoming the main data managers in the world of network connection [5].

The typical batch data processing system is Hadoop platform supporting MapReduce model. MapReduce is a simple but powerful programming model, which can distribute large-scale computing tasks to large commercial PC clusters to run in parallel. Its computing model consists of user-defined Map and Reduce. In the map stage, multiple map programs preprocess the input data in parallel. After that, the data is transferred from the map end to reduce through the shuffle process. Finally, the reduce end processes the data globally and then outputs the data to the storage system (Fig. 2).

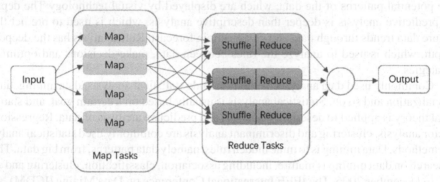

Fig. 2. MapReduce processing model

5.2 Stream Data Processing System

The stream data processing system has a short processing delay, and is suitable for real-time data stream processing, such as real-time log, traffic flow analysis, real-time advertisement positioning and so on. IBM InfoSphere Streams and IBM StreamBase are commercial-grade stream data processing systems. Twitter's Storm and Yahoo's S4 (Simple Scalable Streaming System) are open source streaming computing platforms. Many companies have also launched platforms that combine their own business, such as Puma of Facebook and Dstream of Baidu.

Taking Storm as an example, it is a free and open distributed real-time computing system, which can be easily integrated with the database system, supports multiple programming languages, and is widely used in real-time log processing. Storm's real-time processing performance is excellent, and it can achieve millisecond response. The workflow of Storm is to submit Topology (a real-time application running in streaming) on the client node, and the Nimbus node divides the submitted topology into Tasks, and submits the information related to the task and Supervisor to the Zookeeper cluster, and the supervisor will claim his own task on the Zookeeper cluster and notify his own Worker process to handle the task (Fig. 3).

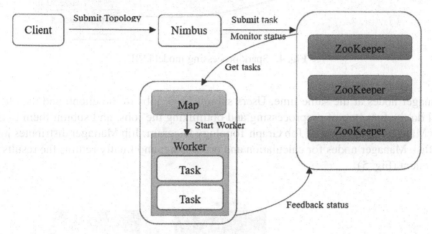

Fig. 3. Storm processing model

5.3 Hybrid Processing System

Hybrid processing system combines the advantages of batch processing and stream processing, and has high system complexity. Typical systems are Spark and Flink.

Spark is another widely used open source computing framework after MapReduce. Spark's programming model is based on the abstract concept called "elastic distributed data set" (RDD), which keeps data objects in memory to reduce the overhead caused by disk and network operations [15], so its performance has been greatly improved. In Spark, the cluster manager manages the cluster, and the Worker is equivalent to the computing node, receiving the master node command and reporting the status; Driver is responsible for controlling the execution of an application. In the execution process of a Spark application, the Driver program is the starting point of application logic execution, which is responsible for job scheduling, that is, Task distribution, and the Worker is used to manage computing nodes and create Executor to process tasks in parallel. In the execution stage, the Driver serializes the file and jar that the Task and the Task depend on and transmits them to the corresponding Worker machine, while the Executor processes the tasks of the corresponding data partition [16] (Fig. 4).

Flink is a real streaming processing engine, and its computing model is dataflow. The final batch processing and real-time flow calculation should be converted into data flow graph for calculation. The Flink runtime starts the Job Manager node and several Task

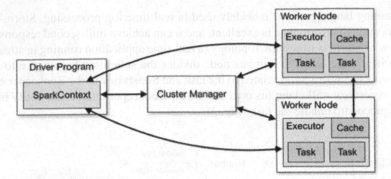

Fig. 4. Spark processing model [18]

Manager nodes at the same time, Users submit Flink jobs to the client, and the client will do the first step of preprocessing and optimizing the jobs, and submit them to the Job Manager in the form of Job Graph Topology Diagram. Job Manager distributes jobs to Task Manager nodes for calculation and processing, and finally returns the results to the client (Fig. 5).

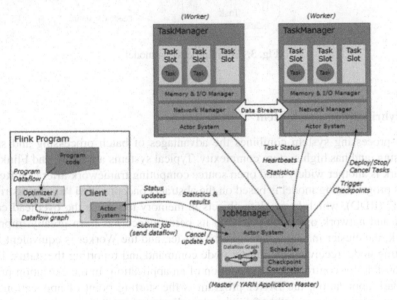

Fig. 5. Flink processing model [18]

Scholars such as Dai Mingzhu evaluated the performance of Spark and Flink under the same conditions, Spark has the best performance, its framework is more mature, and it has advantages in market share and social concern. At the same time, it is pointed out that Flink contains some interesting and novel design concepts, and some design concepts have also been adopted by Spark [19].

5.4   Graph Data Processing System

Graph data processing system is suitable for processing large-scale graph data, and typical systems include Pregel, GraphLab, PowerGraph, GraphChi, GraphX and so on.

Pregel is the earliest system in the field of graph computing, which was developed by Google [20]. Pregel proposed a vertex-centric graph computing programming model, which abstracted each iteration of the algorithm as a computing process that needs to be completed from the perspective of a single vertex, that is, user-defined vertex programs. Each vertex has two States: active and inactive; Only the active vertices need to participate in the calculation in each iteration. In each round, each vertex processes the messages received in the previous round, sends messages to other vertices, and updates its own state and topology. Whether the algorithm can be ended depends on whether all vertices have vote to identify that they have reached halt state. A vertex indicates that it is no longer active by setting its own state to halt. According to the characteristic that graph algorithm usually needs iterative calculation. Pregel avoids the unnecessary overhead of serializing intermediate results to disk repeatedly [22–26] (Fig. 6).

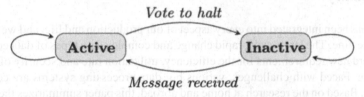

Fig. 6. Pregel processing model [23]

GraphLab is the earliest graph computing system introduced by SELECT laboratory of Carnegie Mellon university at the same time as Pregel. GraphLab is mainly oriented to machine learning/data mining problems. Although it adopts vertex-centered graph computing model, GraphLab is quite different from Pregel in some design decisions: the communication in GraphLab occurs in the state synchronization between different copies of each vertex, rather than the message transmission in Pregel; GraphLab mainly adopts asynchronous computing mode, which ensures the convergence efficiency of the algorithm through various levels of consistency, and Pregel is a typical synchronous computing mode [20]. GraphLab abstracts data into Graph structure, and abstracts the execution process of algorithm based on vertex segmentation into three steps: Gather, Apply and Scatter [21–23].

1. In the gather stage, the edge of the working vertex collects data from the connecting vertex and itself.
2. In the apply stage, mirror sends the calculation results in the gather stage to the master vertex, and the master summarizes and combines the vertex data of the previous step for further calculation, then updates the vertex data of the master and synchronizes it to mirror.
3. In the scatter stage, after the update of the working vertex is completed, update the data on the edge, and inform the neighboring nodes that depend on it of the update status.

As the gather/scatter function takes a single edge as the operation granularity, the gather/scatter function can be called independently by the corresponding nodes for many neighboring edges of a vertex, thus avoiding the problem of Pregel model (Fig. 7).

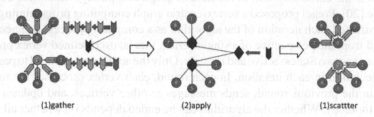

(1)gather   (2)apply   (1)scattter

Fig. 7. GraphLab processing model [22, 23]

6 Summary

Big data has been integrated into every aspect of our production and life, and we generate data all the time. The large scale, rapid change and complex data types of data constantly put forward new requirements for the efficiency, utilization rate and security of our data processing. Faced with challenges, various big data processing systems are constantly emerging. Based on the research at home and abroad, this paper summarizes the big data system framework with the big data life cycle as the main line, and analyzes the typical big data processing systems including batch processing system, stream processing system, batch-stream mixed processing system and graph processing system.

References

1. Canaj, E., Xhuvani, A.: Big data in cloud computing: a review of key technologies and open issues. In: Barolli, L., Xhafa, F., Javaid, N., Spaho, E., Kolici, V. (eds.) EIDWT 2018. LNDECT, vol. 17, pp. 504–513. Springer, Cham (2018). https://doi.org/10.1007/978-3-319-75928-9_45
2. Beniamino, D.M., Rocco, A., Giuseppina, C., Antonio, E., Joanna, K.: Big data (lost) in the cloud. Int. J. Big Data Intell. **1**(1), 3–17 (2014)
3. Chen, M., Mao, S., Liu, Y.: Big data: a survey. Mob. Netw. Appl. **19**(2), 171–209 (2014). https://doi.org/10.1007/s11036-013-0489-0
4. Bello-Orgaz, G., Jung, J., Camacho, D.: Social big data: recent achievements and new challenges. Inf. Fusion **28**, 45–59 (2016)
5. The Digitization of the World: From Edge to Core. https://resources.moredrect.com/white-papers/idc-report-the-digitization-of-the-world-from-edge-to-core. Accessed 27 Nov 2018
6. Big data: the next frontier for innovation, competition, and productivity. https://www.mckinsey.com/business-functions/mckinsey-digital/our-insights/big-data-the-next-frontier-for-innovation. Accessed 1 May 2011
7. Extracting Value from Chaos. https://www.smartdatacollective.com/digital-universe-study-extracting-value-chaos/. Accessed 27 June 2011
8. Liu, C.: Market research and forecast. Mech. Ind. press **8**(1), 84–85 (2017)

9. Zikopoulos, P., Eaton, C.: Understanding Big Data: Analytics for Enterprise Class Hadoop and Streaming Data, 1st edn. McGraw-Hill Osborne Media, New York (2011)
10. 3D Data Management: Controlling Data Volume, Velocity, and Variety. https://www.bibson omy.org/bibtex/742811cb00b303261f79a98e9b80bf49. Accessed 1 Feb 2001
11. Kumar, A., Maskara, S., Chiang, I.: Identifying semantic in high-dimensional web data using latent semantic manifold. J. Data Anal. Inf. Process. **3**(4), 136–152 (2015)
12. Li, X., Gong, H.: Overview of big data system. Sci. China **45**(1), 1–44 (2015)
13. Notice on Printing and Distributing the Action Plan for Promoting Big Data Development. http://www.gov.cn/zhengce/content/2015-09-05/content_10137.html Accessed 05 Sept 2015
14. The digital universe decade-are you ready. https://www.researchgate.net/publication/229124 759_The_Digital_Universe_Decade_-_Are_You_Ready. Accessed 05 Jan 2010
15. Zaharia, M., Chowdhury, M., Franklin, M., Shenker, S. and Stoica, I.: Spark: cluster computing with working sets. In: Proceedings of the 2nd USENIX conference on Hot topics in cloud computing, pp. 10–17. USENIX Association, USA (2010)
16. Apache Spark. http://spark.apache.org/. Accessed 18 Apr 2020
17. Apache Flink. https://flink.apache.org/. Accessed 26 May 2020
18. Yong, T.: Comparative study on calculation models of spark and flink. Comput. Products Circ. **2**(4), 152–153 (2019)
19. Dai, M., Gao, S.: Performance evaluation of large-scale data analysis based on hadoop, spark and flink. J. Chin. Acad. Electron. Sci. **13**(2), 149–155 (2018)
20. We knew the web was big. https://googleblog.blogspot.com/2008/07/we-knew-web-was-big.html. Accessed 25 July 2008
21. Pregel. http://kowshik.github.io/Jpregel/. Accessed 25 July 2009
22. Brief History of Graph Computing System Development. https://zhuanlan.zhihu.com/p/791 69412 . Accessed 21 Oct 2019
23. Comparison of GOD_WAR, GraphX, GraphLab, Pregel. https://blog.csdn.net/young_0609/article/details/101021094Accessed 19 Sept 2019
24. Sun, L., Yu, Q., Peng, D., Subramani, S., Wang, X.: a fog-based framework for disease prognosis based medical sensor data streams. Comput. Mater. Continua **66**(1), 603–619 (2021)
25. Alhroob, A., Alzyadat, W., Imam, A.T., Jaradat, G.M.: The genetic algorithm and binary search technique in the program path coverage for improving software testing using big data. Intell. Autom. Soft Comput. **26**(4), 725–733 (2020)
26. Mirarab, A., Mirtaheri, S.L., Asghari, S.A.: A model to create organizational value with big data analytics. Comput. Syst. Sci. Eng. **35**(2), 69–79 (2020)

Current PHM Surveys for Mechanical Engineering

Jing Tong$^{(\boxtimes)}$

Nanjing Vocational Institute of Mechatronic Technology, Nanjing 211135, China

Abstract. PHM technology has played more and more important in the current mechanical engineering and acted as an intelligent solution to improve the availability of manufacturing systems. PHM consists of system health monitoring, feature extraction, fault diagnosis, and fault prognosis through remaining useful life estimation. With the help of various fault models, artificial intelligence algorithms, monitoring diagnosis, prediction techniques, PHM also uses a large number of condition monitoring data and information to improve the safety and working life of mechanical devices, minimizes the impact of device failures, and avoids the major accidents caused by the mechanical device malfunctions. In this article, several classical PHM surveys and reviews central to nowadays mechanical engineering are studied, ranging from typical PHM frameworks, practical PHM solutions, to concrete PHM approaches. And these related insightful literatures are surveyed and introduced, which could help more readers to better understand the PHM technologies in reshaping the modernization of current mechanical engineering

Keywords: PHM · Mechanical engineering · Intelligent solution

1 Introduction

The acceleration of social and economic construction has put forward higher requirements for industrial production. As vital components in industrial production, mechanical engineering must be analyzed for its service life. The effective analysis can ensure the continuity and rationality of the production process. One solution is to use the prognostics and health management or PHM [1–5] technology, which has played more and more important in the current mechanical engineering and acted as an intelligent solution to improve the availability of manufacturing systems. PHM consists of system health monitoring, feature extraction, fault diagnosis, and fault prognosis through remaining useful life estimation [6]. With the help of various fault models, artificial intelligence algorithms, monitoring diagnosis, prediction techniques, PHM also uses a large number of condition monitoring data and information to improve the safety and working life of mechanical devices, minimizes the impact of device failures, and avoids the major accidents caused by the mechanical device malfunctions. In this article, several classical PHM surveys and reviews central to nowadays mechanical engineering are studied ranging from typical PHM frameworks, practical PHM solutions, to concrete PHM approaches. And these related insightful literatures are also surveyed and introduced,

© Springer Nature Switzerland AG 2021
X. Sun et al. (Eds.): ICAIS 2021, CCIS 1423, pp. 432–440, 2021.
https://doi.org/10.1007/978-3-030-78618-2_35

which could help more readers to better understand the PHM technologies in reshaping the modernization of current mechanical engineering.

2 Related Works

How to enhance the reliability of a mechanical system is a crucial problem in many industrial applications, which requires efficient and effective system health monitoring methods including processing and analyzing large amount of device data to detect anomalies and perform prognosis. Among many promising techniques, deep learning [6–10] has been a rapidly growing field for PHM in terms of interpreting monitoring signals like vibration, acoustics, and pressure. Behnoush Rezaeianjouybari and et al. [5] provided a systematic review of state-of-the-art deep learning-based PHM frameworks. The authors presented the benefits and potentials of state-of-the-art deep neural networks for system health management, and showcased the typical modules of the traditional PHM cycle as presented in Fig. 1 [5].

According to [5] and Fig. 1, the deep learning based PHM model includes:

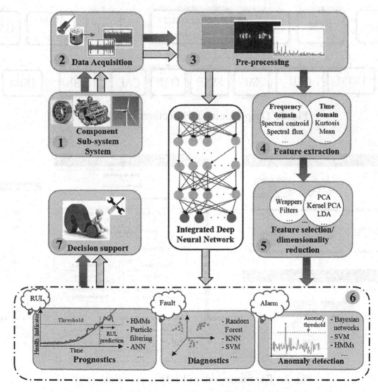

Fig. 1. Deep learning based PHM model [5]

In Fig. 1, the PHM process includes: 1) data accusation which is considered as one of the most important steps in the PHM process because its outcome affects the quality of data and the performance of PHM; 2) data preprocessing in which raw data collected from various sensors can be processed to produce better features; 3) feature extraction which either belongs to physics-based approach or data-driven approach will affect the performance of fault diagnosis and prognosis; 4) fault diagnosis which is mainly used to detect faults or abnormal conditions of systems and identify components that can potentially cause system failures; 5) fault prognosis which is used to predict the remaining time until failure and the time to prevent failure [11–16].

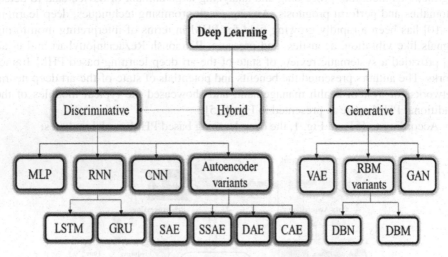

Fig. 2. Deep learning architectures in PHM [5]

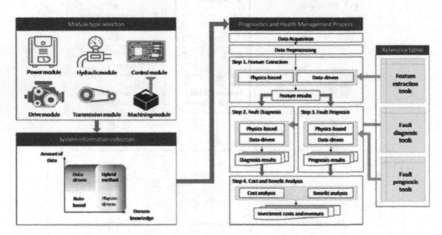

Fig. 3. The framework of PHM applications [16]

Further, the deep learning architectures in PHM was also presented in [5] as is shown in Fig. 2.

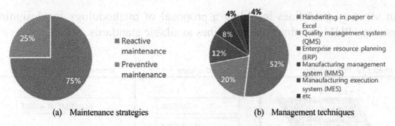

(a) Maintenance strategies   (b) Management techniques

Fig. 4. Maintenance strategies and techniques [16]

The application of PHM to manufacturing systems is a challenging task especially for small and medium-sized enterprises because of the lack of resources for research and development. Insun Shin and et al. [16] developed a framework to provide a readily usable and accessible guideline for PHM applications with regard to manufacturing systems. The authors also presented a survey to gather the current practices in dealing with system failures and maintenance strategies, and a framework was developed for giving a guideline for PHM application based on common core modules across manufacturing systems as is shown in Fig. 3 and the maintenance strategies and techniques as is presented in Fig. 4 [16].

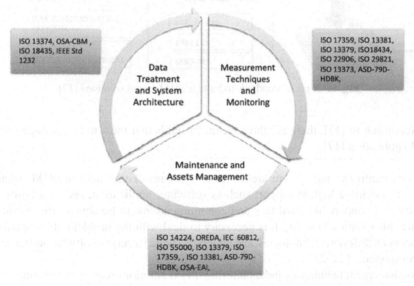

Fig. 5. Typical related standards on PHM solutions [17]

Regarding the mechanical maintenance, PHM is an import factor for reaching more proactive maintenance preparation. The applications of PHM depends on the development of general methodological approaches to guide the design process of maintenance strategies, in which the potential of PHM can be exploited [17]. Antonio J. Guillén and et al. [17] offered a revision of some of the available standards as is shown in Fig. 5

that can serve as guidelines including a proposal of methodology for designing and implementing PHM solutions that combines available standards.

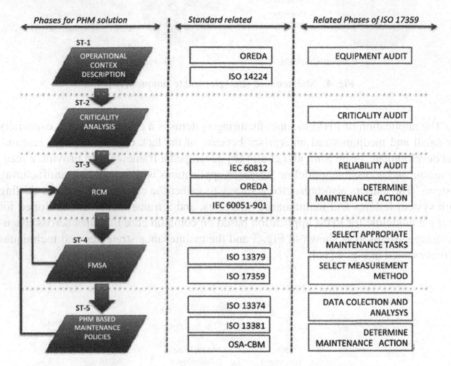

Fig. 6. A set of standards to build a PHM-based solutions [17]

According to [17], there are three technical fields that must to be combined in any PHM application [17]:

1) Data treatment and system architecture. The aim of this field in PHM solutions is to provide a logical support such as software, application, and data bases, and physical support like hardware and communications, to be able to implement and use this solution [18–20]. It is necessary to deal with the problem of compatibility between different technologies, and integrate a wide variety of software and hardware components [21–23].

2) Measurement techniques and monitoring. PHM solutions require monitoring a large number of product parameters to evaluate the health of a product [24–28]. These parameters include operational and environmental loads as well as the performance conditions of the product.

3) Maintenance and assets management. This field includes specific standards to maintenance issues and the standards that address the functional conception of the system and the relation with the rest of the business [29–32].

In addition, the authors in [17] also proposed a practical combined use of standards for PHM-Based solutions including the following 5 steps as is shown in Fig. 6:

1) Step 1: to define the indenture levels and the description of operational contexts;
2) Step 2: to choose the most important systems within the installation, plant or business that are being studied;
3) Step 3: include the two main outputs of the RCM analysis that are the failure mode definition and the election of maintenance activities over every failure mode;
4) Step 4: describe the symptoms of the failure and obtains measures of this symptoms;
5) Step 5: design the related algorithms and PHM policies using the information provided by Step 4.

Finally, there also exist some other PHM methods such as data driven method and a fusion prognostics method as shown in Fig. 7 and 8 that were discussed in [33–38].

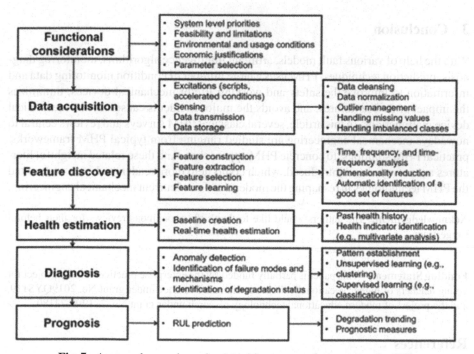

Fig. 7. A general procedure of a data-driven approach to prognostics [33]

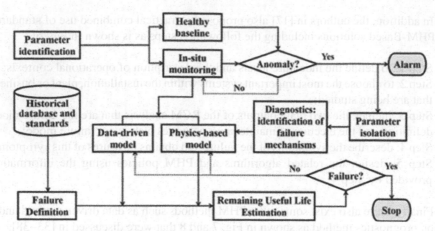

Fig. 8. A fusion prognostics approach [33]

3 Conclusion

With the help of various fault models, artificial intelligence algorithms, monitoring diagnosis, prediction techniques, PHM uses a large number of condition monitoring data and information to improve the safety and working life of mechanical devices, minimizes the impact of device failures, and avoids the major accidents caused by the mechanical device malfunctions. In this article, several classical PHM surveys and reviews central to nowadays mechanical engineering are studied ranging from typical PHM frameworks, practical PHM solutions, to concrete PHM approaches. And these related insightful literatures are surveyed and introduced, which could help more readers to better understand the PHM technologies in reshaping the modernization of current mechanical engineering.

Acknowledgement. The authors would like to thank the anonymous reviews for their helpful suggestions.

Funding Statement. This paper is partially funded by the enterprise practice training project for young teachers of higher vocational colleges in Jiangsu Province under grant No. 2019QYS119, and the project of modern educational technology research under grant No. 2019-R-72180.

References

1. Omri, N., Masry, Z., Mairot, N., Giampiccolo, S., Zerhouni, N.: Industrial data management strategy towards an SME-oriented PHM. J. Manuf. Syst. **56**, 23–36 (2020)
2. Lin, Y., Li, X., Hu, Y.: Deep diagnostics and prognostics: an integrated hierarchical learning framework in PHM applications. Appl. Soft Comput. **72**, 555–564 (2018)
3. Hah, H., Khuntia, J., Kathuria, A., Tan, J.: Rationalizing personal health management (PHM) policy: identifying health IT use patterns via observations of daily living (ODLs) data. Health Policy Technol. **9**(2), 185–193 (2020)
4. Li, R., Verhagen, W., Curran, R.: A systematic methodology for prognostic and health management system architecture definition. Reliab. Eng. Syst. Saf. **193**, 21–32 (2020)

5. Rezaeianjouybari, B., Shang, Y.: Deep learning for prognostics and health management: state of the art, challenges, and opportunities. Measurement **163**, 153–163 (2020)
6. Chen, G., Srihari, S.N.: Revisiting hierarchy: deep learning with orthogonally constrained prior for classification. Pattern Recognit. Lett. **140**, 214–221 (2020)
7. Zhu, Z., Peng, G., Chen, Y., Gao, H.: A convolutional neural network based on a capsule network with strong generalization for bearing fault diagnosis. Neurocomputing **323**, 62–75 (2019)
8. Akinosho, T.D., et al.: Deep learning in the construction industry: a review of present status and future innovations. J. Build. Eng. **32**, 233–255 (2020)
9. Peng, W., Ye, Z.S., Chen, N.: Bayesian deep learning based health prognostics towards prognostics uncertainty. IEEE Trans. Ind. Electron **3**(2), 31–39 (2019)
10. Zhang, J., Wang, P., Yan, R., Gao, R.X.: Long short-term memory for machine remaining life prediction. J. Manuf. Syst **48**, 78–86 (2018)
11. Jin, C., Ompusunggu, A.P., Liu, Z., Ardakani, H.D., Petré, F., Lee, J.: Envelope analysis on vibration signals for stator winding fault early detection in 3-phase induction motors. Int. J. Progn. Health Manag. **6**(1), 1–12 (2015)
12. Hu, C., Smith, W.A., Randall, R.B., Peng, Z.: Development of a gear vibration indicator and its application in gear wear monitoring. Mech. Syst. Signal Process. **76**, 319–336 (2016)
13. An, Q.T., Sun, L., Sun, L.Z.: Current residual vector-based open-switch fault diagnosis of inverters in PMSM drive systems. IEEE Trans. Power Electron. **30**(5), 2814–2827 (2015)
14. Iurinic, L.U., Herrera-Orozco, A.R., Ferraz, R.G., Bretas, A.S.: Distribution systems high-impedance fault location: a parameter estimation approach. IEEE Trans. Power Deliv. **31**(4), 1806–1814 (2016)
15. Li, C., Sanchez, R.V., Zurita, G., Cerrada, M., Cabrera, D.: Multimodal deep support vector classification with homologous features and its application to gearbox fault diagnosis. Neurocomputing **168**, 119–127 (2015)
16. Shin, I., Lee, J., Lee, J.Y., et al.: A framework for prognostics and health management applications toward smart manufacturing systems. Int. J. Precis. Eng. Manuf.-Green Tech. **5**, 535–554 (2018)
17. Guillén, A.J., González-Prida, V., Gómez, J.F., Crespo, A.: Standards as reference to build a phm-based solution. In: Koskinen, K.T., et al. (eds.) Proceedings of the 10th World Congress on Engineering Asset Management (WCEAM 2015). LNME, pp. 207–214. Springer, Cham (2016). https://doi.org/10.1007/978-3-319-27064-7_20
18. Vogl, G.W., Weiss, B.A., Donmez, M.A.: Standards for prognostics and health management (PHM) techniques within manufacturing operations. In: Annual Conference of the Prognostics and Health Management Society, pp. 1–13 (2014)
19. Vachtsevanos, G., Lewis, F., Roemer, M., Hess, A., Wu, B.: Intelligent Fault Diagnosis and Prognosis for Engineering Systems. Wiley, NJ (2006)
20. Waeyenbergh, G., Pintelon, L.: A framework for maintenance concept development. Int. J. Prod. Econ. **77**, 299–313 (2002)
21. Wang, D., Tsui, K., Miao, Q.: Prognostics and health management: a review of vibration based bearing and gear health indicators. IEEE Access **6**, 665–676 (2018)
22. Moubray, J.: RCM II: Reliability-Centred Maintenance. Industrial Press Inc., New York (1997)
23. Sheppard, J.W., Kaufman, M.A., Wilmer, T.J.: IEEE standards for prognostics and health management. IEEE Aerosp. Electron. Syst. Mag. **24**(9), 34–41 (2009)
24. Cheng, S., Azarian, M., Pecht, M.: Sensor systems for prognostics and health management. Sensors **10**, 5774–5797 (2010)
25. Crespo, A., Gupta, J.: Contemporary maintenance management: process, framework and supporting pillars. Omega **34**(3), 313–326 (2006)

26. Guillén, A.J., Gómez, J., Crespo, A., Guerrero, A.: Towards the industrial application of PHM: challenges and methodological approach. In: PHM Society European Conference, pp. 1–10 (2014)
27. Haddad, G., Sandborn, P., Pecht, M.: An options approach for decision support of systems with prognostic capabilities. IEEE Trans. Reliab. **61**(4), 872–883 (2012)
28. Meng, H., Li, Y.: A review on prognostics and health management (PHM) methods of lithium-ion batteries. Renew. Sustain. Energy Rev. **116**, 23–40 (2019)
29. International Organization for Standardization: ISO 13374-1:2003—Condition monitoring and diagnostics of machines—Data processing, communication and presentation—Part 1: General guidelines (2003)
30. International Organization for Standardization: ISO 13381-1:2004—Condition monitoring and diagnostics of machines—Prognostics—Part 1: General guidelines (2004)
31. International Organization for Standardization: ISO 17359:2011—Condition monitoring and diagnostics of machines—General guidelines (2011a)
32. International Organization for Standardization: ISO 13379-1:2012—Condition monitoring and diagnostics of machines—Data interpretation and diagnostics techniques—Part 1: General guidelines (2012b)
33. Varde, P.V., Pecht, M.G.: Prognostics and Health Management. In: Risk-Based Engineering. SSRE, pp. 447–507. Springer, Singapore (2018). https://doi.org/10.1007/978-981-13-0090-5_13
34. Sun, L., Yu, Q., Peng, D., Subramani, S., Wang, X.: Fogmed: a fog-based framework for disease prognosis based medical sensor data streams. Comput. Mater. Continua **66**(1), 603–619 (2021)
35. Sangaiah, A.K., Gaol, F.L., Mishra, K.K.: Guest editorial: special section on big data & analytics architecture. Intell. Autom. Soft Comput. **26**(3), 515–517 (2020)
36. Abdullah, B., Daowd, H., Mallappa, S.: Semantic analysis techniques using twitter datasets on big data: comparative analysis study. Comput. Syst. Sci. Eng. **35**(6), 495–512 (2020)
37. Kwon, D., Hodkiewicz, M.R., Fan, J., Shibutani, T., Pecht, M.G.: IoT-based prognostics and systems health management for industrial applications. IEEE Access **4**, 3659–3670 (2016)
38. Lee, J., et al.: Prognostics and health management design for rotary machinery systems-reviews, methodology and applications. Mech. Syst. Signal Process. **42**(2), 314–334 (2014)

Multi-sensor Fusion Detection Method for Vehicle Target Based on Kalman Filter and Data Association Filter

Xuting Duan[1]($\boxtimes$), Chengming Sun[1], Daxin Tian[1], Kunxian Zheng[1], Gang Zhou[2], Wenjuan E[3,4], and Yundong Zhang[5]

[1] Beijing Advanced Innovation Center for Big Data and Brain Computing, School of Transpotation Science and Engineering, Beihang University, Beijing 100191, China
duanxuting@buaa.edu.cn
[2] Research Institute of Highway, Ministry of Transport of the People's Republic of China, Beijing 100088, China
[3] School of Rail Transportation, Soochow University, Suzhou 215000, China
[4] Suzhou Automotive Research Institute, Tsinghua University, Suzhou 215000, China
[5] State Key Laboratory of Digital Multimedia Chip Technology, Chongqing Vimicro AI Chip Technology Co., Ltd., Chongqing 400722, China

Abstract. Multi-sensor data fusion is an emerging technology, which has been widely used in medical diagnosis, remote sensing, inertial navigation and many other fields. What's more, the implementation and application of automatic driving system rely heavily on target detection technology. Due to the high mobility and unpredictability of vehicle-mounted equipment, for automatic vehicles, it is arduous to achieve real-time and accurate vehicle target detection by a single sensor means, thus it is difficult to reliably guarantee the safety and stability. This paper proposes a novel object detection method based on a multi-sensor fusion mechanism, which considers the real-time sensing data from two types of sensors including radar and camera. It collects multi-vehicle speed and position information efficiently and reliably. Then, it filters and integrates data according to Extended Kalman Filter, Data Association Filter and some other methods. Furthermore, vehicle-borne equipment makes intelligent decision based on the data. In addition to theoretical support, the designed simulation results also show that the multi-sensor fusion mechanism can detect target vehicles efficiently and accurately, and it has superiority in the stability and accuracy of perception than single sensor sensing method.

Keywords: Multi-sensor fusion · Extended Kalman filter · Data Association Filter · Target detection

1 Introduction

In recent years, as the leading direction of the development of transportation science, a cooperative vehicle-infrastructure system (CVIS) relies on various kinds of sensing facilities to sense the state information of vehicles, and realizes the information interaction

© Springer Nature Switzerland AG 2021
X. Sun et al. (Eds.): ICAIS 2021, CCIS 1423, pp. 441–448, 2021.
https://doi.org/10.1007/978-3-030-78618-2_36

and sharing between vehicles and road-side infrastructures through vehicle-to-vehicle (V2V) and vehicle-to-infrastructure (V2I) communication technologies. In this traffic system: on the one hand, for the vehicle-infrastructure system, the red and green indicator light is an important medium of vehicle-infrastructure interaction. The on-board equipment detects its visual information according to its own sensor system, and the vehicle makes an intelligent decision according to the received road information, calculates and obtains the optimal recommended route and the optimal recommended speed, so as to ensure that the vehicle can cross the intersection in a more uniform speed and more optimized time; on the other hand, for the vehicle system, the vehicle intelligently detects the surrounding target vehicles, calculates and analyzes the status information of the surrounding vehicles, such as the location and speed information of the surrounding vehicles, so as to make intelligent decisions and convert the decision results into control signals, control the next attitude of the vehicle, and achieve vehicle collision avoidance, queue following and lane changing overtaking. It can effectively reduce the travel time of drivers and guarantee their life safety to certain extent.

In the CVIS, the perception information of the vehicle to the external environment is one of the important channels to realize the interaction between the vehicle and the external information. The vehicle can accurately and effectively detect the target information, which is the precondition for the vehicle equipment to perceive the external environment. However, due to the high mobility and unpredictability of on-board equipment, a single sensor cannot meet the requirement of real-time and accurate detection of the target. That is, it cannot effectively perceive the external environment, and thus it is difficult to reliably guarantee the safety and stability of the vehicle. In order to make the vehicle accurately and comprehensively detect the surrounding environment, the target detection method that applies the sensor fusion technology to the vehicle sensing equipment arises at the historic moment. There are six kinds of sensors used in vehicle detection, including machine vision, microwave radar, millimeter wave radar, infrared, laser radar and ultrasonic radar. They all have their own advantages and disadvantages. How to integrate their functions and characteristics and optimize the accuracy and accuracy of vehicle detection to the maximum extent is a big challenge.

In the case of a large number of researches on the practical applications of different sensors, simultaneous interpreting of multiple sensors is more robust and more capable of detecting targets in complex environments. In the application of vehicle target detection methods, a wide range of multi-sensor fusion detection methods mainly include the fusion of lidar and machine vision, the fusion of lidar and millimeter wave radar, the fusion of millimeter wave radar and inertial navigation [1]. The common ones are the fusion of lidar and machine vision for the target detection based on AdaBoost algorithm [2]; the research of integrated navigation adopts the fusion of millimeter wave radar and inertial navigation system based on the augmented particle filter algorithm [3]. In this paper, it is considered that in the process of vehicle borne equipment target detection, the camera equipment has high recognition accuracy and high accuracy, but the ranging accuracy is low and the operating distance is short, which is limited by strong light, rain and fog, night and other environments; millimeter wave radar is less affected by the weather, which can measure the relative distance and speed of the accurate workshop, but it is difficult to identify pedestrian, traffic markings and other elements. By fusing the two information, we can learn from each other and optimize the comprehensiveness and reliability of vehicle detection target information. At present, the common target detection and tracking algorithms of multi-sensor fusion technology include target tracking algorithm based on Kalman filter [4], which is mainly applied to a linear Gaussian system based on the estimation of random process; target tracking algorithm based on particle filter [5], which is nonlinear tracking based on a Monte Carlo algorithm; Z.Q. Hou et al. use space and texture information to track the target based on particle filter Color [6]. However, the above algorithm mainly relies on the visual sensor to track the target, which is easy to be affected by the illumination change, occlusion and background interference, and easy to lose the target in the actual tracking process [7]. Moreover, the common tracking algorithm needs to specify the tracking target manually in the initial state, which brings inconvenience in the practical application [8].

Based on machine vision and millimeter wave fusion perception method, this study accurately and efficiently detects the target vehicle, collects the relative speed and position information of the vehicle ahead, and selects and integrates the data based on the extended Kalman filter model and data association filter. The vehicle equipment analyzes the external environment based on the data, and makes an intelligent decision, so as to further guarantee the vehicle queue to follow the safety of galloping and the robustness of collision avoidance.

2   Vehicle Target Detection Theoretical Model

2.1   Extended Kalman Filter Theoretical Model

The extended Kalman filter is an extended form of the standard Kalman filter in the non-linear case, and it is an efficient recursive filter. On account of millimeter wave radar adopts polar coordinate system and camera adopts Cartesian coordinate system, extended Kalman filter is used to estimate the state of detection target (Fig. 1).

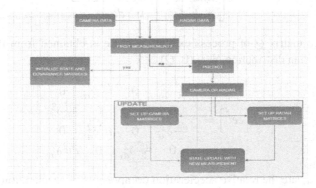

Fig. 1. Sensor fusion steps

First, initialize the monitoring target state x of the camera and millimeter wave radar,

assuming $x = \begin{bmatrix} p_x \\ p_y \\ v_x \\ v_y \end{bmatrix}$.

$$\text{Camera}: \begin{bmatrix} p_x \\ p_y \\ v_x \\ v_y \end{bmatrix} = \begin{bmatrix} 1 & 0 \\ 0 & 1 \\ 0 & 0 \\ 0 & 0 \end{bmatrix} \begin{bmatrix} p_x \\ p_y \end{bmatrix} \tag{1}$$

$$\text{Radar}: \begin{bmatrix} p_x \\ p_y \\ v_x \\ v_y \end{bmatrix} = \begin{bmatrix} \rho\cos\varphi \\ \rho\sin\varphi \\ \dot\rho\cos\varphi \\ \dot\rho\sin\varphi \end{bmatrix} \tag{2}$$

Where p_x is the position parameter of the detection target in the x-axis direction, p_y is the position parameter in the y-axis direction, v_x is the relative speed parameter in the x-axis direction, v_y is the relative speed parameter in the y-axis direction, ρ is the radial distance of the detection target, $\dot\rho$ is the relative radial speed of the detection target and the detection vehicle, and φ is the deviation angle between the detection target and the x-axis.

Since there is always acceleration deceleration relationship between the target vehicle and the detection vehicle, assuming the relative acceleration between them is a, the process excitation noise e can be deduced as follows:

$$e = \begin{bmatrix} \frac{a_x dt^2}{2} \\ \frac{a_y dt^2}{2} \\ a_x dt \\ a_y dt \end{bmatrix} = \begin{bmatrix} \frac{dt^2}{2} & 0 \\ 0 & \frac{dt^2}{2} \\ dt & 0 \\ 0 & dt \end{bmatrix} \begin{bmatrix} a_x \\ a_y \end{bmatrix} \tag{3}$$

The covariance matrix Q of process excitation noise is obtained from the fact that e obeys the Gaussian distribution $N \sim (0, Q)$

$$Q = E\left[ee^T\right] = \begin{bmatrix} \frac{dt^4}{4}\delta_{ax}^2 & 0 & \frac{dt^3}{2}\delta_{ax}^2 & 0 \\ 0 & \frac{dt^4}{4}\delta_{ay}^2 & 0 & \frac{dt^3}{2}\delta_{ay}^2 \\ \frac{dt^3}{2}\delta_{ax}^2 & 0 & dt^2\delta_{ax}^2 & 0 \\ 0 & \frac{dt^3}{2}\delta_{ay}^2 & 0 & dt^2\delta_{ay}^2 \end{bmatrix} \tag{4}$$

Where a_x and a_y are the relative acceleration components of acceleration a in X and Y directions, δ_{ax}^2 and δ_{ay}^2 are the estimated variance of acceleration a_x and a_y respectively.

For radar and camera, the predicted running track of the target vehicle is basically the same. The predicted target state x' and its uncertain state prediction P' are:

$$x' = Fx \tag{5}$$

$$P' = FPF^T + Q \tag{6}$$

Where F is the state transition matrix, F^T is its transition matrix, and P is the known system covariance, and P' is the estimated covariance.

According to the above formula, the target vehicle status at a certain time in the future is predicted, and the actual vehicle status at that time is Z. at this time, the extended Kalman filter method is applied to modify the current values of radar and camera respectively:

Camera $K_c = \frac{PH^T}{HPH^T + R_c}$ Radar : $K_r = \frac{PH_j^T}{H_j PH_j^T + R_r}$

$x_c = x + K_c(z - Hx)$ $x_r' = x + K_r(z - f(x))$

$P_c' = (1 - K_c H)P$ $P_r' = (1 - K_r H_j)P$

Where $f(x) = \begin{bmatrix} \rho \\ \varphi \\ \dot{\rho} \end{bmatrix} = \begin{bmatrix} \sqrt{p_x^2 + p_y^2} \\ arctan\frac{p_y}{p_x} \\ \frac{p_x v_x + p_y v_y}{\sqrt{p_x^2 + p_y^2}} \end{bmatrix}$ $H_j = \frac{\partial f(x)}{\partial x} = \begin{bmatrix} \frac{\partial \rho}{\partial p_x} & \frac{\partial \rho}{\partial p_y} & \frac{\partial \rho}{\partial v_x} & \frac{\partial \rho}{\partial v_y} \\ \frac{\partial \varphi}{\partial p_x} & \frac{\partial \varphi}{\partial p_y} & \frac{\partial \varphi}{\partial v_x} & \frac{\partial \varphi}{\partial v_y} \\ \frac{\partial \dot{\rho}}{\partial p_x} & \frac{\partial \dot{\rho}}{\partial p_y} & \frac{\partial \dot{\rho}}{\partial v_x} & \frac{\partial \dot{\rho}}{\partial v_y} \end{bmatrix}$

K_c and K_r are the respective filter gain matrix, R_c and R_r are the uncertainties of the respective measurements [9].

2.2 Joint Probabilistic Data Association

In the video surveillance of multiple moving targets, it is necessary to match and identify different cloud top targets between consecutive frames according to the data association of detection results, so as to achieve multi-target tracking. In the case of large monitoring range, similar appearance characteristics of moving targets or small target area, this paper adopts JPDA (Joint Probability Data Association). Its basic idea is corresponding to the situation that observation data fall into the intersection area of tracking gate, these observation data may come from multiple vehicles, calculate the association probability between observation data and each vehicle, and consider that all effective echoes may originate from each specific vehicle, but the probability of them coming from different vehicles is different (Fig. 2).

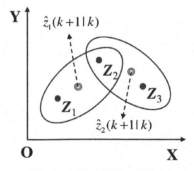

Fig. 2. JPDA design sketch

It is assumed that the false measurements which are not interconnected with the target follow the uniform distribution of volume V, and the measurements which are interconnected with the target follow the normal distribution, Gate probability $P_G = 1$.

$$P\{\theta_i(k)\} = \frac{\varphi(\theta_i(k))}{m_k!} \mu_F(\varphi(\theta_i(k))) \prod_{t=1}^{T} \left(P_D^t\right)^{\delta_t(\theta_i(k))} \left(1 - P_D^t\right)^{(1-\delta_t(\theta_i(k)))} \tag{7}$$

Where $\delta_t(\theta_i(k))$ is target detection indication, $\varphi(\theta_i(k))$ is number of false alarm measurements, P_D^t is the target detection probability, and $\mu_F(\varphi(\theta_i(k)))$ is the probability density function of the number of $\varphi(\theta_i(k))$ false measurements.

$$\widehat{X}^t(k|k) = E\left[\widehat{X}^t(k)|Z^k\right] = \sum_{j=0}^{m_k} \beta_{jt}(k)\widehat{X}_j^t(k|k) \tag{8}$$

Where $\widehat{X}_j^t(k|k)$ is the state estimation of target t by Extended Kalman filter with j measurements at k time [10].

3   Simulation Result of Vehicle Target Detection Module

The simulation in this section is designed that the blue vehicle is the detection vehicle when several vehicles are driving on the same road section with two lanes. A millimeter wave radar and camera detector are installed at the front and rear of the vehicle, and two-millimeter wave radar devices are installed at the left and right respectively to ensure the maximum detection range. The detector detects and tracks the position and speed information of the multi-target vehicle in real time, records the previous historical information, analyzes and integrates the fusion information of the multi-sensor according to the extended Kalman filter and JPDA principle, so that the detection vehicle updates the filtering algorithm and predicts its path selection according to the actual position of the target vehicle at the next time. In this example, red vehicles and purple vehicles are in a stable following state. Yellow vehicles are overtaking vehicles. The blue detection vehicle predicts their future paths according to the historical position and speed information of the Yellow vehicles and update the filtering algorithm according to their changing real-time position information. In the simulation, the detection vehicles predict the paths basically credibly to the driving paths of the target vehicles (Fig. 3).

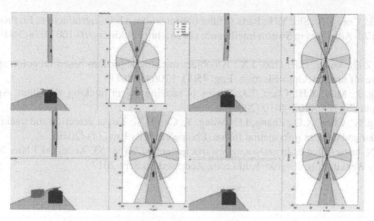

Fig. 3. Target detection simulation

4 Conclusions

A multi-sensor fusion detection method for vehicle target based on Kalman filter and data association filter is proposed and designed in this paper. This paper applies multi-sensor fusion to the vehicle target detection and tracking field. The proposed multi-sensor fusion framework utilizes the extended Kalman filter and joint probabilistic data association to update and forecast target vehicle path, which can make decision in advance according to the target track and speed, so as to avoid the risk of passing in and ensuring the driver's life safety. The simulation results show that our system is capable of constantly updating and accurately predicting the driving information of the target vehicle. However, there may be asymmetry between simulation results and real information. It will be our next research topic to apply the experimental simulation to the real vehicle experiment, and further verify the correctness and accuracy of the theory.

Acknowledgement. This research was supported by the National Key Research and Development Program of China under Grant No. 2017YFB0102502, 2017YFC0804803 and 2018YFB1600500, the Beijing Municipal Natural Science Foundation under Grant No. L191001, the National Natural Science Foundation of China under Grant No. U20A20155 and 61822101, the Newton Advanced Fellow-ship under Grant No. 62061130221.

References

1. Xiang, B.H.: Research on Target Detection Method Based on Vehicle Radar and Camera Information Fusion. Chongqing University (2017)
2. Huang, L., Barth, M.: Vehicle detection, tightly coupled LIDAR and computer vison integration for. In: Intelligent Vehicle Symposium, pp. 604–609. IEEE (2009)
3. Zhao, W., Wang, N., Gao, X.Z.: Research on MMW radar/GPS/INS integrated navigation method based on augmented particle filter algorithm. Electro. Optic Control **6**, 54–59 (2016)
4. Granström, K., Baum, M., Reuter, S.: Extended object tracking: introduction, overview, and applications. J. Adv. Inf. Fusion **12**(2), 139–174 (2017)

5. Liu, B., Cheng, S., Shi, Y.H.: Particle filter optimization: a brief introduction. In: Proceedings of the 7th Advances in Swarm Intelligence (2016). https://doi.org/10.1007/978-3-319-41000-5_10
6. Hou, Z.Q., Wang, L.P., Guo, J.X.: An object tracking algorithm based on color, space and texture inf oration. Opto-Electron. Eng. **45**(5), 170643 (2018)
7. Zhang, J., Mao, X.B., Chen, T.J.: Survey of moving object tracking algorithm. Appl. Res. Comput. **26**(12), 4407–4410 (2009)
8. Chang, X., Chen, X.D., Zhang, J.C., Wang, Y., Cai, H.Y.: Target detection and tracking based on lidar and camera information fusion. Photoelectricity Eng. (7) (2019)
9. CSDN. https://blog.csdn.net/young_gy/article/details/78468153. Accessed 7 Nov 2017
10. Baidu Wenku. https://wenku.baidu.com. Accessed 30 Sept 2019

Research on Crop Growth Period Estimation Based on Fusion Features

Qi Gao[1] and Xing Sun[2](✉)

[1] Ecological and Agricultural Meteorological Center, Shijiazhuang Meteorological Bureau, Shijiazhuang 050000, China
[2] School of Information Science and Engineering, Hebei University of Science and Technology, Shijiazhuang 050000, China

Abstract. Automatic recognition of crop growth period is one of the core parts of precision agriculture support technology. In order to identify different growth periods in real time and obtain crop growth information, a crop growth period estimation method based on fusion features is proposed. First, the crop images are preprocessed to filter out the noise. Then the HOG features, SILTP features and color features are fused. Finally, XQDA is used to measure the similarity to classify and identify the growing period of crops.

Keywords: Estimated crop growth period · Feature fusion · XQDA

1 Introduction

Corn is one of the third cereal crops in planting area. As the most widely used food crop, corn can usually be used as raw material for non-staple food production and feed in animal husbandry. Reprocessing with corn as raw material can also be used in the production of textile, paper, biofuel and cosmetics. As an important part of growth status monitoring, automatic judgment of growth period has increasingly become the focus of attention. The real-time judgment of the growth period can help people analyze the relationship between the growth status of crops and agrometeorology, and provide effective agricultural help to increase the yield of agricultural products. The traditional observation method of crop growth cycle is to manually record the date of the whole growth period from sowing to maturity according to the plant type, morphological changes and other parameters of crops. Manual observation is not only time-consuming and inefficient, but also affected by the technical level of observers, observation standards and other factors, so it is difficult to guarantee the measurement accuracy. At the same time, the growth information of crops can not be provided in real time, which brings a lot of inconvenience to the information development of precision agriculture.

With the continuous development of computer vision technology, image processing technology is widely used in the field of agricultural automation, such as crop and weed identification [1], pest detection [2], crop growth research [3] and so on. However, it is rarely used in the study of crop growth cycle. Lu Ming et al. [4] used RGB color model to extract green pixel value and HSL color model to extract yellow pixel value in identifying

© Springer Nature Switzerland AG 2021
X. Sun et al. (Eds.): ICAIS 2021, CCIS 1423, pp. 449–456, 2021.
https://doi.org/10.1007/978-3-030-78618-2_37

the growth period of summer corn, and divided the growth period of corn according to the different pixel values of corn in each period. Liu Yongjuan [5] conducted image enhancement processing and clustering segmentation on the images of different growth periods of corn to judge the growth period of corn. In the automatic observation of cotton development period, Wu Qian [6] divided the growth period by crop extraction, color segmentation and straight line detection of the number of main stem and lateral stem according to the characteristics of cotton in each period. Quan Wenting et al. [7] used S-G filter to identify wheat returning green stage and heading stage, through the change characteristics of NDVI time series curve on remote sensing images. Sun Huasheng et al. [8] use MODIS data to identify the key growth and development stages of rice according to the EVI variation characteristics of time series, but they are easily affected by environmental factors. KurtulmusF et al. [9] use SVM, classifier to classify the color information of maize male ear to realize image binarization, determine the position of maize male ear, and then eliminate the misclassified position of maize male ear through shape and texture features, and finally determine the position of maize male ear and realize automatic castration.

The rest of this article is organized as follows. In Sect. 2, Image preprocessing. In Sect. 3, HOG features, SILTP features and color features are extracts. In Sect. 4, features are fused, and similarity measurement functions are learned. In Sect. 5, experiments are carried out to verify the effectiveness of the proposed algorithm. Finally, the last section concludes the paper.

2   Image Preprocessing

When crop images are taken directly from farmland, there are some problems, such as uneven light intensity, background and soil interference, which bring noise to the image. These noises are characterized by the blocking of the light of the leaves at the bottom of the crop plant, the interference of weeds and so on. In this paper, the image preprocessing method is used to remove the noise, and the image which can better characterize the characteristics of maize growing period can be obtained. The process of corn image preprocessing is shown in Fig. 1.

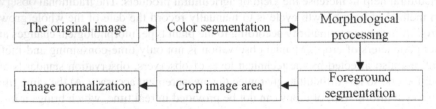

Fig. 1. Image preprocessing flowchart

First of all, the green part of the original image of corn in different growing periods was obtained by color segmentation. Then Grabcut segmentation algorithm is used to distinguish maize plants from similar plants such as other weeds. Finally, the plant image is obtained by morphological processing, eliminating the small noise and keeping the edge of the image intact. The original image and the preprocessed image are shown in Fig. 2.

Fig. 2. Original image and preprocessed image

3 Feature Extraction

3.1 HOG Feature Extraction

HOG (Histogram of Oriented Gradient) feature can better capture edge or shape information, and has good robustness to illumination, and can well describe the contour curve of the target in the image [10].

The implementation process of the HOG feature extraction algorithm is as follows:

(1) Normalization of the color space. Normalization eliminates interference from uncontrollable elements such as the shooting environment, background, and device in the target image.

2) Gradient calculation. Gradients in the horizontal and vertical directions of a pixel point (x, y) in the image are calculated as follows:

$$\begin{cases} G_x(x, y) = I(x + 1, y) - I(x - 1, y) \\ G_y(x, y) = I(x, y + 1) - I(x, y - 1) \end{cases} \tag{1}$$

Then, the gradient and direction of the obtained pixel point are as follows:

$$G(x, y) = \sqrt{G_x(x, y)^2 + G_y(x, y)^2} \tag{2}$$

$$\theta(x, y) = \arctan\left(\frac{G_x(x, y)}{G_y(x, y)}\right) \tag{3}$$

(3) Histogram of gradient direction. The image is divided into many cells (in this paper, $8 \times 8 = 64$ pixels are used as one cell, and there is no overlap between adjacent cells), and all the gradients in each cell are counted, while all the gradient directions are sorted into 9 bins. The gradient amplitudes of each bin are aggregated, and the histogram is finally normalized to obtain the characteristics of each cell.

(4) Normalization of overlapping block histograms. The HOG features of the whole image can be obtained by grouping several cells into one block (in this paper, every 4 cells form a block, thus allowing overlap between blocks), and the feature histograms of all cells in a block are connected in series to form the block feature histogram, while all the block feature histograms are connected in sequence.

The visual image of HOG features are shown in Fig. 3.

Fig. 3. Visual image of HOG features

3.2 Texture Feature Extraction

In terms of texture feature description, LBP (Local binary pattern) operator [11] is widely used because of its multi-scale characteristics, rotation invariance, and low complexity. But the algorithm is sensitive to noise. As shown in Fig. 2, the coding process of the LBP operator, when there is noise interference, will cause small changes in the surrounding pixels, resulting in misjudgment. Therefore, this paper uses the improved operator scale invariant local ternary pattern (Scale Invariant Local Ternary Pattern, SILTP) of LBP feature to extract texture features (Fig. 4).

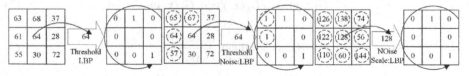

Fig. 4. LBP operator coding process

The SILTP is an improved local binary pattern (LBP) description operator with a good anti-interference ability for noise in the region. When the detection region is dark, covered by shadows or contains a lot of noise, the operator has strong adaptability. Moreover, the SILTP operator exhibits scale invariance, which makes it robust to brightness changes; thus, the SILTP feature will be only slightly affected, even if the illumination suddenly changes from dark to bright. Figure 2 shows the encoding process of the SILTP operator in this algorithm.

Assuming that the pixel position of an image is (x_c, y_c), The SILTP operator uses two thresholds to compare with the central pixel point value and all adjacent pixels with a central pixel radius of R, and divides the comparison results into three cases, as shown in Eq. (4) and Eq. (5).

$$SILTP^t_{Q,R}(x_c, y_c) = \overset{Q-1}{\underset{k=0}{\oplus}} s_t(I_c, I_k) \qquad (4)$$

$$s_t(I_c, I_k) = \begin{cases} 01 \ I_k > (1+t)I_c \\ 10 \ I_k < (1-t)I_c \\ 00 \ others \end{cases} \qquad (5)$$

where I_c is the grayscale value of the image center pixel point, I_k is the grayscale value of the pixel point corresponding to the Q neighborhood with radius R, $\oplus$ connects the binary values of all neighborhoods into character strings, and t is the threshold range. As shown in Fig. 3, the image is binary coded according to Eqs. (4) and (5), and the center point is coded as 0010010100001001 in counterclockwise order. The coding process of the SILTP operator is shown in Fig. 3. Figure 3 reveals that, even if the image contains noise or scale changes within a certain range, the SILTP coding value remains unchanged, which indicates that the operator is robust to problems such as illumination changes (Fig. 5).

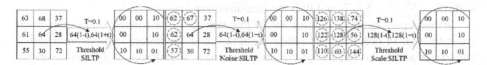

Fig. 5. Encoding process of the SILTP operator

3.3 Color Feature Extraction

Hue-Saturation-Value (HSV), Lightness-A-B (LAB) and Luminance-Chroma: Blue-Chroma: Red (YCbCr) are three complementary color spaces; therefore, describing a given object from different angles can better reflect the differences between samples. This paper extracts features in the HSV, LAB and YCbCr color spaces. Due to light, background and other reasons, it will have a great impact on the extracted color, so before extracting the color feature histogram, the image is enhanced by Retinex image enhancement algorithm to reduce the effect of light on color [12].

For each channel of each color space in the image, the 16-dimensional color histogram features are extracted, and all the color histograms are concatenated together to form the color features of the image. Each image can extract 144-dimensional ($3 \times 3 \times 16$) color features. Using the original 144-dimensional features to directly learn the similarity measurement function requires estimation of $2 \times 144 \times 144$ parameters, which is too much. Therefore, in the experiment, PCA is used to reduce the feature dimension of the image to a specific dimension.

4   Feature Fusion and Similarity Measurement Function

The cross-view quadratic discriminant analysis (XQDA) algorithm [13] is an excellent metric algorithm in learning. Compared with similar algorithms, this algorithm has the advantages of high matching rate, strong robustness and short computing time. Therefore, this paper uses the XQDA to measure the degree of similarity [14–17].

The XQDA method simultaneously performs feature subspace and metric learning and considers the effect of dimension reduction on the metric learning results while reducing the feature dimension. In XQDA, the original feature x_i, $x_i \in R^d$ is mapped to a low-dimensional subspace by learning the mapping matrix. The similarity function is defined in Eq. (6):

$$\delta(x_i, x_j) = (x_i - x_j)^T M \left(\sum_{I}'^{-1} - \sum_{E}'^{-1} \right) M^T (x_i - x_j) \tag{6}$$

where $\sum_I' = M^T \sum_I M, \sum_E' = M^T \sum_E M$, and $\sum_I$ and $\sum_E$ are the covariance matrices of the intraclass and interclass sample difference distributions, respectively. When solving and decomposing the characteristic value of matrix $\sum_I^{-1} \sum_E$, matrix M is composed of eigenvectors corresponding to the first r maximum characteristic values, with $W = \sum_I'^{-1} - \sum_E'^{-1}$, and W is the measurement matrix.

In this paper, the HOG features, SILTP features and color features of the crop image are extracted. In order to fully reflect the differences in feature expression in different spaces and make full use of the complementary advantages of different features, the independent measure learning method is adopted to extract HOG features, SILTP features and color features to learn the measure matrix W_1, W_2, W_3 separately, so that the measurement criteria based on different features can be obtained. On this basis, the similarity of the test samples in different spaces is weighted and fused to get the final similarity.

Using the HOG features, SILTP features and color features of the crop image for learning, 3 measurement matrices W_A, W_B, W_C can be obtained respectively. Through the Eq. (6), the similarity δ_A, δ_B, δ_C of the three features can be obtained. The HOG features, SILTP features, and color features are weighted to get the similarity, such as Eq. (7).

$$\delta(x_i, x_j) = \lambda \delta_A(x_i, x_j) + \beta \delta_B(x_i, x_j) + \gamma \delta_C(x_i, x_j) \tag{7}$$

Among them, λ, β, γ are the similarity degree weight. In the following experiments, the weight values are set to 0.3, 0.3, 0.4, respectively.

5 Experiment and Analysis

According to the application scenario of this paper, the data sets used in the training test are all 2000 corn images actually collected. Corn images are divided into four categories, namely seedling stage, jointing stage, male stage and mature stage. As shown in Fig. 6, the size of each image is normalized to 16×16. This experiment is implemented under the platform of Ubuntu.

Using the features of this paper, the experimental results of classifying the corn image data set are shown in Table 1.

Table 1. Classification and recognition results of Maize growing period

Test sample	Recognition result				
	Seedling period	Jointing period	Tasseling period	Maturity period	Recognition rate/%
Seedling period	500	0	0	0	100
Jointing period	0	476	24	0	95.2
Tasseling period	0	16	454	30	90.8
Maturity period	0	0	32	468	93.6

As can be seen from the table, the recognition rates of seedling stage, jointing stage, Tasseling period and mature stage are 100%, 95.2%, 90.8% and 93.6% respectively, and the average recognition rate of corn growing stage is 94.9%. It achieves a high recognition rate and accuracy.

6 Conclusion

In this paper, a crop growth period estimation algorithm based on fusion features is proposed, which combines HOG, SILTP and color features. The experimental results show that this method can real-time and accurately identify different crop growth periods, obtain crop growth information, and can accurately identify crop growth periods. However, in this paper, in the similarity fusion, the weight coefficient can not adaptively find the direct optimal weight of the feature, and the future work can get the optimal weight under different conditions through learning.

References

1. Zu, Q., Zhang, S.F., Cao, Y., et al.: Research on the identification of weeds in cabbage combined with spectral image technology and SAM classification method. Spectro. Spectral Anal. **35**(2), 479–485 (2015)
2. Li, R.C, Tao, H.B, Zhang, Z.Q., et al.: Research on the monitoring of summer corn population growth based on image processing technology Maize Sci. **18**(2), 128–132(2010)
3. Guo, F., Liu, P., Zhang, C., Chen, W., Han, W., et al.: Research on the law of garlic price based on big data. Comput. Mat. Continua **58**(3), 795–808 (2019)
4. Lu, M., Shen, S.H., Wang, C.Y., et al.: A preliminary study on the identification method of summer corn growth period based on image recognition technology. Chine. Agric. Meteorol. **32**(3), 423–429 (2011)
5. Liu, Y.J.: Research on Recognition of Corn Development Period Based on Computer Vision Technology. Jiangnan University, Wuxi (2017)
6. Wu, Q.: Research on automatic observation of cotton development period based on image processing technology. Wuhan: Huazhong University of Science and Technology. (2013)
7. Quan, W.T., Zhou, H., Li, H.M., et al.: Remote sensing identification and growth mon itoring of winter wheat growth period in Guanzhong area of Shaanxi based on S-G filtering. Chin. Agric. Meteorology. **36**(1), 93–99 (2015)
8. Sun, H.S., Huang, J.F., Peng, D.L.: Using MODIS data to identify key growth and development stages of rice. J. Remote Sens. **13**(6), 1122–1137 (2009)
9. Kurtulmus F, Kavdir.: Detecting com tassels using computer vision and support vector machines. Expert Syst. Appl. **41**(16), 7390–7397 (2014)
10. Dalal, N., Triggs, B.: Histograms of oriented gradients for human de tection. IEEE Comput. Soc. **1**, 886–893 (2005)
11. Zhang J., Xiao, J., Zhou, C., et al.: A multi-class pedestrian detection network for distorted pedestrians. In: 13th IEEE Conference on Industrial Electronics and Applications (ICIEA), pp. 1079–1083 (2018)
12. Nejad, M.B., Shiri, M.E.: A new enhanced learning approach to automatic image classification based on Salp Swarm Algorithm. Comput. Syst. Sci. Eng. **34**(2), 91–100 (2019)
13. Liao, S.C., Hu, Y., Zhu, X.Y.,Li, S.Z.: Person re-identification by local maximal occurrence representation and metric learning. In: Proceedings of the IEEE Conference on Computer Vision and Pattern Recognition, pp. 2197–2206 (2015)
14. Chen, M., Wang, X.J., He, M.S., Jin, L., Javeed, K., Wang, X.J.: A network traffic classification model based on metric learning. Comput. Mater. Continua **64**(2), 941–959 (2020)
15. Li, H., Zeng, W., Xiao, G., Wang, H.: The instance-aware automatic image colorization based on deep convolutional neural network. Intell. Autom. Soft Comput. **26**(4), 841–846 (2020)
16. Wu, H., Liu, Q., Liu, X.: A review on deep learning approaches to image classification and object segmentation. Comput. Mater. Continua **60**(2), 575–597 (2019)
17. Hu, Z. W. et al.: End-to-end multimodal image registration via reinforcement learning. Med. Image Anal. **68**, (2021)

Research and Application of Holographic Portrait Label System Construction for Main Equipment of Distribution Network Based on Big Data

Huifeng Yan[1], Kun Sheng[1], Ying Xiang[1], Jun Yang[1], Yuxiang Xie[2,3], and Dawei Li[2,3(✉)]

[1] State Grid Hunan Electric Power Company Limited, Changsha 410007, China
[2] State Grid Hunan Electric Power Company Limited, Economic and Technical Research Institute, Changsha 410007, China
[3] Hunan Key Laboratory of Energy Internet Supply-Demand and Operation, Changsha 410007, China

Abstract. Relying on the big data platform, based on data mining technology and label profile technology, this paper analyzes the distribution network equipment data in two typical areas of Changsha and Shaoyang in the past two years, and establishes equipment with five dimensions of attributes, benefits, operation, cost, and life. Characteristic index library; analyze the three application scenarios of operation status evaluation, operation benefit evaluation and investment decision support, and build a multi-angle and comprehensive intelligent holographic portrait label system for distribution network equipment; finally select a distribution transformer in Changsha City As an application case, use Python programming combined with machine learning algorithms such as cluster analysis and decision trees to display the holographic image of the device.

Keywords: Label portrait technology · Main equipment of distribution network · Machine learning · Big data mining

1 Introduction

As the final unit of power grid operation, distribution transformer is the carrier of massive data in power grid construction. As the most direct connection equipment between the power grid and the majority of users, distribution transformers directly affect the power supply quality and safety of the entire region. Heavy overload of equipment will cause power outages and other faults, which will seriously disrupt the normal life of residents; in addition, heavy overload of power supply equipment for a long time will accelerate the loss of internal parts of the equipment and bring great risks to the operation of the power supply system. Therefore, heavy overload management is an extremely important part of the power grid.

With the informatization of statistical services and the popularization of smart grid terminals, power grid companies have accumulated multi-level and multi-dimensional physical information and equipment data. The scale of data has developed from TB to PB, and it has moved from single-function informatization to online Shanghua has reached the big data stage represented by PIS 2.0 [1]. Power equipment, as the generator and carrier of massive data, further excavates data on the energy efficiency of power grid equipment such as attributes, operation, efficiency, etc., providing good conditions for deepening the implementation of equipment energy efficiency analysis.

The rapid development of big data technology has enabled all walks of life to tap the value of data with the help of big data technology. Reference [2] shows the concept of smart grid big data, and proposes a smart grid big data research framework and technical development route; reference [3] is based on household electricity data, combined with behavioral theory, house age information, surrounding weather and other data, using correlation Analyze the rules, analyze the energy efficiency of users and put forward power saving suggestions. Domestic power grids have also formulated the 13th Five-Year Plan and Guiding Opinions for the Application of Enterprise Big Data [1].

Portrait technology has a wide range of applications in precision marketing and other aspects. The typical application of portrait technology in the context of big data is to create user portraits for customer groups. For example, China Mobile conducts data analysis through consumption scenarios and needs, builds user portraits, and conducts differentiated marketing based on customer segmentation [4, 5]. Internet e-commerce giants such as Taobao and Dangdang have also built customer portraits based on their own business needs. Currently in the power industry, literature [6] proposes a set of power customer portrait labeling system based on big data theory; literature [7] proposes to use sparse coding model to explore the abnormal power consumption behavior of power users, which can be used to construct abnormal power users Power consumption portrait; Literature [8] builds a risk prediction model of electricity fee recovery based on logistic regression for various voltage residential users. However, the research on the equipment of the distribution network itself is lacking, so the establishment of a standardized power equipment label system and holographic portrait is very important to promote grid planning and lean investment.

Starting from the overall strategy, this research is based on data mining technology and label profiling technology, through the integration of internal and external mass data of distribution network equipment, build a data warehouse for various application scenarios, build a distribution network equipment labeling system, and realize equipment "labeling" "Management and display of holographic portraits, accurately grasp the health status of equipment, play the basic role of equipment portraits, and finally achieve the overall goal of three new, three controls, and one platform, that is, to achieve algorithm innovation, application innovation, evaluation innovation, and monitoring and operation of operating conditions. Benefit control, investment decision control, and issue of overall application platform construction plan for distribution network equipment holographic portrait technology.

2 Overall Structure and Technical Route

Based on the big data platform, establish a high-quality equipment feature index library, analyze the three application scenarios of operation status evaluation, operation benefit evaluation and investment decision support, and construct the equipment intelligent holographic portrait label system, which is mainly divided into the following three steps:

Step 1. Feature index library based on big data extraction equipment

Step 2. Intelligent holographic portrait label system for construction equipment

Step 3. "Three controls and one painting" application based on label system

2.1 Technology Architecture

The overall technical architecture is based on the idea of big data, adopts multi-layer technical architecture design to realize the collection, processing, storage, and calculation of data, and introduces the microservice framework, carries out the microservice design according to the business, and provides the application through a unified service gateway support.

On the whole, the technical architecture includes the original data layer, data processing layer, device data warehouse, public components, service gateway, and device profile application. As shown in Fig. 1.

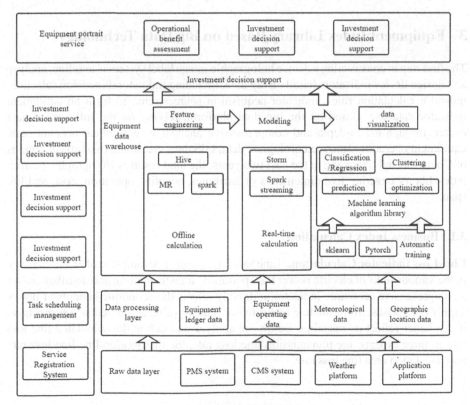

Fig. 1. Overall technical framework of device image application

(1) Data service: It mainly includes the original data layer and data processing layer. The original data layer uses big data technology to collect business data of various business systems, including EMS, CMS, marketing platform, weather platform and other related data items of business systems, The data processing layer preprocesses equipment account data, equipment operation data, weather data, geographic location data, etc. according to data processing rules to ensure data quality meets business needs.

(2) Equipment data warehouse: Use the offline computing engine MapReduce provided by the big data platform and the memory computing Spark framework to realize the non-real-time requirement index calculation in the equipment index library, and use the big data platform real-time analysis engine to realize the time-critical indicators in the equipment index library Calculate, use the self-developed automated AI training platform to automatically train machine learning algorithms, self-dig, self-evolve, and further dig prediction hidden indicators.

(3) Common components: to achieve access control and unified management, and also provide services such as data verification rules and data quality monitoring.

(4) Service Gateway: Controls application access to services, and provides services such as load balancing, routing and forwarding, and black and white lists.

(5) Portrait application: It can support applications such as operation status evaluation, operation benefit evaluation, investment decision support, group/individual equipment portrait analysis, and equipment personalized recommendation.

3 Equipment Index Library Based on Big Data Technology

The first step in constructing a device holographic image label system is to refine, analyze and design device indicators based on big data, including indicator dimension selection, indicator calculation rules, indicator acquisition sources, etc., to form an equipment indicator database. Based on the big data platform, relying on the full-service data center, through the in-depth and comprehensive analysis of equipment account data, equipment operation data, meteorological data, GIS data, etc. in the two typical regions of Changsha and Shaoyang in the past two years, the final result is Holographic portrait index library covering five dimensions of attributes, benefits, operation, cost, and life span.

3.1 Business Index Calculation

Line Loss Indicator Calculation. Line loss refers to the consumption of electric energy in the various links of electric power transportation, transformation, and distribution. As a comprehensive economic indicator, it directly affects the economic benefits of power supply enterprises. Since the line loss rate is a relative value expressed as a percentage, it can better reflect its meaning. Below we analyze and define the calculated line loss rate in three aspects: the transmission line loss rate, the distribution line line loss rate and the station area line loss rate.

(1) Transmission line: Under the balance of busbar, the loss rate of transmission line is:

$$H_t = \frac{s_i - s_0}{s_i} \times 100\% \tag{1}$$

(2) Distribution line: first calculate the input and output power of the distribution line:

Input power:

$$s_i = a_{kv} + a_i + a_0 + a_r \tag{2}$$

Output power:

$$s_0 = a_c + a_t + a_m \tag{3}$$

The line loss rate of the distribution line is:

$$H_d = \frac{s_i - s_0}{s_i} \times 100\% \tag{4}$$

In the formula, a_{kv} is the 10 kV line outgoing power, a_i is the on-grid power of the line power plant, a_0 is the distributed power, a_r is the 400 V reverse on-grid power, a_c is the power of the public transformer connected under the line, a_t is the power of the dedicated substation, and a_m is the reverse Send main network power.

(3) Station area line loss: first find the bottom of the daily frozen table through the station area table, and get the station area total meter electricity; then query the daily supply (sales) electricity of all low-voltage users under the station area (calculate the daily electricity consumption based on today The difference between the 24 o'clock indication and yesterday's 24 o'clock indication shall prevail).

Daily power supply in station area:

$$s_i = a_s + a_r \tag{5}$$

Daily electricity sales in area station:

$$s_0 = a_u + a_m + a_e \tag{6}$$

Daily line loss rate in in area station:

$$H_z = \frac{s_i - s_0}{s_i} \times 100\% \tag{7}$$

In the formula, a_s is the total meter power in the station area, a_r is the distributed power grid power under the station area, a_u is the total meter online power in the station area, a_m is the power sold in the station area, and a_e is the office power consumption.

Operation Indicator Calculation

(1) Load index

The maximum load rate of the main (distribution) transformer:

$$R_m = \frac{P_m}{C_r} \times 100\% \qquad (8)$$

Main (distribution) variable average load rate:

$$R_a = \frac{P_a}{C_r} \times 100\% \qquad (9)$$

The maximum load rate of the line:

$$L_m = \frac{I_m}{I_r} \times 100\% \qquad (10)$$

The load growth rate is:

$$a_u = \frac{R_{m1} - R_{m2}}{R_{ma}} \qquad (11)$$

In the formula, P_m is the main (distribution) transformer maximum power supply load, C_r is the main (distributed) variable rated capacity, P_a average power supply load of main distribution transformer, I_m is the maximum working current of the line, I_r is the maximum allowable transmission current of the line, R_{m1} is the maximum load rate of the equipment at the end of the statistical period, R_{m2} is the maximum load rate of the equipment at the beginning of the statistical period, R_{ma} is the maximum load rate of the equipment at the beginning of the statistical period.

(2) Operational indicators

Operational efficiency is:

$$R_r = \frac{s_3}{a_3} \times 100\% \qquad (12)$$

Equipment utilization is:

$$R_u = \frac{T_{sum} - T_p - T_u - T_m \times 24}{T_{sum}} \times 100\% \qquad (13)$$

In the formula, s_3 is the total power output of a single device in the past three years after it is put into production, a_3 is the average total power output of the company's distribution transformers at the same voltage level in the past three years, T_{sum} is the number of hours during the statistical period, T_p is the planned outage hour, and T_u is the unplanned outage hour, T_m is the number of days when the maximum load rate of the equipment is less than 2%.

(3) Growth indicators

The average annual growth rate of the total scale of transformer capacity of each voltage level during the three years before the statistical date in the assessment area reflects the growth rate of the transformer capacity during the statistical period of the region. The average annual growth rate of the line scale of each voltage level reflects the growth rate of the line scale during the statistical period of the region.

The average annual growth rate of electric capacity is:

$$a_y = \frac{s_t - s_3}{3} \times 100\% \tag{14}$$

The average annual growth rate of line length is:

$$a_l = \frac{L_t - L_3}{3} \times 100\% \tag{15}$$

In the formula, s_t is the capacity of the transformer at the end of the year before the statistical date, s_3 is the capacity of the transformer at the beginning of the previous three years; L_t is the line length at the end of the year before the statistical date, and L_3 is the line length at the beginning of the previous three years.

(4) Cost indicators

The increase in power supply per unit load growth is:

$$T_u = \frac{s_t - s_L}{a_t - a_L} \tag{16}$$

In the formula, s_t is the electricity sold in this year, s_L is the electricity sold in the previous year, a_t is the largest electricity load this year, and a_L is the largest electricity load last year.

4 Device Holographic Portrait Label System

4.1 Label Refinement and Classification

Based on the equipment holographic portrait index library, the equipment tags are refined through logic calculation, text mining, machine learning and other technologies with three types of equipment such as substations, transformers, and lines, and the index thresholds of different intervals are set according to algorithms such as cluster analysis to distinguish the tags. Boundary, according to the characteristics of the equipment and management requirements, in order to form an all-round intelligent holographic portrait model of the equipment, the establishment of the tag library starts from five dimensions:

Basic information (Type A): The inherent properties of the device, such as the voltage level, are static properties of the device, and its value is usually not easy to change and easy to obtain directly.

Operational information (Type B): the dynamic properties of the equipment, the information that the equipment updates over time during operation.

Cost information (Type C): equipment information related to costs.

Life stage (Class D): including operating years and age.

Operating income (Class E): including static and dynamic properties of the equipment, describing the income through utilization and heavy equipment overload.

4.2 Label Generation Process

Data Processing. The label data needs to undergo data processing. The processing is divided into three steps: equipment data cleaning, equipment data fusion and feature extraction processing:

Step 1. Equipment data cleaning: using mean, mode filling, clustering, and regression elimination to process missing data; merge or delete duplicate data; delete data error data according to the clustering algorithm, perform the above processing, and output a high-quality data set.

Step 2. Equipment data integration: equipment-related business systems such as marketing business systems, PMS systems, etc., are integrated through multiple contacts of the same device, including graph-based strong communication and machine learning fuzzy communication, and finally Output data aggregate warehouse data.

Step 3. Feature extraction processing: Feature engineering can transform original data into features, which is a work of transformation and structuring. In this stage, it is necessary to standardize the labels for data standardization judgment.

Through this stage, the data aggregation warehouse is processed, which penetrates the entire data processing layer, and provides robust basic data for the data business layer.

Label Definition and Generation Method. The data is extracted according to different business dimensions. The label data can be divided into three categories: fact labels, model labels, and smart prior labels. The specific hierarchical structure is shown in Fig. 2.

Fact Label: Declarative fact data extracted from the original data in business systems such as PMS. For example, equipment voltage level, equipment line length, transformer type, line nature, manufacturer, etc. If multiple systems have this field, matching, comparison, and selection are required when labeling values.

Model Label: The label calculated by the calculation model according to the established calculation rules. For example, the average annual growth rate of variable (distribution)

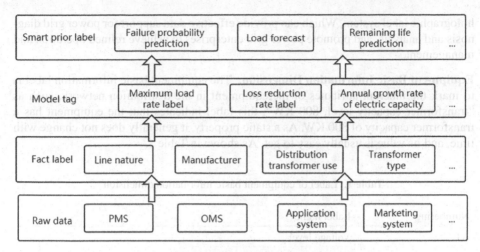

Fig. 2. Data label hierarchy

capacitance, the average annual growth rate of line length, the maximum load rate label, the loss reduction rate label, etc.

Intelligent a Priori Tags: based on artificial intelligence technology and organically combine the business experience of business experts to mine and explore potential business tags. Common methods of artificial intelligence technology are:

(1) Classification analysis: classify the specified attribute features into labels. Commonly used algorithms include Naive Bayes, KNN algorithm, Gradient Boosting, SVM, BP neural network, etc.
(2) Clustering analysis: behavioral label generation methods based on density and distance clustering, such as traditional K-means and mean clustering; for clustering analysis and mining of unclear attributes, hierarchical clustering and fuzzy clustering can be used Class etc.
(3) Regression analysis: mainly linear regression models, as well as multiple nonlinear regression, logistic regression and other techniques. Linear algebraic solution optimized by ordinary least squares and gradient descent.
(4) Association analysis: The purpose of association analysis is to find the hidden association network in the data set, which is the basis of discrete variable causality analysis. Find out the hidden relationship with the prior label through association analysis, and get the relevant basic label coefficients, mainly using the Aprioir algorithm.

4.3 Label System Construction

Mining the association relationship between tags through association relationship and other algorithms, from the four application scenarios of equipment basic information, operating status evaluation, investment decision support, and operation efficiency evaluation, the tags are reasonably defined and assigned scientific weights to construct a device holographic label system, Which can provide effective data support for power grid diagnosis and analysis, and promote power grid enterprises to achieve refined operation and management.

Equipment Basic Information Dimension. The equipment basic information label is to mark the inherent attributes of the equipment in the distribution network, such as "transformer capacity level, 800 KW", this label indicates that the equipment has a transformer capacity of 800 KW. As a static property, it generally does not change with time, and its value is usually easy to get. As shown in Table 1.

Table 1. Label of equipment basic information dimension

Numbering	Label name
A1	Voltage level
A2	Transformer capacity grade
A3	Total line length
A4	Nature of assets
A5	Whether rural network
A6	Transformer category
A7	Operating status
A8	Manufacturer
A9	Line erection method
A10	Line nature
A11	Equipment importance
A12	Equipment status evaluation
A13	Characteristics of the area where the equipment is located

All labels are basic labels, of which the voltage level and total line length label classification standards are classified according to the specific interval specified by the relevant regulations, and the rest can be obtained directly from the system.

Operating Status Evaluation Dimension. The establishment of a holographic portrait of the operating equipment can more accurately monitor the operating status of the equipment. The labels for measuring the evaluation of the operating status are shown in Table 2.

The above labels are all model labels. The interval classification is calculated according to the formula in Sect. 3.1. Some calculation and classification standards are as follows:

The operating life of the equipment (the operating time from the commissioning date of the distribution transformer to the calculation date) is compared with the design life of the distribution transformer to calculate the current life stage of the distribution transformer; the result is: the juvenile equipment: $0 \leq$ the operating life of the distribution

Table 2. Label of operation status evaluation dimension

Numbering	Label name
D1	Operating life
E1	Average monthly input power
B1	Annual growth rate of electric capacity
B2	Line loss rate label
B3	Average annual growth rate of line length
B4	Voltage qualification rate
B5	Distribution transformer capacity per household
B6	Maximum load rate
B7	Load operating status
B8	Average load rate
B9	Load growth
D2	Old equipment
C1	Whether the low voltage station area

transformer ≤ 5; Juvenile equipment: $5 <$ distribution transformer operating life ≤ 10; youth equipment: $10 <$ distribution transformer operating life ≤ 20; middle-age equipment: $20 <$ distribution transformer operating life ≤ 30; elderly equipment: distribution transformer operating life > 30.

The label of the monthly average input power of the equipment is the average monthly input power of the 12 months before the statistical date; the top 10% of the average monthly input power of the same type of equipment: the output is responsible, in the range of 10%–30%, the output is efficient; within 30%–70% Interval, the output is normal; after 70%, the output is inefficient.

For the line loss rate label, refer to the formulas (1), (4) and (7) in Sect. 3.1 to check whether the line loss rate of the equipment of the same voltage level in the area conforms to the normal distribution. If it does, calculate the average line loss rate u and variance σ; The result is high line loss equipment: $u + \sigma \leq \Delta p\%$; higher line loss equipment: $u \leq \Delta p\% \leq u + \sigma$; general line loss equipment: $u - \sigma \leq \Delta p\% \leq u$; low line loss equipment: $0 \leq \Delta p\% \leq u - \sigma$; Negative loss equipment: $\Delta p\% \leq 0$.

The load operating status tab counts what the daily maximum load rate belongs to, and obtains the time proportion of each load situation: negative overload operating time percentage, heavy load operating time percentage, light load operating time percentage, reasonable operating time percentage The final display result is: more than 90% of the whole year and the cumulative time is greater than 30 days are regarded as overload operation; more than 70% and the cumulative time is greater than 30 days (annual) is regarded as heavy operation; the load rate is more than 30% Time less than 30 days is regarded as uneconomical work; the load rate is more than 70% and the time is less than 30 days and the load rate is more than 30% and the time is greater than 30 days is regarded as reasonable work with a relatively high proportion of operating time.

The load growth rate judges the growth of the maximum load rate of the equipment and predicts the growth trend. The calculation refers to the formula (11) in Sect. 3.1.2. The final display result is: less than 0% is a decline, 0% to 7% is slow, and 7% to 12% is medium, more than 12% is faster.

Investment Decision Support Dimension. The formation of the holographic portrait of the equipment can directly show the safe operation level of the power grid equipment, reflect the overall operation status of the regional power grid, provide precise control for the lean investment of the power grid, and assist work decision-making. The labels that measure the dimensions of investment decision support are shown in Table 3.

Table 3. Label of investment decision support dimension

Numbering	Label name	Label classification
E2	Equipment operation efficiency	Efficient, stable, and inefficient
E3	A priori prediction of transformer heavy overload	whether
E4	Priori estimation of line overload	whether
C2	Increase in power supply per unit load growth	High and low efficiency

The operating efficiency of equipment and the increase in power supply per unit load growth are the model tags, and the calculation refers to the formula (12) and (14) in Sect. 3.1. Both transformer heavy-overload a priori prediction and line heavy-overload a priori prediction are smart a priori tags, based on feature sets (historical load, holidays, temperature, humidity, etc.), through intelligent algorithm training prediction, and the key description in the case.

Operational Efficiency Evaluation Dimension. The systematic analysis of equipment operation information and topology information, and obtaining equipment indicators that the planning profession pays attention to, can provide effective data support for power grid diagnosis and analysis, which is conducive to the control of operational benefits. The labels that measure the dimensions of the operational efficiency evaluation are shown in Table 4.

Table 4. Label of operational efficiency evaluation dimension

Numbering	Label name	Label classification
E5	Equipment operation efficiency	High, low, general Responsible, efficient, generally inefficient
E6	A priori prediction of transformer heavy overload	High, low, general Responsible, efficient, generally inefficient

Both labels are model labels, and their intervals are divided as follows:

The unit electricity sales are calculated by the quotient of the equipment's annual (monthly) electricity sales and the equipment capacity (length). The final display result is the ranking of the equipment's annual (monthly) average input electricity in the local city and the monthly average input electricity of the same type of equipment. Accounted for the top 10%: the output is responsible; in the range of 10%–30%, the output is efficient; in the range of 30%–70%, the output is average; after 70%, the output is inefficient.

The equipment utilization rate is used to describe the length of time the equipment can produce economic output. The calculation refers to the formula (9) in Sect. 3.1. The final display result is: the available coefficient ≥ 0.8 is high utilization rate, and the available coefficient ≤ 0.5 is low utilization rate; the rest are General utilization.

5 Device Holographic Portrait Application

This article uses the real equipment data of the Electric Power Co., Ltd., and selects a distribution transformer in Changsha City as a display case. According to the data obtained by the system, the holographic image display table is improved. The label calculation table mainly calculates the device label value of the case equipment and the required. The index value, other tags can be obtained according to the previous content. In this module, we only explain the acquisition of smart a priori tags, and finally perform "three-control" analysis and display the holographic image of the device.

5.1 Smart a Priori Label Refinement

Extract the operating data of a specific transformer M from June 1, 2018 to November 02, 2019. First, the original data is preprocessed by the data processing layer as the source data of the machine learning model variables, and then a variety of machine learning is selected Algorithms and neural network algorithms are compared to train the prediction model, select the optimal model, and finally refine the equipment overload a priori prediction label, as shown in Fig. 3.

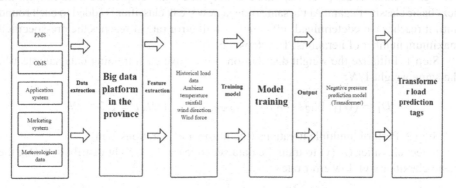

Fig. 3. Heavy overload prior estimate label

Input variables: Short-term heavy-load state prediction is affected by a variety of external factors. At present, the input variables for heavy-load forecast modeling are mainly selected from three aspects: historical heavy load, meteorological conditions and date types. For historical heavy load, the closer the date, the greater the correlation with the heavy load situation of the point to be predicted. Therefore, the forecast time corresponds to the same time in the previous week, 1 time in the previous week, 2 time in the previous week, and The heavy load state at 3 time before 1 week, 4 time before 1 week, 5 time before 1 week and 6 time before 1 week before constitute input variables. At the same time, the heavy load status of different weather conditions and date types have obvious differences, so the temperature and humidity at the forecast time and the types of hours, weeks and holidays are taken as input variables. To sum up, the specific description of the 12-dimensional input variables that can be selected is shown in Table 5.

Table 5. 12 labels selected by input variables

Input variable	Variable composition
x_1-x_7	The corresponding 7 moments of heavy load state
x_8-x_9	Forecast temperature and humidity
x_{10}	Collection point moment
x_{11}	Week type
x_{12}	Holiday type

Related algorithm introduction: Select 9 machine learning algorithms for comparative training, including AdaBoostRegressor, BaggingRegressor, ExtraTreeRegressor, GradientBoostingRegressor, KNeighborsRegressor, RandomForestRegressor, SVM, DecisionTreeRegressor, LinearRegression, among which two are introduced.

AdaBoostRegressor: is an iterative algorithm. In each iteration, a new learner will be generated on the training set. Given a training data set $T = \{(x_1, y_1), (x_2, y_2) \cdots (x_N, y_N)\}$, where instance $x \in X$, and instance space X is R^n, y_i belongs to the label set $\{-1, +1\}$, and the weighted total samples are used to train the next basic classifier again. At the same time, a new weak classifier is added to each round until it reaches a predetermined sufficiently small error rate or reaches the pre-specified maximum number of iterations. The steps are:

Step 1. Initialize the weight distribution. First, give each training data sample W_{1i} the same weight $1/N$:

$$D_1 = (W_{11}, W_{12} \cdots W_{1i} \cdots W_{1N}), W_{1i} = 1/N, i = 1, 2 \ldots N$$

Step 2. Perform multiple iterations (the number of iterations is m)

Select classifier $G_m(x)$ to train the data set to learn the weight distribution D_m, the basic classifier with low error rate:

$$G_m(x) \in \{+1, -1\}$$

Calculate the loss function of $G_m(x)$ on the training data set, which is the average number of misclassified samples

$$loss = \sum_{i=1}^{N} W_{mi} I(G_m(x_i) \neq y_i)$$

Calculate the classification error rate a_m of $G_m(x)$. Among them, when $e_m \leq \frac{1}{2}$, $a_m \geq 0$, and a_m increases as e_m decreases

$$a_m = \frac{1}{2} \log \frac{1 - e_m}{e_m}$$

Update the weight distribution, where the smaller the classification error rate a_m, the higher the weight of the base learner in the final strong learner, and the updated training set is used for the next iteration

$$D_{t+1} = (w_{m+1,1}, w_{m+1,2} \cdots w_{m+1,i} \cdots w_{m+1,N})$$

$$w_{m+1,i} = \frac{w_{mi}}{z_m} \exp(-a_m y_i G_m(x_i)), \ i = 1, 2 \ldots N$$

Where z_m is the normalization factor that makes it a probability distribution

$$z_m = \sum_{i=1}^{N} w_{mi} \exp(-a_m y_i G_m(x_i))$$

Step 3. Until a predetermined small enough error rate or a pre-specified maximum number of iterations is reached, a weighted fusion of the prediction results of multiple weak classifiers is obtained.

$$G(x) = sign\left[\sum_{m=1}^{M} a_m G_m(x) \right]$$

SVM is a support vector machine. The characteristic of its algorithm is to find the optimal decision boundary as much as possible. The steps are as follows:

Step 1. Training is expanded to n-dimensional space according to the distance from the geometric midpoint to the line, and the distance is $W^T x + b = 0$ from $\theta^t x_b = 0$.

$$h = \frac{|W^T x + b|}{\|W\|}, \ \|W\| = \sqrt{W_1^2 + W_2^2 + \cdots + W_n^2}$$

Step 2. When $\frac{|W^T x + b|}{\|W\|} \leq b$, $\forall y^{(i)} = -1$ launch:

$$y^{(i)}(W^T x^{(i)} + b) \geq 1$$

Step 3. Finally get the conditional optimization problem:

$$\min \frac{1}{2} \|w\|^2 \text{ s.t. } y^{(i)}(W^T x^{(i)} + b) \geq 1$$

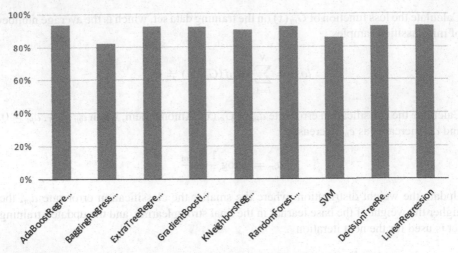

Fig. 4. Precision contrast diagram

Model training results: The model uses the 12 input variables in the above table as the input features of the model. Based on the machine learning algorithm model training, the comparison of 9 algorithms is shown in Fig. 4.

As shown in Fig. 4, the model with the highest accuracy is 93.8%. The prediction control (excerpt) of 96 points in a day on September 4, 2019 in the test set is shown in Table 6.

Table 6. September 4, 2019 forecast control (excerpt)

Numbering	Actual value	Predictive value
['2019-09-04 00-15']	True	True
['2019-09-04 00-30']	True	True
['2019-09-04 00-45']	True	True
['2019-09-04 01-00']	True	True
['2019-09-04 01-15']	True	True
['2019-09-04 01-30']	True	True
['2019-09-04 01-45']	True	True
['2019-09-04 02-00']	True	True
['2019-09-04 02-15']	True	True
['2019-09-04 02-30']	True	True
['2019-09-04 02-45']	True	True
['2019-09-04 03-00']	True	True

(*continued*)

Table 6. (*continued*)

Numbering	Actual value	Predictive value
['2019-09-04 03-15']	False	True
['2019-09-04 03-30']	True	True
['2019-09-04 03-45']	False	False
['2019-09-04 04-00']	True	True

5.2 "Three Controls" Analysis and Data Calculation

The most complicated calculations in the "Three Controls" analysis are the two types of indicators, operating information and operating income, as shown in Tables 7 and 8 respectively.

Table 7. Operation information index calculation

Label calculated value	Index required for label calculation
Slow growth	The average annual growth rate of electric capacity is: 0
General	Line loss rate: 2.54% Average line loss rate in Changsha area: 3.63% The variance is: 87.50
Line loss equipment	Equipment qualified voltage time: 24 Equipment voltage qualification rate: 100%
Voltage pass rate is normal	Maximum load of main distribution transformer: 1323.06 (taken November 17) Maximum load rate of main distribution transformer: 165%
Overload operation	Take 2019 data, The maximum load rate exceeds 90% for a total of 253 days
Overload	Average load of main distribution transformer: 1146.91127787234 (11.17) Average load rate of main distribution transformer: 140%
Run job	Number of low-voltage users: 122 Distribution transformer capacity per household: 6.56
Average load rate is too high	Take 2019.11.02–11.17 data The maximum load rate of the equipment at the beginning of the period: 1.554 The maximum load rate of the equipment at the end of the period: 1.482 Load growth rate: −4.6%

Table 8. Calculation of operation income index

Label calculated value	Index required for label calculation
Input efficient	Average monthly input power: 41852 Ranking: 9419/34336, top 27%
Smooth operation	Equipment operation efficiency: 83%
High utilization	Equipment utilization: 0.92
Efficient output	Unit electricity sales: 52.74 Ranking: 8428/34336, top 24.5%
The probability of heavy overload in the next 3 days is 100%	September 4, 2019: Predict 96 points heavy overload September 5, 2019: Predict 96 points heavy overload September 6, 2019: Predict 96 points heavy overload

6 Conclusion

The construction of a holographic portrait label system for the main equipment of the distribution network based on big data can comprehensively and accurately identify the characteristics of the main equipment of the distribution network; system analysis of equipment operation information and topology information, acquisition of equipment indicators of professional concern for planning, can diagnose the power grid Analysis provides effective data support, which is conducive to the control of operational benefits. The formation of a holographic portrait of equipment can visually show the safe operation level of power grid equipment, reflect the overall operating status of the regional power grid, provide precise control over the lean investment of the power grid, and assist in work decisions.

References

1. Xu, T., Qu, H., Zhang, Y., Zhang, M., Zhang, P.: Research on the application demand of electric power big data. Oper. Manag. **04**, 107–111 (2017)
2. Zhang, D., Miao, X., Liu, L., Zhang, Y., Liu, K.: Study on the development of smart grid big data technology. Proc. Chin. Soc. Electr. Eng. **35**(01), 2–12 (2015)
3. Levine, J., Zhang, D., Ma, W.: Application of energy consumption service based on electricity consumption data analysis by Aoneng Corporation of the United States. Power Supply Use **32**(09), 56–58+49 (2015)
4. Yang, W.: Analysis of big data application in the marketing platform of mobile communication operators. China New Commun. **17**(24), 65–66 (2015)
5. Zhang, L.: Research on user portraits based on big data analysis to help precision marketing. Telecommun. Technol. (01), 61–62+65 (2017)
6. Lin. S., Ouyang, L.: Construction of electric power customer label system based on big data theory. Electr. Technol. (12), 98–101+112 (2016)
7. Zhou, L., Zhao, J., Gao, W.: Application research of sparse coding model in the detection of abnormal power consumption behavior of power users (English). Power Syst. Technol. **39**(11), 3182–3188 (2015)
8. Yin, X., Lin, S., Ouyang, L., Huang, J.: Research on the application of logistic regression model based on market segmentation in the risk forecast of electricity fee recovery. Electr. Demand Side Manag. **18**(04), 46–49 (2016)

9. Zhao, Y., Ma, J., Zhang, K.: Research on label portrait technology based on the life cycle of power assets. Power Syst. Clean Energy **34**(01), 51–58 (2018)
10. Jun, F., Xin, X., Luo, D., Zhu, T., Liu, X.: Research on construction technology of power user behavior profile. Electr. Appl. **37**(13), 18–23 (2018)
11. Liu, W.: Research on smart energy use of energy internet based on the Full-service Unified Data Center of provincial power grid enterprises. In: "Electronic Technology Application" Smart Grid Conference Proceedings, pp. 75–76. China Electric Power Research Institute Co., Ltd., State Grid Power Investment (Beijing) Technology Center (2017)
12. Ren, X., Dai, G., Geng, Z.: Research on power asset portrait technology based on graph database. Power Syst. Clean Energy **33**(11), 59–62+69 (2017)
13. Li, L., Xin, J.: Analysis of user load and power supply strategy of "coal to electricity" in Beijing rural areas. China Electr. Power Enterp. Manag. **10**, 56–58 (2017)
14. Chen, Z., et al.: Research on modeling of precision investment decision in power grid. Econ. Res. Guid. **35**, 17–20 (2018)
15. He, R., Wu, B., Fu, H., Zhang, X., Tao, L., Zhao, L.: Construction of a panoramic view of power customer growth based on big data analysis. Autom. Appl. (10), 70–71 (2018)
16. Zuo, H.: Design of accurate service and early warning system for power grid based on user portrait. China Equip. Eng. **11**, 168–169 (2019)

An Empirical Study on the Tourism Image of Nanjing from the Perspective of International Students

Pu Han[1,2(✉)] ⓘ, Mingtao Zhang[1,2] ⓘ, Mingxiu Yao[1,2], Zhenrong Hui[1,2], and Meitong Chen[1,2]

[1] School of Management, Nanjing University of Posts and Telecommunications, Nanjing 210023, China
hanpu@njupt.edu.cn
[2] Jiangsu Provincial Key Laboratory of Data Engineering and Knowledge Service, Nanjing 210023, China

Abstract. International students are a special group in Chinese cities, and their tourism image perception has important research significance for urban tourism construction. Based on the destination tourism image model proposed by Baloglu and McCleary, the tourism image of Nanjing is divided into three aspects: cognitive image, emotional image and overall image. Aiming at the international student group in Nanjing, the questionnaire survey was used to obtain the perception data of the group's tourism image in Nanjing with SPSS. The empirical research on the tourism image of Nanjing was carried out from three aspects: tourism image perception factor, overall image perception and representative attractions. The study found that in the structured part of the dimension, international students are most satisfied with "urban environment" and least concerned about "attractions". Through the single factor measurement, the most satisfied one is the rich historical and cultural heritage, and the most dissatisfied one is the crowded urban environment. In the unstructured part of the international students on Nanjing tourism image, the overall satisfaction is high, in which the destination image perception of the "delicious food" is the best. In the perception of urban tourism image, the perception of "a beautiful city" is the best. The analysis of the characteristics of social population structure shows obvious individualized difference. Boys tend to Zhongshan mausoleum, and girls are more inclined to Confucius Temple Qinhuai scenery belt.

Keywords: Tourism image · International students · Training tourism · Factor analysis method

1 Introduction

The image of a tourist destination plays an important role in the tourism decision-making of potential tourists. With the implementation of the country's opening-up policy and the increasing influence of China in the world, the number of international students in

© Springer Nature Switzerland AG 2021
X. Sun et al. (Eds.): ICAIS 2021, CCIS 1423, pp. 476–485, 2021.
https://doi.org/10.1007/978-3-030-78618-2_39

China has increased significantly in recent years. According to the statistics of Ministry of Education, in 2017, people from 204 countries and regions studied in 935 colleges and universities of 31 provinces, autonomous regions and municipalities directly under Chinese Central Government in all. The total number of master's and doctoral students was about 75,800, an increase of 18.62% over 2016. As the scale of studying in China continues to expand, China is now the largest destination for study abroad in Asia. For a long time, in the definition of tourists, foreign students are usually listed as non-tourist groups [1], while international students are not residents of the country of study, and their identity is not clearly defined. In recent years, for the special group of international students, their tourism characteristics have once again attracted the attention of the academic community. Specifically, the broad-based study tour refers to all travel activities with the purpose of studying and using tourism as a mean or form. Charlotte [2] believed that although the main purpose of study tour for the international students is learning, its essence is a special kind of tourism behavior, and gave a definition of the study tour: study tourism refers to the sum of all phenomena and relationships caused by learning and life behaviors in the form of tourism, including long-term academic education and short-term non-degree education.

As the special group, the international student not only has the characteristics of travel, curiosity and exploration of tourists, but also has the characteristics of residence and leisure of residents. Based on the existing research, this paper believes that the special group has multi-dimensional attributes, which not only has the characteristics of tourists, but also has the characteristics of residents in the city. The perception of urban tourism image of international students is more mature and stable than that of ordinary tourists, their perception of the city is long-lasting, and they have a certain international perspective. Therefore, through the above analysis, this paper uses questionnaires, literature research and other research methods to explore the tourism perception image of Nanjing from the perspective of international students, and adopts data statistics and factor analysis to make an empirical analysis of urban tourism image from five dimensions and 13 factors.

2 Literature Review

Since Hunt and others first proposed the concept of tourism image in the 1970s, the study of tourist destination image has been an important research field. The academic community generally believes that the tourism image is the overall perception or overall impression of the individual (tourism/scenic area) [3]. Gartner [4] split the perception image of tourism destination into cognitive image, emotional image and intentional image. On the basis of Gartner's research, Son and Pearce [5] studied the tourism international students' views of Australia from the above three aspects by using the questionnaire and factor analysis. Hunter [6] evaluated the tourism image of Seoul by collecting social media data of tourists' evaluation destinations and using text analysis.

From the existing researches, it can be found that the research on tourism image mainly uses questionnaires, interviews and text analysis. By the questionnaires, Chen and Kerstetter [7] examined the image international students at Penn State have of rural travel destinations in the state of Pennsylvania from four distinct image dimensions, "tourism infrastructure", "atmosphere", "natural amenity", and "farm life". Pan and Rasouli [8] used semi-structured interview method to investigate tourist destination choice, focusing on the research question how and to what extent the tourism images of tourists' social network members influence their choice behavior.

The measurement and evaluation of tourism image are mostly based on "structured" and "unstructured" methods. Sultan et al. used the "structured method" to measure and analyze the tourism image of the world's longest sandy sea beach, Cox's Bazar [9]. Yang et al. [10] proposed a systematic method and step for qualitative and quantitative measurement of tourist destination image perception through a comprehensive comparison of structural and non-structural methods. Some literatures combined structural and non-structural methods to study tourism image [11–13]. Some scholars also carried out research on the image of tourist destinations from other perspectives or different methods. For example, Yang [14] introduced the method of implicit association test from the perspective of psychology to the image of tourism destinations.

Based on the existing research, this paper uses questionnaire survey method from the perspective of the combination of structured, unstructured and social demographic characteristics to empirically study the perception of tourism in Nanjing. Exploring the tourism image construction of Nanjing from the perceptual data of international students not only helps to expand the research perspective of tourism image research, but also helps to build a more international, diversified and personalized image of Nanjing tourism.

3 Methods and Data

Based on the existing research, this paper is based on the destination tourism image model proposed by Baloglu and McCleary [15], which divides the tourism image of Nanjing into three aspects: cognitive image, emotional image and overall image, and adopts structure in the questionnaire. The method of structured measurement, unstructured content analysis and social demographic characteristics has designed three corresponding sections.

Structured sections. Firstly, referring to the tourism destination image factor proposed by Baloglu, 13 perceptual factors are extracted for the characteristics of this study (see Table 2); then, through factor analysis, extracting five image perception dimensions of "attractions", "transportation", "social environment", "urban environment" and "social image". These factors basically cover all the elements of tourism image perception of Nanjing. In the development of the scale, in order to better show the degree of tourism perception of the international students, the 5-point Likert scale is used in the measurement (the number "1" stands for "very disagree", "2" stands for "disagree", "3" stands for "general", "4" stands for "agree", and "5" stands for "strongly agree"). The scale is used to measure the perception factors of international students' tourism image of Nanjing, and the semantic difference scale is used to measure the emotional image of international students. In the structured data analysis, SPSS 22.0 validity test, factor analysis and frequency analysis are used to obtain a quantitative evaluation of Nanjing tourism image perceived by international students.

Unstructured sections. The section contains the following five questions: "In the famous scenic spot of Nanjing you have visited, which one are you most satisfied with?",

"In the famous scenic spot of Nanjing you have visited, which one are you most disappointed with?" "Which famous scenic spot would you recommend to friends who come to Nanjing for the first time?", "When you mention Nanjing, what do you think of?", "Please list 3 items (persons, things, events)", "Please summarize your impressions of Nanjing in three words." The first three questions are multiple-choice questions, and the last two questions are fill-in-the-blank questions, which facilitates personalized text analysis.

Social demographic structure features. This section mainly deals with the nationality, gender, age, education, and the school where the international student is studying. In the social demographic structural characteristics section, the differences of tourism image of Nanjing among foreign students with different characteristics are analyzed and evaluated.

4 Result and Interpretation

4.1 Data Acquisition

The questionnaire of this study was published from October to December in 2018. Through the combination of online e-questionnaire and offline paper questionnaire, the questionnaires were distributed to the international students of 13 universities in Nanjing. During the period, a total of 150 questionnaires were distributed and 135 were collected. Due to the language deviation of the international student population, the paper questionnaires were incomplete and resulted in a total of 85 high-quality and effective questionnaires.

4.2 Data Analysis

Structured Analysis. In this paper, the Bartlett spherical test and KMO test method in SPSS 22.0 statistical analysis software are used to measure the validity, and the analysis of whether the 13 Nanjing tourist destination image measurement items are suitable for the extraction factor in the effective questionnaire is analyzed. Shown in Table 1.

Table 1. KMO and Bartlett Accreditation

Kaiser-Meyer-Olkin measure of sampling adequacy		0.818
Bartlett's test of sphericity	About Chi-square Distribution	386.180
	df	78
	Statistical significance	0.000

Table 1 shows that Bartlett's spherical test p = 0, significantly less than the significance level of 0.05, should reject the null hypothesis, the correlation coefficient matrix and the unit coefficient matrix are significantly different, while the KMO value is 0.818, higher than the general level (KMO = 0.7), from which the measurement item can be considered suitable for factor analysis. Since only the first four factors have eigenvalues > 1 and accumulate 66.574% (> 50%), the first four factors are extracted as the main factors, and a 4-factor destination perceptual image structure composed of 13 measurement items is obtained.

Table 2 gives the students' perception of the factors affecting Nanjing's tourism image from five dimensions.

Table 2. The perceived evaluation of the influence factors of international students on the tourism image of Nanjing

Dimensions	Measurements	Average of questionnaire	Mean	Cronbach α Coefficient
Attractions	Nanjing is a world-famous historical capital	3.70	3.56	0.724
	Nanjing's delicious food is unique		3.59	
	Nanjing City has lots of historical and cultural heritage		4.13	
	Nanjing has very folk customs and local characteristics		3.54	
Transportation	Nanjing's overall traffic layout is convenient and reasonable	4.15	4.11	0.5
	I have a good impression of Nanjing Lukou Airport		4.09	
Social environment	Good social security in Nanjing	3.95	4.05	0.5
	The citizens of Nanjing are warm and friendly		3.84	
Urban environment	Nanjing's urban environment is crowded	3.52	3.11	0.492
	Nanjing's city streets are clean and hygienic		4.04	
	Good air quality in Nanjing		3.42	
Social image	Nanjing's tourist attractions tend to be international	3.74	3.55	0.5
	Nanjing's economic is developed		3.93	

Table 2 presents the preference and satisfaction to the elements of Nanjing tourism image by means of descriptive analysis. It can be found that the five image perception dimensions of "attractions", "transportation", "social environment", "urban environment" and "social image", and the above 13 perceptual factors are measured by the Likert scale method. The average value of 13 measurement items exceeds 3, which indicates that foreign students are more satisfied with the overall tourism image of Nanjing. The values of the five dimensions from high to low are "transportation", "social environment", "social image", "attractions" and "urban environment". Among the perceptual factors, foreign students have higher recognition of "Nanjing has rich historical and cultural heritage" and lower recognition of "Nanjing has good air quality".

Unstructured Analysis - Cross Analysis, High Frequency Word Analysis. In order to understand the perception of Nanjing's tourism image more comprehensively and systematically, this study conducted cross-analysis and high-frequency vocabulary analysis. This part explores the differences in perceptions of gender differences for scenic preferences by cross-analysis. The results are shown in Table 3.

Table 3. Cross analysis

In these famous scenic spots in Nanjing	In the famous scenic spot of Nanjing you have been to, your most satisfied scenic spot is:		In the famous your scenic spot of Nanjing you have been to, most disappointed scenic spot is:		When your friend come to Nanjing which famous scenic spot you will recommend:	
	Male	Female	Male	Female	Male	Female
The Sun Yat-sen Mausoleum	13	4	4	3	11	9
Xuanwu Lake	1	2	5	0	3	2
Nanjing Presidential Palace	2	0	3	2	4	0
Yuhuatai Scenic Area	2	0	2	0	3	1
Qixia Mountain	5	3	0	1	3	5
Yuejiang Tower	3	1	3	0	1	1
Niushou Mountain	3	1	0	1	4	2
Nanjing China Green Expo Garden	0	1	1	1	0	0
Tangshan Hot Spring Tourist Resorts	2	0	0	1	1	0
Jiangning Imperial Silk Manufacturing Museum	1	1	1	0	1	0
Stone City Ruins Park of Nanjing	0	0	3	0	1	0
Confucian Temple	10	12	3	1	10	4
East Zhonghua Gate Historical Culture Block	1	3	1	0	1	1
Former Residence of Gan Xi	1	0	2	0	0	2
The Memorial Hall of the Victims in Nanjing Massacre by Japanese Invaders	3	3	2	3	7	4
Others	5	2	22	20	2	2
Total	52	33	52	33	52	33

It can be seen from Table 3 that different genders have obvious differences in satisfaction, disappointment and preference. The most satisfactory scenic spot for boys is Sun Yat-sen Mausoleum. The most satisfying scenic spot for girls is the Confucius Temple Qinhuai scenery belt. In the survey of the most disappointing scenic spots, boys and girls were not the most disappointed with these famous scenic spots. In the survey of recommending scenic spots to friends, 76% recommended the three scenic spots of Sun

Yat-sen Mausoleum, Confucius Temple Qinhuai Scenery Belt and the Memorial Hall of the Nanjing Massacre Victims invading China.

High-frequency word analysis can focus on the main perceptions of urban students' impressions on the city. In order to comprehensively present and reduce sample bias, this paper designs the following topic: "When referring to Nanjing, please write down 3 words you think of? Such as person, things and events". After statistical analysis, the frequency extracted from 40 keywords is no less than 6 high frequency words, representative person/thing/event analysis is shown in Table 4.

Table 4. The representative characters, events and things of international students' perception of Nanjing

Vocabulary	Frequency	Proportion (%)
Delicious food	16	6.27%
Culture	10	3.92%
Sun Zhongshan	7	2.75%
University	6	2.35%
Nanjing Massacre	6	2.35%
Xuanwu Lake	6	2.35%

Table 4 shows that among the representative person/things/events in Nanjing, the most mentioned "person" is Sun Yat-sen, and the most mentioned "event" is the Nanjing Massacre, while the most mentioned "things" are food, culture, university, Xuanwu Lake. In addition to the high-frequency keywords in Table 4, there are also more influential figures, things or events such as "Presidential Office", "Museum", "Jiang Jieshi", "Salt Duck" and "Xinjiekou".

In the same way, through the design of the topic: "Please summarize your impressions of Nanjing in three words" to investigate and acquire the personality and characteristics evaluation for Nanjing so as to obtain the understanding of the integrity and uniqueness of Nanjing's tourism image. Table 5 gives the high-frequency vocabulary of international students' perception of Nanjing tourism image.

Table 5. High-frequency vocabulary of Nanjing tourism image perceived by foreign students

Vocabulary	Frequency	Proportion (%)
A beautiful city	38	19.90%
Peaceful	11	3.92%
Clean and hygienic	11	2.75%
Friendly people	10	2.35%
A long history	10	2.35%
Safe	10	2.35%
Convenient transportation	9	3.53%

The high-frequency words in Table 5 are basically positive descriptions. The psychological feelings of foreign students and the negative descriptions of nature and humanities appear very little, indicating that Nanjing has a relatively high reputation. "A beautiful city", "Convenient transportation", "Clean and hygienic" and "A long history" are positive comments of the tourism environment and transportation of Nanjing, which has a long history. "Peaceful", "Friendly people" and "Safe" reflect that Nanjing is a united and friendly family. In addition, there have also been perceived keywords such as "outstanding", "affordable", "new and old", "interesting" and "unique".

Analysis of the Characteristics of Social Population Structure. This part analyzes the perceived differences of different groups of tourism images by investigating the information of international students, their schools, gender, age, and education. Statistics show that 49.3% of the international students surveyed are from Africa, 44.7% from Asia, 2.4% from Europe, 2.4% from South America, and 1.2% from North America. According to the statistics of age structure, the samples participating in the survey are mainly concentrated between 18 and 24 years old, accounting for 55.3%; the second is the sample of 25–35 years old, accounting for 43.5%; the youngest group is 36–44 years old, accounting for 1.2%. From the gender perspective of the sample of international students, the proportion of male students is 61.2%, and that of female students is 38.8%. The distribution of international students in the university is shown in Fig. 1.

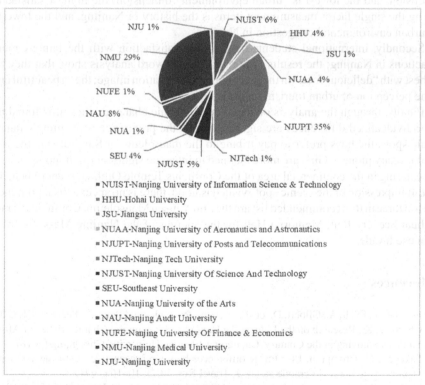

Fig. 1. School distribution of international students

As can be seen from Fig. 1, among the international students who participated in the survey, all of them belonged to Nanjing universities, among which Nanjing University of Posts and Telecommunications accounted for the highest proportion, followed by Nanjing Medical University. The number of international students enrolled in these two universities in recent years was high.

5   Research Analysis

As a special group, foreign students have gradually attracted the attention of researchers in recent years. The perception of tourism image based on the perspective of foreign students is a new field worth exploring. This paper obtains the data of the international students' perception of Nanjing tourism image through questionnaires, and analyzes the international tourism image of Nanjing from three aspects: tourism image perception factor, overall image perception and representative attractions. In this study, nearly two-thirds of the respondents have been studying in Nanjing for more than one year. Their understanding of Nanjing cities and tourist attractions is higher than that of ordinary tourists, and their understanding is relatively stable.

Through research, first of all, among the five dimensions of Nanjing tourism image perception factors, the highest satisfaction of international students is "transportation" dimension, and the lowest is "urban environment" dimension; the highest satisfaction among the single factor measurement items is the history of Nanjing, and the lowest is the urban environmental congestion in Nanjing.

Secondly, international students have higher satisfaction with the famous tourist attractions in Nanjing; the results of high-frequency word analysis show that they feel the best with "delicious food" in the perception of destination image; the "a beautiful city" in the perception of urban tourism image is best.

Finally, through the analysis of social demographic characteristics, it is found that the individualized differences are significant. For the preference of Nanjing's famous scenic spots, the boys prefer to pay tribute to the mausoleum of Sun Yat-sen, the great revolutionary pioneer. Girls are more inclined to integrate sightseeing, shopping, leisure, and catering in the commercial area of the Confucius Temple Qinhuai scenery belt. The overall impression of the scenic spots visited is good, there is no special disappointment. The top three in the recommended list are the Sun Yat-sen Mausoleum, Confucius Temple Qinhuai Scenery Belt, Memorial Hall for the Victims of the Nanjing Massacre by the Japanese Invaders.

References

1. Fletcher, J., Fyall, A., Gilbert, D., et al.: Tourism: Principles and Practice. Pearson, UK (2017)
2. Charlotte, K.: Research on the Influencing Factors and Behavioral Characteristics of African Students Studying in the Country. Chongqing Jiaotong University, Chongqing (2018)
3. Fakeye, P.C., Crompton, J.L.: Image differences between prospective, first-time, and repeat visitors to the lower rio grande valley. J. Travel Res. 30(2), 10–16 (1991)
4. Gartner, W.C.: Image formation process. J. Travel Tourism Mark. 2(3), 191–215 (1993)

5. Son, A., Pearce, P.: Multi-faceted image assessment: international students' views of australia as a tourist destination. J. Travel Tourism Market. **18**(4), 21–35 (2005)
6. Hunter, W.C.: The social construction of tourism online destination image: a comparative semiotic analysis of the visual representation of Seoul. Tour. Manag. **54**(1), 221–229 (2016)
7. Chen, P.J., Kerstetter, D.L.: International students' image of rural Pennsylvania as a travel destination. J. Travel Res. **37**(3), 256–266 (1999)
8. Pan, X., Rasouli, S., Timmermans, H.: Investigating tourist destination choice: effect of destination image from social network members. Tour. Manag. **83**(1), (2021)
9. Sultan, M.T., Sharmin, F., Badulescu, A., et al.: Travelers' responsible environmental behavior towards sustainable coastal tourism: an empirical investigation on social media user-generated content. Sustainability **13**(1), 56 (2021)
10. Yang, Y., Bai, L., Su, Z.: A comparative study on the structured and unstructured measurements of tourist destination image: a case of yangshuo. Guilin. Tourism Tribune **1**(4), 53–57 (2007)
11. Choi, W.M., Chan, A., Wu, J.: A qualitative and quantitative assessment of Hong Kong's image as a tourist destination. Tour. Manag. **20**(3), 361–365 (1999)
12. O'leary, S., Deegan, J.: People, pace, place: qualitative and quantitative images of Ireland as a tourism destination in France. J. Vacation Market. **9**(3), 213–226 (2003)
13. Hem, L.E., Iversen, N.M.: How to develop a destination brand logo: a qualitative and quantitative approach. Scand. J. Hospitality Tourism **4**(2), 83–106 (2004)
14. Yang, J., He, J., Gu, Y.: The implicit measurement of destination image: the application of implicit association tests. Tour. Manag. **33**(1), 1–52 (2012)
15. Baloglu, S., McCleary, K.W.: A model of destination image formation. Ann. Tourism Res. **26**(4), 868–897 (1999)

Anomaly Detection Based on Isolated Forests

Jun-Liang Li[1], Yi-Feng Zhou[1], Zhi-Yang Ying[1], Hong Xu[1], Yuanxi Li[2], and Xiaojie Li[1(✉)]

[1] Chengdu University of Information Technology, Chengdu 610103, China
lixj@cuit.edu.cn
[2] Chengdu Shengdaren Technology Co. Ltd., Chengdu, China

Abstract. Anomaly detection plays an important role in big data, which deals with high dimensional data effectively and quickly. In this paper is going to propose an anomaly detection method based on isolated forests. In the proposed method, the original data set is divided into different initial static blocks to calculate the intra-block density and mean density, respectively; after calculating the intra-block density of static blocks, the data set is simplified with the mean density of the original data set as a threshold (delete such blocks with intra-block density which is bigger than the mean density); for blocks with lower intra-block density, we construct isolated forests with the recursive method of nodes; the corresponding features are extracted and normalized to calculate the spatial position distance between the cluster center point and other points; based on density and distance, the anomaly scores are added to compare with the corresponding threshold. This method can effectively improve the accuracy of anomaly detection algorithm, and greatly reduce the actual amount of data in the process of anomaly detection. Furthermore, our method could save a lot of computing resources, and improve the efficiency of anomaly detection, and enhance the robustness of anomaly detection algorithm.

Keywords: Anomaly detection · Block density · Mean density · Isolated forest · Normalization

1 Introduction

Anomaly detection is a detecting process that finds out its behavior is very different from the expected object [1]. An anomaly is defined by the Hawkins (1980) [2]. An anomaly refers to the data that is different in the data set, which makes people suspect that these data are not random deviations, but are derived from completely different mechanisms. Removal of outliers is helpful to obtain more practical results and improve the accuracy of the algorithm. Abnormal point detection has specific applications in human's manufacture and life, such as credit card fraud, industrial damage detection, image detection and so on [3].

There are many different methods for how to detect anomalies. There are algorithms that take labels as the main criteria, position and density information as the main criteria, and data parameters as the criteria. Among the commonly used anomaly detection algorithms, many classical algorithms conduct anomaly detection from different

© Springer Nature Switzerland AG 2021
X. Sun et al. (Eds.): ICAIS 2021, CCIS 1423, pp. 486–495, 2021.
https://doi.org/10.1007/978-3-030-78618-2_40

angles, such as density-based method, distance-based method, statistics-based method, clustering-based method, classification-based anomaly detection algorithm and so on [4, 5].

The statistical method is to construct a related mathematical model for the original data set and evaluate the data anomaly according to the object fitting model [6]. Then the probability distribution model is found by estimating the parameters. The user determines some parameters to be estimated independently, such as the sum of Gaussian distribution, μ and σ estimates the parameters by using the data set to obtain the prediction $\frac{3}{\sigma}$ model. For example, detect outliers in unary normal distribution, using classical principles. For multivariate normal distribution, the Mahalanobis distance based on covariance matrix is used to detect. However, if there is an error in the model while modeling, the object is likely to be wrongly judged as an anomaly. Moreover, most of the anomaly detection algorithms based on statistics adopt single attributes, which is not mature for multi-attribute data modeling. If there is sufficient prior knowledge of data and test types, statistical-based methods may be very effective for anomaly detection of single attributes. For high dimensional data (multivariate data), the performance of the test may be poor.

A most commonly distance-based anomaly detection method is proposed by Knorr et al. [4-2]. Given a radius ε and a percentage π, DB (distance-based) outliers DB (ε, π) are defined as follows: an object p is considered an outlier if at least π percent of all other points have a distance to p greater than ε. Formally, denote an object p on the original data set S called DB (x,y) outlier, then $|\{p \in S, DB(x, p) > \varepsilon\}| \geq \pi m$, where m is the number of data point and $|\cdot|$ counts the number of elements of the set. Ramaswamy et al. [8] proposed a scoring algorithm based on the distance of a point from its kth nearest neighbor [7]: for each point x, calculating the distance of its k nearest neighbor $D^k(x)$ takes the first n points with a maximum D^k value as an outlier. They also presented a highly efficient partition-based algorithm for mining outliers. For different parameters, the results are also very unstable, and the complexity of the algorithm is high.

The density-based method is generally calculating the relative density to compare the density values of the selected objects with their adjacent regions. The points with lower density are identified as outliers, and the corresponding processing methods of different density selection methods are also different. Breunig et al. [9] proposed a scoring algorithm by comparing the local density of a given point and its surrounding neighbors. Assume that the k is a natural number. The accessible distance p the observation point relative to the o is defined as reach $- distk(p, o) = \max\{K - dis \tan ce(o), d(p, o)\}$. A local reachable density p an observation point is defined as

$$lrd_{MinPts}(p) = \cfrac{1}{\left(\cfrac{\sum\limits_{o \in N_{MinPts}(p)} reach-dist_{MinPts}(p,o)}{|N_{MinPts}(p)|} \right)}$$

a local anomaly factor p an observation point is

$$LOF_{MinPts}(p) = \cfrac{\sum\limits_{o \in N_{MinPts}(p)} \cfrac{lrd_{MinPts}(o)}{lrd_{MinPts}(p)}}{|N_{MinPts}(p)|}$$

If the local anomaly factor p the observation point is larger, it is then closer to the anomaly [7-2].

A classification anomaly detection algorithm based on support vector machine uses the calculation of spatial Euclidean distance [3] between points to determine the corresponding support vector and customize an exception score and threshold [10]. When the abnormal score value of data exceeds the threshold, it is marked as 0, representing abnormal data point. Then the distance between the two support vectors is maximized by the objective function under the constraint condition, and the separation hyperplane can be determined to achieve the purpose of anomaly detection. Of course, the method above is based on the linear separable data set as the model, and the kernel method for the processing of nonlinear separable data sets is derived. Its training set cannot contain abnormal samples, otherwise, it may affect the selection of boundaries during training. In the face of multi-classification, problems cannot be directly dealt with effectively. When dealing with linear inseparability, the kernel method will be used, but this would lead to the data distortion when the kernel selection method is improper.

Outlier anomaly detection algorithm TRAOD uses trajectory to divide lines and uses lines to represent the local characteristics of the trajectory (this is the basic comparison unit), and then uses the line segment Hausdorf to calculate the distance between each two segments to indicate the abnormal trajectory. Moreover, in order to improve the efficiency of the algorithm, TRAOD also provides a two-stage partition method that the starting point and the end point of the trajectory are divided into coarse-grained trajectory fragments to represent the coarse-grained trajectory fragments which are found to be abnormal locally, and then the anomaly trajectory fragments are divided into line segments to find the anomalies RAOD which solves the mismatch between the long trajectories very well.

2   Outlier Detection Based on Isolated Forest

iForest does not need to model the original data set and the training process with labels. So how do we determine that whether the sample point is isolated by iForest [10] is a very efficient method? For the original data space, we randomly select a hyperplane to cut, which can form two sub-space. Then random cutting is carried out between the two subspaces, and the same operation cycle goes on until each subspace contains only one data point [11].

Isolation tree (iTree) [12]: suppose T is a node of an isolated tree, then it is either a leaf node without a child node or an internal node with only two child nodes (Tl,Tr). Each step of segmentation contains feature q and segmentation values p, dividing data with $q < p$ into Tl, and otherwise dividing the data into the Tr.

Given dataset $X = \{x_1, \cdots x_n\}$ with n samples and the dimension of the feature is d. To build an isolated tree, we need to randomly select a feature q and its segmentation value p, and then dividing data sets X recursively until any of the following conditions is met:

(1) The tree reaches the limit height;
(2) There is only one sample on the node;

(3) All features of the sample on the node are the same.

The iForest training ends after obtaining t iTree [12-2], and then we can evaluate the test data with the generated iForest. With a training data x, we make it traverse each tree iTree, then calculate x eventually falling on the first layer of each tree (x at the height of the tree). And then we can get the average height of x in each tree. After obtaining the height average of each test data, we can set a threshold (boundary value), and the test data whose height average is lower than this threshold is abnormal. That is, the anomaly has only a very short average height in these trees

Path Length: the path length x the sample point h (x) is the number of edges passing from the root node of the iTree to the leaf node.

Anomaly Score: given a data set containing n samples, the average path length of the tree is

$$c(n) = 2H(n-1) - \frac{2n-1}{n}$$

where H (i) is the harmonic number, which can be estimated as ln (i)0.5772156649. c_n is the average of the path length when the number of samples is given, it is used to standardize the path length x the sample h (x).

Exception score of x is defined as $s(x, n) = 2^{-\frac{E(h(x))}{c(n)}}$, where E (h (x)) is the expectation of the path length of the sample x in a batch of isolated trees. The relationship between s and E (h (x)) can be seen in the Fig. 1.

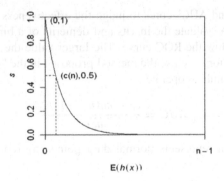

Fig. 1. E (h (x))

Some conclusions can be drawn from the above:

When E (h (x)) → c (n), the average length of the path x of the sample is close to the average path length of the tree.

When E (h (x)) → 0, s → 1, i.e., abnormal score of the x is close to 1, is judged as abnormal.

When E (h (x)) → n−1, s → 0, is judged normal.

Our method is to divide the original data set into initial static average blocks, calculate the intra-block density and mean density, calculate the intra-block density of each static block, and simplify the data set with the mean density of the original data set as the threshold. An isolated forest is constructed by recursive method of nodes. Then an anomaly score is determined by calculating the path length, then the original data set is extracted by feature extraction, and the data is processed the same. Finally, the two outliers are added and compared with the sum of the two means. Data points with a score greater than the mean value are determined as outliers.

Initial static partitioning of the original data set; according to the original data set $\Phi = \{x_1, x_2, \cdots \cdots, x_n\}$ divide the data set Φ into k datasets on a scale, Mark the subscripts of the sub dataset sequentially as $\{\phi_1, \phi_2, \cdots \cdots, \phi_k\}$ constitute a subset of data sets $\{\phi_1, \phi_2, \cdots \cdots, \phi_k\} \subset \Phi$, called basic subdatasets, calculate $\rho_i = \sum_j \chi (d_{ij} - d_c)$ the inner density of the k sub-datasets according to their respective, where the density calculation function is $\chi(x) = \begin{cases} 1, x<0 \\ 0, x\geq 0 \end{cases}$, a custom distance is called a truncated distance d_c, then calculate the mean density of the original data set Φ;

$$\overline{\rho} = \frac{\sum_{i=1}^{n} x_i}{n}$$

Then comparison of calculated intra-block density and mean density result with $\delta_i = \max\{\rho_i, \overline{\rho}\}$ $i = 1, 2, \cdots \cdots, n$, if $\rho_i > \overline{\rho}$, we set the label of the corresponding sub dataset to 1, vice versa.

2.1 Evaluation Measure

We use ROC curves and AUC scores to judge the effectiveness of the algorithm [15]. They are often used to evaluate the merits and demerits of a binary classifier. AUC is defined as the area below the ROC curve. The larger value the AUC is, the better the classification is. Therefore, we use the method proposed in the [16], in which the AUC uses the following formula to operate.

$$AUC = \frac{s_0 - n_0(n_1 - 1)/2}{n_0 n_1}$$

In this formula, n_0 represents normal data points, n_1 represents the number of abnormal points,

$$s_0 = \sum_{i=1}^{n} r_i$$

where r_i represents the rank of normal data in the classification model.

When dataset is divided into positive class (positive) or negative class (negative). For binary classification, there are four situations in practice. If an instance is a positive class and is predicted to be a positive class, it's True Positive (TP); if an instance is a positive class but is predicted to be a negative class, it's False Negative (FN); if an instance is a negative class but is predicted to be a positive class, it's False Positive (FP); if an instance is a negative class but is predicted to be a negative class, that is, it's a true negative class (True Negative TN). Then the Precision (P) is defined as the number of true positives (TP) over the number of true positives plus the number of false positives (FP).

$$P = \frac{TP}{TP + FP}$$

Recall (R) is defined as the number of true positives (TP) over the number of true positives plus the number of false negatives (FN).

$$R = \frac{TP}{TP + FN}$$

Generally speaking, a classifier with good classification effect can sort the actual data more reasonably, even if the recall rate improves its accuracy, it will not be greatly affected and can maintain a high level. The classifier with poor effect often needs to sacrifice accuracy to improve recall rate. Some articles have proposed a new accurate recovery curve to better select the appropriate classifier to process the data, because sometimes the gap between the curves is not particularly obvious, and the numbers can better depict the difference. The following is a more common metric average accuracy, which is equivalent to the area under the precision-recall curve (AUPRC) [17].

$$AP = \sum_{i=1}^{n} (R_n - R_{n-1})P_n$$

where P_n and R_n are the precision and recall at the nth threshold, respectively.

2.2 Data Sets

We selected nine data sets on the UCI, including eight real-word data sets and one synthetic data set. By classifying these data sets, most of the data sets are used for classification tasks. Inspired by [19] this article, we choose the following data processing methods:

1) Delete all instances of the smallest class of all classes directly determined as outliers.
2) Most of these classes (those with higher number of passes) are directly identified as normal data points.

We select two smaller classes from all classes, then arbitrarily select 3% of the data points as abnormal data points. Special, for the "MADELON" data set, we select only one subclass. From these principles above, the data feature information of the eight data sets is shown in Table 1. In the selected column, the number represents the selection of the corresponding principle. Figures in parentheses represent the number of subclasses. And for synthetic data sets, it generates 150 normal points in a standard normal distribution by setting $\mu = 0$, $\sigma = 1$ and 59 outliers obtained from uniform distribution, the range of values is −6 to 6. The information for the eight data sets is seen in Table 1 below.

The description of the "NHL1" dataset is from the National Hockey League, in which we select the percentage of goals, shots and goals, in which we consider ChrisOsgood

Table 1. Data set

Data set	Totol	Normal	Abnormal	Dim	Select
ARRHYTHMIA	452	245	207	279	1
ARTIFICIAL	200	150	50	20	1
MNIST-2D	1797	351	44	2	2 (2,8)
IONOSPHERE	351	225	126	34	1
MADELON	2000	1000	30	500	2
NHL1	855	853	2	3	1
OPTDIGITS	5620	1111	135	64	2 (2,8)
SPAMBASE	4601	2788	1813	57	1

and MarioLemieux as abnormal data, and the dataset contains the corresponding attribute characteristics of 96 players.

We think the "SPAMBASE" data set is an abnormal data value. The standard we think of email information as spam, is whether it has a commercial request. The attributes of the email are mostly related to certain words or characters, which its attribute of running length is to measure the length of a continuous sequence of uppercase letters.

"ARRHYTHMIA" data set is a synthetic data set which contains 279 attribute features, some of which are labeled outliers, and 206 linear data which contains a variety of attribute features. We select features such as height, weight, sex, age, QRs duration, and then group them. Our main task is to distinguish the existence of arrhythmia. We use our algorithm to process each set of data, select two kinds of data—— class two and class eight data—— to evaluate the effectiveness of the algorithm. The results shown in Table 2 and Table 3 prove the effectiveness of our method.

Table 2. AUC score

Data set	OSVM	IF	LOF	RC	MINE
arrhythmia	0.4981	0.6020	0.5888	0.6020	0.8067
artificial	0.8300	0.7000	0.7000	0.7000	0.9874
ionosphere	0.6744	0.6429	0.6305	0.6389	0.8743
madelon	0.5000	0.5515	0.5515	0.5172	0.9654
nhl1	0.7251	0.9508	0.9508	0.9508	0.9508
optdigits	0.5280	0.7719	0.7220	0.7968	0.8642
spambase	0.6461	0.5165	0.4192	0.4544	0.5163
credits	0.4194	0.7321	0.5046	0.6752	0.8735

(continued)

Table 2. (*continued*)

Data set	OSVM	IF	LOF	RC	MINE
maxnum	0.8300	0.9508	0.9508	0.9508	0.9874
minnum	0.4194	0.5165	0.4192	0.4544	0.5163
average	0.6026	0.6835	0.6334	0.6669	0.8548

2.3 AUC Score

In order to prove the effectiveness of the algorithm, we select four common anomaly detection algorithms to compare. The corresponding effects of these methods are shown in Table 2. The parameters we select are the same as the default parameters of the algorithm.

As shown in Table 2, our algorithm has obvious advantages over the four associated anomaly detection algorithms in seven datasets, and the detection results on a dataset are the same. This column of the maximum value shows the effectiveness of our method. For nhl1 data sets, although they don't show our sufficient advantage, the overall efficiency is the same as IF, LOF and RC algorithms. However, our advantages are more obvious on arrhythmia, artificial, ionosphere and optdigits data sets [20]. Our algorithm on spam base dataset is higher than LOF and RC algorithms, which only has the gap of 0.03 with IF algorithm. Considering the effects of maximum, minimum and mean, it can be shown that the stability of our algorithm is better. For high-dimensional data, because of the pretreatment process, our method has good performance characteristics for high dimensional data.

As shown in Table 2, we limit the value range of parameter k from 5 to 5log(m) our this column, we calculate the value of each k as follows, and get the sk score we then averaged all AUC scores to obtain the FIFOAUC scores of our method.

$$s = \frac{\sum_{k=5}^{5\log(m)} sk}{5\log(m) - 5}$$

2.4 AUPRC Score

To demonstrate the effectiveness of our approach more clearly, except for precision-recall curves, we choose the AUPRC score as criteria, and that's more persuasive than AUC. We also use the equation above to calculate the AUPRC average score in the Table 3. For the data analysis in the Table 3, our algorithm has obvious advantages over other common algorithms on six data sets. LOF algorithm has the advantage of 0.0104 on credits and dermatology data set, comparing with the more effective IF algorithms on ionosphere data sets, the gap between us is only 0.0001 which is very close to the best score. Our method and other algorithms behave the same as the whole on the nhl1 data set. Table 3 data shows similar results to Table 2, Table 3 also shows that our algorithm performs well in high-dimensional data.

Table 3. AUPRC scores

Data set	OSVM	IF	LOF	RC	MINE
arrhythmia	0.5412	0.5981	0.5901	0.5981	0.6007
artificial	0.915	0.8333	0.8333	0.8333	0.9433
ionosphere	0.7414	0.7143	0.7073	0.712	0.7142
madelon	0.9709	0.9758	0.9738	0.9709	0.9837
nhl1	0.9987	0.9998	0.9998	0.9998	0.9998
optdigits	0.8971	0.9476	0.9369	0.9522	0.9485
spambase	0.6919	0.614	0.5962	0.585	0.8178
credits	0.9735	0.9876	0.9772	0.985	0.9876
dermatology	0.9737	0.9974	0.9609	0.9788	0.9974

3   Conclusion

Compared with the traditional anomaly detection algorithm, the proposed algorithm is an effective algorithm based on isolated forest. We use parallel processing density relationship to simplify the data volume, construct iTree and then propose the mean density as the threshold. The feature information is used as the criterion to form a double correlation prediction model, which effectively avoids misjudgment. In the preprocessing stage, we can judge the abnormal situation with region density value, and we do not need the training process with label. The calculated AUC and AUPRC scores can confirm the effectiveness of our method. In the process of implementation, we find that our algorithm is more stable than the traditional algorithm for higher dimensional data sets

Acknowledgment. This work was supported by the Sichuan Science and Technology program (2019JDJQ0002, 2019YFH0085, 2018RZ0072).

References

1. Li, X., Lv, J., Zhang, Y.: An efficient representation-based method for boundary point and outlier detection. IEEE Trans. Neural Netw. Learn. Syst. **99**, 1–12 (2016)
2. Hawkins, D.M.: Identifification of outliers. Biometrics **37**(4), 860 (1980)
3. Aggarwal, C.C., Yu, P.S.: Outlier detection for high dimensional data. ACM Sigmod Record **30**(2), 37–46 (2001)
4. Knorr, E.M., Ng, R.T.: Algorithms for mining distance-based outliers in large datasets. In: International Conference on Very Large Data Bases, pp. 392–403 (1998)
5. Li, X., Lv, J.C., Cheng, D.: Angle-based outlier detection algorithm with more stable relationships (2015)
6. Hautamaki, V., Karkkainen, I., Franti, P.: Outlier detection using k-nearest neighbour graph. In: International Conference on Pattern Recognition, vol. 3, pp. 430–433 (2004)
7. Lucic, M., Bachem, O., Krause, A.: Linear-time outlier detection via sensitivity. In: International Joint Conference on Artificial Intelligence, pp. 1795–1801 (2016)

8. Ramaswamy, S., Rastogi, R., Shim, K.: Efficient algorithms for mining outliers from large data sets. In: ACM SIGMOD International Conference on Management of Data, pp. 427–438 (2000)
9. Breunig, M.M.: Lof: identifying density-based local outliers. In: ACM SIGMOD International Conference on Management of Data, pp. 93–104 (2000)
10. Scholkopf, B., Platt, J.C., Shawe-Taylor, J., Smola, A.J., Williamson, R.C.: Estimating the support of a highdimensional distribution. Neural Comput. **13**(7), 1443 (2001)
11. Zhang, T., Ramakrishnan, R., Livny, M.: Birch: a new data clustering algorithm and its applications. Data Min. Knowl. Disc. **1**(2), 141–182 (1997)
12. Liu, F.T., Kai, M.T., Zhou, Z.H.: Isolation forest. In: Eighth IEEE International Conference on Data Mining, pp. 413–422 (2008)
13. Rousseeuw, P.J., Driessen, K.V.: A fast algorithm for the minimum covariance determinant estimator. Technometrics **41**(3), 212–223 (1999)
14. Bentley, J.L.: Multidimensional binary search trees used for associative searching. Commun. ACM **18**(9), 509–517 (1975)
15. Bradley, A.P.: The use of the area under the roc curve in the evaluation of machine learning algorithms. Pattern Recogn. **30**(7), 1145–1159 (1997)
16. Hand, D.J., Till, R.J.: A simple generalisation of the area under the roc curve for multiple class classification problems. Mach. Learn. **45**(2), 171–186 (2001)
17. Goodrich, M., Oliphant, L., Shavlik, J.: Gleaner: creating ensembles of first-order clauses to improve recall-precision curves. Mach. Learn. **64**(1–3), 231–261 (2006)
18. Bache, K., Lichman, M.: Uci machine learning repository (2013)
19. Sugiyama, M., Borgwardt, K.M.: Rapid distance-based outlier detection via sampling. Adv. Neural Inform. Process. Syst. **26**, 467–475 (2013)
20. Laurens, V.D.M.: Accelerating t-sne using tree-based algorithms. J. Mach. Learn. Res. **15**(1), 3221–3245 (2014)

An Information Identification Method
for Venture Firms Based on Frequent
Itemset Discovery

Ning Cao[1], Yansong Wang[2], Xiaoyu Chen[2], Yulan Zhou[2], Mingrui Wu[2],
Xiaofang Li[3], Jianrui Ding[2], and Dongjie Zhu[2(✉)]

[1] College of Information Engineering, Sanming University, Sanming 365000, China
[2] School of Computer Science and Technology, Harbin Institute of Technology,
Weihai 264200, China
zhudongjie@hit.edu.cn
[3] Department of Mathematics, Harbin Institute of Technology, Weihai 264209, China

Abstract. In recent years, the emergence of a large number of venture firms has brought great profits to venture capital firms. However, it is not easy to identify venture firms with investment prospects. Therefore, based on frequent item sets, this paper mainly mines the enterprise text information to identify the venture enterprises with investment prospects. Firstly, we use TF-IDF algorithm to extract keywords from enterprise text; Secondly, the word2VEC model is used to vectorize the text keywords, and cosine similarity is calculated with the word vectors in the keyword database; Finally, we use the Apriori algorithm to find frequent item sets and generate association rules, complete vector weighting calculation of combination keywords, and finally retain the first three words or phrases with the highest weight as the identification keywords of the enterprise, thus determining whether the enterprise is a risk company with potential investment prospects. Experimental results show that the proposed method is effective.

Keywords: Discovery frequency term · TF-IDF · Word2vec · Cosine similarity · Venture firms identification

1 Introduction

Venture firms [1] are the product of the new technological revolution. They have developed rapidly since the 1990s which specialized in high-technology industries [2] with high risks, such as medicine, biological engineering, computer, microelectronics, space technology, Marine technology, new materials, new energy and so on. The emergence of venture enterprises drives venture capital enterprises [3] and their survival, which are closely related, mutually beneficial and mutually beneficial, and each takes what he needs. However, the current market threshold is low, a variety of enterprises mixed, how to detect and identify the potential investment prospects of venture enterprises and their different stages of development, is particularly important for the venture company's investment choice. Therefore, it has become the focus of relevant researchers to mine

© Springer Nature Switzerland AG 2021
X. Sun et al. (Eds.): ICAIS 2021, CCIS 1423, pp. 496–509, 2021.
https://doi.org/10.1007/978-3-030-78618-2_41

enterprise text data, detect and identify the enterprise's research field, development stage, whether it is a risk enterprise and whether it has investment value.

For the mining of a large number of enterprise text data, the text is often divided into several words. Through the selection and comparison of the lexis, some stopwords can be removed, such as mood particles with no practical meaning, and only some important keywords can be left. However, not all of these keywords can represent the theme of the text. On the contrary, a large number of words reduce the efficiency of text feature mining. Therefore, we should determine the weight of keywords in the text, so as to effectively and accurately determine the theme characteristics of the text. Therefore, TF-IDF [4] commonly used in research can be used to calculate the weight in the keyword enterprise text data. As a statistical method, TF-IDF is mainly used to evaluate the importance of a word in a text or a corpus. TF is the number of times a word appears in a text. But some common words do little to highlight the features of the subject. Therefore, simply using TF cannot find out the words that can best characterize the text theme. So, the design of weights must be able to give higher weights to the words with stronger ability to predict theme features. IDF can solve this problem, if a corpus contains less documents of a certain word, the greater the IDF, the stronger the ability to distinguish the word. Finally, by combining TF and IDF, we can get the weight of key words with main features in the text data: TF * IDF.

Keywords in the enterprise information text can only represent the text to a certain extent. How to further judge whether the enterprise is a venture enterprise with invest-ment prospects, the words need to be quantitatively processed, and then compared with the keywords in the lexicon of high-tech enterprises field. Quantitative representation of text documents has long been a challenging task in machine learning, with many meth-ods using the well-known but simplistic bag of word approach (BOW) [5], but the results will be mostly generic because the BOW is not thoughtful in many ways, such as word ordering. Generally speaking, when we use keywords to build some models, it is com-mon to mark keywords or do thermal coding [6], but thermal coding method can make words lose their meaning. The Word2vec [7] algorithm proposed by Google in 2013. The algorithm captures the relationship between words by vectorizing each word. The similarity between words can be calculated by the vector representation between words, and the cosine similarity is commonly used for calculation. By comparing the similarity between keywords in enterprise text and keywords in the lexicon of high-tech industry field, the information of enterprises with potential risks is preliminarily screened out.

The single keyword screening test using TF-IDF algorithm cannot effectively reflect the key degree of words and the distribution of feature words, and it has certain limita-tions for weight adjustment. Especially in similar companies, the disadvantages of this algorithm are obvious. It is simply that the words with low frequency in the text are more important, while the words with high frequency are more useless, so it will cover up the keywords in the same text. Apriori algorithm [8], a highly influential frequent item set algorithm mining Boolean association rules, is used to solve the above problems. Anuja Soni [8] et al. used the Apriori algorithm to discover and study frequent item sets based on the user demand information obtained through interviews and brainstorming, so as to dig out complete and correct requirements and achieve significant results in user satisfaction and software development progress. In this paper, the Apriori algorithm is used to discover the association rules between keywords of a risk enterprise and the combination of key words that may appear at the same time, so as to enhance the weight of keywords reflecting the text characteristics of the enterprise and identify whether the company is a risk company according to the association rules.

This paper uses TF-IDF to obtain the weight of keywords in the text data of enterprises, compares the vectorization of keywords with the lexicon vector in the high-tech industry, calculates the cosine similarity, and preliminarily determines whether it is a venture enterprise with investment prospects. Then suspicious text data using Apriori algorithm for the discovery of frequent itemsets and association rules mining, find out the potential relationship between the combination of the key words, the phrase vector weighted calculation, the weight of keywords to increase risk, finally after frequent itemsets generated association rules to identify the potential risk of enterprise investment prospect.

2 Related Work

In recent years, the target of venture capital is mainly focused on the high-tech industries with small scale, great potential and high investment risk. Due to the advanced technology of high-interest technology industries, it has become the absolute advantage of market competition and has more investment value than the traditional industries. Therefore, once the venture capital enterprise aims at the target investment success, will be able to occupy the market quickly, obtain the huge investment return. Therefore, in recent years, the mining of venture enterprises has become a key target of venture capital enterprises. A large amount of information contained in enterprise text data in network data [9] is of great significance to the detection and identification of venture enterprises, and a large number of researchers are devoted to the work in this field. The extraction of text keyword features is the basic work of enterprise text data mining. In 1957, Hans Peter Luhn [10] concluded that the weight of words in documents is proportional to word frequency (TF), which is the number of times a word appears in a text or a corpus. In 1972, Karen Sparck Jones [11] introduced the inverse text frequency factor, which reduced the weight of words frequently appearing in the document and increased the weight of gifts rarely appearing, and became the inverse text frequency (IDF), which became the basis of TF-IDF algorithm. After that, TF-IDF algorithm is widely popular as the weighted factor of information retrieval and text mining. A survey from 2015 showed that 83% of digital library recommendation systems use TF-IDF algorithms. Yuan [12] et al. used TF-IDF algorithm to perform static detection on Android package (APK) files, calculated the permission value of each permission and the sensitivity of APK, which showed a good effect in detecting malware. In this paper, TF-IDF algorithm is used to extract the key words in enterprise text and calculate the weight of each keyword, so as to provide a basis for preliminary screening of risk enterprises.

For the quantification of keyword data after text preprocessing, word embedding is often used to represent the existing keyword entities as vectors of the real domain, and vector computation is implemented in the continuous low-dimensional network space to express the semantic relations between words [13–15]. The well-known model word bag model (BOW) [5] generally does not consider the ordering between words, and the results are very general. When modeling keywords, it seems reasonable to encode them singly, but the words will lose their meaning. Since Tomas Mikolov [16] of Google proposed word2vec algorithm in 2013, the above problems have been improved. The algorithm inputs a large corpus and uniquely assigns each word in the corpus to the generated vector space of several hundred dimensions in order to calculate the semantic similarity of these word vectors in the vector space. The Word2vec algorithm contains two models: Continuous word bag model (CBOW) is used to predict the current word by the context word, whereas the skip-gram model [17] is on the contrary. The speed of predicting the current word by the context word is much slower than that of CBOW, but it has a higher accuracy for the words that are not often used. Amit Kumar Sharma [18] et al. generated vectors from the pre-trained Word2vec model and used CNN to extract text features and classify them, thus solving the non-uniformity of heterogeneous texts in social networks [19, 20]. In this paper, the pre-trained Word2vec model is used to generate the vector of enterprise text keywords, and cosine similarity is compared with the vector of keywords in the high-tech industry domain, so as to preliminarily judge whether it is a potential risk enterprise.

Due to the limitations of the weight of a single keyword, it has a weak degree of differentiation in the corpus of the same kind. It is not comprehensive to measure the importance of a word simply by "word frequency". Apriori algorithm enhances the weight of a single key word by discovering frequent item sets and mining the rules between frequent item sets, which is of great benefit to the study of this paper. Zhu [21] used Apriori algorithm to mine network alarm information, reducing the number of original alarms, incorporating relevant rules, and improving alarm delay and frequency, etc. In this paper, The Apriori algorithm is used to mine frequent keyword combinations related to high-tech industries in enterprise text data and the rules contained therein. This can further improve the company's suspicious risk weight, and then detect and identify whether a company is a venture capital company's target risk enterprise.

3 Method

In this section, we first introduce the overall process of risk enterprise detection and identification, and then introduce the algorithm technology used in each part of the implementation in detail.

The design is mainly divided into four modules: data acquisition, thesaurus establishment, risk enterprise information detection and data storage. In the enterprise data acquisition module, the text data of LinkedIn, Wikipedia and the official website of the enterprise are crawled to form a fusion data set, and the fusion corpus of enterprise information detection is formed through data preprocessing operations such as repeating words and stopping words. In the field of high and new technology industry, according to the category of high and new technology industry, such as medicine, biological engineering, computer, microelectronics, space technology, Marine technology, new materials, new energy, etc. Keywords constitute the seed word set, and English corpus such as world dictionary is used to expand the word set according to the rules of approximate word set, related word set and substitute word set, thus preliminarily forming the key word set. In the risk enterprise information detection module, TF-IDF algorithm is first used to screen out the key words that can reflect the text characteristics, and the weight of each key word is calculated (Fig. 1).

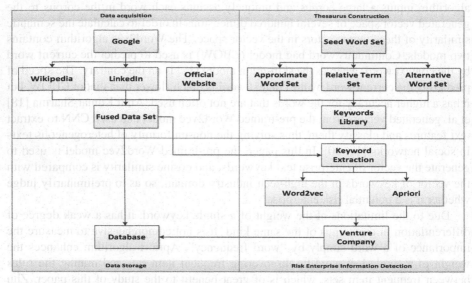

Fig. 1. Overall flow chart of risk enterprise detection and identification.

Secondly, key words vectors generated by using Word2vec model and new and high technology industries thesaurus of the keyword vector, computing the cosine similarity, preliminary screening potential risk of enterprises, after using Apriori algorithm found frequent itemsets, find out the relationship with the combination of key words, dig out the potential association rules between words. Finally, by using association rules, the weighted calculation of single and combined keywords can improve the suspicious degree of risk enterprises, and finally detect the risk enterprises with potential investment value. The data storage module will store the data generated by the enterprise text detection process into the database.

3.1 Construction of Key Words Database in High-Tech Industry Field

The construction of new and high-tech industry keyword database is the basic task of information detection and identification for venture enterprises. An enterprise keyword database with wide coverage and accurate classification should consider: how to select the seed word set with wide coverage and strong distinguishing ability. How to improve the calculation of keyword similarity so that unknown enterprise data can be given higher category weight in order to detect potential risk enterprises. In this paper, terms are extracted from the pre-processed corpus to form the seed word set, which is expanded through the worldwide dictionary, American contemporary English corpus, and Google trillion-word bank. Similar word sets (e.g., biology & Biotechnology), related word sets (e.g., biology & Biotechnology), and alternative word sets (e.g., IT & Information

Technology) are combined to form the key words library of high-tech industry. Figure 2 is the establishment process of the key words database in the high-tech industry:

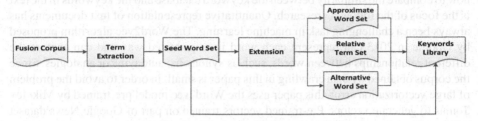

Fig. 2. The construction flow chart of keywords library in high-tech industry field.

3.2 Enterprise Text Keyword Extraction Based on TF-IDF

In the text keyword extraction part of enterprise domain, this paper uses TF-IDF algorithm to filter out the frequently appearing words in the text, and retains a few appearing words in the text. In this method, if a word or phrase appears frequently in the text and rarely in other articles, it is considered that the word has a good degree of differentiation, can well represent the characteristics of the text, and should be given a high weight. In a given file, term frequency (TF) refers to the frequency of a given word appearing in the file. Through normalization processing, to avoid text length influence. For any word t_i in a certain text, the word frequency to measure its importance is expressed by formula (1):

$$\text{tf}_{i,j} = \frac{n_{i,j}}{\sum_k n_{k,j}} \tag{1}$$

$n_{i,j}$ is the number of occurrences of the word in text d_j. The denominator is the sum of the occurrences of all the words in the text d_j.

The inverse Document Frequency (IDF) is a measure of the universal importance of a word. The IDF of a certain word can be obtained by dividing the total number of files by the number of files containing the word, and then taking the logarithm of the quotient, as shown in formula (2):

$$\text{idf}_i = \log \frac{|D|}{|\{j : t_i \in d_j\}|} \tag{2}$$

Where $|D|$ represents the total number of files in the corpus, and $|\{j : t_i \in d_j\}|$ represents the number of files containing the word t_i (namely $n_{i,j} \neq 0$ number of files). If the word is not in the corpus, the denominator will be zero, so in general, the denominator is $|\{j : t_i \in d_j\}| + 1$.

Finally, the product of TF and IDF is calculated as the weight of key words that can reflect the characteristics of enterprise text. After this step, we remove the documents that do not contain the classified keywords in the high-tech industry field, and only retain the documents with keywords, so as to further perform vector quantization and similarity calculation, and then achieve the screening and matching of single keywords.

3.3 Enterprise Data Vectorization Based on Word2vec

After the construction of the keyword database and the extraction of a single keyword, how to compare the similarity between the keyword database and the keywords in the text is the focus of the following research. Quantitative representation of text documents has always been a challenging task in machine learning. The Word2vec algorithm proposed by Google in 2013 can represent each word in a quantized way and can capture the different relationships between words, such as synonyms, antonyms or analogies. Since the corpus obtained by data crawling in this paper is small, in order to avoid the problem of large vectorization error, this paper uses the Word2vec model pre-trained by Mikolov Tomas to generate vectors. Pre-trained vectors trained on part of Google News dataset (about 100 billion words). The model contains 300-dimensional vectors for 3 million words and phrases. In this paper, the pre-processed enterprise text keywords are input into the model to generate vector W_1 for each keyword. The words in the high-tech industry domain are input into the model, and vector W_2 of the words and phrases in the lexicon is generated by vector weighting. Formula (3) is used to calculate the cosine similarity of the two vectors, and the venture enterprises with investment prospects are preliminarily screened out.

$$\cos(\theta) = \frac{a \bullet b}{\|a\| \times \|b\|} = \frac{\sum_{i=1}^{n} x_i y_i}{\sqrt{\sum_{i=1}^{n} (x_i)^2} * \sqrt{\sum_{i=1}^{n} (y_i)^2}} \tag{3}$$

3.4 Discovery of Frequent Item Sets of Enterprises Based on Apriori Algorithm

Although TF-IDF algorithm is relatively simple in the implementation process and can filter and match keywords rapidly, the extraction of keywords by TF-IDF algorithm relies heavily on corpus, so it is necessary to select a corpus of high quality that is consistent with the processed text for training. To solve the above problems, the Apriori algorithm is further adopted in this paper to find the combination of keywords with correlation relationship, namely frequent item sets in the Apriori algorithm, so as to strengthen the weight of combination keywords and further enhance the weight of venture enterprises with investment potential. The core idea of Apriori algorithm is to discover frequent item sets and generate association rules. The implementation steps are as follows:

(1) Find frequent items: That is, find variables that often appear together in the data set. First, scan the database, calculate the number of each keyword, and keep the items that meet the minimum support. Find the set of frequent item sets, which is called L1, then use L1 to find the set L2 of frequent item sets, use L2 to find L3, and then join the pruning loop until you can no longer find the frequent k item set.

(2) Mining association rules: An association rule is an implication expression of the form $X \rightarrow Y$, where X and Y are disjunct item sets, $X \cap Y = \emptyset$. The strength of an association rule can be measured by its support and confidence. The support determination rule can be used to determine how frequently a given dataset occurs, and the confidence level determines how frequently Y appears in the text containing X. Starting with a frequent item set, create a rule list, first generating only one

keyword (such as {information} =>{IT}). Test the rule against the predefined confidence, merge the remaining rules to create a new rule list, and then generate two keywords (such as {information, data} =>{IT}), repeat the above procedure until the rule is empty. At this time, the remaining rules are all strong association rules, and the weight of the related phrase can be calculated, paving the way for further rule-based classification.

4 Experiment

In this part, we will follow the designed risk enterprise identification process step by step to find the venture company with investment potential.

4.1 Datasets

The data set used in this experiment is the crawled corporate profile text data fusion data set. We use data from LinkedIn, Wikipedia, and company profiles on the company's website. These profiles may include the company's history, development, and business scope to help us identify potential venture companies.

When obtaining data, in order to solve problems such as crawling restrictions on websites, we first conducted fuzzy query through Google. You then use Google's advanced search capabilities to qualify your domain name and indirectly crawl your enterprise data from www.linkedIn.com and en.wikipedia.org. Secondly, the original enterprise data was cleaned, special characters such as punctuation were removed, and the text was segmented with whitespace to filter out the stop words. Then, the part of speech labeling and the restoration of the part of speech are carried out, and the key words in the high-tech industry are used for preliminary filtering, and the text data of non-high-tech industries such as traditional enterprises are removed. The high-tech enterprise text after preliminary screening is taken as the data set of the venture enterprise.

4.2 Algorithm Implementation

Keywords Extraction of Venture Enterprise Based on TF-IDF. In order to extract the keywords of venture enterprise text, we use TF-IDF algorithm to implement. We're using the TfidfVectorizer in Python. First, extract all words in the text, count the number of all words, calculate the word frequency and inverse text frequency of each word in the text of each venture enterprise, and calculate the TF-IDF value of each word. By setting the range of n-gram, the top 10 words with the highest TF-IDF value are obtained as the keywords in the text of the venture enterprise. We generate the word cloud from the extracted text keywords, as shown in the Fig. 3. Keywords with high frequency appear in the text data are visually highlighted in the word cloud image, and the rendering of keywords forms a color image similar to the cloud, so that the semantic meaning of the text data can be seen at a glance.

Fig. 3. TF-IDF keywords cloud image.

Taking the first text data as an example, the TF-IDF value of the first 10 keywords is shown in Table 1.

Table 1. Table of top 10 words with the highest TF-IDF value in text 1.

Index	Key words	TF	IDF	TF-IDF
1	Decision	670	3.00	0.41
2	Ambiguity	109	5.40	0.30
3	Scientist	2229	4.01	0.22
4	Innovative	1324	4.01	0.23
5	Integration	1349	2.66	0.22
6	Data	654	2.33	0.19
7	Software	2335	2.31	0.19
8	Computer	524	3.39	0.19
9	Problem	1984	3.20	0.18
10	Team	2477	2.84	0.16

In Table 1, the first column is the index of keywords arranged according to the size of TF-IDF value, the second column is the keywords, and the third column is the word frequency of the keywords. The number of words here serves as TF, the fourth column is the IDF value, and the fifth column is the TF-IDF value. If only relying on TF to judge the importance of a word, the more frequency the word appears in the corpus, the less important the word, and the less important the text one is, the most critical word in the ten keywords is called "team", which judgment will be affected by the length of the text and is one-sidedness. If we use the word "IDF" to measure the degree of key, the greater the value of the word "IDF", the greater the degree of distinction and the stronger the representativeness of the word, and the less important word of the text "Text I" is the word "software". However, this judgment will be affected by the corpus text category, and it also has certain limitations. Therefore, we use the product of the two – TF-IDF value as an indicator to judge the importance of words. This method comprehensively considers the influence of text length and category. Therefore, the top 10 representative keywords of text 1 can be screened out. According to Table 1, we can infer that the company may be an innovative software company by selecting the first ten key words, and these ten key words can represent the characteristics of this text. After that, the next step of vectorization can be performed.

Keyword Vectorization of Venture Enterprise Based on Word2vec. Due to the small data set in this paper, in order to avoid excessive errors after vectorization, this paper uses the Word2vec model pre-trained by Mikolov Tomas to generate vectors. The model covers 100 billion Google news words and phrases, vector dimension for 300d, context window is 5, risk enterprise keyword vector generated by this model and high-yield technology industry keyword vector in the thesaurus, computing the cosine similarity of both, the preliminary judging whether the enterprise with the risk of enterprise investment prospect.

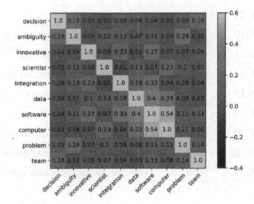

Fig. 4. Keyword vector and glossary vector correlation coefficient matrix thermal diagram take text 1 as an example.

In order to prove the effectiveness of the method, this paper takes Text 1 as an example and draws the correlation thermal diagram of keyword vectors by using correlation coefficient matrix according to the similarity between the two keywords, as shown in Fig. 4. In Fig. 4, both horizontal and vertical axis coordinates are the keywords of text 1 extracted by using TF-IDF. According to the value range of correlation coefficient $[-1, 1]$, when the correlation coefficient is -1, the color of square in the heat map is set as black; when the correlation coefficient is 1, the color of square in the heat map is light yellow; other square colors vary between black and light yellow according to the value of correlation coefficient. According to the actual situation, in order to better show the effect of the heat map, the color card in the figure only shows the color range between $[-0.4, 0.6]$. The value in each square is the correlation coefficient between any two keywords. The greater the correlation coefficient is, the stronger the correlation between the two keywords will be. According to the color range of Square in Fig. 4, a keyword extracted from the text is positively correlated, which can effectively represent the main content of text 1. By calculating the cosine similarity between the keyword vector extracted from the text and the keyword vector in the high-tech industry field, if the keyword extracted from the text is not in the lexicon, the weight of the keyword is denoted as 0; otherwise, the weight of each keyword is calculated.

After that, the weights of TF-IDF and similarity degree calculated are weighted to obtain the weights of top10 keywords. Take text 1 as an example, and the weighted results are shown in Table 2. The first column is the keyword index of text 1, the second column is the keyword, the third column is the weight of the keyword TF-IDF, the fourth column is the similarity weight, the fifth column is the similar words in the lexicon, and the last column is the weight calculated by TF-IDF and similarity weight. Therefore, the keyword with the highest weight after weighting is "data", and the keyword with the lowest weight is "problem".

Table 2. Table of top 10 words with the highest weighting value in text 1

Index	Key words	TF-IDF	Similarity	Similar words	Weighting
1	Data	0.19	1.00	Data	0.76
2	Integration	0.22	0.89	Data integration	0.69
3	Software	0.19	0.79	Data visualization technology	0.62
4	Decision	0.41	0.67	Office policy development	0.60
5	Scientist	0.22	0.72	Social science information study	0.57
6	Innovative	0.23	0.71	Interactive data discovery	0.57
7	Computer	0.19	0.71	Science technology security	0.55
8	Ambiguity	0.30	0.65	Data interpretation utilization	0.55
9	Team	0.16	0.70	Defense contract management agency	0.54
10	Problem	0.18	0.68	Defense threat reduction agency	0.53

Frequent Item Discovery of Risk Enterprises Based on Apriori. In order to improve the problem of low keyword discrimination in similar TF-IDF documents, this paper further uses Apriori algorithm to discover frequent item sets among keywords and generate association rules. In this algorithm, the degree of support is the ratio of the number of keywords M and N appearing at the same time to the number of words in the corpus, and the degree of confidence is the ratio of the degree of support of keywords M and n appearing at the same time to the degree of support of keywords M appearing in the conditional probability. Set the minimum support to 0.2 and the minimum confidence to 0.7, and the output association rules are all greater than or equal to the preset minimum support and confidence.

Input minimum support and minimum confidence into the database and define a variable k as the number of items in the frequent item set. The data type is integer and the initial value is set to 1. In the database scan text search in the first place, from a single keyword list of itemsets began circulating searching process, each time to remove does not meet the minimum support keyword itemsets, after connection, pruning, and scan again, until can't find more keywords end when the frequent itemsets, final output keywords of frequent itemsets. The item sets of frequently occurring keywords found when the support degree is 0.2, 0.4, 0.6 and 0.8 are shown in Table 3:

Table 3. Table of frequent items with different support settings

Frequent item	Counts	Support
{Business, Technology, Biology, Material … [Software, Computer] … [Software, Computer, Engineer] … [Software, Computer, Solution, Technology]}	3507	0.2
{Technology, Biological … [Software, Computer, Solution, Technology]}	1529	0.4
{[Biology, Engineer] … [Software, Computer, Solution, Technology]}	287	0.6
{[Marine, Technology] … [Software, Solution, Technology]}	62	0.8

Table 3 shows that through the connection pruning of Apriori, the database scale is greatly reduced and the operational efficiency is improved. According to the frequent items found by Apriori algorithm, the text keyword is weighted by another step. Take text 1 as an example, the lexicon similarity words corresponding to the first three words that retain the highest weight after weighted calculation are adopted as the recognition label of the text, as shown in Table 4.

Table 4. Text 1 top3 keywords weight tag table

Key Words	Weighting	Weighted value	Text tags
Data	0.76	0.84	Data
Integration	0.69	0.75	Data integration
Software	0.61	0.67	Data visualization technology

5 Conclusion

In this paper, TF-IDF algorithm is used to extract key words of enterprise text, and the weight of the top ten keywords with the highest TF-IDF value is calculated. Then, the key words database in the field of high and new technology industry is constructed. By using word2vec model, the vectorial representation of the two keywords is carried out, and the cosine similarity of the two keywords is compared and analyzed to preliminarily screen out the venture enterprises with potential investment prospects. Then, this paper uses Apriori algorithm to discover frequent item sets of enterprise texts, and finds out the combinations of key words that may appear at the same time. After weighting calculation, the association rules generated by frequent item sets are used to retain the top three words or phrases with the highest weight, so as to improve the keyword weight of risk enterprises. Two-thirds of the companies in the experimental data set were effectively identified, and the phrases in the thesaurus and weighted weights were used to label the companies. Finally identify the potential investment prospects of the venture enterprises. Experimental results show that this method has certain recognition effect.

Acknowledgement. This work is supported by State Grid Shandong Electric Power Company Science and Technology Project Funding under Grant no. 520613200001, 520613180002, 62061318C002, the Fundamental Research Funds for the Central Universities (Grant No. HIT. NSRIF.201714), Weihai Science and Technology Development Program (2016DX GJMS15) and Key Research and Development Program in Shandong Provincial (2017GGX90103).

References

1. 김은혜, F.: The influence of venture firm's internal capabilities and external resource utilization on the level of internationalization: the expansion of resource-based view. J. Strateg. Manag. **23**(1), 1–23 (2020)
2. Wolf, M.: The high-tech industry, what is it and why it matters to our economic future. Beyond Numbers **5**, 8 (2016)
3. Wang, X.H.: Venture capital agglomeration and high-tech industrial innovation: the mediating role of industry-university knowledge flow and the regulating role of relationship orientation. Journal of Xi'an Jiaotong University (Social Science edition), pp. 1–16 (2020)
4. Beel, J.: Research-paper recommender systems: a literature survey. Int. J. Digit. Libr. **17**, 305–338 (2016)
5. Sivic, J.: Efficient visual search of videos cast as text retrieval. IEEE Trans. Pattern Anal. Mach. Intell. **31**(4), 591–605 (2009)
6. Harris, D.: Digital Design and Computer Architecture. Morgan Kaufmann, San Francisco, Calif, vol. 129 (2012)
7. Tomas, M.: Efficient estimation of word representations in vector space, vol. 1301, p. 3781 (2013)
8. Soni, A.: A methodological approach for mining the user requirements using Apriori algorithm. J. Cases Inform. Technol. **22**(4), 1–30 (2020)
9. Zhu, D., Du, H., Sun, Y., Cao, N.: Research on path planning model based on short-term traffic flow prediction in intelligent transportation system. Sensors (Basel) **18**(12), 4275 (2018)
10. Hans Peter, L.: A statistical approach to mechanized encoding and searching of literary information. IBM J. Res. Dev. **1**(4), 309–317 (1957)
11. Spärck Jones, K.: A statistical interpretation of term specificity and its application in retrieval. J. Documentation **28**, 11–21 (1972)
12. Yuan, H.L.: A detection method for android application security based on TF-IDF and machine learning. Plos One **15**(9), e0238694 (2020)
13. Zhu, D., Sun, Y., Du, H., Baker, T.: HUNA: a method of hierarchical unsupervised network alignment for IoT. IEEE Internet Things J. **10**(1109), 1 (2020)
14. Zhu, D., Sun, Y., Li, X.: MINE: a method of multi-interaction heterogeneous information network embedding. Comput. Mater. Continua **63**(3), 1343–1356 (2020)
15. Zhu, D., Sun, Y., Cao, N.: BDNE: a method of bi-directional distance network embedding. In: 2019 International Conference on Cyber-Enabled Distributed Computing and Knowledge Discovery (CyberC), pp. 158–161. IEEE, Guilin (2019)
16. Tomas, M.: Distributed representations of words and phrases and their compositionality. Adv. Neural Inform. Process. Syst. **1310**, 4546 (2013)
17. Huang, X.D.: The SPHINX-II speech recognition system: an overview. Comput. Speech Lang. **7**(2), 137–148 (1992)

18. Amit Kumar, S.: Sentimental short sentences classification by using CNN deep learning model with fine tuned Word2Vec. Procedia Comput. Sci. **167**, 1139–1147 (2020)
19. You, C., Zhu, D., Sun, Y.: SNES: social-network-oriented public opinion monitoring platform based on elastic search. CMC-Comput. Mater. Continua **61**(3), 1271–1283 (2019)
20. Zhu, D., Wang, Y., You, C.: MMLUP: multi-source & multi-task learning for user profiles in social network. Comput. Mater. Continua **61**(3), 1105–1115 (2019)
21. Zhu, L.H.: Implementation of web log mining device under Apriori algorithm improvement and confidence formula optimization. Int. J. Inform. Technol. Web Eng. **15**(4), 53–71 (2020)

Design of Abnormal Behavior Detection System in the State Grid Business Office

Xueming Qiao[1], Weiyi Zhu[2], Dan Guo[1], Ting Jiang[1], Xiuli Chang[3], Yulan Zhou[4], Dongjie Zhu[4(✉)], and Ning Cao[5]

[1] State Grid Weihai Power Supply Company, No.23, Kunming Road, Weihai 204209, China
[2] State Grid Shandong Electric Power Company, Jinan 250000, China
[3] Shandong Institute of Shipbuilding Technology, Weihai 264209, China
[4] School of Computer Science and Technology, Harbin Institute of Technology, Weihai 264209, China
zhudongjie@hit.edu.cn
[5] School of Internet of Things and Software Technology, Wuxi Vocational College of Science and Technology, Wuxi 214028, China

Abstract. Nowadays, with the popularization of electricity, the status of grid business office in people's lives has become more and more important. Grid business office often have a large flow of people, so it becomes very necessary for abnormal detection of grid business offices. Traditional video surveillance has a lot of problems. This paper uses various computer vision technologies to improve traditional video surveillance. First, the YOLO v3 algorithm is introduced to detect the number of people in the business office, and then the motion foreground extraction algorithm is used to calculate the contour of the human body. The contour judges whether there is an abnormal situation currently, and finally introduces the concept of image entropy to judge whether there is intense movement currently. Finally, in the end of the paper, the current work is summarized and the future word is prospected.

Keywords: Abnormal detection · Computer vision technology · Motion foreground extraction · Image entropy

1 Introduction

1.1 Research Background and Significance

In today's home life, no family can do without the use of electricity, and the power grid business office, as the main place for residents to handle electricity business, often has a large flow of people. However, due to the limited space in the business office, excessive flow of people may make it difficult to guarantee the service quality of the business office. Residents have a long queue time and at the same time the grid counter employees cannot get a reasonable rest. And due to the large flow of people [1], it is difficult for traditional manual video surveillance methods to respond to sudden situations in time. When the crowd is overcrowded, there is a stampede, or when the old and infirm fainted alone,

© Springer Nature Switzerland AG 2021
X. Sun et al. (Eds.): ICAIS 2021, CCIS 1423, pp. 510–520, 2021.
https://doi.org/10.1007/978-3-030-78618-2_42

or other vicious violent incidents occur, if they are not detected in time and dealt with accordingly, it may endanger the lives of the people.

Therefore, it is very important to provide a safe and reliable service environment for the grid business office. Although at present, the power grid business office has a relatively complete video monitoring system [2], which can achieve monitoring coverage of most areas. But traditional video surveillance still has many shortcomings:

1) High maintenance costs. The monitoring center usually monitors many video images at the same time. To achieve real-time monitoring, a certain amount of manpower is required for long-term monitoring, and the manpower cost is high.

2) Easy to miss inspection. Human attention is limited and due to normal physiological needs, it is difficult to ensure that they are always on duty, so it is easy to miss inspections, resulting in failure to detect abnormalities in time.

3) Difficulty in investigation and evidence collection. Criminal behaviors or other abnormal behaviors often last for a short period of time, and the amount of monitoring data saved is large. Therefore, the investigation and evidence collection of videos generally requires viewing a large amount of video images, which greatly increases the difficulty of investigation and evidence collection.

1.2 Current Research Status at Home and Abroad

After years of development, image analysis and deep learning algorithms are now relatively mature and have been widely used in the field of intelligent video surveillance [3]. Through the blessing of algorithms, today's video surveillance has many advanced functions such as pedestrian detection, vehicle detection, and dense crowd detection.

In the current foreign smart video research, the SSS (Smart Surveillance System) system developed by IBM has realized the automatic monitoring function of the scene. At the same time, the database is used to manage the monitoring data and search for specific content, and it can also realize remote alarm based on network protocol or full tracking of specific targets [4].

The ADVIDOR system, jointly researched by a number of institutions in the UK, is a system for monitoring crowded places. The system recognizes whether pedestrians are in a company, analyzes pedestrian behavior, and recognizes abnormal behaviors to respond to possible terrorist attacks.

In addition, the human body tracking and behavior understanding system Pfinder developed by the Massachusetts Institute of Technology, the crowd and personal behavior recognition project developed by the University of Reading, etc., build a human body model by extracting the characteristics of various parts of the human body, or use the shape and color of the human body and the environment Distinguish, achieve the purpose of automatic detection, tracking and monitoring of human targets [6–8].

In the industry, there are still many technology companies engaged in intelligent monitoring. Hikvision is a video-centric intelligent IoT solution and big data service provider. Its business focuses on integrated security, big data services and smart business. Its products and solutions are based on cloud computing technology and video big data processing technology, applied in more than 150 countries and regions, and played an important role in major projects such as the G20 Hangzhou Summit, the Beijing Olympics, and the Shanghai World Expo.

1.3 Main Research Content

Definition of Abnormal Conditions. This paper takes the abnormal behavior recognition in the power grid business office as the main research content. For different application scenarios, the definition of abnormal behavior will be different. Considering the actual situation of the power grid business office, in this study, the following two abnormal events are mainly considered:

1) A single fall event. When a single person falls, the state of the whole person will change from a standing (vertical) state to a lying (horizontal) state, and the overall body contour will change significantly. This feature can be used to detect a single person's fall.
2) Multiplayer fights. Under normal circumstances, due to the high density of people in the power grid business office, people's movements tend to be smooth, and when there is a fight, the movement is more intense and faster, and the movement contains greater kinetic energy. Use this feature to detect violent fights.

Research Content. The research goal of this paper is to realize the detection and early warning of abnormal behavior in the power grid business office. Therefore, this article takes the power grid business office as an application scenario, and conducts related research on the detection of abnormal events that may occur to users in the business office.

This paper decides to choose the surveillance camera installed in the power grid business office as the sensor and image input. First, in order to accurately estimate the number of people in the office, this paper introduces the YOLO v3 algorithm to estimate the number of people in the screen. In order to detect the movement of the target more accurately, an improved motion foreground extraction algorithm based on the ViBe algorithm is also introduced. Finally, by constructing a movement history graph to depict the energy state of human movement to determine whether the user is in a state of intense exercise and give corresponding warnings.

1.4 Chapter Arrangement

Section 1 mainly introduces the research background and significance of this article, and describes the current research and development status in the field of intelligent video surveillance at home and abroad, and finally makes a corresponding introduction to the research content and objectives of this article.

Section 2 first introduces the YOLO v3 algorithm, combined with the specific application scenarios of the power grid business office, and explains how to use the algorithm to estimate the number of people.

Section 3 aim at the actual scene and real-time requirements of the power grid business office, a motion foreground extraction algorithm based on the ViBe algorithm is proposed. The contour of the human body is calculated by the algorithm, and finally the fall behavior is judged based on the contour. For the abnormal situation of multiple people, a motion history map is introduced, and the image entropy is further calculated according to the motion history map, so as to determine whether an abnormal situation has occurred currently.

Section 4 summary and Prospects, summarizes the main content and results of the research in this article, and elaborates the deficiencies of this research and the prospects for future research work.

2 People Estimation Model Based on YOLO v3 Algorithm

Before counting the number of people in the power grid business office, it is first necessary to identify the target in the video screen through the target detection algorithm and mark it for further processing. In recent years, the target detection algorithm has made great breakthroughs. The more popular algorithms can be divided into two categories [8]. One is the R-CNN algorithm based on Region Proposal (R-CNN, Fast R-CNN, Faster R-CNN, etc.), they are two-stage algorithms. The target candidate frame, that is, the target position, needs to be generated by the algorithm first, and then the candidate frame is classified and regressed through the convolutional neural network. The other type is one-stage algorithms such as YOLO and SSD, which only use a convolutional neural network CNN to directly predict the categories and positions of different targets [9]. Compared with two-stage algorithms, the speed is faster but the accuracy is lower. Among them, the YOLO algorithm [10] is a typical one-stage target detection algorithm. The overall idea of the algorithm is to use the entire image as the input of the network, and directly return to the position of the bounding box (recognition box, denoted as box) and bounding box in the output layer belonging to the category, so as to achieve the goal recognition as a regression problem to solve. This detection method is very fast and can meet the requirements of real-time detection [11].

This article comprehensively considers the decision to use the YOLO v3 algorithm [12] to estimate the number of people present in the screen.

The general flow of the YOLO v3 algorithm is as follows:

1) Resize the input image first, adjust the size
2) Input the image into the CNN network for feature extraction and prediction
3) Filter the box through non-max suppression to obtain the image of the calibration target

We use part of the COCO data set as training samples to train the YOLO v3 network. The COCO data set is a large and rich object detection, segmentation and captioning data set. This data set aims at scene understanding, which is mainly intercepted from complex daily scenes. The target in the image is calibrated by precise segmentation. The images include 91 types of targets, 328,000 images and 2,500,000 labels are the largest dataset with semantic segmentation so far. There are 80 categories provided, with more than 330,000 images, of which 200,000 are labeled, and the number of individuals in the entire dataset is more than 1.5 million.

After the training process is completed, we use the monitor video collected from power grid business office to test the model.

As shown in the Fig. 1, the YOLO v3 algorithm can effectively detect pedestrians appearing in video surveillance.

Fig. 1. Multi-scene detection results.

3   Abnormal Behavior Detection of Power Grid Business Office

3.1   Single Person Falls

This article regards a single person falling in the power grid business office as an abnormal situation. First, before the fall behavior is detected, the fall behavior is systematically analyzed. When people lose their balance and fall, their overall shape will change significantly in a short period of time (from a vertical state to a horizontal state), and the corresponding overall outline has also undergone major changes. The difference between the individual's body shape and the posture after a fall, this paper chooses the circumscribed rectangle of the human body as the detection target.

In order to accurately extract the contours of the human body, this paper introduces the ViBe algorithm for motion foreground extraction, and obtains the binarized image through motion foreground extraction [13]. The ViBe algorithm is an image processing algorithm that builds a background model by collecting background samples [14]. Its working principle is to establish a sample set of pixels by extracting the pixel values around the pixel (x, y) and the previous pixel values, and then combine the pixel value at another frame (x, y) with the pixel value in the sample set For comparison, if the distance from the pixel value in the sample set is greater than a certain threshold, the pixel is considered as a foreground pixel, otherwise it is a background pixel. The ViBe algorithm [15] can be initialized only with a single frame of image, and it occupies small memory, runs fast, and has strong anti-interference ability, which can well meet the requirements of real-time detection.

The Vibe algorithm can be roughly divided into the following three parts:

1) Initialize the background model. Create a sample set for pixels
2) Foreground and background matching. Match the pixels in the video frame to be detected
3) Update the background model. Through the random background update method and the Gaussian mixture model, the change process of each pixel over time is simulated after extracting the motion foreground through the ViBe algorithm, the binarized image is obtained and the outline of the human body is marked. As shown in Fig. 2, when the human body is standing, the overall outline of the human body is vertical, and the corresponding circumscribed rectangle is a vertical cuboid. When the human body falls down and lies down, the overall outline of the human body is horizontal, and the corresponding circumscribed rectangle becomes a horizontal cuboid.

(a) standing figure   (b) falling figure

Fig. 2. Illustration of standing and falling.

The fall detection flow chart of the entire system is shown in the Fig. 3:

Set the height of the circumscribed rectangle of the human body to H and the width to W. It is easy to know from the figure that under normal circumstances, the aspect ratio of a person when standing must be greater than 1, and when the human body falls, the aspect ratio must be less than 1, and because the human body moves more smoothly when standing, and the aspect ratio change is small, this feature can be used to accurately determine whether the human body falls in a timely and accurate manner.

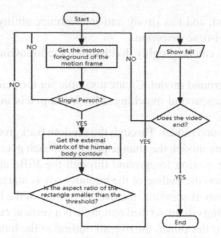

Fig. 3. Flow chart of people fall detection.

3.2 Multiplayer Fight

Due to the high density of people in the business office of the power grid, after entering the business office, people are usually in a state of queuing, moving slowly and working at window counters. The movement range is small and the momentum is small. When fighting or other intense exercise occurs, people's movement range Larger and greater momentum, you can use this feature to establish a corresponding energy model, set the corresponding threshold according to the number of people currently detected, and then judge the user's behavior according to the calculated energy value [16] (see Fig. 4).

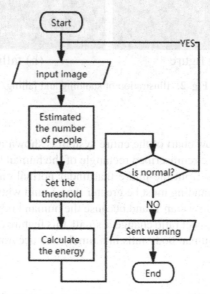

Fig. 4. Flow chart of multi-person violence detection.

Feature Extraction. The motion energy [17] map performs motion-based object recognition by describing how the object moves and where the motion occurs in space, which shows the outline of the motion and the spatial distribution of energy. The motion history map is developed on the basis of the motion energy map. The motion history map uses a vision-based template method to calculate the pixel changes at the same position within a time period, and express the target motion in the form of image brightness. The gray value of each pixel represents the recent motion of the pixel at that position in a group of video sequences. The closer the motion occurs, the higher the gray value, and the longer the time interval, the lower the gray value of the motion [18]. In this way, the temporal and spatial characteristics of the motion are retained.

Let H be the intensity value of the pixel of the motion history image, H (x, y, t) can be calculated by the update function:

$$H_\tau(x, y, t) = \begin{cases} \tau \ if \ \psi(x, y, t) \\ \max(0, H_t(x, y, t-1) - \delta \ otherwise \end{cases} \tag{1}$$

In the formula, (x, y) and t are the position and time of the pixel; τ is the duration, which determines the time range of the movement from the perspective of the number of frames; delta is the decay parameter. $\Psi(x, y, t)$ is the update function, which can be defined by multiple methods such as inter-frame difference, image difference or optical flow, among which the inter-frame difference method is the most commonly used [19]:

$$\Psi(x, y, t) = \begin{cases} 1 \ if \ D(x, y, t) \geq \xi \\ 0 \ otherwise \end{cases} \tag{2}$$

Where ξ is the artificially set threshold, D (x, y, t) is the difference image, which can be calculated by the following formula

$$D(x, y, t) = |I(x, y, t) - I(x, y, t \pm \Delta)| \tag{3}$$

In the formula, I (x, y, t) is the intensity value of the pixel at the t-th frame coordinate (x, y) of the video image sequence, delta is the distance between frames [20].

Energy Function. According to the characteristics of people's small motion range under normal circumstances, the concept of picture entropy is introduced, and the calculation formula of picture entropy is used as the energy function for judging whether people are in intense exercise.

In the field of image recognition, image entropy is similar to other entropy concepts to express the degree of confusion of the information contained in the image. When the image is blurry, that is, the color difference in more areas is smaller, and the edges are blurry, then the image entropy value is smaller. If the picture is clear, the entropy value is larger.

The calculation formula of picture entropy is as follows:

$$\text{Entropy} = -\sum_{i=0}^{255} p(i)\log_2 p(i) \tag{4}$$

Where I (x, y, t) is the pixel value at (x, y) at time t, and Δ is the time difference between frames.

Discrimination Rules. After calculating the picture entropy of the entire picture, it is necessary to gather the number of people in the current business office for comprehensive judgment. Because when the flow of people in the business office is small, people's movement is less restricted and the range of movements may be larger. On the contrary, when the flow of people is large, people's movements are relatively smooth and tend to be static due to other reasons such as queuing. Therefore, the threshold of abnormal behavior needs to be changed according to the number of people.

According to this characteristic, True Color designed a calculation method based on the estimated energy threshold of the number of people:

$$T_{all} = 1$$
$$T_{eve} = \begin{cases} 0.4, \ h > 1 \\ 0.5, \ h = 1 \end{cases} \tag{5}$$

Where T_{all} is the global energy threshold, T_{eve} is the average energy threshold of a single person, and h is the number of people detected. See below for the judgment of abnormality:

$$Warning = \begin{cases} 0, \ E_{all} < T_{all} \ \& \ E_{eve} < T_{exe} \\ 1, \ else \end{cases} \tag{6}$$

When the global energy value is greater than the global threshold, it is determined to be an abnormal situation, and other states are determined to be normal.

4   Summary and Outlook

4.1   Summary

Based on the research of computer vision and deep learning, this research takes the detection of abnormal behavior in the power grid business office as the goal, and conducts in-depth analysis and research on the abnormal conditions and safety detection problems that may occur in the power grid business office. This article has conducted an in-depth study of video-based abnormal event detection in power grid business offices. First, it defines the possible abnormal situations according to the actual situation, and then introduces the YOLO algorithm, foreground extraction algorithm and VIBE algorithm to help real-time detection of the number of business offices and whether abnormal situations occur. And finally complete the whole system construction. Finally, the contents of this research are summarized as follows:

1) Analyzed the possible abnormal behaviors of the power grid business office and the problems that smart video surveillance should be able to solve and the goals achieved, and made a certain introduction to the commonly used target detection algorithms, and based on the business characteristics, chose the YOLOv3 algorithm for more In-depth research, finally realized the detection of the number of people in the business office

2) Introduced the VIBE algorithm to achieve a motion foreground extraction method suitable for power grid business offices, and use this method to achieve the depiction of human contours
3) Calculate the information entropy contained in the picture through the motion history graph, thereby expressing the kinetic energy of the picture, and use this parameter to determine whether abnormal behavior is currently occurring.

4.2 Outlook

Due to the huge difference between the experimental environment and the actual environment, there are still many situations that have not been considered, which are summarized as follows:

1) There may be many abnormal situations in the real world. This study only considers two abnormal situations, and a lot of supplements are needed in further research in the future.
2) The computer vision and deep learning technologies involved in this research are in a stage of rapid development, and better algorithms can bring higher precision and efficiency breakthroughs to the system. In future research, we need to continuously explore better algorithms to make greater progress.
3) The research in this article only considers the scenario of abnormal behavior detection. In the future, we can further dig out more functions of intelligent video surveillance, such as using real-time detection of the current number of people in the business office to reasonably allocate the current service window number.

Acknowledgement. This work is supported by State Grid Shandong Electric Power Company Science and Technology Project Funding under Grant no. 520613200001,520613180002, 62061318C002, Weihai Scientific Research and Innovation Fund (2020) and the Grant 19YG02, Sanming University.

References

1. Held, C., Krumm, J., Markel, P.: Intelligent video surveillance. Computer **45**(3), 83–84 (2012)
2. Collins, R.T., Lipton, A.J., Kanade, T.: A system for video surveillance and monitoring. VSAM final report 2000, pp. 1–68 (2000)
3. Mabrouk, A.B., Zagrouba, E.: Abnormal behavior recognition for intelligent video surveillance systems: a review. Expert Syst. Appl. **91**, 480–491 (2018)
4. Zhu, D., Du, H., Sun, Y., et al.: Research on path planning model based on short-term traffic flow prediction in intelligent transportation system. Sensors **18**(12), 4275 (2018)
5. Zhu, D., Du, H., Cao, N., Qiao, X., Liu, Y.: SP-TSRM: a data grouping strategy in distributed storage system. In: Vaidya, J., Li, J. (eds.) ICA3PP 2018. LNCS, vol. 11334, pp. 524–531. Springer, Cham (2018). https://doi.org/10.1007/978-3-030-05051-1_36
6. Zhu, D., Du, H., Sun, Y., et al.: Massive files prefetching model based on LSTM neural network with cache transaction strategy. Comput. Mater. Continua **63**(2), 979–993 (2020)

7. Zhu, D., Du, H., Wang, Y., et al.: An IoT-oriented real-time storage mechanism for massive small files based on Swift. Int. J. Embedded Syst. **12**(1), 72–80 (2020)
8. Wang, H., Yang, G., Li, E.: High-voltage power transmission tower detection based on faster R-CNN and YOLO-V3. In: Proceedings of the 38th Chinese Control Conference (2019)
9. Lee, Y.H., Kim, Y.: Comparison of CNN and YOLO for object detection. J. Semicond. Display Technol. **19**, 85–92 (2020)
10. Siebel, N.T., Maybank, S.: The advisor visual surveillance system. In: ECCV 2004 Workshop Applications of Computer Vision (ACV) (2004)
11. Ahmad, T., Ma, Y., Yahya, M.: Object detection through modified YOLO neural network. Hindawi Sci. Program. **10**, 8403262 (2020)
12. LeCun, Y., Bengio, Y., Hinton, G.: Deep learning. Nature **521**(7553), 436–444 (2015)
13. Zhang, Y.Z., Xu, S.S., Gao, L.: Research on people counting based on stereo vision. Appl. Mech. Mater. **373–375**, (619-623) (2013)
14. Mukilan, P., Wahi, A.: An efficient multiple human and moving object detection scheme using threshold technique and modified PSO (IPSO) algorithm. Res. J. Appl. Sci. Eng. Technol. **10**(2), 169–176 (2015)
15. Wei, S., Du, H., Ma, G.: Moving vehicle video detection combining ViBe and inter-frame difference. Int. J. Embedded Syst. **12**(3), 371–379 (2020)
16. Barnich, O., Van Droogenbroeck, M.: ViBe: a universal background subtraction algorithm for video sequences. IEEE Trans. Image process. **20**(6), 1709–1724 (2010)
17. Zhichao, L., Jianguo, W., Yubian, W.: Improved algorithm of the video moving object detection based on ViBE. Recent Adv. Comput. Sci. Commun. **13**(4), 781–789 (2020)
18. Hong, B., Yufang, S., BoVideo, X.: Based abnormal behavior detection. In: ICCC 2011: Proceedings of the 2011 International Conference on Innovative Computing and Cloud Computing (2011)
19. Monzón, N., Salgado, A., Sanchez, J.: Regularization strategies for discontinuity-preserving optical flow methods. IEEE Trans. Image Process. **25**(4), 1580–191 (2016)
20. Zuo, J., Jia, Z., Yang, J.: Moving object detection in video sequence images based on an improved visual background extraction algorithm. Multimedia Tools Appl. **79**, 29663–29684 (2020)

Research on the Application of Intelligent Detection Technology in Business Hall System

Xueming Qiao[1], Xiaohui Liu[1], Pengfei Zheng[1], Yingxue Xia[1], Haifeng Sun[1], Rongning Qu[2], Weiguo Tian[3], and Dongjie Zhu[3(✉)]

[1] State Grid Weihai Power Supply Company, Weihai 264200, China
[2] Department of Mathematics, Harbin Institute of Technology, Weihai 264209, China
[3] School of Computer Science and Technology, Harbin Institute of Technology, Weihai 204209, China
zhudongjie@hit.edu.cn

Abstract. The existing offline business halls are unable to accurately identify customers for accurate marketing, and lack effective detection mechanisms for some abnormal behaviors, and cannot assist security personnel such as security personnel in the security work. The successful application of face recognition technology in the payment field makes it feasible to apply it in offline systems of business halls, and the development of behavior detection technology based on computer vision also makes us actively explore its application in offline scenarios of business halls. Therefore, we researched the application of intelligent detection technology including dynamic face recognition technology and behavior detection technology in offline systems of business halls, designed and implemented a prototype system based on this technology, and tested it in real scenarios. The experimental results show that it is feasible to apply the intelligent detection technology to the offline service system of the business hall.

Keywords: Face recognition · Behavior detection · Business hall system

1 Introduction

The rapid development of mobile Internet has greatly improved the efficiency of people's business handling, but there are still some businesses that can only be handled through offline business halls [1]. The existing business hall business under the Internet model cannot completely abandon the offline business platform. The development of face recognition technology [2] is generally believed to have started in an article published in Nature in the 1880s. Since the late 1990s, due to the development of various other related support technologies, face recognition methods have made breakthroughs, and face recognition has truly entered the primary application stage. During the same period, some important methods were born, such as the face recognition method based on the illumination cone model with multiple poses and multiple illumination conditions, etc. Until now, after years of development, considerable progress has been made, and many representative technologies have emerged, such as geometric feature facial recognition

© Springer Nature Switzerland AG 2021
X. Sun et al. (Eds.): ICAIS 2021, CCIS 1423, pp. 521–529, 2021.
https://doi.org/10.1007/978-3-030-78618-2_43

method [5], eigenface-based facial recognition method, neural network facial recognition method [6], elastic graph matching technology (EGM) face recognition method [7], support vector machine (SVM) face recognition method [8]. Nowadays, many countries around the world have scientific research institutions dedicated to the study of face recognition and related applications, and there are many gains.

In addition to the development of face recognition technology, human action and behavior recognition [3] has always been one of the hot research topics in the field of computer vision, which is widely used in security monitoring systems, medical diagnostics and monitoring, human-computer interaction and so on [16]. The purpose of human behavior recognition is to analyze and understand individual actions and interactions among multiple people in videos. As a hotspot of computer vision research, the research on human behavior recognition has important academic significance. At the same time, human behavior recognition technology has application value in security monitoring systems, medical diagnosis and monitoring, human-computer interaction and other fields [17–19].

Accurate identification of customers in offline business halls can facilitate the front desk and security guards to carry out targeted marketing work. At the same time, timely identification of abnormal dangerous behaviors of personnel in the business hall [9] can assist security guards in safety protection work. Nowadays, security has always been an important issue that cannot be ignored in work scenarios where there are interactive operations such as business halls. The traditional security that relies heavily on manpower, whether it is offline security or online surveillance security personnel, cannot avoid the occurrence of visual fatigue. Therefore, through the application of artificial intelligence technology, the processing of surveillance video or image and when Early warning when abnormal behavior occurs is particularly important. In addition to the detection and recognition of abnormal human behaviors, face recognition technology has gradually matured. It is used to assist marketers such as the front desk to complete fixed-point marketing and follow-up corresponding tasks, which can greatly reduce the work intensity and difficulty of employees. Based on this, we researched the application of face recognition technology and action recognition technology in offline business hall systems and verified the feasibility of the scheme through experiments.

2 Design

Our design includes 5 modules, namely the login and registration module, customer information management module, employee information management module, face recognition module, and dangerous behavior recognition module. Strict authority management settings are carried out in the system, and different roles have different operation authority to the system after logging in to the system through the login and registration module. The customer information management module is used to assist administrators in modifying customer information and staff to view customer information. The employee information management module is mainly used to assist administrators in managing employee information. These three modules already exist in the traditional offline business hall management system, and they are not the focus of our research. We mainly design and research the face recognition module and the dangerous behavior recognition module. The following is the overall module diagram of the system (see Fig. 1).

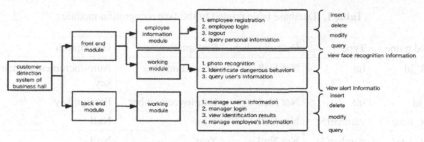

Fig. 1. Overall modules of the system.

2.1 Face Recognition Module

The face recognition module is responsible for the collection and viewing of face information and the entry of information into the business hall system. After passing the login verification, the employee enters the customer's photo for a query and then performs face recognition and living body recognition detection on the photo. If the verification fails, then a reminder, if the detection passes, then a face search. Existing research believes that when the match between the face to be detected and all faces in the face database is less than 75%, it is considered that the face is not registered in the database. If the match is successful, the query result will be displayed and the identified situation will be stored in the database record. The following is the operation flow of the recognition module (see Fig. 2).

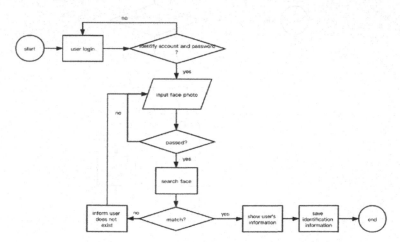

Fig. 2. Operation flow of the recognition module.

The database table related to the face recognition module is the custom record table, which is used to record the customer's face recognition information (see Table 1).

Table 1. Database table related to the face recognition module

Field name	Type	Default value	Explanation	Description
WR_id	int	Not Null	Record number	Auto-increment primary key
SI_id	int	Not Null	Employee number	Foreign key
WR_time	varchar(5)	Not Null	Time	Null
WR_year	varchar(5)	Not Null	Year	Null
WR_month	varchar(5)	Not Null	Month	Null
WR_day	varchar(5)	Not Null	Day	Null

2.2 Dangerous Behavior Recognition Module

The dangerous behavior recognition module is mainly responsible for analyzing and viewing dangerous behaviors. After the employee's login verification is passed, the recorded video is entered into the system for analysis. If dangerous behavior is identified, an early warning message will be issued and recorded in the database for archiving; if no dangerous information is identified, it will be directly recorded in the database for archiving (see Fig. 3).

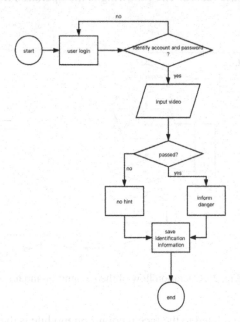

Fig. 3. Operation flow of the behavior recognition module.

The database table related to dangerous behavior recognition is the warning table, which is used to record abnormal behavior detection information (see Table 2).

Table 2. Database table related to the behavior recognition module

Field name	Type	Default value	Explanation	Description
CR_id	int	Not Null	Record number	Auto-increment primary key
CI_id	int	Not Null	Employee number	Foreign key
CR_time	date	Not Null	Time	Null
CR_year	varchar(5)	Not Null	Year	Null
CR_month	varchar(5)	Not Null	Month	Null
CR_day	varchar(5)	Not Null	Day	Null

3   Implementation and Testing

According to the design ideas of the above two modules, we have implemented a prototype system for the application of face recognition and abnormal behavior detection
in business hall business, so as to carry out feasibility analysis and verification of the
scheme. We use Spring [10], SpringMVC [11], and Mybatis [12] framework to build
the back-end platform of the entire prototype system so that the prototype system can
be quickly built; the database uses MySQL [13] version 5.7; the front-end is developed
based on Android [14] SDK.

3.1   Customer Information Identification Module

The customer information identification information module mainly operates the
database through CusRecordMapper, CusRecordService processes tasks, CusRecord-
Controller responds to operations sent back from the front end, and CusRecord
encapsulates customer identification, information classes (see Fig. 4).

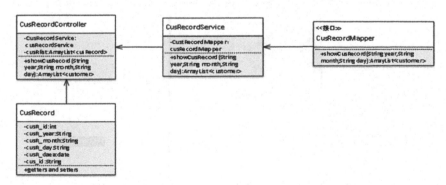

Fig. 4. Database tables of the customer information identification module.

3.2 Hazard Identification Information Module

The dangerous behavior information identification module mainly operates the database through WarnRecordMapper, WarnRecordService processes tasks, WarnRecordController responds to the operations sent back from the front end, and WarnRecord encapsulates customer identification, information classes (see Fig. 5).

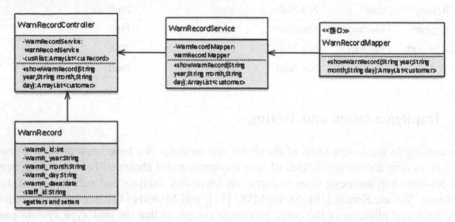

Fig. 5. Database tables of the hazard identification information module.

Our test server host is configured with an Intel i7 series processor, 8 GB RAM, 138 GB SSD, the system kernel version is CentOS [15] Linux release 7.7.1908, and the client APP runs on Android 8.0. The focus of our test is the functional design of face recognition and abnormal behavior detection, so we did not consider the slow response of the client that may be caused by network delay issues. The following is the test operation interface (see Fig. 6).

Fig. 6. Front end operation interface.

As shown in the Fig. 7, in order to recognize the live face data, it is necessary to enter the customer's face photo in advance so that the system can make a judgment based on the physical picture. In addition to being able to detect live photos, our design can also identify and detect dangerous behaviors based on the video situation. The following is the result of the dangerous behavior recognition operation (see Fig. 8).

Fig. 7. Operation interface of the customer recognition module.

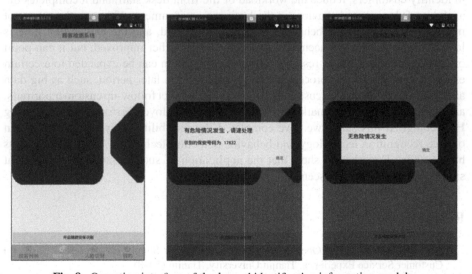

Fig. 8. Operation interface of the hazard identification information module.

In order to test the system in detail and find out the existing or potential system vulnerabilities, we use black box testing and white box testing methods to test the prototype system. According to the black and white box test results, we basically completed the original design of the system. All functions are slightly inferior in performance. It takes about 5 s to wait for the face to be stored in the database. The speed of face recognition can meet the demand. The recognition of dangerous behaviors is worse. It takes 6–10 s of recognition processing time for a video with a time length of 5 s to get a response. The concurrency of the system has not reached our expectations for the time being. This may be the result of many factors. For example, the system does not use a database caching mechanism to cache hot data, and the identification request is submitted in a synchronous manner will also affect the overall concurrency of our system ability, this is the key breakthrough goal of our next research.

4 Conclusion

This paper focuses on the application feasibility of face recognition technology and behavior detection technology in the business hall system and develops a prototype system that meets our needs based on the SSM (Spring + SpringMVC + MyBatis) architecture. Due to the rapid development of artificial intelligence technology, it is inevitable to facilitate people's lives through artificial intelligence technology. The existing business hall system has an increasing demand for the use of facial recognition technology for precision marketing and the use of behavior detection technology to assist security systems. The value of existence will gradually be reflected. Our prototype system implements the modules mentioned in the system design.

The system can meet the needs of assisting the front desk staff in the business hall to identify customers, reduce the workload of the front desk staff, and it completes the analysis of dangerous behaviors in the business environment. Although there are not many types of dangerous behaviors currently supported, and the recognition time is long, and the recognition accuracy rate needs to be further improved, but it can point out the direction for future research. Besides, the system can be expanded to a certain extent, and new business processes can be added in the later period, such as big data analysis in accordance with customer identification, perfect follow-up customer portraits, and complete fixed-point marketing write-offs and employee performance accounting Happening. At this stage, we have completed the feasibility study of the application of face recognition technology and behavior detection technology in offline business hall systems. Experiments show that the application of such technologies is of great significance in the current scenario.

References

1. Niewei, F.: Research on Operation Mode of New Power Supply Business Hall Based on Customer Service Experience, Tianjin University, Tianjin (2018)
2. Yu Dayong, F., Zhenwei, S.: Application of face recognition technology of specific foreign personnel in fine management. Communication World, pp. 60–61 (2019)

3. Xingjian, Z.: Recognition and development of human behavior. Journal of Shanghai University of Electric Power, pp. 102–106 (2017)
4. Wang, Y., Wu, S., Tian, L., Shi, L.: SSM: a high-performance scheme for in-situ training of imprecise memristor neural networks. Neurocomputing **407**, 270–280 (2020)
5. Li, J., Lei, L., Li, H., et al.: Dynamic face recognition based on geometric features. Science Technology and Engineering (2010)
6. Zhong, J., Shan Hu, S., Yu, Y.J.: A face recognition method based on the Bp neural network. Journal Of Computer Research and Development (1999)
7. Hai-Zhou, F., Xuellai, F.: Real-time face recognition based on elastic graph matching in videos. Computer Science (2003)
8. Wei, J., Jian-Qi, Z., Xiang, Z.: Face recognition method based on support vector machine and particle swarm optimization. Expert Syst. Appl. **38**(4), 4390–4393 (2011)
9. Yinghe, D., Guosheng, H.: Abnormal behavior detection and recognition in video surveillance system. Mechanical Design and Manufacturing Engineering, pp. 66–70 (2020)
10. Spring Homepage. https://spring.io/. Accessed 21 Aug 2020
11. Spring MVC Homepage. https://spring.io/guides/gs/serving-web-content/. Accessed 30 Aug 2020
12. Mybatis Homepage. http://mybatis.org/spring-boot-starter/mybatis-spring-boot-test-autoco nfigure/. Accessed 1 Act 2020
13. Mysql Homepage. https://www.mysql.com/. Accessed 11 Act 2020
14. Android Homepage. https://developer.android.google.cn/. Accessed 21 Act 2020
15. Centos Homepage. https://www.centos.org/. Accessed 31 Act 2020
16. Zhu, D., Du, H., Sun, Y., et al.: Research on path planning model based on short-term traffic flow prediction in intelligent transportation system. Sensors **18**(12), 4275 (2018)
17. Zhu, D., Du, H., Cao, N., Qiao, X., Liu, Y.: SP-TSRM: a data grouping strategy in distributed storage system. In: Vaidya, J., Li, J. (eds.) ICA3PP 2018. LNCS, vol. 11334, pp. 524–531. Springer, Cham (2018). https://doi.org/10.1007/978-3-030-05051-1_36
18. Zhu, D., Du, H., Sun, Y., et al.: Massive files prefetching model based on LSTM neural network with cache transaction strategy. Comput. Mater. Continua **63**(2), 979–993 (2020)
19. Zhu, D., Du, H., Wang, Y., et al.: An IoT-oriented real-time storage mechanism for massive small files based on Swift. Int. J. Embed. Syst. **12**(1), 72–80 (2020)

Study on Freshness Indicator Agent of Natural Plant Dyes

Y. G. Huang, G. Y. Wang(✉), K. X. Qi, and P. F. Fang

College of Engineering and Technology, Northeast Forestry University, Harbin 150040, China
wangguiying@nefu.edu.cn

Abstract. Natural plant dye is selected as the pH sensitive agent of the freshness indicators, and the solvent is used to extract the dyes from six kinds of plants-Xinlimei radish, mulberry, red raisin peel, pitaya peel, red carnation and purple onion peel. The color change in solution with different pH value shows that most plant dyes are very sensitive to change in pH value-red in acid solution and blue in alkaline solution. According to the pH change of the spoilage process of chilled meat, low-temperature smoked sausage, fruits and vegetables, appropriate plant dyes are selected as the freshness indicator agent. The test result shows that Xinlimei radish dye is more suitable as a pH indicator agent for chilled meat and high-acid fruits. The purple onion skin pigment indicator agent can be used for fresh fish and neutral vegetables. The mulberry pigment indicator agent can be used for medium-acid fruits. And the theoretical design of the natural color food freshness indicator label is given.

Keywords: Freshness indicator · Food spoilage · Plant pigment

1 Introduction

With the continuous development of materials science, computer technology, modern control technology, artificial intelligence and other related technologies, the traditional manufacturing industry is constantly changing to intelligent manufacturing. In the future, with the development and in-depth integration of new technologies such as printed electronics, RFID (radio frequency identification), flexible display, and 5G communications, especially the rapid development and application of various sensing technologies such as electronic tags and QR codes, it will bring the traditional packaging industry with a brand-new transformation and upgrading to realize the development of the internet of everything. Smart packaging is widely used in all fields and industries, such as food, beverages, electronic goods, medicine, and daily necessities [1–8].

Traditional commodity packaging mainly has the functions of protecting products, facilitating storage & transportation and beautifying commodities, etc. [9]. But it is not sufficient for the commodity quality with the growing concerns of consumers with the food safety and quality. In recent years, with people paying more attention to food safety, how to quickly and accurately identify the freshness of food has gradually become a research hotspot in the food field. Intelligent indicator is a kind of visual indicator,

X. Sun et al. (Eds.): ICAIS 2021, CCIS 1423, pp. 530–540, 2021.
https://doi.org/10.1007/978-3-030-78618-2_44

which can characterize the quality change of products in packaging according to the change of environmental parameters such as temperature and food storage period, and directly provides the freshness information to consumers [10]. For many food products, when they spoiled, their pH value would change [11], numerous efforts have been made to develop visual pH indicator sasone type of intelligent food packaging system for its small size, great sensitivity and low costs [12]. Some chemical reagents such as bromophenol blue and chlorophenol red can be used as pH sensitive indicators [13], however they are harmful to human beings for food application. Since natural dyes are easy to prepare and safe for food application, they can be used as the natural pH sensing dyes for intelligent food packaging systems [14–16]. In 2004, New Zealand Pro-Pressive Enterprises Supermarket launched a Ripe SenceTM label for pear by detecting the natural aroma components produced by pear ripening [17]. At present, this intelligent packaging label has been widely applied to fruit packaging. However, the application of intelligent food labels in China is still in the development stage. Among the plant-based natural dyes, anthocyanins have a sensitive color reaction to wide pH change. The main principle is that the dyecolor changes obviously when pH changes. Fang Rongmei et al. [18] studied the pH indicator effect of red radish pigment and corn poppy pigment. The results showed that the pH indicator ranges of the two dyes were 6.8–8.2 and 6.33–8.25, among which the color of red radish dye changed from pink to purple and the color of corn poppy pigment changed from purple to brown. Lu Yuzhen [19] studied that the valid pH indication range of purple cabbage dye was form 6.8 to 7.8 and the color changed from purple red to green. Zou Xiaobo et al. [20] studied that the pH indicator range of Roselle dye. When pH value changed from 2 to 6, the color gradually turned from red to pink. When the pH value changed from 7 to 9, the color was blue. When the pH value changed from 9 to 14, the color gradually turned from yellow to green due to the decomposition of anthocyanin in strong alkaline conditions. Choi et al. [21] developed a purple sweet potato anthocyanin pH indicator film to monitor the freshness of pork. Uranga et al. [22] found that anthocyanin was a natural nontoxic dye widely found in fruits and vegetables, which is sensitive to the change of pH value and has potential application in food spoilage monitoring. In addition, anthocyanins have strong oxidation resistance, which could be released from the packaging film and extend the shelf life of food. Therefore, the intelligent packaging systems with anthocyanins extracted from purple sweet potato, purple grapes, red grape, bluberry, purple cabbages and eggplant used to indicate pH changes were also reported [11, 23–28]. But indicator agent with anthocyanins extracted from Xinlimei radish, mulberry, red raisin peel, pitaya peel, red carnation and purple onion peel have not yet been studied.

In this paper, pH-sensitive freshness indicator agent was studied. Plant dyes extracted with four different extraction solvents were selected as pH-sensitive agent from purple onion peel, mulberry, red raisin peel, Xinlimei radish, red carnation and pitaya peel. The extraction effect of different solvents on the same dye was investigated and the best extraction solvent for each dye was determined. The color change of six different plant dyes at different pH values was tested to determine their color variation range, and the suitable pH indicator agent was selected according to the spoilage process of fresh fruits and cooked foods.

2 Experimental Part

2.1 Materials and Instruments

Xinlimei radish, mulberry, red raisin, pitaya and purple onion were all purchased at Harbin Carrefour Supermarket; red carnations were purchased at Harbin Flower Market. The instruments included: AJ5003- electronic balance (Shanghai Sunny Hengping Scientific Instrument Co., Ltd.), AZ8692- pH test pen (Taiwan Hengxin Technology Co. Ltd.), DK-98-II-electric heating constant temperature water bath, (Tianjin Test Instrument Co. Ltd.).

2.2 Experimental Method

Preparation of Standard Solution:

1) Preparation of 1 mol/L NaOH standard solution. 10 g of NaOH solid was weighed with a balance and diluted and dissolved with distilled water to 250 mL. It is stirred and shook evenly and then transferred to a reagent bottle for later use. With phenolphthalein as indicator, the NaOH solution was titrate the dand calibrated with potassium hydrogen phthalate until the solution was pink and did not fade within half a minute. The formula for calculating the concentration of NaOH standard solution was as follows:

$$C = 1000\,m/MV \qquad (1)$$

Where: m-the mass of potassium hydrogen phthalate (g); M: the relative molecular mass of potassium hydrogen phthalate (g/mol); V: the amount of sodium hydroxide standard titration solution (mL).

2) Preparation and calibration of 1 mol/L HCl standard solution. 20.9 mL of concentrated hydrochloric acid was measured with a graduated cylinder, diluted to 250 mL with distilled water, stirred with a glass rod and then transferred to a glass stopper reagent bottle for storage. With methyl orange as an indicator, the HCl solution was titrated and calibrated with anhydrous sodium carbonate until the solution turns from orange to red. The calculation formula for the concentration of the HCl standard solution was as follows:

$$C = 2000\,m/MV \qquad (2)$$

Where: m-the mass of anhydrous sodium carbonate (g); M-the relative molecular mass of anhydrous sodium carbonate (g/mol); V-the amount of hydrochloric acid standard titration solution (mL).

3) Preparation and calibration of 1 mol/L HAc standard solution. 14.4 mL of glacial acetic acid was measured with a graduated cylinder, diluted to 250 mL with distilled water, stirred with a glass rod and then transferred to a glass stopper reagent bottle for storage. With phenolphthalein as an indicator, the HAc standard solution was

titrated and calibrated with NaOH standard solution until the solution turns red. The calculation formula for the concentration of the HAc standard solution was as follows:

$$C = 500C_1V_1M/V \tag{3}$$

Where: C_1-the concentration of NaOH solution (mol/L); V_1-the volume of NaOH solution (mL); M-the relative molecular mass of HAc (g/mol); V-the volume of HAc solution (mL).

4) Preparation and calibration of 1 mol/L ammonia standard solution. 18.9 mL of concentrated ammonia was measured with a graduated cylinder, diluted to 250 mL with distilled water, stirred with a glass rod and then transferred to a glass stopper reagent bottle for storage. With methyl orange as an indicator, the ammonia standard solution was titrated and calibrated with HCl standard solution until the solution turns from orange to red.

$$C = 1.703C_1V_1/V \tag{4}$$

Where: C_1-the concentration of HCl solution (mol/L); V_1- the volume of HCl standard solution consumed (mL); V-the volume of ammonia solution (mL).

Preparation of pH Series Solution. The prepared 1 mol/L NaOH, 1 mol/L HCl, 1 mol/L CH_3COOH, 1 mol/L NH_3H_2O standard solutions was used to prepare a solution of the specified pH value and the prepared solutions was put into labeled reagent bottles for use. The dosage used for preparing the solution of different pH value is shown in Table 1 below.

Table 1. Reagent volume required to prepare pH series solution

Number	Required volume of solution					pH theoretical value
	NaOH (mL)	HCl (mL)	CH_3COOH (mL)	$NH_3.H_2O$ (mL)	H_2O (mL)	
1	–	2.0	–	–	18	1
2	–	0.2	–	–	19.8	2
3	–	–	1.2	–	18.8	3
4	2.6	–	17.4	–	–	4
5	7.8	–	12.2	–	–	5
6	9.8	–	10.2	–	–	6
7	9.9	–	10.1	–	–	6.7
8	10.0	–	10.0	–	–	6.8
9	–	–	10.0	10.0	–	7
10	–	9.8	–	10.2	–	8
11	–	7.8	–	12.2	–	9
12	–	2.6	–	17.4	–	10

(*continued*)

Table 1. (*continued*)

Number	Required volume of solution					pH theoretical value
	NaOH (mL)	HCl (mL)	CH$_3$COOH (mL)	NH$_3$.H$_2$O (mL)	H$_2$O (mL)	
13	–	–	–	1.2	18.8	11
14	0.2	–	–	–	19.8	12
15	2.0	–	–	–	18	13
16	20	–	–	–	–	14

Study on the Best Extraction Solvent of Dyes. Among the four main natural dyes, phenolic dyes, carotenoids dyes, pyrrole dyes and quinone dyes, anthocyanins belonging to phenolic dyes is most sensitive to pH value variation. It are easily soluble in organic solvents, so the extraction process is simple. In this experiment, 6 plants with high anthocyanins content, such as Xinlimei radish, mulberry, purple onion peel, red raisin peel, red carnation and pitaya peel are selected. The solvent extraction method was adopted in this experiment. The specific steps are as follows:

Raw materials → washing → air drying → chopping → weighing → grinding → adding solvent → leaching → filtering → pigment leaching solution.

A proper amount of Xinlimei radish, red raisin peel, pitaya peel, red carnation, purple onion peel and mulberry were washed with clear water, dried and chopped. Four samples were taken from each material, each of which was 5 g. After the samples were ground, different solvents were added and stirred evenly, and soaked at 30 °C for 3 h. According to the extraction method of plant pigment, 95% ethanol, 50% ethanol, 0.05 ml/l hydrochloric acid and distilled water were added to each pigment, and soaked at room temperature for 30 min to observe the dissolution of pigment. The results were shown in Table 2.

Table 2. Dissolution of plant pigments in different solvents

Plant	Solvent			
	95% C$_2$H$_6$O	50% C$_2$H$_6$O	0.05ml/l HCl	H$_2$O
Xinlimei Radish				
Red raisin peel				
Pitaya peel				
Red carnation				
Purple onion peel				
Mulberry				

It can be seen from the above table that the dye of Xinlimei radish with 0.05 ml/l hydrochloric acid is darker, so 0.05 ml/l hydrochloric acid is selected as the best extraction solvent for Xinlimei radish dye. Similarly, the best extraction solvent for red raisin peel, pitaya peel and red carnation is distilled water. The best extraction solvent for purple onion skin and mulberry is 50% ethanol.

Discoloration of Each Pigment in Different pH Solutions. Take two pieces of 12-hole white drip plates, drip 6 drops of solution with pH value of 1–14 into the 14 holes of the drip plates, then add 3 drops of leaching solution of the same dye, rest for 1 min, observe and record the color change of the solution, and other dye test methods were the same as above. According to the color change of six plant dyes under different pH conditions, compared with the standard color card, three repeated experiments were carried out. The final color development of six plant dyes in solutions with different pH values was as shown in Table 3.

Table 3. Color development of plant pigments in different pH solutions

Plant	Color of extract	pH value												
		1	2	3	4	5	6	7	8	9	10	11	12	13	14
Purple onion peel															
Xinlimei Radish															
Red carnation															
Pitaya peel															
Mulberry															
Red raisinpeel															

3 Results and Analysis

3.1 Analysis of Experimental Results

It can be seen from Table 3 that different plant dyes have different color changing range under different acid and base solution. The color changing variation is shown in Table 4.

Design of Freshness Indicator Label. The indicator label was mainly composed of a carrier coated with a pH indicator, a transparent component and a substrate. The indicator used in the freshness indicator label designed was an extract of plant dyes.

Table 4. Discoloration range of several plant dyes

Plant	Color variation
Purple onion peel	1–5 Pink fades 6 Colorless 7–12 Yellow gets darker 13–14 Green
Xinlimei Radish	1–2 Orange red 3–6 Pink fades 7–9 Purple fades
	10 Grey 11–14 Yellow
Red carnation	1–2 Orange 3–7 Pink fades 8–14 Yellow gets darker
Pitaya peel	1–2 Magenta 3–6 Pink gets darker 7 Fuchsia 8–11 Purple gets darker
	12 Grayish purple 13 Tan 14 Yellow
Mulberry	1–3 Orange 4–7 Pink 8–12 Purple gets darker 13 Navy blue 14 Dark green
Red raisin peel	1–4 Pink fades 5 Colorless 6–7 Pink 8–11 Purple 12 Pink 13–14 Yellow

The transparent component served as the outer layer of the freshness indicator label, and the color changed on the inner carrier can be clearly observed through the outermost transparent component. In order to adapt to the complex circulation environment, transparent materials must have excellent heat and high temperature resistance, so cast polypropylene film (CPP) was used as the transparent component of the freshness indicator label.

The substrate is in direct contact with the food. To ensure that the material was safe and non-toxic, white filter paper is selected as the substrate of the freshness indicator label and cut into rectangular pieces of 15 mm × 40 mm in size. The indicator was coated in an "X" shape. Cloth to ensure that the indicator was distributed as evenly as possible on the indicator card substrate to achieve a better color rendering effect.

3.2 Determination of pH Sensitizers for Different Food Types

Selection of pH Sensitizer for Chilled Meat. The main reasons for the spoilage of chilled meat included fat oxidation, microbial contamination and growth [22]. Fresh meat was rich in nutrients, such as protein, fat, sugars, vitamins, organic acids, etc., with a pH value of 5.7 to 6.5 and high free water content. It was suitable for the growth and reproduction of microorganisms and resulted in the reduction of the quality of fresh meat and the production of TVB-N, CO_2, sulfide and other metabolites [29, 30]. Dainty [31] found that meat spoilage usually occurs when the pH greater than 6.0, and the meat spoiled when the pH exceeded 6.7. It could be seen from the experimental results that Xinlimei radish was magenta when the pH was 6.7, and yellow when the pH was 6.8, with a mutation in color. Therefore, Xinlimei radish could be used as a pH sensitive agent for cold meat freshness indicator label.

Selection of pH Sensitive Agent for Fresh Fish. It should be noted that the pH value has a close relationship with the freshness of fish samples. Generally, during storage, volatile compounds containing $(CH_3)_3N$ (trimethylamine or TMA), $(CH_3)_2NH$ (dimethylamine or DMA) and NH_3 (ammonia) are produced in foods by microbial degradation, and their concentrations are steadily increased in the headspace of an enclosed food package, resulting in a pH increase over time. The headspace is a source of information about its freshness. Previous investigation [32] evidenced that the onset of spoilage was detected in the region of 12 h after milkfish (Chanos chanos) samples were kept at room temperature, its pH 5.8 and total volatile basic nitrogen (TVBN) value 9 mg N/100 g; after 16 h storage, fish spoilage was at "mid-point" with pH 6.2, and point saturation was about 22 h, with pH > 6.9 and TVBN value 22 mg N/100 g. From their same report, it could be found that the threshold of bacteria spoilage for the milkfish sample was 12 h, and the sample reached its full spoilage at 23 h storage (maximum bacteria population) at room temperature (25 °C), pH with 6.2 and 7.0 were estimated corresponding to the storage time (12 and 23 h). X.H. Zhang et al. [33] used pigments extracted from Bauhinia flowers to prepare a pH sensor film. They found that for fish samples, the color of the sensor film changed from purple to brown stably after about 12 h. Then it changed from brown to green after 16 h at 25 °C. When the storage time exceeds 20 h, the color of the sensing film changes to green, indicating that the pH of the fish sample begins to change. After the fish samples were stored for 24 h, the color of the sensing film completely changed to green, indicating that the pH value of the samples had changed significantly. It can be seen from Table 3 that the purple onion peel has a significant color change between pH 5 and 7, so it can be used as a pH sensitive agent for fish freshness indicator cards.

Selection of pH Sensitive Agents for Fruits and Vegetables. Fruits and vegetables had a lot of carbohydrates. During the spoilage process, due to the action of microorganisms and their own enzymes, carbohydrates underwent a series of reactions, and finally carbon dioxide and water was formed. Because carbon dioxide was acidic, the pH value in the system decreased [34].

For neutral vegetables such as lettuce and peas, the pH is between 6.0 and 7.0. Li Chunhai [35] indicated that pH is one of the indicators to measure the content of organic acids. Vegetables usually contain a certain amount of organic acids, and the type and content of organic acids directly affect the taste of vegetables. In the storage process, as the aging process accelerates, the organic acids of vegetables reduced due to their participation in metabolism. Mehran Moradi et al. [36] developed a new intelligent pH sensor indicator based on bacterial nanocellulose and black carrot anthocyanin. They studied the color changes of anthocyanin solution and indicator at different pH and found the indicator when the pH was 7, it appeared bright blue, and when the pH was lower than 6, the indicator turned pink. It can be seen from Table 3 that when the pH value is lower than 6, the pigment of purple onion peel changes from yellow to pink. Therefore, the sensitizer for neutral vegetables can be purple onion peel.

The pH value of high-acid fruits such as plums, lemons, strawberries, etc., is between 3.0 and 4.0. J.J Zhang [37] combined roselle anthocyanins to prepare a smart indicator film. When the pH was lower than 3, the Anthocyanins mainly existed in the form of yellow salt ions, and the solution was dark red. When the pH value was 4.0–6.0, their structure gradually changed to quinone type, and the solution gradually became colorless. It can be seen from Table 3 that Xinlimei radish and red carnations are orange-red at pH 1–2, and pink at pH 3–6. Therefore, Xinlimei radish or red carnations can be selected as the pH indicator of high-acid fruits. In the same way, it can be seen that the color of mulberries changes obviously between pH 1–3 and 4–7, which is relatively suitable to indicate the medium-acid fruits with pH values between 3 and 5.

4 Conclusion

In this experiment, we used 4 kinds of solvents to extract pigments from 6 kinds of plants and measured the color development of different plant pigments under different pH condition. The following conclusions are as follows:

The solubility of different pigments in the same solvent is different, and the solubility of the same plant pigment in different solvents was also quite different. This was caused by the different nature of the pigments contained in plants. The different pigments needed to select a suitable solvent to achieve a better extraction effect. According to the color development of the 6 pigments under different pH conditions, mulberries basically conform to the law of red or purple when exposed to acid and blue when exposed to alkali, which shows that the content of anthocyanin in mulberries is the most.

When choosing pH indicators for different types of foods, in addition to satisfying the basic requirements of obvious discoloration and sensitive discoloration reaction, appropriate plant pigments should be selected as the pH sensitive agents of the indicator labels based on the characteristics of the food spoilage process. Different from natural pigment as an acid-base indicator, it is not that the wider the color range, the more suitable it is to be a pH indicator for food freshness indicator label, as long as its color changes significantly with the change of pH in a certain range.

The six pigments selected in this experiment were all water-soluble pigments, which were used as the pH sensitive agent of the freshness indicators, so that consumers could intuitively judge the freshness of the food by the color change on the indicators. The natural pigments had a wide variety, were safe and non-toxic, and the extraction process was relatively simple. Therefore, the use of natural pigments as a pH sensitive agent for food freshness indicators has broad application prospects and development potential, but the preservation methods of natural pigments need further research and investigation.

Acknowledgments. The authors thank for the financial supports by the Basic Scientific Research Project2572020DF01 of Northeast Forestry University.

Fund Projects. Basic Scientific Research Project2572020DF01 of Northeast Forestry University.

Conflicts of Interest. The authors declare that we have no conflicts of inter- est to report regarding the present study.

References

1. Sheu, J., Chen, I., Liao, Y.: Realization of internet of things smart appliances. Intell. Autom. Soft Comput. **25**(2), 395–404 (2019)

2. Chu, C., Huang, Z., Xu, R., Wen, G., Liu, L.: A cross layer protocol for fast identification of blocked tags in large-scale RFID systems. Comput. Mater. Continua **64**(3), 1705–1724 (2020)
3. Sehrai, D.A., Muhammad, F., Kiani, S.H., Abbas, Z.H., Tufail, M., et al.: Gain-enhanced metamaterial based antenna for 5G communication standards. Comput. Mater. Continua **64**(3), 1587–1599 (2020)
4. Wang, Q., Yang, C., Wang, Y., Wu, S.: Application of low cost integrated navigation system in precision agriculture. Intell. Autom. Soft Comput. **26**(6), 1433–1442 (2020)
5. Kim, S.K., Köppen, M., Bashir, A.K., Jin, Y.: Advanced ICT and IoT technologies for the fourth industrial revolution. Intell. Autom. Soft Comput. **26**(1), 83–85 (2020)
6. Zhang, W., Fang, W., Zhao, Q., Ji, X.: Energy efficiency in internet of things: an overview. Comput. Mater. Continua **63**(2), 787–811 (2020)
7. Xu, Z., Zhou, Q., Yan, Z.: Special issue on recent advances in artificial intelligence for smart manufacturing – part II. Intell. Autom. Soft Comput. **25**(4), 1–3 (2019)
8. Xu, Z., Zhou, Q., Yan, Z.: Special section on recent advances in artificial intelligence for smart manufacturing – part I. Intell. Autom. Soft Comput. **25**(4), 693–694 (2019)
9. Sai, W.: Application of intelligent packaging technology. Printing Quality and Standardization, no. 1, pp. 28–31 (2015)
10. Sheng G.: A new classic of food intelligent packaging (2012). http://news.pack.cn/hydt/xzyc/2007-02/2007020211002659.shtml
11. Pereira, V.A., de Arruda, I.N.Q., Stefani, R.: Active chitosan/PVA films with anthocyanins from Brassica oleraceae (Red Cabbage) as time-temperature indicators for application in intelligent food packaging. Food Hydrocolloids **43**, 180–188 (2015)
12. Gupta, B.D., Sharma, S.: A long-range fiber optic pH sensor prepared by dye doped sol–gel immobilization technique. Opt. Commun. **154**(5–6), 282–284 (1998)
13. Dong, S., Luo, M., Peng, G., Cheng, W.: Broad range pH sensor based on sol–gel entrapped indicators on fibre optic. Sens. Actuators B-Chem. **129**(1), 94–98 (2008)
14. Pavai, M., Mihaly, J., Paszternak, A.: pH and CO_2 sensing by curcumin coloured cellophane test strip. Food Anal. Methods **8**(9), 2243–2249 (2015)
15. Yoshida, C.M.P., Maciel, V.B.V., Mendonca, M.E.D., Franco, T.T.: Chitosan biobased and intelligent films: monitoring pH variations. LWT-Food Sci. Technol. **55**(1), 83–89 (2014)
16. Calogero, G., Yum, J.-H., Sinopoli, A., Di. Marco, G., Grätzel, M., Nazeeruddin, M.K.: Anthocyanins and betalains as light-harvesting pigments for dye sensitized solar cells. Sol. Energy **86**(5), 1563–1575 (2012)
17. Ripesense: The next revolution in fresh produce marketing (2012). http://www.ripesen-se.com/
18. Yuzhen, L., Xunmo, Y.: A natural indicator-purple cabbage pigment. Guizhou Sci. **3**, 53–57 (1996)
19. Xiaobo, Z., et al.: Preparation of a double-layer smart film and its application in indicating salmon freshness. Food Sci. **40**(23), 206–212 (2019)
20. Choi, I., Lee, J.Y., Lacroix, M., Han, J.: Intelligent pH indicator film composed of agar/potato starch and anthocyanin extracts from purple sweet potato. Food Chem. **218**(9), 122–128 (2017)
21. Uranga, J., Etxabide, A., Guerrero, P., de la Caba, K.: Development of active fish gelatin films with anthocyanins by compression molding. Food Hydrocolloids **84**(6), 313–320 (2018)
22. Peng, J.: Research on quality and safety control technology of cold fresh meat. M.S. dissertation, Department of Food Processing and Safety, Wuhan University of Light Industry, Zhengzhou (2014)
23. Golasz, L.B., Silva, J.D., Silva, S.B.D.: Film with anthocyanins as an indicator of chilled pork deterioration. Food Sci. Technol. (Campinas) **33**, 155–162 (2013)

24. Chen, X., Gu, Z.T.: Absorption-type optical pH sensitive film based on immobilized purple cabbage pigment. Sens. Actuators B-Chem. **178**, 207–211 (2013)

25. Silva-Pereira, M.C., Teixeira, J.A., Pereira-Júnior, V.A., et al.: Chitosan/corn starch blend films with extract from Brassica oleraceae (red cabbage) as a visual indicator of fish deterioration. LWT - Food Sci. Technol. **61**(1), 258–262 (2015)

26. Abolghasemi, M.M., Sobhi, M., Piryaei, M.: Preparation of a novel green optical pH sensor based on immobilization of red grape extract on bioorganic agarose membrane. Sens. Actuators B Chem. **224**, 391–395 (2016). https://doi.org/10.1016/j.snb.2015.10.038

27. Andretta, R., Luchese, C.L., Tessaro, I.C., Spada, J.C.: Development and characterization of pH-indicator films based on cassava starch and blueberry residue by thermocompression. Food Hydrocolloids **93**, 317–324 (2019). https://doi.org/10.1016/j.foodhyd.2019.02.019

28. Bilgiç, S., Söğüt, E., Seydim, A.C.: Chitosan and starch-based intelligent films with anthocyanins from eggplant to monitor pH variations. Turk. J. Agric. Food Sci. Technol. **7**(Suppl. 1), 61–66 (2019). https://doi.org/10.24925/turjaf.v7isp1.61-66.2705

29. Mutwaki, L.: Meat spoilage mechanisms and preservation techniques: a critical review. Am. J. Agric. Biol. Sci. **6**(4), 486–510 (2011)

30. Nychas, G.J.E., Skandamis, P.N., Tassou, C.C., et al.: Meat spoilage during distribution. Meat Sci. **78**(6), 77–89 (2008)

31. Dainty, R.H.: Chemical/biochemical detection of spoilage. Int. J. Food Microbiol. **33**(1137), 19–33 (1996)

32. Kuswandi, B., Restyana, A., et al.: A novel colorimetric food package label for fish spoilage based on polyaniline film. Food Control **25**(10), 184–189 (2012)

33. Zhang, X., Sisi, L., Chen, X.: A visual pH sensing film using natural dyes from Bauhinia blakeana Dunn. Sens. Actuators B Chem. **198**(2), 268–273 (2014)

34. Jiang, J., Hu, W.: Microbial contamination of fresh-cut fruits and vegetables and its sterilization technology. Food Ind. Sci. Technol. **30**(6), 319–324 (2009)

35. Guilian, W., Xinling, W., Hongyang, Y., Si Yanjiao, L., Yongjie, Z.L.: Research and design of a strawberry freshness indicator label. Sci. Technol. Innov. Guide **11**(33), 185–186 (2014)

36. Moradi, M., Tajik, H., Almasi, H., et al.: A novel pH-sensing indicator based on bacterial cellulose nanofibers and black carrot anthocyanins for monitoring fish freshness. Carbohydr. Polym. **222**(11), 115030 (2019)

37. Zhang, J., Zou, X., Zhai, X., et al.: Preparation of an intelligent pH film based on biodegradable polymers and roselle anthocyanins for monitoring pork freshness. Food Chem. **272**(8), 306–312 (2018)

Multi-dimensional Visualization and Simulation Analysis of COVID-19 Outbreak

Wu Zeng, YingGe Zhang(✉), Kun Hu, and YingXiang Jiang

Department of Electrical and Electronic Engineering, Wuhan Polytechnic University,
Hubei 430023, China

Abstract. The progression of the global COVID-19 epidemic situation is the
main focus of attention of all countries in the world. Due to characteristics, such
as multi-origins, huge amount, and inaccessibility, of the existing data, an all-round
analyzation of the epidemic situation, which is in dire need, is impeded. The aim
of the following study is to provide a multi-dimensional analysis of COVID-19
through visualization and dynamic simulation of data. In order to achieve this goal,
the study collected related data though multiple platforms and used tools such as
Echarts and Java Swing to visualize the data, and then dynamically simulated
the transmission model. Moreover, the data of Wuhan has been applied to the
SEIR model to study the effect of quarantine on the transmission of COVID-19.
Ultimately, the study hopes to demonstrate an effective method of data analyzation
that can be applied to prevent and contain similar outbreak in the future.

Keywords: COVID-19 · Echarts · Java Swing · Visualization · SEIR model
prediction

1 Introduction

Public health incidents are public undertakings closely related to national security and
people's lives and health, and epidemic prevention and control is one of its most important contents [1]. In December 2019, a cluster of pneumonia of unknown cause appeared
in Wuhan, Hubei Province, which was later confirmed to be an acute respiratory infectious disease caused by the "2019 novel Coronavirus" (2019-NCOV). The World Health
Organization named it the new type of coronavirus pneumonia (referred to as COVID-
19) [2]. With the outbreak of COVID-19 around the world, the development trend of the
epidemic has quickly become the focus of global attention.

The presentation of the epidemic situation and the deployment of prevention and control require the support of relevant information, which mainly comes from various data.
However, the huge amount of data, complicated information and real-time changing data
characteristics increase the difficulty for users to analyze and interpret the content of the
epidemic data. Epidemic data visualization extracts structured data content through data
mining and transformation, and presents epidemic information in a more understandable
visual form and expresses the internal laws of epidemic data [3]. The application of data
visualization in the spread of the epidemic, on the one hand, can help people understand

© Springer Nature Switzerland AG 2021
X. Sun et al. (Eds.): ICAIS 2021, CCIS 1423, pp. 541–553, 2021.
https://doi.org/10.1007/978-3-030-78618-2_45

and analyze the new coronavirus pneumonia epidemic in a more accurate and intuitive way, such as the distribution of infected people and the route of virus transmission. On the other hand, it provides scientific reference for the medical departments in disease monitoring, medical resource allocation, personnel flow management, etc., so that the government can take reasonable measures to reduce the epidemic infection rate [4].

Researchers across the globe have done a lot of research on data visualization of the novel coronavirus pneumonia epidemic, which mainly includes two aspects: showing the development trend of the epidemic and predicting the future trend of the epidemic.

The presentation of the epidemic situation generally uses various types of infographics, such as the work "Barometer of Epidemic Change" by the Visualization and Visual Analysis Laboratory of Peking University [5], which focuses on incremental data, collects statistics on daily historical data, and Use color saturation to give visual hints to the degree of infection; another work "Epidemic Dimension" uses "graphics" and "colors" and supplemented by digital production methods. By clicking on the boxes of each province, you can view the national epidemic situation Switching between the two and the epidemic situation of the whole province, the macroscopic situation of the epidemic situation is showing. Jiang Fuling et al. [6] analyzed the epidemiological characteristics of the proportion of confirmed cases, gender distribution, and case types in various districts (counties) of Chongqing through statistical chart visualization. Yixian Zhang et al. [7] analyzed the Chinese sentiment of the COVID-19 public opinion environment through data visualization, and clearly displayed various sentiment categories, keywords, hot topics, and other information, and comprehensively and intuitively reflected the epidemic's impact on public sentiment Changes.

The analysis and prediction of the development trend of the COVID-19 epidemic usually use classic disease transmission models based on complex networks, including SI models, SIR models, SIS models, SEIR models, etc. [8]. Recently, Yu Zi et al. [9] have revised the SIR model, using the susceptible reproduction number, the daily infection rate, and the latent infection rate to solve the virus evolution dynamics equation and use time-varying parameters to predict the development of the epidemic. Provide certain theoretical support for epidemic intervention decision-making. Cao Shengli et al. [10] established a modified SEIR infectious disease dynamics model, conducted a retrospective study on the epidemic situation in Hubei Province, assessed and verified the key impact of prevention, control, isolation, and centralized treatment on the rapid decline of the peak number of infections. Fan Ruguo et al. [11] used the SEIR model to analyze the spread of the epidemic in Wuhan, and evaluated the peak and turning points of the epidemic under different virus incubation period scenarios, and achieved good prediction results.

It can be seen that many scholars have done data visualization analysis on the new crown pneumonia epidemic, but they are biased towards a certain aspect of research, and there is a relative lack of multi-dimensional visualization analysis of epidemic data.

This study analyzes the visualization of epidemic data. We first realize the visual presentation of epidemic information from the perspective of spatial distribution and timing characteristics; then use Java Swing technology to simulate the development trend of the epidemic from the flow of people to verify the rationality of travel restrictions to curb the spread of the epidemic; finally establish a SEIR transmission dynamics model of the COVID-19 epidemic with an incubation period to predict and analyze the spread of the new coronavirus and its inflection point, and according to the degree of conformity between the SEIR prediction model and the simulation results, the correctness of the theoretical model built is verified.

2 Data Collection and Processing

Develop Python's Scrapy crawler framework to crawl Tencent's real-time epidemic data [12], including new cases, confirmed cases, cured cases and deaths. At the same time, data were manually obtained from platforms such as the National Health Commission, dxy.cn, the Website of Hopkins University and the online website of the World Health Organization (WHO), striving for data integrity and accuracy. In addition, according to the demographic data published on the website of Wuhan Municipal People's government [13], by the end of 2019, the number of permanent residents in Wuhan is 11.212 million.

Then, Excel, Python and other tools are used to preprocess the acquired data. Clean the obvious abnormal data, modify the format error, and make up 0 for the vacant value, to prepare the data for the following data visualization and model simulation prediction.

3 Visual Analysis of the Epidemic

Visualization is the most intuitive way to express the epidemic. Authoritative websites at home and abroad, such as the Hopkins University website and the Visualization and Visual Analysis Laboratory of Peking University, express and visually display the COVID-19 epidemic. According to the content and method of visualization, the existing public platforms can be roughly divided into three categories: digital visualization of epidemic situation, real-time map of epidemic situation and visualization analysis of the epidemic situation. In this visualization program, the epidemic situation is analyzed visually in terms of spatial and temporal distribution.

3.1 Analysis of Spatial Distribution Characteristics

Population density reflects the multi-dimensional "distance" between people, including physical distance, social distance, etc. [14]. Theoretically speaking, areas with densely distributed populations will allow more face-to-face communication between residents, which makes these areas likely to become hot spots for the rapid spread of infectious diseases; at the same time, areas with densely distributed populations Possibly easier access to health care facilities and better implementation of social distancing policies and practices [15]. This study first considers the impact of population density in a region on the number of confirmed cases, and performs a series of conversions and calculations on the collected data. Figure 1 selects some representative (epidemic development trends) countries from all continents in the world, shows the distribution of population density and the number of confirmed these countries histogram (as Beijing standard time on December 16, 2020).

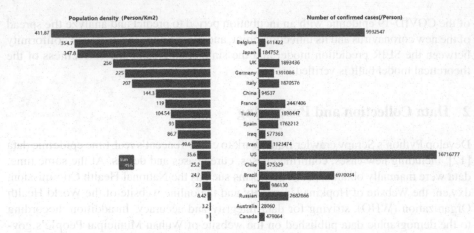

Fig. 1. Relationship between population density and the number of confirmed cases

In Fig. 1, the population density of India is 411.87 (person/km^2), the number of confirmed people has reached 9932547, the population density of Belgium is 354.7 (person/km^2), the number of confirmed people is 611422, and the population density of Japan is 347.8 (person/km^2), the number of confirmed people is 184752, the population density difference of three places is not large, but the number of confirmed is quite different. The United States has a population density of 34.86 (person/km^2) and Brazil has a population density of 24.76 (person/km^2), but the number of confirmed cases reached 16716777 and 6970034, respectively. Therefore, population density may be a factor that affects the development of the epidemic in an area, but it is not a decisive factor.

Novel Coronavirus showed different propagation efficiency at different temperatures [16]. Different geographical conditions may result in different climates [17]. Figure 2 shows the cumulative number of confirmed cases in the top 30 countries in the world at the deadline (considering that the statistics of the epidemic in Africa are not very timely, the populations of countries in Oceania are small, so the main statistics are the Americas, Europe, and Asia.).

In the red bar in Fig. 2, there are 9 countries in the Americas, namely, the United States, Brazil, Argentina, Colombia, Mexico, Peru, Belgium, Chile and Canada. The yellow bar shows the Asian region, there are 9 countries: India, Iran, Indonesia, Iraq, Bangladesh, Philippines, Pakistan, Israel and Saudi Arabia. The blue shows the European region, there are 12 countries: Russia, France, Turkey, UK, Italy, Spain, Germany, Poland, Czechia, Romania and Switzerland. Therefore, there is no significant gap between continents in the epidemic situation, and the geographical environment is also not a decisive factor affecting the development of the epidemic.

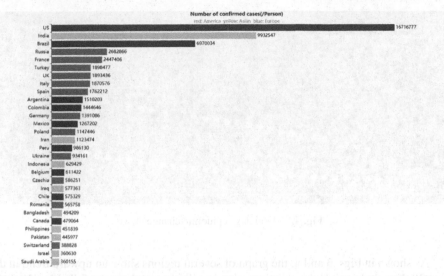

Fig. 2. Top 30 countries with the cumulative number of confirmed cases worldwide (Color figure online)

3.2 Analysis of Timing Characteristics

Time series analysis is a method based on time series to study the development process of things and predict possible targets in the future time domain [18]. Through time series analysis, this paper studies the changes of new coronavirus pneumonia in different countries and regions over time, so as to confirm the impact of population mobility on the epidemic. Figure 3 randomly selected five countries or regions: Hubei Province, Italy, India, the United Kingdom, and Russian (Hubei Province is the main outbreak area of the epidemic in China, so Hubei Province is selected here for comparison), and displays the curves of the cumulative number of confirmed cases in 1–30 days and 31–60 days, respectively.

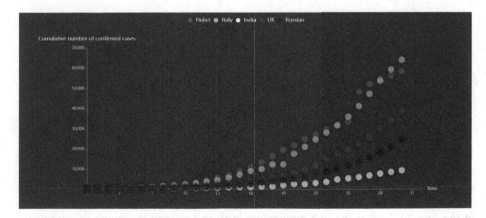

Fig. 3. 1–30 days epidemic change curve

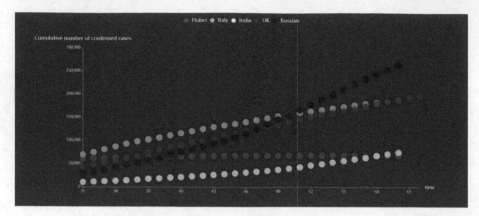

Fig. 4. 30–60 days epidemic change curve

As shown in Figs. 3 and 4, the graph of several regions show an upward trend in the first 30 days. Italy and Hubei province are very similar, while in the following 30 days, only Hubei province stabilized. The remaining 4 regions are all on the rise.

Considering that Hubei Province is the region where the epidemic first break out in China, and Italy is the country where the epidemic first break out in Europe. The total population of both places is about 60 million. Therefore, we will take Hubei Province and Italy as examples to focus on comparing and analyzing the trend of the epidemic situation in the two places over time.

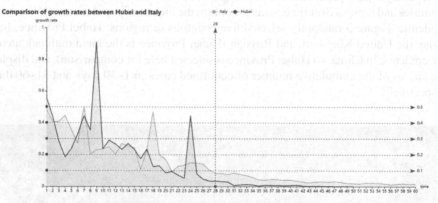

Fig. 5. The daily growth rate of the previous epidemic in Hubei province and Italy

In Fig. 5, the cumulative number of confirmed cases in Hubei and Italy is just over 100 as the first day, and the daily growth rate of the two places is analyzed to study the epidemic situation in the two places. The cumulative number of confirmed cases in Hubei Province is just over 100 on January 19, 2020, and the cumulative number of confirmed cases in Italy on February 24, 2020 exceeds 100. The daily growth rates in the first 30 days of the two regions are high or low, and the graph of cumulative confirmed Numbers is very similar. However, due to the closed management of almost all cities in Hubei Province on January 26, 2020, the daily growth rate of Hubei Province continue to decline in the following 30 days. Of course, Italy take measures late and also achieve certain results. Therefore, the implementation of urban quarantine measures to restrict the movement of people can reduce the daily growth rate to a relatively low value, effectively controlling the spread of the epidemic, and having obvious effects on the spread of the epidemic.

4   Epidemic Simulation and Model Prediction

4.1   Propagation Dynamic Simulation

The activity of the novel coronavirus is closely related to the season. The experiment of Shane Riddell et al. [19] show that infectious SARS-CoV-2 can remain on a non-porous surface for at least 28 days under ambient temperature and humidity (20 °C and 50% RH). Increasing the temperature while maintaining humidity can greatly reduce the survival time of the virus. In an environment of 40 °C, the survival time of the virus is only 24 h. Cory Merow et al. [20] establish a statistical model base on fine weather data and global infection reports. Base on the analysis of weather factors such as ultraviolet rays, it is predicted that COVID-19 will temporarily decrease in summer, rebound in autumn, and reach a peak in winter.

The autumn and winter rebound of COVID-19 has begun, and the second wave of COVID-19 outbreak has begun [21]. Based on Java Swing technology, the dynamic simulation of epidemic spread is carried out to prove the important impact of crowd flow control on the epidemic. Java Swing technology is mainly used to build cross-platform desktop Window program, it is a graphical component library technology written in Java language on the basis of AWT (Abstract Window Toolkit) [22]. Swing components include a variety of containers and basic components. Containers are mainly used to contain and arrange basic components, and they can also contain corresponding containers [23]. The container used this time is mainly JFrame, which is used to simulate the city, and the components used are dots to simulate the random distribution of people. White dots represent healthy people, yellow dots represent latent people, and red dots represent confirmed patients. The dots move from static to dynamic, simulating the flow of real people.

As shown in Fig. 6, it is assumed that one of the two regions restricts travel and the population mobility is small, and the other is not restricted, so the population mobility is high. while controlling other conditions (total population, initial number of infections, transmission rate, etc.) to be the same. As can be clearly seen from the figure, with the change of time, there are obviously more red and yellow dots in areas with no travel restrictions than areas with restricted travel, and the epidemic situation is more serious.

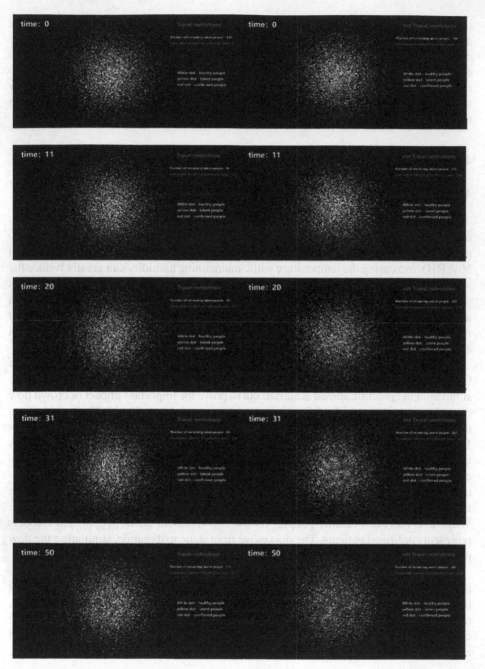

Fig. 6. Simulation of the epidemic situation in different population flow states

4.2 SEIR Model Prediction

Considering that recent research results indicate that COVID-19 is infectious during the incubation period, which is consistent with the basic SEIR SEIR epidemic dynamics model [24], as shown in Fig. 7. This paper proposes a modified SEIR model on the basis of the existing model. The new model takes into account the risk of transmission of patients in the incubation period, and also considers the impact of prevention, control and isolation on the evolution of the epidemic.

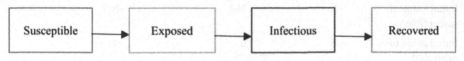

Fig. 7. Basic SEIR model

Based on the assumptions established: the impact of asymptomatic infections is not considered; the impact of population inflows and outflows on the model is not considered; the impact of natural mortality and natural population growth rate is not considered; and it is believed that the rehabilitated R class members will not become S class members again. The SEIR differential equation in the natural propagation state can be established as Formulas (1), (2), (3) and (4):

$$\frac{dS}{dt} = \frac{-r_1 \beta IS}{N} + \frac{-r_2 \beta_2 ES}{N} \tag{1}$$

$$\frac{dE}{dt} = \frac{r_1 \beta IS}{N} + \frac{r_2 \beta_2 ES}{N} - \alpha E \tag{2}$$

$$\frac{dI}{dt} = \alpha E - \gamma I \tag{3}$$

$$\frac{dR}{dt} = \gamma I \tag{4}$$

The iterative equation is shown in Formulas (5), (6), (7) and (8):

$$S_n = S_{n-1} - \frac{r_1 \beta I_{n-1} S_{n-1}}{N} - \frac{r_2 \beta_2 E_{n-1} S_{n-1}}{N} \tag{5}$$

$$E_n = E_{n-1} + \frac{r_1 \beta I_{n-1} S_{n-1}}{N} - \alpha E_{n-1} + \frac{r_2 \beta_2 E_{n-1} S_{n-1}}{N} \tag{6}$$

$$I_n = I_{n-1} + \alpha E_{n-1} - \gamma I_{n-1} \tag{7}$$

$$R_n = R_{n-1} + \gamma I_{n-1} \tag{8}$$

The main parameter settings of the modified SEIR model are shown in Table 1. What needs to be stated is that if the prevention and control isolation measures are implemented on the 20th day, the parameters need to be reset: $r_1 = 10$, $r_2 = 10$, $\beta = 0.02$, $\beta_2 = 0.02$.

Table 1. Parameters in modified SEIR model

Model parameter	Model parameter	Wuhan (in natural state)	Wuhan (under isolation measures)
Total population	N	11212000	11212000
Initial value of exposed	E	0	12 point, bold
Initial value of infectious	I	10	10
Initial value of susceptible	S	N-I	N-I
Initial value of recovered	R	0	0
Daily contact rate of infected persons	r_1	20	10
Daily contact rate of exposed persons	r_2	20	10
Infection rate of infected persons contacting susceptible persons	β	0.03	0.02
Infection rate of exposed persons contacting susceptible persons	β_2	0.03	0.02
The probability of an exposed person turning into an infected person	α	0.1	0.1
Daily recovery rate	γ	0.1	0.1

In the MATLAB programming environment, the modified SEIR model is used to evaluate the impact of isolation measures on the evolution of epidemic situation in Wuhan.

As shown in Fig. 8, in the natural state of Wuhan without quarantine measures, many people will be infected according to the model. If quarantine measures are taken from the 20th day, as shown in Fig. 9, the time of the high-incidence period will be extended later and the peak number of disease will drop significantly. It is found by comparison that the control measures implemented in advance by Wuhan City are effective, which will bring the inflection point of the epidemic to 1 to 2 months earlier, thus effectively reducing the consumption of social resources.

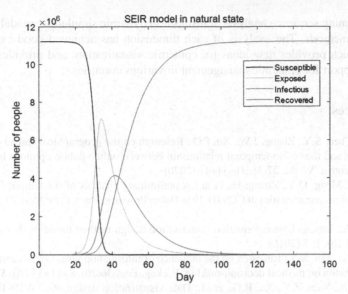

Fig. 8. SEIR model in the natural state

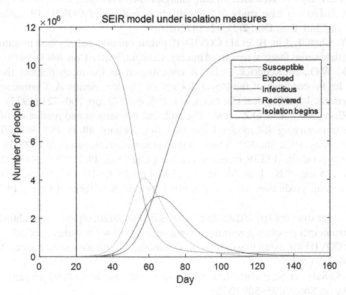

Fig. 9. SEIR model under isolation measures

5 Summary

This paper uses the method of data visualization to conduct a detailed discussion on the geographical distribution and population density distribution under the epidemic situation, the time node of epidemic development and the dynamic visualization process. The collected data will be visually displayed through spatial distribution characteristics analysis, timing sequence analysis, transmission dynamic simulation, model prediction and other methods. The analysis of each dimension has achieved good experimental results, which provides new ideas for epidemic visualization, and provides decision-making support for epidemic management in various countries.

References

1. Li, J., Chen, S.Y., Zhang, J.W., Xu, P.G.: Research on the geographical spread of epidemic diseases and the spatio-temporal relationship between online public opinions based on big data. Geomat. World. **27**(3), 31–34+41 (2020)
2. Liu, X., Meng, Q.Y., Zhang, H., et al.: A preliminary analysis of the temporal and spatial distribution characteristics of COVID-19 in Hubei Province. Pract. Prev. Med. **27**(8), 902–905 (2020)
3. Liu, Z.X.: Research on information visualization design method based on demand. Packag. Eng. **37**(16), 1–5 (2016)
4. Wang, X., Xin, X.Y.: Research on the influence of information visualization and knowledge visualization on medical decision-making. Packag. Eng. **36**(20), 8–11+33 (2015)
5. Sun, Y.B., Wen, Z.Y., Xu, R.G., et al.: Data visualization design of COVID-19 epidemic. Youth J. **40**(8), 51–62 (2020)
6. Jiang, F.L., Wang, Y.: Research on data analysis and expression methods in epidemic visualization design – a case study of "visualization analysis of COVID-19 epidemic data in Chongqing." Ind. Eng. Des. **2**(2), 32–38 (2020)
7. Zhang, Y., Chen, J., Liu, B., et al.: COVID-19 public opinion and emotion monitoring system based on time series thermal new word mining. Comput. Mater. Con. **64**(3), 1415–1434 (2020)
8. Kermack, W.O., McKendrick, A.G.: A contribution to the mathematical theory of epidemics. In: Proceedings of the Royal Society of London. Series A, Containing Papers of A Mathematical and Physical Character, vol. 115, no. 772, pp. 700–721 (1927)
9. Yu, Z., Zhang, G.Q., Liu, Q.Z., et al.: The outbreak assessment and prediction of COVID-19 based on time-varying SIR model. J. Electron. Sci. Technol. **49**(3), 357–361 (2020)
10. Cao, S.L., Feng, P.H., Shi, P.P.: Study on the epidemic development of COVID-19 in Hubei province by a modified SEIR model. J. Zhejiang Univ. Sci. **49**(2), 178–184 (2020)
11. Fan, R.G., Wang, Y.B., Luo, M., et al.: SEIR-based COVID-19 transmission model and inflection point prediction analysis. J. Univ. Electron. Sci. Technol China **49**(3), 369–374 (2020)
12. Tencent's real-time epidemic data. https://news.qq.com/zt2020/page/feiyan.htm?#/
13. Wuhan municipal people's government homepage. http://www.wuhan.gov.cn/
14. Tim, C.: COVID-19: extending or relaxing distancing control measures. Lancet Public Health **5**(5), 236–237 (2020)
15. Hamidi, S., Sabouri, S., Ewing, R.: Does density aggravate the COVID-19 pandemic? J. Am. Plann. Assoc. **86**(4), 495–509 (2020)
16. Aboubakr, H.A., Sharafeldin, T.A., Goyal, S.M.: Stability of SARS-CoV-2 and other coronaviruses in the environment and on common touch surfaces and the influence of climatic conditions: a review. Transbound. Emerg. Dis. **68**(2), 296–312 (2020)
17. Zeng, W., Jiang, Y., Huo, Z., Hu, K.: Clustering analysis of extreme temperature based on K-means algorithm. In: Sun, X., Wang, J., Bertino, E. (eds.) ICAIS 2020. LNCS, vol. 12240, pp. 523–533. Springer, Cham (2020). https://doi.org/10.1007/978-3-030-57881-7_46
18. Zhang, X., Lin, H., Zhu, C.M., et al.: Spatiotemporal characteristics and dynamic process analysis of epidemic diagnosis time of COVID-19 at early stage in Chinese Mainland. Geomat. Inf. Sci. Wuhan Univ. **45**(6), 791–797 (2020)

19. Riddell, S., Goldie, S., Hill, A., et al.: The effect of temperature on persistence of SARS-CoV-2 on common surfaces. Virol. J. **17**(1), 145 (2020)
20. Merow, C., Urban, M.C.: Seasonality and uncertainty in COVID-19 growth rates (2020)
21. Chen, B., Liang, H., Yuan, X., et al.: Roles of meteorological conditions in COVID-19 transmission on a worldwide scale. MedRxiv (2020)
22. Zhang, D.D.: Analysis of Java Swing component form design. Comput. Knowl. Technol. **16**(21), 160–161 (2020)
23. Appert, C., Beaudouin-Lafon, M.: SwingStates: adding state machines to Java and the Swing toolkit. J. Softw. Softw. Pract. Exper. **38**(11), 1149–1182 (2008)
24. Tang, B., Wang, X., Li, Q., Bragazzi, N.L.: Estimation of the transmission risk of the 2019-nCoV and its implication for public health interventions. J. Clin. Med. **9**(2), 462 (2020)

Enterprise Electricity Consumption Forecasting Method Based on Federated Learning

Qianhui Zhai[1], Xin Zhang[1], and Jianchun Cheng[2(✉)]

[1] Marketing Service Center, State Grid Jiangsu Electric Power Co., Ltd., Nanjing, China
[2] Nanjing University of Information Science and Technology, Nanjing, China

Abstract. With the development of intelligence and data construction of electric power system in China, a large amount of data accumulated by electric power enterprises provide a data base for the fine prediction of electric power consumption. High-precision power forecasting model has far-reaching influence on urban planning and construction, smart grid development and so on. The problem of power big data privacy leads to the phenomenon of Power Data Island, which leads to the shortage of the accuracy of the current power forecasting methods. Federal learning breaks the long-standing Data Island phenomenon in power industry, and satisfies the privacy and security requirements of power data in application. This paper presents a high-precision federal learning method for enterprise electricity consumption forecasting, which takes into account weather conditions and enterprise tax information. Based on the FATE platform, this method combines the enterprise electricity consumption data with the tax data, and uses the third party coordinator to conduct encryption training, then constructs the enterprise electricity consumption forecast model based on the SecureBoost algorithm. The simulation results show that the federated learning method can effectively improve the accuracy of enterprise electricity consumption forecasting model.

Keywords: Federated learning · Enterprise electricity consumption forecasting · Power big data · FATE

1 Introduction

With the development of intelligent and data-based power system in China, the amount of data generated by power network operation, power equipment monitoring, power enterprise marketing and management has increased exponentially [1], these data have the characteristics of big data in terms of data quantity, diversity, speed and value. The effective application of power big data can provide a large number of high value-added services within and outside the industry. By using the data resources of electric power production, trade and consumption, we can analyze the change of energy structure, study the development trend of enterprises, and assist the government to make accurate decision. It can realize the value realization of marketing power data outside the industry. For government agencies, it can conduct dynamic economic analysis and prediction of the industry and region, can also provide support for government decision-making. For financial institutions, it can provide dynamic risk assessment of enterprise loans and decision-making basis for investment. Face with enterprise users, it can improve enterprise power efficiency and enhance the level of comprehensive energy services. The effective application of power big data plays an important role in decision support for energy enterprise management, research and development of energy-saving and environmental protection products, and comprehensive service provision of energy data [2]. But at present, the application of big data in power industry is still in the primary stage, a large number of marketing power data is in a sleeping state, the commercial value of data needs to be mined urgently.

Against the background of the further development of big data, data privacy protection and data security have become the focus of attention, the world's data regulatory trends, laws and regulations [3] tend to be more stringent, comprehensive and intensive. In 2018, the European Union formally introduced the "General Data Protection Regulation" (GDPR) to strengthen the Data security and the privacy Protection. China has also promulgated the "Network Security Law of the People's Republic of China" and the "information security technology personal information security standard" in order to maintain the integrity, confidentiality and availability of data. It regulate the use and sharing of personal information in the requirements. In 2019, the "law of the People's Republic of China on network data security" has entered the formulation stage and will further clarify the legal responsibilities for data security. Therefore, the problem of "isolated data island" [4, 5] existing universally in the world restricts the external value output of power data. because the power big data involves the privacy of many power users, it puts forward higher requirements for information security. With the emphasis on data security and the introduction of the Privacy Protection Act, the previous extensive data sharing has been challenged. Each data owner has returned to the status of isolated data island and the phenomenon will not disappear. Instead, it will become the new normal, even within large groups, as well as between different companies and organizations. In the future, we will have to face the fact that if we want to make better use of data and do more meaningful things with big data and AI, we must to share data across organizations or between companies and users, this sharing requires the privacy and security of the data. But, traditional machine learning and deep learning can not meet the requirements of user privacy protection, data security and government regulation.

Federated-Learning was first proposed by Google [6–8] to solve the problem of end-users for updating their models locally on android phones. Research is currently being done on federal learning security [9] and on promoting federal learning personalization [10]. The research direction of federated learning [11] includes simplifying communication mechanism, enhancing privacy and security, optimizing federated Algorithm and adapting to various application scenarios. Yang K et al. [12] realized the logical regression in vertical federal learning under the federal learning framework with central servers. Liu Y et al. [13] put forward the method of realizing random forest under the same framework —— Federal Forest. Hartmann et al. [14] proposed a method to deploy the support vector machine (SVM) in the federal learning, which guarantees the data privacy and security mainly through Feature Hashing and update block. LSTM networks have also been used by many scholars to predict the characters [15, 16] in the Federated Language Model. In terms of applications, Alibaba's Ant Financial platform solves the problems of data sharing and privacy protection in e-commerce by integrating ant's own business scenario features. Ping An Group applies federal learning to the medical industry to solve the problem of insufficient data for Smart Medical Training. As the first industry-level federal learning platform in the world, Federated AI Technology Enabler (FATE), is an open source project initiated by the AI Department of WeBank. Fate has already launched a number of applications in credit risk management, Customer Equity Pricing, and Regulatory Technology.

In this paper, a novel power prediction algorithm based on Federated Learning was proposed by using the FATE platform, named FL-Enterprise Electricity Consumption Forecasting Algorithm, which is designed to meet the requirements of power data privacy and security, using artificial intelligence technology to improve the accuracy of power forecasting and solving the problem of data sharing in power enterprises.

2 Related Work

2.1 Forecasting Method of Enterprise Electricity Consumption

Electric consumption forecasting can assist decision-making for scientific planning of generation and transmission, and help to reduce the waste of resources. At home and abroad, a lot of research has been done on the methods of electric quantity forecasting. The common forecasting methods include regression analysis, elasticity coefficient method, neural network method, grey system method and combination forecasting method and so on. Wang YL et al. [17] proposed a medium-and long-term electrical load forecasting model based on Partial least squares regression. Wang HZ et al. [18] using Wavelet Transform and CNN to predict Photovoltaic power. Zhang Qian et al. [19] based on iForest-LSTM Photovoltaic Power Generation Prediction, it improves the utilization of photovoltaic power generation. Min Xu et al. [20] provide a short-term regional power consumption forecasting based on residual autoregressive method. Wu Jiamao et al. [21] proposed a short-term electricity consumption forecasting method based on rough set-chaotic time series Elman neural networks. Liu Ming et al. [22] adopt the method of weighted moving average to forecast the daily electricity quantity, which does not consider the short-term meteorological conditions, and only apply to the scenario where the electricity quantity changes smoothly. Liu Ye et al. [23] used the time-sharing prediction method, also did not fully consider the impact of meteorological and other factors on the short-term changes in electricity trends, prediction accuracy has further room for improvement. Lv Kun et al. [24] used the actual power supply and meteorological data to show that temperature, relative humidity and hours of sunshine are significantly correlated with power consumption. The traditional method of electric power forecasting can not be modeled by multi-data sets, and the accuracy of electric power forecasting is low, so it is difficult to get the ideal effect, at the same time, it can not fully meet the privacy and security requirements of power big data.

2.2 Federated Learning

With the development of the research on Federated Learning, the projects of federated learning in various application scenarios are coming to the ground. Guorun Chen et al.

[25] proposed a communication fraud detection model based on federal learning, which makes it possible for the federation to jointly model the data sets of the telecom operators and the Public Security Bureau. In view of the new coronavirus pneumonia, Xu Ping et al. [26] used edge learning and federal learning techniques to design a management model for the prevention and control of the new coronavirus pneumonia epidemic in colleges and universities, and rapidly analyzed the data of teachers and students collected by colleges and universities, in order to arrange the corresponding preventive measures in time to avoid the spread of new pneumonia. According to the current data operation situation of banks and other financial institutions, Lizhi Zheng [27] actively explores the application of "federal learning + financial recommendation" and "federal learning + micro enterprise loan risk management". Chunkai Wang et al. [28] also take the insurance industry as the background, under the premise of legal compliance, to build a data fusion architecture based on federal learning and applicable privacy protection tools. Federal Learning has been applied in finance, insurance, medical and other fields. For the power industry, considering the privacy and security of power data, it is very important to apply federal learning to power big data. Feng Xie et al. [29] Aiming at the practical problems and policy bottlenecks in the implementation of cross-industry and cross-business line data centralized training in the ubiquitous power Internet of Things, based on the architecture of ubiquitous power Internet of Things, the strategy and basic process of using federated learning in the design of various application scenarios are described. In order to solve the privacy and data diversity challenges related to smart grid short-term load forecasting, Afaf Taik et al. [30] propose a household load forecasting model based on edge computing and joint learning technology was proposed.

Fate is a safety computing framework based on federated learning technologies developed by the WeBank (China). The model sample matching is based on the Secure multi-party computation scheme, and Paillier [31–33] is used to encrypt the data, which ensures the security of the data owner. At present, the AI team of WeBank has successfully promoted the application in the field of credit risk controlling, customer equity pricing on FATE, solving the problems of insurance personalized pricing and micro-enterprise credit risk management. We also explore with AI company to reshape the machine vision market, the equipment manufacturing industry, IOT, smart security and other industries. Relying on federal learning, they broaden the scene of the visual market and help the Federal Vision apply to urban management.

3 Enterprise Electricity Consumption Forecasting Algorithm Based on Federated Learning

3.1 Introduction to the FATE Framework

As an industrial-level federal learning framework, FATE aims to provide a secure computing framework to support joint AI ecosystems. It not only provides a series of out-of-the-box federated learning algorithms, but also most of the traditional algorithms can be adapted to the federated learning framework. At the same time, through the modularized and extensible modeling pipeline, clear visual interface and flexible scheduling system, enterprises and organizations can cooperate with AI under the premise of protecting data security and data privacy.

The following is a brief introduction to the major modules of FATE. The Federation module provides a Federated Communication Api for the exchange of intermediate encrypted data. The Meta-Service module provides node information for storing metadata services and configuring the cluster. Proxy provides a routing service when multiple parties interact. Roll provides the Basic Api for computing and storage. Fate-Flow is a task pipeline management module for Scheduling Algorithm Component Execution. Fate-board is a visualization module, which is responsible for displaying the status of the task execution, viewing the log, and so on. Serving-server is the core module of the prediction function, which provides the algorithm components to realize the prediction.

Usually, a complete federated learning modeling process, Including data upload, ID alignment, feature pre-processing and selection, joint modeling and model evaluation process. Firstly, writing the upload data profile, and then, executing the script to upload the local data to the server. Next, configuring the DSL and Configure file submission tasks for model training. Finally, the results are viewed in the visual interface by querying the job ID, and the evaluation results for the model can be viewed by using the Evaluation component.

3.2 FL-Enterprise Electricity Consumption Forecasting Algorithm

In this paper, federal learning for data security and privacy protection is applied to the field of power big data, and a new federal learning enterprise power consumption forecasting method is proposed. With the combination of multi-data (such as weather data and enterprise tax data), the method can improve the accuracy of electric power forecasting greatly, and solve the security problem of cross-industry data sharing in the field of electric power big data. The Algorithm Framework is shown in Fig. 1:

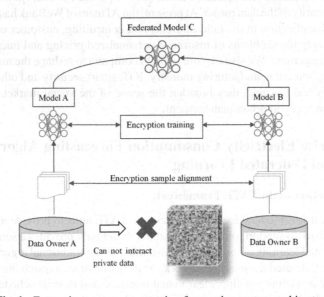

Fig. 1. Enterprise power consumption forecasting system architecture.

The main steps of the system architecture are as follows:

Step 1: Choosing the vertical federal learning method between power company A and I.R.S. B, using encryption-based sample alignment to extract data from shared users because their data samples do not exactly coincide, and in the process, the system does not expose non-overlapping users.

Step 2: These data can be used to train the model after the shared user has been identified. In order to guarantee the confidentiality of data in the training process, it is necessary to use central Server C for encryption training.

In the training phase, vertical SecureBoost algorithm is used to train based on FATE platform. SecureBoost is a federated learning algorithm proposed by the WeBank (China), which essentially models the XGBoost algorithm using federated learning. The XGBoost Algorithm, known as eXtreme Gradient Boosting, is an improvement on the Gradient Boosting Decision Tree Algorithm (GBDT). The XGBoost algorithm balances the performance of the model and the speed of computation. It reduces the complexity of the model and avoids over-fitting by adding regularization term to the objective function. The XGBoost objective function is as follows Eq. (1):

$$Obj = \sum_{i=1}^{m} l(y_i, \hat{y}_i) + \sum_{k=1}^{K} \Omega(f_k) \tag{1}$$

$\hat{y}_i$ is prediction value, y_i is true value, l is a loss function, $\Omega(f_k)$ is a regular term and f_k is a decision tree. The first item represents the traditional loss function, which measures the difference between the true value and the predicted value. The second item represents the complexity of the model, which represents a formula for measuring the complexity of the tree model from its structure, as shown in Eq. (2):

$$\Omega(f_k) = \gamma T + \frac{1}{2}\lambda \sum_{j=1}^{T} \omega_j^2 \tag{2}$$

γ and λ is the parameters of artificial setting, ω is the weight of leaf node, T is the number of leaf nodes.

The XGBoost algorithm also uses a second order Taylor expansion, assuming that the loss function for the t th time is:

$$Obj^{(t)} = \sum_{i=1}^{n} l\left(y_i, \hat{y}_i^{(t-1)} + f_t(x_i)\right) + \Omega f(t) \tag{3}$$

For the Second Order Taylor expansion:

$$Obj^{(t)} \cong \sum_{i=1}^{n} \left[y_i, \hat{y}_i^{(t-1)} + g_i f_t(x_i) + \frac{1}{2}h_i f_t^2(x_i) \right] + \Omega f(t) \tag{4}$$

Where $g_i = \partial_{\hat{y}^{(t-1)}} l(y_i, \hat{y}_i^{(t-1)})$, $h_i = \partial_{\hat{y}^{(t-1)}}^2 l(y_i, \hat{y}_i^{(t-1)})$.

Where the g_i is first derivative and h_i is the second derivative. By Second Order Taylor expansion, the convergence rate of the model can be accelerated and the global optimal solution can be obtained. As can be seen from Eq. (4), the value of the objective function is nearly dependent on g_i and h_i.

To optimize our objective function each time we add a tree, we introduce the structure of the tree into the objective function:

$$Obj^{(t)} = \sum_{i=1}^{n} \left[G_j\omega_j + \frac{1}{2}(H_j + \lambda)\omega_j^2 \right] + \gamma T \qquad (5)$$

$G_j = \sum_{i \in I_j} g_i$ is the first derivative of the leaf node, and $H_j = \sum_{i \in I_j} h_i$ is the second derivative of the leaf node. From the above formula, we can see that one of the advantages of XGBoost over other algorithms is that it can change the sample traversal into the leaf node traversal, which improves the operation speed.

The final objective function is a quadratic function with respect to ω_j, such that its minimum point and minimum value are:

$$\omega_j^* = -\frac{G_j}{H_j + \lambda} \qquad (6)$$

$$Obj^* = -\frac{1}{2} \sum_{j=1}^{T} \frac{G_j^2}{H_j + \lambda} + \gamma T \qquad (7)$$

Equation (8) is the standard to measure the quality of the tree structure. When we specify the loss function, we can find g and H, and then we can get the minimum of the objective function. The optimal segmentation is determined according to the Eq. (9), and the segmentation with the largest fraction is chosen as the optimal segmentation.

$$Gain = \frac{1}{2} \left[\frac{G_L^2}{H_L + \lambda} + \frac{G_R^2}{H_R + \lambda} + \frac{(G_L + G_R)^2}{H_L + H_R + \lambda} \right] - \gamma \qquad (8)$$

4   Comparison and Analysis of Experimental Results

4.1   Experimental Setup

The data of power consumption characteristics of enterprises in the experiment come from the quarterly power consumption information of 1000 enterprises in a certain area of Jiangsu Province, the enterprises belong to eight major industries, covering the period from January 2010 to December 2015, including industry, transportation, commerce, manufacturing, accommodation and catering, warehousing and postal services. The data includes 8 dimensions, which are enterprise code, voltage level, active power, reactive power, maximum load, maximum load utilization hour, average daily load and quarterly power consumption.

In addition, we should also consider the impact of meteorological factors related to the region where the enterprise is located on the accuracy of the enterprise electricity consumption forecasting model. The weather data comes from the quarterly real-time data recorded by the automatic weather station in the region of the enterprise, and the time span is also from January 2006 to December 2016. We select the six main influencing factors in the weather data as the experimental data, they are average temperature, average maximum temperature, average minimum temperature, average relative humidity, average wind speed and precipitation. The Electric Power Characteristic Data and mete-orological information data are combined to construct the electric power information data set D_A, which contains 14 dimensions.

The experimental data of enterprise tax payment comes from a local tax bureau in Jiangsu Province. The data set D_B of enterprise tax payment information is constructed by selecting 6 dimensions of the data, they are enterprise code, value added tax, value added tax rate, enterprise income tax, enterprise business tax rate, enterprise business tax. Business Tax and value added tax are the two major types of tax in China, the scope of collection is different. For Different Industries, the tax items that need to be paid are different, and the corresponding tax rates are also different. From this, we can judge that the nature of the enterprise, the nature of the enterprise and the amount of electricity consumption are closely related, taking into account the nature of the enterprise in the training model can greatly improve the accuracy of the enterprise electricity consumption forecasting model. The number of enterprise income tax reflects the operation of the enterprise in a period of time, and is an important basis for forecasting the electricity consumption of the enterprise.

Considering the advantages of federally learning power forecasting method in mod-eling multi-party data under the premise of protecting data privacy and security, the original training sample set is formed with 20 dimensions of enterprise electricity con-sumption data set D_A and enterprise tax information data set D_B as input and quarterly electricity consumption as output. We divide the data into training set and test set, 70% of the data is used as training model, 30% of the data is used as test model effect, in the experiment setting SecureBoost training parameter, the learning rate learning is 0.3, the maximum number of trees, num is 8, the number of ITERATIONS is 5, the canonical term is 1, and the loss function is used to do regression prediction for the least square error loss, and then an enterprise power consumption prediction model based on vertical SecureBoost algorithm is established. We use the FATE platform to train the model to simulate two data holders, one with enterprise electricity and weather data and the other with enterprise tax data, performing a script to upload the data and submit it to a task to initiate federal learning, go to the visualization page by prompting the URL to see the results. Fate's experimental environment is shown in Table 1:

Table 1. Experimental environment of FATE.

Configuration	8 core/16G memory/500G hard disk
Operating system	Version: CentOS Linux release 7
Docker version	118.09.0-3.el7
Docker-compose version	1.24.0
FATE version	standalone-fate-master-1.5.0_preview

In order to verify the effectiveness of federated learning SecureBoost algorithm in forecasting enterprise power consumption model, the traditional machine learning XGBoost algorithm training model is used in the same sample set without privacy protection, the experimental results show that the precision of the federated learning SecureBoost method is slightly different from that of the traditional machine learning XGBoost method, but to the extent that we can accept it, we call federal learning intact.

To compare the predictive power of the Federated Learning SecureBoost model, we establish the Support vector machine (support vector machine) predictive model. SVM is a general machine learning theory based on statistics proposed by Vapnik and others, which can solve the problems of finite sample, nonlinearity, dimension disaster and local minimum, and has global convergence and simple structure, it is widely used in the field of state prediction. Because SVM can not combine the enterprise tax data, the enterprise electricity information data set is used as the input of the forecasting model. We use Sklearn as the basic machine learning database, and use SVM algorithm in python 3 to train the data to get the basic comparison model.

We use the Precision, root mean square error (RMSE), mean absolute error (MAE), and Decision Coefficient (R Squared) to evaluate the predictive performance of the model. We take the average of all the data precision as the precision of the model, and RMSE measures the deviation between the predicted value and the true value. Mae represents the average of the absolute error between the predicted value and the true value, this shows that the prediction model has better accuracy. The limitation of RMSE and Mae is that it is difficult to compare the effects of different categories, such as predicting student's grades and predicting house prices. The RMSE and Mae results are not comparable. But r Squared is the answer, so we introduce the most important metric, r Squared, which measures the accuracy of the prediction model. The closer it is to 1, the better it is. Their formula is as follows:

$$RMSE = \sqrt{\frac{1}{m}\sum_{i=1}^{m}(y_i - \hat{y}_i)^2} \tag{9}$$

$$MAE = \frac{1}{m}\sum_{i=1}^{m}|y_i - \hat{y}_i| \tag{10}$$

$$R\,Squared = 1 - \sum_{i=1}^{m}(y_i - \hat{y}_i)^2 \Big/ \sum_{i=1}^{m}(y_i - \overline{y}_i)^2 \tag{11}$$

y_i represents the true value, $\hat{y}_i$ is the predicted value, $\overline{y}_i$ is the average value of the true value, m is the amount of data.

Finally, we use different data sizes to predict the difference between the SecureBoost model and the SVM model under different data sizes. The Mean Absolute Percentage Error (APE) is used as the evaluation index, and the value of MAPE is smaller, it shows that the prediction model has better accuracy. The formula is as follows:

$$MAPE = \frac{100\%}{m}\sum_{i=1}^{m}\left|\frac{y_i - \hat{y}_i}{y_i}\right| \tag{12}$$

4.2 Analysis of Experimental Results

The method of multi-training in horizontal federated learning is partly similar to traditional machine learning. The advantage of federated learning over machine learning with centralized data is that it solves problems which traditional machine learning approaches can not solve in functional scenarios where you need to use some data that cannot be left out of the local area.

For Federated Learning, The word 'Federal', can be substitute with another word—'Commonwealth'. That is to say, Federated Learning can also be called 'Commonwealth Learning', and not just for modelling purposes, also for the multiple meanings of the participants' mutual benefit. Participants are independent and autonomous individuals in the federal learning, which requires reasonable incentive mechanism and benefit distribution mechanism to motivate participants to actively participate in the federal learning. This doesn't exist in traditional machine learning.

For Federated Learning, the first is that the working node in horizontal federated learning represents the data owner of model training. It has full autonomous authority over local data and can decide when to join the federation learning for modeling. In contrast to traditional distributed machine learning, the central node is always dominant. Thus, federated learning is faced with a more complex learning environment. Secondly, federal learning emphasizes the protection of the data owner's data privacy in the process of model training, which is an effective measure to deal with the protection of data privacy. It can better cope with the future of more stringent data privacy and data security regulatory environment.

In this paper, we use the traditional machine learning XGBoost algorithm and the Federated Learning SecureBoost algorithm to model the same data samples without considering the data privacy, the results of the experiment are shown in Table 2:

Table 2. Comparison of XGBoost and SecureBoost model experiment results.

	XGBoost	SecureBoost
Precision	0.864	0.862
RMSE	188.04	190.25
MAE	148.33	149.98
R Squared	0.88	0.88

Comparing the experimental results, we can find that the accuracy of the model trained by the traditional machine learning XGBoost algorithm and the Federated Learning SecureBoost algorithm is similar. Federated Learning can achieve the same level of accuracy as traditional machine learning methods through multiple training rounds, and the loss of accuracy is within acceptable range.

In contrast to the traditional machine learning approach, because federated learning can combine multiple data sets for modeling training while ensuring data privacy, we simulate the differences between the two data holders' data sets, federated learning combines data from multiple dimensions to compare the differences in the accuracy, RMSE, Mae, and R Squared of models trained by different methods. To see the results more clearly, we present the data as a bar graph, see Figs. 2 and 3:

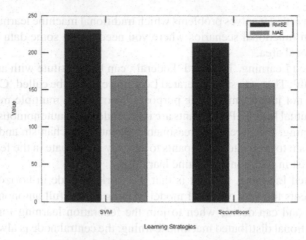

Fig. 2. Comparison of RMSE and MAE.

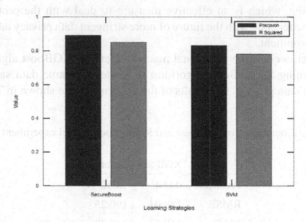

Fig. 3. Comparison of precision and R squared.

By analyzing the above data, the Federated Learning SecureBoost model combines two-party data and outperforms SVM model in model accuracy. The more training data satisfied, the more accurate forecasting results. From the error aspect, RMSE and Mae of SecureBoost model are obviously smaller than those of SVM model, and have lower error.

To further illustrate the validity of SecureBoost prediction model, we divide the sample data into 25 enterprise groups, and use the method above to model 25 groups separately. The error of power consumption prediction is compared as shown in Fig. 4. It shows that for 25 enterprise groups, the size of the prediction and the true value affects the MAPE value when the data is small, for example, when the true value = 100, the prediction value = 1, Mae = 99, MAPE = 99%; and when the true value = 1, the prediction value = 100, Mae = 99, MAPE = 9900%, you can see that MAPE is amplified if the predicted value is larger than the true value. On the whole, with the increase of population size, the distribution of the mean absolute percentage error obeys normal distribution, MAPE of SecureBoost model is obviously smaller than SVM model. As a result, the Federated Learning SecureBoost prediction model is statistically more accurate.

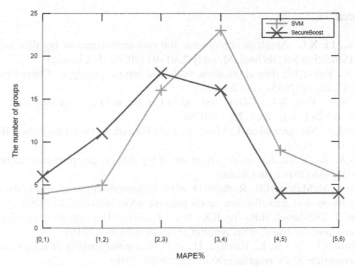

Fig. 4. Comparison of forecasting errors of electricity consumption.

Based on the overall experimental results, the power consumption prediction under the federal learning scenario can guarantee and improve the precision of model training and the accuracy of power consumption prediction under the condition of data privacy and security.

5   Conclusion

This paper combines the privacy and security requirements of electric power big data and the development trend of artificial intelligence technology, analyzes the consistency of federated learning in the field of electric power big data, and proposes a high precision enterprise electricity consumption forecasting method based on the FATE framework. What the electric power industry needs is a computing architecture that can ensure that data is not transmitted outside and can conduct data interaction securely based on the current federated learning technology. This architecture enables the joint construction of cross-organizational models of marketing power data, which not only improves the accuracy of power business models, but also makes it possible to output the commercial value of marketing power data with the help of the absolute safety of data learned by federation. Federated learning is a powerful, accurate, safe, and robust method. Although all technical issues have not been resolved, we do believe that its potential impact on the power industry and the prospect of ultimately realizing commercial realization of marketing power data are very broad. In addition, through the model of federated learning, the power industry can further unite financial institutions, Internet service providers and other fields to establish a federated ecosystem in the future, break industry data barriers, and train more high-quality, high-precision models to promote the realization of usable and easy-to-use social big data applications.

References

1. Qin, F.K., Li, X.L.: Application problems and countermeasures of big data technology in China. Pioneering Sci. Technol. Monthly **2**, 91–94 (2020). (In Chinese)
2. Sun, Y.X.: Power big data application mode and prospect analysis. China Power Enterp. Manag. **17**, 22–24 (2015). (In Chinese)
3. Houser, K.A., Voss, W.G.: GDPR: the end of Google and Facebook or a new paradigm in data privacy. Rich. J. L. Tech. **25**, 1 (2018)
4. Mehmood, A., Natgunanathan, I., Xiang, Y., et al.: Protection of big data privacy. IEEE Access **4**, 1821–1834 (2016)
5. Fang, B.X., Jia, Y., Li, A.P., et al.: Overview of big data privacy protection technology. Big Data **2**(1), 1–18 (2016). (In Chinese)
6. Konečný, J., McMahan, H.B., Ramage, D., et al.: Federated optimization: distributed machine learning for on-device intelligence. arXiv preprint arXiv:1610.02527 (2016)
7. Konečný, J., McMahan, H.B., Yu, F.X., et al.: Federated learning: strategies for improving communication efficiency. arXiv preprint arXiv:1610.05492 (2016)
8. McMahan, H.B., Moore, E., Ramage, D., et al.: Federated learning of deep networks using model averaging. arXiv preprint arXiv:1602.05629 (2016)
9. Zhao, Y., Li, M., Lai, L., et al.: Federated learning with non-IID data. arXiv preprint arXiv: 1806.00582 (2018)
10. Geyer, R.C., Klein, T., Nab, M.: Differentially private federated learning: a client level perspective. arXiv preprint arXiv:1712.07557 (2017)
11. Li, T., Sahu, A.K., Talwalkar, A., et al.: Federated learning: challenges, methods, and future directions. IEEE Sig. Process. Mag. **37**(3), 50–60 (2020)
12. Yang, K., Jiang, T., Shi, Y., et al.: Federated learning via over-the-air computation. IEEE Trans. Wireless Commun. **19**(3), 2022–2035 (2020)
13. Liu, Y., Liu, Z., et al.: Federated forest. IEEE Trans. Big Data 1 (2020)
14. Hartmann, V., Modi, K., Pujol, J.M., et al.: Privacy-preserving classification with secret vector machines. In: Proceedings of the 29th ACM International Conference on Information & Knowledge Management, pp. 475–484 (2020)
15. Chilimbi, T., Suzue, Y., Apacible, J., et al.: Project ADAM: building an efficient and scalable deep learning training system. In: 1st USENIX Symposium on Operating Systems Design and Implementation, pp. 571–582. ACM Press, New York (2014)
16. Liu, Y., Muppala, J.K., Veeraraghavan, M., et al.: Data Center Networks: Topologies, Architectures and Fault-Tolerance Characteristics, p. 75. Springer, Cham (2013). https://doi.org/10.1007/978-3-319-01949-9
17. Wang, Y.L., Wu, M.L.: Medium and long term load forecasting model based on partial least square regression under new normal economy. Electr. Power Autom. Equip. **38**, 133–139 (2018)
18. Wang, H.Z., Yi, H., Peng, J., et al.: Deterministic and probabilistic forecasting of photovoltaic power based on deep convolutional neural network. Energy Convers. Manage. **153**, 409–422 (2017)
19. Zhang, Q., Ma, Y., Li, G.L.: Applications of frequency domain decomposition and deep learning algorithms in short-term load and photovoltaic power forecasting. Proc. CSEE **39**(8), 2221–2230 (2019)

20. Min, X., Ye, Q., Cai, G.Y.: Short-term regional power consumption forecasting based on residual autoregressive method. Technol. Econ. **38**(6), 119–124 (2019). (In Chinese)
21. Wu, J.M., Li, Y., Fu, Y.J.: Short-term electricity consumption prediction based on rough set-chaotic time series Elman Neural Network. Power Syst. Prot. Control **47**(3), 23–30 (2019). (In Chinese)
22. Liu, M., Li, H., Fu, X.Y., et al.: Research on short-term power forecasting in Lianyungang. In: Proceedings of the Smart City Power Technology Forum (2014). (In Chinese)
23. Liu, Y.: Study and application of time-sharing forecasting model for electric power forecasting. Ph.D. dissertation, Jiangsu University, Zhenjiang (2016). (In Chinese)
24. Lv, K., Jiang, S., Shen, J., et al.: Relationship between electricity supply and meteorological elements in Huizhou City and its prediction model. Guangdong Meteorol. **41**(4), 51–53 (2019). (In Chinese)
25. Chen, G.R., Mu, M.R., Zhang, R., et al.: Realization of communication fraud identification model based on federated learning. Telecommun. Sci. **36**(S1), 304–310 (2020). (In Chinese)
26. Xu, P., He, J.J., Yue, X.Y.: Study on management model of prevention and control of new coronary pneumonia (COVID-19) in colleges and universities based on marginal learning and federal learning. Forum Contemp. Educ. **2**, 76–82 (2020). (In Chinese)
27. Zheng, L.Z.: The exploration of data security based on federal learning in banking. China Financ. Comput. 9 (2020). (In Chinese)
28. Wang, C.K., Feng, J.: An applied study of federal learning in the insurance industry. J. Vocat. Insur. Coll. **1**, 13–17 (2020). (In Chinese)
29. Xie, F., Bian, J.L., Wang, N., et al.: Application of federated learning in the field of artificial intelligence for Power IoT. China Hi-tech **59**(23), 20–23 (2019). (In Chinese)
30. Taïk, A., Cherkaoui, S.: Electrical load forecasting using edge computing and federated learning. In: ICC 2020–2020 IEEE International Conference on Communications (ICC), pp. 1–6. IEEE (2020)
31. Gentry, C.: Fully homomorphic encryption using ideal lattices. In: Proceedings of the Forty-First Annual ACM Symposium on Theory of Computing, pp. 169–178 (2009)
32. Brakerski, Z.: Fully homomorphic encryption without modulus switching from classical GapSVP. In: Safavi-Naini, R., Canetti, R. (eds.) CRYPTO 2012. LNCS, vol. 7417, pp. 868–886. Springer, Heidelberg (2012). https://doi.org/10.1007/978-3-642-32009-5_50
33. Fan, J., Vercauteren, F.: Somewhat practical fully homomorphic encryption. IACR Cryptol. ePrint Arch. 144 (2012)

Cloud Computing and Security

Revisit Raft Consistency Protocol on Private Blockchain System in High Network Latency

Ning Cao[1], Dianheng Jiang[2], Yang Liu[2], Yulan Zhou[2], Haiwen Du[3], Xueming Qiao[4], Yingxue Xia[4], Dongjie Zhu[2(✉)], Fang Yu[5], and Wenbin Bi[6]

[1] College of Information Engineering, Sanming University, Sanming 365000, China
[2] School of Computer Science and Technology, Harbin Institute of Technology,
Weihai 264209, China
zhudongjie@hit.edu.cn
[3] School of Astronautics, Harbin Institute of Technology, Harbin 150001, China
[4] State Grid Weihai Power Supply Company, No. 23, Kunming Road, Weihai 264200, China
[5] College of Information Engineering, Qingdao Binhai University, Qingdao 266555, China
[6] Department of Internet of Things Engineering, School of Computer and Software, Dalian
Neusoft University of Information, Dalian 116033, China

Abstract. Raft's good performance in the CFT system makes it a mainstream implementation solution for the consistency of the private chain system. However, we found in practice that Raft's performance degradation is very serious when the network latency is greater than 1 ms. Therefore, we simulated the blockchain network environment and tested the TPS performance of Raft and Multi-raft. The results show that when the TPS is the same, Multi-raft reduces network traffic by 30% compared with Raft's leader, and the CPU load increases slightly. Based on the experimental results, we discussed the optimization scheme of Raft on the geographically distributed system, and provided ideas for future research.

Keywords: Consistency model · Network latency · Private chain · Raft

1 Introduction

As a new generation of information security communication and confidentiality technology, bloc kchain has become a popular solution to the trust problem of transaction participants, especially in IoT fields [1, 2]. However, the blockchain system needs faster transaction processing speed, and adapts to high-concurrency data services by allowing blockchain participating nodes to reach a consensus on data changes faster [3, 4]. As we know, consensus protocols such as proof of work (PoW) and delegated proof of stack (DPoS) [5], which are widely used in public chains, are mainly used in an anonymous and open environment. In order to ensure the security of the blockchain, the efficiency of reaching a consensus is low, and it cannot meet the business requirements in a high-concurrency environment. Therefore, how to improve the efficiency of achieving data consistency of blockchain nodes has become a key issue that is difficult for blockchain systems to be widely used.

© Springer Nature Switzerland AG 2021
X. Sun et al. (Eds.): ICAIS 2021, CCIS 1423, pp. 571–579, 2021.
https://doi.org/10.1007/978-3-030-78618-2_47

However, a large number of business scenarios that require blockchain to ensure data security, their business participants are non-anonymous [6]. This makes transaction processing performance loss caused by consensus algorithms such as PoW a meaningless burden on the system. Therefore, the private chain architecture is proposed by researchers, which uses a consensus protocol based on CFT to improve the transaction processing speed of the system. Although this reduces the ability of the blockchain system to resist malicious attacks, since all network participating nodes are certified by certificates, any malicious behavior will be directly traced. In such business scenarios, the issue of transaction processing speed optimization has become the focus of researchers' attention.

Existing CFT protocols such as Paxos [7] and Raft [8] are mainly designed for distributed systems in low-latency environments. The application scenario of blockchain is geographically distributed, and nodes need to cross multiple layers of routing for data communication [9]. Although the existing consensus protocol can still work in this environment, due to the network delay caused by cross-regions, a large number of threads are waiting in the data communication process. This enables the system to maintain a large number of remote procedure call (RPC) connections at the same time during the log replication process, which seriously affects the amount of concurrent transaction processing. At present, the optimization method for CFT protocol concurrency is mainly aimed at low-latency environments. Therefore, this makes the current private chain system insufficient support for high concurrency scenarios.

We explained the development of consensus protocol and blockchain technology in Sect. 2. In the third section, we analyze the performance problems of the raft protocol in a high-latency environment. In the fourth section, based on the open source Hyperledger blockchain system, we conduct transaction concurrency experiments under different network delays for the Raft protocol it uses, and discuss the performance impact caused by the delay. In the fifth section, we also put forward suggestions for improving Raft in the blockchain system. We summarize the paper in Sect. 6.

2   Related Works

2.1   Blockchain System

The concept of blockchain was proposed by Satoshi Nakamoto in 2008 and realized the first blockchain-based application Bitcoin [10]. Bitcoin uses the PoW formula mechanism to design an accounting rights competition model based on hash collisions, and uses computing power to ensure that the blockchain cannot be tampered with. In fact, the node that obtains the accounting right in the Bitcoin network is the leader node of the log replication process in the distributed system. For the Bitcoin network, all transaction objects are hash addresses and will be destroyed after one use. Therefore, there is no concept of an account in the Bitcoin network. During the transaction, the account used by the user is a logical structure, that is, the sum of bitcoins contained in the valid hash address held by the user. Currently, the industry refers to this blockchain architecture as blockchain 1.0.

The excellent data security demonstrated by the blockchain 1.0 system has attracted the attention of many industries. However, the blockchain 1.0 system cannot meet the needs of data services in complex scenarios due to a single transaction object. Therefore, the researchers proposed a blockchain 2.0 system represented by Ethereum [11]. It applies the PoS consensus mechanism, which reduces the cost of a large number of computing resources in the process of obtaining accounting rights. In addition, it supports the development of more complex data structures and smart contracts, making it more customizable. Although this type of system can meet most application scenarios involving transactions, it still lacks a design for the security of the data itself. In addition, it has insufficient support for environments where the number of transaction parties is greater than two. Therefore, it is still not suitable for more complex application scenarios.

In order to expand the application scenarios of blockchain, the blockchain 3.0 system represented by Hyperledger was proposed [12]. Unlike the previous blockchain system, Hyperledger is geared towards private chain business and uses CFT models such as Raft and Kafka to implement transaction replication. In addition, it introduces an endorsement strategy, which can flexibly introduce any business participants to complete transactions involving multiple parties. However, the CFT model is mainly used in a low-latency distributed cluster environment, and the participating organizations and nodes of the blockchain are cross-regional. In an unstable network environment, how to ensure the high efficiency of transaction consistency is still a problem that needs to be tacked.

2.2   CFT vs. BFT

The BFT protocol can tolerate the emergence of malicious nodes in the cluster. Therefore, it is widely used in the public chain architecture. Due to PoW, PoS and other protocol transactions that compete for the right to issue transactions, the processing efficiency is low. Therefore, the current BFT protocol on the private chain platform is generally implemented by PBFT [13]. However, for a large number of nodes, the BFT protocol consumes more resources. This is because BFT-type agreements need to check malicious nodes when reaching a consensus, which will cause the network to generate N^2 network traffic. However, in the private chain architecture, all transactions are traceable. This allows illegal transactions submitted by malicious nodes to be directly recorded and tracked. Therefore, in the private chain system, the security improvement in exchange for the additional overhead caused by the use of BFT-type protocols is less effective.

Unlike byzantine fault tolerance (BFT), the CFT protocol cannot handle malicious borrowing. However, its improvement in transaction processing capabilities makes it more in line with the requirements of modern business scenarios for blockchain systems. Private chain platforms represented by Hyperledger are increasingly turning their own consensus protocols to CFT, such as Raft and Paxos. However, when the node scale is large, the high load of the Leader node is also the concurrency bottleneck faced by the CFT protocol. Therefore, researchers have proposed optimization methods such as Multi-raft, which reduce the load of the leader in the CFT protocol by decentralizing transaction publishing rights, thereby increasing the amount of concurrency. However, the CFT protocol is designed for low-latency distributed clusters. Its transaction processing efficiency in a distributed blockchain environment still needs to be tested and verified.

3 Protocol Analysis

In this chapter, we analyze the Raft log replication process and discuss its possible performance problems. We will analyze from two aspects: network delay and Leader load. Since Raft's Leader replacement strategy is simple enough, our work does not involve performance problems caused by network partitions.

3.1 Network Latency

During the log replication process of the Raft protocol, all new log append requests are initiated by the leader. As long as the Leader's Term and Log index comply with the rules, the follower will write the corresponding Log into its own Log and apply it to the state machine. Therefore, Follower does not have the right to publish Log, and all RPCs received by Follower from the client will be directly forwarded to Leader (see Fig. 1).

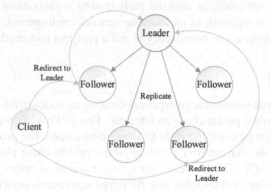

Fig. 1. Follower forwarding and Leader log replication process of Raft protocol.

Subsequently, the Leader will assign an Index to the log and write it to its own log. When the log is written, Leader will immediately check the Index recently received by each Follower. Subsequently, it will use RPC to synchronize the logs that follower has not responded to in the order of Index (see Fig. 2).

But when the last log synchronization operation is not completed, Leader still needs to maintain the RPC communication connection with Follower. This makes it easy for Leader to fail to obtain the log replication status of Follower in time when the network delay is large. Therefore, the load generated by the leader mainly comes from two points: 1) The huge number of RPC connections that the leader will maintain increases the request delay and makes log replication more likely to time out. 2) Leader repeatedly sends a large number of logs known by Follower but has not responded in time, which increases network traffic consumption.

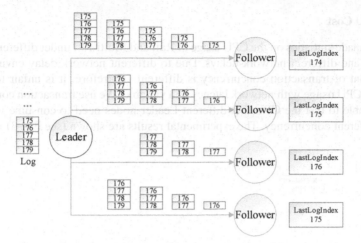

Fig. 2. Log retransmission caused by network latency.

3.2 Leader Overhead

In a Raft cluster, for Leader, all logs will be replicated to each node through it. Therefore, this will cause Leader to generate a lot of network traffic. Since each node has the same opportunity in Leader election, this makes all consensus nodes must meet the maximum network load. However, the bandwidth required by Follower during operation is much lower than that of the Leader node, resulting in a waste of bandwidth resources. Unlike the local area network, the bandwidth cost of the public network is relatively high. This will also greatly increase the cost of network construction.

On the other hand, in an environment with a large amount of concurrent transactions, the CPU load generated by the Leader when scheduling threads and executing log copy operations is also a key issue that Raft faces. Among them, when performing log copy operations, Raft needs to traverse the state of other nodes and cyclically encapsulate their logs behind themselves. As mentioned in Sect. 3.1, during the cross-regional network delay process, other nodes may lag behind their own logs by more. This makes Raft need to perform more cycles to encapsulate the log.

4 Experiments

In order to verify our ideas, we use the open source raft-java project on Github for implementation. It is an opportunity to realize brpc's raft and obtain 800+ stras. In the experimental environment, we use multiple servers to run this architecture.

All nodes are deployed on three servers with a Xeon E5-2620 v4 CPU, 64 GB of RAM, 4 TB, 7200 RPM SATA disk. The system runs CentOS Linux release 7.5.1804, 64 bit, with Linux kernel Version 3.10.0. We designed an environment with node sizes of 5 and 7. The client uses 40 threads to call the additional log interface of the Raft cluster in a loop. We use Linux tc command to set the network card latency from 0.1 ms to 30 ms to simulate the data transmission latency in the physical environment.

4.1 CPU Cost

We have made statistics on the CPU usage of Raft and Multi-raft under different number of nodes and different network delays. Due to different network delay environments, the amount of transaction concurrency is different. Therefore, it is unfair to directly compare CPU usage with network latency as a variable. We use transaction concurrency as a variable to test the CPU that different Leader nodes need to consume when they reach different concurrency. The experimental results are shown (see Fig. 3).

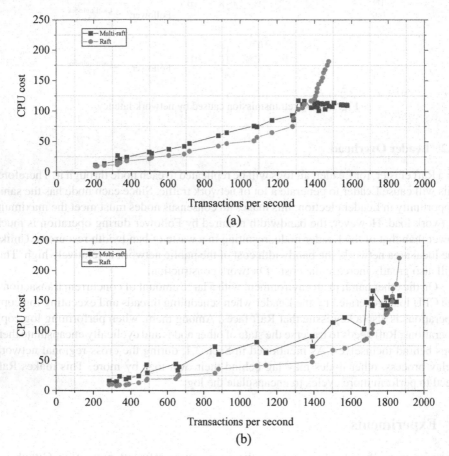

Fig. 3. CPU cost of Raft and Multi raft in the same TPS environment. (a) is collected from 5 node sized cluster, (b) is collected from 9 node sized cluster.

We can see that at a lower transaction processing speed, Raft is better than Multi-raft in terms of CPU latency. With the increase in transaction processing speed, Raft's Leader node bears a greater CPU load.

4.2 Network Traffic

As with the CPU load, we also use the test method that uses TPS as an independent variable for network traffic. Among them, for Multi-raft, we measure the average network traffic consumption of all nodes. For Raft, we measured the network traffic consumption of Leader and Follower nodes. The experimental results are shown (see Fig. 4).

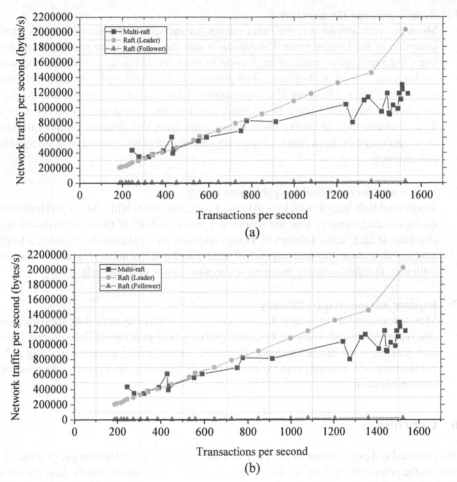

Fig. 4. Network traffic of Raft and Multi raft in the same TPS environment. (a) is collected from 5 node sized cluster, (b) is collected from 9 node sized cluster.

We see that Raft's network traffic consumption is basically higher than Multi-raft in terms of transaction concurrency. However, in an environment with low TPS, the network traffic reduction effect brought by Multi-raft is not obvious. This is because a large number of message retransmissions still exist. In addition, the network traffic of Leader and Follower in the Raft protocol is very different. This is because Follower only needs to reply to Leader's request and does not need to actively send data to Leader.

5 Discussion

We conducted performance tests on the blockchain consensus protocol Raft under different delays to illustrate the possible problems in the cross-regional environment. In view of our analysis and experimental results of the Raft protocol, we believe that it still has room for improvement in the following aspects.

1) Reduce message retransmission
   Message retransmission is the main reason for increasing the network traffic consumption of the Leader node. The reason is that the Leader node cannot obtain the latest log replication status of each node in time. In addition, in order to improve the response rate of the log replication process, Leader will replicate all nodes after any log is written. However, if a large number of messages are merged and copied, the client connection cannot be released, causing some requests to wait for a long time to obtain their log submission status. Therefore, the dynamic combination of messages is one of the means to reduce message retransmissions and increase system concurrency.

2) Reasonably decentralized log publishing power
   Traditional Raft transfers all logs to Leader for replication, while Multi-raft balances all logs to each node to lead the replication process. Both of these methods are too absolute. In fact, in the Internet of Things and specific application scenarios, a large amount of transaction-free dependent data can be dynamically synchronized by Follower, thereby avoiding frequent re-election issues in Multi-raft.

3) Improve message reuse efficiency
   Message multiplexing is an effective means to improve system data transmission efficiency. Multi-raft without RPC multiplexing will generate N^2 level data links and generate a lot of useless load. Therefore, in the use of decentralized log publishing methods, message reuse is also one of the potential directions to improve log synchronization.

6 Conclusion

We analyzed and experimented on the performance of the Raft protocol in geographically distributed private blockchain scenarios. Experimental results show that the Raft protocol in this environment has a large performance overhead in terms of CPU and network traffic consumption, which affects the concurrent performance of the system. Finally, based on the analysis and experimental results, we put forward recommendations for optimization of the Raft consensus protocol based blockchain system.

Acknowledgement. This work is supported by State Grid Shandong Electric Power Company Science and Technology Project Funding under Grant no. 520613200001, 520613180002, 62061318C002, Weihai Scientific Research and Innovation Fund (2020) and the Grant 19YG02, Sanming University.

References

1. Zhu, D., Du, H., Wang, Y., Peng, X.: An IoT-oriented real-time storage mechanism for massive small files based on Swift. Int. J. Embed. Syst. **12**(1), 72–80 (2020)
2. Zhu, D., Du, H., Sun, Y., Cao, N.: Research on path planning model based on short-term traffic flow prediction in intelligent transportation system. Sensors **18**(12), 4275 (2018)
3. Zhu, D., et al.: An access prefetching strategy for accessing small files based on Swift. Procedia Comput. Sci. **131**, 816–824 (2018)
4. Zhu, D., et al.: Massive files prefetching model based on LSTM neural network with cache transaction strategy. Comput. Mater. Continua **63**(2), 979–993 (2020)
5. Mingxiao, D., Xiaofeng, M., Zhe, Z., Xiangwei, W., Qijun, C.: A review on consensus algorithm of blockchain. In: 2017 IEEE International Conference on Systems, Man, and Cybernetics (SMC), pp. 2567–2572. IEEE (2017)
6. Li, H., Huang, H., Tan, S., Zhang, N., Fu, X., Tao, X.: A new revocable reputation evaluation system based on blockchain. Int. J. High Perform. Comput. Networking **14**(3), 385–396 (2019)
7. Lamport, L.: Paxos made simple. ACM SIGACT News **32**(4), 18–25 (2001)
8. Ongaro, D., Ousterhout, J.: In search of an understandable consensus algorithm. In: 2014 {USENIX} Annual Technical Conference ({USENIX}{ATC} 14), pp. 305–319 (2014)
9. Papadis, N., Borst, S., Walid, A., Grissa, M., Tassiulas, L.: Stochastic models and wide-area network measurements for blockchain design and analysis. In: IEEE INFOCOM 2018-IEEE Conference on Computer Communications, pp. 2546–2554. IEEE (2018)
10. Nakamoto, S.: Bitcoin: a peer-to-peer electronic cash system. Manubot (2019)
11. Wood, G.: Ethereum: a secure decentralised generalised transaction ledger. Ethereum Project Yellow Paper **151**, 1–32 (2014)
12. Androulaki, E., et al.: Hyperledger fabric: a distributed operating system for permissioned blockchains. In: Proceedings of the thirteenth EuroSys conference, pp. 1–15 (2018)
13. Sukhwani, H., Martínez, J.M., Chang, X., Trivedi, K.S., Rindos, A.: Performance modeling of PBFT consensus process for permissioned blockchain network (hyperledger fabric). In: 2017 IEEE 36th Symposium on Reliable Distributed Systems (SRDS), pp. 253–255. IEEE (2017)

Privacy-Preserving Outsourced Nash Equilibrium Computation in Cloud Computing

Dongao Zhang[1], Ziyan Cheng[1], Peijia Zheng[1,2](✉), Lin Chen[1], and Weiqi Luo[1]

[1] School of Computer Science and Engineering, Guangdong Key Laboratory of
Information Security Technology, Sun Yat-Sen University, Guangzhou 510006, China
{zhangdao,chengzy5}@mail2.sysu.edu.cn,
{chenlin69,luoweiqi}@mail.sysu.edu.cn
[2] State Key Laboratory of Information Security, Institute of Information
Engineering, Chinese Academy of Sciences, Beijing 100093, China

Abstract. In a non-cooperative game, the Nash equilibrium is computed by the game players with the payoff matrix. With the obtained Nash equilibrium, game players can analyze equilibrium strategies and make optimum decisions. In cloud computing, the computation of Nash equilibrium may be outsourced to the cloud due to the constrained resources of players. However, the payoff matrix may be sensitive and needs to protect against the cloud server. In this paper, we propose a cloud-based framework to secure outsourcing the task of computing mixed-strategy Nash equilibria. In our framework, the payoff matrix is encrypted with additive homomorphic encryption before uploaded and stored in the cloud. By combining secure multi-party computing techniques, we enable the cloud server to compute Nash Equilibria on the encrypted data without disclosing sensitive users' data. We conduct experiments to verify the effectiveness, evaluate the precision, and then analyze the computational complexities.

Keywords: Game theory · Nash equilibria · Privacy preserving ·
Homomorphic encryption · Cloud computing

1 Introduction

With the advent of the era of big data, large-scale data are being generated tremendously in many areas, e.g., surveillance videos, personal image databases, and financial data, etc. The computational task of making use of these abundant data is also becoming highly expensive for resource-constrained data owners. Regarding the massive storage overhead, large computational workload, and tedious data management, the data owner is preferable to outsource the data storage and processing tasks to the cloud due to the fast development of cloud computing. For example, several investors can join their assets and financial intelligence and ask the cloud to make the optimal investment decision, which is

X. Sun et al. (Eds.): ICAIS 2021, CCIS 1423, pp. 580–592, 2021.
https://doi.org/10.1007/978-3-030-78618-2_48

theoretically the solution of a game involving more players, e.g., the Nash equilibrium [12]. Although outsourcing the storage and computation tasks is convenient and beneficial for data owners, it raises privacy concerns and interest disputes when their data are uploaded without any protection measures. There has been some work on these studies, such as [9,10,14,15]. For example, many financial data with investment decisions are private sensitive and of personal economic interests. Encryption methods can effectively protect data security and personal privacy; however, it also makes the cloud very difficult or even impossible to perform conventional processing approaches on ciphertexts. Thus, it is challenging and meaningful to enable secure and effective computation of Nash equilibria for the cloud over encrypted data.

There are already many applications proposed for privacy-preserving computation on encrypted data. Some basic operations have been implemented in the encrypted domain, such as secure comparison [8], secure sorting over encrypted cloud data [18]. In [16], Sreekumari *et al.* presented a privacy-preserving keyword search scheme over encrypted cloud data. There are also some works on data hiding in the encrypted domain. In [19], Huang *et al.* proposed a framework with block partition and steam encryption to enable applying existing reversible data hiding to encrypted images directly. In [2,5–7], the authors developed some methods to train neural networks over encrypted data using encryption methods for deep learning network models. However, according to our best knowledge, there is no report on solving the Nash equilibrium in Game theory in the encrypted domain before.

Game theory [11] focus on the research of mathematical models in rational decision strategic interaction, which is widely used in the fields of economic science, social science, computer science, etc. We can group games into simultaneous games and sequential games. In simultaneous games, both players move simultaneously. If they do not move simultaneously, it is assumed that the later players are unaware of the earlier players' actions. In sequential games (or dynamic games) are games where later players have some knowledge about earlier actions. We can also divide games into cooperative games and non-cooperative games. In a cooperative game, the players can form binding commitments externally enforced. While in a non-cooperative game, players cannot form alliances, or all agreements need to be self-enforcing. In the following, we focus on the Nash equilibrium, which is the solution of a non-cooperative game.

Game theory has been used in some scenarios of multimedia applications. In [4], Fu *et al.* focused on the problem of autonomous wireless stations (WSTAs) deployed by various non-collaborative and strategic users. The author used a game-theoretic pricing mechanism to enforce WSTAs to declare their resource requirements truthfully and to act in a socially optimal way instead of allocating public resources equally to each user. However, the information is exchanged before resources are allocated, and it can lead to the disclosure of information. Most of the existing optimization-based methods heuristically determine their weights, such as minimizing the weighted sum of the distortions or maximizing the weighted sum of the peak signal-to-noise ratios (PSNRs). In [1],

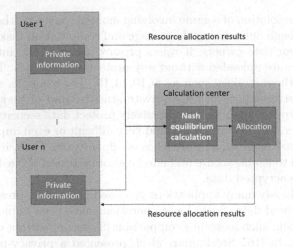

Fig. 1. The conventional framework

Chen *et al.* proposed a game-theoretic framework. The utility/payoff function of each user/player is jointly determined by the characteristics of the transmitted video sequence and the allocated bit-rate. By using the personal information provided by each user, a center calculates the Nash equilibrium. We summary the conventional model in Fig. 1, where the optimal decision (the Nash equilibrium) is computed with the multi-party information aggregation and is then returned to every party. However, the privacy issue is not considered in these models.

To solve this problem, we propose a privacy-preserving outsourced framework to compute mixed-strategy Nash equilibria in cloud computing. The sensitive data of each player is encrypted with homomorphic encryption before stored in the cloud. By relying on the additive homomorphic property and secure multi-party computing techniques, we propose a protocol to enable the cloud to solve the Nash equilibrium without decrypting the ciphertexts. The encrypted form of the Nash equilibrium is then sent back to the players. With the proposed scheme, both the original data and the Nash equilibrium is protected from the cloud.

The rest of this paper is organized as follows. In Sect. 2, we introduces some preliminaries on our system model, Paillier encryption, and the Nash equilibrium. The proposed secure protocol is detailed in Sect. 3. Section 4 provides the experimental results and some theoretical analyses. The paper is concluded in Sect. 5.

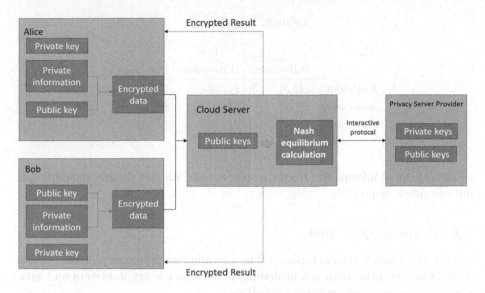

Fig. 2. The proposed framework

2   Preliminaries

2.1   System Model

There are four parties, the two players Alice and Bob, the cloud server, and the privacy service provider in our system. The privacy service provider provides the cryptographic service for the system. In particular, the privacy service provider will generate a pair of public encryption key $\mathcal{PK}$ and private decryption key $\mathcal{SK}$ during the system initialization. The privacy service provider will send $\mathcal{PK}$ to the two players and the cloud server and deliver $\mathcal{SK}$ only to the two players in a secure channel. Alice and Bob encrypt their data with $\mathcal{PK}$ and upload ciphertexts to the cloud server. The cloud server provides data storage service and is responsible for solving the Nash equilibrium when receiving the players' request. During the Nash equilibrium computation, the cloud server will a $\mathcal{SK}$ for assistance from the privacy service provider. We show our system framework in Fig. 2.

2.2   Threat Model

In the proposed system, we consider that cloud server and privacy service provider are two independent servers, such as Google, Microsoft, Amazon, etc. They are assumed to be not colluded with each other. This non-colluding assumption is reasonable since the service providers are commercial corporations that have to consider their reputation and financial interests.

We also assume cloud server and privacy service provider are semi-honest, following the existing privacy-preserving applications [8,16]. Under this assumption, the cloud server follows and executes the protocol honestly, and tries to

Table 1. Payoff matrix

Alice	Bob		
	B_decision$_1$	B_decision$_2$	B_decision$_3$
A_decision$_1$	ξ_1^1, β_1^1	ξ_2^1, β_2^1	ξ_3^1, β_3^1
A_decision$_2$	ξ_1^2, β_1^2	ξ_2^2, β_2^2	ξ_3^2, β_3^2
A_decision$_3$	ξ_1^3, β_1^3	ξ_2^3, β_2^3	ξ_3^3, β_3^3

learn additional information from the encrypted data and the intermediate outputs as much as possible.

2.3 Cryptographic Tool

We use the Paillier cryptosystem [13] as the additive homomorphic encryption.
The Paillier cryptosystem is a probabilistic asymmetric cryptosystem and satisfies the following homomorphic properties.

- The product of two ciphertexts is an encrypted value of the sum of their
  corresponding plaintexts.

$$D\left(\llbracket m_1 \rrbracket \cdot \llbracket m_2 \rrbracket\right) = m_1 + m_2 \tag{1}$$

  where m_1, m_2 are two plaintexts, $\llbracket \cdot \rrbracket$ and $D(\cdot)$ denote the encryption and
  decryption operations, respectively.
- A ciphertext raised to an integer k is an encrypted value of the product of
  the corresponding plaintext and k.

$$D\left(\llbracket m_1 \rrbracket^k\right) = k m_1 \tag{2}$$

We refer to [13] for more details of the encryption algorithm, decryption algorithm, and security analysis.

2.4 Nash Equilibrium

As for the two-player game in this paper, we focus on the case that each
player has three decisions to choose. We show the payoff matrix of this
case in Table 1, where {A_decision$_1$, A_decision$_2$, A_decision$_3$} and {B_decision$_1$,
B_decision$_2$, B_decision$_3$} are the sets of decisions of Alice and Bob, respectively.
If Alice chooses A_decision$_i$ and Bob choose B_decision$_j$, then Alice will get the
payoff ξ_j^i and Bob will get the payoff β_j^i. For convenience, we use P_A to denote
Alice's payoff matrix, that is $P_A = \{\xi_j^i\}_{i,j}$. Similarly, P_B is used to denote Bob's
payoff matrix, i.e., $P_B = \{\beta_j^i\}_{i,j}$.

We consider the computation of mixed-strategy Nash equilibria. Suppose
that the probability that Alice chooses A_decision$_i$ is x_1, and the probability

that Bob chooses B_decision$_j$ is y_j. The decision spaces of Alice and Bob are then $S_A = (x_1, x_2, x_3)$ and $S_B = (y_1, y_2, y_3)$, respectively. We have

$$x_1 + x_2 + x_3 = 1, \tag{3}$$
$$y_1 + y_2 + y_3 = 1. \tag{4}$$

Based on the above notations, we can compute Alice's revenue function E_A as

$$
\begin{aligned}
E_A &= S_A \times P_A \times S_B^\top \\
&= \begin{bmatrix} x_1 & x_2 & x_3 \end{bmatrix} \begin{bmatrix} \xi_1^1 & \xi_2^1 & \xi_3^1 \\ \xi_1^2 & \xi_2^2 & \xi_3^2 \\ \xi_1^3 & \xi_2^3 & \xi_3^3 \end{bmatrix} \begin{bmatrix} y_1 \\ y_2 \\ y_3 \end{bmatrix} \\
&= \sum_{j=1}^{3} y_j \sum_{i=1}^{3} \left(\xi_j^i x_i \right)
\end{aligned}
\tag{5}
$$

The derivative of E_A with respect to x_i can be computed as

$$
\frac{\partial E_A}{\partial x_i} = y_1 \left(\xi_1^i - \xi_1^3 - \xi_3^i + \xi_3^3 \right) + y_2 \left(\xi_2^i - \xi_2^3 - \xi_3^i + \xi_3^3 \right) + \left(\xi_3^i - \xi_3^3 \right) \tag{6}
$$
$$ i = 1, 2 $$

By setting the above function equal to 0, we can easily solve the equation and obtain the stationary point (y_1, y_2, y_3). That is

$$
y_1 = \frac{(\xi_2^1 - \xi_1^3 - \xi_3^1 + \xi_3^3)(\xi_3^2 - \xi_3^3) - (\xi_3^1 - \xi_3^3)(\xi_2^2 - \xi_2^3 - \xi_3^1 + \xi_3^3)}{(\xi_1^1 - \xi_1^3 - \xi_3^1 + \xi_3^3)(\xi_2^2 - \xi_2^3 - \xi_3^2 + \xi_3^3) - (\xi_1^2 - \xi_2^3 - \xi_3^2 + \xi_3^3)(\xi_2^1 - \xi_1^3 - \xi_3^1 + \xi_3^3)}, \tag{7}
$$

$$
y_2 = \frac{(\xi_1^1 - \xi_1^3 - \xi_3^1 + \xi_3^3)(\xi_2^2 - \xi_3^3) - (\xi_3^1 - \xi_3^3)(\xi_1^2 - \xi_1^3 - \xi_3^2 + \xi_3^3)}{(\xi_2^1 - \xi_1^3 - \xi_3^1 + \xi_3^3)(\xi_1^1 - \xi_1^3 - \xi_3^1 + \xi_3^3) - (\xi_1^1 - \xi_1^3 - \xi_3^1 + \xi_3^3)(\xi_2^2 - \xi_2^3 - \xi_3^2 + \xi_3^3)}, \tag{8}
$$

$$ y_3 = 1 - y_1 - y_2. \tag{9}$$

(y_1, y_2, y_3) is the optimal decision for Bob in this game. For Bob's revenue function E_B, we have

$$
E_B = S_B \times P_B \times S_A^\top = \sum_{i=1}^{3} x_i \sum_{i=j}^{3} \left(\beta_j^i y_j \right) \tag{10}
$$

Similarly with Eq. (7), we can obtain the stationary point (x_1, x_2, x_3) of E_B, which is Alice's optimal decision in this game.

3   Proposed Scheme

In this section, we propose a privacy-preserving outsourced scheme to compute Nash equilibria in cloud computing, relying on the techniques of homomorphic encryption and secure multiparty protocols [3]. With our protocol, the two players Alice and Bob, receive the encrypted form of the Nash equilibrium from the cloud by outsourcing the computing task to the cloud. We take the outsourced computation of y_1 as an example as follows. The outsourced computation of $\{y_j\}_{j=2,3}$ and $\{x_i\}_{i=1,2,3}$ y_1 can be obtained similarly.

3.1   Data Encryption

Since the elements in the payoff matrix are not necessary integers, the players need to convert them into integers before encryption. Specifically, all the xi_j^i and β_j^i are multiplied by a positive integer $Q \in \mathbb{N}$ and then rounded to the near integers, i.e.,

$$\lambda_j^i = \lceil Q\xi_j^i \rfloor \tag{11}$$
$$\gamma_j^i = \lceil Q\beta_j^i \rfloor \tag{12}$$

where $\lceil Q \cdot \rfloor$ denotes the rounding operation. After obtaining $\{\lambda_j^i\}$ and $\{\gamma_j^i\}$, the two players encrypt them with Paillier encryption and upload the ciphertexts $\{[\![\lambda_j^i]\!]\}$ and $\{[\![\gamma_j^i]\!]\}$ to the cloud server.

3.2   Computation in the Cloud

After receiving the encrypted payoff matrix, the cloud server firstly computes several ciphertexts to facilitate the subsequent computation, i.e.,

$$[\![a]\!] = [\![\lambda_1^1]\!][\![\lambda_1^3]\!]^{-1}[\![\lambda_3^1]\!]^{-1}[\![\lambda_3^3]\!] \tag{13}$$
$$[\![b]\!] = [\![\lambda_2^1]\!][\![\lambda_1^3]\!]^{-1}[\![\lambda_3^1]\!]^{-1}[\![\lambda_3^3]\!] \tag{14}$$
$$[\![c]\!] = [\![\lambda_3^1]\!][\![\lambda_3^3]\!]^{-1} \tag{15}$$
$$[\![d]\!] = [\![\lambda_1^2]\!][\![\lambda_2^3]\!]^{-1}[\![\lambda_3^2]\!]^{-1}[\![\lambda_3^3]\!] \tag{16}$$
$$[\![e]\!] = [\![\lambda_2^2]\!][\![\lambda_2^3]\!]^{-1}[\![\lambda_3^2]\!]^{-1}[\![\lambda_3^3]\!] \tag{17}$$
$$[\![f]\!] = [\![\lambda_3^2]\!][\![\lambda_3^3]\!]^{-1} \tag{18}$$

From the above results, the cloud server then compute the ciphertexts $[\![b \cdot f]\!]$, $[\![c \cdot e]\!]$, $[\![a \cdot e]\!]$, and $[\![b \cdot d]\!]$. To compute the product in the encrypted domain from two ciphertexts, the cloud server resorts to the following secure multiplication protocol.

Secure Multiplication Protocol. Let us take the computation of $[\![bf]\!]$ from $[\![f]\!]$ and $[\![b]\!]$ as an example. The cloud server runs the secure multiplication protocol with the assistance of the privacy service provider.

1) The cloud server generates two random integers r_1 and r_2 that are much larger than f and b.
2) The cloud server computes $[\![f + r_1]\!] = [\![f]\!][\![r_1]\!]$ and $[\![b + r_2]\!] = [\![b]\!][\![r_2]\!]$.

3) The cloud server sends $[\![f + r_1]\!]$ and $[\![b + r_2]\!]$ to the privacy service provider.

4) The privacy service provider decrypts $[\![f+r_1]\!]$ and $[\![b+r_2]\!]$ and then calculates $(f + r_1)(b + r_2) \triangleq g$.

5) The privacy service provider encrypts g and obtains the ciphertext $[\![g]\!]$. The privacy service provider sends $[\![g]\!]$ to the cloud server.

6) The cloud server computes

$$[\![c]\!][\![f]\!]^{-r_2}[\![b]\!]^{-r_1}[\![r_1 r_2]\!] = [\![(f + r_1)(b + r_2) - r_2 f - r_1 b - r_1 r_2]\!]$$
$$= [\![bf]\!] \tag{19}$$

By employing this secure multiplication protocol, the cloud server can obtain the other three encrypted products $[\![ce]\!]$, $[\![ae]\!]$, and $[\![bd]\!]$, respectively. The cloud server then computes

$$[\![bf]\!][\![ce]\!]^{-1} = [\![bf - ce]\!] \triangleq [\![m_1]\!], \tag{20}$$
$$[\![ae]\!][\![bd]\!]^{-1} = [\![ae - bd]\!] \triangleq [\![m_2]\!]. \tag{21}$$

It is noticed that m_1 and m_2 are the approximate scaled numerator and denominator, respectively.

3.3 Secure Division Protocol

To obtain the encrypted quotient of m_1 and m_2 based on the two ciphertexts $[\![m_1]\!]$ and $[\![m_2]\!]$, the cloud server runs the secure division protocol with the assistance of the privacy service provider. We detail the underlying division protocol as follows.

1) The cloud server randomly generates two larger integers r_1 and r_2, and then computes $R = r_1 r_2$.

2) The cloud server disturb m_2 with the random integer r_2 in the encrypted domain, i.e.,

$$[\![m_2]\!]^{r_2} = [\![m_2 r_2]\!] \triangleq [\![m_2']\!]. \tag{22}$$

3) The cloud server sends $[\![m_1]\!]$, $[\![m_2']\!]$, and R to the privacy service provider.

4) The privacy service provider decrypt $[\![m_2']\!]$ and obtain the corresponding plaintext $m_2' = m_2 r_2$.

5) The privacy service provider divides R by m_2' to obtain

$$m_2'' = \left\lceil \frac{R}{m_2'} \right\rceil = \left\lceil \frac{r_1 r_2}{m_2 r_2} \right\rceil = \left\lceil \frac{r_1}{m_2} \right\rceil. \tag{23}$$

6) The privacy service provider computes the product of m_1 and m_2'' in the encrypted domain, i.e.,

$$[\![m_1]\!]^{m_2''} = [\![m_1 m_2'']\!] = \left[\!\left[m_2 \left\lceil \frac{r_1}{m_2} \right\rceil \right]\!\right] \triangleq [\![y_1']\!]. \tag{24}$$

7) The privacy service provider sends $[\![y_1']\!]$ to the cloud server.

After receiving the ciphertext $[\![y'_1]\!]$, the cloud server sends $[\![y'_1]\!]$ as well as r_1 to Bob. Bob decrypts $[\![y'_1]\!]$ to obtain the plaintext y'_1. Bob then divides y'_1 by r_1 and obtains $\tilde{y}_1 = y'_1/r_1$ that is the approximate value of y_1. Similarly, Bob can obtain the approximate value $\tilde{y}_2$ of y_2 with the help of the cloud server. The approximate value of y_3 is then computed as $\tilde{y}_3 = 1 - \tilde{y}_1 - \tilde{y}_2$. Hence, Bob can obtain his best decision as $(\tilde{y}_1, \tilde{y}_2, \tilde{y}_3)$. Similarly, Alice can compute her best decision as $(\tilde{x}_1, \tilde{x}_2, \tilde{x}_3)$, where $\tilde{x}_1$, $\tilde{x}_2$, and $\tilde{x}_3$ are the corresponding approximate values of x_1, x_2, and x_3, respectively.

4   Experimental Results and Analysis

We have implemented the proposed scheme in JAVA. We conducted experiments to evaluate the effectiveness and precision. We then analyzed the computational complexity and compared the running time with related works. The experimental results were generated on a 64-bit Windows 10 PC with Intel Core i7-7700HQ CPU @2.80 GHz and 16 GB memory

4.1   Precision

To evaluate the effectiveness, we compare the Nash equilibria obtained with our scheme and those obtained with the conventional method in the plaintext domain. We represent the Nash equilibria obtained by Alice and Bob in homomorphic encrypted domain as $(\tilde{x}_1, \tilde{x}_2, \tilde{x}_3)$ and $(\tilde{y}_1, \tilde{y}_2, \tilde{y}_3)$, respectively. The Nash equilibria obtained by Alice and Bob in the plaintext domain are denoted by (x_1, x_2, x_3) and (y_1, y_2, y_3), respectively. We assess the difference between the Nash equilibria obtained in the encrypted and plaintext domains with the following metric

$$\text{Error} = \sum_{i=1}^{2} \left(\left| \frac{\tilde{x}_i - x_i}{\tilde{x}_i + x_i} \right| + \left| \frac{\tilde{y}_i - y_i}{\tilde{y}_i + y_i} \right| \right). \tag{25}$$

During the data encryption step, we set the scaling factor $Q = 10^l$, where l is a positive integer. We vary the value of l from 0 to 6. For each value of l, we generate 1,000 random payoff matrices, compute their Errors, and sum them up to obtain the total errors. We plot the curve of the total errors for different scale factors in Fig. 3, which is plotted on a logarithmic scale. We can see that the precision is increased as the scaling factor becomes large.

4.2   Computational Complexity

The main factor affecting the computational complexity of our scheme is the algebraic operations caused by Paillier encryption. We group these operations into encryption, decryption, modular multiplication (MM), modular inversion (MI), and modular exponentiation (ME). The computational complexity of our scheme can be approximately evaluated by the numbers of these operations since the computational complexity in the plaintext domain is negligible. The size of

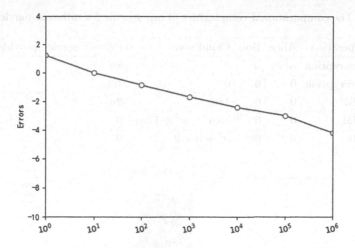

Fig. 3. The total errors for different scaling factors.

the payoff matrix is denoted by $n \times n$. Since we only consider the 3×3 payoff matrix, we focus on the computational complexity of this case in the following.

The cloud server will calculate $2n$ intermediate variables like Eq. (13). For each intermediate variable, it costs $2(n-1)n+2$ MMs and $4n-2$ MIs. There are $4n$ pairs of numerator and denominator as Eq. (20). The cloud server in total needs to perform $4n$ MMs, $2n$ MIs, and run $8n$ secure multiplication protocols with the privacy service provider. In each secure multiplication protocol, the cloud server has to perform five MMs and two MEs, and the privacy service provider has to perform one decryption and one encryption. To get the final result, the cloud server and the privacy service provider need to run $2n$ secure division protocols in total. In each secure division protocol, the cloud server performs one ME, and the privacy service provider performs one ME and one decryption. We show the computational complexities of our scheme for different parties in Table 2.

4.3   Comparison of Running Time

One of the critical sub-protocol in our scheme is the division protocol. There are already some previous works on the encrypted domain division, such as the two methods proposed by Veugen *et al.* in [17]. We use *ted* and *tad* to represent the exact division method and the approximate division method in [17], respectively. We replace the division sub-protocol in the proposed scheme with the two encrypted-domain division methods and obtain another two schemes to solve Nash equilibria. We compare the running time of our scheme with those of the above two schemes. We randomly generate 100 payoff matrices and compute the average times to solve Nash equilibria for the three schemes. The comparison

Table 2. The computational complexities of our scheme for different parties. $n = 3$.

Operation	Alice	Bob	Cloud sever	Privacy service provider
Encryption	n^2	n^2	0	$8n$
Decryption	0	0	0	$10n$
ME	0	0	$18n$	$2n$
MM	0	0	$4(n^3 - n^2 + 12n)$	0
MI	0	0	$n^2 + n + 2$	0

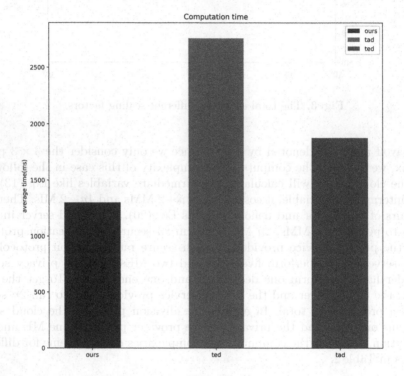

Fig. 4. Comparison of running time.

results are shown in Fig. 4. The running times of our scheme, ted, and tad, are 1310 ms, 2757 ms, and 1877 ms, respectively. Thus, the proposed scheme outperforms the compared schemes.

5 Conclusions

In this paper, we have proposed a secure cloud-based framework to solve the Nash equilibria over encrypted cloud data. By using the additive homomorphic encryption and secure multi-party computation techniques, we enable the game players to securely outsource the computational task of Nash equilibria to a public cloud without revealing their sensitive data. During the execution of the proposed protocol, the cloud server cannot learn the original sensitive information and the Nash equilibria results. The proposed scheme can be used in the application scenario of cloud computing, where game players need to protect their privacy.

Acknowledge. This work was supported in part by the Natural Science Foundation of Guangdong (2019A1515010746, 2019A1515011549), in part by the SYSU Youth Teacher Development Program (19lgpy218), in part by the National Science Foundation of China (61972430).

References

1. Chen, Y., Wang, B., Liu, K.R.: Multiuser rate allocation games for multimedia communications. IEEE Trans. Multimedia **11**(6), 1170–1181 (2009)
2. Dong, D., Wu, Y., Xiong, L., Xia, Z.: A privacy preserving deep linear regression scheme based on homomorphic encryption. J. Big Data **1**(3), 145 (2019)
3. Erkin, Z., et al.: Protection and retrieval of encrypted multimedia content: when cryptography meets signal processing. EURASIP J. Inf. Secur. **2007**, 17 (2007)
4. Fu, F., Stoenescu, T.M., van der Schaar, M.: A pricing mechanism for resource allocation in wireless multimedia applications. IEEE J. Sel. Top. Sig. Process. **1**(2), 264–279 (2007)
5. Gilad-Bachrach, R., Dowlin, N., Laine, K., Lauter, K., Naehrig, M., Wernsing, J.: CryptoNets: applying neural networks to encrypted data with high throughput and accuracy. In: International Conference on Machine Learning, pp. 201–210 (2016)
6. Hesamifard, E., Takabi, H., Ghasemi, M.: CryptoDL: towards deep learning over encrypted data. In: Annual Computer Security Applications Conference (ACSAC 2016), Los Angeles, California, USA, vol. 11 (2016)
7. Jiang, X., Kim, M., Lauter, K., Song, Y.: Secure outsourced matrix computation and application to neural networks. In: Proceedings of the 2018 ACM SIGSAC Conference on Computer and Communications Security, pp. 1209–1222. ACM (2018)
8. Kaghazgaran, P., Sadeghyan, B.: Secure two party comparison over encrypted data. In: 2011 World Congress on Information and Communication Technologies, pp. 1123–1126, December 2011. https://doi.org/10.1109/WICT.2011.6141405
9. Kim, D., Kim, H., Kwak, J.: Secure sharing scheme of sensitive data in the precision medicine system. CMC-Comput. Mater. Continua **64**(3), 1527–1553 (2020)
10. Le Nguyen, B., et al.: Privacy preserving blockchain technique to achieve secure and reliable sharing of IoT data. CMC-Comput. Mater. Continua **65**(1), 87–107 (2020)
11. Luce, R.D., Raiffa, H.: Games and Decisions: Introduction and Critical Survey. Courier Corporation, Chelmsford (1989)
12. Osborne, M.J., Rubinstein, A.: A Course in Game Theory. MIT Press, Cambridge (1994)
13. Paillier, P.: Public-key cryptosystems based on composite degree residuosity classes. In: Stern, J. (ed.) EUROCRYPT 1999. LNCS, vol. 1592, pp. 223–238. Springer, Heidelberg (1999). https://doi.org/10.1007/3-540-48910-X_16
14. Shang, T., Pei, Z., Chen, R., Liu, J.: Quantum homomorphic signature with repeatable verification. Comput. Mater. Continua **59**(1), 149–165 (2019)

15. Shi, W., Wang, J., Zhu, J., Wang, Y., Choi, D.: A novel privacy-preserving multi-attribute reverse auction scheme with bidder anonymity using multi-server homomorphic computation. Intell. Autom. Soft Comput. **25**(1), 171–181 (2019)
16. Sreekumari, P.: Privacy-preserving keyword search schemes over encrypted cloud data: an extensive analysis. In: 2018 IEEE 4th International Conference on Big Data Security on Cloud (BigDataSecurity), IEEE International Conference on High Performance and Smart Computing, (HPSC) and IEEE International Conference on Intelligent Data and Security (IDS), pp. 114–120, May 2018. https://doi.org/10.1109/BDS/HPSC/IDS18.2018.00035
17. Veugen, T.: Encrypted integer division. In: 2010 IEEE International Workshop on Information Forensics and Security, pp. 1–6. IEEE (2010)
18. Vidhyalakshmi, M.S., Acharya, S.: Multi-keyword based sorted querying over encrypted cloud data. In: 2015 International Conference on Futuristic Trends on Computational Analysis and Knowledge Management (ABLAZE), pp. 23–27, February 2015. https://doi.org/10.1109/ABLAZE.2015.7154961
19. Yin, B., Chen, F., He, H., Yan, S.: Separable reversible data hiding in encrypted image with classification permutation. In: 2017 IEEE Third International Conference on Multimedia Big Data (BigMM), pp. 201–204, April 2017. https://doi.org/10.1109/BigMM.2017.48

Efficient Multi-receiver Certificate-Based Proxy Re-encryption Scheme for Secure Cloud Data Sharing

Jinmei Tian, Yang Lu(✉), Fen Wang, and Xuanang Yu

School of Computer and Electronic Information,
Nanjing Normal University, Nanjing 210046, China

Abstract. Sharing data through clouds has never been more economical and easier than now. To guarantee the confidentiality of the data stored in the cloud storages, the data owners should encrypt their sensitive data before uploading them to the clouds. But, traditional encryption paradigm makes it difficult for flexibly sharing encrypted data between different users. The paradigm of proxy re-encryption (PRE), which can securely delegate the decryption right from one user to another, offers an effective solution to the encrypted data sharing in the clouds. To share the encrypted data with multiple users efficiently and securely, we extend certificate-based PRE into the multi-receiver setting and put forward the notion of multi-receiver certificate-based PRE (MR-CBPRE). By using MR-CBPRE, a data owner can securely distribute his encrypted data to a group of users though public clouds in an efficient manner. We first formalize the syntax and security definition of MR-CBPRE, and then design a concrete MR-CBPRE scheme. In the random oracle model, the proposed scheme is proven to be chosen-ciphertext secure. To demonstrate the merits of our scheme, we analyze its performance by comparing it with the previous certificate-based PRE schemes which consist of only single receiver. As far as we know, it is the first certificate-based PRE scheme in the multi-receiver setting to date.

Keywords: Public cloud · Encrypted data sharing · Multi-receiver ·
Certificate-Based proxy Re-Encryption · Random oracle model ·
Chosen-Ciphertext security

1 Introduction

Today, public cloud storage is gaining popularity and there is an emerging trend that increasingly more users are beginning to use public cloud storage for online data storing and sharing. However, these data applications are obstructed by some security issues, such as data confidentiality and information leakage. Once the users upload their private data to the cloud storage, they will lose the direct control of their data and have to trust the third-party cloud service provider (CSP). However, the CSPs are usually untrusted and the users' data may be compromised. Therefore, it has been widely recognized that data confidentiality should be mainly relied on cloud users instead of CSPs. A typical

© Springer Nature Switzerland AG 2021
X. Sun et al. (Eds.): ICAIS 2021, CCIS 1423, pp. 593–605, 2021.
https://doi.org/10.1007/978-3-030-78618-2_49

approach for data confidentiality protection is to encrypt the sensitive data before upload-ing them to the cloud storage. But, traditional encryption paradigm makes it difficult for flexibly sharing encrypted data between different users. To share the encrypted data with a friend, the data owner has to download the encrypted data from the cloud, decrypt them, re-encrypt them using his friend's public key and then re-upload the re-encrypted data to the cloud. Clearly, this way will be extremely inefficient due to the heavy overhead at the data owner. In addition, it also loses the value of cloud storage.

Proxy re-encryption (PRE), introduced by Blaze *et al.* in Eurocrypt 1998 [1], offers us an effective solution to encrypted data sharing in public clouds. The main goal of PRE is to solve the problem of secure delegation of the decryption right from a delegator to a delegate. In a PRE system, a semi-trusted third party called proxy is employed by the delegator so that it can convert a ciphertext encrypted under the delegator's public key into a new ciphertext of the same message encrypted under the delegate's public key without learning the underlying message. More specifically, a PRE system works in the following way: the delegator creates a re-encryption key and sets it in the proxy; when receiving a ciphertext intended for the delegator, the proxy uses the re-encryption key to convert it into a ciphertext for the delegate; when receiving the re-encrypted ciphertext, the delegate recovers the underlying message using his own private key. Obviously, PRE can be employed as a fundamental building block to implement the secure and effective data sharing applications in clouds. By using a PRE scheme, a data owner can flexibly delegate the access rights of the sharing data to others so that they can access these data from the cloud directly. Furthermore, PRE introduces minor overhead on cloud users by eliminating any direct interaction between the data owners and the authorized receivers.

Since the introduction of PRE, a number of PRE schemes have been proposed. However, most of them were constructed over either traditional public-key cryptography (PKC) (*e.g.* [2–6]) or identity-based cryptography (IBC) (*e.g.* [7–10]). It is well known that traditional PKC suffers from the heavy certificate management problem and IBC has the inherent key escrow problem. To solve the key escrow problem in identity-based PRE while keeping the implicit authentication property, Sur et al. [11] put forward the notion of certificateless PRE (CLPRE) by extending PRE into certificateless public-key cryptography (CLPKC) introduced by Al-Riyami and Paterson in Asiacrypt 2003 [12]. In their proposal, every user independently generates a private key by combining the partial private key from a partially trusted authority named key generation center (KGC) with the secret value chosen by the user himself. In this way, KGC does not know any user's private key. Therefore, there is no key escrow problem in CLPRE. Following Sur *et al.*'s work, several CLPRE schemes [13–16] have been proposed. However, CLPRE inevitably suffers from the key distribution problem, as the KGC needs to send partial private keys to users over secure channels. Hence, the applications of CLPRE may be limited in public clouds.

To overcome the problems in the previous PRE approaches, Sur *et al.* [17] proposed certificate-based PRE (CBPRE) following the idea of certificate-based encryption (CBE) introduced by Gentry [18]. CBE is a new paradigm that has attracted great interest in recent years [19–25]. It provides an interesting balance between traditional public-key encryption (PKE) and identity-based encryption (IBE). In CBE, each user generates a public/private key pair and sends the public key to a trusted certificate authority (CA) to request a certificate. The certificate has all of the functionality of a traditional PKI certificate and also acts as a partial decryption key. This functionality supplies an implicit certificate property so that a user needs to use both his certificate and private key to decrypt the received ciphertext, while other users need not obtain the fresh information on the status of this user's certificate. Thus, CBE eliminates the third-party query problem and simplifies the certificate revocation problem in traditional PKE. Furthermore, as CA does not know any user's private key and the certificates can be sent to the users publicly, CBE overcomes both the key escrow and distribution problems in IBE. As far as we know, three CBPRE schemes have been proposed. In [17], Sur *et al.* formalized the concept of CBPRE and designed the first provably secure CBPRE scheme. Subsequently, another two CBPRE schemes were proposed by Li *et al.* [26] and Lu [27] respectively.

In practice, a same message often needs to be sent to a group of receivers in a secure manner. Simply encrypting the message for each receiver individually requires a very long transmission and high computation cost. To efficiently send a single message to multiple receivers, the paradigm of multi-receiver PKE (MR-PKE) was proposed [28]. In a MR-PKE scheme, a sender can apply a multi-receiver encryption algorithm to a message and a group of receivers' public keys for generating a multi-receiver ciphertext, while each authorized receiver can decrypt the multi-receiver ciphertext using his own private key. Due to the nature of MR-PKE, MR-PKE can be applied to many applications closely related to secure contents distribution. Since its advent, MR-PKE has received a great attention from the research community [29–34]. However, to our knowledge, no related research has been done in the PRE setting.

The goal of this paper is to design an efficient CBPRE scheme in the multi-receiver setting. Let us consider a scenario where a data owner wants to share his encrypted data with a group of users. The previous PRE schemes consist of only single receiver. If using these schemes, the data owner has to generate a re-encryption key for each authorized receiver while the proxy has to re-encrypt this data owner's encrypted data to each authorized receiver individually. In this case, it will be highly inefficient and quite inconvenience, especially for a large number of receivers. Therefore, it is necessary and interesting to provide an effective solution to this problem. Inspired by the idea of MR-PKE, a natural question we may ask is whether there exists a MR-PRE scheme that can distribute the encrypted data to multiple receivers with a high-level of computational efficiency while retaining security. In this paper, we answer this question by providing a provably secure multi-receiver CBPRE (MR-CBPRE) scheme, by which a data owner can produce a re-encryption key for a set of authorized receivers and the proxy can use the re-encryption key to convert the data owner's encrypted data into a multi-receiver re-encrypted data intended for all the authorized receivers so that each authorized receiver can decrypt the re-encrypted data using his own private key and certificate.

The contributions of paper are twofold. Firstly, we formalize the notion of MR-CBPRE and its security model. A reasonable and elaborated security model is necessary for constructing provably secure cryptographic schemes. Based on the security models of CBE [18], CBPRE [17] and MR-PKE [28], we formally define the security model of MR-CBPRE schemes. Secondly, we design a concrete MR-CBPRE scheme. In the random oracle model [35], the proposed scheme is strictly proved to be indistinguishable against adaptive chosen-ciphertext attacks under the hardness of the 1-bilinear

Diffie-Hellman inversion problem and the modified bilinear Diffie-Hellman inversion for q-values problem. In addition, we analyze its performance by comparing it with the previous single-receiver CBPRE schemes. The performance comparison shows that our scheme is efficient and practical.

Paper Organization. The rest of this paper is organized as follows. In Sect. 2, we briefly review some background definitions related to our paper. In Sect. 3, we provide the definition of MR-CBPRE. The proposed MR-CBPRE scheme is described in Sect. 4 and analyzed in Sect. 5 respectively. Finally, we draw our conclusions in Sect. 6.

2   Bilinear Pairing and Complexity Problems

Let k be a security parameter and p be a k-bit prime number. Let G be an additive cyclic group of prime order p, G_T be a multiplicative cyclic group of the same order and P be a generator of G. A bilinear paring is a map $e\colon G \times G \to G_T$ satisfying the following properties:

- Bilinearity: For any $P_1, P_2 \in G$ and $a, b \in Z_p^*$, we have $e(aP_1, bP_2) = e(P_1, P_2)^{ab}$;
- Non-degeneracy: $e(P, P) \neq 1$;
- Computability: For any $P_1, P_2 \in G$, $e(P_1, P_2)$ can be efficiently computed.

The security of our scheme is based on the following two complexity problems.

Definition 1 [36]. The 1-bilinear Diffie-Hellman inversion (1-BDHI) problem in (G, G_T) is, given $(P, \alpha P) \in G^2$ for unknown $\alpha \in Z_p^*$, to compute $e(P, P)^{1/\alpha} \in G_T$.

Definition 2 [37]. The modified bilinear Diffie-Hellman inversion for q-values (q-mBDHI) problem in G is, given $(P, \alpha P, (\omega_1 + \alpha)^{-1}P,..., (\omega_q + \alpha)^{-1}P, \omega_1,..., \omega_q)$ $\in G^{q+2} \times (Z_p^*)^q$ for unknown $\alpha \in Z_p^*$, to compute $e(P, P)^{(\omega^* + \alpha)^{-1}}$ for some value ω^* $\in Z_p^- \{\omega_1,..., \omega_q\}$.

3   Definition of Multi-receiver Certificate-Based Proxy Re-encryption

A MR-CBPRE scheme is composed of eight algorithms: (1) System setup algorithm *Setup*, which is performed by a CA to generate a master secret key and a set of public parameters; (2) User-key generation algorithm *UserKeyGen*, which is performed by the user to generate a pair of private key and public key; (3) Certification algorithm *Certify*, which is performed by a CA to generate a certificate for each user; (4) Encryption algorithm *Encrypt*, which is performed by the data owner to produce the original ciphertexts of his data; (5) Original ciphertext decryption algorithm *Decrypt1*, which is performed by the data owner to decrypt his original ciphertexts; (6) Re-encryption key generation algorithm *ReKeyGen*, which is performed by the data owner to generate the re-encryption keys for any multiple receivers; (7) Re-encryption algorithm *ReEncrypt*, which is performed by a proxy to translate the original ciphertexts into the multi-receiver re-encrypted ciphertexts; (8) Re-encrypted ciphertext decryption algorithm *Decrypt2*, which is performed by any authorized receiver to decrypt the re-encrypted ciphertexts for him.

A more formal definition of a MR-CBPRE scheme is as follows:

- *Setup(k)*: On input a security parameter k, this algorithm outputs a master secret key *msk* and a list of public parameters *params*.
- *UserKeyGen(params)*: On input the public parameters *params*, this algorithm outputs a private/public key pair (SK_U, PK_U) for a user U.
- *Certify(params, msk, τ, ID_U, PK_U)*: On input the public parameters *params*, the master key *msk*, an index τ of a time period, a user U's identity ID_U and public key PK_U, this algorithm outputs a certificate $Cert_U^\tau$ for the user U.
- *Encrypt(params, M, τ, ID_O, PK_O)*: On input the public parameters *params*, a plaintext M, an index τ of a time period and a data owner's identity ID_O and public key PK_O, this algorithm outputs an original ciphertext C_O^τ.
- *Decrypt1(params, C_O^τ, ID_O, SK_O, $Cert_O^\tau$)*: On input the public parameters *params*, an original ciphertext C_O^τ and a data owner's identity ID_O, private key SK_O and certificate $Cert_O^\tau$, this algorithm outputs a plaintext M or an error symbol $\perp$.
- *ReKeyGen(params, ID_O, SK_O, $Cert_O^\tau$, $\mathcal{ID}_R$, $\mathcal{PK}_R$)*: On input the public parameters *params*, a data owner's identity ID_O, private key SK_O and certificate $Cert_O^\tau$, a list of the receivers' identities $\mathcal{ID}_R = (ID_{R_1}, ID_{R_2}, \ldots, ID_{R_n})$ and a list of the corresponding public keys $\mathcal{PK}_R = (PK_{R_1}, PK_{R_2}, \ldots, PK_{R_n})$, this algorithm outputs a re-encryption key $RK_{O \to R}^\tau$.
- *ReEncrypt(params, C_O^τ, $RK_{O \to R}^\tau$)*: On input the public parameters *params*, an original ciphertext C_O^τ and a re-encryption key $RK_{O \to R}^\tau$, this algorithm outputs a multi-receiver re-encrypted ciphertext C_R^τ.
- *Decrypt2(params, C_R^τ, ID_{R_i}, SK_{R_i}, $Cert_{R_i}^\tau$, $\mathcal{ID}_R$)*: This algorithm is run by any receiver with identity $ID_{R_i} \in \mathcal{ID}_R$. On input the public parameters *params*, a multi-receiver re-encrypted ciphertext C_R^τ, a receiver's identity $ID_{R_i} \in \mathcal{ID}_R$, private key SK_{R_i} and certificate $Cert_{R_i}^\tau$ and a list of the receivers' identities $\mathcal{ID}_R$, this algorithm outputs a plaintext M or an error symbol $\perp$.

For correctness, it is required that:

1) If $C_O^\tau = Encrypt(params, M, \tau, ID_O, PK_O)$, then $Decrypt1(params, C_O^\tau, ID_O, SK_O, Cert_O^\tau) = M$;
2) If $RK_{O \to R}^\tau = ReKeyGen(params, ID_O, SK_O, Cert_O^\tau, \mathcal{ID}_R, \mathcal{PK}_R)$ and $C_R^\tau = ReEncrypt(params, C_O^\tau, RK_{O \to R}^\tau)$, then $Decrypt2(params, C_R^\tau, ID_{R_i}, SK_{R_i}, Cert_{R_i}^\tau, \mathcal{ID}_R) = M$ for each $ID_{R_i} \in \mathcal{ID}_R$.

4 Description of the Proposed Scheme

In this section, we present a concrete MR-CBPRE scheme which is mainly based on the multi-receiver IBE scheme proposed by [30] and the CBE scheme proposed by Lu *et al.* [21]. The detailed description of the scheme is as follows:

- *Setup(k)*: To generate the public parameters *params* and the master secret key *msk*, this algorithm does the following steps:

  - Choose a k-bit prime number p, generate two cyclic groups G and G_T of order p such that there exists a bilinear paring map $e: G \times G \to G_T$;
  - Choose a generator $P \in G$ and compute $g = e(P, P)$;
  - Choose a random value $\alpha \in Z_p^*$ and compute $Q = \alpha P$;
  - Select five hash functions $H_1: \{0,1\}^* \times G \times G \to Z_p^*$, $H_2: \{0,1\}^l \to \{0,1\}^m$, $H_3: \{0,1\}^* \to Z_p^*$, $H_4: G_T \times G_T \to \{0,1\}^m$ and $H_5: G_T \times G_T \to Z_p^*$, where m and l denote the bit-length of a message and a random bit string respectively;
  - Output $params = \{p, G, G_T, e, m, l, P, Q, g, H_1, H_2, H_3, H_4, H_5\}$ and $msk = \alpha$.

- *UserKeyGen(params)*: To generate a private key and public key pair (SK_U, PK_U) for a user U, this algorithm chooses a random value $x_U \in Z_p^*$ as the private key SK_U and then computes the corresponding public key $PK_U = (PK_U^{(1)}, PK_U^{(2)}) = (x_U P, x_U Q)$.
- *Certify(params, msk, τ, ID_U, PK_U)*: To generate a certificate $Cert_U$ for a user U with identity ID_U and public key PK_U, this algorithm computes $Cert_U^\tau = (h_U + msk)^{-1}P = (h_U + \alpha)^{-1}P$ where $h_U = H_1(\tau, ID_U, PK_U)$.
- *Encrypt(params, τ, M, ID_O, PK_O)*: To encrypt a message $M \in \{0,1\}^n$ using a data publisher's identity ID_S and public key $PK_O = (PK_O^{(1)}, PK_O^{(2)})$, this algorithm performs as follows:

  - Randomly choose $\delta \in \{0,1\}^l$ and compute $U = M \oplus H_2(\delta)$;
  - Compute $r = H_3(M, \delta, \tau, ID_O, PK_O)$;
  - Compute $V = \delta \oplus H_4(g^r)$ and $W = r(h_O PK_O^{(1)} + PK_O^{(2)})$, where $h_S = H_1(\tau, ID_O, PK_O)$;
  - Output $C_O^\tau = (U, V, W)$ as the original ciphertext.

- *Dencrypt1(params, C_O^τ, ID_O, SK_O, $Cert_O^\tau$)*: To decrypt an original ciphertext $C_O^\tau = (U, V, W)$, a data owner with identity ID_O, private key SK_O and certificate $Cert_O^\tau$ does the following:

  - Compute $\delta' = V \oplus H_4(e((SK_O)^{-1}Cert_O^\tau, W))$ and then $M' = U \oplus H_2(\delta')$;
  - Check whether $W = r'(h_O PK_O^{(1)} + PK_O^{(2)})$ holds, where $h_O = H_1(\tau, ID_O, PK_O)$ and $r' = H_3(M', \delta', \tau, ID_O, PK_O)$. If it does, accept the message M'; otherwise reject the decryption.

- *ReKeyGen(params, ID_O, SK_O, $Cert_O^\tau$, $\mathcal{ID}_R$, $\mathcal{PK}_R$)*: To generate a proxy re-encryption key $RK_{O \to R}^\tau$, a data owner with identity ID_O, private key SK_O and certificate $Cert_O^\tau$ does the following:

  - For each $ID_{R_i} \in L_{ID}$, choose a random value $s_i \in Z_p^*$, compute $RK_{O \to R_i}^{(1)} = s_i(h_i P + Q)$ and $RK_{O \to R_i}^{(2)} = t_i(SK_O)^{-1} Cert_O^\tau$, where $h_i = H_1(\tau, ID_{R_i}, PK_{R_i})$ and $t_i = H_5(e(PK_{R_i}^{(1)}, s_i P))$;

- Output $RK^{\tau}_{O\rightarrow R} = (RK^{(1)}_{O\rightarrow R_1}, RK^{(2)}_{O\rightarrow R_1}, \ldots, RK^{(1)}_{O\rightarrow R_n}, RK^{(2)}_{O\rightarrow R_n})$.

- *ReEncrypt(params, C^{τ}_O, $RK^{\tau}_{O\rightarrow R}$)*: To convert an original ciphertext $C^{\tau}_O = (U, V, W)$ under the identity ID_O and the public key PK_O into a multi-receiver re-encrypted ciphertext C^{τ}_R using the proxy re-encryption key $RK^{\tau}_{O\rightarrow R}$, the proxy does the following:

  - Set $U' = U$ and $V' = V$ respectively;
  - Set $X_i = RK^{(1)}_{O\rightarrow R_i}(i = 1,\ldots, n)$ and compute $Y_i = e(W, RK^{(2)}_{O\rightarrow R_i})\ (i = 1,\ldots, n)$. It is easy to deduce that $Y_i = e(r(h_O PK^{(1)}_O + PK^{(2)}_O), t_i(SK_O)^{-1} Cert^{\tau}_O) = e(rx_O(h_O + \alpha)P, t_i(x_O)^{-1}(h_O + \alpha)^{-1}P) = g^{rt_i}$.
  - Set $C^{\tau}_R = (ID_O, U', V', X_1, Y_1, \ldots, X_n, Y_n)$ as the re-encrypted ciphertext.

- *Decrypt2(params, C^{τ}_R, ID_{R_i}, SK_{R_i}, $Cert^{\tau}_{R_i}$, $\mathcal{ID}_R$)*: To decrypt a multi-receiver re-encrypted ciphertext $C^{\tau}_R = (ID_O, U', V', X_1, Y_1, \ldots, X_n, Y_n)$, a receiver with identity $ID_{R_i} \in \mathcal{ID}_R$ performs as follows:

  - Compute $t'_i = H_5(e(X_i, SK_{R_i} Cert^{\tau}_{R_i}))$;
  - Compute $\delta' = V' \oplus H_4((Y_i)^{1/t'_i})$ and then $M' = U' \oplus H_2(\delta')$;
  - Compute $r' = H_3(M', \delta', \tau, ID_O, PK_O)$;
  - Check whether $Y_i = g^{r't'_i}$. If the check holds, output M'; otherwise, output $\bot$.

In our scheme, a re-encrypted ciphertext C^{τ}_R consists of two parts. The first part (ID_O, U', V') is same to all the receivers and the second part $(X_1, Y_1, \ldots, X_n, Y_n)$ can be viewed as an n-tuple where the i-th component (X_i, Y_i) is specific to the receiver with identity ID_{R_i}. When decrypting a re-encrypted ciphertext C^{τ}_R, the receiver with identity ID_{R_i} only needs to download the first part (ID_O, U', V') and the i-th component (X_i, Y_i) of the second part from the cloud and then runs the *Decrypt2* algorithm.

5 Analysis of the Proposed Scheme

5.1 Correctness

The correctness of the proposed scheme can be verified as follows:

- *Original ciphertext decryption*: If C^{τ}_O is a valid original ciphertext, then $C^{\tau}_O = (U, V, W) = (M \oplus H_2(\delta), \delta \oplus H_4(g^r), r(h_O PK^{(1)}_O + PK^{(2)}_O))$. Therefore, we have $\delta' = V \oplus H_4(e((SK_O)^{-1}Cert^{\tau}_O, W)) = \delta \oplus H_4(g^r) \oplus H_4(e((SK_O)^{-1}Cert^{\tau}_O, r(h_O PK^{(1)}_O + PK^{(2)}_O))) = \delta \oplus H_4(g^r) \oplus H_4(e(x_O^{-1}(h_O + \alpha)^{-1}P, r(h_O x_O P + x_O \alpha P))) = \delta \oplus H_4(g^r) \oplus H_4(g^r) = \delta$. Thus, we have $M' = U \oplus H_2(\delta') = M \oplus H_2(\delta) \oplus H_2(\delta) = M$.
- *Multi-receiver re-encrypted ciphertext decryption*: If C^{τ}_R is a valid multi-receiver re-encrypted ciphertext, then $C^{\tau}_R = (ID_O, U', V', X_1, Y_1, \ldots, X_n, Y_n)$, where $U' = U = M \oplus H_2(\delta)$, $V' = V = \delta \oplus H_4(g^r)$, $X_i = RK^{(1)}_{O\rightarrow R_i} = s_i(h_i P + Q)\ (i = 1,\ldots, n)$ and $Y_i = e(W, RK^{(2)}_{O\rightarrow R_i}) = g^{rt_i}(i = 1,\ldots, n)$. Therefore, we have $t'_i = H_5(e(X_i, SK_{R_i} Cert^{\tau}_{R_i}))$

$$= H_5(e(s_i(h_iP + Q), SK_{R_i}(h_i + \alpha)^{-1}P)) = H_5(e(PK_{R_i}^{(1)}, s_iP)) = t_i \text{ and } \delta' = V' \oplus$$
$$H_4((Y_i)^{1/t_i'}) = \delta \oplus H_4(g^r) \oplus H_4((g^{rt_i})^{1/t_i}) = H_4(g^r) = \delta. \text{ Thus, we have } M' = U' \oplus$$
$$H_2(\delta') = M \oplus H_2(\delta) \oplus H_2(\delta) = M.$$

5.2 Security

The security of our scheme can be proved by the following two theorems.

Theorem 1. Assume that a Type-I adversary $\mathcal{A}_I$ has an advantage ε against our scheme when asking at most q_{cu} queries to the oracle $O^{CreateUser}$, q_{pk} queries to the oracle $O^{RevealPrivateKey}$, q_{cer} queries to the oracle $O^{RequestCertificate}$, q_{rk} queries to the oracle $O^{RevealReKey}$, q_{ren} queries to the oracle $O^{ReEncrypt}$, q_{dec1} queries to the oracle $O^{Decrypt1}$, q_{dec2} queries to the oracle $O^{Decrypt2}$ and q_i queries to the random oracles H_i ($i = 1, 2, 3, 4, 5$) respectively, then there exists an algorithm $\mathcal{B}$ who can solve the $(q_1 - 1)$-mBDHI problem with advantage

$$\varepsilon' \geq \frac{\varepsilon}{q_1 q_4}(1 - \frac{q_{ren}}{2^k})(1 - \frac{q_{dec1}}{2^k})(1 - \frac{q_{dec2}}{2^k}). \tag{1}$$

Theorem 2. Assume that an Type-II adversary $\mathcal{A}_{II}$ has an advantage ε against our scheme when asking at most q_{cu} queries to the oracle $O^{CreateUser}$, q_{pk} queries to the oracle $O^{RevealPrivateKey}$, q_{rk} queries to the oracle $O^{RevealReKey}$, q_{ren} queries to the oracle $O^{ReEncrypt}$, q_{dec1} queries to the oracle $O^{Decrypt1}$, q_{dec2} queries to the oracle $O^{Decrypt2}$ and q_i queries to the random oracles H_i ($i = 1, 2, 3, 4, 5$), then there exists an algorithm $\mathcal{B}$ who can solve the 1-BDHI problem with advantage

$$\varepsilon' \geq \frac{\varepsilon}{q_{cu} q_4}(1 - \frac{q_{ren}}{2^k})(1 - \frac{q_{dec1}}{2^k})(1 - \frac{q_{dec2}}{2^k}). \tag{2}$$

Due to space limitation, the proofs of the above theorems will be given in the full version of the paper.

5.3 Performance Comparison

To evaluate the performance of our MR-CBPRE scheme, we compare the computation costs and the ciphertext sizes of our scheme with those of the previous CBPRE schemes [17, 26, 27].

Considering that all the previous CBPRE schemes consist of only single receiver, we compare our scheme with the naive extension of them for multi-receiver setting. In the computation cost comparison, we consider four atomic operations: pairing, exponentiation in G_T, scalar multiplication in G and map-to-point hash. For simplicity, we denote these operations by P, E, M and H respectively. As usual, the computation costs of the general hash function are ignored. In addition, if G is a multiplicative group, the scalar multiplication in G is then called the exponentiation correspondingly. In the comparison of the ciphertext sizes, m denotes the bit-length of the plaintext; l denotes the bit-length of the random string used in the encryption algorithm, which should be at least 160 in order to obtain a reasonable security. The details of the compared schemes are listed in Table 1.

Table 1. Performance of the compared schemes (n receivers).

Compared items	Ours	Sur *et al.*'s [17]	Li *et al.*'s [26]	Lu's [27]
Encrypt	$E+2M$	$2P+2E+3M+3H$	$3P+2E+3M+3H$	$2P+2E+M+2H$
ReKeyGen	$n(P+4M)$	$n(2P+2E+3M+4H)$	$n(2P+E+5M+4H)$	$n(P+2M+3H)$
ReEncrypt	nP	$n(7P+H)$	$n(5P+H)$	nP
Decrypt1	$P+E+2M$	$2P+E+2M+H$	$4P+2M+2H$	$P+2M+H$
Decrypt2	$P+2E+M$	$4P+E+M+3H$	$4P+E+M+2H$	$2P+2M+H$
Original ciphertext	$|G|+m+l$	$3|G|+m+l$	$2|G_T|+2|G|+m$	$|G_T|+|G|+m$
Re-encrypted ciphertext	$n(|G_T|+|G|)+m+l$	$n(2|G_T|+2|G|+m+l)$	$n(2|G_T|+2|G|+m)$	$n(|G_T|+|G|+m)$

The efficiency of a pairing-based cryptographic scheme depends on the chosen curve. In [38], Boyen provides the estimated relative time for all atomic asymmetric operations and representation sizes for group elements when instantiated in super-singular curves with 80 bits security (SS/80) and MNT curves with 80 bits security (MNT/80). In Table 2, we recall the relative data from [38]. To make a much clearer comparison, Table 3 and Table 4 compute the concrete values of the computation costs in terms of the operation M and the ciphertext sizes for the compared schemes according to Table 2. To facilitate comparison, we assume that the SHA-1 hash function is used to encrypt the plaintext in all compared schemes. Thus, the bit-length of a plaintext (*i.e.*, the value of m) is 160. In addition, the value of l is also assumed to be 160. The comparison shows that our scheme has obvious advantage in the whole performance. Therefore, it is more practical than the previous CBPRE scheme.

Table 2. Relative time of atomic operations and representation of group elements in bits.

Curves	Relative time				Representation size (bits)	
	P	E	M	H	$|G|$	$|G_T|$
MNT/80	150	36	1	1	171	1026
SS/80	20	4	1	1	512	1024

Table 3. Comparison of the schemes in MNT/80.

Compared items	Ours	Sur et al.'s [17]	Li et al.'s [26]	Lu's [27]
Encrypt	38 M	378 M	528 M	375 M
ReKeyGen	154 nM	377 nM	345 nM	155 nM
ReEncrypt	150 nM	1051 nM	751 nM	150 nM
Decrypt1	188 M	339 M	604 M	153 M
Decrypt2	223 M	640 M	639 M	303 M
Original ciphertext	491	833	2554	1357
Re-encrypted ciphertext	1197n+320	2714n	2554n	1357n

Table 4. Comparison of the schemes in SS/80.

Compared items	Ours	Sur et al.'s [17]	Li et al.'s [26]	Lu's [27]
Encrypt	6 M	54 M	74 M	51 M
ReKeyGen	24 nM	51 nM	53 nM	25 nM
ReEncrypt	20 nM	141 nM	101 nM	20 nM
Decrypt1	26 M	47 M	84 M	23 M
Decrypt2	29 M	88 M	87 M	43 M
Original ciphertext	832	1856	3232	1696
Re-encrypted ciphertext	1536n+320	3392n	3232n	1696n

6   Conclusions

In this paper, we introduce the notion of multi-receiver certificate-based proxy re-encryption (MR-CBPRE) and propose a concrete MR-CBPRE scheme that can re-encrypt the encrypted data for multiple receivers with a high-level of efficiency. The proposed scheme is formally proved to be chosen-ciphertext secure in the random oracle model. Compared with previous single-receiver CBPRE schemes, our scheme enjoys better performance in the whole performance. Considering that certificate-based schemes and certificateless schemes share similarities in many aspects, we believe that one may also construct a multi-receiver certificateless proxy re-encryption scheme using a similar technique presented in this paper, which will be our future work. In addition, it would be interesting to construct a MR-CBPRE scheme with constant-sized re-encrypted ciphertext.

Acknowledgments. This work was supported in part by the National Natural Science Foundation of China under Grant Nos. 61772009, 61972095, 62072104 and U1736112, the Natural Science Foundation of Jiangsu Province under Grant No. BK20181304.

References

1. Blaze, M., Bleumer, G., Strauss, M.: Divertible protocols and atomic proxy cryptography. In: Nyberg, K. (ed.) EUROCRYPT 1998. LNCS, vol. 1403, pp. 127–144. Springer, Heidelberg (1998). https://doi.org/10.1007/BFb0054122
2. Ateniese, G., Fu, K., Green, M., Hohenberger, S.: Improved proxy re-encryption schemes with applications to secure distributed storage. ACM Trans. Inf. Syst. Secur. 9(1), 1–30 (2006)
3. Canetti, R., Hohenberger, S.: Chosen-ciphertext secure proxy re-encryption. In: 14th ACM Conference on Computer and Communications Security, pp. 185–194. ACM (2007)
4. Deng, R.H., Weng, J., Liu, S., Chen, K.: Chosen-ciphertext secure proxy re-encryption without pairings. In: Franklin, M.K., Hui, L.C.K., Wong, D.S. (eds.) CANS 2008. LNCS, vol. 5339, pp. 1–17. Springer, Heidelberg (2008). https://doi.org/10.1007/978-3-540-89641-8_1
5. Libert, B., Vergnaud, D.: Unidirectional chosen-ciphertext secure proxy re-encryption. In: Cramer, R. (ed.) PKC 2008. LNCS, vol. 4939, pp. 360–379. Springer, Heidelberg (2008). https://doi.org/10.1007/978-3-540-78440-1_21
6. Shao, J., Cao, Z.: CCA-secure proxy re-encryption without pairings. In: Jarecki, S., Tsudik, G. (eds.) PKC 2009. LNCS, vol. 5443, pp. 357–376. Springer, Heidelberg (2009). https://doi.org/10.1007/978-3-642-00468-1_20
7. Green, M., Ateniese, G.: Identity-based proxy re-encryption. In: Katz, J., Yung, M. (eds.) ACNS 2007. LNCS, vol. 4521, pp. 288–306. Springer, Heidelberg (2007). https://doi.org/10.1007/978-3-540-72738-5_19
8. Chu, C.-K., Tzeng, W.-G.: Identity-based proxy re-encryption without random oracles. In: Garay, J.A., Lenstra, A.K., Mambo, M., Peralta, R. (eds.) ISC 2007. LNCS, vol. 4779, pp. 189–202. Springer, Heidelberg (2007). https://doi.org/10.1007/978-3-540-75496-1_13
9. Matsuo, T.: Proxy re-encryption systems for identity-based encryption. In: Takagi, T., Okamoto, T., Okamoto, E., Okamoto, T. (eds.) Pairing 2007. LNCS, vol. 4575, pp. 247–267. Springer, Heidelberg (2007). https://doi.org/10.1007/978-3-540-73489-5_13
10. Luo, S., Shen, Q., Chen, Z.: Fully secure unidirectional identity-based proxy re-encryption. In: Kim, H. (ed.) ICISC 2011. LNCS, vol. 7259, pp. 109–126. Springer, Heidelberg (2012). https://doi.org/10.1007/978-3-642-31912-9_8
11. Sur, C., Jung, C.D., Park, Y., Rhee, K.H.: Chosen-ciphertext secure certificateless proxy re-encryption. In: De Decker, B., Schaumüller-Bichl, I. (eds.) CMS 2010. LNCS, vol. 6109, pp. 214–232. Springer, Heidelberg (2010). https://doi.org/10.1007/978-3-642-13241-4_20
12. Al-Riyami, S.S., Paterson, K.G.: Certificateless public key cryptography. In: Laih, C.-S. (ed.) ASIACRYPT 2003. LNCS, vol. 2894, pp. 452–473. Springer, Heidelberg (2003). https://doi.org/10.1007/978-3-540-40061-5_29
13. Zhu, J., Zhang, F., Song, X.: A new certificateless proxy re-encryption scheme. In: 2010 International Conference on Web Information Systems and Mining, pp. 53–58. IEEE (2010)
14. Xu, L., Wu, X., Zhang, X.: CL-PKE: A certificateless proxy re-encryption scheme for secure data sharing with public cloud. In: 7th ACM Symposium on Information, Computer and Communications Security, pp. 87–88. ACM (2012)
15. Yang, K., Xu, J., Zhang, Z.: Certificateless proxy re-encryption without pairings. In: Lee, H.-S., Han, D.-G. (eds.) ICISC 2013. LNCS, vol. 8565, pp. 67–88. Springer, Cham (2014). https://doi.org/10.1007/978-3-319-12160-4_5
16. Wang, L., Chen, K., Mao, X., Wang, Y.: Efficient and provably-secure certificateless proxy re-encryption scheme for secure cloud data sharing. J. Shanghai Jiaotong University (Science) 1(9), 398–405 (2014)
17. Sur, C., Park, Y., Shin, S.U., Rhee, K.H., Seo, C.: Certificate-based proxy re-encryption for public cloud storage. In: 7th International Conference on Innovative Mobile and Internet Services in Ubiquitous Computing, pp. 159–166. IEEE, Heidelberg (2013)

18. Gentry, C.: Certificate-based encryption and the certificate revocation problem. In: Biham, E. (ed.) EUROCRYPT 2003. LNCS, vol. 2656, pp. 272–293. Springer, Heidelberg (2003). https://doi.org/10.1007/3-540-39200-9_17
19. Galindo, D., Morillo, P., Ràfols, C.: Improved certificate-based encryption in the standard model. J. Syst. Softw. **81**(7), 1218–1226 (2008)
20. Liu, J.K., Zhou, J.: Efficient certificate-based encryption in the standard model. In: Ostrovsky, R., De Prisco, R., Visconti, I. (eds.) SCN 2008. LNCS, vol. 5229, pp. 144–155. Springer, Heidelberg (2008). https://doi.org/10.1007/978-3-540-85855-3_10
21. Lu, Y., Li, J., Xiao, J.: Constructing efficient certificate-based encryption with pairing. J. Comput. **4**(1), 19–26 (2009)
22. Shao, Z.: Enhanced certificate-based encryption from pairings. Comput. Electr. Eng. **37**(2), 136–146 (2011)
23. Wu, W., Mu, Y., Susilo, W., Huang, X., Xu, L.: A provably secure construction of certificate-based encryption from certificateless encryption. Comput. J. **55**(10), 1157–1168 (2012)
24. Yao, J., Li, J., Zhang, Y.: Certificate-based encryption scheme without pairing. KSII Trans. Internet Inf. Syst. **7**(6), 1480–1491 (2013)
25. Hyla, T., Maćków, W., Pejaś, J.: Implicit and explicit certificates-based encryption scheme. In: Saeed, K., Snášel, V. (eds.) CISIM 2014. LNCS, vol. 8838, pp. 651–666. Springer, Heidelberg (2014). https://doi.org/10.1007/978-3-662-45237-0_59
26. Li, J., Zhao, X., Zhang, Y.: Certificate-based conditional proxy re-encryption. In: Au, M.H., Carminati, B., Kuo, C.-C.Jay (eds.) NSS 2014. LNCS, vol. 8792, pp. 299–310. Springer, Cham (2014). https://doi.org/10.1007/978-3-319-11698-3_23
27. Lu, Y.: Efficient certificate-based proxy re-encryption scheme for data sharing in public clouds. KSII Trans. Internet Inf. Syst. **9**(7), 2703–2718 (2015)
28. Bellare, M., Boldyreva, A., Micali, S.: Public-key encryption in a multi-user setting: security proofs and improvements. In: Preneel, B. (ed.) EUROCRYPT 2000. LNCS, vol. 1807, pp. 259–274. Springer, Heidelberg (2000). https://doi.org/10.1007/3-540-45539-6_18
29. Kurosawa, K.: Multi-recipient public-key encryption with shortened ciphertext. In: Naccache, D., Paillier, P. (eds.) PKC 2002. LNCS, vol. 2274, pp. 48–63. Springer, Heidelberg (2002). https://doi.org/10.1007/3-540-45664-3_4
30. Baek, J., Safavi-Naini, R., Susilo, W.: Efficient multi-receiver identity-based encryption and its application to broadcast encryption. In: Vaudenay, S. (ed.) PKC 2005. LNCS, vol. 3386, pp. 380–397. Springer, Heidelberg (2005). https://doi.org/10.1007/978-3-540-30580-4_26
31. Sur, C., Jung, C.D., Rhee, K.H.: Multi-receiver certificate-based encryption and application to public key broadcast encryption. In: 2007 ECSIS Symposium on Bio-inspired, Learning, and Intelligent Systems for Security, pp. 35–40. IEEE (2007)
32. Fan, C., Tsai, P., Huang, J., Chen, W.T.: Anonymous multi-receiver certificate-based encryption. In: 2013 International Conference on Cyber-Enabled Distributed Computing and Knowledge Discovery, pp. 19–26. IEEE (2013)
33. Hafizul Islam, S.K., Khan, M.K., Al-Khouri, A.M.: Anonymous and provably secure certificateless multireceiver encryption without bilinear pairing. Secur. Commun. Netw. **8**(13), 2214–2231 (2015)
34. Hung, Y.H., Huang, S.S., Tseng, Y.M., Tsai, T.T.: Efficient anonymous multireceiver certificateless encryption. IEEE Syst. J. **11**(4), 2602–2613 (2017)
35. Bellare, M., Rogaway, P.: Random oracles are practical: a paradigm for designing efficient protocols. In: 1st ACM Conference on Communications and Computer Security, pp. 62–73. ACM (1993)
36. Boneh, D., Boyen, X.: Efficient selective-ID secure identity-based encryption without random oracles. In: Cachin, C., Camenisch, J.L. (eds.) EUROCRYPT 2004. LNCS, vol. 3027, pp. 223–238. Springer, Heidelberg (2004). https://doi.org/10.1007/978-3-540-24676-3_14

37. Selvi, S.S.D., Vivek, S.S., Shukla, D., Rangan Chandrasekaran, P.: Efficient and provably secure certificateless multi-receiver signcryption. In: Baek, J., Bao, F., Chen, K., Lai, X. (eds.) ProvSec 2008. LNCS, vol. 5324, pp. 52–67. Springer, Heidelberg (2008). https://doi.org/10.1007/978-3-540-88733-1_4

38. Boyen, X.: The BB1 identity-based cryptosystem: a standard for encryption and key encapsulation. http://grouper.ieee.org/groups/1363/IBC/submissions/Boyen-bb1_ieee.pdf. Accessed 6 Jan 2021

Identity Authentication Technology in Edge Computing Environment: Vision and Challenges

Yuanyuan Peng[1], Sule Ye[2], Tao Qin[3(✉)], and Meng Li[4]

[1] Beijing Commsat Technology Development Co., LTD, Beijing 100000, China
[2] University of Science and Technology Beijing, Beijing 100083, China
[3] National Computer Network Emergency Response Technical Team/Coordination Center of China, Beijing 100000, China
qintao@cert.org.cn
[4] Beijing University of Posts and Telecommunications, Beijing 100876, China

Abstract. In the era of the Internet of Everything, the number of terminal devices connected to the network is increasing day by day, and the amount of data at the edge of the network has increased dramatically. Under this background, network applications have put forward higher requirements on network bandwidth and network delay. The centralized cloud computing model can no longer meet network requirements. Edge computing emerged as a supplement and extension of cloud computing. To ensure the security of edge computing communications, efficient and reliable identity authentication technology is particularly important. To this end, first introduced the generation of edge computing, and at the same time analyzed and elaborated several major identity authentication technologies, combined with the demand characteristics of edge computing, analyzed the development direction of identity authentication technology in the edge computing environment.

Keywords: Edge computing · Security requirements · Identity authentication

1 Introduction

Cisco predicts that the future will be the era of the Internet of Things technology. With the rapid development of the Internet of Things technology and its widespread application in the field of actual production and life, the number of network terminals has also increased dramatically. This application trend has brought about a sharp increase in the amount of data generated by the terminal. At the same time, due to the promotion of cloud services, the cloud computing paradigm is not enough to cope with the problems facing the network now [1]. Therefore, to supplement cloud computing, the concept of edge computing is proposed.

In recent years, edge computing has attracted more and more investment and research interest in the industry. In early 2013, Nokia and IBM jointly launched a cloud server for radio applications, which is an edge computing platform for 4G/LTE networks. In 2014, the standardization of mobile edge computing started under the auspices of the European Telecommunications Standards Institute (ETSI) [2]. In June 2015, Vodafone, Intel,

© Springer Nature Switzerland AG 2021
X. Sun et al. (Eds.): ICAIS 2021, CCIS 1423, pp. 606–613, 2021.
https://doi.org/10.1007/978-3-030-78618-2_50

Huawei and Carnegie Mellon University jointly launched the Open Edge Computing Initiative (OEC). In October 2016, the first IEEE/ACM Edge Computing Workshop was held in Washington, DC. Today, edge computing plays a central role in the upcoming 5G technology.

However, edge computing faces many key issues in practical applications. The primary condition for the successful implementation of edge computing is security. In the edge computing paradigm, the network edge is in a highly dynamic and heterogeneous complex environment, which leads to extremely difficult network security protection, which brings new network security challenges [3–7].

In an edge computing environment, edge servers, cloud servers, and users play the roles of providing services and accessing resources, respectively, and are in different trusted domains. The low latency requirements of edge computing and the mobility of end users make identity authentication a difficulty. In the process of edge computing communication, it is necessary to make sure that the identity of each communication object is true and effective, which is of great significance to the security of edge computing.

2 Secure Key Technology for Edge Computing

So far, in order to solve the identity authentication in the communication process in the edge computing environment, researchers have proposed many related technologies.

2.1 Identity Authentication Technology Based on Cryptography

The two parties involved in the authentication confirm the identity of the other party by sending encrypted information about the identity. The method of encrypting the message may use symmetric encryption technology or asymmetric encryption technology. The author uses symmetric encryption technology to encrypt the message, and combines the Hash function to verify the authenticity of the other party's identity during the challenge response, and finally realizes the two-way identity authentication of the fog server and fog user [8, 9]. On the basis of [8], a virtual ID is established for the edge user, which achieves the goal of anonymous authentication and reduces the risk of user privacy leakage during the authentication process. The security of cryptography mainly relies on reliable key distribution, management and maintenance mechanisms. This feature leads to the limitation of its application performance in the wireless transmission environment under dynamic movement and the edge computing scenarios with limited resources [10]. In general, if you want the encryption algorithm to be more secure, the key size should be larger, but it requires a larger key storage space. Therefore, terminals with limited resources cannot meet the key storage requirements of traditional complex encryption algorithms.

2.2 Identity Authentication Scheme Based on Biometrics

For each biological individual, it has unique, stable and reliable biometrics. The biometric-based identity authentication scheme uses biometrics as the identification, and combines image analysis technology and pattern recognition technology to identify and identify the authentication object Identity, more common face recognition, finger-print recognition and voice verification. In the literature, Liu Shuhua and others used Kinect cameras to obtain RGB and infrared radiation images of human faces, and used multi-task cascaded convolutional networks to crop and align the collected images. Next, the processed data was used to train the CNN model for activity detection. The FaceNet model is trained with RGB images for face recognition, and finally an anti-spoofing identity authentication scheme based on face recognition is realized [11]. P. Punithavathi et al. Proposed a lightweight cloud-based cancelable biometric authenti-cation system framework. They used random projection transformation technology to convert the obtained fingerprint into multiple templates, and then performed authenti-cation based on Euclidean distance The template matching operation between objects completes the identity authentication process. In this scheme, the converted template is used to replace the real fingerprint information, which has the effect of being replaceable and anonymous [12]. Although the biometrics-based identity authentication scheme has high reliability, it requires a large amount of calculation and requires a large amount of memory to store biometric data. At the same time, this scheme requires expensive and precise identification equipment, which does not meet the requirements of edge computing Low-cost, low-power application requirements.

2.3 Password-Based Identity Authentication Scheme

Both parties in identity authentication agree and store a private password in advance. When authentication is required, the user submits the password and the other party checks it to complete the identity authentication. Password authentication is simple and easy to implement, but the security is weak, and it is easy to be cracked by exhaustive attacks and dictionary attacks.

The method of hash chain is abandoned, and the two-way password authentication is realized with a single hash function. This authentication algorithm is more flexible and reduces the amount of calculation [13]. In addition to traditional text passwords, there are graphic passwords. In modern people's lives, touch screen technology is widely used in smart terminals. By randomly changing the position of the digital graphic on the touch screen, the user can draw different graphic unlocking procedures according to the unique or backup PIN password each time. This method makes it more complicated and more difficult for an attacker to steal user information, thereby increasing the user Information security [14].

2.4 Identity Authentication Scheme Based on Physical Layer

This is a new type of identity authentication technology in recent years, which is differ-ent from other traditional identity verification methods to ensure secure communication within the network. This scheme uses physical signals or hardware characteristics of the device to identify the identity. The two types of physical layer attributes used for device authentication are mainly composed of the mutual channel characteristics of wireless transceivers and some analog front end (AFE) defects [15]. Aiming at the asymmet-ric resource edge computing system, a physical layer identity authentication scheme based on clustering is proposed in [5]. This scheme combines lightweight cryptography technology and CSI based physical layer authentication technology to realize two-way identity authentication between edge devices and terminals. Confirm the identity of the other party by analyzing the statistical characteristics of the channel state information (CSI) [16]. Run-Fa Liao et al. Proposed a deep learning-based physical layer authentication framework for industrial wireless sensor networks [17], they obtain CSI and preprocess the data to form a training data set, and use the training data and corresponding tags to train the deep neural network (DNN), convolutional neural network (CNN) and convolutional preprocessing neural network (CPNN). Get a deep learning model. In the identity authentication stage, CSI is used as the input of the model, and the output is the identity authentication result. The physical layer-based authentication scheme has the irreplaceable advantages of other traditional methods. The specific physical layer characteristics are directly affected by the equipment and environment during the communication process, and it is difficult for an attacker to simulate counterfeiting. However, the instability of fast time-varying channels often reduces the performance of physical layer authentication. In addition, the performance of AFE defect-based authentication technology is limited by the low reliability of AFE defect estimation [18].

In recent years, deep learning [19] has received many effective improvements and demonstrated its good application performance. Therefore, it has received widespread attention from researchers in various fields. The application of machine learning and deep learning algorithms to identity authentication schemes has become a kind of trend. In [20], the author proposes a physical layer identity authentication scheme based on CSI, which uses a convolutional neural network to extract a set of features that are stable with respect to rotation from the original CSI measurement data, and then compares the user's previous CSI with the CSI received by the heart To determine whether the user's identity is legal and valid. This scheme can achieve the effect of identity authentication, but because every authentication must traverse all users in the system, resulting in lower authentication efficiency.

3 Development Direction of Identity Authentication Technology in Edge Computing Environment

Through the research and summary of the identity authentication technology in the edge computing environment, in order to achieve a safe and reliable identity authentication effect, in the future research, the identity authentication technology in the edge computing environment should develop in the following aspects.

3.1 Technology Migration

So far, the identity authentication technology has made many important achievements, with various authentication methods, and also has considerable effects in security. However, most of the current research on identity authentication is still focused on other computing paradigms. The research on identity authentication technology specifically for edge computing is relatively small. The characteristics of edge computing are not fully considered. The identity authentication technology that is really applicable to edge computing is still in place in the exploration stage [21].

Therefore, we can consider migrating from identity authentication schemes applied to other computing paradigms to edge computing, such as cloud computing, mobile edge computing, and fog computing. However, the technical solution cannot be applied to the edge computing environment, but the characteristics of the edge computing terminal, such as limited computing / storage resources and low latency requirements, should be considered to appropriately improve the identity authentication scheme.

Password-based identity authentication technology is often used in other computing paradigms. Among them, Kerberos [22] is a typical password authentication system, which belongs to a symmetric password system. The Kerberos authentication system uses a trusted third-party authentication scheme, and its database stores the authentication server and the user's key. Therefore, the authentication system can complete the function of authenticating the identity of another entity for one entity. However, Kerberos has the risk of the old authentication code being reused, and because its server needs to store a large number of keys, the key management problem will become an unfavorable factor restricting its best performance in edge computing. Therefore, the shortcomings of Kerberos can be improved to enhance the effectiveness and security of identity authentication in the edge computing environment. For example, in order to solve the weakness of excessive key storage, it can be combined with the public key cryptosystem, and the Kerberos system no longer needs to store keys, so that the key management problem can be solved, and the efficiency of identity authentication is also improved.

3.2 Integration of Multiple Identity Authentication Technologies

Through the analysis of multiple identity authentication technologies, it is found that these technical solutions have their advantages, but at the same time there are many shortcomings. For example, the hardware cost of identity authentication technology based on machine learning is too high, and the amount of calculation data required is too large; the identity authentication technology based on cryptography has problems such as key management, key length size, and security that are difficult to balance; in biometric authentication The collected biometric data may cause data distortion due to interference noise. On the other hand, when the research technology is applied to solve practical problems, due to environmental factors or human factors, the application effect will be poor, and the security will not meet expectations.

Considering the above reasons, multiple technologies can be organically combined to learn from each other. This identity authentication scheme is a good idea to be applied in the edge computing environment. Combining the advantages of multiple technologies can improve the reliability and reliability of edge computing identity authentication effectiveness.

As a whole, the password-based authentication method is the simplest and easy to perform, but it is easy to be attacked by attackers; the cryptography-based authentication technology is the most mature, widely used, with various solutions and stable performance; smart cards can store secret information and provide hardware encryption, High security; due to the uniqueness of biometrics, it is not easy to be forged, so the authentication technology based on biometrics is the most secure. If the advantages of these technologies can be properly combined, it can make up for the shortcomings of some of these solutions and improve the actual availability of the overall identity authentication scheme in the edge computing environment.

For example, the most common thing today is to combine biometric authentication with deep learning. Chaoran Liu et al. Adopted the fusion feature of local binary mode and oriented gradient histogram, and used unsupervised convolution constraint Boltzmann machine to train the gait energy map, and proposed a kind of input from gait energy map to gait recognition the result of the program. This algorithm framework that integrates deep learning into gait recognition can obtain efficient gait recognition results based on a small amount of gait images, which improves the efficiency and accuracy of recognition [23].

3.3 Unified Identity Authentication Mechanism

With the continuous development of edge computing, there are more and more edge computing applications. When a user needs to access edge computing resources, the user needs to perform multiple identity authentication operations, and the data containing private information will be repeatedly input during multiple identity authentication, which will bring huge privacy risks to users. In addition, the edge server needs to create a large number of user databases, so managing and maintaining the database will be an extremely complex and difficult problem. Considering these factors, it is very important to study a unified identity authentication technology suitable for edge computing.

In the edge computing environment, the identity management between different edge servers can be regarded as authentication between different trust domains. If a unified identity authentication method is used for resource access requests, users can achieve cross-platform through only one identity authentication, Cross-domain operations.

There are many well-known unified identity authentications at present, For example, IBM's WebSphere solution [24], Net Passport developed by Microsoft [25].

Zhang Fuyou and others proposed a unified identity authentication scheme based on biometrics. When the user performs a single sign-on operation, the scheme can simultaneously provide users with security and convenience through the biometrics identification device of the mobile terminal device and the trusted environment Authentication function. When users request access to the service, they will use their biometrics instead of user names and passwords to pass identity authentication, so users do not need to frequently input messages containing private information, and the risk of user privacy leakage will be significantly reduced [26].

4 Conclusions

Edge computing occupies a core position in the rapidly developing Internet of Things technology and has broad practical application prospects. However, edge computing also faces many new security challenges. Efficient and reliable identity authentication is an important way to solve security problems, which can greatly reduce the risk of user privacy leakage. According to the characteristics of edge computing with low latency and limited terminal resources, research on lightweight identity authentication technology is the main challenge. At the same time, in order to better explore the identity authentication technology that is highly suitable for edge computing, it is a research direction worthy of attention to migrate from other computing paradigms to develop identity authentication technology; faced with the advantages and disadvantages of many different identity authentication technologies, many The concept of technology fusion has certain practical significance; with the increasing use of edge computing, unified identity authentication technology is an inevitable development trend. In general, how to form an identity authentication technology that truly meets the needs of edge computing needs in-depth research.

Acknowledgement. This work is supported by the National Natural Science Foundation of China under Grant (No. 61971032), Fundamesntal Research Funds for the Central Universities (No. FRF-TP-18-008A3).

Conflicts of Interest. The authors declare that they have no conflicts of interest to report regarding the present study.

References

1. IBM and Nokia Siemens Networks Announce World's First Mobile Edge Computing Platform #MWC13, Press Release, Nokia, 25 February 2013. company.nokia.com/en/news/press-releases/2013/02/25/ibm-and-nokia-siemens-networks-announce-worlds-frst-mobile-edge-computing-platform-mwc13
2. Antipolis, S.: ETSI announces first meeting of new standardization group on mobile-edge computing, The Standard, European Telecommu-nications Standards Inst., 30 October 2014. www.etsi.org/news-events/news/838-2014-10-news-etsi-announces-first-meeting-of-new-standardization-group-on-mobile-edge-computing
3. Li, H., Zhou, C., Haitao, X., Lv, X., Han, Z.: Joint optimization strategy of computation offloading and resource allocation in multi-access edge computing environment. IEEE Trans. Veh. Technol. **69**(9), 10214–10226 (2020)
4. Hong, X., Wang, Y.: Edge computing technology: development and countermeasures. Strateg. Study Chin. Acad. Eng. **20**(2), 20–26 (2018)
5. Rodrigues, T.G., Suto, K., Nishiyama, H., et al.: Hybrid method for minimizing service delay in edge cloud computing through VM migration and transmission power control. IEEE Trans. Comput. **66**(5), 810–819 (2017)
6. Shi, W., Sun, H., Cao, J., et al.: Edge computing: a new computing model in the era of internet of everything. Comput. Res. Dev. **1** (2017)
7. Varghese, B., Wang, N., Barbhuiya, S., et al.: Challenges and opportunities in edge computing. In: 2016 IEEE International Conference on Smart Cloud (SmartCloud), pp. 20–26. IEEE (2016)
8. Ibrahim, M.H.: Octopus: an edge-fog mutual authentication scheme. IJ Netw. Secur. **18**(6), 1089–1101 (2016)
9. Amor, A.B., Abid, M., Meddeb, A.: A privacy-preserving authentication scheme in an edge-fog environment. In: IEEE/ACS 14th International Conference on Computer Systems and Applications (AICCSA), pp. 1225–1231. IEEE (2017)
10. Liu, H., Wang, Y., Liu, J., et al.: Practical user authentication leveraging channel state information (CSI). In: Proceedings of the 9th ACM Symposium on Information, Computer and Communications Security, pp. 389–400 (2014)

11. Liu, S., Song, Y., Zhang, M., et al.: An identity authentication method combining liveness detection and face recognition. Sensors **19**(21), 4733 (2019)
12. Punithavathi, P., Geetha, S., Karuppiah, M., et al.: A lightweight machine learning-based authentication framework for smart IoT devices. Inf. Sci. **484**, 255–268 (2019)
13. Ling, C.H., Lee, C.C., Yang, C.C., et al.: A secure and efficient one-time password authentication scheme for WSN. IJ Netw. Secur. **19**(2), 177–181 (2017)
14. Shen, S.S., Kang, T.H., Lin, S.H., et al.: Random graphic user password authentication scheme in mobile devices. In: 2017 International Conference on Applied System Innovation (ICASI), pp. 1251–1254. IEEE (2017)
15. Zeng, K., Govindan, K., Mohapatra, P.: Non-cryptographic authentication and identification in wireless networks. Netw. Secur. **1,** 3 (2010)
16. Chen, Y., Wen, H., Wu, J., et al.: Clustering based physical-layer authentication in edge computing systems with asymmetric resources. Sensors **19**(8), 1926 (2019)
17. Liao, R.F., Wen, H., Wu, J., et al.: Deep-learning-based physical layer authentication for industrial wireless sensor networks. Sensors **19**(11), 2440 (2019)
18. Wang, X., Hao, P., Hanzo, L.: Physical-layer authentication for wireless security enhancement: current challenges and future developments. IEEE Commun. Mag. **54**(6), 152–158 (2016)
19. Pouyanfar, S., Sadiq, S., Yan, Y., et al.: A survey on deep learning: algorithms, techniques, and applications. ACM Comput. Surv. (CSUR) **51**(5), 92 (2019)
20. Yazdani Abyaneh, A., Pourahmadi, V., Hosein Gharari Foumani, A.: CSI-based authentication: extracting stable features using deep neural networks. Trans. Emerg. Telecommun. Technol. **31**(2), e3795 (2020)
21. Zhang, J., Zhao, Y., Chen, B., Hu, F., Zhu, K.: Survey on data security and privacy-preserving for the research of edge computing. J. Commun. **39**(3), 1–21 (2018)
22. Neuman, B.C., Ts'o, T.: Kerberos: an authentication service for computer networks. IEEE Commun. Mag. **32**(9), 33–38 (2002)
23. Liu, C., Wq, Y.: Gait recognition using deep learning. In: Handbook of Research on Multimedia. Cyber Security (2020)
24. Camargo, C., Martens, H.: IBM Websphere Portal 8: Web Experience Factory and the Cloud. Packt Publishing (2012)
25. Deng, Y., Cheng, X.H.: System design of mobile cross-domain single sign-on. Comput. Eng. Des. **31**(8), 1667–1672 (2010)
26. Fuyou, Z., Wang, Q., Song, L.: Research on unified identity authentication system based on biometric recognition. Inf. Netw. Secur. (09), 86–90 (2019)

Research on Security Mechanism and Forensics of SQLite Database

Chengdu Zhang and Jie Yin[✉]

Jiangsu Police Institute, Nanjing 201101, China
yinjie@jspi.edu.cn

Abstract. With the rapid development of information technology and wireless communication technology, SQLite database has been widely used in various occasions in peacetime. SQLite database, as a relatively common database in the Android operating system, usually contains a series of key information such as call records and short messages. Research on SQLite database has a certain positive effect on public security electronic evidence collection. This article hopes to study the security mechanism and cracking method of SQLite database, the encryption and decryption mechanism and operation method of open source software such as SQL Cipher, and the actual forensic operation of WeChat as an example to conduct the research of SQLite database forensic analysis.

Keywords: SQLite database · Embedded database · Forensic analysis · AES encryption algorithm

1 Introduction

1.1 Research Background

With the continuous advancement of information technology, smart phones have become a type of work assistant that most people cannot give up, and they play an extremely important role in their various types of work. In order to meet the diverse usage requirements of users, the working capabilities of smart phones are improving day by day. Based on the background that smart phones are used in various fields and occasions, smart phones will inevitably store a large amount of user information. Smart phones have become an important auxiliary tool for people's work and life, and they have also become exposed to people's social life. Information database of information such as contacts, outings, etc. As smart phones are widely used nowadays, digital forensics technology for smart phones has also developed. Digital forensics, as a means of using information technology to extract and analyze the required information from various electronic information equipment, has great room for development in the contemporary era of rapid development of information technology. By analyzing the information stored in smart phones, it is not difficult to find that whether it is mobile phone address book, call history, SMS or a series of commonly used apps such as browser, WeChat, and maps, the data in it is often stored in the form of SQLite database [1]. As a mini-database, SQLite can use

X. Sun et al. (Eds.): ICAIS 2021, CCIS 1423, pp. 614–629, 2021.
https://doi.org/10.1007/978-3-030-78618-2_51

less resources, has high 2system compatibility, supports multiple computer languages, and processes instructions and data at a high speed. Therefore, the application scenarios of SQLite database are very extensive. Based on the background of the wide application of SQLite database in smart phones, the security mechanism and forensic research of SQLite database is particularly important.

1.2 Research Significance

For the public security forensic work, obtaining evidence from smart phones is a must. A number of information stored in the smart phone, including but not limited to the user's basic personal information, communication records. Such information can often play an important auxiliary role in the work of public security. A considerable number of criminal cases can be analyzed by collecting evidence from smartphones.

After analyzing the structure of the SQLite database, not only the data content that has not been cleared but still retained in the SQLite database can be obtained, but the data content that has been cleared can also be retrieved to a certain extent. However, because the SQLite database in a smart phone is often not in an unencrypted state, to achieve forensics, you need to obtain the SQLite password. In most cases, it is difficult to obtain the SQLite password directly. Therefore, the security mechanism of SQLite is required, especially the encryption mechanism. Conduct understanding and research, find out the method to obtain the encryption and decryption keys of the SQLite database, and then realize the forensic analysis of the SQLite database.

2 SQLite Security Mechanism and Principle

2.1 The Architecture of SQLite Database

Features of SQLite Database. SQLite database is different from other databases, it is light enough, about 130,000 lines of code, about 4.43M. Although SQLite is very small, it has complete functions and the advantages of ACID. When the transaction is in progress, the uninterruptibility of the transaction is guaranteed, and the occurrence of some operations is avoided. At the same time, it ensures that the database status is the same before and after the execution, and there is no case that partial changes are saved after the transaction is interrupted. For multiple transactions running at the same time, they are isolated from each other and do not interfere with each other. Once the transaction is completed, the changes made in the database will be retained. Even in unexpected situations such as system crashes or physical power cuts, the data can be preserved intact. The SQLite database does not require configuration and loading, and supports the database SQL92 standard. Including indexes, constraints, triggers and viewing, etc. and contains simple and easy-to-use APIs.

SQLite is designed to fit embedded systems. SQLite is not a single program that interacts independently with the program, but integrates itself into the program and becomes an important module of the program. Therefore, the communication rules 3reached between SQLite and other programs are application program interface calls made directly within program statements. This call operation reduces consumption, reduces delays, and reduces overall difficulty. At present, many embedded products have used SQLite, including a series of applications under the Adobe system company, Firefox browser, Thunderbird mailbox, Google and many other applications, as well as many applications of the Android system [2]. Most of the time, the memory that SQLite needs to occupy is too low to imagine. In some embedded systems, it only needs to provide less than 1M of memory resources. Although the SQLite database is so small, its load capacity is also considerable. The designer underestimated its load capacity, thinking that it can withstand about 10,000 website clicks, but in actual testing, this data may increase by 9 times.

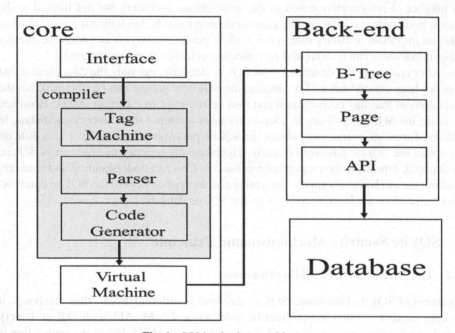

Fig. 1. SQLite database architecture

SQLite Modular Design. SQLite is a modular database. When constructing a SQLite database, it first displays the structure and workflow of the database in the form of a framework, and then defines the relationship between the frameworks. It is composed of three main parts, each part is also subdivided into multiple modules. As shown in Fig. 1.

The internal structure of the SQLite database can be described by these four components: core, SQL compiler, backend, and accessories [3]. With the assistance of the virtual machine, SQLite reduces the difficulty of debugging the SQLite core and improves the operability and efficiency. All SQL statements used by SQLite are easy to understand. After these source statements are compiled, the generated target program can also be run in a virtual machine. SQLite has relatively broad restrictions on the size of the database, and the data is stored in the form of a B-tree.

SQLite Architecture. Each module in the SQLite database architecture has corresponding functions [4], and the SQLite database architecture is shown in Fig. 2.

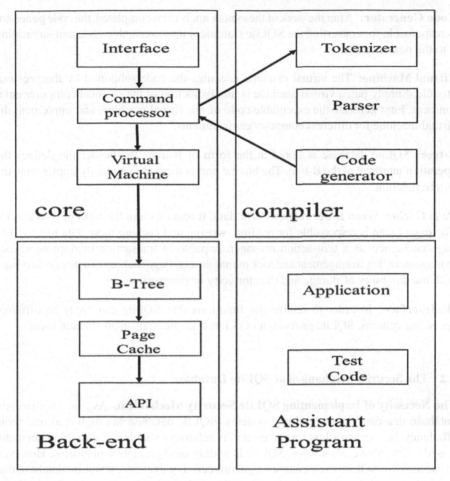

Fig. 2. SQLite database architecture

Interface: As a C language library, it is mainly used to receive user commands. Whether it is a program or a dynamic language, it needs to establish a connection with SQLite through an interface.

Tokenizer: When a string with SQL statements is received, the interface will forward it to the tokenizer. The tokenizer is responsible for dividing it into multiple tokens and passing these tokens to the parser. In different design methods, there are cases where the tokenizer calls the grammar analyzer, and there are also cases where the grammar analyzer calls the tokenizer, but the designer is considering the higher efficiency of the tokenizer calling the grammar analyzer, and more choose the former.

Parser: The function of the parser is to give the tokens specific meaning after receiving the tokens segmented by the tokenizer. That is, these tags are converted into complete SQL statements.

Code Generator: After the work of the syntax analyzer is completed, the code generator is responsible for converting the SQLite statement into executable code and submitting it to the next module.

Virtual Machine: The virtual machine executes the code submitted by the previous module. Simply put, a virtual machine is an abstraction of the physical computer environment. First generate the executable code of the virtual machine, and implement the virtual machine for different computer environments.

B-tree: SQLite database is stored in the form of B-tree. The header file defines the operation interface of the B-tree. The btree.c part is the part that mainly implements the B-tree function.

Page Cache: When B-tree requests disk data, it requests it in the form of data blocks. The page cache is responsible for reading, writing and caching these data blocks. The page cache acts as a transaction manager, capable of transaction management, data management, log management and lock management. Page caching can be said to ensure both the durability of storage and the atomicity of transactions.

OS Interface: In order to realize the functions that SQLite can apply to different operating systems, SQLite provides an OS interface through an abstraction layer.

2.2   The Security Mechanism of SQLite Database

The Necessity of Implementing SQLite Security Mechanism. As a lightweight database that can support multiple systems, SQLite database has high read and write efficiency, but occupies less resources, and is relatively simple and easy to understand. Based on the above advantages, SQLite is widely used on mobile platforms. However, the security of SQLite itself cannot be guaranteed. For example, a SQLite database that does not use any security measures, regardless of whether it is a user of the database, as long as the file can be accessed, and the simplest notepad software can also open the database. And see the data stored in it [5]. Therefore, in order to ensure the security of the SQLite database, the security mechanism of the SQLite database needs to be implemented.

Types of SQLite Security Mechanisms. To implement the SQLite database security mechanism, in fact, it is necessary to ensure the security of the data information in the SQLite database, that is, to meet the security features proposed above. At present, the user authentication function can be realized by encrypting the database, and the role-based permission control can be implemented [6].

One type of security mechanism is the user authentication mechanism. User authentication means that the user must submit a user name and password to the system when using the database. The system determines whether the user can access the system by checking whether the user name and password are legal. The SQLite database itself is a binary file that does not support user authentication. To realize the user authentication mechanism, you need to create a system database and embed the user authentication function into the system database.

Another type of security mechanism is role-based permission control. Permission control is to restrict the permissions of users who have entered the system within the system to prevent users from unauthorized access and operations. Compared with the autonomous control method and the mandatory permission control method, the rolebased permission control is more flexible, reduces the difficulty of permission assignment, and conforms to the high efficiency of SQLite database operation [7].

2.3 Encryption Algorithm Comparison

In addition to user authentication mechanisms and permission control mechanisms, strong encryption protection for specific databases used by mobile devices is currently one of the most common database security methods. Data encryption is to transform the manifestation of data information through a transformation method. Transform information that conforms to people's reading habits into random codes that seem to be irregular. When the data is needed, it is converted back to its original form. In the process of data storage and transmission, data encryption can effectively protect data content and is a practical and effective security mechanism [8].

For database encryption, there are two commonly used methods. One is to find out the content data to be encrypted and encrypt the content data. Then write the encrypted data obtained after encryption into the database. This method is simple to understand and implement. When writing data into the database and extracting useful content from the database, you only need to encrypt the current content to be operated accordingly. And decryption operation is enough. This method solves the problem of expressing data content directly in plain text at a certain level of security, but the method of content encryption is not safe, and there is no operation on the database skeleton. Only the content and data are encrypted. The structure of the table has not changed, so this information can be easily analyzed. In addition, one of the uses of the database is data retrieval. After the content is encrypted, the retrieval of the requested content is also a big problem. The second is to encrypt the entire database, which is to encrypt the generated library files. This method can generally reduce the possibility of database security threats [9]. The currently commonly used SQLite database encryption is based on the second method.

Encryption Algorithm Comparison. According to the types of keys, encryption algorithms can be divided into two categories. One is a symmetric encryption algorithm, which is characterized by the same key used in the encryption and decryption process. Both the sender and receiver of the information need to know this key to be able to communicate. This kind of encryption algorithm has a higher operating speed. And if you want to ensure security, you can use a long key. The keys used in the encryption and decryption process of asymmetric encryption algorithms are inconsistent. Public keys can be published, but private keys are the opposite. These two keys need to be used together [10]. This kind of encryption algorithm has a high demand for calculation. Due to the fast speed of symmetric encryption, it is suitable for large data volume encryption. Considering the high efficiency of the SQLite database and the actual situation of storing large amounts of data in the database, the symmetric encryption algorithm is a better

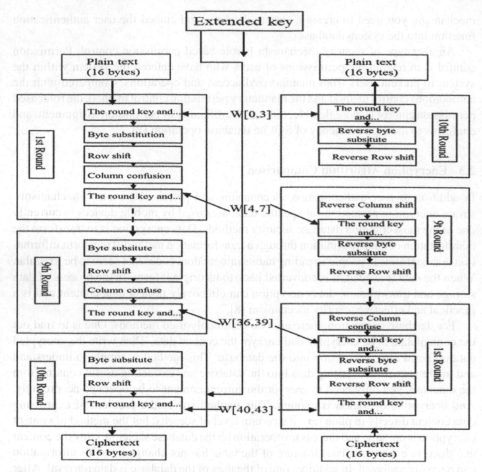

Fig. 3. AES encryption process Show.

choice. Therefore, the currently widely used SQL cipher encryption method is the AES encryption algorithm.

AES Encryption Algorithm. AES encryption is a commonly used encryption algorithm, which can be divided into 128-bit, 192-bit or 256-bit according to the key length, depending on the encryption level requirements. In use, the encryption function module is called by inputting the plaintext and the key as parameters at the same time, and the encryption result is obtained after the operation. The AES encryption process first splits the target plaintext into 16 parts, which are described by a square matrix. Then, each plaintext block is encrypted into a ciphertext block. Finally, combining all the ciphertext blocks is the final output encryption result. The conversion of plaintext to ciphertext using AES encryption is not completed at one time.

The encryption process is shown in Fig. 3.

From a security perspective, the encryption method is designed to be multiple rounds of encryption. In order, the first round of encryption is 1 time, after N ordinary rounds of encryption, and then the final round is 1 time. The key used in AES supports three lengths, which are 128 bits, 192 bits, and 256 bits. The intensity is getting higher and higher. The number of rounds of encryption is determined by the selected key length. Subtracting the number of rounds occupied by the first round of encryption, 128 bits, 192 bits, and 256 bits correspond to 10 rounds, 12 rounds, and 14 rounds respectively [11].

In different stages of encryption, the round has different steps. The first round has only one step—round key addition, while the ordinary round uses byte replacement, row shift, column confusion, and round key addition. And execute multiple times according to the key length. The final round cancels the column confusion step, reserves bytes instead, row shift and round key plus three steps.

Byte Replacement. Byte substitution is to replace each byte of the plaintext block with another byte. The 16-byte plaintext block is arranged in a square matrix pattern during each processing. The byte substitution relies on the S box. The S box is a 16X16 two-dimensional array for permutation calculation in the symmetric key algorithm. When the byte is replaced, the byte is divided into row value and column value, corresponding to each row and column, find the value in the S box and output it.

Row Shift. Row shift is to shift the 16-byte plaintext block by column, as shown in Fig. 4.

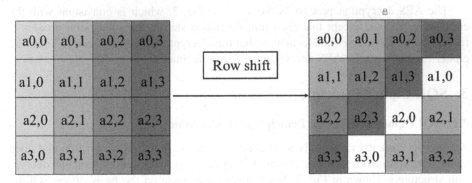

Fig. 4. Row shift process

The first row remains the same, the second row a1.0, a1.1, a1.2, and a1.3 modules are shifted to the left by one byte in turn, and the three or four rows are moved by analogy.

Column Confusion. Column confusion is implemented after row shifting. Multiply the row-shifttransformed matrix with the column confusion matrix to obtain the result of the column confusion transformation.

Round Key Addition. The round key addition is one of the keys used in the four transformations. In this step, the AES keys used are also formed into a 4 * 4 square matrix, and the input matrix to be encrypted corresponds to the key matrix one by one in rows and columns. The corresponding value is XORed to get the output value. The keys used in different rounds are not the same, which involves the concept of extended keys. The extended key is located in the AES source code, and an array W with a length of 4 * 4 * (10 + 1) bytes is used to store the keys of all rounds. Taking AES128 as an example, the value of W{0–15} is the value of the initial key, which is used for the initial round of encryption. In the W array, W{0–15} is used for the initial round of processing, W{32–47} is used for the second round of processing, until W{160–175} is used for the 10th round (final round) of processing.

AES Decryption Process. The AES decryption process is the reverse operation of the AES encryption process, and the plaintext can be obtained by inputting the ciphertext and key as parameters into the decryption functions.

Reverse Byte Substitution. AES defines the S-box as well as the inverse S-box. There is no process difference between reverse byte substitution and byte substitution, only the difference between using the reverse S-box.

Reverse Row Shift. The process of reverse row shift is similar to that of row shift, except that the direction of movement is opposite. That is, the first line remains as it is, the second line is rotated by one byte to the right, and the third and fourth lines are so on.

Reverse Nematic Confusion. Inverse nematic confusion is also realized in the form of multiplication with a matrix. The matrix used for inverse nematic confusion and the matrix used for column confusion are mutually inverse, and the result of the multiplication of the two is the identity matrix.

The AES decryption process is the same as Fig. 3, which is consistent with the encryption process, except that each transformation step in the encryption process is replaced with an inverse transformation, but this decryption method needs to know the ciphertext and key after AES encryption at the same time.

3   SQL Cipher Principle

3.1   SQLCipher Encryption Principle and Algorithm

Among the currently commonly used encryption tools, SQLCipher is a free and open source encryption tool that uses 256-bit AES encryption, and its encryption and decryption structure is shown in Fig. 5. Since this tool is made on the basis offree SQLite, the encryption interface it uses is consistent with SQLite. SQLCipher as an Android application. The third-party library for creating "encrypted database" is very simple to use. It is the same as the SQLite used internally in the Android SDK, except that the corresponding import is replaced.

Using SQLCipher to create a new database, you will get an encrypted database, and for the old database without encryption, SQLCipher provides the sqlcipher_export() function, which can easily import an ordinary database into the SQLCipher encrypted database. Encryption of the database. Decryption is the reverse operation of the encryption process. It also calls the function provided by SQLCipher. Decryption is to import the encrypted database of SQL Cipher into a database that has not been encrypted. Encrypting the existing database actually generates a copy of the original database, and the database file generated after the copy has the encryption function.

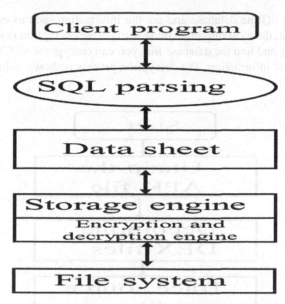

Fig. 5. Database encryption and decryption structure

3.2 SQL Cipher Decryption Principle and Algorithm (Take WeChat as an Example)

The encryption tool represented by SQLCipher uses the AES-256 encryption algorithm to encrypt and decrypt database files for the SQLite storage module. This method has high security and good performance. To crack SQLCipher, you cannot use brute force cracking. The key length of AES-256 is 256 bits, and brute force cracking is to use each key for decryption attempts until the only key that can complete the decryption is obtained. Referring to the example of brute force cracking, there are short-term brute-force cracking cases, and there are also cases that take a long time. But in general, to try out the correct key, the average number of keys to be tried is about one-half of the total number of keys. The longer the key length, the greater the total number of keys. Take AES-256 as an example. The number of AES-256 keys is 2 to the 256th power, which is $1.2*10^{77}$. To brute force AES-256, the time required is immeasurable, and the cost is also an astronomical figure. There is no type of encrypted information that is worth the time and money costs of this magnitude. Therefore, to crack AES-256, brute force cracking cannot be used. But this does not mean that AES cannot be cracked. It should be recognized that AES is a symmetric encryption algorithm used for encryption and decryption. SQLCipher uses an overall encryption scheme instead of encrypting tables or columns. In other words, you only need to get an encryption key, which is equivalent to obtaining the decryption key for SQLCipher encrypted database files.

WeChat SQLCipher Decryption Ideas. Take WeChat database encryption as an example. The WeChat encryption database uses SQL Cipher encryption, which means that WeChat is equivalent to publishing its own encryption algorithm, AES-256. The way to ensure the security of the WeChat database is to keep the used keys secret. To open the WeChat SQLite database and get the information such as contacts and chat records stored in it, the most important thing is to get the encryption key. As long as you can obtain the key and find the database file, you can encrypt the WeChat database and extract the required information. The decryption process is shown in Fig. 6.

Fig. 6. Decryption process.

Get WeChat SQL Cipher Encryption Guidelines. To obtain the encryption key of the WeChat SQLite database file, you need to start with the source code. The package of the installer in the Android system is an apk file. Find the WeChat-related file with the suffix apk in the file manager of the smart phone and decompress it. You can find a series of files with the suffix dex. In actual analysis, six files with dex as the suffix were found from classes to classes6. This is the key file to find the encryption key of the WeChat SQLite database file. The file ending with dex is a special data format, similar to the jar format file, which belongs to the optimized exe file of the Android version. In fact, dex files are ubiquitous in the apk installation package. This file contains all operating instructions and runtime data of the mobile APP. By analogy with the PC side, running a *.dex file on the Android system is equivalent to running a .class file on the PC side. After the Java program is compiled into a class file, the class file is generally integrated to improve compactness and reduce redundancy. After this integration, the generated dex file is often half the size of the general jar file.

Since the dex file contains all the app code, the Java source code can be obtained by decompiling. To crack WeChat passwords using static methods, we must first find the key points [12], and import the source code obtained by decompilation into Eclipse. Using a database in Android will definitely involve the SQLiteDatabase class. You can first search for this class globally in Eclipse. Through a global search, it was found that SQLiteDatabase appeared in the file with the dex suffix. Check the dex file and check its openDatabase method. Follow up through the methods called inside the file, and finally found that the j method was called to construct a string and take the first seven Bit. By parsing the j method, it is found that this string is generated by concatenating the IMEI value and the uin value and performing MD5 calculation. In other words, the key to encrypt the database file of WeChat using SQLCipher is to concatenate the IMEI value of the mobile phone and the uin value given to the user by WeChat to form a string. After MD5, a 32-bit string is generated, and the first seven digits are taken in lowercase. enter.

4 Practical Application of SQLite Database Forensic Analysis

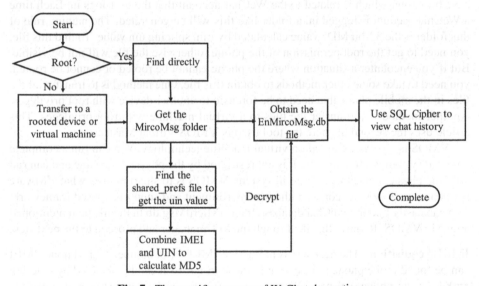

Fig. 7. The specific process of WeChat decryption

The encryption structure of SQLCipher is introduced above, and the encryption guidelines for WeChat database files are also introduced. If you know the guidelines, you can manually decrypt the WeChat database files. After decryption, you can view the chat records and other information stored in it. Although the WeChat database files are encrypted, users do not need to enter the database key when viewing their chat records when using WeChat, indicating that WeChat decrypts the database files when the user uses the APP. When we turn off the data connection or wireless network of the mobile phone, or turn on the airplane mode of the mobile phone, the user can still see the previous chat history of WeChat. This shows that WeChat not only saves the database files locally, but also stores the strings needed to decrypt the WeChat database. Therefore, the WeChat database file and the string used for encryption can be found in the memory of the smartphone, and then the WeChat database file encryption guidelines can be applied to obtain the decryption key. The specific decryption process is shown in Fig. 7.

4.1 Manually Decrypt the WeChat Database

Manual decryption of the WeChat database means that the WeChat database is not cracked by code or software. Manual cracking is based on the premise of knowing the encryption guidelines for WeChat database files. After obtaining the WeChat database file, IMEI serial number and uin value, the WeChat database can be decrypted. This method can be used to crack the chat records of a small number of WeChat accounts.

Obtaining WeChat Database Files. To decrypt the WeChat database file, you first need to get the database file EnMicroMsg.db [13]. The path of this file is \data\data\com.tencent.mm\MicroMsg\<usermd5>\EnMicroMsg.db. The user-md5 is a 32-bit string, which is related to the WeChat account that the user logs in. Each time a WeChat account is logged in, a folder like this will be generated. The naming rule of this folder is the 32-bit MD5 value calculated by mm splicing uin value. To find this file, you need to get the root permission of the phone, otherwise the file will not be visible. But if you encounter a situation where the phone cannot be rooted or cannot be rooted, you need to take some other methods to obtain this file. One method is to transfer all the files in the mobile phone that need to be forensic to another device with root privileges. Another method is to transfer the files to a virtual machine with root privileges. This article uses the second method, the tool used is VMOS Virtual Master.

VMOS is a software based on virtual machine technology. You can run a complete Android system in this software. It is not restricted by the physical machine and can run with the physical machine's Android system. VMOS is to smart phones what VMware is to computers. VMOS comes with root environment and supports xposed framework. You can easily find the WeChat database file EnMicroMsg.db in the file path mentioned above in VMOS. Remove the file through the MT manager and proceed to the next step.

IMEI Acquisition. The next step is to find the IMEI serial number of the phone. IMEI can be found in the phone information in the settings, or it can be obtained by entering *#06# on the phone dial page. Since some software on the network can also use the method of importing the MicroMsg folder to decrypt the WeChat database, it can be seen that there are also files in the folder that record the IMEI serial number of the mobile phone. Generally speaking, this serial number is recorded in the CompatibleInfo.cfg file.

UIN Acquisition. The last step is to obtain the uin value, which is stored in the auth_info_key_prefs.xml file in the \data\data\com.tencent.mm\shared_prefs folder. Use Notepad to open the file with the xml suffix, and find int name="_auth_uin" value="1373161555", which is the uin value given to users by WeChat.

After obtaining the WeChat database file EnMicroMsg.db, the IMEI serial number of the mobile phone and the WeChat uin value, combine the IMEI serial number and uin to find the MD5 value and take the first seven digits. Use SQL Cipher to open the file, enter a seven-digit string, you can unlock the WeChat database file, open the database file in SQL Cipher, select Browse Data, select the message form, you can see that all the WeChat accounts have not been deleted The chat history [14], the screenshot of opening the WeChat database file in SQL Cipher is shown in Fig. 8.

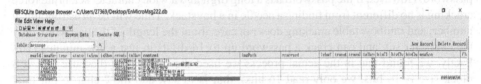

Fig. 8. Screenshot of WeChat database file decryption

Reasons for Decryption Failure. But in actual operation, some problems are often encountered. For example, some smart phones may have multiple IMEI serial numbers, and only one of the serial numbers is called in the encryption, and it needs to be tried to exclude invalid serial numbers. WeChat may also call the MEID or even the IMSI serial number of the SIM card, or it may use the serial number of the mobile phone used for WeChat registration. In another case, although the IMEI number of the machine is used during encryption, it is not fully used. IMEI numbers are mostly 15 digits, but only 14 of them may be used in encryption. Although WeChat, in order to protect the user experience and prevent users from not being able to see the old chat records, it will not modify this encryption rule. But even if the correct phone serial number is obtained, if the string called by the encryption algorithm itself is not obtained, there is still no way to manually decrypt the WeChat database. In the face of these situations, another cracking method can be adopted.

4.2 Brute Force Cracking of WeChat Database Files

Although the AES-256 encryption used by SQL Cipher is actually impossible to be brute-forced, using SQL Cipher to open the WeChat database file only needs to use the first 7 characters of the 32-bit characters calculated by MD5. It is feasible to brute force the 7-bit characters. The speed of brute force cracking using the CPU can only reach 200 per second, but the actual operation is relatively difficult. At present, the technical content of GPU (graphics processing unit) is getting higher and higher, and the computing speed is increasing. Using GPU cracking, although the operation difficulty is higher than CPU cracking, the speed can be greatly improved, and the cracking speed can even reach 300,000 per second [15]. To implement GPU brute force cracking operations, you can download a processing tool called SQLCipher Password Cracker OpenCL from GitHub and build an OpenCL+CUDA environment to brute force the WeChat database files.

Directly Use GPU to Accelerate Cracking. Using GPU to accelerate cracking, the speed is very impressive. The worst time for my RTX2060 Mobile to crack is 14 min. Most speeds exceed 300 K Passphrase/s. If multiple GPUs are used to crack at the same time, the time can be greatly shortened.

Use a Rainbow Table-Like Approach. According to the cracking mechanism, it can be divided into rainbow table cracking and brute force cracking. Brute force cracking uses the same encryption algorithm as the password, which is equivalent to guessing the password. However, if the password has a long digit and a wide character set, brute force cracking is no different from finding a needle in a haystack. Time will be an astronomical number; and rainbow table cracking does not care about the length of the password, only the character set, and can crack a password up to 14 digits in just a few minutes [16]. Factly, we found that in the actual process we used the first 4 char (because the AES block size is 16 bits, we only read 16 bits), that is to say, add the 7 char to our total length of 11 char, all The possible solution space is 16^11, which is 17, 592, 186, 044, 416. Only by recording these 11 bits and the result of the iteration, you can directly judge whether the password is correct or not. Omit the iteration process, then we can imagine searching for us on multiple machines at the same time The correct password will be obtained instantly (of course, these are based on our sufficient understanding of the encryption).

5 Summary and Outlook

With the rapid development of information technology, smart phones have gradually penetrated into all aspects of people's lives. Since most software in smart phones often use SQLite database, the security mechanism and forensics research of SQLite database is particularly important. This article briefly introduces the application status of SQLite database, describes the structure and characteristics of SQLite database, and introduces and discusses the security mechanism of SQLite database.

At the same time, this article gives a brief introduction to the encryption tool SQL Cipher, and uses WeChat as an example to introduce its cracking method. This article also uses mobile phone WeChat forensics as an example to actually show how to obtain mobile phone WeChat database file encryption keys and forensics for mobile phone WeChat SQLite database. At the same time, we must also realize that with the continuous development of technology, the challenges we face will continue to be updated. This article only discusses the cracking method of WeChat SQLite database in smart phone, and briefly introduces SQL Cipher, a commonly used encryption tool for SQLite database. Due to time and equipment constraints, no research has been conducted on how to recover deleted WeChat chat records, nor has it been researched on the records of other types of apps used in smartphones, such as Baidu Maps, QQ, and mobile browsers. Not only that, but also understand that technology is constantly advancing, and SQLite databases and corresponding security mechanism implementation tools will continue to improve and develop. There is more research space for SQLite security mechanisms and forensic analysis.

References

1. Bei, H.: Research and application of SQLite database. Nanjing University of Posts and Telecommunications, Nanjing (2019)
2. Pereira, M.T.: Forensic analysis of the firefox 3 internet history and recovery of deleted SQLite records. Digit. Invest. **5**, 93–103 (2009)
3. Yongen, L.: Research on the application of sqlite database in embedded system. Mod. Comput. **000**(7), 60–62 (2015)
4. Xuan, L.: Design and Implementation of SQLite Embedded Database Management System. Xidian University, Xi'an (2009)
5. Wen, L.: Database security technical analysis and security research review. Caizhi **1**, 249 (2018)
6. Lin, L.: Research on the Security of Embedded Database SQLite. Kunming University of Science and Technology, Kunming (2010)
7. Liu, H.-y., Yang, J.-k., Cai, H.-l., Wang, D.-y.: Analysis and design of the security mechanisms of embedded database SQLite. J. Acad. Armored Force Eng.**05**, 64–67 (2009)
8. Liao, S., Le, J.: Analysis and research on SQLite encryption method of embedded database. Comput. Appl. Softw. **025**(10), 70–71, 89 (2008)
9. Chunbo, W.: Analysis and design of security mechanism of embedded database SQLite. Comput. CD Softw. Appl. **05**, 279–280 (2014)
10. Ming, G.: Talking about the application of symmetric encryption algorithm and asymmetric encryption algorithm. Electron. World **477**(15), 65–66 (2015)
11. Guang, Y.: Research and implementation of the principle of advanced encryption standard AES Algorithm. Digit. World **1**, 141 (2019)
12. Weibing, W., Wen Bocong, W., Qi. : Research on android version of WeChat forensics method under complex conditions. Netw. Secur. Technol. Appl. **8**, 170–174 (2017)
13. Yanjiao, Z.: Research on Key Technologies of Smart Phone Forensics Based on Android Platform. Strategic Support Force Information Engineering University, Henan (2018)
14. Qinghua, Z.: Design and Implementation of Frensics System Based on Android Phone SQLite. Dalian University of Technology, Dalian (2015)
15. Distributed Multi-core CPU and GPU WPA/WPA2-PSK High-speed Cracking. Nanjing University of Posts and Telecommunications, Nanjing
16. Wang, Z.-y., Zhao, W., Tian Y., et al.: Application of rainbow table in password cracking. Inf. Secur. Commun. Priv. (11), 54–55, 58 (2010)

Research on Software Defined Programmable Strategy of Fireworks Model Oriented to Edge Computing Nodes

Yi-Qin Bao and Hao Zheng(✉)

College of Information Engineering of Nanjing XiaoZhuang University, Nanjing 2111711, China
Zhenghao@njxzc.edu.cn

Abstract. In cloud computing, since the program only runs in the cloud, it can be written in a programming language and compiled in a specific target platform. Due to the heterogeneous nature of the edge node platform, many tasks are migrated from the cloud to the edge terminal. So it is not easy to realize the edge computing programming, and the maintenance cost is also high. In order to solve this problem, this paper designs a set of software definable programming strategy through Hypertext Marked Language (HTML) format (independent of the operating system) file, and realizes the programming of the fireworks node of Internet of things (IoT) gateway under the edge computing, which is applied in the remote automatic monitoring system. Compared with the same system under the cloud computing, it is convenient for the user's programming, enhances the real-time performance, and greatly. It reduces the communication data flow, saves the data transmission cost, relieves the overall pressure of the system, and reduces the power consumption due to data transmission data storage.

Keywords: Edge computing · Fireworks model · Cloud computing · RTU · Modbus · Software definition

1 Introduction

The unprecedent development of the Internet of Things (IoT) and the popularization of 5G network, has significantly increased the number of network edge devices. The centralized big data processing technology with cloud computing model as the core is not able to efficiently process the data generated by edge devices. Therefore, the edge data processing with the edge computing model as the core emerges as the need of the hour. The former generates a small amount of data computing, which is consistent with the existing centralized data processing with the latter as the core, and better solves the problems existing in the era of IoT.

In the cloud computing model, users write applications and deploy them to the cloud. User programs are usually written and compiled on the target platform, run on the cloud server, save or transfer data to the cloud, and finally process in the cloud. Based on this kind of centralized data processing model, there are batch processing [1–5] and flow processing [6–12] ways. Applications are processed centrally under the cloud platform,

© Springer Nature Switzerland AG 2021
X. Sun et al. (Eds.): ICAIS 2021, CCIS 1423, pp. 630–641, 2021.
https://doi.org/10.1007/978-3-030-78618-2_52

which is an advantage of application development under the cloud computing model [13].

However, in the edge computing model, some or all of the computing tasks are migrated from the cloud to the edge nodes, while the edge nodes are mostly heterogeneous platforms, and the running environment of each node may be different. Therefore, when deploying user applications under the edge computing model, programmers will encounter great difficulties, while the traditional programming methods, such as MapReduce and sparkt, are not suitable A new programming method based on edge computing is studied [14]. In order to realize the programmability of edge computing, a concept of computing flow is proposed. Computing flow is a series of computing / functions performed on the data along the data transmission path. Computing/functions can be all or part of the functions of an application program, which occurs on the data transmission path that allows the application application to perform computing. The computing flow belongs to the category of software defined computing flow It is mainly used in the device end, edge node and cloud computing environment of source data to achieve efficient distributed data processing.

At present, edge computing has been applied in many industries. Wu Hongjie et al. [15] proposed a state perception model of building equipment based on edge computing. Zhan Xiong et al. [16] made a study on the safety risk assessment method based on edge computing in the national grid. P. Liu et al. [17] proposed a model transfer framework for CNNS on low-resource edge computing node. Zhang Quan et al. [18] proposed a new programming model based on edge computing fireworks model. Among these programming models, fireworks model is an object-oriented programming model, which has good generality. It extends the visualization boundary of data, and provides a new programming model for data processing in collaborative edge environment (CEE). However, fireworks model is an abstract programming model, which needs to be used with a rest of programming strategies and applications.

Aiming at the programming of fireworks model under the edge computing architecture, this paper designs a set of software definable programming strategy through HTML format (independent of the operating system) file, and realizes the programming of IoT gateway (edge node). Its application in the remote automatic monitoring platform system realizes the software definable programming of remote terminal unit (RTU), It enhances the system function, facilitates the maintenance of users and the expansion of system function, reduces the communication data flow and reduces the power consumption due to data transmission.

Section 2 introduces the fireworks model structure under the edge computing architecture; Sect. 3 defines the programmable strategy for the fireworks model software of the edge node; Sect. 4 tests and compares the systems under three different architectures; finally, summarizes the full text.

2 Fireworks Model Structure

In the era of Internet of things, many data production and consumption need to be transferred from the cloud to the edge devices, which increases the requirements for the distributed sharing and processing of big data. Therefore, a fireworks model is proposed, which can realize the distributed sharing and processing of big data, and enable private data to be processed on the devices of data stakeholders (such as fireworks nodes).

Fireworks model is a programming model based on edge computing, which mainly includes two parts: firework manager and firework node, as shown in Fig. 1. Fireworks model promotes geographically distributed data sources by creating virtual shared data views, while data stakeholders (fireworks model nodes) provide a level of predefined functional interface for end users to access with notes.

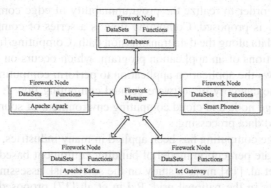

Fig. 1. Overall structure of fireworks model

The interface form of fireworks model is a set of data sets and functions, as shown in Fig. 1. The function is bound with the data set. The data processing of fireworks model is closer to the data producer, avoiding the long-distance data transmission from the network edge device to the cloud center, and reducing the subject delay. In the fireworks model, all the data use the relevant devices (fireworks model nodes) need to register their own data sets and corresponding functions to abstract into a unified data view.

3 Programmable Strategy of Firework Node

3.1 Firework Node

The fireworks model is mainly composed of firework manager and firework node, as shown in Fig. 1. One of the fireworks node is IoT gateway. The fireworks model should be applied to the specific project, corresponding to the remote automatic monitoring system based on cloud platform, which is designed as the remote automatic monitoring system based on edge computing. The definition of firework node is IoT gateway. It is RTU, as shown in Fig. 2.

The remote automatic monitoring system based on the cloud platform mainly integrates the real-time information, user information and geographic information of the distribution network by using modern automation control technology and wireless communication technology, so as to realize the normal operation of the distribution network and the monitoring and control of the distribution management in case of accidents. The system mainly consists of RTU (remote terminal unit) [19], RCU (remote control unit), wireless data transmission, cloud platform, etc., as shown in Fig. 2. RTU is a high-performance measurement and control device integrated with analog signal input and output, switch value input and output, count and communication. RTU is connected with many signal input / output modules (such as DI switch input, DO switch output, AI analog input, AO analog output), but the internal logic relationship between them needs to be programmed according to the site conditions, and even if multiple RTUs want to achieve linkage, they need to realize the PLC (programmable logic controller) through the method defined by software Function.

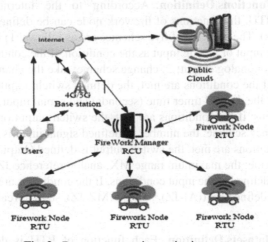

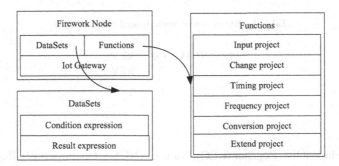

Fig. 2. Remote automatic monitoring system

3.2 Interface of Firework Node

Firework Node		Functions
DataSets	Functions	Input project
Iot Gateway		Change project
		Timing project
DataSets		Frequency project
Condition expression		Conversion project
Result expression		Extend project

Fig. 3. IoT gateway firework node interface

The interface form of fireworks model is a set of datasets and functions. The specific functions of firework node RTU are defined as five scheme types, which constitute five functions. According to the functional requirements of PLC, the following five schemes can be defined (not limited to this, expandable): 1) input scheme 2) change scheme 3) timing scheme 4) times scheme 5) conversion scheme, as shown in Fig. 3. Each scheme has a set of datasets. Each scheme is composed of scheme expression, which consists of two parts: condition expression and result expression. Condition / result expression consists of multiple linked lists or a single linked list, and multiple linked lists consist of a single linked list. Therefore, as long as a single linked list is defined, the firework node interface can be defined.

Firework Node Functions Definition. According to the internal logic function requirements of RTU, the functions of firework node can be defined by five schemes (not limited to this). The contents of five schemes are as follows: 1) input scheme: take the defined switch input or analog input as the condition, if the condition is met, define the switch output or analog output; 2) change scheme: take the change of switch input as the condition, If the conditions are met, the defined switch output or analog output; 3) timing scheme: the defined timer time (seconds) and signal input are used as timing and input conditions; if the conditions are met, the switch output or analog output are defined; 4) frequency scheme: the number of defined signal input is used as input conditions; if the conditions are met, the switch output is defined Output or analog output; 5) conversion scheme: the maximum range MX, analog reference JZ and analog range reference MZ are defined as the input conditions. If the conditions are met, the output of analog quantity is defined as $(((AI-JZ) * MX) / (MZ-JZ)$, so as to realize the conversion function.

Firework Node Datasets Definition. Each function of RTU is defined by scheme expression, and the datasets of firework node corresponds to scheme expression. The scheme expression consists of condition expression and result expression. The condition/result expression consists of multiple linked lists or a single linked list, and multiple linked lists consist of a single linked list. A single linked list is defined as follows:

Table 1. Bytes of the single linked list data field

EG	NUM	OP	REV REV
1	1	1	2

1. A single linked list: Register (REG), Number (NUM), Operator (OP), Register value (REV), as shown in Fig. 4.
2. The single linked list has 5 bytes in total, and the number of bytes in each data field of the single chain table is shown in Table 1. The multi linked list consists of n single linked lists with a total of 5 * N bytes.
3. The single linked list data field definition:

   a) Register (REG) definition, as shown in Table 2.

Table 2. Definition of REG

Name	Meaning	Value
DI	Switching value input	0
AI	Analog input	1
DO	Switching value output	2
AO	Analog output	3
TM	Timer	4
CS	Switching input times	5
MX	Maximum of analog	6
JZ	Analog reference	7
MZ	Analog range reference	8

Table 3. Definition of OP

OP	Representative	Value
=	Equal	0
>	Greater	1
<	Less	2
!	Not equal	3

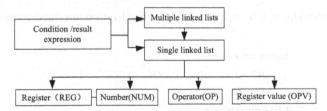

Fig. 4. Condition expression and result expression

b) Number (NUM) definition. The range from 0 to 255.
c) Operator (OP) definition, as shown in Table 3.
d) Register value (REV) definition. The range is 0-0xffff, occupying 2 bytes, from low to high.

3.3 Software Definition of Firework Node

HTML file definition scheme is adopted, which has the characteristics of good visualization and independent of the operating system. The scheme definition is realized by an HTML file, which can be edited by a text editor and opened and browsed by a browser. The scheme corresponding to each node is an HTML file, and each scheme is a table table. Each table stores the scheme expression, which is composed of condition expression and result expression. Both condition expression and result expression are composed of linked list expression. The head and tail of condition expression are contained by tags <th> and < / th >, the head and tail of result expression are contained by tags < td > and < / td >. The condition and result expression are composed of linked list expressions, which contain four fields: register, number, operator, register value. The register defines the input and output modules of RTU (such as DI, DO, AI, AO, etc.). The format of linked list expression: REG + NUM + : + OP + REV.

3.4   Software Definition of Firework Node

Python is a big data programming language, which is well used for web crawler and feature extraction. The expression data of fireworks node can be extracted by extracting scheme features of HTML file with Python program. Feature extraction is mainly divided into three steps:

1) According to the HTML tag table, extract the scheme name. The python regular expression is:
   pattern_scheme = r' <table> (. + ?) </table>'
2) According to the tag th, extract the conditional expression. The python regular expression is:
   pattern_th = r' <th> (. +) </th>'
3) According to the tag TD, extract the result expression. The python regular expression is:
   pattern_td = r'value = (. + ?) > </td>'

For example: Through IE, open the HTML visualization interface, as shown in Fig. 5:

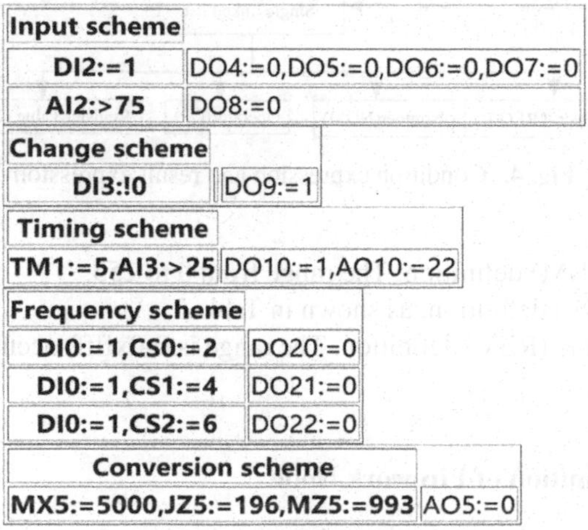

Input scheme	
DI2:=1	DO4:=0,DO5:=0,DO6:=0,DO7:=0
AI2:>75	DO8:=0

Change scheme	
DI3:!0	DO9:=1

Timing scheme	
TM1:=5,AI3:>25	DO10:=1,AO10:=22

Frequency scheme	
DI0:=1,CS0:=2	DO20:=0
DI0:=1,CS1:=4	DO21:=0
DI0:=1,CS2:=6	DO22:=0

Conversion scheme	
MX5:=5000,JZ5:=196,MZ5:=993	AO5:=0

Fig. 5. Software definable interface example

3.5 Data Packaging of Firework Node

1) Modbus communication protocol

RTU has the electrical characteristics of serial interface and Ethernet interface, which conforms to the Modbus specification. The Modbus protocol is shown in Table 4.

Table 4. Modbus protocol format

Address	Function code	Scheme number	Scheme data block	CRC check code

RTU implements five function scheme, each scheme corresponds to a function code, as shown in Table 5

2) Generate scheme data block

Composition of scheme data block:condition expression number of single linked list + condition expression data + result number of single linked list + result expression data. Condition expression data and result expression data are composed of a single linked list data, as shown in Fig. 4.

Table 5. Definition of Function code

Function code	Scheme type
0x81	Input scheme
0x82	Change scheme
0x83	Timing scheme
0x84	Frequency scheme
0x85	Conversion scheme

3) Package into MODBUS message

According to the scheme name and condition / result expression of feature extraction, corresponding to function code and scheme data type, the Modbus message is composed.
For example.
scheme Name: conversion scheme.
Conditional expression:
<th> MX5: = 5000,JZ5: = 196,MZ5: = 993 </th>
Result expression:
<td> AO5: = 0 </td>

The corresponding projec tdata block:
03 06 05 00 88 13 07 00 00 C4 00 08 00 00 E1 03 01 03 05 00 00 00.
Modbus message:
01 85 01 03 06 05 00 88 13 07 00 00 C4 00 08 00 00 E1 03 01 03 05 00 00 00 F6 FF.
Corresponding to Modbus protocol, as shown in Table 6.

Table 6. Message parsing

Address	Function code	Scheme number	Scheme data block	CRC
01	85	01	03 06 05 00 88 13 07 00 00 C4 00 08 00 00 E1 03 01 03 05 00 00 00	F6 FF

3.6 Programmable Implementation of Firework Node

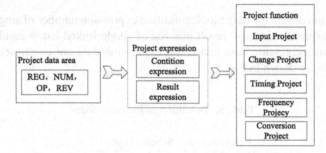

Fig. 6. Process From Data to Function of RTU

RTU receives the Modbus message of the master station through the network port, reads the data in the scheme data area, and translates it into the scheme condition expression and result expression in turn. RTU judges that when the condition expression is met, the result expression will be executed automatically, thus realizing the function of software definable programming. The process from data to function of RTU is shown in Fig. 6.

4   Testing and Comparison

Combined with the traditional cloud architecture system and the edge computing architecture system, the system using fireworks model is compared with them. First, the definition is: the total number of edge node RTUs is N, the number of changing RTUs (indicating that the state changes) is K, the average number of changes is k1, the number of linked RTUs (indicating that the state changes need to be linked) is G, and the average number of links is g1. Set the system to run for 3 days and poll once in 5 min, then the polling times are 24 * 12 * 3 = 864 times, the data flow of each status packet is L = 50 bytes, and the total data flow of heartbeat packet is H = 24 * 6 * 10 * 3 =

4320 (heartbeat once in 10 min, heartbeat six times in one hour, heartbeat message 10 bytes). The communication data flow formula of three systems running for three days is as follows:

1) The communication data flow formula under the traditional cloud computing architecture (due to the constant polling of cloud computing, no heartbeat is required):

$$Z1 = (N * 864 + G * g1) * L \tag{1}$$

2) The communication data flow formula under edge computing architecture:

$$Z2 = (K * k1 + G * g1) * L + H \tag{2}$$

3) The communication data flow formula of fireworks model is applied:

$$Z3 = K * k1 * L + H \tag{3}$$

Table 7. Comparison of data flow test of three architectures

Residential	RTU (Number)	Change RTU		Linkage RTU		Cloud (Mb)	Edge (Mb)	Firework (Mb)
		K	k1	G	g1			
TianRun	182	120	50	63	45	8.342	1.020	0.540
QiaoBai	95	81	56	57	51	4.371	0.534	0.268
ChuangYi	125	90	66	71	53	5.738	0.705	0.367
XinJaiKo	168	150	55	80	45	7.648	0.885	0.495
Total:	727	636	323	583	316	33.247	3.923	2.084

Because K is less than n (not all RTU states change), K1 is less than 864 (RTU state changes are few in 5 min), H value is not very large, from (1) and (2), Z2 value is less than Z1; from (2) and (3), Z3 value is far less than Z2. Therefore, under the edge computing fireworks model architecture, the data flow will be lower than the traditional edge computing architecture and edge computing architecture. In the remote automatic monitoring system test, the same hardware and software and network environment, through the upgrade and transformation of the three architectures, respectively run the test, statistics of the data transmission flow in three days, the statistical results are shown in Table 7.

According to the test results in Table 7, draw the comparison curve of the three architectures, the number of RTUs in operation corresponding to the X axis and the corresponding data transmission flow corresponding to the Y axis, as shown in Fig. 7:

From the comparison curve Fig. 7, it can be seen that the data flow of edge computing and fireworks model is greatly reduced, indicating the importance of edge computing;

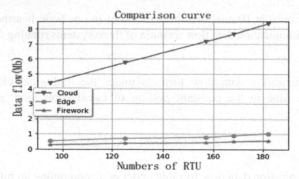

Fig. 7. Data flow comparison curve of three architectures

from the summary of statistical results in Table 7, cloud computing flow: 33.247 mb, edge computing: 3.923 mb, fireworks model: 2.084 mb, edge computing system data flow is 11.8% of cloud computing system, fireworks model system data flow is 53.1% of edge computing system, fireworks model architecture system data flow is the lowest.

5   Conclusions

This paper designs a set of software programmability strategy based on HTML format (independent of operating system), solves the problem of edge node programmability, and makes a concrete application to realize the remote automatic monitoring system based on edge computing fireworks model. The test results show that compared with the centralized data processing of cloud computing architecture, the programmable data processing of fireworks model greatly reduces the communication data flow. Compared with the traditional edge computing data processing, it increases the programmability of edge nodes and reduces the programming difficulty. Fireworks model software can define programming strategy, which has been well applied in the remote automatic monitoring system, and can provide good programming ideas and methods for other edge computing systems. However, to achieve a common programming platform for all edge computing systems needs further research.

Acknowledgement. This work is supported by Natural Science Foundation Project of China (61976118), key topics of the '13th five-year plan' for Education Science in Jiangsu Province (B-b /2020/01/18).

References

1. Dean, J., Ghemawat, S.: Mapreduce: simplified data processing on large clusters. Commun. ACM **51**(1), 107–113 (2008)
2. Isard, M., Budiu, M., Yu, Y., Birrell, A., Fetterly, D.: Dryad: distributed data-parallel programs from sequential building blocks. ACM SIGOPS Oper. Syst. Rev. **41**(3), 59–72 (2007)

3. Saha, B., Shah, H., Seth, S., Vijayaraghavan, G., Murthy, A., Curino, C.: Apache tez: a unifying framework for modeling and building data processing applications. In: Proceedings of the 2015 ACM SIGMOD International Conference on Management of Data, pp. 1357–1369. ACM (2015)
4. Zaharia, M., Chowdhury, M., Franklin, M.J., Shenker, S., Stoica, I.: Spark: cluster computing with working sets. In: Proceedings of the 2nd USENIX Conference on Hot Topics in Cloud Computing, vol. 10, p. 10 (2010)
5. Shvachko, K., Kuang, H., Radia, S., Chansler, R.: The hadoop distributed fifile system. In: 2010 IEEE 26th Symposium on Mass Storage Systems and Technologies (MSST), pp. 1–10. IEEE (2010)
6. Qian, Z., et al.: Timestream: reliable stream computation in the cloud. In: Proceedings of the 8th ACM European Conference on Computer Systems, pp. 1–14. ACM (2013)
7. Akidau, T., et al.: Millwheel: fault tolerant stream processing at internet scale. Proc. VLDB Endowment 6(11), 1033–1044 (2013)
8. Apache storm. https://storm.apache.org/. Accessed 20 Apr 2016
9. Neumeyer, B., Robbins, A.N., Kesari, A.: S4: distributed stream computing platform. In: 2010 IEEE International Conference on Data Mining Workshops (ICDMW), pp. 170–177. IEEE (2010)
10. Kulkarni, S., et al.: Twitter heron: stream processing at scale. In: Proceedings of the 2015 ACM SIGMOD International Conference on Management of Data, pp. 239–250. ACM (2015)
11. IBM: Ibm infosphere streams. www.ibm.com/software/products/en/infosphere-streams. Accessed 20 Apr 2016
12. Zaharia, M., Das, T., Li, H., Hunter, T., Shenker, S., Stoica, I.: Discretized streams: fault-tolerant streaming computation at scale. In: Proceedings of the Twenty-Fourth ACM Symposium on Operating Systems Principles, pp. 423–438. ACM (2013)
13. Liu, Z., Yang, Y., Gu, W., Xia, J.: A multi-tenant usage access model for cloud computing. Comput. Mater. Continua 64(2), 1233–1245 (2020)
14. Shi, W.-S., Sun, H., Cao, J., Zhang, Q., Liu, W.: Edge computing: a new computing model in the age of Internet of things. Comput. Res. Dev. 54(5), 907–924 (2017)
15. Wu, H., et al.: State perception model and application of building equipment based on edge computing. Comput. Res. Dev. 54(5), 907–924 (2017)
16. Jia, Y., et al.: Task migration and collaborative load balancing mechanism based on mobile edge computing. Comput. Sci. 46(12), 126–131 (2019)
17. Liu, P., Ren, H., Shi, X., Li, Y., Cai, Z., et al.: Motransframe: model transfer framework for CNNS on low-resource edge computing node. Comput. Mater. Continua 65(3), 2321–2334 (2020)
18. Zhang, Q., Zhang, X., Zhang, Q., et al.: Firework: big data sharing and processing in collaborative edge environment. In: Proceedings of IEEE/ACM Symposium on Edge Computing (SEC2016), pp. 81–82. IEEE, Piscatawqy (2016)
19. Wu, Z.-G., Zhang, C.-Y., Deng, Q.-G.: Remote terminal design of new electric power dispatching automation system. Comput. Appl. 26(4), 771–773 (2006)

Boolean Functions with a Few Walsh Transform Values

Wengang Jin, Xiaoni Du$^{(\boxtimes)}$, Jinxia Hu, and Yanzhong Sun

College of Mathematics and Statistics, Northwest Normal University,
Lanzhou 730070, Gansu, People's Republic of China

Abstract. Boolean functions have been extensively studied in coding theory, cryptography, sequence design and graph theory. By adding two products of three linear functions to some known bent functions, in this paper, we construct a class of bent functions and obtain their dual functions. In the meantime, a class of semi-bent functions and some classes of five-valued Walsh spectra are given.

Keywords: Boolean functions · Bent functions · Semi-bent functions · Walsh transform · Five-valued Walsh spectra

1 Introduction

Boolean functions are widely used in cryptography, error correction codes [2] and signal sequence design [7]. Their applications in cryptographic systems have been studied for more than three decades. Some important properties of these functions, including balance, nonlinearity and algebraic immunity, are obtained. Walsh transform is a powerful tool to study the properties of Boolean functions in the application of cryptography and coding theory. The Walsh transform of a Boolean function, a discrete Fourier transform, can be used to express the cryptographic properties of a Boolean function.

Bent functions proposed by [14] are Boolean functions with two different Walsh transform values and implements the maximum Hamming distance function to all the affine Boolean functions. Bent functions exist only with even number of variables. Bent functions have been extensively studied because of their interesting algebraic and combinatorial properties and it have received a lot of attention in the literature on communications, because of their multiple applications in cryptography [1], the fields of coding theory [8] and sequence design [13].

No bent function is balanced. As generalizations of bent functions, [5] introduced the concept of semi-bent functions and obtained the balancedness and good nonlinearity in both even and odd number of variables. Moreover, [17,18] proved that bent functions and semi-bent functions are particular cases of the so-called plateaued functions. Like bent functions, semi-bent functions are also widely studied in cryptography. Because they have low Walsh transform values which can provide protection against fast correlation attacks [12] and linear

X. Sun et al. (Eds.): ICAIS 2021, CCIS 1423, pp. 642–655, 2021.
https://doi.org/10.1007/978-3-030-78618-2_53

cryptanalysis [9], they can possess desirable properties such as low autocorrelation, propagation criteria, resiliency, and high algebraic degree. Several new families of semi-bent functions were proposed by [3,4,6,10,15].

In 2014, [11] provided several new effective constructions of bent functions, and then gave several new infinite families of bent functions by adding a product of two linear functions to some known bent functions and their duals. After that, by adding a product of three linear functions to some known bent functions, [16] presented several classes of bent functions. Inspired by those results, in this paper, we firstly add a product of three linear functions to some known bent functions, and then add another product of three linear functions to which one (the added two products are related each other), so we obtain a class of bent functions and their duals. On the other hand, we promote a class of semi-bent functions and some classes of Boolean functions with five-valued Walsh spectra. Finally, a spectrum distribution of some class of Boolean functions with five-valued Walsh spectra is presented.

The paper is organized as follows. In Sect. 2, we introduce some notations and preliminaries. In Sect. 3, we present some bent functions, semi-bent functions and some functions with five-valued Walsh spectra. In Sect. 4, a spectrum distribution of the Boolean functions obtained in Sect. 3 is given. Section 5 concludes the paper.

2   Preliminaries

For a positive integer n, let $\mathbb{F}_{2^n}$ be the finite field with 2^n elements, $\mathbb{F}_{2^n}^* = \mathbb{F}_{2^n} \setminus \{0\}$. Tr_1^n denotes the absolute trace function from $\mathbb{F}_{2^n}$ onto $\mathbb{F}_2$

$$Tr_1^n(x) = x + x^2 + \cdots + x^{2^{n-1}}, \text{ for all } x \in \mathbb{F}_{2^n}.$$

Thus the Walsh transform of a Boolean function f on $\mathbb{F}_{2^n}$ is defined by

$$\hat{f}(a) = \sum_{x \in \mathbb{F}_{2^n}} (-1)^{f(x) + Tr_1^n(ax)}, \text{ for all } a \in \mathbb{F}_{2^n}.$$

Let N_i be the number of $\alpha \in \mathbb{F}_{2^n}$ such that $\hat{f}(\alpha) = v_i$, i.e., $N_i = |\{\alpha \in \mathbb{F}_{2^n} : \hat{f}(\alpha) = v_i\}|$, where $1 \leq i \leq t$ and t is a positive integer. By the properties of Walsh transform, we have the following system of equations:

$$\begin{cases} \sum_{i=1}^{t} N_i = 2^n, \\ \sum_{i=1}^{t} N_i v_i = 2^n (-1)^{f(0)}, \\ \sum_{i=1}^{t} N_i v_i^2 = 2^{2n}, \end{cases} \tag{1}$$

A Boolean function $f : \mathbb{F}_{2^n} \to \mathbb{F}_2$ (n even) is said to be bent if $\hat{f}(\omega) = \pm 2^{\frac{n}{2}}$ for all $\omega \in \mathbb{F}_{2^n}$. Bent functions occur in pair. In fact, given a bent function f

over $\mathbb{F}_{2^n}$, we define its dual function, denoted by $\tilde{f}$, when considering the signs of the values of the Walsh transform $\hat{f}(x)(x \in \mathbb{F}_{2^n})$ of f. More precisely, $\hat{f}$ is defined by

$$\hat{f}(x) = 2^{\frac{n}{2}}(-1)^{\tilde{f}(x)}. \tag{2}$$

A Boolean function $f : \mathbb{F}_{2^n} \to \mathbb{F}_2$ is said to be semi-bent if $\hat{f}(\omega) \in \{0, \pm 2^{\frac{n+2}{2}}\}$ and if $\hat{f}(\omega) \in \{0, \pm 2^{\frac{n+1}{2}}\}$ for all $\omega \in \mathbb{F}_{2^n}$ corresponding to n even and n odd, respectively. It is well known that the algebraic degree of a bent or semi-bent function defined on $\mathbb{F}_{2^n}$ is at most $\frac{n}{2}$ [2].

Let $n = 2m$ be a positive even integer and h be the monomial Niho quadratic function

$$h(x) = Tr_1^m(\lambda x^{2^m+1}), \tag{3}$$

with $\lambda \in \mathbb{F}_{2^m}^*$. It is well known that h is bent, and its dual function $\tilde{h}$ is given (see [11]) by

$$\tilde{h}(x) = Tr_1^m(\lambda^{-1}x^{2^m+1}) + 1. \tag{4}$$

Below we always let $n = 2m$ be an even and $\lambda \in \mathbb{F}_{2^m}^*$.

3 Infinite Families of Bent, Semi-bent and Five-Valued Functions from Monomial Bent Functions

In this section, we give a class of bent functions, its dual function, a class of semi-bent functions and some classes of five-valued Walsh spectra.

We begin with the result presented by [11] that plays an important role. Let f_1, f_2 and f_3 be three pairwise distinct Boolean functions. Then define $g : \mathbb{F}_{2^n} \to \mathbb{F}_2$:

$$g(x) = f_1(x)f_2(x) + f_1(x)f_3(x) + f_2(x)f_3(x). \tag{5}$$

Lemma 1. *[11] Let f_1, f_2 and f_3 be three pairwise distinct bent functions over $\mathbb{F}_{2^n}$ such that $\psi = f_1 + f_2 + f_3$ is bent. Let g be a Boolean function defined by Eq. (5). Then g is bent if and only if $\tilde{f}_1 + \tilde{f}_2 + \tilde{f}_3 + \tilde{\psi} = 0$. Furthermore, if g is a bent function, then $\tilde{g}$ is given by*

$$\tilde{g}(x) = \tilde{f}_1(x)\tilde{f}_2(x) + \tilde{f}_2(x)\tilde{f}_3(x) + \tilde{f}_3(x)\tilde{f}_1(x), \text{ for all } x \in \mathbb{F}_{2^n}.$$

[11] provides several new effective constructions of bent functions based on Eq. (5). Let $f_i, 1 \leq i \leq 3$ be three bent functions given by

$$f_i(x) = Tr_1^m(\lambda x^{2^m+1}) + Tr_1^n(a_i x), a_i \in \mathbb{F}_{2^n}^*,$$

where a_1, a_2 and a_3 are pairwise distinct elements of $\mathbb{F}_{2^n}^*$. After a simple calculation, Mesnager obtained that the Boolean function $g(x) = f_1(x)f_2(x) + f_1(x)f_3(x) + f_2(x)f_3(x) = Tr_1^m(\lambda x^{2^m+1}) + Tr_1^n(ax)Tr_1^n(bx) + Tr_1^n(a_1 x)$, where $a = a_1 + a_3, b = a_1 + a_2$. In the next lemma, Mesnager pointed out that $g(x)$ is a bent function under some conditions.

Lemma 2. *[11] Let $(a, b) \in \mathbb{F}_{2^n}^* \times \mathbb{F}_{2^n}^*$ such that $a \neq b$ and $Tr_1^n(\lambda^{-1}b^{2^m}a) = 0$. Then the Boolean function g defined on $\mathbb{F}_{2^n}$ as $g(x) = Tr_1^m(\lambda x^{2^m+1}) + Tr_1^n(ax)Tr_1^n(bx)$, it is a bent function of algebraic degree 2 and its dual function $\tilde{g}$ is given by*

$$\tilde{g}(x) = 1 + Tr_1^m(\lambda^{-1}x^{2^m+1}) + \left(Tr_1^m(\lambda^{-1}a^{2^m+1}) + Tr_1^n(\lambda^{-1}a^{2^m}x)\right)$$
$$\cdot \left(Tr_1^m(\lambda^{-1}b^{2^m+1}) + Tr_1^n(\lambda^{-1}b^{2^m}x)\right).$$

Then one constructs a new class of Boolean functions and invests their properties by the two lemmas above. Let

$$f_i(x) = Tr_1^m(\lambda x^{2^m+1}) + Tr_1^n(ax)Tr_1^n(a_ix),$$

where a, a_1, a_2, a_3 are pairwise distinct elements of $\mathbb{F}_{2^n}^*$. Hence by Eq. (5), one can obtain

$$\begin{aligned} f(x) &= f_1(x)f_2(x) + f_2(x)f_3(x) + f_1(x)f_3(x) \\ &= Tr_1^m(\lambda x^{2^m+1}) + Tr_1^n(ax)Tr_1^n(a_1x)Tr_1^n((a_2+a_3)x) \\ &\quad + Tr_1^n(ax)Tr_1^n(a_2x)Tr_1^n(a_3x). \end{aligned} \tag{6}$$

Motivated by [16, Lemma 1], we get the following result.

Lemma 3. *Let $h(x)$ be a Boolean function on $\mathbb{F}_{2^n}$, and a, a_1, a_2, a_3 are pairwise distinct elements of $\mathbb{F}_{2^n}^*$. If $f(x)$ is defined as follows*

$$f(x) = h(x) + Tr_1^n(ax)Tr_1^n(a_1x)Tr_1^n((a_2+a_3)x) + Tr_1^n(ax)Tr_1^n(a_2x)Tr_1^n(a_3x),$$

then for any $b \in \mathbb{F}_{2^n}$,

$$\hat{f}(b) = \frac{1}{4}\left(2\hat{h}(b) + \sum_{i=1}^{3}\hat{h}(b+a_i) - \hat{h}(b+\sum_{i=1}^{3}a_i) + 2\hat{h}(a+b)\right.$$
$$\left. - \sum_{i=1}^{3}\hat{h}(a+b+a_i) + \hat{h}(a+b+\sum_{i=1}^{3}a_i)\right).$$

Proof. For any $(\varepsilon_1, \varepsilon_2, \varepsilon_3) \in \mathbb{F}_2^3$, we define the set

$$T(\varepsilon_1, \varepsilon_2, \varepsilon_3) = \{x \in \mathbb{F}_{2^n}|Tr_1^n(a_1x) = \varepsilon_1, Tr_1^n(a_2x) = \varepsilon_2, Tr_1^n(a_3x) = \varepsilon_3\}$$

and integer

$$S_{(\varepsilon_1,\varepsilon_2,\varepsilon_3)}(b) = \sum_{x \in T(\varepsilon_1,\varepsilon_2,\varepsilon_3)} (-1)^{h(x)+Tr_1^n(bx)}.$$

Then for any $b \in \mathbb{F}_{2^n}$ and $(\varepsilon_1, \varepsilon_2, \varepsilon_3) \in \mathbb{F}_2^3$, we have

$$
\begin{aligned}
\hat{f}(b) &= \sum_{x \in \mathbb{F}_{2^n}} (-1)^{f(x) + Tr_1^n(bx)} \\
&= \sum_{x \in \mathbb{F}_{2^n}} (-1)^{h(x) + Tr_1^n(ax) Tr_1^n(a_1 x) Tr_1^n((a_2 + a_3)x)} \\
&\quad \cdot \sum_{x \in \mathbb{F}_{2^n}} (-1)^{Tr_1^n(ax) Tr_1^n(a_2 x) Tr_1^n(a_3 x) + Tr_1^n(bx)} \\
&= \sum_{wt(\varepsilon_1, \varepsilon_2, \varepsilon_3) \leq 1} S_{(\varepsilon_1, \varepsilon_2, \varepsilon_3)}(b) + \sum_{2 \leq wt(\varepsilon_1, \varepsilon_2, \varepsilon_3)} S_{(\varepsilon_1, \varepsilon_2, \varepsilon_3)}(a + b) \\
&= \hat{h}(b) - \sum_{2 \leq wt(\varepsilon_1, \varepsilon_2, \varepsilon_3)} \left(S_{(\varepsilon_1, \varepsilon_2, \varepsilon_3)}(b) - S_{(\varepsilon_1, \varepsilon_2, \varepsilon_3)}(a + b) \right), \qquad (7)
\end{aligned}
$$

One can immediately have $wt(\varepsilon_1, \varepsilon_2, \varepsilon_3)$ is the Hamming weight of the vector $(\varepsilon_1, \varepsilon_2, \varepsilon_3)$.

From the definitions of $S_{(\varepsilon_1, \varepsilon_2, \varepsilon_3)}(b)$ we have

$$
\begin{aligned}
8 S_{(\varepsilon_1, \varepsilon_2, \varepsilon_3)}(b) &= 8 \sum_{x \in \mathbb{F}_{2^n}} (-1)^{h(x) + Tr_1^n(bx)} \prod_{i=1}^{3} \frac{1 + (-1)^{\varepsilon_i + Tr_1^n(a_i x)}}{2} \\
&= \hat{h}(b) + \sum_{\substack{d_i \in \mathbb{F}_2 \\ 1 \leq i \leq 3}} (-1)^{\sum_{i=1}^{3} d_i \varepsilon_i} \hat{h}\left(b + \sum_{i=1}^{3} d_i a_i\right), \qquad (8)
\end{aligned}
$$

for $2 \leq wt(\varepsilon_1, \varepsilon_2, \varepsilon_3)$, substitute $a + b$ for b in the above equation, we get

$$
8 S_{(\varepsilon_1, \varepsilon_2, \varepsilon_3)}(a + b) = \hat{h}(a + b) + \sum_{\substack{d_i \in \mathbb{F}_2 \\ 1 \leq i \leq 3}} (-1)^{\sum_{i=1}^{3} d_i \varepsilon_i} \hat{h}\left(a + b + \sum_{i=1}^{3} d_i a_i\right). \qquad (9)
$$

Applying Eqs. (8) and (9) to Eq. (7), and after a simple calculation, we get

$$
\begin{aligned}
4 \hat{f}(b) &= 2\hat{h}(b) + \sum_{i=1}^{3} \hat{h}(b + a_i) - \hat{h}\left(b + \sum_{i=1}^{3} a_i\right) + 2\hat{h}(a + b) \\
&\quad - \sum_{i=1}^{3} \hat{h}(a + b + a_i)) + \hat{h}\left(a + b + \sum_{i=1}^{3} a_i\right).
\end{aligned}
$$

This completes the proof. □

In the following, we assume that $A = Tr_1^m(\lambda^{-1} b^{2^m + 1})$. Replace $h(x)$ with $Tr_1^m(\lambda x^{2^m + 1})$ in Lemma 3, which happens to be Eq. (6), then after a tedious calculation by using Eqs. (2)–(4), we obtain

$$\hat{f}(b) = \frac{1}{4}(-2^m)(-1)^A \left(2 + \sum_{i=1}^{3}(-1)^{c_i} - (-1)^{\sum_{i=1}^{3}(c_i+t_i)} + 2(-1)^{c_4} \right.$$

$$\left. - \sum_{i=1}^{3}(-1)^{c_i+c_4+t_{i+3}} + (-1)^{\sum_{i=1}^{4}c_i+\sum_{i=1}^{6}t_i} \right), \tag{10}$$

where

$c_i = Tr_1^m(\lambda^{-1}(b^{2^m}a_i + ba_i^{2^m} + a_i^{2^m+1})), c_4 = Tr_1^m(\lambda^{-1}(b^{2^m}a + ba^{2^m} + a^{2^m+1})),$
$t_1 = Tr_1^n(\lambda^{-1}a_1^{2^m}a_2), \qquad\qquad t_2 = Tr_1^n(\lambda^{-1}a_2^{2^m}a_3),$
$t_3 = Tr_1^n(\lambda^{-1}a_3^{2^m}a_1), \qquad\qquad t_{i+3} = Tr_1^n(\lambda^{-1}a^{2^m}a_i),$

for $1 \leq i \leq 3$.

Remark 1. In fact, since a, a_1, a_2, a_3 are pairwise distinct elements of $\mathbb{F}_{2^n}^*$, if a, a_1, a_2, a_3 are linear dependent over $\mathbb{F}_2$, we have the following two cases holds:

(1) If $a + a_i + a_j = 0, i \neq j$, then the three cases are corresponding to the result with [11].

(2) If $\sum_{i=1}^{3} a_i = 0$ or $a + \sum_{i=1}^{3} a_i = 0$, then the two cases are the same with the result of [16].

Below we always put $t_0 = \sum_{i=1}^{3} t_i$ modulo 2.

Now we discuss the properties of the function defined in Eq. (6).

Theorem 1. *With the notation as above. Let a, a_1, a_2, a_3 are linear independent over $\mathbb{F}_2$. If $(t_4, t_5, t_6) = (0, 0, 0)$, then $f(x)$ in Eq. (6) is a bent function if and only if $t_0 = 0$. Furthermore, the dual function $\tilde{f}(x)$ of the bent function $f(x)$ in Eq. (6) is given by*

$$\tilde{f}(x) = \tilde{f}_1(x)\tilde{f}_2(x) + \tilde{f}_2(x)\tilde{f}_3(x) + \tilde{f}_1(x)\tilde{f}_3(x)$$

$$= 1 + Tr_1^m(\lambda^{-1}x^{2^m+1}) + \left(Tr_1^n(\lambda^{-1}a^{2^m}x) + Tr_1^m(\lambda^{-1}a^{2^m+1}) \right)$$

$$\left(\sum_{1 \leq i < j \leq 3} \left(Tr_1^n(\lambda^{-1}a_i^{2^m}x) + Tr_1^m(\lambda^{-1}a_i^{2^m+1}) \right) \right.$$

$$\left. \cdot \left(Tr_1^n(\lambda^{-1}a_j^{2^m}x) + Tr_1^m(\lambda^{-1}a_j^{2^m+1}) \right) \right).$$

Proof. Let $\varphi(x) = \sum_{i=1}^{3} f_i(x) = Tr_1^m(\lambda x^{2^m+1}) + Tr_1^n(ax)Tr_1^n(\sum_{i=1}^{3} a_i x)$. Since $t_4 = t_5 = t_6 = 0$, i.e., $Tr_1^n(\lambda^{-1}a^{2^m}a_i) = 0$ for $1 \leq i \leq 3$, by Lemma 2 we find that f_1, f_2, f_3, φ are all bent functions and their dual functions $\tilde{f}_1, \tilde{f}_2, \tilde{f}_3, \tilde{\varphi}$ are given by

$$\tilde{f}_i(x) = 1 + Tr_1^m(\lambda^{-1}x^{2^m+1}) + Tr_1^m(\lambda^{-1}a^{2^m+1})$$

$$+ Tr_1^n(\lambda^{-1}a^{2^m}x)\left(Tr_1^m(\lambda^{-1}a_i^{2^m+1}) + Tr_1^m(\lambda^{-1}a_i^{2^m}x) \right),$$

and

$$\tilde{\varphi}(x) = 1 + Tr_1^m(\lambda^{-1}x^{2^m+1}) + Tr_1^m(\lambda^{-1}a^{2^m+1}) + Tr_1^n(\lambda^{-1}a^{2^m}x)$$

$$\left(Tr_1^m(\lambda^{-1}(\sum_{i=1}^{3}a_i)^{2^m+1}) + Tr_1^n(\lambda^{-1}(\sum_{i=1}^{3}a_i)^{2^m}x)\right).$$

Assume that $0 = \sum_{i=1}^{3}\tilde{f}_i(x) + \tilde{\varphi}(x)$, which is equivalent to

$$\left(Tr_1^n(\lambda^{-1}a^{2^m+1}) + Tr_1^n(\lambda^{-1}a^{2^m}x)\right)\left(\sum_{i=1}^{3}Tr_1^m(\lambda^{-1}a_i^{2^m+1})\right.$$

$$\left. + Tr_1^m(\lambda^{-1}(\sum_{i=1}^{3}a_i)^{2^m+1})\right) = 0,$$

for all $x \in \mathbb{F}_{2^m}$, hence the equation holds if and only if $Tr_1^n(\lambda^{-1}(a_1^{2^m}a_2 + a_1^{2^m}a_3 + a_2^{2^m}a_3)) = 0$. Thus the result follows from Lemma 1.

The dual function $\tilde{f}$ of the bent function $f(x)$ then follows from Lemmas 1–2. □

Remark 2. The condition $t_0 = 0$ in Theorem 1 implies that $(t_1, t_2, t_3) \in \{(1,1,0), (0,1,1), (1,0,1), (0,0,0)\}$. Thus, if $(t_1, t_2, t_3) = (0,0,0)$, then Theorem 1 can be easily obtained by [19, Corollary 4.2]. Even though the function constructed in Eq. (6) is contained in the function in [19, Corollary 4.2], where the other three cases are not discussed.

Theorem 2. *Let* a, a_1, a_2, a_3 *are linear independent over* $\mathbb{F}_2$. *If* $(t_0, t_4, t_5, t_6) = (0,1,1,1)$, *then* $f(x)$ *in Eq. (6) is a semi-bent function.*

Proof. If $(t_0, t_4, t_5, t_6) = (0,1,1,1)$, then Eq. (10) can be written as

$$\hat{f}(b) = \frac{1}{4}(-2^m)(-1)^A\left(2 + 2(-1)^{c_4} + \sum_{i=1}^{3}(-1)^{c_i} - (-1)^{\sum_{i=1}^{3}c_i}\right.$$

$$\left. - \sum_{i=1}^{3}(-1)^{c_i+c_4+1} + (-1)^{\sum_{i=1}^{4}c_i+1}\right).$$

So if $c_4 = 0$, we have

$$\hat{f}(b) = \frac{1}{2}(-2^m)(-1)^A(2 + \sum_{i=1}^{3}(-1)^{c_i} + (-1)^{\sum_{i=1}^{3}c_i+1})$$

$$= \begin{cases} -2^{m+1}(-1)^A, & wt(c_1, c_2, c_3) \leq 1, \\ 0, & 2 \leq wt(c_1, c_2, c_3), \end{cases}$$

and if $c_4 = 1$, we have

$$\hat{f}(b) = \frac{1}{4}(-2^m)(-1)^A(0) = 0.$$

According to the definition of semi-bent function, we find that $f(x)$ is a semi-bent function.   □

Theorem 3. *With the notation defined as above, we have*

(1) *If $(t_0, t_4, t_5, t_6) = (1,1,1,1)$, then $f(x)$ in Eq. (6) is five-valued and the Walsh spectrum of f is $\{0, \pm 2^m, \pm 3 \cdot 2^m\}$.*

(2) *If $(t_0, t_4, t_5, t_6) \in \mathbb{F}_2^4 \backslash \{(0,0,0,0), (0,1,1,1), (1,1,1,1)\}$, then $f(x)$ is five-valued and the Walsh spectrum of f is $\{0, \pm 2^m, \pm 2^{m+1}\}$.*

Proof. We only give the proof for the case of (1) since the other case can be proved in the same manner.

(1) If $(t_0, t_4, t_5, t_6) = (1,1,1,1)$, then Eq. (10) can be reduced as

$$\hat{f}(b) = \frac{1}{4}(-2^m)(-1)^A \left(2 + 2(-1)^{c_4} + \sum_{i=1}^{3}(-1)^{c_i} - (-1)^{\sum_{i=1}^{3} c_i + 1}\right.$$
$$\left. - \sum_{i=1}^{3}(-1)^{c_i + c_4 + 1} + (-1)^{\sum_{i=1}^{4} c_i}\right).$$

Thus if $c_4 = 0$, we have

$$\hat{f}(b) = \begin{cases} 3 \cdot 2^m (-1)^{A+1}, & wt(c_1, c_2, c_3) = 0, \\ 2^m (-1)^A, & wt(c_1, c_2, c_3) = 3, \\ 2^m (-1)^{A+1}, & \text{otherwise.} \end{cases}$$

And if $c_4 = 1$, we have

$$\hat{f}(b) = \frac{1}{4}(-2^m)(-1)^A (0) = 0.$$

The remaining cases of proof are similar to that of $(t_0, t_4, t_5, t_6) = (1,1,1,1)$, so we omit it here.   □

Let $m = 6$ and ξ be a primitive element in $\mathbb{F}_{2^6}$ such that $\xi^6 + \xi^4 + \xi^3 + \xi + 1 = 0$.

Example 1. Let $\lambda = a = 1, a_1 = \xi, a_2 = \xi^5, a_3 = \xi^7$. Then we have $(t_0, t_4, t_5, t_6) = (0,0,0,0)$ and it was verified by a Magma program that

$$f(x) = Tr_1^3(x^9) + Tr_1^6(x)Tr_1^6(\xi x)Tr_1^6((\xi^5 + \xi^7)x) + Tr_1^6(x)Tr_1^6(\xi^5 x)Tr_1^6(\xi^7 x)$$

is a bent function. This is consistent with our result in Theorem 1.

Example 2. Let $\lambda = a = 1, a_1 = \xi^3, a_2 = \xi^6, a_3 = \xi^{12}$. Then we have $(t_0, t_4, t_5, t_6) = (0,1,1,1)$ and it was verified by a Magma program that

$$f(x) = Tr_1^3(x^9) + Tr_1^6(x)Tr_1^6(\xi^3 x)Tr_1^6((\xi^6 + \xi^{12})x) + Tr_1^6(x)Tr_1^6(\xi^6 x)Tr_1^6(\xi^{12} x)$$

is a semi-bent function. This is consistent with our result in Theorem 2.

Example 3. (1) If $\lambda = 1, a = \xi, a_1 = \xi^3, a_2 = \xi^9, a_3 = \xi^{13}$, then we have $(t_0, t_4, t_5, t_6) = (1, 1, 1, 1)$ and it was verified by a Magma program that

$$f(x) = Tr_1^3(x^9) + Tr_1^6(\xi x)Tr_1^6(\xi^3 x)Tr_1^6((\xi^5 + \xi^{13})x) + Tr_1^6(\xi x)Tr_1^6(\xi^5 x)Tr_1^6(\xi^{13} x)$$

has $\{0, \pm 2^3, \pm 3 \cdot 2^3\}$ five-valued Walsh spectra.

(2) If $\lambda = a = 1, a_1 = \xi, a_2 = \xi^2, a_3 = \xi^4$, then we have $(t_0, t_4, t_5, t_6) = (1, 0, 0, 0)$ and it was verified by a Magma program that

$$f(x) = Tr_1^3(x^9) + Tr_1^6(x)Tr_1^6(\xi x)Tr_1^6((\xi^2 + \xi^4)x) + Tr_1^6(x)Tr_1^6(\xi^2 x)Tr_1^6(\xi^4 x)$$

has $\{0, \pm 2^3, \pm 2^4\}$ five-valued Walsh spectra.

4   The Walsh Spectrum of the Functions Given in Section 3

In this section, we give a spectrum distribution of the Boolean functions proposed in Sect. 3 with five-valued Walsh spectra.

Theorem 4. *Let a, a_1, a_2, a_3 are linear independent over $\mathbb{F}_2$. Then for $f(x)$ given by Eq. (6), the following statements hold:*

(1) If $(t_0, t_4, t_5, t_6) = (1, 1, 1, 1)$, then the spectrum distribution of $f(x)$ is

$$\hat{f}(b) = \begin{cases} (-1)^A 3 \cdot 2^m, & 2^{n-5} + (-1)^A 2^{m-4}(1 + \sum_{i=1}^{3}(-1)^{t_i}) \text{ times,} \\ (-1)^A 2^m, & 7 \cdot 2^{n-5} + (-1)^A 2^{m-4}(5 - 3\sum_{i=1}^{3}(-1)^{t_i}) \text{ times,} \\ 0, & 2^{n-1} \text{ times.} \end{cases}$$

(2) If $(t_0, t_4, t_5, t_6) = (1, 0, 0, 0)$, then the spectrum distribution of $f(x)$ is

$$\hat{f}(b) = \begin{cases} (-1)^A 2^{m+1}, & 2^{n-4} \text{ times,} \\ (-1)^A 2^m, & 2^{n-2} + (-1)^A 2^{m-1} \text{ times,} \\ 0, & 3 \cdot 2^{n-3} \text{ times.} \end{cases}$$

(3) For other cases, the spectrum distribution of $f(x)$ is

$$\hat{f}(b) = \begin{cases} (-1)^{A+1} 2^{m+1}, & 2^{n-4} + (-1)^{A+1} 2^{m-3}(1 - (-1)^\delta) \text{ times,} \\ (-1)^A 2^m, & 2^{n-2} + (-1)^A 2^{m-2}(1 + (-1)^\delta) \text{ times,} \\ 0, & 3 \cdot 2^{n-3} \text{ times,} \end{cases}$$

with

$$\delta = \begin{cases} t_1, & \text{if } (t_0, t_4, t_5, t_6) = (0, 0, 0, 1), \\ t_2, & \text{if } (t_0, t_4, t_5, t_6) = (0, 1, 0, 0), \\ t_3, & \text{if } (t_0, t_4, t_5, t_6) = (0, 0, 1, 0), \\ t_1 + 1, & \text{if } (t_0, t_4, t_5, t_6) \in \{(0, 1, 1, 0), (1, 0, 0, 1), (1, 1, 1, 0)\}, \\ t_2 + 1, & \text{if } (t_0, t_4, t_5, t_6) \in \{(0, 0, 1, 1), (1, 1, 0, 0), (1, 0, 1, 1)\}, \\ t_3 + 1, & \text{if } (t_0, t_4, t_5, t_6) \in \{(0, 1, 0, 1), (1, 0, 1, 0), (1, 1, 0, 1)\}. \end{cases}$$

Proof. We only prove $(t_0, t_4, t_5, t_6) = (0, 0, 0, 1)$, i.e., $\delta = t_1$ in (3), since the other cases can be proved in the same method. If $(t_0, t_4, t_5, t_6) = (0, 0, 0, 1)$, then from Eq. (10) we have

$$\hat{f}(b) = \frac{1}{4}(-2^m)(-1)^A \left(2 + 2(-1)^{c_4} + \sum_{i=1}^{3}(-1)^{c_i} + (-1)^{\sum_{i=1}^{3} c_i + 1}\right.$$

$$\left. + \sum_{i=1}^{2}(-1)^{c_i + c_4 + 1} + (-1)^{c_3 + c_4} + (-1)^{\sum_{i=1}^{4} c_i + 1}\right).$$

So if $c_4 = 0$, we have

$$\hat{f}(b) = \begin{cases} 2^m(-1)^{A+1}, & (c_1, c_2, c_3) \in \{(0,0,0), (0,0,1), (1,1,0), (1,1,1)\}, \\ 2^{m+1}(-1)^{A+1}, & (c_1, c_2, c_3) \in \{(1,0,0), (0,1,0)\}, \\ 0, & (c_1, c_2, c_3) \in \{(1,0,1), (0,1,1)\}, \end{cases} \quad (11)$$

and if $c_4 = 1$, we have

$$\hat{f}(b) = \begin{cases} 2^m(-1)^{A+1}, & (c_1, c_2) = (0,0), \\ 2^m(-1)^A, & (c_1, c_2) = (1,1), \\ 0, & (c_1, c_2) \in \{(0,1), (1,0)\}. \end{cases} \quad (12)$$

Now we figure out the number of $b \in \mathbb{F}_{2^n}$ such that $\hat{f}(b) = 2^{m+1}$, i.e., $c_4 = 0, A = 1$. Let N_1 denote the number of $b \in \mathbb{F}_{2^n}$ such that $(c_1, c_2, c_3, c_4, A) \in \{(1,0,0,0,1), (0,1,0,0,1)\}$. Then we have

$$N_1 = \sum_{b \in \mathbb{F}_{2^n}} \left(\frac{1 + (-1)^{c_4}}{2} \cdot \frac{1 + (-1)^{c_1 + 1}}{2} \cdot \frac{1 + (-1)^{c_2}}{2} \cdot \frac{1 + (-1)^{c_3}}{2} \cdot \frac{1 + (-1)^{A+1}}{2} \right.$$

$$\left. + \frac{1 + (-1)^{c_4}}{2} \cdot \frac{1 + (-1)^{c_1}}{2} \cdot \frac{1 + (-1)^{c_2 + 1}}{2} \cdot \frac{1 + (-1)^{c_3}}{2} \cdot \frac{1 + (-1)^{A+1}}{2} \right)$$

$$= \frac{1}{2^5} \sum_{\substack{d_i \in \mathbb{F}_2 \\ 1 \leq i \leq 4}} \sum_{b \in \mathbb{F}_{2^n}} \left((-1)^{\sum_{i=1}^{4} d_i c_i + d_1} + (-1)^{\sum_{i=1}^{4} d_i c_i + d_2} \right.$$

$$\left. + (-1)^{\sum_{i=1}^{4} d_i c_i + d_1 + A + 1} + (-1)^{\sum_{i=1}^{4} d_i c_i + d_2 + A + 1} \right).$$

To calculate N_1, we first consider $N_{11} = \sum_{\substack{d_i \in \mathbb{F}_2 \\ 1 \leq i}} \sum_{b \in \mathbb{F}_{2^n}} (-1)^{\sum_{i=1}^{4} d_i c_i + d_1}$ and $N_{12} =$

$\sum_{\substack{d_i \in \mathbb{F}_2 \\ 1 \leq i}} \sum_{b \in \mathbb{F}_{2^n}} (-1)^{\sum_{i=1}^{4} d_i c_i + d_2}$, from the definitions of $c_i, 1 \leq i \leq 3$, we have

$$N_{11} = \sum_{\substack{d_i \in \mathbb{F}_2 \\ 1 \le i \le 4}} \sum_{b \in \mathbb{F}_{2^n}} (-1)^{\sum\limits_{i=1}^{3} Tr_1^m(d_i \lambda^{-1}(b^{2^m} a_i + b a_i^{2^m} + a_i^{2^m+1}))}$$

$$\cdot (-1)^{Tr_1^m(d_4 \lambda^{-1}(b^{2^m} a + b a^{2^m} + a^{2^m+1})) + d_1}$$

$$= \sum_{\substack{d_i \in \mathbb{F}_2 \\ 1 \le i \le 4}} (-1)^{Tr_1^m(\lambda^{-1}(\sum\limits_{i=1}^{3} d_i a_i^{2^m+1} + d_4 a^{2^m+1})) + d_1}$$

$$\cdot \sum_{b \in \mathbb{F}_{2^n}} (-1)^{Tr_1^m(\lambda^{-1}(b^{2^m}(\sum\limits_{i=1}^{3} d_i a_i + d_4 a) + b(\sum\limits_{i=1}^{3} d_i a_i + d_4 a)^{2^m}))}$$

Note that a_1, a_2, a_3 and a are linear independent, that is, we have $\sum\limits_{i=1}^{3} d_i a_i + d_4 a \ne 0$ if and only if $(d_1, \cdots, d_4) \ne (0, \cdots, 0)$. If $(d_1, \cdots, d_4) \in \mathbb{F}_2^4 \setminus \{(0, \cdots, 0)\}$, then we have

$$\sum_{b \in \mathbb{F}_{2^n}} (-1)^{Tr_1^m(\lambda^{-1}(b^{2^m}(\sum\limits_{i=1}^{3} d_i a_i + d_4 a) + b(\sum\limits_{i=1}^{3} d_i a_i + d_4 a)^{2^m}))} = 0$$

since $\lambda \ne 0$. Therefore, we obtain

$$N_{11} = \begin{cases} 2^n, & (d_1, \cdots, d_4) = (0, \cdots, 0), \\ 0, & \text{otherwise.} \end{cases}$$

Then by a similar argument, we can also have $N_{12} = N_{11}$.

Now we considered $N_{13} = \sum\limits_{\substack{d_i \in \mathbb{F}_2 \\ 1 \le i \le 4}} \sum\limits_{j=1}^{2} \sum\limits_{b \in \mathbb{F}_{2^n}} (-1)^{\sum\limits_{i=1}^{4} d_i c_i + A + d_j + 1}$, then we have

$$N_{13} = \sum_{\substack{d_i \in \mathbb{F}_2 \\ 1 \le i \le 4}} \sum_{j=1}^{2} \sum_{b \in \mathbb{F}_{2^n}} (-1)^{\sum\limits_{i=1}^{3} d_i Tr_1^m(\lambda^{-1}(b^{2^m} a_i + b a_i^{2^m} + a_i^{2^m+1}))}$$

$$\cdot (-1)^{d_4 Tr_1^m(\lambda^{-1}(b^{2^m} a + b a^{2^m} + a^{2^m+1}))} \cdot (-1)^{Tr_1^m(\lambda^{-1} b^{2^m+1}) + d_j + 1}$$

$$= \sum_{\substack{d_i \in \mathbb{F}_2 \\ 1 \le i \le 4}} \sum_{j=1}^{2} (-1)^{\sum\limits_{i=1}^{2} Tr_1^n(\lambda^{-1} d_i d_{i+1} a_{i+1}^{2^m}) + Tr_1^n(\lambda^{-1} d_3 d_1 a_3^{2^m} a_1)}$$

$$\cdot (-1)^{\sum\limits_{i=1}^{3} d_i Tr_1^n(\lambda^{-1} d_i d_4 a_i^{2^m} a) + d_j + 1} \cdot \sum_{b \in \mathbb{F}_{2^n}} (-1)^{Tr_1^m(\lambda^{-1}(b + \sum\limits_{i=1}^{3} d_i a_i + d_4 a)^{2^m+1})}.$$

Note that $\displaystyle\sum_{b\in \mathbb{F}_{2^n}} (-1)^{Tr_1^m(\lambda^{-1}(b+\sum_{i=1}^{3} d_i a_i+d_4 a)^{2^m+1})} = -2^m$ from the bentness of $Tr_1^m(\lambda^{-1}x^{2^m+1})$. Thus, one can obtain that N_{13} can expressed as

$$N_{13} = \sum_{\substack{d_i\in \mathbb{F}_2 \\ 1\leq i\leq 4}} \sum_{j=1}^{2} 2^m(-1)^{\sum_{i=1}^{2} d_i d_{i+1} t_i + d_1 d_3 t_3 + \sum_{i=1}^{3} d_4 d_i t_{i+3}+d_j}.$$

So we get

$$N_1 = \frac{1}{2^5}(N_{11} + N_{12} + N_{13})$$

$$= 2^{n-4} + 2^{m-4}\Big(3 - (-1)^{t_4} + \sum_{i=5}^{6}(-1)^{t_i} - (-1)^{t_3} - (-1)^{t_1} + (-1)^{t_2}$$

$$-(-1)^{t_3+t_4+t_6} - (-1)^{t_0} + (-1)^{t_2+t_5+t_6} - (-1)^{t_1+t_4+t_5} - (-1)^{\sum_{i=1}^{6} t_i}\Big)$$

$$= 2^{n-4} + 2^{m-3}(1 - (-1)^{t_1}).$$

Let N_2 denote the number of $b \in \mathbb{F}_{2^n}$ such that $\hat{f}(b) = 0$. It then follows from Eqs. (11) and (12) that $\hat{f}(b) = 0$ for any $(c_1, c_2, c_3, c_4) \in \{(1,0,1,0), (0,1,1,0), (0,1,0,1), (0,1,1,1), (1,0,0,1), (1,0,1,1)\}$. It is the same as the calculation of N_{11}, we have

$$N_2 = \frac{1}{2^4}\sum_{\substack{d_i\in \mathbb{F}_2 \\ 1\leq i\leq 4}}\sum_{b\in \mathbb{F}_{2^n}} \Big((-1)^{\sum_{i=1}^{4} d_i c_i+d_1+d_3} + (-1)^{\sum_{i=1}^{4} d_i c_i+d_2+d_3} + (-1)^{\sum_{i=1}^{4} d_i c_i+d_2+d_4}$$

$$+(-1)^{\sum_{i=1}^{4} d_i c_i+d_2+d_3+d_4} + (-1)^{\sum_{i=1}^{4} d_i c_i+d_1+d_4} + (-1)^{\sum_{i=1}^{4} d_i c_i+d_1+d_3+d_4}\Big)$$

$$= \frac{1}{2^4}(2^n + 2^n + 2^n + 2^n + 2^n + 2^n)$$

$$= 3 \cdot 2^{n-3}.$$

Let $n_1 = |\{b \in \mathbb{F}_{2^n} : \hat{f}(b) = 2^m\}|, n_2 = |\{b \in \mathbb{F}_{2^n} : \hat{f}(b) = -2^m\}|$, and $n_3 = |\{b \in \mathbb{F}_{2^n} : \hat{f}(b) = -2^{m+1}\}|$. Then from Eq. (1) we have

$$\begin{cases} 2^n = n_1 + n_2 + n_3 + 2^{n-4} + 2^{m-3} - 2^{m-3}(-1)^{t_1} + 3 \cdot 2^{n-3}, \\ 2^n = 2^m \cdot n_1 - 2^m \cdot n_2 - 2^{m+1} \cdot n_3 + 2^{m+1} \cdot (2^{n-4} + 2^{m-3} - 2^{m-3}(-1)^{t_1}), \\ 2^{2n} = (2^m)^2 \cdot (n_1 + n_2) + (-2^{m+1})^2 \cdot n_3 + (2^{m+1})^2 \\ \quad \cdot (2^{n-3} + 2^{m-3} - 2^{m-3}(-1)^{t_1}). \end{cases}$$

After a simple calculation, we have

$$\begin{cases} n_1 = 2^{n-4} + 2^{m-3} + 2^{m-3}(-1)^{t_1}, \\ n_2 = 2^{n-4} - 2^{m-3} - 2^{m-3}(-1)^{t_1}, \\ n_3 = 2^{n-4} - 2^{m-3} + 2^{m-3}(-1)^{t_1}. \end{cases}$$

$\square$

5   Conclusion

In this paper, a class of bent functions and their dual functions are constructed according to [11]. In addition, we obtain a class of semi-bent functions and some classes of five-valued Walsh spectra. Then according to the Magma program, we can see that the conclusion is consistent with our result in this paper.

References

1. Canteaut, A., Carlet, C., Charpin, P., Fontaine, C.: On cryptographic properties of the cosets of r(1, m). IEEE Trans. Inf. Theory **47**(4), 1494–1513 (2001). https://doi.org/10.1109/18.923730
2. Carlet, C.: Boolean functions for cryptography and error correcting codes. In: Crama, Y., Hammer, P. (eds.) Chapter of the Monography Boolean Models and Methods in Mathematics, Computer Science, and Engineering, pp. 257–397 (2010)
3. Carlet, C., Mesnager, S.: On semibent Boolean functions. IEEE Trans. Inf. Theory **58**(5), 3287–3292 (2012). https://doi.org/10.1109/TIT.2011.2181330
4. Charpin, P., Pasalic, E., Tavernier, C.: On bent and semi-bent quadratic Boolean functions. IEEE Trans. Inf. Theory **51**(12), 4286–4298 (2005). https://doi.org/10.1109/TIT.2005.858929
5. Chee, S., Lee, S., Kim, K.: Semi-bent functions. In: Pieprzyk, J., Safavi-Naini, R. (eds.) ASIACRYPT 1994. LNCS, vol. 917, pp. 105–118. Springer, Heidelberg (1995). https://doi.org/10.1007/BFb0000428
6. Khoo, K., Gong, G., Stinson, D.R.: A new characterization of semi-bent and bent functions on finite fields. Des. Codes Cryptogr. **38**(2), 279–295 (2006). https://doi.org/10.1007/s10623-005-6345-x
7. Khoo, K.: Sequence design and construction of cryptographic Boolean functions. Ph. D. Thesis, University Waterloo (Canada) (2004)
8. MacWilliams, F.J., Sloane, N.J.A.: The Theory of Error Correcting Codes. North-Holland, New York (1977)
9. Matsui, M.: Linear cryptanalysis method for DES cipher. In: Helleseth, T. (ed.) EUROCRYPT 1993. LNCS, vol. 765, pp. 386–397. Springer, Heidelberg (1994). https://doi.org/10.1007/3-540-48285-7_33
10. Mesnager, S.: Semi-bent functions from Dillon and Niho exponents, Klooster-man sums, and Dickson polynomials. IEEE Trans. Inf. Theory **57**(11), 7443–7458 (2011). https://doi.org/10.1109/TIT.2011.2160039
11. Mesnager, S.: Several new infinite families of bent functions and their duals. IEEE Trans. Inf. Theory **60**(7), 4397–4407 (2014). https://doi.org/10.1109/TIT.2014.2320974
12. Meier, W., Staffelbach, O.: Fast correlation attacks on stream ciphers. In: Barstow, D., et al. (eds.) EUROCRYPT 1988. LNCS, vol. 330, pp. 301–314. Springer, Heidelberg (1988). https://doi.org/10.1007/3-540-45961-8_28
13. Olsen, J., Scholtz, R.A., Welch, L.: Bent-function sequences. IEEE Trans. Inf. Theory **28**(6), 858–864 (1982). https://doi.org/10.1109/TIT.1982.1056589
14. Rothaus, O.S.: On bent functions. J. Comb. Theory Ser. A **20**(3), 300–305 (1976). https://doi.org/10.1016/0097-3165(76)90024-8
15. Wolfmann, J.: Special bent and near-Bent functions. Adv. Math. Commun. **8**(1), 21–33 (2014). https://doi.org/10.3934/amc.2014.8.21

16. Xu, G., Cao, X., Xu, S.: Several classes of Boolean functions with few Walsh transform values. Appl. Algebra Eng. Commun. Comput. **28**(2), 155–176 (2016). https://doi.org/10.1007/s00200-016-0298-3
17. Zheng, Y., Zhang, X.-M.: Plateaued functions. In: Varadharajan, V., Mu, Y. (eds.) ICICS 1999. LNCS, vol. 1726, pp. 284–300. Springer, Heidelberg (1999). https://doi.org/10.1007/978-3-540-47942-0_24
18. Zheng, Y., Zhang, X.-M.: Relationships between bent functions and complementary plateaued functions. In: Song, J.S. (ed.) ICISC 1999. LNCS, vol. 1787, pp. 60–75. Springer, Heidelberg (2000). https://doi.org/10.1007/10719994_6
19. Zheng, L., Peng, J., Kan, H., Li, Y.: Several new infinite families of bent functions via second order derivatives. Cryptogr. Commun. **12**(6), 1143–1160 (2020). https://doi.org/10.1007/s12095-020-00436-0

Research on Automation Strategy of Coq

Hanwei Qian[✉]

Jiangsu Police Institute, Nanjing 210013, China
qianhanwei@jspi.edu.cn

Abstract. Formal verification technology based on theorem proving assistant is the only way to strictly guarantee the correctness of the program system. The theorem proof assistant expresses the theorems and the proof process in high-order logic as high-level strategies, but human experts must manually construct proofs by inputting the strategies into the proof assistant. In this article, we propose the use of machine learning and concurrent search methods to improve the degree of automation of theorem proofs, which can help theorem assistants find suitable proof strategies faster and reduce the workload of constructing proofs. Our solution can generate effective tactics and can be used to prove theorems by automated methods more quickly.

Keywords: Automation strategy · Proof assistant · Machine learning · Parallel search

1 Introduction

Formal verification technology is the only way to strictly guarantee the correctness of the program system, especially the theorem proving method. Because it overcomes the problem of the state explosion in model checking, it has good scalability. In the past ten years, many universities and research institutions around the world have carried out formal design and verification studies using Coq [1] and other theorem proving assistants as tools. Some operating systems, compilers and other large-scale basic software verification work have achieved a series of important Results. At present, the correctness of kernel functions of operating system software such as CertiKOS [2] and seL4 [3] have been effectively proved.

Although the current formal verification work has made considerable progress, the formal verification technology based on theorem proof still faces considerable challenges. On the one hand, the workload of formal verification is very large. In the verification process, theorem proving requires a lot of manual participation. Especially in large-scale software such as operating systems, the problem of verification workload is more prominent. For example, in the CertiKOS project, the proof of about 6,500 lines of C code involves 900,000 lines of Coq script code [4]. The μC/OS-II system kernel uses 1400 lines of C code with 220,000 lines of Coq script code. At the same time, some source code changes may cause a huge workload of re-verification [5]. On the other hand, the labor cost of formal verification is very high. Verification assistants such as Coq have very high requirements for verifiers, requiring them to have a deep formal theoretical foundation and a deep understanding of the verified software. In the process of software development practice, formal methods such as Coq theorem assistants cannot be used for software development. It is widely accepted by the authors that these factors severely restrict the application of formal methods to the process of verifying more large-scale important software.

2 Automation in Automated Theorem Provers

2.1 The Evolution of Automatic Strategies

At present, the theorem prover used in formal verification is mainly tools such as Coq and Isabelle [6]. Isabelle is a high-order logic-based prover jointly developed by Paulson of the University of Cambridge in the United Kingdom and Nipkow of the Technical University of Munich in 1986. Isabelle is written in functional language ML and uses natural deduction rules to prove theorems. The proof verification work is carried out under the framework provided by meta-logic, so it can support multiple logic systems. Coq is a high-level logic-based prover developed by the French National Institute of Information Technology (INRIA), written by OCaml code and a small amount of C code. Originally derived from a comprehensive dependent type and polymorphic type system developed by Coquand [7], it was later expanded to add some good properties of the axiomatization of inductive data type algorithms, forming an inductive construction calculus.

In order to reduce the verification script workload of the theorem prover and reduce the cost of formal verification, CSIRO's data61 developed a series of related tools for formal verification based on Isabelle, covering all stages of software verification work [8], such as C Parser [9] and AutoCorres[10] tools can automatically convert C programs into higher-level monadic representations with consistent semantics, simplifying the formal verification of C code and reducing the manual workload in the verification process.

Iris [11] is a high-level concurrent separation logic library of Coq, which encapsulates the verified modules or commonly used proof conclusions into a theorem library, reuses the proved results, reduces the workload of manual participation, and reduces the difficulty of proof. SmtCoq is a constraint solver implemented in Coq [12]. Coqsmtcheck can prove simple mathematical propositions related to real numbers [13]. Smt4coq is an automatic proof strategy for proving mathematical propositions related to 32-bit machine integers in Coq. It improves the degree of automation of Coq by calling the constraint solver Z3 in Coq. The proof of some propositions is converted to the problem of solving SAT [14], Satisfiability is automatically given by the machine, which reduces the overhead of the user's manual verification program and greatly reduces the proof scripts for integer math propositions. VST-Floyd first automatically compiles the C program into the corresponding abstract syntax tree, and generates Verifiable C code that is more in line with the Coq syntax rules, helping users to use the functional correctness proof of the C program [15]. During the certification process, VST-Floyd provided a set of semi-automatic Coq strategies.

2.2 Auto Strategy Mechanism of Coq

Automatic proof auto strategy is the most used strategy in Coq. Through auto strategy, Coq can help realize automatic proof of some theorems conveniently, without manual giving. If there is no proof, it will always take the same time from the beginning of the search strategy in Coq to the prompt failure. Because all strategy combinations within a given depth have been tried, regardless of the order in which strategies are used, the time required by the system is always the sum of the strategy time. When there is a proof, the optimal situation is that the strategy selected every time is correct, and the worst situation is that the correct strategy is finally selected. The difference between the optimal situation and the worst situation is relatively large, so modifying the proof strategy or searching the theorem is preferred. The level may greatly affect the solution speed of the auto strategy.

In fact, for many specific types of problems, such as the extensive application of basic inductive definitions of natural numbers in the proof process of number theory, the proof process follows certain fixed patterns. In this case, if the automatic proof strategy has a choice, heuristic search is used Technology, can greatly improve the efficiency of automatic proof search strategy. Through machine learning reinforcement learning and rule learning algorithms, using a large number of existing proof scripts for a specific application scenario as a data set, train a proof model that meets the characteristics of certain theorem proving scenarios, and let the theorem proving assistant Coq according to the code and The logical feature intelligently selects the proof strategy and application, improves the speed of automatic proof, strengthens the ability of automatic proof, and reduces the process of manual participation in the proof.

3 Automatic Proof Strategy Learning

3.1 Scripting Code Strategy Language Model

Through data analysis and training of specific scenario proof scripts, learn the optimal search strategy for automatic theorem proving in specific scenarios. Make full use of hardware computing power, increase the concurrency of Coq's strategy search through multi-threading and other technologies, and thereby further improving the automatic proof ability of Coq's auto strategy. Design a suitable neural network for training, learn the optimal search strategy according to the existing theorem proof script of a specific scenario, and assign the most reasonable priority to each theorem.

Similar to the language model in natural language processing, the probability distribution between different words is different, and the probability distribution between different theorems is also different. The language model is the modeling of the probability distribution of sentences. According to the C-H isomorphism, the proof calculus of the natural reasoning system has the same structure as the λ-calculus of the functional programming model, and the process of theorem proving is also the process of constructing a program. Take the proposition imp_trans as an example.

$$imp\_trans \,:\, (P-> Q)-> (Q-> R)-> P-> R \tag{1}$$

$$fun\ imp\ :\ (H : P->Q)\ (H' : Q->R)(p : P) => H'(H\,p) \qquad (2)$$

The imp_trans is a λ-term fun imp, the proof of Q is obtained by applying H to p, and then the proof of H' applying on Q gets the proof of R. This reasoning method is often used in the proof According to the syllogism method, the probability of the connection between the theorem H and H is obviously much higher than the connection between H and other theorems.

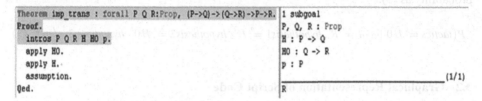

Fig. 1. Proof of imp_trans in Coq.

Theorem proving in Coq is a backward process. The user starts with the theorem itself as the initial goal and repeatedly apply tactics to decompose the goal into a list of sub goals. The proof is complete when there are no sub-goals left. Proving is a process of trial and error; the user may try a tactic to decompose the current goal, analyze the feedback from Coq, and backtrack to the previous step to try a different tactic.

Each step of the proof is to choose an appropriate strategy all in the current environment, transform the goal or theorem, and make the hypothesis get closer and closer to the goal. As shown in Fig. 1, it is known that under the premise of the current environment (H, H0, p) and the target R, the probability of selecting the apply H0 strategy for reasoning should be the highest.

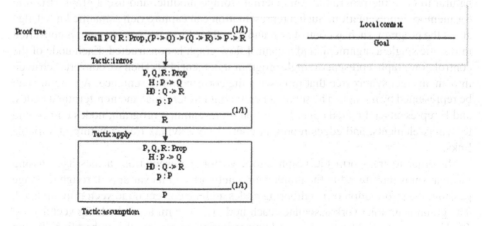

Fig. 2. Proof tree of imp_trans.

A successful Coq proof implicitly generates a proof tree whose root is the original theorem and whose nodes are goals, see Fig. 2. All goals share the same environment, but have a unique local context with premises local to each goal. The edges of the proof tree are tactics; they can be simple strings, can have arguments at various positions, and can be combined into compound tactics.

From the perspective of neural network training, the learning task is to input the environment and target value in a certain proof process, and the network is required to correctly predict the use of the strategy apply H0, that is, to maximize the probability as (3).

$$P\left(tactics =' H0'|goal =' R', hypothesis1 =' H', hypothesis2 =' H0', hypothesis3 =' p'\right) \quad (3)$$

3.2 Graphical Representation of Script Code

The complexity of the script code is not conducive to understanding and analysis. Graphical representation programs such as proof trees, abstract syntax trees, control flow, and data flow are conducive to further analysis, and it is also convenient to vectored graphics and use neural networks for training [19, 20]. These program diagrams not only encode the program text, but also encode semantic information, which can be obtained through standard compilation tools. The proof tree is a tree graph generated by the theorem proof process, where each node corresponds to the application of a certain proof strategy, the top node comes from the current environment and current context of Coq, and each subtree corresponds to the need to solve a sub-objective Proof strategy [21].

We encodes the current goal and premises into vectors. We include the entire local context and up to 10 premises in the environment, excluding a large number of premises imported from libraries [22]. A model could be more powerful if it is capable of selecting relevant premises from the entire environment, but that is left for future research.

The reasoning proves to be carried out in the given context of the program. It is natural to code the program as an external storage module, and use a graph structure for memory representation. Such a representation can capture rich semantic knowledge about the program, such as control flow and data flow. First, a given program is converted into static single assignment, and a control flow graph is constructed. Each node of the control flow graph represents a single program statement [17]. Then we convert each node into an abstract syntax tree that represents the corresponding sentence. A program can be represented by a graph. The set of nodes V contains terminal and non-terminal nodes, and E represents a directed edge. In a graph representing a program, nodes correspond to syntax elements, and edges represent control flow, syntax tree structure or variable links.

In order to transform the graph into a vector representation, a message passing mechanism is introduced in the graph neural network and its variants, through message passing, the information of neighboring nodes and the current node vector are updated. The graph neural network associates each node $v \in V$ with an embedding vector $\mu_v \in R^d$. Use general neighborhood embedding to iteratively update the embedding. Taking x in a graph neural network as an example, the adjacent nodes x_1, x_2, and x update their vector as (4).

$$\mu_v^{(l+1)} = h\left(\left\{\mu_v^{(l)}\right\}_{u\in N^k(v), k\in\{1,2,\dots,K\}}\right) \qquad (4)$$

Through the messages sent by x_1, x_2. Where h is a nonlinear function, repeat this process for L steps, and use it to aggregate neighborhood information to update the embedding. $N^k(v)$ is the set of neighbor nodes connected to v with edge type k. The parameterization takes the edge types into account. The specific parameterization used is shown (5) (6) below.

$$\mu_v^{(l+1),k} = \sigma\left(\sum_{u\in N^k(v)} W_2\mu_v^{(l+1)}, \forall k \in \{1, 2, \dots, K\}\right) \qquad (5)$$

$$\mu_v^{(l+1)} = \sigma\left(W_3\left[\mu_v^{(l+1),1}, \mu_v^{(l+1),2}, \dots, \mu_v^{(l+1),K}\right]\right) \qquad (6)$$

If x_v represents the syntax information of node v, such as token or constant value in the program. Matrices W_3 are learnable model parameters, and σ is some nonlinear activation function. The model parameters are learnable matrices, and the model function is a nonlinear activation function. The model parameters are trained through information such as the edge type of the program graph and the connection between nodes, and the finally trained node and edge parameters are the vectored representation of the graph. Matrices W_1 is initialized to zero.

$$\mu_v^{(0)} = W_1 x_v \qquad (7)$$

3.3 Training and Inference

We train the model on the proof steps extracted from the script code. When expanding a node using a production rule, we apply the cross-entropy loss to maximize the likelihood of the ground truth production rule. However, when the model emits a tactic argument, there may be no corresponding argument in the ground truth; because the model might have generated a different tactic from the ground truth. For example, the model may output 'apply H' with an argument H, while the ground truth may be split without any argument.

To apply a reasonable loss in this scenario, we could train the model with forcing learning. During the sequential generation of a tactic AST, the model outputs how to expand the partial tree, but the tree grows following the ground truth, not the model's output [23]. Then the arguments generated by the model must correspond to those in the ground truth, and we can apply losses normally.

During testing, we combine the model with depth-first search for fully-automated theorem proving. At each step, the model samples a few tactics via beam search, which are used to search for a complete proof via DFS [24]. We prune the search space by backtracking when a duplicate proof state is detected.

All of these automated tactics either prove the goal completely or leave the goal unchanged; they do not decompose the goal into sub-goals. We combine the tactics with them as follows: At each step, the agent first uses an automated tactic to see if it can solve the current goal [25]. If not, the agent executes a tactic from tactics to decompose the goal into sub-goals.

4 Parallel Search in Automatic Strategy

4.1 Parallel Search Feasibility

Decompose the large search task into small tasks that can be executed in parallel, and design a multi-threaded framework to replace the existing auto strategy search process. On the one hand, Coq's automatic proof capability is limited by the depth of the strategy search. As the depth deepens, the search space grows exponentially, causing the explosion of the search space [26]. On the other hand, the performance of Coq's automated search is limited by the concurrency of the system, so automated proof capability of Coq has not been effectively improved with the substantial increase in hardware capabilities. The principle of Auto strategy is to use a strategy library to act on the initial target, and loop until all the targets are proven. If there is a sub-goal that cannot be proven, the action process is cancelled and the initial target is returned [27]. That is to say, the second strategy can only be carried out after the first strategy is determined and the strategy is applied to the target. Repeatedly, the use of the latter strategy is completely dependent on the previous strategy, which proves that the dependence between strategies is determined [28]. The serialization of the proof process. Like Post's problem, the theorem proving reasoning is an undecidable problem. The reasoning steps in the theorem proving can be infinite [16], so the space for the theorem proving is also infinite, and there is no fixed algorithm to prove the theorem. Derive through manual participation.

In fact, in most program verification, most of the reasoning problems involved in the nature of the program we care about are deduced within a limited number of steps. In most projects, the proof of each theorem does not exceed hundreds of lines. Therefore, if the total number of proof steps is fixed, the theorem we want to prove is a decidable problem under the premise that the proof exists [29]. There are combinations of automatic search in the strategy library with the theorem number n and the search depth d. The limited search space is reasonably divided, and the search task is divided into multiple small tasks to run in different threads [30]. The strategy library is searched by different threads to improve the concurrent processing efficiency and performance of Coq.

4.2 Parallel Framework Design

Coq is written by OCaml code and a small amount of C code, but the current main version of OCaml does not really support multi-core programs. Domainslib is a domain-level parallel programming library [18], which extends the multi-core of OCaml and provides the control and data structure in parallel programming using domains. For example, channels can be used in multiple senders and Process communication is shared among receivers, and the task structure is a work-stealing pool with asynchronous/waiting parallel processing.

The domainslib concurrent programming library, decompose the search strategy task into multiple small tasks that are not re-combined and sent, and search for suitable theorem proving strategies. Make full use of the hardware computing power, preprocess the combination of theorem strategies in advance, and use the Hash function as the K-V form to save the repeated results and equivalent theorems, reduce repeated searches, and narrow the search space [31, 32].

5 Conclusion

Research on methods and techniques such as modular verification and theorem reuse, develop and improve new Coq and other theorem proving assistants and verification tools, improve the degree of automation in the formal verification process, reduce the process of manual participation, reduce the difficulty of verification personnel, and control verification cost.

Theorem prover is currently used to prove complex mathematical theorems and verify large-scale software systems, but the formalization of theorem prover is not mature enough. There are still deficiencies in the theorem prover technology. It is necessary to better support the theorem library for automatic proof, which can allow better knowledge sharing between the theorem proving systems, the multi-core calculation and verification of the theorem, and better support for machine learning and depth Mining technology for proof guidance and automation, these problems are being solved by more researchers. The improvement and maturity of verification technology and tools based on theorem proof prove that the popularization and application of engineering industry will become possible, and the correctness and safety of some safety-critical software systems such as operating systems will also be fundamentally solved.

References

1. Coq Homepage. http://coq.inria.fr/. Accessed 21 Dec 2020
2. CertiKOS Homepage. http://flint.cs.yale.edu/certikos/. Accessed 21 Dec 2020
3. Klein, G., et al.: seL4: formal verification of an OS kernel. In: Proceedings of the ACM SIGOPS 22nd Symposium on Operating Systems Principles, pp. 207–220. ACM, New York (2009)
4. Gu, R., et al.: CertiKOS: an extensible architecture for building certified concurrent OS kernels. In: 12th Symposium on Operating Systems Design and Implementation, pp. 653–669. USENIX, Berkeley (2016)
5. Xu, F., Fu, M., Feng, X., Zhang, X., Zhang, H., Li, Z.: A practical verification framework for preemptive OS kernels. In: Chaudhuri, S., Farzan, A. (eds.) CAV 2016. LNCS, vol. 9780, pp. 59–79. Springer, Cham (2016). https://doi.org/10.1007/978-3-319-41540-6_4
6. Isabelle Homepage. https://isabelle.in.tum.de/. Accessed 21 Dec 2020
7. Brauer, W., Salomaa, A., Rozenberg, G., Paulin-Mohring, C.: Coq'Art: the calculus of inductive constructions. Springer, Berlin. (2004). https://doi.org/10.1007/978-3-662-07964-5
8. Proof-engineering Homepage. https://ts.data61.csiro.au/projects/TS/proof-engineering/. Accessed 21 Dec 2020
9. C Parser Homepage. https://github.com/seL4/l4v/tree/master/tools/c-parser. Accessed 21 Dec 2020
10. Greenaway, D., Andronick, J., Klein, G.: Bridging the gap: Automatic verified abstraction of C. In: Beringer, L., Felty, A. (eds.) ITP 2012. LNCS, vol. 7406, pp. 99–115. Springer, Heidelberg (2012). https://doi.org/10.1007/978-3-642-32347-8_8
11. Iris project Homepage. https://iris-project.org/. Accessed 21 Dec 2020
12. SMTCoq Homepage. https://smtcoq.github.io/. Accessed 21 Dec 2020
13. Coq-smt-check Homepage. https://github.com/gmalecha/coq-smt-check. Accessed 21 Dec 2020

14. Armand, M., Faure, G., Grégoire, B., Keller, C., Théry, L., Werner, B.: A modular integration of SAT/SMT solvers to Coq through proof witnesses. In: Jouannaud, J.-P., Shao, Z. (eds.) CPP 2011. LNCS, vol. 7086, pp. 135–150. Springer, Heidelberg (2011). https://doi.org/10.1007/978-3-642-25379-9_12

15. Cao, Q., Beringer, L., Gruetter, S., Dodds, J., Appel, A.W.: VST-Floyd: a separation logic tool to verify correctness of C programs. J. Autom. Reason. **61**(1), 367–422 (2018)

16. Huth, M., Ryan, M.: Logic in Computer Science: Modelling and reasoning about systems. Cambridge University Press, Cambridge (2004)

17. Si, X., Dai, H., Raghothaman, M., Naik, M., Song, L.: Learning loop invariants for program verification. In: Neural Information Processing Systems, December 2018

18. Domainslib Homepage. https://github.com/ocaml-multicore/domainslib. Accessed 21 Dec 2020

19. Wenzel, M., Wiedijk, F.: A comparison of Mizar and Isar. J. Autom. Reason. **29**(3), 389–411 (2002)

20. Urban, J., Hoder, K., Voronkov, A.: Evaluation of automated theorem proving on the Mizar Mathematical Library. In: Fukuda, K., Hoeven, J. van der, Joswig, M., Takayama, N. (eds.) ICMS 2010. LNCS, vol. 6327, pp. 155–166. Springer, Heidelberg (2010). https://doi.org/10.1007/978-3-642-15582-6_30

21. Shiraz, S., Hasan, O.: A library for combinational circuit verification using the HOL theorem prover. IEEE Trans. Comput. Aided Des. Integr. Circuits Syst. **37**(2), 512–516 (2017)

22. Blanchette, J.C., Böhme, S., Paulson, L.C.: Extending Sledgehammer with SMT solvers. J. Autom. Reason. **51**(1), 109–128 (2013)

23. Hong, W., Nawaz, M., Zhang, X., Li, Y., Sun, M.: Using Coq for formal modeling and verification of timed connectors. In: Cerone, A., Roveri, M. (eds.) SEFM 2017. LNCS, vol. 10729, pp. 558–573. Springer, Cham (2018). https://doi.org/10.1007/978-3-319-74781-1_37

24. Gauthier, T., Kaliszyk, C., Urban, J., Kumar, R., Norrish, M.: TacticToe: learning to prove with tactics. J. Autom. Reason. **65**(2), 257–286 (2020). https://doi.org/10.1007/s10817-020-09580-x

25. Faithfull, A., Bengtson, J., Tassi, E., Tankink, C.: Coqoon. In: Chechik, M.., Raskin, J..-F. (eds.) TACAS 2016. LNCS, vol. 9636, pp. 316–331. Springer, Heidelberg (2016). https://doi.org/10.1007/978-3-662-49674-9_18

26. Eén, N., Sörensson, N.: An extensible SAT-solver. In: Giunchiglia, E., Tacchella, A. (eds.) SAT 2003. LNCS, vol. 2919, pp. 502–518. Springer, Heidelberg (2004). https://doi.org/10.1007/978-3-540-24605-3_37

27. Ekici, B., et al.: SMTCoq: a plug-in for integrating SMT solvers into Coq. In: Majumdar, R., Kunčak, V. (eds.) CAV 2017. LNCS, vol. 10427, pp. 126–133. Springer, Cham (2017). https://doi.org/10.1007/978-3-319-63390-9_7

28. Czajka, L., Kaliszyk, C.: Hammer for Coq: automation for dependent type theory. J. Autom. Reason. **61**(1), 423–453 (2018)

29. Cohen, C., Rouhling, D.: A formal proof in Coq of LaSalle's invariance principle. In: Ayala-Rincón, M.., Muñoz, C.A. (eds.) ITP 2017. LNCS, vol. 10499, pp. 148–163. Springer, Cham (2017). https://doi.org/10.1007/978-3-319-66107-0_10

30. Boldo, S., Lelay, C., Melquiond, G.: Formalization of real analysis: a survey of proof assistants and libraries. Math. Struct. Comput. Sci. **26**(7), 1196–1233 (2016)

31. Boldo, S., Lelay, C., Melquiond, G.: Coquelicot: a user-friendly library of real analysis for Coq. Math. Comput. Sci. **9**(1), 41–62 (2015)
32. Brown, C.E.: Reducing higher-order theorem proving to a sequence of SAT problems. J. Autom. Reason. **51**(1), 57–77 (2013)

A Model Design of Blockchain-Based Data Storage for E-Government Application

Jizhou Chen[1,2], Xianghui Liu[3(✉)], Wenbao Han[2], and Jieren Cheng[2]

[1] Guangdong Provincial Administration of Government Service and Data, Guangzhou, China
[2] School of Computer and Cyberspace Security, Hainan University, Haikou, China
[3] Telecommunications Planning and Design Institute Co., Ltd., Changsha, China

Abstract. E-government is a gradual system engineering, which needs to integrate new information technology. In e-government application scenarios, a large number of data (i.e. text, audio, video, graphics and animation) are managed by platforms maintained by data providers, which usually adopt centralized architecture design. However, this centralized architecture may lead to a single point of failure and data ownership disputes. It is difficult to ensure the integrity of the data and track the trusted traceability of data usage. In order to solve these problems, this paper proposes a cost-effective blockchain data storage framework for e-government data management. Generally speaking, in the field of e-government data management, the application trend of blockchain can be summarized into two aspects: one is to lay the foundation for the development of public services and government management through the establishment of identity authentication system based on blockchain; the other is to make use of the characteristics of blockchain, which can not be tampered with and has full historical records, so that the information resources of different institutions can be connected, which can achieve the goal Now the definition of data ownership and the traceability of data access.

Keyword: Blockchain · Data storage · E-government application

1 Introduction

Since the emergence of E-government in the 1990s, there are many definitions of e-government, which are constantly updated with the development of practice.

The economic and Social Council of the United Nations defines e-government as a way for the government to organize public management through the intensive use of information and communication technology and strategic application. It aims to improve efficiency, enhance the transparency of the government, improve financial constraints, improve the quality of public policies and the scientificity of decision-making, and establish good inter governmental, governmental and social, community, and government and citizen In order to improve the quality of public services and win extensive social participation.

The world bank believes that e-government is mainly concerned about the use of information technology (such as the world wide web, the Internet and mobile computing) by government agencies to give government departments unique capabilities to transform their relationships with citizens, enterprises and government departments. These technologies can serve different purposes: to provide more effective government services to citizens, to improve the relationship between government and enterprises and industries, to better fulfill citizenship through the use of information, and to increase the efficiency of government management. The resulting revenue can reduce corruption, provide transparency, facilitate government services, increase government revenue or reduce government operating costs.

E-government is a systematic project, which should meet three basic conditions.

First E-government is a comprehensive service system that must rely on electronic information hardware system, digital network technology and related software technology; hardware part: including internal LAN, external Internet, system communication system and dedicated lines; software part: large database management system, information transmission platform, authority management platform, document formation and approval upload system, news There are dozens of systems, such as publishing system, service management system, policy and regulation release system, user service and management system, personnel and file management system, welfare and housing provident fund management system, etc.

Second, e-government is an integrated system dealing with public affairs and internal affairs related to the government. It includes not only the administrative affairs within the government, but also the management affairs of the legislative, judicial and other public organizations, such as procuratorial affairs, judicial affairs and community affairs.

Third, e-government is a new, advanced and revolutionary administrative system. E-government is not simply to move the traditional government management affairs to the Internet, but to restructure its organizational structure and business process. Therefore, there are significant differences between e-government management and traditional government management.

In the application of blockchain, it is a new topic in the field of e-government to combine it with government governance and public services. The government digital transformation planning based on blockchain technology is of great significance to reshape the data sharing, transparency and trust between the government and citizens. At present, in the field of E-government in China, there have been theoretical exploration and practical cases of blockchain application. Based on the actual situation of China's e-government, this paper explores the specific use cases of blockchain technology in China's e-government, and analyzes its application effect.

2 Blockchain-Based Data Storage

In this section, we present our data storage approach for e-government applications using blockchain technology. First, the data storage process is analysed. Secondly, the overall architecture design is presented to give a systematic view of blockchain-based data storage. Thirdly, the identity management and access control mechanisms are proposed.

2.1 Data Storage Process

The data of e-government consist of different data types, including diagrams, text, videos, audios, etc. Figure 1 illustrates the data storage process of e-government applications, in which each task indicates the services that should be supported in a data storage platform.

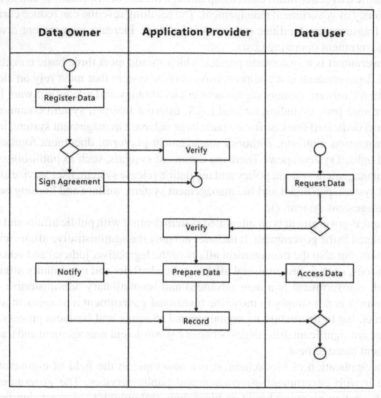

Fig. 1. Data of e-government process

Combined with the actual scenario of e-government application, we simplify the roles into three categories: data owner, application provider and data user.

The first is the data registration process. Data owners register through the platform provided by application providers, while application providers rely on the platform for data verification and data storage services.

Then there is the use of data. The data user submits the data use request, the application provider verifies the request and data, and then prepares the data to feed back to the data user, notifies the owner of the data access information, and records the data request and access for future data audit and tracking.

It should be emphasized that the above simplified data processing process also depends on the sharing of government information resources. The sharing of government information resources is a mechanism of using information resources within the government and between the government and the outside of the government on the basis of certain policy system, incentive measures and security. The purpose is to improve the level of public management and public service. The content and purpose of government information resource sharing are different at different levels of demand. In practice, to formulate reasonable goals and strategies according to different levels of demand, we need more certain policy guarantee and economic incentive measures, otherwise it is difficult to achieve government information resource sharing in practice. The sharing of government information resources involves the most basic data storage issues, as well as related data ownership, trusted traceability and other issues, which is the application point of the close combination of blockchain technology and e-government applications.

2.2 Model Design

In the blockchain system, the node as a complete node stores complete blockchain data, which can effectively ensure the data security of the blockchain [32], that is, the data security of the blockchain is guaranteed through the high redundancy storage mechanism. This section will design the basic model and key technologies of blockchain storage by combining with the typical bitcoin model with high redundancy storage mechanism. The storage model of blockchain can be abstracted into two layers, namely data layer and network consensus layer. Blockchain network is essentially a P2P network, the node status is the same. After the miner node calculates the correct nonce value, the miner node broadcasts it to the whole blockchain network. After receiving the block, other nodes verify it and link the new block to their own stored blockchain.

Data Layer. A complete block consists of a block head and a block body. The block head contains the version number and the hash value of the previous block; the difficulty of the current block, the random value nonce of the current block solved by POW; the time stamp of the current block and the Merkle root of all transactions in the current block. The block body contains the number of transactions in the current block and all verified transactions.

Chain structure is the core of blockchain data structure. When new blocks are generated, miners add them to the end of the blockchain. Blocks are linked in turn to form complete blockchain data, Merkle root is an important part to connect the block head and block body. Merkle root can quickly summarize and check the existence of transactions in the block and the integrity of the block. First, all transactions in the block are grouped and hashed; then, the calculated hash values are inserted into the Merkle tree; then, these hash values are grouped and hashed again, The time stamp indicates the generation time of the current block, so all blocks in the blockchain are arranged in chronological order. The time stamp can be used as a proof of the existence of blocks, which improves the unforgeability and tamperability of the blockchain, Hash function has good properties such as unidirectionality, easy calculation and anti-collision.in addition, the data generated by hash function has fixed length hash value. These characteristics make hash function very suitable for application in blockchain. Encryption technology, especially asymmetric encryption, is used to protect the security of blockchain data.

Network Consensus Layer. The network consensus layer includes the composition of blockchain network, message propagation mechanism, data verification mechanism and consensus mechanism. The nodes in bitcoin and other public chain networks are distributed and can enter and leave freely, so the P2P network is used to form the blockchain network. In P2P network, each node has the same status, and each node has the same function, Message propagation mechanism means that when a new block is generated, its miners will be broadcast to other nodes in the blockchain network for verification. Data verification means that any node will listen to the transactions broadcast in the blockchain network and the new block at any time. After receiving the transactions broadcast by other nodes, the node will broadcast to other nodes for verification. To verify its effectiveness: if the transaction is valid, it will be added to the transaction pool to store the valid transactions that have not been added to the block; if the transaction is invalid, it will be deleted. Consensus mechanism is the core of the network consensus layer in the storage model, which can make the nodes in the blockchain network reach consensus efficiently and maintain the consistency of the blockchain. In order to solve a mathematical problem which is difficult to calculate but simple to verify, the node who first solves the problem has the right of accounting and can get a certain economic reward.

2.3 Protocols for Data Storage

This section describes key protocols designed for data storage, including DIDmanagement process, access notifying process, access granting process, and version control process. Please note that in this study, we focus on the on-chain business logic as the traditional data storage scheme are mature.

DID Management for Self-Sovereign Identity. Each user needs to register through DIDand use blockchain account to register did. The registered DIDrepresents the identity of the user in the platform. Note that when this service is called, a blockchain transaction is created to send DDoS to the blockchain. After successful registration, record the DIDand its corresponding DDO in the DIDregistry.

Registered DIDcan be viewed through DIDparsing to demonstrate DDO to users. DDO contains the user's public key, which is used to verify the user's digital signature and the service endpoint for personal interaction. If the DDO data changes, the user can call the DDO update to upload the new information. Finally, when the DIDis useless, it can be revoked, and then the stored DDO can be removed from the DIDregistry. Please note that DDO update and DIDrevocation can only be performed by the DIDowner who has control over the relevant blockchain account, and any other malicious operation of forging DIDwill be rejected.

Access Notifying. User interaction through data storage. The data owner uploads the sensitive information of the data to the data registry through data registration, while the original file is stored in the off chain data repository, because the current blockchain technology does not support the storage of large or complex data (documents, images, videos). Registration needs to be checked by the application provider. The application provider can manually verify whether the data meets the requirements in some e-government links, or apply its existing automatic procedures. At the same time, the data accessed by the data user will be recorded for later data audit, ownership traceability and use tracking.

Offline Storage. Offline storage is a method to transfer the data content from the original block body to the offline storage system. Only the "pointer" and other non data information pointing to these data are stored in the block body to solve the scalability problem of blockchain storage. When the complete data needs to be stored, the original data is saved to the non blockchain system, and at the same time, The unique identification of the data is generated according to certain rules and returned to the blockchain system; when the complete data needs to be accessed, the original data is searched in the non blockchain storage system through the unique identification of the data.

In the off chain storage mode, the block head or important data is still stored in the blockchain ledger, and the original block and other data are stored by the off chain storage system. In the new block, the access records and other information of accessing the off chain storage system can be stored, while the "pointer" information pointing to the off chain storage system can be stored in the new block, According to the structure of bitcoin blocks, the size of a block is about 1 m, while the size of the block head of a block is 80 byte. Therefore, from the perspective of storage efficiency, offline storage can greatly reduce the pressure of block storage.

3 Implementation

3.1 Architecture

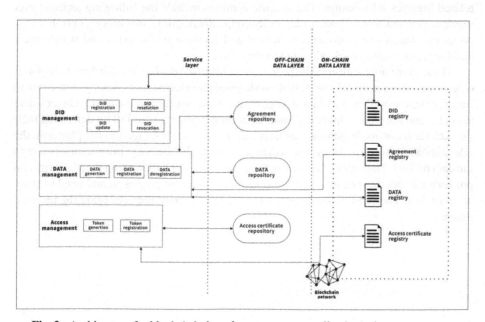

Fig. 2. Architecture for blockchain-based e-government application's data management

Figure 2 shows the overall architecture design of the system from the perspective of platform users, including data owners, service providers and end users, and analyzes the above management process. The architecture consists of three layers: service layer, off chain data layer and on chain data layer. Firstly, the service layer consists of different management services: did management, data management and access management. Each type of service is provided by at least one smart contract to achieve different functions. Each platform user should have at least one did to identify himself through did management, and each did is bound with a blockchain account to pre serve uniqueness. Data service protocol and data registration are implemented through data management, and access management grants and verifies specific access rights. Secondly, the data layer outside the chain stores the original data files and documents, and accesses the certificate containing the authorization information of specific data rights. Finally, in the architecture design, the blockchain network and smart contract are used to process the data and business logic on the chain.

3.2 Use Case

In the feasibility evaluation, we choose the government internal logistics service as the use case. Generally speaking, flow refers to the whole process of planning, implementation and management of raw materials, semi-finished products, finished products or related information from different addresses by means of transportation, storage and distribution in order to meet the needs of information and material flow within the government.

In the existing government logistics system, the components of logistics include transportation, storage, packaging, handling, circulation, processing, distribution and related logistics information. The specific contents include the following aspects: user service, demand forecasting, order processing, distribution, inventory control, transportation, warehouse management, layout and location of factories and warehouses, handling, purchasing, packaging and information.

Through the application of the proposed architecture design, the third-party logistics enterprises share most of the actual work through information docking, but need to transfer some workflow and data storage to the smart contract on the chain. Government agencies and third-party logistics companies should first register DIDto determine their blockchain accounts. When the business information is exchanged to the platform, the relevant data is stored in the off chain data repository, and the basic information is sent to the data registry. Data users should also have their own DIDwhen using the platform, and put forward specific data access requirements for different purposes, and need to share access token. They can access logistics related information after verifying the received token.

3.3 Feasibility

The application of blockchain technology generates records of data transactions. As important vouchers for institutional activities and social individuals, these records involve a large number of personal privacy and public interests, and need to be properly kept for long-term reference. Should the files generated in the blockchain be stored in the blockchain system or transferred to another management system? How to solve the problem of long-term preservation of these documents? At present, the research and practice of blockchain is more focused on the current value it can play, and less attention is paid to these issues about long-term preservation. In the practice of Chancheng District, all data changes or transactions in the blockchain are recorded on a cloud system. However, there is no clear solution to the problems such as how to transfer the subsequent data to the archives department, how to identify, destroy or keep it for a long time.

The biggest difference between blockchain technology and other information technology lies in its decentralized account book mode, and the corresponding changes will appear in each application link, which also leads to the difference between its file management mode and the existing one. Therefore, for the long-term preservation of data, we should study it from the perspective of file management at the beginning of its application in e-government management, which can be explored from a macro perspective Discuss the feasibility of blockchain technology application, from the generation to long-term preservation of the whole life cycle of its research, is conducive to better consider its feasibility; also can from the perspective of archives management for long-term preservation of archives to ensure that the archives have authenticity, integrity, long-term availability of the construction needs of the introduction of blockchain application, make for blockchain application system The construction of the system will be more comprehensive.

3.4 Experiment

In this paper, the proposed data management mechanism for e-government applications is implemented on the blockchain system Fabric to verify the effectiveness of the proposed method. The experiment is carried out on a cluster composed of two machines, each of which is equipped with Intel i7 10700k CPU, 256 GB RAM and 4 TB hard disk. The blockchain system runs on Ubuntu 20.0.4, and the blockchain adopts the tendermint consensus, and the consensus time is set to. We test the data management performance of using dictionary tree and linear scan to find incremental records. The experimental results show that the performance of data management method using dictionary tree is always better than that of linear scan incremental record buffer method. When more table names and more incremental records are maintained, the difference between the two methods is larger. This is because dictionary tree only needs one string comparison to get the location of incremental record set. Without dictionary tree, the system needs to traverse the whole incremental record buffer every time it gets the incremental record set (Fig. 3).

Number of Tables	Time Consumption	Using Trie	Linear Scanning
100	100	226	248
120	200	247	279
140	300	267	309
160	400	288	340
180	500	308	371
200	600	328	403
220	700	349	436
240	800	370	470
260	900	390	504
280	1000	412	538
300	1100	433	574

Fig. 3. Experiment result table for blockchain-based data management

4 Conclusions

The government's management activities involve the basic rights and interests of citizens and the normal operation of society, and the requirements for the reliability and security of information are very high. In the process of government management, a lot of information closely related to citizens' life will be produced, and the requirements for the proper storage and rational use of these information are also very high. How to provide more efficient, higher quality, more fair public services, how to provide more reliable, more transparent, more comprehensive information resources, is an important problem for the government to carry out e-government activities. The chain data structure provided by blockchain, which can not be tampered with and can be recorded in the whole process, just meets the needs of information security and reliability in government information disclosure. At the same time, it also provides a new audit idea for administrative examination and approval. From the audit of conditions to the audit of social individual credit data chain, the combination of the characteristics of blockchain and the development needs of e-government can not only promote the deepening of e-government Development can also promote the construction of social credit system.

First, individual identity authentication. Blockchain is built on the basis of the Internet. Individual related certificates, assets, supporting documents, and even various public records can be migrated to the blockchain. New encryption authentication technology and network wide consensus mechanism are used to form a "digital ID card". Using the complete, distributed and tamperable continuous account database of blockchain, individuals and institutions can form their own identity cards, and can use the data information verified by multiple parties in the whole network for "self certification", without relying on the authentication of a third party. This new type of credit relationship can further promote the demand of simple and clean government in the development of e-government. On the one hand, when individuals apply for public services, they no longer need to travel between different institutions to collect the required certification materials, and the government departments do not need to repeatedly verify the authenticity and reliability of the data when approving. Through the digital ID card in the blockchain system, they can obtain reliable and complete information such as personal basic information and credit information, which will greatly improve administrative efficiency; on the other hand On the one hand, the non tamperability of digital ID card and the change of administrative examination and approval from conditional examination and approval to performance examination and approval can urge social individuals to cherish their credit information and pay more attention to their own performance in social activities, which will help the government improve its governance efficiency. Therefore, the construction and development of individual ID card is in line with the demands of simplicity, integrity and efficiency in e-government, which will be a major direction of block chain application in E-government in the future.

Second, production process supervision. With the advancement of the process of government information disclosure, citizens' demand for information closely related to their lives is growing. Through the contract mechanism, blockchain technology can connect the information of different industries and organizations, without building different management systems according to different information disclosure needs, and can form a complete data chain, such as monitoring information in the process of grain and oil circulation; at the same time, it can ensure that the information in this process can not be tampered with.

Third, government information disclosure. Hash processing and other encryption algorithms of blockchain can desensitize some data to protect sensitive personal privacy content. Through fine authorization, it is conducive to the establishment of horizontal data circulation mechanism, and also makes more government information available. It not only reduces the construction cost of information disclosure, but also ensures the reliability and integrity of information. It not only meets the public's right to know and the right to supervise government work, but also increases the strength and depth of government information disclosure, which is conducive to the construction of "sunshine government". At the same time, as a "timeline database" arranged in chronological order, blockchain can avoid the collection and cleaning of effective data and greatly reduce the cost of data collection. Combined with big data technology, we can deeply mine and analyze the massive data in the blockchain, which will greatly enhance the value and use space of blockchain data. Blockchain can play a huge role in government information interconnection, openness, deep mining and rational utilization.

References

1. Huggahalli, R., Iyer, R., Tetrick, S.: Direct cache access for high bandwidth network I/O. In: ISCA (2005)
2. Tang, D., Bao, Y., Hu, W., et al.: DMA cache: using on-chip storage to architecturally separate I/O data from CPU data for improving I/O performance. In: HPCA (2010)
3. Liao, G., Zhu, X., Bhuyan, L.: A new server I/O architecture for high speed networks. In: HPCA (2011)
4. León, E.A., Ferreira, K.B., Maccabe, A.B.: Reducing the impact of the memory wall for I/O using cache injection. In: 15th IEEE Symposium on High-Performance Interconnects (HOTI 2007), August 2007
5. Kumar, A., Huggahalli, R., Makineni, S.: Characterization of direct cache access on multi-core systems and 10GbE. In: HPCA (2009)
6. Liao, G.,Bhuyan, L.: Performance measurement of an integrated NIC architecture with 10GbE. In: 17th IEEE Symposium on High Performance Interconnects (2009)

7. Foong, A., et al.: TCP performance re-visited. In: IEEE International Symposium on Performance Analysis of Software and Systems, March 2003
8. Clark, D., Jacobson, V., Romkey, J., Saalwen, H.: An analysis of TCP processing overhead. IEEE Commun. Mag. **27**(6), 23–29 (1989)
9. Doweck, J.: Inside Intel Core microarchitecture and smart memory access. Intel White Paper (2006)
10. Kumar, A., Huggahalli, R.: Impact of cache coherence protocols on the processing of network traffic (2007)
11. Hu, W., Wang, J., Gao, X., et al.: GODSON-3: a scalable multicore RISC processor with x86 emulation. IEEE Micro **29**(2), 17–29 (2009)
12. Cadence Incisive Xtreme Series. http://www.cadence.com/products/sd/xtreme_series
13. Synopsys GMAC IP. http://www.synopsys.com/dw/dwtb.php?a=ethernet_mac
14. Miller, D.J., Watts, P.M., Moore, A.W.: Motivating future interconnects: a differential measurement analysis of PCI latency. In: ANCS (2009)
15. Binkert, N.L., Saidi, A.G., Reinhardt, S.K.: Integrated network interfaces for high-bandwidth TCP/IP. In: Proceedings of the 12th International Conference on Architectural Support for Programming Languages and Operating Systems (ASPLOS) (2006)
16. Liao, G., Bhuyan, L.: Performance measurement of an integrated NIC architecture with 10GbE. In: HotI (2009)

Offloading Method Based on Reinforcement Learning in Mobile Edge Computing

Shen Liu, Li Ma$^{(\boxtimes)}$, Dongchao Ma, Yingxun Fu, and Ailing Xiao

School of Information Science and Technology, North China University
of Technology, Beijing 100144, China
mali@ncut.edu.cn

Abstract. Mobile Edge Computing (MEC) has the potential to enable computation-intensive applications in 5G networks. MEC can extend the computational capacity at the edge of a wireless network by offloading computation-intensive tasks to the MEC server. This paper considers a multi-mobile equipment (Mobile Equipment, ME) MEC system, where multiple mobiles -equipment can perform computational offloading via a wireless channel to a MEC server. To reduce the total cost during the offloading process, an algorithm based on reinforcement learning, Pre-Sort Q, is proposed. First, the transmission delay and calculation delay that computation jobs may experience, the transmission energy and computation energy that the computing system would consume were modeled. Then, the weighted sum of the delay and energy consumption and use preprocessing to determine the offloading decision to minimize system cost. Pre-Sort Q can reduce the weighted sum of delay and energy consumption through experimental simulation analysis and comparison compared with three benchmarks and one method.

Keywords: Mobile edge computing · Reinforcement learning · Computing offload · Offloading strategy · Resource allocation

1 Introduction

With the popularity of wireless communication, new computing-intensive mobile applications sensitive to delay are emerging, such as augmented reality, virtual reality, and car networking [1]. These new applications usually require many computing resources to meet the requirements of low latency. However, due to the limited battery power and computational capacity, mobile terminal equipment resources are limited, which can hardly meet the needs above applications' needs [2]. Mobile Cloud Computing (Mobile Cloud Computing, MCC) is considered an effective way to offload computing tasks to solve the contradiction between mobile equipment and applications. Its computational capacity can significantly reduce latency. However, offloading computing tasks to a cloud center in space away from ME will result in higher transmission latency and increased energy

© Springer Nature Switzerland AG 2021
X. Sun et al. (Eds.): ICAIS 2021, CCIS 1423, pp. 677–689, 2021.
https://doi.org/10.1007/978-3-030-78618-2_56

consumption. For issues such as high transmission delays during the offloading of cloud computing, mobile edge computing appears at the right time.

The core idea of MEC is to migrate the computing and storage resources of the server to the vicinity of ME to enhance the computational capacity at the edge of the mobile network, which can reduce transmission delay, processing delay, and energy consumption of computing tasks [3]. MEC servers are densely distributed close to ME, and mobile equipment can offload computing tasks to MEC servers through wireless channels. By computing shunting, mobile users can significantly reduce the latency encountered by the application and improve service quality (Quality of Service, QoS). Therefore, as the key point of MEC system, the topic of computing offloading and computing resource allocation has aroused great interest [4].

Researchers have proposed some topics about computing offloading for different design objectives in recent years and made a breakthrough. These studies aim to explore the best offload decisions to reduce latency and save energy on ME. The work in reference [5] puts forward general guidelines to make offloading decisions to minimize energy consumption, in which case it is easy to assume that the communication link has a fixed rate. In [6], three algorithms based on heuristic search, reconstruction linearization and semi-deterministic relaxation are used to study the tradeoff between delay and reliability in the mobile edge computing environment minimize system delay unload failure rate. The resource allocation problem in the mobile edge computing offload system composed of multiple users is studied in reference [7]. The optimal resource allocation problem is expressed as a convex optimization problem to minimize the energy consumption of ME while meeting the delay requirements. Literature [8] proposes a method of allocating edge computing resources to priority services, assigning priorities based on business value, and assigning weighted resources to tasks with different priorities to reduce business execution time and energy consumption. The above studies on computing offloading have achieved good results, such as reducing waiting time or reducing energy consumption. However, there are still some shortcomings. Firstly, the traditional optimization algorithms (such as minimum mean square error, semi-deterministic relaxation algorithm, and convex optimization algorithm) have high complexity and often need multiple iterations to obtain results, which leads to high running time cost. Furthermore, it cannot meet the timeliness requirements. Secondly, the task's dynamic arrival in the uninstall system is not considered (that is, the arrival time of the task is uncertain). Therefore, these uninstall strategies do not applicable to the actual situation.

Due to its low algorithm complexity and maximum long-term benefit, reinforcement learning (Reinforcement Learning, RL) agents can adjust their strategies to achieve the best long-term goals and timeliness requirements, which is very important in time-varying systems. As the basic RL theory, Markov's data process (Markov Decision Process, MDP) theory is widely used by researchers. In [9], a task scheduling strategy with an optimal delay of a single terminal is designed based on MDP theory, which controls the buffer queue length of local processing and transmission tasks according to the channel state. In order to further optimize the computational delay and energy consumption, the problem of minimizing the long-term average execution consumption of a single terminal is considered in [10], and a semi-MDP framework is proposed to jointly control the local CPU frequency, modulation scheme, and data transmission rate. However, the methods proposed in the above research rely too much on environmental information. In [11], Markov chain theory is used to analyze the delay of a given computing task, and a one-dimensional search algorithm is used to find the offloading strategy with minimum delay. Most of the above research on computing offload in the MEC environment focuses on the offloading scenario of single-device computing tasks, which cannot meet the actual situation. Given the actual costs and benefits, the MEC server should serve multiple mobile equipment scenarios.

In this paper, we are committed to designing an RL-based method for a multi-device MEC computing offload system. An algorithm Pre-Sort Q based on Q learning is proposed to replace MDP. According to the general offloading problem, the optimization objective of minimizing the weighted total cost of the system is established. The constraints are formulated; the RL agent's status, reward and action are defined in detail, while this action contains only one parameter in other papers. Besides, it is proposed to prejudge the decision type before learning the algorithm. Simulation results show the effectiveness of the proposed method.

The rest of this article is arranged as follows. The second section, introduces the system model, including the network model, the task model and the computing model. In the third section, describes the formulation of the optimization problem. In the fourth section, proposes a pretreatment method in detail. In Section V, we show the simulation results. Finally, we summarize this study in Section VI.

2 System Model

2.1 Network Model

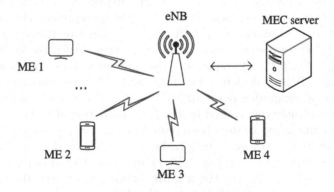

Fig. 1. System model

Figure 1 shows the network model. We consider a scenario of one small cell. There is one eNodeB (eNB) and N ME in the cell. A MEC server is deployed with the eNB.

The set of ME is denoted as $M = \{M_1, M_2, \ldots, M_N\}$. We assume that each ME has a computation-intensive task to be completed. Each ME could offload the task to the MEC server through wireless or execute it locally. The MEC server's capacity is limited and may not be sufficient for all ME to offload tasks.

We define B as the bandwidth of the wireless channel. There is only one base station in a unit, so interval interference is neglected. Assuming that multiple ME select the offloaded task simultaneously, the wireless bandwidth will be evenly allocated to the ME uploaded data calculated by the offload. According to [12], the achievable upload data rate for ME_n is:

$$R_n = \frac{B}{L} \log \left(1 + \frac{P_n h_n}{\frac{B}{L} N_0} \right) \tag{1}$$

L is to calculate the number of unloaded ME, P_n is the ME_n transmission power when uploading data, h_n is the channel gain of ME_n in the wireless channel, and N_0 is problematic Gaussian variance channel noise.

2.2 Task Model

We assume that each ME n has a computation-intensive task or delay-sensitive task, defining Z_n as the calculation task, $Z_n = \{d_n, c_n, d_n^o, p^u, p^d, \vartheta_n\}$, Among them, d_n is the amount of data input by the calculation task, including code blocks, hyperparameters, etc.; c_n refers to the amount of calculation of the task, that is, the total number of CPU cycles required to execute and complete the task; d_n^o refers to the amount of data when the task is calculated and output, the unit is bit; p^u, p^d are the power required for uploading/unloading when ME interacts with the MEC server. It is worth noting that the total number of CPU cycles represents the resources required for calculation. In addition, ϑ_n represents the maximum tolerable delay for the completion of the computing task. As a constraint on the delay, it is very important to satisfy the service experience. Define the two-tuple $ES = \{c^e, f^e\}$ to represent the edge server, where c^e represents the number of CPU cycles required by the server to process 1-bit data; f^e represents the computing power of the server. For mobile devices, $ME_n = \{c_n^{loc}, f_n^{loc}, p_n^m\}$, c_n^{loc} represents the number of CPU cycles used by the mobile device ME to calculate 1-bit data, and f_n^{loc} represents the nth mobile device The local computing power of ME is different between different MEs; p_n^m is the energy consumption caused by the local execution of tasks.

Define the unloading strategy represented by the vector y to distinguish which tasks are executed locally and which tasks will be migrated to the MEC server. The vector $y = \{y_1, y_2, \ldots, y_n\}, y \in \{0, 1\}$ means n The unloading strategy of the ME; $y_n = 0$ indicates that the nth ME chooses to execute the task locally; $y_n = 1$ indicates that the ME chooses to offload the computing task to the server for execution.

2.3   Local and Offloading

Local Execution. If ME_n chooses to execute its task Z_n locally, then the local computing time of Z_n can be expressed as:

$$T_n^{loc} = \frac{C_n c_n^{loc}}{f_n^{loc}} \tag{2}$$

The total energy consumption calculated locally can be expressed as:

$$E_n^{loc} = T_n^{loc} p_n^m \tag{3}$$

Offloading Computing. If ME n chooses to execute task Z_n by offloading computing, then the overall during the offloading process is:

$$T_n^{off} = \frac{d_n}{R_n} + \frac{c_n c^e}{f^e} + \frac{d_n^o}{R_n} \tag{4}$$

Choosing to offload means that the task will go through three processes. One is that ME n uploads the calculation data to the edge server through the wireless transmission medium (the eNB transmits the data to the MEC server deployed together). Then the server runs the computing task, and then returns the output data of the task to the ME again through the wireless transmission medium. The time delay experienced in these three processes corresponds to the three parts of formula (4). At this time, the energy consumption of the first step can be calculated by:

$$E_{n,1}^o = \frac{d_n}{R_n} p^u \tag{5}$$

It is worth noting that the above energy consumption is the energy consumption when transmitting 1-bit data. When the server is processing computing tasks, the device itself is in a spatial state and still has energy consumption, so the power consumption in the idle state is defined as P_n^0, and the energy consumption corresponding to the second step is expressed as follows (server energy consumption is not considered):

$$E_{n,2}^o = P_n^0 \frac{c^e}{f^e} \tag{6}$$

For the last step of calculating the offloading task, the time required is the download delay of the returned result after processing, and the corresponding energy consumption can be calculated in the same way:

$$E_{n,3}^o = p^d \frac{d_n^o}{R_n} \tag{7}$$

However, according to the literature [13], the download rate is much higher than the upload rate, and the amount of processed data is often much smaller than the amount of input data, so the delay and energy consumption of the download step are ignored. In summary, the total energy consumption for uninstalling is:

$$E_n^{off} = \frac{d_n}{R_n} p^u + P_n^0 \frac{c^e}{fe} \tag{8}$$

Our optimization goal is to achieve the smallest weighted sum of execution time and energy consumption, which is regarded as the total system cost of the MEC system in both the local and off-load execution scenarios. Therefore, the objective function is defined as

$$\Lambda = \delta \sum_{i=1}^{N} T + (1 - \delta) \sum_{i=1}^{N} E \tag{9}$$

where E represents the total energy consumption of the mobile device in the local or unloading phase, and T represents the total delay of processing computing tasks in different phases; δ is the delay weight coefficient, and $(1-\delta)$ is the energy weight coefficient. In fact, the weight coefficient can be adjusted according to the application scenario. For example, the weight value can be appropriately increased for the delay sensitivity calculation task, and the energy consumption coefficient is also the same.

From the above, we know the delay and energy consumption of ME in the local and offloading modes, then the total system cost for calculating the delay and ME energy consumption is

$$\Lambda = \delta \left[\sum_{i=1}^{N} T_n^{loc} + \sum_{i=1}^{N} T_n^{off} \right] + (1 - \delta) \left[\sum_{i=1}^{N} E_n^{loc} + \sum_{i=1}^{N} E_n^{off} \right] \tag{10}$$

We have formulated the offloading of the MEC system as an optimization problem. The purpose is to reduce the total cost of computing delay and energy consumption of all mobile devices in the MEC system as much as possible. It also requires the maximum tolerable delay of the task and the respective computing resources of the ME and the MEC server. Based on the constraints, the optimization problem is expressed as follows:

$$\min_{y,f} \Lambda = \delta \left[\sum_{i=1}^{N} T_n^{loc} + \sum_{i=1}^{N} T_n^{off} \right] + (1 - \delta) \left[\sum_{i=1}^{N} E_n^{loc} + \sum_{i=1}^{N} E_n^{off} \right]$$
$$\beta 1 : y_n \in \{0, 1\}, \forall n \in N$$
$$\beta 2 : T_n^{loc}, T_n^{off} \leq \vartheta_n, \forall n \in N$$
$$\beta 3 : 0 \leq f_n \leq F_e, \forall n \in N$$
$$\beta 4 : \sum_{i=1}^{N} f_n \leq F_e, \forall n \in N \tag{11}$$

Restriction $\beta 1$ represents the decision classification of each ME for computing tasks; restriction $\beta 2$ represents that the time delay for local execution or offload execution of the task should not exceed the maximum tolerable delay of the task; restriction $\beta 3$ refers to the MEC server in the cell allocated to the ME The computing resources of is less than the total resources of the server. The restriction condition $\beta 4$ ensures that all allocated computing resources do not exceed all the computing resources of the MEC.

3   The Key Elements of Reinforcement Learning

This section mainly introduces the three essential elements of reinforcement learning-state, action, reward, and their embodiment, and puts forward the Pre-sort Q method based on reinforcement learning.

3.1   Three Key Elements for RL

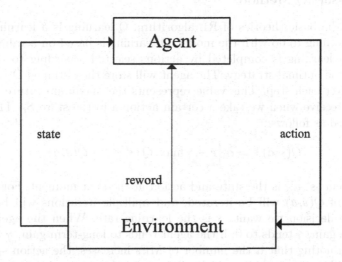

Fig. 2. reinforcement learning model

As shown in Fig. 2, in a typical reinforcement learning model, the agent continuously interacts with the environment's state, action, and reward information. After several iterative learning, the agent finally gets the optimal strategy.

In the optimization problem that this article focuses on, state, action, and reward are defined as follows:

State: The system state consists of two parts $s_t = (C_t, F_t^e)$. Define C_t as the total cost of the entire system, that is, the current state of the system is composed of the weighted sum of delay and energy consumption, which is the expected goal; F_t^e is the available calculation amount of the MEC server, which represents the idle resources in the current state.

Action: In the system model, the action is the direction selected by the agent based on the environmental information, which is mainly composed of two parts, that is, the offloading strategy $y = \{y_1, y_2, \ldots, y_n\}$ and resource allocation $f = \{f_1^e, f_2^e, \ldots, f_n^e\}$ of all ME. Combining 1 and 2 gives the action vector $\{y_1, y_2, \ldots, y_n, f_1^e, f_2^e, \ldots, f_n^e\}$.

Reward: After performing each action, the agent will get a corresponding reward in the current state S_t. Generally speaking, the reward should be related to the goal, it is the evaluation of the profit obtained by the action in the previous state. The goal of reinforcement learning is to obtain the largest reward/benefit, and we have established an optimization index that minimizes the total cost of the system, so the reward of reinforcement learning is defined as the negative correlation function of the optimization objective.

3.2   Pre-sort Q Method

As one of the basic theories of RL algorithm, Q learning is a learning method that has nothing to do with the model. Q learning is based on a value function, and finally learning is completed by actions selected according to the current state and the optimal strategy. The agent will store the obtained Q value in the Q table after each step. This value represents the maximum future reward we expect to receive when we take a certain action a in the state S_t. The Q value is calculated as follows:

$$Q(s,a)+ = \alpha \left[r + \gamma \max_a Q\left(s',a'\right) - Q(s,a) \right] \tag{12}$$

Among them (s',a') is the state and action at the next moment. For each step, the value of $Q(s,a)$ will be iterated, and multiple iterations will be made to obtain the decision we want. γ is the learning rate. When the agent pursues short-term gain, γ tends to 0; if the agent tends to long-term gain, γ tends to 1. It is worth noting that if the number of MEs increases, the action space for Q learning will increase rapidly, which will increase the traversal time, and may not be able to traverse all the Q values and cause the Q value to be overestimated. In order to reduce the size of the space, the unloading decision can be preprocessed before the learning process.

For ME_n, if the local calculation cannot meet the delay constraint, the task can only be uploaded to the MEC server for calculation. Then during this decision-making period $y_n = 1$ is fixed, and the computing resources allocated by the MEC server to the task should satisfy $f_n^e \succeq \frac{c^n}{\vartheta^n - \frac{d_n}{R_n}}$, thereby reducing the possible value of decision-making and computing resource allocation. Algorithm 1 is the Pre-sort Q algorithm process.

Algorithm 1. Pre-sort Q
Initialize $s, Q(s, a) = 0$
Set up γ and reward matrix
for each episode:
Judge the delay constraint, choose whether to offload and meet the resource requirements
for each step of episode
Choose an action a from all possible actions of state s
Execute this possible a, observe reward and s'
Get maximum Q value for this next state based on all possible actions
$Q(s, a) \leftarrow Q(s, a) + \alpha \left[r + \gamma max_{a'} Q\left(s', a'\right) - Q(s, a)\right]$
Let $s \leftarrow s'$
until s is terminal
end for

4   Simulation Result

This section, presents the simulation results to estimate the performance of the proposed theme. In the simulation, we assume that a scenario is as follows. We consider a single cell using the bandwidth $B = 10$MHz, and eNB with the MEC server deployed is located in the center. The ME is randomly distributed within a 200 m distance away from the eNB. The MEC server's computation capacity is $f^e = 10$ GHz/s the CPU frequency of each ME is $f_n^{loc} = 1$ GHz/sec. The ME's transmission power and idle power are set to be $P_n^m = 500$ mW and $P_n^0 = 200$ mW. The number of CPU cycles c_n (in Megacycles) obeys the uniform distribution between (900, 1200). Set up δ as 0.8.

We compare the proposed algorithm with the other four methods in the following parameters:

"Local computing" means that all ME perform tasks through local computing. "Edge server computing" means that ME offloads all computing tasks to the MEC server, and the MEC server allocates resources equally to all tasks. "Q-learning" refers to the original Q-learning algorithm, applied to the scenario assumed in this article.

"SSDOA" is a modification of the uninstall algorithm [14], which restricts that all subtasks on mobile equipment must be offloaded to the same edge server (if you choose to offload), so it cannot benefit from the edge server network mentioned in the original context. It is worth noting that the DAG scheduling strategy is proposed regarding the classical HEFT algorithm in OS scheduling. Because the algorithm proposed in this paper regards the ME as an indivisible task, and SSDOA considers the advantage of parallel processing of multiple subtasks, we set the DAG subtask of each ME to 1 to isolate the influence of multiple subtasks.

Figure 3 shows the performance comparison of the Q-learning algorithm, SSDOA algorithm, Pre-sort Q algorithm, local computing, and offloading computing in the case of an increasing number of ME. In a single edge server

environment, we increased the number of mobile equipment from 10 to 50. With
the continuous increase in the number of ME, the total cost shows an upward
trend. The "Edge server computing" method grows much faster when there is
more ME.

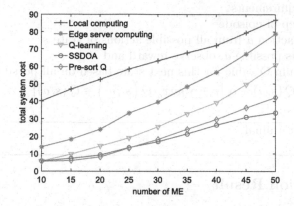

Fig. 3. Total system cost versus the number of ME

It is worth noting that when the number of ME is less than 25, the Pre-sort
Q method proposed in this paper can get the best results. This is because, in
the parallel advantage of subtasks, SSDOA also needs to offload tasks to edge
servers, which avoids the consumption of local computing, but at the cost of
increasing delay. Reinforcement learning makes preprocessing judgments at the
beginning of task offloading, which reduces the number of decision steps and
the number of possible values stored in the Q table, thereby reducing the total
cost. However, the cost gap between SSDOA and Pre-sort Q increases with the
number of ME.

The results show that the increase of the number of ME leads to a sharp
increase in Q-table storage, so it is not easy to obtain enough samples to traverse
each state, while SSDOA improves the parallel processing ability of different
tasks. In the equipment-intensive scene, the task execution delay and energy
consumption at the same time are better than the proposed method in this
paper.

Figure 4 shows the system's total cost when the task workload is between
[200, 1000]-setting the number of ME to 5. When the computational capacity of
local devices and edge servers remains unchanged, even if there is no resource
contention between ME, the increase in the number of tasks will inevitably lead
to longer transmission time and execution time, resulting in a corresponding
increase in energy consumption, and increase the total system cost. The growth
trend of the proposed Pre-sort Q method is slower than that of other methods.

Figure 5 shows the change in the system's total cost when the MEC server's
computational capacity is between [1, 10]. Set the number of ME to 5. As can

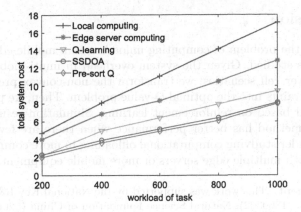

Fig. 4. Total system cost versus the workload of a task

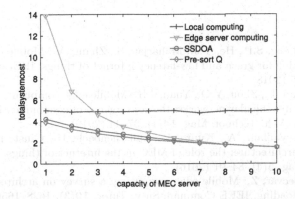

Fig. 5. Total system cost versus the capacity of MEC server

be seen from the figure, with the improvement of the MEC server's computational capacity, the local computing method's total system cost curve is almost unchanged because all computing tasks are performed on the local equipment and do not use the computing resources of MEC. The other three curves show a downward trend. In the case of a given number of ME, the stronger the computational capacity, the more abundant computing resources allocated to the ME, thus reducing the processing time and energy consumption. Moreover, the richer the MEC server's computing resources, the lower the total cost of unloading computing, SSDOA, and Pre-sort Q, and the performance of these offloading methods is almost the same.

5   Conclusion

In this paper, the problem of computing unloading in a mobile edge computing environment is studied. Given the system overhead in multi-mobile equipment and single-server cell scenarios, we transform the non-convex problem of optimization constraints into the optimal Q-value problem. Then, we propose a Presort Q method based on reinforcement learning. Simulation results show that the proposed method has better performance when there are few ME. Future work will consider studying computational offloading in more complex scenarios, such as ME with multiple edge servers or more mobile equipment.

Acknowledgment. This work was supported by the National Key R&D Program of China (2018YFB 1800302), Natural Science Foundation of China (62001007), Beijing Natural Science Foundation (KZ201810009011, 4202020, 19L2021).

References

1. Zhang, K., Leng, S.P., He, Y.J., Maharjan, S., Zhang, Y.: Mobile edge computing and networking for green and low-latency internet of things. IEEE Commun. Mag. **56**(5), 39–45 (2018)
2. Qi, Y.L., Tian, L., Zhou, Y.Q., Yuan, J.H.: Mobile edge computing assisted admission control in vehicular networks: the convergence of communication and computation. IEEE Veh. Technol. Mag. **14**(1), 37–44 (2019)
3. Sabella, D., Vaillant, A., Kuure, P., Rauschenbach, U., Giust, F.: Mobile-edge computing architecture: the role of MEC in the internet of things. IEEE Consum. Electron. Mag. **5**(4), 84–91 (2016)
4. Mach, P., Becvar, Z.: Mobile edge computing: a survey on architecture and computation offloading. IEEE Commun. Surv. Tutor. **19**(3), 1628–1656 (2017)
5. Kumar, K., Lu, Y.H.: Cloud computing for mobile users: can offloading computation save energy? Compute **43**(4), 51–56 (2010)
6. Liu, J.H., Zhang, Q.: Offloading ScheME in mobile edge computing for ultra-reliable low latency communications. IEEE Access **6**, 12825–12837 (2018)
7. You, C.S., Huang, K.B.: Multiuser resource allocation for mobile edge computation offloading. In: IEEE Global Communications Conference (GLOBECOM), Washington, DC, USA, pp. 1–6. IEEE (2016)
8. Wang, Y., Ge, H.B., Feng, A.Q., Li, W.H., Liu, L.H., Jiang, H.B.: Computation offloading strategy based on deep reinforcement learning in cloud-assisted mobile edge computing. In: 2020 IEEE 5th International Conference on Cloud Computing and Big Data Analytics, Chengdu, China, pp. 108–113. IEEE (2020)
9. Liu, J., Mao, Y.Y., Zhang, J., Letaief, K.B.: Delay-optimal computation task scheduling for mobile-edge computing systems. In: 2016 IEEE International Symposium on Information Theory (ISIT), Barcelona, Spain, pp. 1451–1455 (2017)
10. Hong, S.T., Kim, H.: QoE-aware computation offloading scheduling to capture energy-latency tradeoff in mobile clouds. In: 13th Annual IEEE International Conference on Sensing, Communication, and Networking (SECON), London UK, pp. 1–9 (2017)
11. You, C., Huang, K.: Multiuser resource allocation for mobile edge computation offloading. In: IEEE Global Communications Conference (GLOBECOM), Washington, DC, USA, pp. 1–6. IEEE (2016)

12. Zhao, P.T., Tian, H., Qin, C., Nie, G.F.: Energy-saving offloading by jointly allocating radio and computational resources for mobile edge computing. IEEE Access **5**, 11255–11268 (2018)
13. Chen, X., Jiao, L., Li, W.Z., Fu, X.M.: Efficient multi-user computation of loading for mobile-edge cloud computing. IEEE/ACM Trans. Netw. **24**(5), 2795–2808 (2016)
14. Han, Y.P., Zhao, Z.W., Mo, J.W., Shu, C., Min, G.Y.: Efficient task offloading with dependency guarantees in ultra-dense edge networks. In: 2019 IEEE Global Communications Conference (GLOBECOM), Waikoloa, HI, USA, pp. 1–6. IEE (2019)

A Dynamic Decision-Making Method for Endorser Node Selection

Ning Cao[1], Hao Han[2], Yixuan Lu[2], Junliang Liu[2], Weiguo Tian[2], Xiaofang Li[3], Hao Hu[2], and Dongjie Zhu[2(✉)]

[1] College of Information Engineering, Sanming University, Sanming 365000, China
[2] School of Computer Science and Technology, Harbin Institute of Technology, Weihai 204209, China
zhudongjie@hit.edu.cn
[3] Department of Mathematics, Harbin Institute of Technology, Weihai 264209, China

Abstract. The proposal of the blockchain 3.0 architecture represented by Hyperledger Fabric simplifies the process of each node participating in the blockchain network so that a large number of IoT devices can be quickly integrated into the network. However, the participating institutions in the field of power Internet of Things are complex, the performance of participating nodes is not uniform, and the load imbalance caused by it makes it impossible to meet the transaction throughput requirements of the business. In this paper, we established a Zookeeper-based endorser node performance monitoring module and replaced the original random selection strategy with a dynamic endorser node selection strategy based on the available resources of the node, effectively alleviating the endorsement pressure of a single node in high concurrency scenarios, thereby improving the overall concurrent processing capabilities. It is worth noting that our optimization is pluggable and does not make any changes to the interface of the Hyperledger Fabric, and it does not weaken the usability of the system. By comparing the existing architecture with our design, it is found that this dynamic decision-making endorser node selection strategy can help select more appropriate nodes for endorsement according to the node's system resources and real-time load conditions, thus improving the concurrency of the system.

Keywords: Hyperledger fabric · Endorser node selection · Concurrency · Zookeeper

1 Introduction

Distributed ledger technology [1] allows transactions to be conducted in a secure and verifiable manner without the participation of trusted third-party institutions. The proposal of the blockchain 3.0 architecture [2] represented by the Hyperledger Fabric [3, 4] not only meets the decentralization requirements of the business, but also has the characteristics that data cannot be tampered with, and the data can be shared and isolated [3–5]. Therefore, the blockchain is considered to be a kind of technology affecting various industries. However, the blockchain technology must have a TPS (Transactions per

© Springer Nature Switzerland AG 2021
X. Sun et al. (Eds.): ICAIS 2021, CCIS 1423, pp. 690–699, 2021.
https://doi.org/10.1007/978-3-030-78618-2_57

Second) equivalent to the existing database management systems to be able to provide transaction guarantees to meet the availability requirements. However, in the field of power Internet of Things, many terminal devices collect a large amount of small data, which needs to be stored in the blockchain ledger [6–8]. The data submitted by the client can only be submitted to the orderer node for sorting after obtaining the endorsement of a specified number of endorser nodes, and then can be submitted to each peer node in the blockchain. The existing endorser node [6, 8] selection mechanism is difficult to fully utilize the available resources of different nodes and the selection of appropriate nodes for endorsement based on real-time load conditions not only cause a waste of node resources but also make endorser nodes a bottleneck that limits the overall concurrency of the system.

Therefore, we have proposed a dynamic decision-making endorser node selection method based on the problems of the endorsement module in the Hyperledger Fabric 2.0 architecture. The decision module implemented based on this method can select the endorser node according to the real-time load of the node, thereby improving the overall concurrency of the system performance. During the experiment, we gradually changed the initial resource allocation of each peer node, and then compared the transaction concurrency under the two architecture modes. Experiments show that the greater the difference in node system resource allocation, the greater the improvement in system transaction processing capabilities brought about by this dynamic decision-making method. This proves that this dynamic decision-making method of endorser node selection can effectively relieve the pressure of endorser nodes, thereby improving the overall transaction processing capability of the system. Our specific contributions are as follows:

- Established a zookeeper-based [9] endorser node performance monitoring module, where the available resource status information and load information of peer nodes can be released to in real time.
- Modified the selection logic of the endorser node in the SDK, and replaced the original random node selection method with the endorser node selection method based on the dynamic characteristics of the node.
- A non-invasive optimization of the original architecture, this method coexists with the random endorser node selection strategy, and has a higher priority. Even if the zookeeper cluster is unavailable, it can still be downgraded to adopt a random selection method without affecting the availability of the system.

2 Fabric Architecture

Hyperledger Fabric is a distributed ledger solution initiated by the Linux Foundation. The platform is based on a modular architecture and provides a high degree of confidentiality, flexibility, and scalability. The core of the blockchain network is a distributed ledger. Each participant in the network holds a complete copy of the ledger. Even if some nodes in the network maliciously tamper with the data of the local ledger, they still cannot affect other nodes in the network, therefore the blockchain system is also called a decentralized system. Below is a schematic diagram of the distributed ledger (see Fig. 1).

In order to maintain the consistency of the ledger and provide functions including query and transaction, the blockchain network uses smart contracts [10] to control access

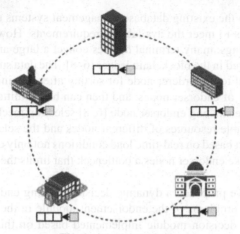

Fig. 1. Distributed ledger.

to the ledger. The client's read and write operations on the ledger data are all done by smart contracts. The advantage is that the business rules recognized by most nodes can be pre-defined to regulate the behavior of the client. The following figure shows how the smart contract interact with the ledger(see Fig. 2).

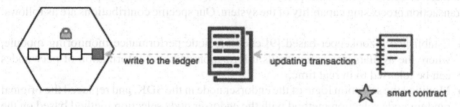

write to the ledger   updating transaction

smart contract

Fig. 2. Access the ledger with smart contract.

The modification of the ledger is synchronized to each node through the consensus algorithm. Through the consensus algorithm [11], it can be ensured that the transaction can only be updated to the ledger state after the specified participant agrees, and that the transaction is executed on the peer node in the same order.

2.1 Node Type

The client initiates a read and write request to the Fabric node. There are only two types of nodes in the Fabric, namely the peer node and the orderer node. Each peer node maintains a local ledger, which can submit blocks to the local ledger and modify the state database accordingly. The client selects a part of peer nodes as endorser nodes to verify the transaction according to the rules defined by the chain code. The orderer node is responsible for sorting the transactions to ensure that each peer node verifies and submits the transactions to the local ledger in the same order.

2.2 Execution Flow

Different from the order-execute execution process of other blockchains, the transaction in the Fabric adopts the execute-order-commit execution process. The transaction process can be divided into the following steps:

(1) The client uses the API provided by the corresponding SDK to construct a transaction proposal and submit it to the corresponding endorser node. The transaction proposal includes channel information, chaincode information that will be called, timestamp, the client's signature, and transaction-related information.

(2) The endorser node verifies the received transaction proposal request. After the verification is passed, the chain code is called to simulate the transaction, and the transaction result of the read-write set is endorsed with the response value and sent to the client. Note that this is a simulation execution, and the data in the ledger will not be modified.

(3) After the client receives enough messages and endorsement signatures, if it is a read request, the client will check the response result; if it is a write request, the client will check whether the specified endorsement policy is met, and then construct a legal transaction request and the transaction request is broadcast to the orderer node.

(4) After the orderer node receives the transaction request, it does not need to check the specific data of the transaction, but sorts the received transaction request and creates a transaction block, and then broadcasts the transaction block to each peer node of the channel.

(5) The peer node verifies the transaction and modifies the local ledger after the verification is passed.

The figure below shows the transaction flow of Hyperledger Fabric before our optimization (see Fig. 3).

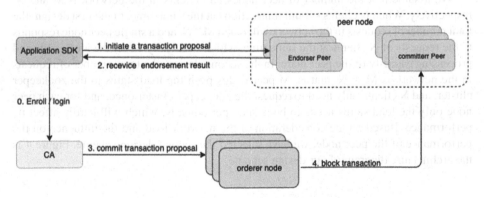

Fig. 3. Execution flow of Hyperledger Fabric.

3 Design

This part shows our optimization of the Fabric 2.2.0 version of the architecture. As can be seen from the description of the Fabric execution process in the previous part, the client's transaction request needs to be sent to the endorser node for endorsement, and the client can proceed to the next submission operation after receiving the endorsement result of the endorser node. This process is synchronous, so the endorsement capability of the endorser node has a great impact on the transaction processing capability of the entire system, which is the premise for us to propose this design. The endorsement capability of a node is not only related to the static host configuration of the node, but also the current load of the node. Therefore, it is inappropriate to specify the endorser node statically. It can neither make full use of the static resource configuration of the node nor can it make a dynamic adjustment based on the current load situation of the node. Therefore, we propose a new design, that is to add an endorser node decision module on the client-side, which is responsible for node selection according to the real-time load status of the node, meanwhile, the corresponding node status report module is also designed on the blockchain node, which is responsible for obtaining the status of the node and for reporting the status.

To achieve this goal, we considered two designs. The first design is to set up a separate process on each peer node to respond to the client. When the client selects the endorser node, it first requests all peer nodes to obtain the load status of each node, and then makes a judgment and decision to choose the appropriate one. The node becomes the endorser node. The second design also needs to set up a separate process on the peer node. The difference is that this process does not passively respond to client requests but regularly pushes its load status to a monitoring cluster. We selected zookeeper as the monitoring cluster. Before making an endorsement decision, the client first obtains the load status pushed by the peer node from the zookeeper cluster and then makes a decision.

We assume that the number of peer nodes and clients in the network is M and N, respectively. When N clients submit transactions at the same time, in the first design, the total number of requests in the network will reach M * N, and a single peer node responds to the requests of N clients at the same time, which will badly affect the load status and processing capacity of the peer node. In the second design, the total number of requests in the network is M + N, that is, M peer nodes push the load status to the zookeeper cluster, and N clients only need to request the zookeeper cluster once, and for each peer node only the load status needs to be pushed periodically, which will hardly affect its performance. Based on the consideration of the network load and the influence on the performance of the peer node, we have selected the second design scheme. Figure 4 is the architecture diagram of our design scheme.

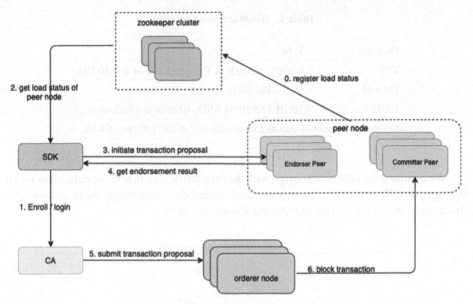

Fig. 4. Execution flow of our new architecture

Based on the original architecture, we introduced the zookeeper cluster to monitor the load status of peer nodes. Each peer node regularly pushes the node load status to the zookeeper cluster. The client program first obtains the load status of the peer node from the zookeeper cluster before sending transaction proposals. Based on the load status of each node, the appropriate peer node is selected as an endorser node and the endorsement process is performed, to achieve the purpose of optimizing the use of the available resources of the peer node and improve the overall transaction processing capability of the system.

4   Experiment

In order to verify the performance of our proposed new architecture, we built a prototype system based on Hyperledger Fabric version 2.2.0. In the experiment, docker 19.03.13 was used to run each node. There were 12 nodes in the whole system, including 3 orderer nodes, 3 CA nodes, and 3 peer nodes in each organization. These nodes were connected to the overlay type two-layer network created by docker swarm. The default LevelDB [12] database was used in the underlying layer of each peer node.

On the 12 node blockchain network, we created an application channel to share data between the two organizations, and deployed fabcar chain code in the channel to simulate the process of adding new cars. On the client side, we use the API of fabric gateway java version 2.2.0 to interact with the blockchain network, and use multithreading to simulate high concurrency scenarios. In order to reduce data access conflicts, UUID is used as the key every time a car is created. The following Table 1 shows the hardware environment used in our experiment.

Table 1. Hardware environment.

Property	Type
CPU	Intel(R) Xeon(R) CPU E5–2620 v4 @2.10 GHz
DRAM	1GB 2400 MHz
HDD	10GB 7200RPM SSD, 4096-byte-block-size
Operation System	CentOS Linux release 7.8.2003 (Core), 64-bit

We compare the optimized design with the original design in four aspects: transaction throughput, CPU utilization, memory utilization and disk page swapping in and out. The differences in transaction throughput are shown as Fig. 5.

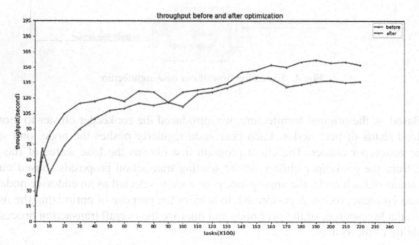

Fig. 5. Throughput of the two architectures.

In the optimized design, the transaction throughput is improved, but the improvement is not significant. The following Fig. 6 shows the CPU utilization of the two designs, and you can see that the CPU utilization is significantly reduced.

The following Fig. 7 shows the memory consumption. The memory consumption in the two architectures remains stable during transaction processing, but the optimized design takes up more memory than the design before optimization. This is because each node needs to obtain and upload the load status of this node to the zookeeper cluster on a regular basis.

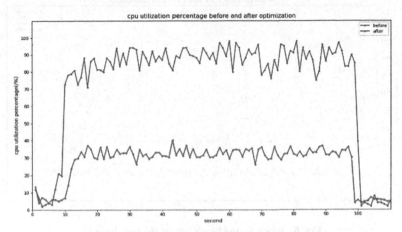

Fig. 6. CPU utilization of the two designs.

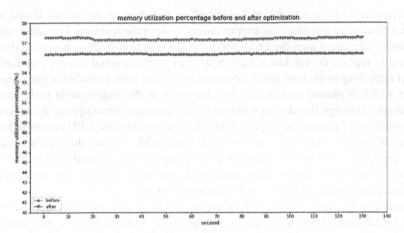

Fig. 7. Memory utilization of the two designs

The following Fig. 8 shows the difference between the two designs when reading and writing disk blocks. The number of read disk blocks per second in the two designs is basically the same, but the number of disk blocks written per second in the optimized design is significantly reduced.

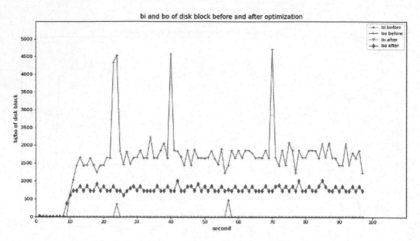

Fig. 8. Block in and block out of the two designs

5   Result

The correctness of the new design is verified by the above experiments. Based on the original design, we introduce zookeeper cluster to save the real-time load status of each peer node. The client uses the endorsement node selection strategy based on dynamic decision to replace the random selection strategy in the original design, calculates the weight according to the load status information of each node recorded in the zookeeper cluster which is pushed periodically, and then selects the endorsement node based on the weight. Although this design will bring extra memory consumption, it can improve the throughput of transaction request, and effectively reduce the CPU consumption, the number of writing disk blocks and network bandwidth consumption. Compared with these, the extra memory consumption is acceptable. This method effectively alleviates the problem of excessive endorsement node pressure, and improves the transaction concurrent processing ability of the blockchain network.

There is still room for improvement in our design. In our current design, the weight ratio of each load item is set manually on the client, which cannot be well applied to all application scenarios. Therefore, if we can dynamically adjust the weight proportion of different load items according to different scenarios, we can make better decisions for different scenarios. In the next research, we will consider introducing a machine learning module, which takes the data set of a specific scene as the input and the weight proportion of load items suitable for the scene as the output, and transfers the output parameters to our proposed dynamic decision-making module for weight calculation of different peer nodes, to optimize the selection process of endorser nodes.

Acknowledgement. This work is supported by State Grid Shandong Electric Power Company Science and Technology Project Funding under Grant no. 520613200001,520613180002, 62061318C002, Weihai Scientific Research and Innovation Fund (2020) and the Grant 19YG02, Sanming University.

References

1. Mills, D.C.F., Wang, K.S., Malone, B.T., et al.: Distributed ledger technology in payments, clearing, and settlement (2016)
2. Androulaki, E.F., Barger, A.S., Bortnikov, V.T., et al.: Hyperledger Fabric: a distributed operating system for permissioned blockchains. In: Proceedings of the thirteenth EuroSys Conference, pp. 1–15 (2018)
3. Maesa, F., Damiano Di Francesco, S., and Paolo Mori, T.: Blockchain 3.0 applications survey. J. Parallel Distrib. Comput. 99–114 (2020)
4. Zhu, D.F., Du, H.S., Wang, Y.T., et al.: An IoT-oriented real-time storage mechanism for massive small files based on Swift. Int. J. Embedded Syst. 12(1), 72–80 (2020)
5. Zhu, D.F., Du, H.S., Sun, Y.T., et al.: Research on path planning model based on short-term traffic flow prediction in intelligent transportation system. Sensors 18(12), 4275 (2018)
6. Zhu, D.F., Du, H.S., Qiao, X.T., et al.: An access prefetching strategy for accessing small files based on swift. Procedia Comput. Sci. 131, 816–824 (2018)
7. Zhu, D.F., Du, H.S., Sun, Y.T., et al.: Massive files prefetching model based on LSTM neural network with cache transaction strategy. Comput. Mat. Continua 63(2), 979–993 (2020)
8. Androulaki, E.F., De Caro, A.S., Neugschwandtner, M.T., et al.: Endorsement in hyperledger fabric. In: 2019 IEEE International Conference on Blockchain (Blockchain), Atlanta, pp. 510–519. IEEE (2019)
9. Hunt, P.F., Konar, M.S., Junqueira, F.P.T., et al.: Zookeeper: wait-free coordination for internet-scale systems. In: Paul Barham, F., Timothy Roscoe, S., USENIX Annual Technical Conference 2010, USENIX ATC 2010, Boston, Massachusetts, vol. 8, no. 9 (2010)
10. Buterin, V.F.: A next-generation smart contract and decentralized application platform. white paper 3(37) (2014)
11. Ongaro, D.F., Ousterhout, J.S.: In search of an understandable consensus algorithm. In: 2014 {USENIX} Annual Technical Conference ({USENIX}{ATC} 14), Philadelphia, pp. 305–319. USENIX (2014)
12. Dent, A.F.: Getting started with LevelDB. Packt Publishing Ltd (2013)

A Proxy Node Resource Load Balancing Strategy Based on the Swift System

Yingying Wang[1], Zhixin Huo[2], Dongge Fu[3], Jingrui Wen[2], Yundong Sun[4], Xueming Qiao[5], Yao Tang[5], and Dongjie Zhu[2(✉)]

[1] College of Information Engineering, Qingdao Binhai University, Qingdao 266555, China
[2] School of Computer Science and Technology, Harbin Institute of Technology, Weihai 264209, China
zhudongjie@hit.edu.cn
[3] School of Information Science and Engineering, Harbin Institute of Technology, Weihai 264209, China
[4] School of Astronautics, Harbin Institute of Technology, Harbin 150001, China
[5] State Grid Weihai Power Supply Company, Weihai 264200, China

Abstract. The internet of Things (IoT) uses wireless sensor devices to build a huge network transmission center, the data is increasing, and the data types have diverse characteristics. Such data raise a certain challenge for data storage and resource scheduling in cloud platforms. Swift can solve the needs of massive data storage capacity, but it is impossible to effectively achieve load balancing and waste resources. Therefore, according to the resource load status of the proxy node, this paper proposes a node resource load balancing strategy based on Linux Virtual Server (LVS). Through the study of scheduling algorithms, a dynamic feedback load balancing algorithm based on a weighted minimum connection is proposed. Experimental results show that the dynamic feedback load balancing algorithm based on a weighted minimum connection can effectively solve the resource scheduling problem.

Keywords: Swift · Cloud storage · Load balance · LVS

1 Introduction

With the rapid development of the Industrial Internet of Things, a large amount of data is generated by different devices. For example, smart glasses take up a lot of storage space, and storing all the data locally on the device is unrealistic. Therefore, utilizing cloud storage to solve IoT device data storage has become a solution. IDC statistics show that in 2018, the global data storage capacity has reached 33ZB, and it is expected that the total global data will reach 175ZB by 2025 [1]. Nearly half of the data is generated by public clouds. Data growth is a serious challenge for storage technology. Existing SAN and NAS technologies have been unable to meet the needs of massive data storage, so a file system with flexible expansion capabilities is needed to meet the storage capacity requirements [2]. In the traditional network file system and stand-alone file system, the data of a file system must be stored on the same physical device, and there is no data redundancy storage function, their concurrent read and write capabilities, scalability and fault tolerance are difficult to meet big data requirements for storage. Therefore, low-cost, highly scalable, safe, and reliable data storage services have become the focus of attention in the industry.

Cloud storage is easy to deploy and allows rapid configuration of unlimited storage services [3]. Users store data on off-site storage systems maintained by third parties and believe that they have unlimited storage space. And there is no need to carry a storage device with you, users can access data anytime and anywhere through the network, which brings great convenience and flexibility. The goals of the cloud storage system mainly include [4]:

(a) Scalability: The scalability of the system can meet the rapid growth of data storage, but the data transmission capacity should also be maintained while increasing the storage capacity.
(b) Throughput and data access: Throughput is important in the system. Data can be quickly accessed without knowing the specific storage location.
(c) Data sharing: Data sharing allows members with a sharing relationship to communicate data and improve collaboration efficiency.

To improve the performance of cloud platforms and system load balancing, many researchers use scheduling algorithms to increase the utilization of system resources [5]. However, the scheduling algorithm they proposed is only for the system load in specific scenarios. The Opportunistic Load Balancing algorithm uses a free sequence method to assign tasks to idle nodes [6]. This method is simple and can effectively improve load balancing. But the disadvantage is that it does not consider the task completion cycle time, resulting in a low system throughput rate.

The architecture in SAN and NAS cannot solve the problem of long waiting times caused by insufficient resources. Related scholars have proposed load balancing algorithms to improve system throughput. Jiexi Zha et al. [7] proposed a performance monitoring scheme to distribute resources equally in sub-regions, reduce resource tilt, and achieve load balancing.

According to the migration mode, the dynamic load balancing algorithm can be divided into the direct method and iterative method. The direct method collects the load information of all nodes, finds the overload nodes and idle nodes among them, and assigns the tasks of the overload nodes to the idle nodes. The iterative method finds the nodes with lighter load adjacent to the overloaded node and distributes the load to these nodes. This method can enable the system to achieve global load balancing and improve throughput. Destanoglu O [8] proposed a method of the randomized hydrodynamic load balancing, using both direct and iterative methods. Using load migration as a direct method solves the problem of excessive system load in an instant and assigns the task of the node with the excessive load to the relatively idle node. It uses the fluid power method as the iterative method, consumes fewer system resources, and achieves global load balancing.

The weighted minimum connection algorithm considers the performance differences between servers in the server cluster and assigns a weight to each server to represent its processing power. At the same time, it also considers that different requests consume different resources of the server, resulting in different response times of the server to different tasks. In the weighted minimum connection algorithm, once the weight of the server is given, the entire system will not change during operation. Then, a server with a high weight may receive many requests and cause a significant drop in processing power, which will affect the entire performance of the cluster. If the weight can be dynamically changed according to the load of the server, the effect will be better. At the same time, the weighted minimum connection algorithm uses the index of the number of connections on the server to represent the current load of the server, which does not represent the load condition of the server well. CPU utilization, memory utilization, and network utilization can be better of the server's load status.

In the Swift cloud storage system, the authentication node provides identity authentication services, and the proxy node is responsible for processing user requests [9]. It is the entrance to external access to the cloud storage system. When the request comes, the proxy service will be obtained through the account ring, container ring, and object ring. Request the storage location of the object, and then forward the request to the storage node. The proxy service also handles a large number of failures. For example, when the storage service node of the storage object is unavailable, the proxy service will obtain another storage service node through the query loop and forward the request to the new storage service node. Storage nodes are used to store data. Each storage node runs account services, container services, and object services, providing management of accounts, containers, and objects, respectively. The Swift cloud storage system deployment architecture is shown in Fig. 1.

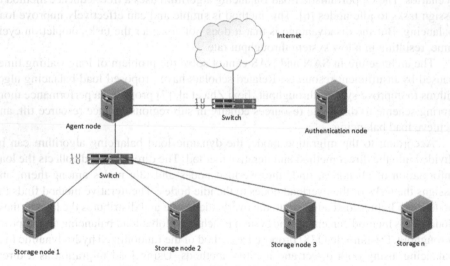

Fig. 1. The architecture of the Swift cloud storage system.

The proxy node is the external access to the Swift cloud storage system. All requests are first processed by the proxy node, and the proxy service also handles many failed nodes. For example, when the storage service node of the storage object is unavailable.

The proxy service will obtain another storage service node through the loop check and forward the request to the new storage service node. At the same time, the data requested by the user and the server response result pass through the agent node. The agent node is responsible for these functions, so it needs to have good performance. The cloud storage system is mainly for data storage and acquisition. When the user request volume is very large, the load is too high, which will result in a long response time of the system and poor availability. At this time, the proxy node will become the system bottleneck of the entire cloud storage system.

Therefore, we study the scheduling algorithm and propose a dynamic feedback load balancing algorithm based on a weighted minimum connection. And apply dynamic feedback load balancing algorithm based on weighted minimum connection to the Swift cloud storage system.

2 Design

2.1 Overall Design

When multiple agent nodes are introduced, it is a challenge to properly distribute the load. However, there is no load balancing function of agent nodes in swift. The user request needs to be authenticated by the authentication module first, then it reaches the agent node, and then the agent node processes the request. When the user access is large, the agent node will become the performance bottleneck and single point of failure of the system. To do this, multiple agent nodes need to be deployed to share user requests. At this time, it is necessary to balance the load of these agent nodes to avoid the high load of some agent nodes and the low load of other agent nodes, which not only causes the waste of resources, but also affects the overall performance of the system. After the load balancing scheduler is added to the system, after the user request passes the authentication, it will be forwarded to the load balancing scheduler first, then the load balancing scheduler selects the agent node according to the load balancing scheduling

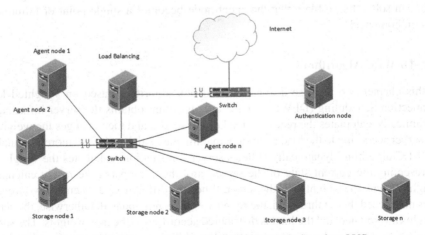

Fig. 2. Architecture of swift cloud storage system based on LVS.

algorithm, and then the load balancing scheduler forwards the user request to the agent node for processing. The system architecture is shown in Fig. 2.

The swift cloud storage system based on LVS load balancing mainly includes identity authentication module, load balancing module, proxy service module and storage service module. The relationship between the modules is shown in Fig. 3.

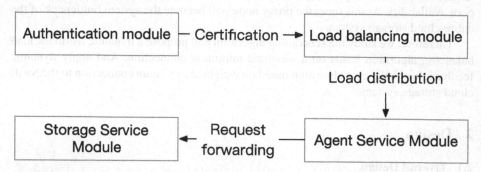

Fig. 3. Relationship between modules of the system.

The proxy service is provided by the proxy node, which is the external access to the swift cloud storage system. All requests are processed by the proxy node first. The proxy service also deals with a large number of failures. For example, when the storage service node of the storage object is not available, the proxy service will get another storage service node through ring lookup and forward the request to the new storage service node. At the same time, both the data requested by the user and the data flow of the response result of the backend real server need to flow through the proxy node. In swift cloud storage system, agent node is easy to become a single point of failure and system bottleneck. For this reason, it is necessary to expand the agent node horizontally. The user request is submitted to the load balancer, and then the load balancer allocates the user request to the agent node according to the load balancer scheduling algorithm. This can solve the problem that the agent node becomes a single point of failure and system bottleneck.

2.2 DFWLC Algorithm

In this chapter, we propose a dynamic feedback algorithm based on weighted least Connection Scheduling (DFWLC). DFWLC algorithm obtains the server information dynamically, calculates the real-time load of the server, and then changes the weight of the server according to the load condition, making the load distribution more reasonable. DFWLC algorithm dynamically collects server information, calculates the weight W' representing the current state of the server, and then compares the newly calculated weight W' with the weight W in the server. When the difference between the two weights does not exceed the set threshold, the server weight is not updated. Otherwise, the server weights are updated and the load is distributed according to the new weights. The server weight reflects the real-time processing ability of the server. It changes according to the change of the load. The load distribution changes with the change of the weight, so the load distribution will become more reasonable with the change of the load.

The algorithm of load distribution is described as follows:

Suppose a server set $S = \{S_0, S_1, \ldots, S_{n-1}\}$, the weight of server S_i is represented by $W(S_i)$, the current number of connections is represented by $C(S_i)$, and the current total number of connections is $C_{sum} = \sum C(S_i)$, $(i = 0, 1, \ldots, n)$. New connection requests are assigned to the server numbered m, and S_m must satisfy the following conditions:

$$(C(Sm)/CSUM)/W(Sm) = \min\{(C(Si)/CSUM/W(Si)\}$$
$$(i = 0, 1, \ldots, n - 1)$$
(1)

Since division consumes more CPU resources than other operations, and the Linux kernel does not support floating point arithmetic, the judgment condition $C(S_m)/W(S_m) = C(S_i)/W(S_i)$ can be optimized to $C(S_m) * W(S_i) = C(S_i)/W(S_m)$, The core code of the load distribution algorithm is shown in Fig. 4:

```
for(m = 0; m < n; m++){
    if(W(Sm) >0){
        for(i = m+1; i < n; i++){
            //Select the server with the least weight
            if(C(Sm)*W(Si) > C(Si)*W(Sm))
                m = i;
        }
        return Sm;
    }
}
return NULL;
```

Fig. 4. Core code of load distribution algorithm.

How to collect necessary server information efficiently is also a challenge. Because the real-time collection of server information is to consume a part of server resources, the collection of too much information is not of great significance but will affect the performance of the server. However, it is necessary to collect a small amount of critical information, and the consumption of resources is also small. If the sacrifice of a small amount of resources can lead to better use of resources, then the cost is worth it. The server represents the proxy node. In swift, the proxy node is the entry of cloud storage system services. The user request needs to be processed by the proxy node first. When the user uploads or downloads data, the data flow will flow through the proxy node, but the proxy node is only responsible for forwarding the data flow without caching the data. CPU, memory and network are the main factors that affect the processing capacity of agent nodes. So, this paper mainly collects the CPU, memory and network information of the agent node. The collected indicators include performance indicators and load indicators, including CPU performance, memory performance and network performance; load indicators mainly include CPU utilization, memory utilization and network utilization.

The larger the weight, the more requests the server should allocate; the smaller the weight, the less requests the server should allocate. The higher the load, the less requests the server should allocate; the lower the load, the more requests the server should allocate. So, the higher the load is, the smaller the weight should be. The lower the load is, the larger the weight should be.

Weight calculation includes performance Weight calculation and LoadWeight calculation. As shown in Eq. (2), Eq. (3) and Eq. (4).

$$PerfWeight = \mu_1 * P_{cpu} + \mu_2 * P_{memory} + \mu_3 * P_{network} \tag{2}$$

$$LoadWeight = k_1 * (1 - U_{cpu}) + k_2 * (1 - U_{memory}) + k_3 * (1 - U_{network}) \tag{3}$$

$$Weight = PerfWeight * LoadWeight \tag{4}$$

Among them, P_{cpu} is CPU performance, P_{memory} is memory performance, $P_{network}$ is network card performance, U_{cpu} is CPU utilization, U_{memory} is memory utilization, and $U_{network}$ is network utilization. $\mu_1, \mu_2, \mu_3, k_1, k_2, k_3$ are the influence factors, representing the influence of CPU, memory, and network respectively, where $\mu_1 + \mu_2 + \mu_3 = 1$, $k_1 + k_2 + k_3 = 1$.

Assuming that *Weight* is the weight of the current server, *Weight'* is the new weight calculated according to the real-time load of the server, and threshold is the Threshold value of the weight change:

$$Weight = \begin{cases} Weight & |Wight' - Weight| \leq Threshold \\ Weight & |Wight' - Weight| > Threshold \end{cases} \tag{5}$$

3 Experiments

3.1 Server Configuration

In the experiment of this paper, four machines are used in total, and the configuration of the machines is shown in Table 1.

The experimental scenarios are divided into the experimental environment without agent node load balancing and the experimental scenario with agent node load balancing. Only one copy of the data is stored in the experiment.

The experimental deployment scheme without load balancing includes authentication node, agent node, storage node and test client. The experimental environment is shown in Table 2.

The experimental deployment scheme of agent node load balancing includes authentication node, load balancing node, agent node, storage node and test client. The experimental environment is shown in Table 3.

Traditional performance testing tools are mainly used to test the performance of Web sites. Because cloud storage is a new technology rising in recent years, its special test

Table 1. Machine configuration information in the experiment.

Machine IP	CPU	Internal storage	Network card speed	OS	Core	Disk
172.29.132.51	Intel@Core™2 CPU 6320 @1.86 GHz	1 GB	100 Mb/s	Ubuntu 12.04 LTS	3.11.0-15-generic	HDS728080PLA380
172.29.132.52	Intel@Core™2 CPU 6320 @1.86 GHz	1 GB	100 Mb/s	Ubuntu 12.04 LTS	3.11.0-15-generic	HDS728080PLA380
172.29.132.53	Intel@PentiumCPU G840 @2.80 GHz	5.7 GB	100 Mb/s	Ubuntu 12.04 LTS	3.11.0-15-generic	WD2500AAKX-753CA1
172.29.132.55	AMD A6-3420M APU 1.5 GHZ	2 GB	100 Mb/s	Ubuntu 12.04 LTS	3.11.0-15-generic	HTS547550A9E384

Table 2. No load balancing experimental environment of agent nodes.

Machine IP	Deploy the service	Instructions
172.29.132.51	Proxy server	The agent node
172.29.132.53	Keystone, object server, container server, account server	Authentication node, storage node
172.29.132.55		Test client

Table 3. Experimental environment for load balancing of agent nodes.

Machine IP	Deploy the service	Instructions
172.29.132.51	Proxy server	The agent node
172.29.132.52	Proxy server	The agent node
172.29.132.53	Keystone, LVS, object server, container server, account server	Authentication nodes, load balancing nodes, storage nodes
172.29.132.54	Virtual IP	Virtual IP

benchmark and performance test tools are very few. The cloud object storage benchmark developed by Intel [10] is specially used for stress testing of cloud object storage, and plays an important role in the field of performance testing of cloud object storage. This paper uses COSbench to test the performance of swift cloud storage system. COSench is a distributed system including controller and driver, which has good scalability. The controller provides the entry of the system. The user configures the test scenario on the controller, and then submits the configuration file. The controller will assign the task to each driver according to the configuration file information and the current system topology. The task is finally executed on the driver. COSbench provides a friendly web user interface. Users can easily configure test scenarios, where Worker Count represents the number of concurrent users, and Rampup time represents the warm-up time, which is for the stability of the test. Its information is not the result of the test. The Runtime represents the time of the test run.

According to the different importance of CPU, memory, and network in Swift cloud storage system, in the weight calculation formula of DFWLC algorithm in this paper, the coefficient of CPU utilization is set to 6, the coefficient of memory utilization is set to 2, and the coefficient of network utilization is set to 2. The threshold value for weight change is set to 50.

We use DFWLC as the load balancing scheduling algorithm of the agent node proposed in this paper to simulate the process of 20, 40, 60, 80, 100 users downloading 1 MB to 10 MB random size files at the same time. In order to ensure enough time to stabilize the test results , each test is preheated for 100 s and run for 300 s. The load information is collected and uploaded to the load balancing scheduling node every 10 s. In addition, the results are compared with the weighted least connection algorithm (WLC) used by the proxy node as the load balancing scheduling algorithm and the cloud storage system without load balancing. The performance of the proposed strategy is verified from three aspects: response time, throughput and network bandwidth.

A. **Based on response time analysis results.**

Figure 5 compares the response times of the above-mentioned different cloud storage systems. It can be found that the response times of the three systems are on the rise with the increasing number of concurrent users. For the same number of concurrent users, the response time of DFWLC is about 4% shorter than that of WLC, and 8% shorter than that of none. In addition, the response time of WLC is about 4% shorter than that of none. Therefore, the load balancing strategy proposed in this paper can effectively shorten the response time of the system.

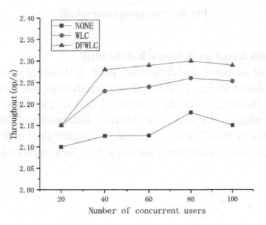

Fig. 5. Response time test result.

B. **Based on throughput analysis results.**

Figure 6 compares the throughput and change trend of different systems according to the number of concurrent users. It is obvious that with the continuous growth of the number of concurrent users, the throughput of the three systems increases. When the number of concurrent users reaches more than 80, the throughput will drop slightly. For the same number of concurrent users, the throughput of DFWLC is about 3% higher than that of WLC, 7% higher than that of NONE, and the throughput of WLC is about 4% higher than that of NONE. Therefore, the use of load balancing algorithm can improve throughput, and the load balancing strategy proposed in this paper is more effective in increasing throughput.

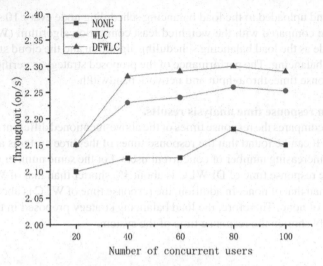

Fig. 6. Throughput test results.

C. Analysis results based on network bandwidth.

The influence of the number of concurrent users in different systems on the network bandwidth is shown in Fig. 7. The network bandwidth will increase first and then decrease with the increase of the number of concurrent users. When the number of concurrent users is the same, the network bandwidth of DFWLC is basically the same as that of WLC, which is about 4% higher than that of NONE. Among them, the bandwidth is maintained between 11.3 mb/s and 11.4 mb/s without load

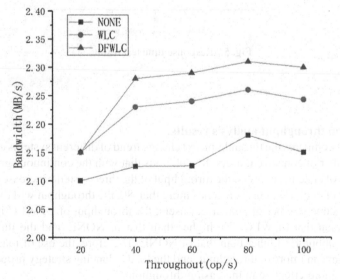

Fig. 7. Experimental results of network bandwidth.

balancing, while the bandwidth of WLC and DFWLC is between 11.7 mb/s and 11.9 mb/s. Therefore, the strategy proposed in this paper can increase the network bandwidth to a certain extent.

The network card of the server in the system is 100 Mbps, and the theoretical maximum network speed is 12.5 mb/s. The network speed in the experiment can hardly be improved because it is close to the theoretical network speed of the network card, which has become an important factor restricting the improvement of the system performance.

In conclusion, compared with the system without load balancing, WLC system performance table is better, which proves the effectiveness of load balancing for agent nodes. For different load balancing strategies, DFWLC proposed in this paper performs better than WLC, so the effectiveness of DFWLC in load balancing algorithm is proved.

4   Conclusions

The rapid development of the Internet and the Internet of Things has driven the development of the intelligent industry, and a large amount of information interaction has increased the burden on the agent nodes in the cloud storage system. For this reason, it is particularly important to use multiple proxy nodes to share requests and achieve load balancing. However, there is no load balancing mechanism for proxy nodes in Swift. This paper proposes a load balancing scheduling algorithm and applies this algorithm to a multi-agent node cloud storage system based on LVS load balancing. It dynamically obtains server resource information and reallocates system resources according to load status. The experimental results show that the performance of the Swift cloud storage system with proxy node load balancing has improved in response time, throughput, and network bandwidth compared to the swift system without load balancing. At the same time, the dynamic feedback algorithm based on the minimum connection further improves the performance of the system.

Acknowledgement. This work is supported by State Grid Shandong Electric Power Company Science and Technology Project Funding under Grant no. 520613200001, 520613180002, 62061318C002, Weihai Scientific Research and Innovation Fund (2020).

References

1. Data Age 2025. https://www.seagate.com/files/www-content/our-story/trends/files/data-age-2025-white-paper-simplified-chinese.pdf. Accessed 06 Mar 2021
2. Westphal, R.E., OMalley, D.M.: Fusion of locomotor maneuvers, and improving sensory capabilities, give rise to the flexible homing strikes of juvenile zebrafish. Front. Neural Circuits 7, 108 (2013)
3. Zeng, W.F., Zhao, Y.S., Ou, K.T., et al.: Research on cloud storage architecture and key technologies. In: 2nd International Conference on Interaction Sciences: Information Technology, pp. 1044–1048. ACM, New York (2009)

4. Snell, A.F.: Solving big data problems with private cloud storage. Intersect360 Research, Cloud Computing in HPC: Usage and Types (June 2011)
5. Li, W.F., Shi, H.S.: Dynamic load balancing algorithm based on FCFS. In: 2009 Fourth International Conference on Innovative Computing, Information and Control (ICICIC), pp. 1528–1531. IEEE, Kaohsiung (2009)
6. Wang, S.C.F., Yan, K.Q.S., Liao, W.P.T., et al.: Towards a load balancing in a three-level cloud computing network. In: 2010 3rd International Conference on Computer Science and Information Technology, pp. 108–113. IEEE, Chengdu (2010)
7. Zha, J.F., Wang, J.S., Han, R.T., et al.: Research on load balance of service capability interaction management. In: 2010 3rd IEEE International Conference on Broadband Network and Multimedia Technology (IC-BNMT), pp. 212–217. IEEE, Beijing (2010)
8. Destanoglu, O.F., Sevilgen, F.E.S.: Randomized hydrodynamic load balancing approach. In: 2008 International Conference on Parallel Processing-Workshops, pp. 196–203. IEEE, Eugene (2008)
9. Zhao, Y.F., Hategan, M.S., Clifford, B.T., et al.: Swift: fast, reliable, loosely coupled parallel computation. In: 2007 IEEE Congress on Services, pp. 199–206. IEEE, Salt Lake City (2007)
10. Zheng, Q.F., Chen, H.S., Wang, Y.T., et al.: COSBench: a benchmark tool for cloud object storage services. In: 6th International Conference on Cloud Computing, pp. 998–999. IEEE, Washington (2012)

Research on the Picture Database of Minority Emotion

Zongnan Wang[(✉)] ⓘ, Xueting Wei ⓘ, Demeng Wu ⓘ, and Huiping Jiang ⓘ

Brain Cognitive Computing Lab, School of Information Engineering,
Minzu University of China, Beijing 100081, China

Abstract. Since ancient times, our country has been a collection of multi-ethnic coexistence. The diversified cultural differences, the regionality of educational background, and the very different living environment have caused different ethnic groups to have different emotions and attitudes towards the same things. Dealing with these problems will cause a lot of unnecessary trouble. In order to better understand and understand the emotional changes of various ethnic groups, promote ethnic integration, enhance national identity, and strengthen the sense of community of the Chinese nation. Therefore, the establishment of a library of ethnic minority emotions is very necessary for ethnic research. In this paper, we first developed an ethnic minority emotional picture tagging system, which uses the form of a network questionnaire to collect data on emotional pictures in the database. Then use SPSS18 to perform statistical analysis on the data, label each emotion picture, build a library of ethnic minority emotion pictures, and provide quantitative services for subsequent ethnic research.

Keywords: Emotion computing · Multi-ethnic emotion picture · Database

1 Introduction

Emotional computing is an advanced stage of artificial intelligence research. Professor Picard of the MIT Media Lab first proposed the concept of affective computing in 1997 [1]. Affective computing is related to emotion, which comes from emotion or calculations that can affect emotions. The goal of emotional computing is to give computers the ability to perceive, understand, and express, to communicate more actively and friendly with people. In the field of affective computing, some scholars use emotion as an independent variable to study emotion-induced behaviors, such as aggressive behavior and helping behavior. Other scholars use emotion as a dependent variable to study related phenomena, such as subjective experience, facial expression behavior, individual differences in nervous system response and emotional response, etc. [2–4]. The subjective characteristics of emotion increase the difficulty of experimental control, which directly affects the measurement and analysis of emotion-related phenomena. Therefore, it is very important to select appropriate emotion-induced experimental materials. Pictures can induce a variety of different emotions. For most people, pictures can induce emotions with high intensity, and the emotions induced by pictures have high consistency with the

X. Sun et al. (Eds.): ICAIS 2021, CCIS 1423, pp. 713–726, 2021.
https://doi.org/10.1007/978-3-030-78618-2_59

subjects. At present, the international standardized emotional material library is mainly based on the International Affective Picture System (IAPS) compiled by Lang et al., which is used for the research of emotion, cognition, and electrophysiology. Although the International Emotional Picture System (IAPS) [5] has good international versatility, due to the differences in factors such as culture, personality, and so on, Luo Jialiang and others have compiled a localized Chinese Emotional Picture System (CAPS) [6]. However, China is a multi-ethnic community. In the process of ethnic integration, different ethnic groups have different demands and expectations. Their diverse opinions lead to different emotional expressions and emotional experiences of different ethnic groups. The emotional differences between different ethnic groups can not be ignored. It is very important to construct the emotional picture database of ethnic minorities for the study of ethnic issues, especially the social mental, and behavioral characteristics of different ethnic groups. This paper studies the emotional picture tagging system nationalizes a large number of emotional pictures and builds a library of ethnic minority emotional pictures. And use SPSS software to evaluate and analyze the effect of the emotional picture library.

2 Related Work

2.1 Emotion Picture Library

The most commonly used emotion-inducing picture system in the world is a set of emotional picture stimulation system developed by the national mental health center of the United States. This system is aimed at the needs of emotion and attention research. Based on the research results of Osgood et al. From different perspectives of emotion analysis, the subjects scored the pleasure, arousal, and control of pictures by self-report method, and then constructed a highly standardized emotional picture stimulation system.

After a long-term research, Professor Zhou Renlai from the school of psychology of Beijing Normal University revised the three dimensions of the international emotional picture system in China. Professor of Psychology (Luo Yuejia, etc.) of the Chinese Academy of Sciences also revised the IAPS system. Under the trend of multi-ethnic integration in our country, the differences between various ethnic groups cannot be ignored. To improve the study of ethnic emotions, it is necessary to establish the emotional picture system of ethnic minorities. Among them, the most important link in the effectiveness of the picture stimulation material. The effectiveness of emotion induction will be affected by the material of the emotion picture library. Therefore, it is necessary to do some nationalized revision work before applying the localized emotional picture library.

2.2 Eysenck Personality Questionnaire

Eysenck's personality theory [7] is put forward by British psychologist eisenk, which is based on the theory of personality dimensions and the three-factor model. In the Eysenck Personality Questionnaire, there are four test questions on the scale, and the scoring standards for the test questions on different scales are different [8]. According to the total scores obtained by the respondent on the E, P, N, and L scales, the standard score T is calculated by the formula (1):

$$T = 50 + 10 * (x - m)/sd \tag{1}$$

x is the testee's score, m is the average of all subjects, and sd is the standard deviation. The specific score description sees Appendix 1. This system uses the Eysenck Personality Questionnaire to test the subjects' personalities.

2.3 Reliability and Validity

Reliability. Reliability refers to the reliability of test tools. The investigator used the same method to repeat the test on the same group of subjects, analyzed and compared the results obtained, and observed the degree of correlation between the two test results [9]. The reliability expressed by the formula is defined as the ratio of the true value variance to the actual value variance, as shown in formula (2):

$$R = t/x \tag{2}$$

Where R represents the reliability, t and x represent the variance of the true value and the actual value, respectively. The true value represents the score obtained by a test object according to the expected test objective, and the actual value is the score obtained during the actual test. In practice, the true value cannot be obtained, so if you want to calculate the level of reliability, you must rely on the reliability coefficient.

The reliability coefficient ranges from 0 to 1. The reliability coefficient is directly proportional to the reliability; otherwise, the reliability is lower. Generally speaking, the reliability coefficient between 0.7 and 0.9 indicates that the test results are more reliable [10]. Reliability analysis methods include retest method, duplicate method, half method, and so on. In this system, we use the test-retest reliability method; that is, two weeks after the first questionnaire survey, use the ethnic minority emotion picture labeling system to continue the questionnaire test on the same group and compare the correlation between the two survey results.

Validity. Validity refers to the degree of correlation between the actual results of the test tool and the characteristics to be measured. Validity also tests whether the experiment can achieve the investigator's purpose, that is, the validity and correctness of the questionnaire. The purpose of the questionnaire is to obtain efficient results that meet the requirements of the investigator. Therefore, the higher the validity, the more effective the questionnaire is. For example, a weight scale is effective for measuring weight, but it is not effective for measuring height. In this questionnaire system, we use a large number of publicly searchable pictures to test emotions, but there are also some pictures with a high degree of controversy and low consistency [11]. Therefore, SPSS is used to process the data, and the average and standard deviation are used to compare the concentration and volatility. For the extremes of the mean, pictures with larger variances are deleted.

The questionnaire survey evaluation system in this article is shown in Fig. 1.

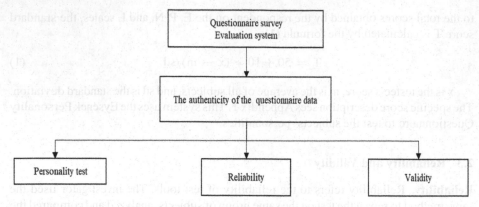

Fig. 1. Questionnaire survey evaluation system

3   Minority Emotion Picture Annotation System

This paper uses the method of online questionnaire survey for practical verification, collects the questionnaire survey data from respondents, and nationalizes the three-dimensional parameters of each picture based on statistical analysis, constructing an emotional picture labeling system for ethnic minorities. The system framework is shown in Fig. 2.

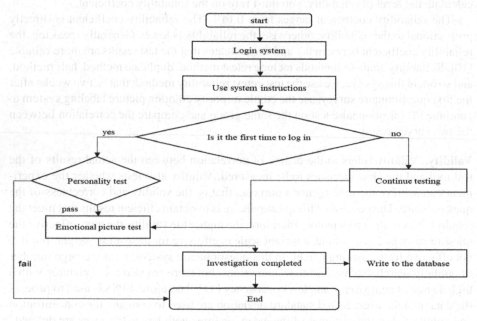

Fig. 2. System architecture

3.1 Login Interface

First, the testee logs in to the survey website [12]. After inputting personal information in the login interface, a permission consent window about privacy protection will pop up, and click agree to enter the personality test interface.

3.2 Personality Test System

Personality can be explained as a human character or all of its psychological characteristics. When we are at different times and places, personality will affect our psychological characteristics and behavior patterns, causing us to show different emotional responses. To judge whether the personality of the testee is extreme or normal, the personality test system is a necessary link. The system refers to setting the test subject in a specific environment and testing the personality characteristics of the test subject through different test questions. Only by passing the personality test can you proceed to the next step.

3.3 Emotional Picture Survey

After the testee gets his score, click the OK button to enter the ethnic minority picture emotion survey interface, which will present a large number of publicly visible pictures retrieved in sequence [13]. In this system, a total of 852 public images are retrieved, all with clear content and resolution, including human emotions like happiness, sadness, horror, anger, threats, charm, ugliness, or various objects, nudes, homes, works of art, daily necessities, houses, sexual contact, and death, public hazards, pollution, urban landscape, seascape, sports scenes, war disasters, news magazines, medical treatment, etc. On the right side of the test interface, there are three dimensions of image display: potency, arousal, and dominance, with nine levels from left to right, increasing in sequence. Because of the limitation of the length of the article, five items are listed. As shown in Fig. 3:

Fig. 3. Sentiment survey interface

Participants who passed the personality test were subjected to emotional picture surveys [14]. Each question listed in this system is a publicly retrieved picture. On the right side of the test interface, pictures are showing the three dimensions of pleasure, arousal, and control, which are 9 levels from left to right, increasing in turn. The subjects selected the corresponding data quantification levels in turn, as shown in Fig. 4. Pleasure is the degree of a person's happiness, ranging from unhappy to happy, arousal is the intensity of the emotional state, ranging from weak to strong, and control is the strength of self-control. The range is from weak to strong. Participants need to choose the answer according to their living habits. After completing the picture test questions, it can end.

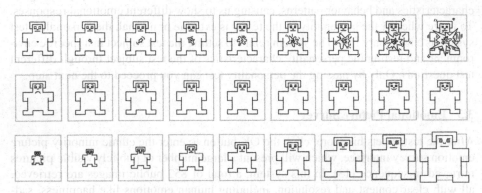

Fig. 4. Picture display of each dimension (respectively arousal, pleasure, control)

Take the level of pleasure as an example. For example, 1 = very unpleasant, 3 = a little unpleasant, 5 = moderate, 7 = a little pleasant, 9 = very pleasant. Among them, 2, 4, 6, 8 provide the participants with the level and degree Interlace more subtle determination and selection.

3.4 Compile a Picture Library of Ethnic Minority Emotions

According to the results of statistical data, the pictures with low emotion-induced consistency are eliminated, and the remaining pictures are nationalized with three-dimensional parameters, to establish and improve the ethnic emotion picture library [15].

This article mainly searches through a large number of publicly visible pictures, selects pictures with obvious emotional characteristics as the evaluation sample, conducts personality tests on minority universities from different ethnicities, different ages, and different genders, and uses self-reporting for those who meet the requirements. In the form of a 9-point scale, emotional pictures are scored from the perspectives of pleasure, arousal, and control. Finally, SPSS software is used to analyze the data of different dimensions, integrate the survey results of the testees, and improve the ethnic emotional picture library from a variety of emotional perspectives, and finally compile a set of ethnic emotional picture survey system.

4 Data Analysis

To verify whether the annotation data of the ethnic minority emotional picture library is valid. A total of 40 subjects from 10 ethnic groups including Han, Hui, Manchu, Tibetan, Mongolian, Miao, Yi, Yao, Kazakh, and Naxi nationalities were selected, of which 20 are male and female: the ages are between 20–24. All 40 subjects passed the personality test. Next, SPSS software was used to analyze the three-dimensional dimension data. The subjects are classified according to different nationalities, genders, and ages, calculate the average and standard deviation of the three-dimensional quantitative data for each test question picture and label the pictures, and establish and improve the ethnic emotion picture library by comparing the consistency of the data [16]. The process is shown in Fig. 5:

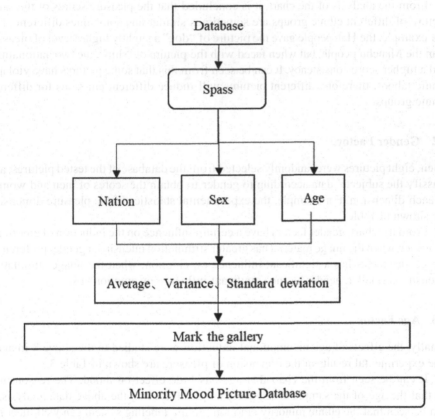

Fig. 5. Data statistics process

The purpose of this article is to nationalize the emotional image library. Therefore, in the statistical data, the score data of the subjects on each dimension of the pictures are classified according to the ethnic groups of the subjects, and the emotional differences of each ethnic group are analyzed and compared, and the result data is stored in the database for reference in future experiments. Besides, this article also studies the influence of gender and age on emotions and analyzes the changing factors of emotions from multiple angles.

4.1 Ethnic Factors

First, the data in the bdo.tb_answer database is classified by ethnicity, and the quantitative values of emotions of different nationalities in each dimension are counted respectively, and the pictures are labeled with nationalization through comparative analysis. For example, from the perspective of the basic emotions of various ethnic groups, eleven representative images were selected from the dbo.photo database to display. For example, in the case of scoring the dimension of pleasure, the experimental results are shown in Table 1:

From the analysis of the chart, it is concluded that the pleasure scores of the same picture of different ethnic groups are sometimes similar and sometimes different [17]. For example, the Han people gave the picture of "dog" a slightly higher level of pleasure than the Manchu people, but when faced with the picture of "ship", the two nationalities had a higher score consistency. It can be seen from this that some pictures have violated ethnic taboos, therefore, different pictures will induce different emotions for different ethnic groups.

4.2 Gender Factors

Then, eight pictures were randomly selected from the database of the tested pictures, and classify the subjects' data according to gender to obtain the scores of men and women in each dimension. For example, the experimental statistics of the pleasure dimension are shown in Table 2:

From the chart, gender factors have a certain influence on the induction of emotions. However, when the image material has greater stimulation intensity or gender preference, the gender factor has a significant influence on emotion; when the image stimulation intensity is smaller, gender has no significant influence on emotion [18].

4.3 Age Factor

Finally, the effects of age on emotional induction were studied in the above 8 images. The experimental results of the dimension of pleasure are shown in Table 3.

It can be seen from the chart that age has little effect on mood. The reason may be that the age of the sample is relatively single. Based on the above data analysis, it can be seen that the ethnic minority emotion picture labeling system can well meet the predetermined system requirements so that the three-dimensional parameters of each emotion picture have national attributes, which lays the foundation for the compilation of ethnic minority emotion picture libraries.

Table 1. Score of pleasure

Ple	Avg											Std										
Sub	Pig	Dog	Hor	Cat	Sn	Sh	Fish	Don	Baby	Ship	Vio	Pig	Dog	Hor	Cat	Sn	Sh	Fish	Don	Baby	Ship	Vio
Han	5.25	5.00	4.50	6.00	5.50	5.75	5.75	4.25	5.50	5.00	5.25	0.96	1.15	0.58	1.15	1.73	0.96	0.50	0.50	1.29	0.82	0.96
Hui	2.00	1.75	1.50	2.75	3.25	4.50	3.75	2.25	4.25	2.25	4.00	0.00	0.96	0.58	1.50	3.20	2.65	1.26	0.50	3.40	1.89	2.71
Mc	6.25	1.50	6.75	4.50	3.75	6.50	4.75	6.75	6.00	4.25	5.00	0.96	0.58	2.50	3.11	3.59	2.38	3.77	1.50	2.16	2.87	2.94
Ti	4.00	4.00	3.75	5.00	4.00	2.50	4.25	3.75	4.00	3.25	5.00	0.82	1.15	0.50	1.83	2.58	1.29	0.50	0.50	1.83	1.71	1.83
Mg	3.00	5.00	4.50	4.50	5.75	4.50	4.00	6.00	3.25	3.50	6.25	2.16	1.63	3.11	2.08	2.87	3.51	0.00	2.83	2.22	2.38	1.71
Mi	5.00	2.50	5.50	4.75	5.50	2.50	4.75	5.25	4.75	4.25	5.75	3.37	1.29	2.38	3.30	3.00	0.58	1.89	1.71	2.06	2.87	2.75
Yi	6.75	2.75	1.75	4.00	3.50	3.75	3.75	5.50	7.00	4.50	5.00	2.22	0.96	0.96	1.83	0.58	3.40	3.10	3.11	1.15	1.00	3.65
Yao	6.50	2.75	4.75	2.75	2.25	5.25	4.25	5.25	6.50	5.50	6.00	1.29	0.96	1.71	0.96	0.50	3.40	2.50	1.71	1.91	1.91	1.41
Ka	2.25	3.75	6.25	4.25	5.00	3.75	4.50	2.25	4.25	5.75	3.75	0.96	1.26	2.22	2.36	2.94	2.75	2.08	1.26	3.30	2.06	2.87
Nax	5.25	3.00	5.75	6.75	3.00	4.50	4.00	5.50	5.25	4.75	5.25	1.71	1.15	2.75	3.20	1.83	1.29	2.94	3.70	2.36	1.89	2.36

Table 2. Score of pleasure

Ple	Ave								Std							
Sub	Spi	Coc	Sha	Wom	Butterfly	Icecream	Judge	Hospital	Spider	Cockroach	Shark	Woman	Butterfly	Icecream	Judge	Hospital
Male	3.25	3.25	3.25	3.25	3.25	3.25	3.25	3.25	0.96	0.96	0.96	0.96	0.96	0.96	0.96	0.96
Female	2.25	2.25	2.25	2.25	2.25	2.25	2.25	2.25	0.96	0.96	0.96	0.96	0.96	0.96	0.96	0.96

Table 3. Score of pleasure

Ple	Ave										Std									
Subjet	Spider	Coc	Shark	Woman	Butterfly	Icecream	Judge	Hospital			Spider	Coc	Shark	Woman	Butterfly	Icecream	Judge	Hospital		
20	3.00	3.25	3.25	5.50	7.00	6.75	4.50	3.50			0.82	0.96	1.26	0.58	0.82	0.50	0.58	0.58		
21	2.75	3.50	3.00	6.75	6.25	6.25	5.00	4.75			0.96	0.58	0.82	0.50	0.96	0.96	0.82	0.50		
22	3.75	3.50	3.00	6.25	6.50	6.75	4.75	4.00			0.96	0.58	0.82	0.96	1.29	0.50	0.50	0.82		
23	3.50	2.75	3.25	5.75	6.00	6.33	4.75	3.50			0.58	0.96	1.71	0.96	0.82	1.53	0.50	0.58		
24	3.25	2.75	3.00	6.75	6.00	6.50	5.00	3.25			0.96	0.96	0.82	0.50	0.82	1.29	0.82	0.50		

5 Conclusion

Based on the international general emotional picture library, this paper establishes an ethnic emotional picture labeling system to label a large number of publicly searchable pictures with the attributes of each ethnic group, providing good materials for the nationalization of pictures in my country. The national emotional picture library has enriched the psychological research of ethnic minorities and has promoted the progress of the research on emotion-induced by Chinese emotional pictures. Through in-depth research on the survey results, the following conclusions are drawn:

1. The influence of ethnic factors is more prominent. For pictures involving religious beliefs, different ethnic groups show different emotional changes in terms of pleasure, arousal, and dominance.
2. The influence of gender is limited. In the face of different kinds of pictures, there are differences in the mood changes of boys and girls, and there are similarities in performance. For example, when facing cockroach pictures, boys and girls have lower levels of pleasure; in terms of arousal, girls have stronger emotions; in terms of control, boys show better control [19].
3. The influence of the age factor has little effect. Among the 5 ages between 20 and 24, the scores of the same pictures fluctuated little in all ages, indicating that the emotional impact was low in the age range of the experimental test.
4. To make the questionnaire more reliable, a second test should be performed on the subjects. After 14 days from the first experiment, the same questionnaire test was conducted on the same 40 students. By comparing the two data before and after, it is found that the test results have a higher correlation, which means that the test content is highly reliable and the questionnaire is reliable.
5. In terms of validity, through statistical analysis of data, each picture can achieve the purpose of measurement, so there is no need to delete pictures.

The establishment of the ethnic minority emotion picture tagging system integrates much negative theoretical knowledge and technical research, but it still needs to be improved in practical applications, and the performance of all aspects needs to be improved to make the testing process more efficient and convenient, and the image attributes are more accurate and effective. In this system, there are the following shortcomings:

1. The range of the tested population is small and the number is small. In the actual experiment, the subjects participating in the survey were limited to the National University, and the age difference was small, so they could not be well represented.
2. There are too many pictures in the questionnaire. When filling in the questionnaire, due to a large number of pictures, the subjects are prone to feelings of boredom and exhaustion during the answering process, which affects the quality of the answers.
3. The length of the interval also has a certain impact on the results of the test. The longer the time, the more likely the subjects are to fluctuate greatly, but if the time is shorter, the subject will have a certain memory of the last test, which will affect the

judgment ability of this time. Due to unable to accurately estimate the appropriate interval time, will have a certain impact on the experimental results [20].

The questionnaire evaluation system of this article is to first conduct a personality test on the subjects through the Eysenck personality questionnaire. This step is mainly to judge whether the personality of the testee is extreme. Then under the premise of ensuring the authenticity and validity of the questionnaire data, the reliability and validity are considered. On the other hand, the ethnic minority emotion picture labeling system mainly uses the online questionnaire survey method for practical verification, collects questionnaire survey data from respondents, and nationalizes the three-dimensional parameters of each picture based on statistical analysis, thereby constructing an emotional picture annotation system for ethnic minorities. To verify the validity of the annotation data of the ethnic minority emotion image database, we selected 40 subjects from 10 ethnic groups. Then SPSS software was used to statistically analyze the three-dimensional parameter annotation data of the subjects. The subjects are classified according to different standards, and the average and standard deviation of the three-dimensional quantitative data of each test question picture are calculated and the pictures are marked, and the ethnic minorities are established and improved by comparing the consistency of the data Emotional ·picture library [21]. This article mainly promotes the research on the nationalization of the emotional picture library in our country and provides quantitative services for the psychological research of ethnic minorities, and at the same time promotes the progress of the research on the emotion induced by emotional pictures in China. The most important thing is to promote national unity and enhance national identity. However, it needs to be continuously improved in practice. The future direction of improvement will mainly focus on gradually expanding the number of testers and increasing the gap between all age groups. This requires us to go deep into ethnic minority areas and cannot rely solely on online questionnaires. Form, to have a better representation. And in practice, due to the large age gap, it will inevitably involve busy working groups. To better carry out the work, it is necessary to select a more appropriate amount of pictures and shorten the test duration.

References

1. Picard, R.W.: Affective Computing. MIT Press, London (1997)
2. Zeng, Z., Pantic, M., Roisman, G.I., et al.: A survey of affect recognition methods: audio, visual, and spontaneous expressions. IEEE Trans. Pattern Anal. Mach. Intell. 31(1), 39–58 (2008)
3. Phillips, M.L., Drevets, W.C., Rauch, S.L., Lane, R., et al.: Neurobiology of emotion perception I: the neural basis of normal emotion perception. Biol. Psychiatry 54(5), 504–514 (2003)
4. Tamietto, M., De. Gelder, B.: Neural bases of the non-conscious perception of emotional signals. Nat. Rev. Neurosci. 11(10), 697–709 (2010)
5. Lang, P.J., Bradley, M.M., Cuthbert, B.N.: International affective picture system (IAPS): technical manual and affective ratings. NIMH Cent. Study Emot. Atten. 1, 39–58 (1997)
6. Bai, L., Ma, H., Huang, Y.X., et al.: Development of Chinese emotional picture system. Chin. J. Ment. Health 19(11), 719–722 (2005)

7. Ryan, J.J., Dai, X.Y., Zheng, L.: Psychological test usage in the People's Republic of China. J. Psychoeduc. Assess. **12**(4), 324–330 (1994)
8. Liu, Y., Tao, L.M., Fu, X.L.: The analysis of PAD emotional state model based on emotion pictures. J. Image Graph. **14**(5), 753–758 (2009)
9. Liu, X.N., Xu, A.X., Zhou, R.L.: Native research of international affective picture system: assessment in university students. Chin. J. Clin. Psychol. **17**(6), 687–689,692 (2009)
10. Zhang, H., Xu, D.: Ethnic painting analysis based on deep learning. Scientia Sinica (Inf.) **49**(2), 204–215 (2019)
11. Zhang, Y.P., Li, G.Y., Li, Y.: Survey of application of deep learning in image recognition. Comput. Eng. Appl. **55**(12), 20–36 (2019)
12. Xu, S.W., Chen, S.Y.: Image classification method based on deep learning. Appl. Electron. Tech. **44**(6), 116–119 (2018)
13. Liu, S.Y.: Research on perception-oriented image scene and emotion categorization. Ph.D. dissertation, Beijing Jiaotong University, China (2010)
14. Zhou, S.R.: Analysis and research of facial expression recognition algorithm. Ph.D. dissertation, Central South University, China (2009)
15. Yang, Z.Z., Kuang, N., Fan, L., Kang, B.: Review of image classification algorithms based on convolutional neural networks. J. Signal Process. **34**(12), 1474–1489 (2018)
16. Li, Z.Y., Xu, H.K., Duan, B.: Research on image emotion feature extraction based on deep learning CNN model. Libr. Inf. Serv. **63**(11), 96–107 (2019)
17. Jing, C.K., Song, T., Zhuang, L., Liu, G., Wang, L., Liu, K.L.: A survey of face recognition technology based on deep convolutional neural networks. Comput. Appl. Softw. **35**(1), 223–231 (2018)
18. Hu, E.L., Feng, R.: Image retrieval system based on deep learning. Comput. Syst. Appl. **26**(3), 8–19 (2017)
19. Liu, R.M., Meng, X.Z.: Emotional analysis of multimedia pictures based on deep learning. e-Educ. Res. **39**(1), 68–74 (2018)
20. Liu, Y.L., Guo, Q.H.: The application of deep learning in image recognition. China Comput. Commun. **32**(7), 28–30 (2020)
21. Wang, W.N., Li, L.M., Huang, J.X., Luo, J.B., Xu, X.M.: A multi-level deep convolutional neural network for image emotion classification. J. South China Univ. Technol. (Nat. Sci.) **47**(6), 39–50 (2019)

Instant Messaging Application Traffic Recognition

Pu Wang[1], Xinrun Lyu[2], Xiangzhan Yu[1], and Chong Zhang[2(✉)]

[1] School of Cyberspace Science, Harbin Institute of Technology, Harbin 150001, China
[2] National Computer Network Emergency Response Technical Team/Coordination Center of China, Beijing 100032, China
zhangchong@cert.org.cn

Abstract. As a basic work of network security, network traffic recognition plays an important role in network resource management and abnormal network traffic monitoring. At present, network traffic identification has become one of the hottest issues in academic research. In the past research, network traffic analysis was mainly done by Port Matching, Deep Packet Inspection. However, these methods are not perfect, and they are not suitable for today. This paper implements a traffic recognition method based on deep learning and machine learning. Besides, this paper implements unsupervised clustering of traffic. On the UNB ISCX data set, the experimental results are quite good.

Keywords: Network traffic recognition · Deep learning · Machine learning · Unsupervised clustering

1 Introduction

Network traffic is a measure of the data interaction of various nodes in the network and can be used as a basis for the evaluation of network operation status. By recognizing the network traffic and mastering the change law of the network traffic, the network status can be evaluated, whether there are abnormal events in the network, and the normal operation of the network can be maintained. As a basic work of network security, network traffic analysis plays an important role in network resource management and abnormal traffic monitoring.

At the same time, instant messaging software represented by QQ and WeChat has developed rapidly and has become a new way of life for people. People's lives are increasingly inseparable from these software, which also occupy most of the entrance of network traffic. So this paper will focus on the flow analysis of instant messaging software. Instant messaging software usually adopts encryption and tunneling transmission technology for security protection, such as Secure Sockets Layer [21] (SSL), Secure Shell [22] (SSH) protocol, Virtual Private Network (VPN) etc. The encrypted traffic data lacks obvious protocol characteristics, which increases the difficulty of classification.

In recent years, deep learning and machine learning have achieved very competitive performance in the fields of computer vision and natural language processing, greatly

© Springer Nature Switzerland AG 2021
X. Sun et al. (Eds.): ICAIS 2021, CCIS 1423, pp. 727–738, 2021.
https://doi.org/10.1007/978-3-030-78618-2_60

improving productivity. Therefore, we try to introduce deep learning models and methods into the traffic analysis problem. For traffic, data is transmitted in a byte stream on the network, and the value range of each byte is [0,255]. This coincides with the pixel value range of the grayscale image. In other words, the traffic data and image data are consistent to some extent, and we may be able to convert the traffic into images for further processing. In this paper, the main contributions of this work are as follows.

1. Unsupervised traffic clustering based on DBSCAN.
2. Traffic recognition based on machine learning.
3. Traffic recognition based on deep learning.

The paper is organized as follows: Sect. 2 presents the related work. Section 3 describes the overall experimental plan, followed by some experimental results in Sect. 4. Finally, we summarize the research in Sect. 5 with a discussion of the future work.

2 Related Work

2.1 Traditional Traffic Recognition

From the perspective of technological development, network traffic recognition technology has roughly gone through two stages: the first stage is from the emergence of the Internet to the end of the last century. Traffic analysis technology is mainly distributed by the global Internet Assigned Numbers Authority [1] (IANA) To the fixed application port. In the second stage, from the end of the last century to the past few years, research directions represented by deep packet inspection and deep flow inspection technologies have emerged.

Port Match. Port-based protocol recognition is often based on the port protocol comparison table provided by the IANA. After analyzing the port number information of the data packet, it is inferred that the network traffic belongs to the protocol type. IANA stipulates that the system application port number ranges from 0 to 1 023, the user application port number ranges from 1024 to 49151, and the dynamic port number ranges from 49152 to 65535.

However, with the rapid development of network applications, many applications provide users with the function of customizing ports. Users can set the ports used by network applications according to their own preferences. In addition, point applications such as Peer-to-Peer (P2P) and IP-based voice transmission (Voice over Internet Protocol, VoIP) use dynamic port technology to avoid operator monitoring. In order to evade firewall detection, some botnet programs introduced port masquerading technology, by changing the communication port to a recognized port to deceive an intrusion detection system based on port filtering. With the advent of these technologies, port-based recognition methods are no longer reliable. Moore et al. [2] and Madhukar et al. [13] respectively confirmed through experiments that the recognition accuracy of the port-based protocol recognition method has been reduced from the initial 70% to less than 20%. However, due to the simple implementation and high running speed of such methods, it is often used as an auxiliary means for protocol recognition.

DPI Technology. DPI technology is a flow detection and control technology based on the application layer, which is called "deep packet inspection". In addition to ordinary packet detection, DPI technology also adds application layer analysis to identify various applications and their content. When IP data packets, TCP or UDP data streams pass through a management system based on DPI technology, the system reorganizes the application layer information in the OSI seven-layer protocol by in-depth reading of the content of the IP packet payload, thereby obtaining the entire application program Content, and then recognize the traffic based on the characteristics.

However, typical deep packet inspection methods have the following three problems: 1) It is difficult to extract protocol identification features, and the feature database needs to be maintained continuously. The extraction of protocol identification features relies on expert domain knowledge and needs to be manually determined; and when the protocol version is upgraded or new protocols appear, the features need to be stored in the feature library in time; in the face of the rapid development of the network, the feature library needs to be continuously updated and maintained. 2) The scope of application is limited, and this method cannot be applied to encrypted traffic and network traffic with unknown protocol specification information. The encryption of traffic will make network data show randomness and uncertainty, making it difficult to extract protocol features. For some private protocols, because the protocol specification information is unknown, no feature matching it can be found in the feature library.

DFI Technology. Deep Flow Inspection (DFI) technology is an improvement of DPI technology, and its inspection granularity extends from a single data packet to a complete data flow. DFI technology is an identification technology based on flow behavior, that is, the flow status of different types of flow data is different. Compared with DPI technology, DFI can identify unknown traffic and encrypted traffic; but overall, the recognition accuracy of this technology is lower than that of DPI technology [13]. Combining the advantages of DPI and DFI, Wang et al. [14] proposed a new P2P traffic recognition system based on DPI and DFI. This system has a wider recognition range and independent learning ability than a single DPI or DFI recognition system.

2.2 Traffic Recognition Method Based on Deep Learning and Machine Learning

This paper attempts to recognize instant messaging software traffic based on deep learning and machine learning. This subsection will give a brief introduction to the methods used.

DBSCAN Algorithm. The full name of DBSCAN [2] is Density-Based Spatial Clustering of Applications with Noise, which is a very typical density clustering method. The traditional K-Means [4] and BIRCH5 clustering algorithms are only suitable for convex sample sets, while the DBSCAN algorithm can be applied to both convex sample sets and non-convex sample sets.

For samples belonging to the same category, it is assumed that they are closely connected, which means that there must be samples of the same category distributed here not far from any sample of a certain category. By dividing the clustered and connected samples into the same category, a cluster division is obtained. Furthermore, by dividing each group of closely connected samples into different categories, the DBSCAN algorithm finally obtains the clustering of all samples. The DBSCAN algorithm can divide data into tasks the clusters of intentional shapes, so as to avoid human subjective mistakes.

For unsupervised clustering algorithms, silhouette coefficient [6] is the main evaluation index. The silhouette coefficient combines two factors, cohesion and resolution. It can be used on the basis of the same original data. The above is used to evaluate the impact of different algorithms or different operating modes of the algorithms on the clustering results.

We define S_i as the evaluation index of the clustering result of sample i, and the mean value of S_i of all samples is called the contour coefficient of the clustering result, which is a measure of whether the clustering is reasonable and effective. The calculation method of S_i is shown in formula 1.

$$S_i = \frac{b_i - a_i}{\max\{b_i - a_i\}} \tag{1}$$

a_i is the dissimilarity within the cluster of sample i, and a i is obtained by calculating the average distance between sample i and other samples in the same cluster. The smaller a_i is, the more sample i should be clustered into this cluster.

b_i is the dissimilarity between clusters of sample i. Define the average distance between sample i and all samples of some other cluster C_j as b_{ij}, which is called the dissimilarity between sample i and cluster C_j, $b_i = \min\{b_{i1}, b_{i2}, \ldots, b_{ik}\}$.

For S_i, S_i is close to 1, indicating that the clustering of sample i is reasonable; S_i is close to -1, it means that sample i should be classified into another cluster; if si is approximately 0, it means that sample i is at the boundary of two clusters on.

Machine Learning Algorithm. In this paper, the machine learning algorithms that mainly use are KNN and SVM [7]. This section will give a brief introduction to it.

KNN classifies by calculating the "distance" between different data. Its basic idea is: if most of the k most similar (the nearest neighbors in the feature space) samples of a sample in the feature space belong to a certain category, then the sample also belongs to this category, where K is usually not an integer greater than 20. When determining the category, the KNN algorithm requires that all training data in the feature space have been correctly classified. Compared with the previous classification, KNN is based on most of the K nearest neighbor objects to perform roles, avoiding the contingency of single object judgment, which is also the advantage of the KNN algorithm [8].

In KNN, a very important point is how to calculate the distance between data and measure the similarity between objects. In practical applications, the distance generally uses Euclidean distance [16] or Manhattan distance [17], as shown in the following formula 2 and 3. Among them, x and y represent different objects, and k represents different dimensions on the objects. In this paper, we choose Euclidean distance as the distance formula for data similarity measure.

$$d(x, y) = \sqrt{\sum_{k=1}^{n} (x_k - y_k)^2} \tag{2}$$

$$d(x, y) = \sqrt{\sum_{k=1}^{n} |x_k - y_k|} \tag{3}$$

SVM (Support Vector Machine) is a machine learning method that uses statistical laws to learn classifiers. Before the advent of deep learning, SVM was considered the most successful and best performing algorithm in machine learning in the past ten years. The algorithm complexity of the trained model is determined by the number of support vectors, not by the dimensionality of the data. So SVM is not easy to produce overfitting. Besides, it can still obtain a classifier with higher classification accuracy even when the number of samples in the training set is small [10].

Deep Learning Algorithm. Given the good performance of CNN [15] in image recognition, we introduce it to the field of traffic recognition. Next, the following will briefly introduce CNN.

CNN consists of input and output layers and multiple hidden layers. The hidden layers can be divided into convolutional layers, pooling layers, RELU layers, and fully connected layers. The convolutional layer is the core of CNN. The parameters of the layer are composed of a set of learnable filters or kernels. During the feedforward period, each filter convolves the input, calculates the dot product between the filter and the input, and generates a two-dimensional activation map of the filter (the input is generally a two-dimensional vector, but may have a height. Simply, the convolutional layer is used to convolve the input layer to extract higher-level features.

Usually, the maximum value of the four pixels in each neighborhood becomes one pixel in the pooling layer. Why can this be done? This is because the convolution has extracted the features, and the features of the adjacent regions are similar and almost unchanged. This is because pooling only selects the pixels that can characterize the features, reducing the amount of data while retaining the features. The role of the pooling layer can be described as blurring the image, losing some of the less important features.

Deep learning has more network layers. Although this effect is very good, it can easily lead to overfitting. Generally, L2 regularization or reduction of network size is used to solve this problem. However, Geoff Hinton [11] believes that overfitting can be alleviated by preventing the synergy of certain features. In order to prevent overfitting, use dropout = 0.5 to make only half of the neurons participate in training each time. In this way, a neural unit is forced to work together with other neural units selected at random, eliminating and weakening the joint adaptability between neuron nodes and enhancing the generalization ability.

3   Overall Experimental Plan

The overall experimental plan is shown in Fig. 1.

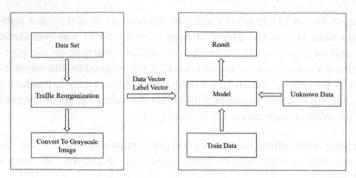

Fig. 1. Overall experimental plan.

3.1 Data Preprocessing Module

Based on experience, the content load of traffic, such as pictures and text, does not contribute to traffic identification. So we don't need to convert all traffic into images. So we need to determine an image size, which can achieve a higher accuracy rate without wasting computing resources.

Combining the feature value distribution of traffic and the characteristics of CNN, we take the first 28*28 = 784 bytes as the image size, which is also the classic CNN image size. For traffic files, the unsigned value represented by one byte is used as the pixel value of the image. According to this method, the pcap [23] file is converted into a grayscale image. At the same time, it should be noted that for the traffic that is less than 200 bytes, it is discarded, and for the traffic that is greater than 200 bytes but less than 784 bytes, the zero-fill operation is performed, and then it is converted into a grayscale image.

Besides, in order to improve the training performance of the model, the number of each group is normalized [24], which turns into [0–1]. Considering that the data of traffic bytes are between [0–255], so each group of data can be divided by 255.

3.2 Data Set

We first used the UNB ISCX dataset, which is the Canadian National Cyber Security Research provides network traffic data. This data set contains the traffic of many web applications. In this experiment, we select Facebook, Hangouts, and Skype as the experimental data. In addition, in order to expand the data set, we restocked the traffic of Zello and Wickr me, and processed the traffic in the same way.

In addition, the data set must contain counterexample data. We captured a lot of free traffic at the network center of Harbin Institute of Technology. Because the positive data are selected foreign instant messaging applications, and these applications are rarely used in China. Therefore, we can use these data as counterexample data.

The data set is shown in Table 1.

Table 1. Data set.

Application	Data size
Wickr me	237 MB
Zello	135 MB
Facebook	112 MB
Hangout	282 MB
Skype	341 MB
Other	248 MB

4 Experimental Result

4.1 DBSCAN Clustering Results

In the experiment, we change the value of the parameter (ϵ, MinPts) and perform a clustering experiment on the flow data. The parameter ϵ describes the neighborhood distance threshold of a sample, and the parameter MinPts describes the threshold of the number of samples in the neighborhood where the distance of a sample is ϵ. The results in Table 2 contain two experimental data, one is the number of clusters, and the other is the contour system.

Table 2. DBSCAN clustering results.

Parameters	MinPts = 3	MinPts = 6	MinPts = 10	MinPts = 20
$\epsilon = 1.5$	$(17, -0.238)$	$(2, -0.217)$	$(1, 0.040)$	$(1, 0.040)$
$\epsilon = 1.0$	$(13, -0.240)$	$(1, 0.240)$	$(1, 0.240)$	$(1, 0.240)$
$\epsilon = 0.5$	$(7, 0.113)$	$(1, 0.240)$	$(1, 0.240)$	$(1, 0.240)$

After comparison, we found that in the case of $\epsilon = 0.5$, MinPts $= 3$, the clustering effect is 7 categories, which is close to the real data. But similarly, we should also find that the contour coefficient is only 0.113, which is close to 0, indicating that the flow data in the cluster category tends to be classified into other categories. This also shows that traffic data's similarity is high and it is not easy to classify.

4.2 Experimental Results Based on Machine Learning

KNN and SVM algorithms are implemented based on the sklearn library in python. After data processing, the next step is to split the data set using the function train_test_split imported from the sklearn package. We use 85% of the data set as the training set and the remaining 15% as the test set.

For KNN we use the KNeighborsClassifier function of sklearn. In the KNeighborsClassifier function, we only change the number of neighbors and store the classification results of the optimal K value for each data set. All other parameters are set to default. For SVM we use the SVC function. The maximum number of iterations is 1000, and the category weight is set to "balanced".

In the course of the experiment, we did not train all the data at once, but added the data types in stages. It is convenient to verify the impact of data types on the accuracy of the model by this way. The experimental results are shown in Table 3.

Table 3. Experimental results based on machine learning.

Number of data types	KNN			SVM
2	K = 1 0.9078	K = 3 0.8754	K = 5 0.8777	0.8581
3	K = 2 0.8119	K = 3 0.8220	K = 5 0.8299	0.7139
4	K = 3 0.6963	K = 3 0.7194	K = 5 0.7226	0.5931
5	K = 4 0.5036	K = 3 0.5594	K = 5 0.5384	0.4461
6	K = 4 0.3912	K = 3 0.3748	K = 5 0.3934	0.3223

In 2 classification, the performance of the machine learning algorithm is acceptable, but the data categories increase, KNN and SVM perform worse and worse.

4.3 Experimental Results Based on Deep Learning

In this experiment, we are going to simulate the types of traffic in the entire network environment. Instant messaging traffic only accounts for a small part. In the past, model evaluation often used the correct rate as the evaluation index, but for data sets with unbalanced data of different categories, we need to add an additional recall rate as an evaluation index. Recall Rate [19] is the ratio of the number of retrieved related documents to the number of all related documents in the document library, and it measures the recall rate of the retrieval system. The formula for calculating the recall rate is shown in formula 4.

$$R = \frac{TP}{TP + FN} \tag{4}$$

Among them, TP means predicting the original positive class as a positive class, and FN means predicting the original positive class as a negative class. In multi-category, the overall recall rate is the average of the recall rates of each category.

Because deep learning will often have over-fitting phenomenon, so we divide 15% from the training set as the verification set [18] to decide whether to stop training. We designed the batch size [20] for model training to be 64, which reduced the gradient calculations, and conducted a total of 30 epochs of training on the data (Table 4).

Table 4. Experimental results based on deep learning.

Number of data types	LOSS	ACC	RECALL
2	0.054	0.9984	0.9999
3	0.062	0.9863	0.9979
4	0.087	0.9482	0.9918
5	0.204	0.9234	0.9816
6	0.318	0.9086	0.9804

The training results on the test set are shown in Table 3. Through the experimental results, we can find that compared to machine learning algorithms, deep learning performance is better. In 6 classification, the accuracy rate can still reach 90%, and the recall rate is also high, which is trustworthy.

In the 6 classification task, the model's loss entropy, accuracy rate, and recall rate on the training set and validation set change with the number of epochs as shown in Figs. 2, 3 and 4.

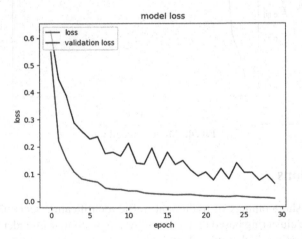

Fig. 2. Model's loss entropy.

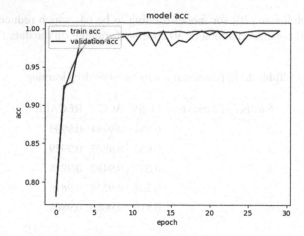

Fig. 3. Model's accuracy rate

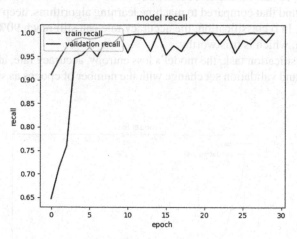

Fig. 4. Model's recall rate.

5 Conclusions

Aiming at the shortcomings of traditional traffic identification technology, this paper proposes traffic clustering based on the DBSCAN algorithm, traffic identification based on machine learning, and traffic identification based on deep learning. The specific method is to first convert the traffic file into a gray image, and then use the algorithm model to identify and classify. In this way, the problem of traffic identification analysis is transformed into an image classification problem.

For unsupervised learning traffic clustering, the clustering effect is general. The final experimental results show that KNN and SVM are effective in identifying a flow separately. But with the increase of traffic types, when the traffic reaches 6 types, the correct rate of KNN is only 39%, and the effect of SVM is even worse, the correct rate is only 32%. However, CNN has a better effect through multiple rounds of iterative learning, and the winning rate is still 90% in 6 classification.

In the future, we will try to identify the behavior of traffic, such as whether the traffic is text messages, voice messages, or video messages. Compared with application recognition, behavior recognition is undoubtedly more challenging.

References

1. Touch, J., Mankin, A., Kohlere, et al.: Service name and transport protocol port number registry [EB/OL] [2019-04-14]. https://www.iana.org/assignments/service-names-port-num bers/service-names-port-numbers.xhtml

2. Moore, A.W., Zuev, D.: Internet traffic classification using Bayesian analysis techniques. ACM SIGMETRICS Perform. Eval. Rev. 33(1), 50–60 (2005)

3. Tran, T.N., Drab, K., Daszykowski, M.: Revised DBSCAN algorithm to cluster data with dense adjacent clusters. Chemom. Intell. Lab. Syst. 120, 92–96 (2013)

4. Jain, A.K.: Data clustering: 50 years beyond K-means. Pattern Recogn. Lett. 31(8), 651–666 (2010)

5. Dong, J., Wang, F., Yuan, B.: Accelerating BIRCH for clustering large scale streaming data using CUDA dynamic parallelism. In: Yin, H., Tang, Ke., Gao, Y., Klawonn, F., Lee, M., Weise, T., Li, B., Yao, X. (eds.) IDEAL 2013. LNCS, vol. 8206, pp. 409–416. Springer, Heidelberg (2013). https://doi.org/10.1007/978-3-642-41278-3_50

6. Aranganayagi, S., Thangavel, K.: Clustering categorical data using silhouette coefficient as a relocating measure, pp. 13–17 (2007)

7. Vita, G., Kamboj, P.: Content based image processing approach on colored images using KNN classifier. Int. J. Emerg. Trends Technol. Comput. Sci. 36(4), 183–191 (2016)

8. Chang, B.M., Tsai, H.H., Yen, C.Y.: SVM-PSO based rotation-invariant image texture classification in SVD and DWT domains. Eng. Appl. Artif. Intell. 52, 96–107 (2016)

9. Guo, G., Wang, H., Bell, D., Bi, Y., Greer, K.: KNN model-based approach in classification. In: Meersman, R., Tari, Z., Schmidt, D.C. (eds.) OTM 2003. LNCS, vol. 2888, pp. 986–996. Springer, Heidelberg (2003). https://doi.org/10.1007/978-3-540-39964-3_62

10. Hao Zhang, J.M., Berg, A.C., Maire, M.: SVM-KNN: Discriminative nearest neighbor classification for visual category recognition. In: IEEE Computer Society Conference on Computer Vision and Pattern Recognition, vol. 2, pp. 2126–2136 (2006)

11. Hinton, G.E., Srivastava, N., Krizhevsky, A., et al.: Improving neural networks by preventing co-adaptation of feature detectors. Comput. Sci. 3(4), 212–223 (2012)

12. Madhukar, A., Williamson, C.: A longitudinal study of P2P traffic classification. In: Proceedings of the 14th International Symposium on Modeling, Analysis, and Simulation, pp. 179–188. IEEE, Piscataway (2006)

13. Chen, H., Hu, Z., Ye, Z., et al.: A new model for P2P traffic identification based on DPI and DFI. In: Proceedings of the 2009 International Conference on Information Engineering and Computer Science, pp. 1–3. IEEE, Piscataway (2009)

14. Wang, C., Zhou, X., You, F., et al.: Design of P2P traffic identification based on DPI and DFI. In: Proceedings of the 2009 International Symposium on Computer Network and Multimedia Technology, pp. 1–4. 'IEEE, Piscataway (2009)

15. Li, Y., Qi, H., et al.: Joint embeddings of shapes and images via CNN image purification. ACM Trans. Graph. 34(6), 1–12 (2015)

16. Yu, K., Guo, G.-D., Li, J., Lin, S.: Quantum algorithms for similarity measurement based on Euclidean distance. Int. J. Theor. Phys. 59(10), 3134–3144 (2020). https://doi.org/10.1007/s10773-020-04567-1

17. Suwanda, R., Syahputra, Z., Zamzami, E.M.: Analysis of Euclidean distance and Manhattan distance in the K-means algorithm for variations number of centroid K. J. Phys. Conf. Ser. **1566**(1), 012058 (6pp) (2020)
18. Mahsereci, M., Balles, L., Lassner, C., et al.: Early stopping without a validation set (2017)
19. Sumkin, J.H., Ganott, M.A., Chough, D.M., et al.: Recall rate reduction with tomosynthesis during baseline screening examinations: an assessment from a prospective trial. Acad. Radiol. **22**, 1477–1482 (2015)
20. Choi, M.: An empirical study on the optimal batch size for the deep Q-network. In: Kim, J.-H., Myung, H., Kim, J., Xu, W., Matson, E.T., Jung, J.-W., Choi, H.-L. (eds.) RiTA 2017. AISC, vol. 751, pp. 73–81. Springer, Cham (2019). https://doi.org/10.1007/978-3-319-784 52-6_8
21. Freier, A., Karlton, P., Kocher, P.: The Secure Sockets Layer (SSL) protocol version 3.0. The syncretic religion of Lin Chao-en, Columbia University Press (2011)
22. Mclane, T.L., Mullen, S.P., Tenginakai, J.B.: Secure shell used to open a user's encrypted file system keystore: US (2013)
23. Ando, R.: Asura: a huge PCAP file analyzer for anomaly packets detection using massive multithreading. In: DEFCON26 (2018)
24. Chen, H.N., Chung, K.L., Hung, J.E.: Novel fractal image encoding algorithm using normalized one-norm and kick-out condition. Image Vis. Comput. **28**(3), 518–525 (2010)

Author Index

Printed in the United States
by Baker & Taylor Publisher Services

Printed in the United States
by Baker & Taylor Publisher Services